D0024263

SELLING DESTINATIONS
Geography for the
Travel Professional

Third Edition

Online Services

Delmar Online
To access a wide variety of Delmar products
and services on the World Wide Web, point your
browser to:
      http://www.delmar.com
      or email: info@delmar.com

A service of

SELLING DESTINATIONS
Geography for the Travel Professional

Third Edition

Marc Mancini, PhD
Department of Travel
West Los Angeles College

Delmar Publishers

an International Thomson Publishing company **I**(**T**)**P**®

Albany • Bonn • Boston • Cincinnati • Detroit • London • Madrid
Melbourne • Mexico City • New York • Pacific Grove • Paris • San Francisco
Singapore • Tokyo • Toronto • Washington

NOTICE TO THE READER

Publisher does not warrant or guarantee any of the products described herein or perform any independent analysis in connection with any of the product information contained herein. Publisher does not assume, and expressly disclaims, any obligation to obtain and include information other than that provided to it by the manufacturer.

The reader is expressly warned to consider and adopt all safety precautions that might be indicated by the activities herein and to avoid all potential hazards. By following the instructions contained herein, the reader willingly assumes all risks in connections with such instructions.

The publisher makes no representation or warranties of any kind, including but not limited to, the warranties of fitness for particular purpose or merchantability, nor are any such representations implied with respect to the material set forth herein, and the publisher takes no responsibility with respect to such material. The publisher shall not be liable for any special, consequential, or exemplary damages resulting, in whole or part, from the readers' use of, or reliance upon, this material.

Cover design: Joseph Villanova
Delmar Staff:

Publisher: Susan Simpfenderfer
Acquisitions Editor: Jeff Burnham
Editorial Assistant: Judy Roberts

Production Manager: Wendy Troeger
Production Editor: Elaine Scull
Marketing Manager: Katherine M. Hans

Copyright © 1999
By Delmar Publishers
an International Thomson Publishing Company I(T)P®

The ITP logo is a trademark under license
Printed in the United States of America

For more information contact:

Delmar Publishers
3 Columbia Circle, Box 15015
Albany, New York 12212-5015

International Thomson Publishing Europe
Berkshire House
168-173 High Holborn
London, WC1V7AA
United Kingdom

Nelson ITP, Australia
102 Dodds Street
South Melbourne,
Victoria, 3205 Australia

Nelson Canada
1120 Birchmont Road
Scarborough, Ontario
M1K 5G4, Canada

International Thomson Publishing France
Tour Maine-Montparnasse
33 Avenue du Maine
75755 Paris Cedex 15, France

International Thomson Editores
Seneca 53
Colonia Polanco
11560 Mexico D. F. Mexico

International Thomson Publishing GmbH
Königswinterer Strasße 418
53227 Bonn
Germany

International Thomson Publishing Asia
60 Albert Street #15-01
Albert Complex
Singapore 189969

International Thomson Publishing Japan
Hirawaka-cho Kyowa Building, 3F
2-2-1 Hirakawa-cho, Chiyoda-ku,
Tokyo 102, Japan

ITE Spain/Paraninfo
Calle Magallanes, 25
28015-Madrid, Espana

All rights reserved. No part of this work covered by the copyright hereon may be reproduced or used in any form or by any means—graphic, electronic, or mechanical, including photocopying, recording, taping, or information storage and retrieval systems—without the written permission of the publisher.

1 2 3 4 5 6 7 8 9 10 XXX 04 03 02 01 00 99

Library of Congress Cataloging-in-Publication Data
Mancini, Marc, 1946–
    Selling destinations : geography for the travel professional /
Marc Mancini. — 3e [ed.]
      p. cm.
    Includes index.
    ISBN 0-7668-0848-3
    1. Tourist trade. 2. Geography. I. Title
G155.A1M263 1999
338.4'791—dc21   98-49624
                            CIP

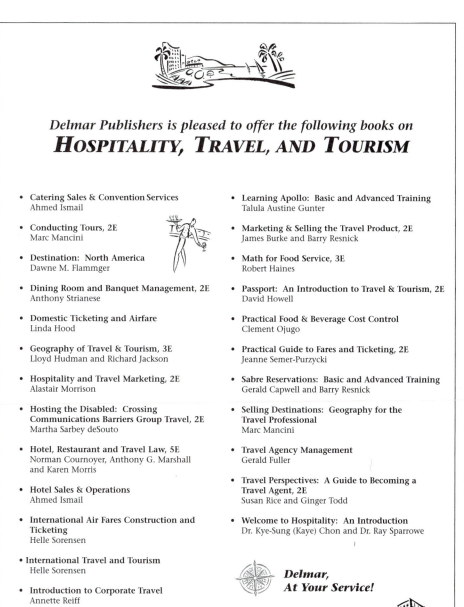

Delmar Publishers *is pleased to offer the following books on*

HOSPITALITY, TRAVEL, AND TOURISM

- **Catering Sales & Convention Services**
  Ahmed Ismail

- **Conducting Tours, 2E**
  Marc Mancini

- **Destination: North America**
  Dawne M. Flammger

- **Dining Room and Banquet Management, 2E**
  Anthony Strianese

- **Domestic Ticketing and Airfare**
  Linda Hood

- **Geography of Travel & Tourism, 3E**
  Lloyd Hudman and Richard Jackson

- **Hospitality and Travel Marketing, 2E**
  Alastair Morrison

- **Hosting the Disabled: Crossing Communications Barriers Group Travel, 2E**
  Martha Sarbey deSouto

- **Hotel, Restaurant and Travel Law, 5E**
  Norman Cournoyer, Anthony G. Marshall and Karen Morris

- **Hotel Sales & Operations**
  Ahmed Ismail

- **International Air Fares Construction and Ticketing**
  Helle Sorensen

- **International Travel and Tourism**
  Helle Sorensen

- **Introduction to Corporate Travel**
  Annette Reiff

- **Learning Apollo: Basic and Advanced Training**
  Talula Austine Gunter

- **Marketing & Selling the Travel Product, 2E**
  James Burke and Barry Resnick

- **Math for Food Service, 3E**
  Robert Haines

- **Passport: An Introduction to Travel & Tourism, 2E**
  David Howell

- **Practical Food & Beverage Cost Control**
  Clement Ojugo

- **Practical Guide to Fares and Ticketing, 2E**
  Jeanne Semer-Purzycki

- **Sabre Reservations: Basic and Advanced Training**
  Gerald Capwell and Barry Resnick

- **Selling Destinations: Geography for the Travel Professional**
  Marc Mancini

- **Travel Agency Management**
  Gerald Fuller

- **Travel Perspectives: A Guide to Becoming a Travel Agent, 2E**
  Susan Rice and Ginger Todd

- **Welcome to Hospitality: An Introduction**
  Dr. Kye-Sung (Kaye) Chon and Dr. Ray Sparrowe

***Delmar,
At Your Service!***

Delmar Publishers

an International Thomson Publishing company **I(T)P**®

Contents

Preface

Does the sheer volume of things the travel industry expects you to know about the world overwhelm you? Do you ever wonder how that knowledge can be translated to real, everyday sales experience? Then *Selling Destinations*—whether you're a student, trainee, or working professional—is written with you in mind.

How This Book Is Unique

Selling Destinations is a very different sort of geography book:

- **It approaches geography from a travel industry perspective.** Important touristic destinations receive detailed treatment in chapters of their own. Secondary destinations merit several pages or paragraphs in special "Potpourri" chapters. Facts and places that travel industry personnel rarely deal with are given only a passing reference (though the Appendices direct you to other reference sources to get the information you'll need).

- **It treats geography as something the travel industry sells.** To be able to match clients to destinations and services is the key to travel industry success. *Selling Destinations* underscores precisely how you can do this in your day-to-day work.

- **It makes reading about destinations fun.** This text uses a breezy, magazine-style prose to make learning about these places an enjoyable experience.

- **It uses many educational devices to make sure you remember what you read.** The biggest problem with most books is that you remember only about 30 percent of what you read. First, *Selling Destinations* limits itself to what you *need* to know to be a travel professional; it won't clutter your mind with obscure details. Second, its two-color highlighting, lists, headings, subheadings, graphs, tables, photos, and application activities serve to clarify and reinforce information. The result: You absorb a far greater percentage of what you read.

What Major Graphic Elements Are Used

Selling Destinations features nearly 300 visual elements to enliven the information that it presents:

- You'll find more than one hundred **maps**. As you read the text, you'll be able to follow along on the map; that way you'll instantly know where the place talked about is situated geographically. The maps are simplified to give special attention to cities and areas that tourists frequent.

Some chapter maps contain symbols. Following is a key to the symbols you will encounter.

MAP LEGEND:

✪ capital city ▲ attraction

✈ major air gateway ʌʌ mountains

- In many chapters, you'll be able to consult a "**For Your Information**" box that summarizes geographic facts about a major destination, such as population, area, currency, languages spoken, history, and even on which side of the road you should drive.
- "**Climate at a Glance**" charts will enable you to rapidly determine the typical temperature, rainfall, and tourist season patterns of major world destinations.
- "**Qualifying the Client**" grid boxes will enable you to identify the types of people who are attracted to major destinations.
- "**Travel Trivia**" boxes and "**Margin Notes**" give you unusual, entertaining, or surprising bits of information about tourism that help flesh out your understanding of the industry and of the world.

How This Book Is Organized

Selling Destinations' part and chapter structure is dictated by travel and touristic concerns:
- **The book is divided into six major parts.** Part I lays a sturdy geographic and sales foundation for all information to come. Parts II through VI cover the world's principal geographic areas: North America, Latin America, Europe, Africa and the Middle East, Asia, Australia and the South Pacific.
- **A short introductory overview** opens each of Parts II through VI. This is followed by several **in-depth chapters** on major touristic centers. (There are 24 such chapters in the book, each focusing on those destinations most visited by North American tourists.) Each part finishes with a **potpourri chapter** that gathers together those remaining destinations not covered in an in-depth chapter.
- **Four useful appendices** lists typical lengths of time spent by tourists in major cities; the addresses of tourist bureaus; research resources—including the phone numbers and addresses of major video distributors and descriptions of other reference books; and movies. A detailed **index** follows.
- **Pronunciation guides** follow place-words that are especially difficult. They're set off in brackets and spelled phonetically.

How Each Chapter Is Organized

The organizational subheadings of *Selling Destinations* are critical to the book's sales-geography philosophy:
- An **introduction** gives a historical, cultural, or client perspective on the destination. It also lists major geographic features, patterns of tourism, and languages spoken.
- **How Travelers Get There** discusses modes of transportation, national airlines (with airline codes), major airports (also with codes), and traveling times from North America, if relevant.
- **Weather Patterns** analyzes seasonal weather and touristic patterns.
- **Getting Around** focuses on internal modes of transportation, both in broad sub-regions and within major cities.

- **Important Places** discusses touristic highlights and day-trip possibilities from central hub cities.
- **Possible Itineraries** lays out typical daily client travel patterns within the destination area.
- **Lodging Options** enumerates the lodging choices of a destination, including principal hotel chains and landmark hotels.
- **Allied Destinations** suggests the typical places that are easily combined with the primary destination as part of a larger client itinerary.
- **Margin Notes** provide intriguing tangents to the place being covered, including tips for travelers and bits of information that may help you better understand each destination.
- **Cultural Patterns** (where applicable) examines the local cultural behaviors of which travelers should be aware.
- **Factors That Motivate Visitors** analyzes why a person typically travels to the destination covered.
- **Possible Misgivings** enumerates those psychological barriers to a destination—perhaps valid, perhaps not—that a person may have, and how or if they should be countered for an effective sale.
- **Sales Strategies** lists the services that a person may wish to arrange in advance—the kinds that yield extra profits to the seller of travel.
- **Activities** close each chapter. A **Map Activity** tests your knowledge of geographic places and their attractions. A **Case Study** permits you to apply your knowledge to hypothetical travelers. A **Creative Activity** challenges you to take a hypothetical situation in the travel industry and turn it into an innovative solution. The goal is to help you marshal all you know, to tap into your creativity—and to have *fun.* These Creative Activities also lend themselves readily to group solutions.

Who Should Use This Text

Selling Destinations is a geography book targeted to those who sell, or who plan to sell, places. At first glance, it may seem to be primarily a study or reference work for travel agents, and it is certainly that. But it will prove equally useful to you even if you're in another segment of the travel industry, and for two reasons. First, you need to know how travel counselors deal with geography, since you depend on their salesmanship. Second, everyone in the travel industry, in one way or another, sells places. The insights and strategies that this book gives can be used by anyone who deals with the traveling public. *Selling Destinations* can be a quick way of bringing yourself up to speed on most major destinations. It can be a powerful and rapid reference tool. And it can become a springboard to other, more specialized treatments of destination geography.

What Isn't Included

Selling Destinations deliberately avoids information that can become rapidly outdated or should more appropriately be looked up in standard, frequently revised sources (most of which are listed for you in the Appendices). Such information includes money conversion rates, visa requirements, and the like. This book also gives minimal attention to destinations that regularly suffer from political turmoil, terrorism, epidemics, and similar factors that make a place difficult or inadvisable to sell. Since a destination's touristic climate can change abruptly, we suggest that you consult the Citizen's Emergency Center, U.S. Department of State, Washington, D.C. 20520, 202-647-5225 or http://travel.state.gov.

To the Instructor or Trainer

Selling Destinations is a combined textbook-workbook that has been created with your pragmatic needs in mind. It can serve as your primary textbook; the many features listed above make it extremely effective when you're dealing with students or trainees who must round out their checkered knowledge of world geography. Or it may be used as a sales-application supplement to more conventional texts. It's well suited for compressed, one-semester geography programs, yet it easily lends itself to longer-term classes and even on-line, distance learning applications.

To further encourage your flexibility in using this book, each chapter is independent from the others. You can present chapters in whatever order you prefer. Note that "Part" sections, however, set the stage for what's to come and are, therefore, less adaptable to shifting.

A feature that will be especially useful to you is the *Instructional Resource Manual,* which amplifies the book and makes your teaching much easier. Among its contents: a set of behavioral objectives, teaching tips, answers to all textbook activities, supplementary research activities, blank maps for reproducing and for quizzing students, and a test bank of more than 80 quizzes with answers.

One other important and unique feature of *Selling Destinations* is a set of five videotapes that reinforce and amplify information contained in the book. For ordering information, please see the Introduction of the Instructor's Resource Guide.

For those of you who have taught from this book before, you'll notice some format changes in this third edition. Travel tips have been moved to the margins, along with additional travel trivia information. A new, challenging exercise, **Pulling It All Together**, can be found in the Potpourri chapters; these Connections games can serve as an effective way to review an entire section.

Information given in this textbook has been cross-checked in multiple sources, all of which are cited in the Appendices. Whenever possible, first-hand experience—that of the author or of various destination experts—has been used to buttress content.

To Our Canadian Educators

A special Canadian version of *Selling Destinations,* with fifty-eight extra pages on Canada and other Canada-specific content, can be ordered from Nelson Canada.

Acknowledgments

The author wishes to acknowledge the following people for their careful reading of this text; they all helped ensure the book's accuracy and completeness: Becky Emerson, Libby Corydon, David Hallal, Beatrice Aduo, Lyn Smith, Sue Soldoff (of Sue's Safaris), and Anna Maria Nassif. The author also would like to thank the following reviewers:

William Buckler
Assistant Professor, Geography Dept.
Youngstown State University
Youngstown, Ohio

Rene C. Gabriel
Assistant Professor, Travel-Tourism/
    Hospitality Management
State University of New York
    at Morrisville
Morrisville, New York

Jerry Fuller, CTC
Training for Tomorrow
Minneapolis, Minnesota

Peggy Mercer
McConnell School, Inc.
Minneapolis, Minnesota

And a special thanks to my research assistants, Robert J. Elisberg (first edition), Karen Fukushima (second and third editions), and Charlene Ambrose (third edition), for their efficient, thorough, and enthusiastic support throughout this project.

Marc Mancini

About the Author

Dr. Marc Mancini is one of the travel industry's best known speakers, educators, and consultants. He is the creative force behind three highly praised travel certification programs: those of CLIA, AAA, and the NTA. His client list includes such prestigious companies as Seabourn, Marriott, Holland America, American Express, Carlson Wagonlit, and Lufthansa, as well as the tourist offices of France, Hawaii, Los Angeles, Scandinavia, the Bahamas, and Switzerland. He has authored nine books, fourteen videos, three CD-ROMs, two Web sites, and over a hundred articles. His works have been syndicated by both the *L.A. Times* and *Prodigy*.

Currently a Professor of Travel at West Los Angeles College, Dr. Mancini has appeared on CNN, ABC's *Good Morning America,* and *Showtime*. He was named "Educator of the Year" by the International Society of Travel and Tourism Educators.

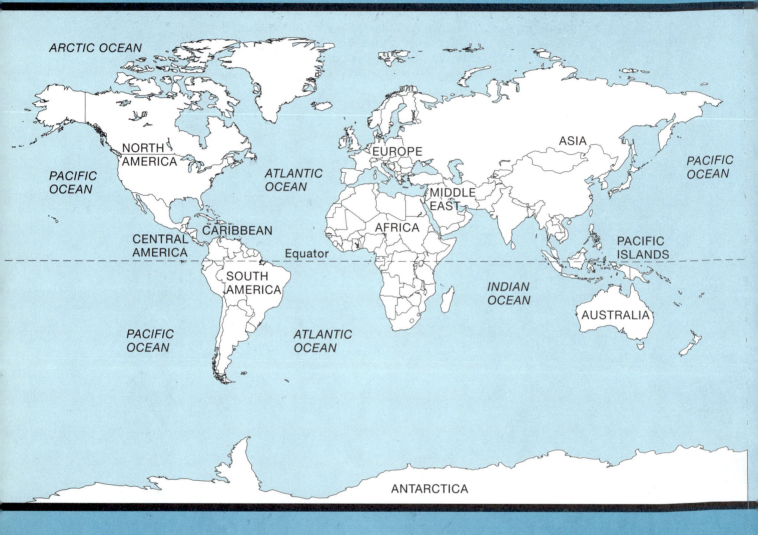

Basic Ingredients
Geography and How to Sell It

Here's a surprise: If you're in the travel business, you don't sell travel. What you sell is *geography*. For example, if you're a travel agent, your client may insist on a specific airline, with a flight at a certain time and price. Yes, that is selling *travel: the act of going from one place to another.* But the act of traveling in an aircraft holds little pleasure. No, the reason your client is traveling is to get to a place, and places are what geography is all about.

To perform any travel-related sales job in a professional manner, you must be aware of at least some aspects of the places travelers favor. Corporate travel managers, incentive operators, convention and meeting planners, tourist bureau representatives, hotel sales and reservation staff, tour planners, cruise personnel, and airline employees—they all have to know their geography to do their job right.

The most obvious sellers of destinations, however, are travel agents. That's why this book often examines the world through their eyes. But even if you're not a travel agent, you still need to know how *they* deal with geography, for virtually every person who serves the travel industry must depend on the salesmanship of travel agents.

No matter what segment of the industry you're in, though, you'll profit enormously from a deep and lasting familiarity of the world you sell, the kind that the chapters that follow will give you. And don't forget that word *sell.* The object is not to simply inform people about a destination, which is worthwhile in itself, but to motivate them to *buy* that destination—with their hearts as well as with their wallets.

Basic Concepts of Destination

Selling a place is a genuine art. It requires knowledge of the destination *and* of the traveler. The following five strategies will help you maximize your ability to sell a place.

You Must Know
All the Relevant Facts about a Destination

Travel geography differs from all other forms of geography in this way: It concentrates on those features about a destination that affect travel and tourism. To know that people in Burundi speak Kirundi, that Burkina Faso's principal crop is groundnuts, and that Montana is America's leading producer of zinc may make you more culturally literate and certainly a winner at Trivial Pursuit. But will this knowledge help you in the travel industry? Probably not. The likelihood is very low that anyone will ever ask you about Kirundi, groundnuts, or zinc. (For that matter, it's improbable that you'll ever encounter anyone going to Burundi or to Burkina Faso.)

On the other hand, to know that many Swedes speak English, that a good place to lodge New York City–bound clients is just south of Central Park, and that opals are a good buy in Sydney *are* useful geographic facts. Climate, transportation options, itinerary routings, hotel locations, and key attractions—these are things you need to know to motivate a person's interest, to help shape the travel experience, and to achieve an effective sale.

You Must Know What Kind of Client Favors a Destination

What's the biggest mistake that travel professionals make? To believe that what they like, everyone else will like. Maybe you're the type of person who adores classical music but hates lying on the beach. So you tend to recommend such destinations as Vienna and Milan, but not Hawaii or the Caribbean. After all, doesn't everyone enjoy a concert by the Vienna Boys Choir or an opera at Milan's La Scala? No. Each place attracts its own type of visitor. Matching destination with type is the key to a sensitive, efficient, and profitable sale.

How many "types" of travelers are there? What motivates them to travel? There are countless ways to slice the tourist "pie." One way is to separate them into **leisure** travelers (those who travel for pleasure) and **business** travelers. You can further subdivide each of these broad categories. Business travelers, for example, may go somewhere to attend a convention or to conduct business; they may even add on a vacation component to their trip.

Tourists whose primary motivation is leisure, in turn, can be subdivided into many types. Another approach categorizes leisure travelers into 12 groups:

- **History buffs** primarily desire to learn about a destination's past. They see travel as a way to experience what they've studied and read about.

- **Culture-seekers** are fascinated by different ways of life. They're intrigued by how other people express their culture via distinctive customs, food, art, and so on.

- **Ethnic travelers** are like culture-seekers, but they wish, above all, to explore the culture from which their *ancestors* came.

- **Religious pilgrims** seek an experience tied to their spiritual beliefs.

- **Environmental travelers** are drawn to scenery and the beauty of places. Two important subsets: "ecotourists," who wish to see places, such as the Brazilian rain forest, where flora and fauna are endangered; and campers, who like to experience a natural place (though it might be from a well-insulated RV).

- **Recreational travelers** wish to participate in such "mass-appeal" sports as golf, tennis, or skiing.

- **Adventure-seekers** prefer more demanding and hardy sports or activities, such as white-water rafting, surfing, mountain hiking, or diving—frequently in off-the-beaten-path places. Their tastes can even run to true physical challenges, such as mountain climbing or parasailing. This is called "hard" adventure travel, in contrast to more mainstream "soft" adventure tourism.

- **Entertainment-seekers** are drawn to activities such as dancing, partying, gambling, and night-club shows. Their tastes can also run to more "serious" entertainment, such as theater and concert performances.

- **Shoppers** love to buy things on trips, and are perhaps a subset of the previous categories, since they view purchasing as entertainment or adventure.

Figure I-1 The Matterhorn, Swiss Alps
Photo by C. J. Ghormley

- **Sensual travelers** wish to indulge their senses via, say, gourmet dining, sun-bathing, or a stay at a spa.
- **Status-seekers** travel to trendy, often expensive destinations, and sometimes bring back significant purchases. They define themselves—both to themselves and to others—by the places they visit.
- **Interpersonal travelers** voyage primarily to socialize and meet people. An important subcategory: people who travel to visit family and friends—and often stay with them. Surprisingly, this motivation accounts for the largest number of personal trips.

   As you read this listing, did you think of a place that fits each kind of traveler? Did you think of someone you know who is the "type" described? Good, you're already thinking like a true travel professional. And did you imagine individuals who combine the traits of several or many categories? Great, because most people do travel for multiple reasons, even though one *primary* motivator may control their destination choices.

To try your hand at matching client-types to destinations, turn to the end of the chapter and do Activity 1.

You Must Know the Individual Client You Are Serving

Imagine, now, that you are a travel agent. You do understand what kind of client favors a place. But are you able to identify that type of client when he or she comes to you for advice? In sales, the act of analyzing a client's needs and wants is called **qualifying** or **interviewing**. This is usually achieved by asking open-ended questions, called **probes**. Asking the right questions and listening carefully to the client's answer is the key to effective qualifying.

What kind of questions will you ask? At first, of course, you must determine the basics, such as name, possible destinations, dates, budget restrictions, and so on. But then, you can probe, for example, to find out what the person does for a living. That might provide a clue. A college history professor, say, might really enjoy the thought of going to Europe, but an Orlando vacation might leave him or her cold. Other possible probes: "Is your trip for business or pleasure?" (Business clients usually have much more focused travel plans.) "Are you an active outdoor person?" "Do you like adventurous places?" "Is this a family vacation?" "What was your favorite vacation and why?" A good way to probe is via contrasting questions: "Do you want to rest on your vacation or be active?" "Do you want to visit someplace exotic or a more familiar kind of culture?"

Note that such questions help you determine what client-type you're dealing with—an essential step to match client needs with your recommendations. Failing to do so can lead to a client/destination or client/service mismatch—something sure to lead to dissatisfaction, complaints, or worse.

Several points bear discussion:

- Don't expect people who are thinking about a vacation to know exactly where they want to go. One study concluded that half of all travelers start out with only the vaguest idea of where to spend their vacation. The others *do* have a rather specific destination in mind, but they hope that you, as a travel professional, will do the work of efficiently assembling the trip for them and perhaps enhance it through your in-depth knowledge.

- A person's primary motivation can change from one trip to the next. On one vacation, Mr. Jones may want to visit every major museum in Europe, but on the next he'll want to kick back at an isolated beach resort.

- Qualifying should be limited to productive minutes; it shouldn't be an excuse to gab.

- Always review a client's needs with him or her before going on to make your recommendations. This tests whether you understand the client's needs and permits the client to add anything forgotten.

- When recommending, explicitly describe how a destination satisfies the client's wishes. It's not enough to say, "The Cayman Islands is where I think you should go." Put it this way: "You wanted to do some diving, not travel too far, and go in April. The Caymans have great diving, are only a two-hour flight away, and usually have great weather in April."

- Your recommendations should also convey a sense that you know the place intimately. Travelers realize that a travel professional can't have visited every place on the globe. But they *do* hope that in the absence of actual experience, you still "know your stuff," that you have the equivalent of first-hand experience.

- Sprinkling little "insider tips" into your recommendations will help establish you as the professional that you are.

You Must Be Ready to Answer a Client's Misgivings

Your descriptions of a place may be so powerful that to close the sale right there will be easy. But sometimes matching a client to a place isn't enough. Fears, either rational or emotional, may stand in the way: "A trip to Tokyo sounds great, but how will I be able to communicate with the Japanese?" "I'd like to go to New York City, but isn't it awfully expensive?" "An African wildlife safari sounds wonderful, but isn't it dangerous?"

Faced with such objections, a travel professional, when appropriate, provides sales-building responses, or **counters**. You should tell the client who worries about communicating in Japan that many of Tokyo's tourist-industry personnel speak some English. You should recommend less expensive hotels or weekend hotel packages to your New York–bound clients. An African wildlife safari is less intimidating if you counsel your client to travel as part of a tour offered by a reputable tour operator.

To allay misgivings isn't always the proper approach. Sometimes the objections a client brings up are so valid—say, the country really *is* dangerous or is totally inappropriate for that client—that you must say so and counter with a completely different destination. To simply dismiss an objection without thought is unprofessional, unethical, and could even trigger a lawsuit later on.

You Must Search for Opportunities to Increase Profits

Three general strategies permit you to increase your profits from a client's trip:

- **Selling-up** allows you to improve the quality of the client's vacation while generally increasing your profits. Some examples: superior-category hotel rooms, first-class seats on a flight, a full-size car rental instead of a compact one, a longer **FIT** for your client. (*FIT* stands for foreign independent travel, but it often refers to any itinerary created from scratch.) Always start by recommending the best product that is reasonably appropriate to your client's needs, then work down. To start with budget recommendations and work up is a poor sales and service approach.

- **Cross-selling** requires you to offer allied services to your client. Many people may contact you only to book their flight. They haven't thought about anything else; they may even wait until they get to their destination to set up other services. This deprives you and your employer of potential income and your client of possible savings or convenience. Always offer to book hotels, car rentals, train trips, theater tickets, city tours, meal plans, boat charters, travel insurance, airport-to-hotel transfers, and whatever else seems appropriate. Underscore the benefits of these services to your client's vacation plans. And point out the advantage of booking these things in advance.

  Cross-selling is much more simple than it used to be: Computers now allow you to access and book all sorts of services. Further, **all-inclusive packages**—combinations of services that can be booked with one call—have made cross-selling easy. Independent tour packages, escorted tours, all-inclusive resorts, and cruises enable you to draw commission from virtually everything your client does, including eat and drink.

- A **follow-up** conversation with a client enables you to find out how a trip went. It can also deepen your destination knowledge. For example, a client could return from St. Martin and tell you that he really had to rent a car to get around the island. In the future, you will know to recommend a car rental to a St. Martin–bound tourist. Follow-up also cements the client-seller relationship, offers an opportunity to make amends for problems experienced during the trip, and opens the door to selling future trips to the client.

Are cross-selling, selling-up, or a follow-up sale manipulative? They can be, but only when you pressure someone into buying something he or she doesn't want or shouldn't have. Travelers often have vague, low, or unrealistic limits on what they want. Your job: to focus their plans, to suggest ways to genuinely improve their vacation, and perhaps to even save them a few dollars (since services arranged in advance or as part of a package are often less costly).

How Other Travel Professionals Sell Places

The five sales and service tactics we've examined primarily address the needs of a travel agent. But if you're contemplating some other career in the industry, these sales techniques will work for you, too:

- A cruise activities director may offer shore excursion tours.
- Airline reservationists can sell-up a caller to the comfort of business class on a long overseas flight.
- A car rental representative can suggest a convertible for the client's tropical vacation.
- A hotel clerk or concierge can make shopping, restaurant, and nightlife arrangements for the hotel guest.
- Flight attendants often answer questions about that flight's destination or explain the many places that their airline flies (a key consideration for members of frequent-flyer mileage programs).
- A tour conductor relates all sorts of facts about the cities the tour group will visit.
- An incentive trip planner can show a corporate client how certain add-on activities will enhance their employees' experience.
- A representative from a convention and tourist bureau can show an audience how their destination fulfills their expectations.

So, the ultimate purpose of both sales and service in the travel field is this: to create the perfect match between the desires of a client-traveler and the assets of a place. But to do this, you must not only love places, you must *know* them.

Geography—The Great Unknown

Gil Grosvenor, the president of the National Geographic Society, tells of a couple who once told him that they might be taking a cruise to Las Vegas, a completely desert-bound city. Writer S. J. Perelman relates that he once told a student that, on graduating from college, she should travel around the world. Her response: "I know, but there are so many places I'd rather see first!" Travel agents have made embarrassing mistakes, too. A traveler was once found wandering around Oakland, California, airport, asking where the New Zealand immigration officials were. His travel agent had mistakenly booked him on a flight to Oakland, instead of Auckland, his intended destination.

A *USA Today* poll discovered that one of seven Americans can't find the United States on a world map. One of five is unable to identify a single country on a map of Europe. One of four can't find the Pacific Ocean, even though it covers one-third the surface of the globe.

To be living in this century and to be ignorant of the world creates a rather shameful indictment of our education system. But to be a travel professional and not to know geography is something else. Would you trust a physician who didn't know anatomy, a builder who didn't know how to read blueprints, or a bank teller who didn't understand math? Should the general public trust travel professionals who can't read maps, who don't know that summer comes to Australia in December, or who book clients bound for the nation of Colombia to the city of Columbia, South Carolina? That has happened, too.

But you *can* make a difference. You can decide to know the world you sell. And it starts right now with a commitment to understand the underpinnings of travel geography itself.

The Kinds of Maps

Maps are the blueprints of travel. Dozens of types of maps exist; here are the ones travel professionals work with the most:

Flat Maps.   Standard flat maps are those we're most familiar with. They come in many varieties: Mercator projections (see Figure I-2), stereographics, mollweides, and lamberts (don't worry about these labels).

Because you can't flatten out our curving earth, flat maps are all somewhat distorted, especially when the whole world is displayed; extreme northern and southern areas may become grossly magnified. In Figure I-2, a typical map, Greenland appears larger than the United States. In reality, the United States is more than four times larger than Greenland. Remember: Maps that can lie flat, lie.

Flat maps mislead in a second way. If you draw a trip on such a map as a straight line—which seems logical—you'll be making a grave error. On most flat

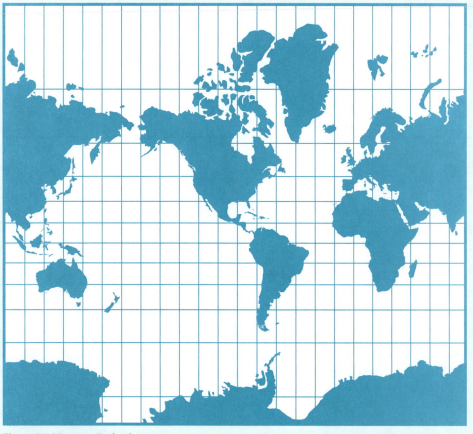

Figure I-2 Mercator Projection

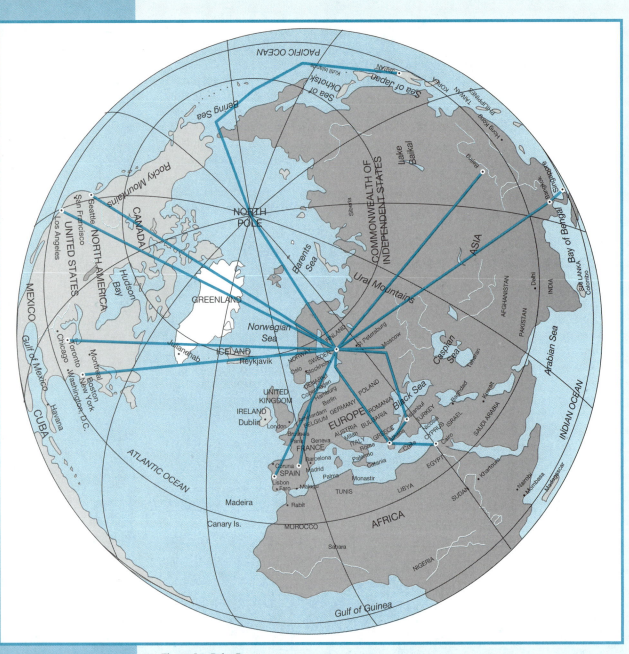

Figure I-3 Polar Routes
Source: Courtesy of Finnair

maps, the shortest distance between two geographic points should be traced out as a *curved* line (often called a great circle route and always arcing toward polar regions). For example, the shortest route from Los Angeles to Cairo might appear, on a flat map, to be on Alitalia Airlines via Rome or Paris. But if you look at a polar projection map (see Figure I-3), or trace the route on a globe, you'll see that going on Finnair via Helsinki will be a bit shorter. Another surprise: From New York, the shortest way to Bangkok, Singapore, and Beijing is via Helsinki. So when looking at world maps, remember that curved routes are usually the most direct.

Route Maps. These are useful reference tools. Each airline often distributes a map that shows all the routes that it flies. This can be a handy visual aid if you're trying to keep a client on one airline for a trip, either for fare reasons or to help build up frequent-flyer miles. AAA also produces superb route maps, including some that give car traveling times between major cities.

Globes. Even though globes are awkward to use and lack detail, they're the most accurate maps around. Keep one handy. They're fun to play with and often help you plot out intricate itineraries.

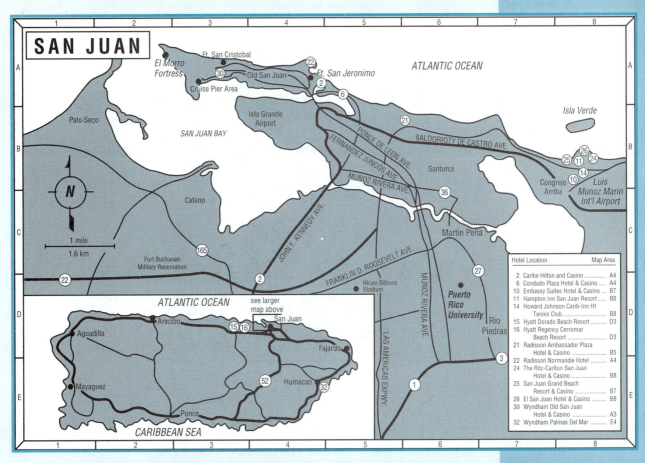

Figure I-4 Locator Map, San Juan, Puerto Rico
Source: Hotel and Travel Index/Reed Travel Group

Locator Maps. These are often found in travel industry reference books. Usually representing a small area, say, a city, they help you find the locations of attractions and hotels. Locator maps indicate places through a grid of numbers and letters rather than with the degrees of a conventional map (see Figure I-4).

Mental Maps. A mental map represents the way you picture geography in your mind. A deceiving feature of mental maps: The farther away a destination is, the more simple, closer together, and more error-prone those features mentally become. For instance, a client who has never been to Europe may imagine that he or she can drive around and see most of its major cities in a week or two, that Paris is a day's drive from Rome, that a cruise on the Danube takes only a few days. In reality, Europe is bigger than the entire United States, Rome is nearly a thousand-mile trip from Paris, and the Danube is so long that most cruises last more than a week. For a well-known, amusing illustration of what a distant place seems like mentally, see Figure I-5.

Other Map Considerations

Several other map-related components have an impact on a travel professional's sales experience.

Hemispheres. Everything north of the equator is called the **Northern Hemisphere**, and everything south, the **Southern Hemisphere** (see Figure I-6). Seasons in the Northern Hemisphere are familiar to us: January comes in winter, and July in summer. But in the Southern Hemisphere, January has summer

Figure I-5 A Perspective

weather, July, winter weather. When selling clients a Southern Hemisphere destination, keep these reversed seasons in mind. Remember, too, that the world is also often divided into a **Western Hemisphere** (North and South America) and an **Eastern Hemisphere** (everything else).

Latitude. Latitude is the distance measured north and south of the equator (expressed in standard geography as degrees). The farther away from the equator your destination, the greater the variations will be between seasonal temperatures and between hours of night and day.

For example, Point Barrow, a north-shore Alaskan town at a **polar latitude**, is an intriguing destination for clients in June and July. Why? Because it's when temperatures there are warmest and daylight is longest. Indeed, the summer midnight sun is a unique attraction. But December and January would be a terrible time for a Point Barrow visit, for darkness and bitter cold prevail. Remember that these seasonal days are exactly the opposite in the Southern Hemisphere: A trip to Antarctica, an exotic and increasingly popular journey, would be best in December or January, worst in June or July.

As one gets closer to the equator, seasonal and daylight differences become less pronounced. For instance, Nairobi, Kenya (in Africa), sits just south of the equator. Unlike Point Barrow, where the average temperatures fluctuate more than seventy degrees between summer and winter, Nairobi—at a **tropical latitude**—sees a yearly fluctuation of only about eight degrees and minimal variation of daylight. Areas between tropical and polar latitudes are called **temperate latitudes** and have neither pronounced nor minimal variations. Because of the absence of extremes, most major industrialized nations lie within this temperate zone.

By the way, most maps represent latitude lines (also known as parallels) as horizontal lines, measured in degrees. A good memory trick: LATitude lines are FLAT.

Longitude. Longitude is the distance east and west of an arbitrary line, called the prime meridian, that passes through the Old Royal Observatory in Greenwich, England. Represented as vertical lines on most maps, longitude lines

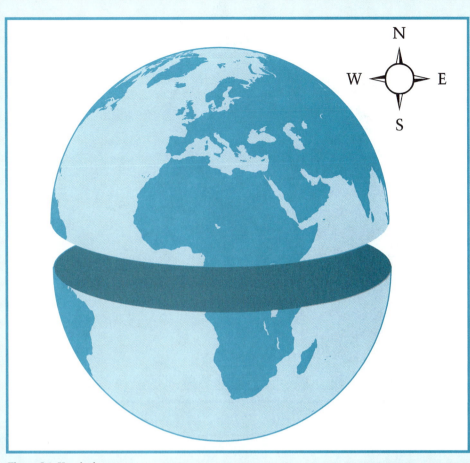

Figure I-6 Hemispheres

(like latitudes) are measured in degrees. Longitude will have less of an impact on your selling destinations, except in one respect: Time zones tend to parallel longitude lines (also known as meridians). Before the late 1800s, each city had its own time determined by the sun-caused shadows on a sundial. Railroads found it next to impossible to create accurate schedules or timetables. So, in 1884, the world's major nations agreed to create twenty-four standard time zones, each extending over about 15 degrees of longitude (see Figure I-7). Because the prime meridian is located there, Greenwich, England, became the reference point. If it's 1 P.M. in Greenwich, it's five hours earlier, that is, 8 A.M., in Washington, D.C. (expressed as −5); conversely, in Tokyo, it's 10 P.M. (expressed as +9).

Time zones aren't all that regular. For example, China—even though it extends through four theoretical time zones—observes only one time, that closest to Beijing, the capital. In other places, the zone's boundaries zig and zag around cities, islands, lakes, or mountains. India should have two time zones but has averaged the two together. Instead of being, say, two o'clock in the west and three o'clock in the east, it's *two-thirty* across the entire country. Daylight savings time, when clocks are set forward to extend daylight into evening hours, complicates things even more. (Arizona, Hawaii, and parts of Indiana don't even observe daylight savings time.)

A trip that crosses many time zones creates that tired feeling called **jet lag** and could affect your client in many other ways. A flight from Los Angeles to Miami takes about five hours, but the passenger, because of the time zones, arrives at a time that's about eight hours later. For example, a passenger leaving Los Angeles at noon flies five hours and arrives at 8 P.M., Miami time. So it's best to book clients on an eastward transcontinental flight for a morning departure; otherwise,

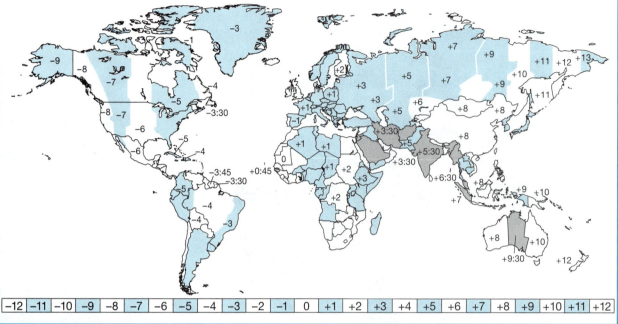

Figure I-7 Time Zones

they'll arrive at their destination late in the evening. For westbound travel, the problem is less serious: A client leaving Miami for Los Angeles could leave at 1:30 P.M., fly for about five hours, yet arrive at 3:30 P.M., Los Angeles time. Because it stretches out their workday, many business clients count on this.

The International Date Line.   A rather challenging bit of time zone figuring involves the international date line, a vertical zigzagging line that bisects the Pacific Ocean (see Figure I-8). Crossing it requires a bit of complicated thinking, usually expressed as gaining a day or losing a day. Remember the following, and you won't be bewildered: (1) When a client crosses the line traveling westward, the day changes to the next day—Tuesday immediately becomes Wednesday, for example, and (2) when a client crosses the line traveling eastward, the day changes to the previous day—Thursday becomes Wednesday, for example. The time of the day (except at midnight) means nothing. A client could cross at 2 P.M., 7 A.M., or 10 A.M. It's all the same. The day changes (but the hour remains the same).

Let's look at an example. If you booked clients to travel from Honolulu westward to Tokyo on a Monday morning departure, they would arrive after about a nine-hour flight. But it would be Tuesday, because they crossed the date line. In turn, if they flew from Tokyo on a Saturday morning, they would arrive in Honolulu on Friday, again because they crossed the date line, this time west to east.

Because the flight is long and many time zones are crossed, the complications can be even greater. If you were to leave Honolulu for Tokyo at 11 P.M. on Wednesday, it would become Thursday an hour after departure, and you haven't even crossed the date line yet. A little later, you would cross the date line on Thursday, at which point it would become Friday! So, you left on Wednesday and arrived on Friday, even though you flew only nine hours.

Confused? Don't worry. Airline schedules give arrival times that are already adjusted for time-zone crossings and for lost or gained days (indicated by some sort of code). You won't have to do the complicated equations. But *do* make sure

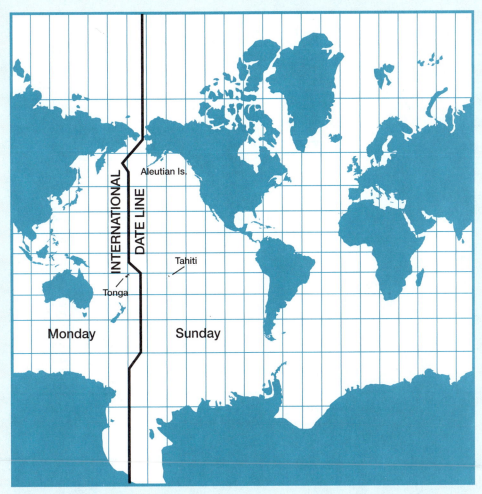

Figure I-8 International Date Line

that you know which day a client will be arriving, or you may book his or her hotel stay for the wrong day.

Elapsed Flying Time and the Twenty-Four Hour Clock.   One thing clients often ask about that's not always given in airline timetables: How long will a flight take? First, you must understand that time in the travel business is often expressed as a four-digit number: 7:00 A.M. is 0700, 11:25 A.M. is 1125, noon is 1200. Afternoon continues up to the digit 24: 1:00 P.M. is 1300, 7:30 P.M. is 1930, midnight is 2400.

To figure out elapsed flying time, simply subtract the departure time of a flight from the arrival time, as long as no time zones are crossed. If a flight leaves Paris at 0800 and arrives in Lyon at 0900, the flight took one hour. If a plane leaves San Diego at 1520 and lands in San Francisco at 1645, the flight took one hour, twenty-five minutes.

What happens when time zones are crossed? Then it gets a bit more difficult. Many travel reference books give charts that enable you to figure out complex, elapsed flying-time problems. Fortunately, airline reservation systems compute elapsed flying time automatically.

Landforms

All destinations you sell relate, in some way, to a landform. Let's now look at the principal landforms and how they're linked to the destinations you'll sell.

Continents.   Continents are the major land masses of the earth (see Figure I-9). There are seven continents. You'll likely deal most with **North America** and

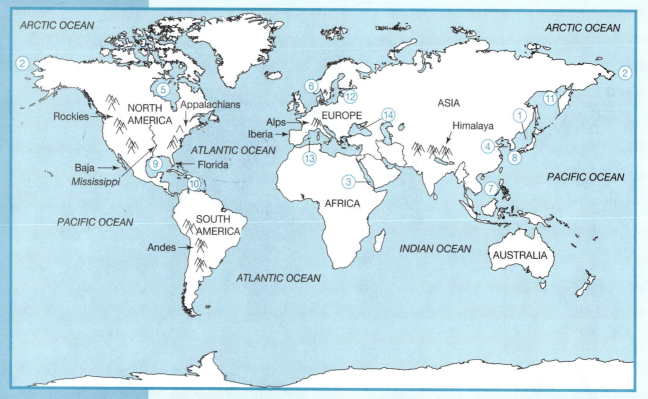

Figure I-9 Landforms and Waterways of the World: 1—Sea of Japan; 2—Bering Sea; 3—Red Sea; 4—Yellow Sea; 5—Hudson Bay; 6—North Sea; 7—South China Sea; 8—East China Sea; 9—Gulf of Mexico; 10—Caribbean; 11—Sea of Okhotsk; 12—Baltic Sea; 13—Mediterranean Sea; 14—Black Sea.

Europe, but **Asia**, **Australia**, **South America**, and **Africa** all boast destinations you may someday sell. Even **Antarctica** has become a destination for tourists via cruises from Chile, Argentina, South Africa, and New Zealand.

Islands.   Because of their natural, isolated beauty, islands are often major destinations. Thousands of them cover the earth, but the most popular groupings are found in the **Caribbean**, the **Mediterranean** (especially southeast of Greece), and throughout the **Pacific** (see Figure I-9).

Cays.   Also called keys, cays are sandy coral islands that are low and small. Examples: the **Cayman Islands** and the **Florida Keys**. Atolls are also small coral islands, but they're usually ringlike and partially or totally enclose a lagoon.

Peninsulas and Capes.   These are both projections of land into the water. Generally, peninsulas are longer than capes. Among the peninsulas that are popular destinations are **Baja**, Mexico; the **Iberian Peninsula** (which contains Spain and Portugal); and **Florida**. Some touristically important capes are **Cape Cod**, Massachusetts; and **Cape Canaveral**, Florida (see Figure I-9).

Reefs.   Reefs are ridges of land that rise to or near the surface of water. They are often found just offshore. Composed of sand, rock, and coral, reefs can offer superb diving opportunities. Major reef-diving and snorkeling areas lie off Australia's northeast coast; off the east coasts of Africa and Brazil; and throughout the Caribbean, the South Pacific, Indonesia, and the Philippines.

Mountains

Mountains profoundly affect travel. Their dramatic beauty impresses virtually every kind of client. Their snow-covered slopes attract skiers. Their forbidding heights can make travel slow and indirect. And volcanic mountains often put on quite a show (and pose an ever-present danger).

Figure I-10 Tropical Island Wind Patterns

Mountains also affect climate. When moisture-bearing winds strike a mountain, precipitation often results at its peak and on its **windward** side. On the opposite side of the mountain, the **leeward** side, it's often much drier (see Figure I-10). For example, the winds that strike the Hawaiian Islands, and their volcanic peaks, generally come from the east and northeast. As a result, they create clouds, rain, and strong waves on the windward shores. On the other hand, most Hawaiian beach resorts are along the islands' western and southwestern shores, where it's most likely to be sunny. Another example: The westerly winds that flow into the Pacific Northwest often bring clouds and rains to Seattle and Vancouver—both of which are on the windward side of the Cascade Mountain Range. The area just east of these mountains (the leeward side) is more dry and sunny.

There are all kinds of mountains: rugged ones, like North America's **Rockies**, Europe's **Alps**, South America's **Andes**, and Asia's **Himalaya**; old, worndown ones, like the U.S. East Coast's **Appalachians**; and volcanic ones, like those of Hawaii, the Caribbean, Iceland, Central Africa, Japan and, the most volcanic nation of all: Indonesia.

Closely allied to the concept of a mountain is that of a **plateau**. A plateau is a broad, flat area that rises above the surrounding land and, because of its elevation, typically has cooler weather. (Mexico City is a prime example.) **Mesas** are smaller, steeper-sided versions of plateaus; **buttes** are even smaller, towerlike versions. The dramatic mesas and buttes of the American Southwest attract many tourists to that region's national parks.

Bodies of Water

Stop and think: Can you name one popular destination that's *not* near water? Not easy, is it? The vast majority of the places you'll sell are near bodies of water.

Gulfs.   Gulfs are large areas of ocean that penetrate into land. A good example is the **Gulf of Mexico**. **Bays** are similar to gulfs but generally smaller and less enclosed by land; **Chesapeake Bay**, in Virginia and Maryland, is an example. **Fjords** [FE-OHRDZ] are also inlets from the ocean or the sea; they are usually long, narrow, and lined with steep cliffs. The most dramatic ones notch into the coastlines of Norway, New Zealand, Chile, and Argentina.

Figure I-11 The *Spirit of '98* ship cruising through a fjord, Alaska
Courtesy of Alaska Sightseeing/Cruise West

Tourist sites are often associated with gulfs, bays and fjords: Beach resorts line the Gulf of Mexico's shores, and ships commonly cruise through the fjords of Norway.

Rivers. Rivers provide significant cruise opportunities for you to sell. Currently, the most popular are North America's **Mississippi**, Europe's **Rhine** and **Danube**, Africa's **Nile**, and for the more adventurous, South America's **Amazon**. A **glacier** is a sort of "river" of solid ice that flows very slowly across near-polar regions and eventually can tumble into the water, creating icebergs. Glaciers are often imposing tourist attractions, most notably in Alaska, Canada, Switzerland, Peru, and New Zealand. (When a mass of ice sits, like a lake, over a broad area, it's called an **ice sheet** or **ice field**.)

Waterfalls. These dramatic cascades of water are magnets for tourists. Both **Niagara Falls** and Germany's **Rhine Falls** have been major attractions for centuries, while more remote ones—such as South America's **Iguazu Falls** and Africa's **Victoria Falls**—are becoming increasingly popular destinations.

Seas. Seas are large bodies of water, usually salty but sometimes fresh. They can be a region of water within an ocean, but usually some sort of land boundaries, such as islands or continental shoreline, partly or almost fully enclose a sea. Like gulfs, seas are often the site of resorts, cruises, and water-sport activities. Geographers count more than fifty seas. Among those most associated with tourism are the **Caribbean** and the **Mediterranean**.

Lakes.   Lakes are smaller than seas, are usually fresh, and are mostly or fully encircled by land. They, too, often feature resort and recreation facilities. A few large, saltwater lakes have been labeled seas, like the **Caspian Sea** and the **Dead Sea**.

Lagoons.   These are shallow bodies of water, generally situated in tropical areas and separated from the ocean by reefs or atolls.

Bayous.   Bayous are marshy or swampy areas. Those in Louisiana have become tourist attractions.

Deltas.   Deltas are the low, V-shaped areas at the mouths of rivers. Many important port cities, such as New Orleans, Louisiana, and Alexandria, Egypt, are located at deltas.

Geysers.   Geysers are jets of steaming water that shoot high into the air. New Zealand, Iceland, and (in the United States) Yellowstone Park have geysers that are tourist attractions.

Springs.   Springs occur where water flows naturally to the earth's surface. European spa resorts are often located near springs.

Oceans.   These are the greatest bodies of water. There are four oceans: the **Atlantic**, the **Pacific**, the **Indian**, and the **Arctic** (see Figure I-9). Ocean water sports, whether off a continental area (such as Florida) or around an island (such as Tahiti), attract many tourists.

One thing that's useful to those who sell travel is how to predict ocean water temperatures. This information can't be found in popular reference books, yet clients who look forward to swimming ask about it all the time. Three factors determine ocean water temperature at resort areas: season, latitude (the nearer the equator, the warmer the ocean is likely to be), and ocean currents. This last factor is one of the hardest to predict. Yet knowing something about the **Coriolis effect** will help you make that prediction with greater confidence.

The Coriolis effect, among other things, makes oceans circulate in a clockwise fashion in the Northern Hemisphere and a counterclockwise manner in the Southern Hemisphere. The resulting currents enable water to pick up heat at the equator and carry it along; conversely, in the polar regions, the currents chill down and carry cold water away for some distance. If you look at Figure I-12, you'll

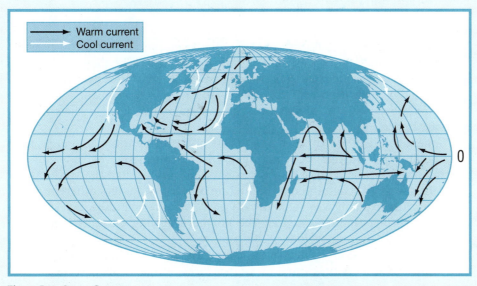

Figure I-12 Ocean Currents

Figure I-13 Old Faithful Geyser, Yellowstone National Park, Wyoming
Photo by C. J. Ghormley

see why ocean water off California is surprisingly cool, yet along the southeastern U.S. coast, it's comparatively warm. A significant variation: The shape of the north Atlantic permits warm water to flow along a **Gulf Stream** from near the equator all the way to Great Britain. (That's one reason why London in the winter only occasionally gets really cold, while parts of Alaska and Canada, at the same latitude, are frozen.)

Generally, ocean water on the east coast of a continent tends to be warmer than ocean water on the west coast of that same continent. The water off, say, Australia's eastern Gold Coast resort area is much warmer than that off Perth, on Australia's western coast, though the two are only a few degrees different in latitude. That also explains why the water off the Galapagos Islands (which sit on the equator) is cooler than you expect. The northern-flowing currents carry water from the frigid Antarctic region.

Does the Coriolis effect determine temperatures in smaller bodies of water? Not really. The water temperatures of, say, the Mediterranean, are governed almost exclusively by the seasons. Its water is chilly in the winter, but sunlight heats it up rapidly as summer approaches.

Two facts also worth knowing: 1) Seacoast locations have fewer extremes of temperature than those farther inland; 2) regions that border cool ocean currents (for example, Southern California) tend to be dryer than those along warmer ocean waters (for example, Florida).

Winds

Winds are among the most unpredictable of the geographically related events. If you've ever sailed a boat, you know that firsthand. But there are general earth-wide patterns, especially for the prevailing winds that stream above the capricious surface breezes (see Figure I-14). Following are some of the major wind flows that affect the destinations you sell.

The Westerlies. The westerlies are winds that tend to blow around the globe from west to east, in temperate areas between 30 and 60 degrees latitude, both in the Northern and Southern Hemispheres. The United States, Canada, and Europe lie within this belt. Now you know why weather maps on the evening news display weather flowing from west to east.

How do the westerlies affect travel? First, the high-altitude, high-velocity core of these westerlies, the **jet stream**, is responsible for making east-to-west flights take longer. (A flight from New York to San Francisco, for example, takes at least thirty minutes longer than one from San Francisco to New York.) Second, western coastal regions, mostly within a 40-degree-to-60-degree belt tend to be rainier than the eastern coastal regions, especially where mountains are involved. Some examples of regions with rainy west coasts: Oregon, Washington State, British Columbia, the Alaskan Panhandle, southern Chile, Ireland, Portugal, Croatia, and New Zealand.

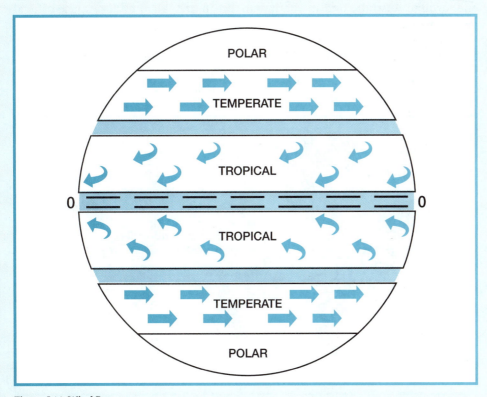

Figure I-14 Wind Patterns

Terrain, ocean temperatures, seasons, and many other factors conspire to create many exceptions to the above. To determine the rainfall patterns for key destinations, consult the "Climate at a Glance" charts that are sprinkled throughout the book.

The Trade Winds.   The trade winds are humid breezes that tend to flow from east to west. These winds are most pronounced in the tropical band between about 25 degrees north and 25 degrees south. There is also some slight trade-wind shifting that can occur, depending on the hemisphere. North of the equator, trade winds often come from the northeast instead of the east, and south of the equator, they frequently come from the southeast. For complicated reasons, much of Africa and some tropical parts of Asia (especially India) don't follow the east-to-west trade-wind pattern. But it does hold for Central and South America, for a good part of Australia, and especially for tropical islands.

When a tropical island is mountainous, the western coast is almost always leeward and therefore drier. This is where you should lodge your clients (see Figure I-10). Because there are no mountains to squeeze out the rain from the trade winds, flat islands are usually breezy and relatively dry. (A good example is Aruba, a flat coral island in the Caribbean.)

Storms

Storms often disrupt your clients' travel plans. Sometimes you can know when they're more likely to occur and thus recommend to your clients the best time to travel to certain destinations.

Hurricanes.   Hurricanes are among the most violent of storms. Usually born near the equator, hurricanes migrate in rather unpredictable patterns (see Figure I-15). They can cover hundreds of square miles with high winds (74 mph or above) and heavy rains for a day or two in one place before moving on. When they're born near the Caribbean or Mexico, they're called hurricanes; when they originate in the western Pacific, they're called **typhoons**; the southward-heading ones around Australia and in the Indian Ocean are called **cyclones**, the official generic name for all such storms.

Hurricanes generally occur from June to November in the Northern Hemisphere, with about 80 percent of them coming in August, September, and

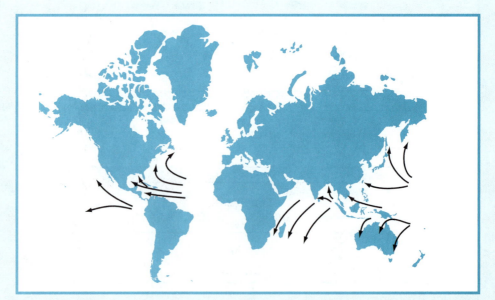

Figure I-15 Hurricane Areas

October. (Of course, hurricane season brings not only the chance of vacation-damaging storms, but also bargain rates.) Cyclones almost never affect Europe, South America (except occasionally on its Caribbean shoreline), Africa (except for the region around Madagascar and Mozambique), or the western coast of the United States and Canada. Hurricanes also rarely maintain strength if they move far inland over a continent; instead, they degenerate into large rainstorms.

Monsoons.   Each year around summertime, in certain parts of the world, winds reverse in such a way as to cause a lengthy, distinct, and heavy rainy season. This monsoon condition can dampen any client's trip. India has torrential monsoon rains from June to September; China's less intense season comes from May to September; and Korea sees quite a bit of rain in July and August. Northern Australia, Indonesia, and Singapore have monsoon-like conditions from December through March, whereas the south-facing parts of west Africa have a monsoon weather pattern from May to October.

Cloudbursts.   Cloudbursts are heavy showers that occur suddenly. They're a major factor in the tropics. A typical pattern is for the morning to be sunny, the afternoon to be partly cloudy, and for a heavy downpour to occur in the late afternoon or early evening. Clients bound for tropical destinations should be warned to start the day as early as possible if they want to avoid the possibility of getting wet.

Other Aspects of Climate

There's a saying among meteorologists: "Climate is what you expect, weather is what you get." That does point out an important distinction: *Weather* refers to what's going on in the atmosphere at a given time and place; *climate* refers to the weather that prevails typically in a region at a certain time of the year. When you tell your clients that Acapulco is usually warm, dry, and sunny in January, you're talking about climate. When they return to tell you that it rained and was chilly for three of the seven days they were down there, they're talking about the weather.

Travel professionals can't be expected to predict the weather. But they should know what climate will prevail. Climate is a critical client concern; knowledge of it can help to clinch a satisfying sale. Here are three facts you should keep in mind:

- **The higher a destination is, the cooler it will be.** Mexico City, which sits on a plateau, reaches an average high of only 73 degrees in July, whereas Manzanillo, a Mexican beach resort at virtually the same latitude (but at sea level) is typically in the high 80s in the same month. In a more extreme example, it can be snowing at Lake Arrowhead, a California mountain resort at a high altitude, while twenty miles away, at a much lower altitude in Palm Springs, vacationers are baking by their hotel pools.

- **The windier it is, the colder it will feel.** It could be 20 degrees Fahrenheit in Moscow, but if it's not windy, the climate won't feel too uncomfortable. But if it's 40 degrees and the wind is whipping, it'll seem much colder. On the other hand, windy days can also be helpful to clients. The trade winds in Hawaii can make an 85-degree day feel absolutely wonderful.

- **When arranging a flight in which a stop or connection is involved, consider what the climate at the stopover city will be.** If it's a January itinerary, it might, if practical, be advisable to connect via a warm-weather city, such as Phoenix, Dallas, or Atlanta, rather than via Denver, Minneapolis, or Chicago, where winter weather could interfere with jet travel. Conversely, in August, northerly cities may make better stopovers than southerly ones, where thunderstorms are more common.

Two other important points about determining the climate bear mentioning. First, any climate tables or graphs you use should be studied carefully. Do they give rainfall in inches, as do those in this book? Do they list days with rain or days with no rain? Are temperatures given as average highs and lows, record highs and lows, or as the average of the entire day? Second, make sure you find out if temperatures are measured in Fahrenheit (used in the United States) or in Celsius (used in most other countries).

Just for the record, to convert Celsius to Fahrenheit, multiply the Celsius number by 9, divide by 5, and add 32. Or, to simplify things, memorize the following: 30°C is hot (86°F), 22°C is pleasant (72°F), 15°C is chilly (59°F), and 0°C is freezing (32°F). That way you can gauge most other Celsius temperatures by comparison.

Human Geography

Most of what you've read in this chapter has to do with **physical geography**, the study of the earth's land, air, and water. But studying the peoples of the earth, an equally noble discipline, is usually called **human** or **cultural geography**. Religion, food, politics, language, national boundaries, art, agriculture, economics, and even history all in some way affect geography. In the chapters that follow, we often bring up one or more of these considerations, for tourism is, after all, an activity of people, not of rocks or ocean currents.

One part of human geography that may bear some scrutiny right now is touristic patterns. People want to go to places because of many reasons; climate, vacation time, and school holidays seem to be the largest determining factors. When tourism is buzzing in a place, it's called **high** or **peak season**. (It's also the most expensive season.) When tourists are fewest, it's called **low** or **off season**. (Real vacation bargains can also be had.) And times in between, when neither a great many people nor a very few people are visiting, are called **shoulder seasons**.

In most places, fall and spring are shoulder seasons; some of the most satisfying vacations take place during shoulder season because the weather may be very good, rates aren't at their highest, and crowds are seldom seen. In temperate or arctic regions, high season usually takes place in the summer, but tropical resorts peak in winter (with all those travelers wanting to get away from the cold). Conversely, for temperate and arctic areas, winter is the low season. One exception: ski resorts, which thrive at this time.

Holidays also profoundly affect travel patterns. In most countries, people don't like to take regular vacations during family holidays, such as Thanksgiving, Passover, or Christmas. (They do like to fly to stay with families around these times. The result: Air fares are high, but hotels are usually empty and offering bargains.) One other interesting pattern: Travel falls sharply a few days after New Year's Day; January is bargain month in many places. But other holidays, such as the U.S. Fourth of July or Japan's Golden Week (April 29 to May 5), set off massive peaks of tourism. Most French and Italians leave their cities en masse in August for Riviera or Alpine vacations; thus, a sort of shoulder season exists in Paris and Rome at summer's end—when most business travel halts and when almost only foreign tourists are left to stay in these cities' hotels.

Make sure to consult each chapter's "Climate at a Glance" chart. These charts show, in detail, what a destination's tourism patterns are, in addition to its climate.

One final—and odd—factor that affects tourism profoundly: the **"event" effect**. An event—either positive or negative—can create a strong, often disproportionate impact over a wide geographic area, and for a long time. Negative events produce the most dramatic (and often irrational) effects. The 1991 Gulf War wiped out tourism in Egypt, Morocco, even Europe, though all three places were hundreds, even a thousand miles away. The 1989 San Francisco earthquake reduced tourism for months across all of California. The 1993 flooding of the Mississippi dampened tourism in places hundreds of miles from any water. And much of this is attributable to one factor we've discussed throughout this chapter: the public's misunderstanding of geography.

Fortunately, the event effect can also be positive: The Olympics, a world's fair, or the Super Bowl can enhance tourism for years, not only at its venue city, but also for the entire state or country.

Reference Tools

The twenty-nine chapters that follow focus more precisely on the most popular places clients want to visit. But even if you memorize every word in this book, there will be times when someone asks a question that you can't answer. For the most useful reference tools that you can go to for the sticky questions, be sure to consult Appendix C of this book.

Summary

Here's a summary of the most important sales-enhancing geographic facts in this chapter:

- Think "curved line" when you're deciding what route or airline to put your clients on for a long flight.
- Seasons in the Southern Hemisphere are the reverse of those in the Northern Hemisphere.
- If a client crosses the international date line from east to west, it becomes the following day; from west to east, it becomes the previous day.
- Winds called the *westerlies* flow west to east in most temperate parts of the globe, affecting weather and jet travel time.
- The trade winds flow more or less from east to west in the tropics.
- Mountainous tropical islands are usually drier on the western coast.
- Ocean water on the east side of a continent tends to be warmer than ocean water at the same latitude on the west side.
- Hurricane (cyclone) season in most places peaks in August, September, and October.
- Areas with monsoon conditions usually get rain during their summer season.
- The higher (in altitude) a destination is, the cooler it will be.

Travel Trivia

Things Geographers Don't Agree On

- Which is the world's longest river, the Nile or the Amazon
- Whether Australia is an island or a continent
- Whether the world's highest mountain should be measured from sea level (it would be Mt. Everest) or from the ocean bottom (it would be Mauna Kea, Hawaii)
- What exactly is the difference between a lake, a sea, and a gulf
- Whether Europe and Asia form one continent or two
- What distinguishes a cape from a peninsula

Activity 1: Qualifying the Client

Based on your current knowledge of geography, name one place, anywhere in the world, that you think might appeal to the client-type named below:

TYPE	PLACE	TYPE	PLACE
1. History buff	——————	7. Adventure-seeker	——————
2. Culture-seeker	——————	8. Entertainment-seeker	——————
3. Ethnic traveler	——————	9. Shopper	——————
4. Religious pilgrim	——————	10. Sensual traveler	——————
5. Environmental traveler	——————	11. Status-seeker	——————
6. Recreational traveler	——————	12. Business traveler in the garment industry	——————

Turn back to page 4 to continue with the sales portion of the text.

Activity 2: Reading a Hotel Locator Map

Study the locator map of Downtown Chicago, then answer the following questions:

1. Which museum is at I-6 on the map?

2. Your client has business at the Sears Tower. Which hotel is closest to it, Sheraton Chicago or Allegro Hotel?

3. It seems easier to lodge clients near which of the following: the University of Illinois or Northwestern University?

4. Your client will be driving from the Hyatt Regency to Milwaukee, a city to the north. Which street and highways will he or she have to take?

5. Your client wants to see the famous Water Tower. At which map coordinates is it?

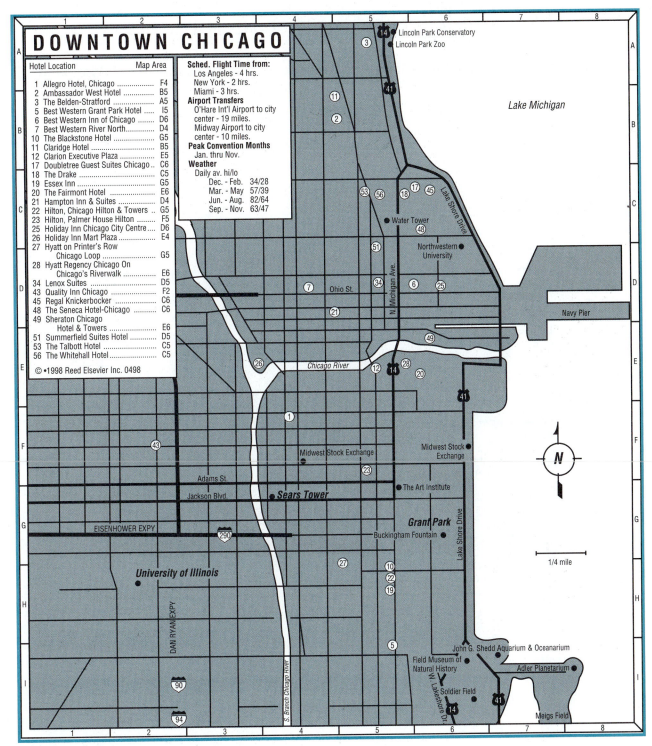

DOWNTOWN CHICAGO

Hotel Location	Map Area
1 Allegro Hotel, Chicago	F4
2 Ambassador West Hotel	B5
3 The Belden-Stratford	A5
5 Best Western Grant Park Hotel	I5
6 Best Western Inn of Chicago	D6
7 Best Western River North	D4
10 The Blackstone Hotel	G5
11 Claridge Hotel	B5
12 Clarion Executive Plaza	E5
17 Doubletree Guest Suites Chicago	C6
18 The Drake	C5
19 Essex Inn	G5
20 The Fairmont Hotel	E6
21 Hampton Inn & Suites	D4
22 Hilton, Chicago Hilton & Towers	G5
23 Hilton, Palmer House Hilton	F5
25 Holiday Inn Chicago City Centre	D6
26 Holiday Inn Mart Plaza	E4
27 Hyatt on Printer's Row Chicago Loop	G5
28 Hyatt Regency Chicago On Chicago's Riverwalk	E6
34 Lenox Suites	D5
43 Quality Inn Chicago	F2
45 Regal Knickerbocker	C6
48 The Seneca Hotel-Chicago	C6
49 Sheraton Chicago Hotel & Towers	E6
51 Summerfield Suites Hotel	D5
53 The Talbott Hotel	C5
56 The Whitehall Hotel	C5

© •1998 Reed Elsevier Inc. 0498

Sched. Flight Time from:
Los Angeles - 4 hrs.
New York - 2 hrs.
Miami - 3 hrs.
Airport Transfers
O'Hare Int'l Airport to city center - 19 miles.
Midway Airport to city center - 10 miles.
Peak Convention Months
Jan. thru Nov.
Weather
Daily av. hi/lo
Dec. - Feb.   34/28
Mar. - May   57/39
Jun. - Aug.   82/64
Sep. - Nov.   63/47

Source: Hotel and Travel Index/Reed Travel Group

Activity 3: Identifying Geographic Features

Below is a rendition of an imaginary tropical island in the Pacific. Letters identify the various geographic features. Match the features with the letter.

1. A peninsula: ———

2. The coolest area: ———

3. A bay: ———

4. A rainier, windward area: ———

5. A cape: ———

6. A dry, leeward area: ———

7. A lake: ———

8. A coral reef: ———

9. A river: ———

10. A fjord-like feature: ———

Activity 4: Reading Climate at a Glance Charts

Examine the four charts on the next two pages, then answer the following questions:

1. Which season would probably provide the best overall weather for a business traveler to visit Calcutta?

2. Which of the four cities has the widest range between summer and winter temperatures?

3. Without looking at a map, determine which of the cities is clearly a Southern Hemisphere destination.

4. Which of the cities has the *least* monthly variation in rainfall?

5. Without looking at a map, which of these four cities would probably be closest to the equator?

6. In which month does Melbourne have its coolest temperatures?

7. Which city is the most likely to have snow in the winter?

8. Which two cities seem to have the greatest variation between daytime and nighttime temperatures?

9. What factor probably accounts for Quito's relatively low temperatures?

10. In one of these cities, it goes down to around 15°C at night in February. Which city is it?

11. What probably accounts for Calcutta's off-season for tourists?

12. Which month in Chicago will probably provide the best weather and temperatures without hordes of tourists?

Climate at a Glance
CALCUTTA, INDIA

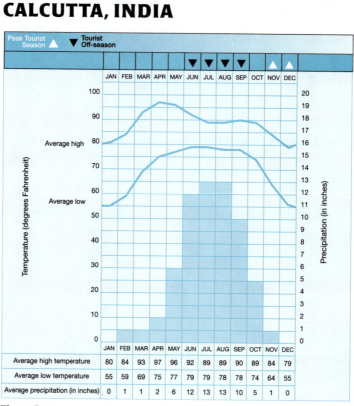

	JAN	FEB	MAR	APR	MAY	JUN	JUL	AUG	SEP	OCT	NOV	DEC
Average high temperature	80	84	93	97	96	92	89	89	90	89	84	79
Average low temperature	55	59	69	75	77	79	79	78	78	74	64	55
Average precipitation (in inches)	0	1	1	2	6	12	13	13	10	5	1	0

Figure I-18

Climate at a Glance
QUITO, ECUADOR

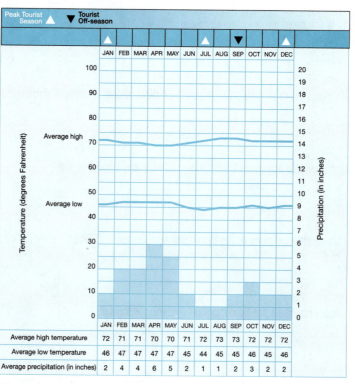

	JAN	FEB	MAR	APR	MAY	JUN	JUL	AUG	SEP	OCT	NOV	DEC
Average high temperature	72	71	71	70	70	71	72	73	73	72	72	72
Average low temperature	46	47	47	47	47	45	44	45	45	46	45	46
Average precipitation (in inches)	2	4	4	6	5	2	1	1	2	3	2	2

Figure I-19

Climate at a Glance
MELBOURNE, AUSTRALIA

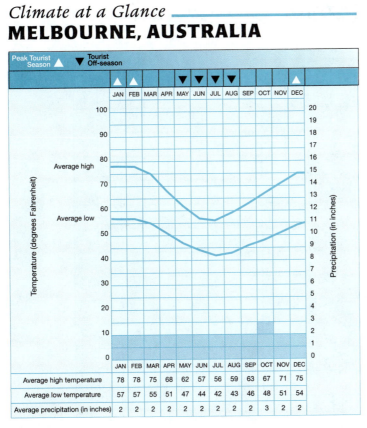

	JAN	FEB	MAR	APR	MAY	JUN	JUL	AUG	SEP	OCT	NOV	DEC
Average high temperature	78	78	75	68	62	57	56	59	63	67	71	75
Average low temperature	57	57	55	51	47	44	42	43	46	48	51	54
Average precipitation (in inches)	2	2	2	2	2	2	2	2	2	3	2	2

Figure I-20

Climate at a Glance
CHICAGO, ILLINOIS

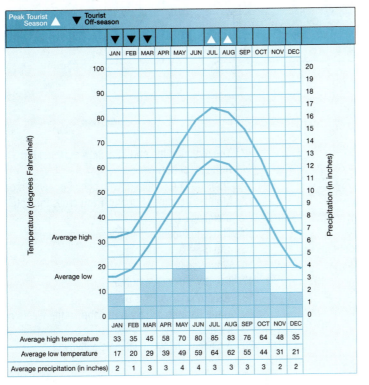

	JAN	FEB	MAR	APR	MAY	JUN	JUL	AUG	SEP	OCT	NOV	DEC
Average high temperature	33	35	45	58	70	80	85	83	76	64	48	35
Average low temperature	17	20	29	39	49	59	64	62	55	44	31	21
Average precipitation (in inches)	2	1	3	3	4	4	3	3	3	3	2	2

Figure I-21

Activity 5: A Geographic Crossword Puzzle

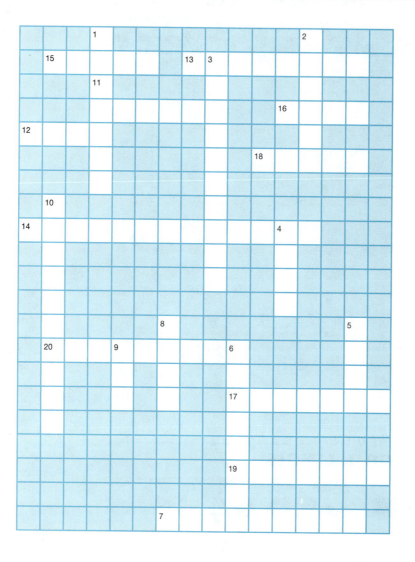

Down

1. A map with an A, B, C, 1, 2, 3 grid.
2. A state without daylight savings time.
3. The least-visited continent.
4. A European mountain range.
5. The number of oceans in the world.
6. The Gulf Stream is in the . . .
7. Thirty-two degrees Fahrenheit equals . . . degrees Celsius.
8. A hotel reference book.
9. A hotel reference book.
10. Tropical winds.

Across

7. The direction the north Pacific's currents turn.
11. A month of hurricanes.
12. The side of a continent with cooler ocean temperatures.
13. Monday becomes Sunday if you cross the date line traveling . . .
14. The longitude line that passes near London.
15. The most accurate map.
16. What Cod is.
17. The dry side of a mountain.
18. You cruise down this river.
19. In the Caribbean it's a hurricane; in the western Pacific it's a . . .
20. A place with lots of volcanic activity.

Activity 6: Putting It All Together

Examine the world map below, then answer the questions by giving the letter or location on the map. You may use each letter only once; there will be some letters you won't use.

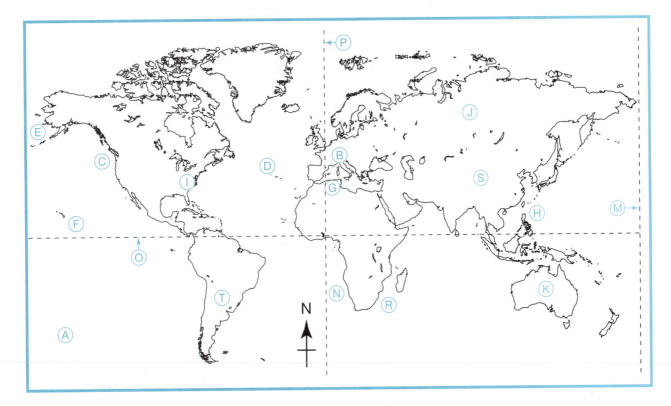

———— 1. An area that, because of prevailing winds, has high rainfall.

———— 2. An ocean where currents flow counterclockwise.

———— 3. An area with many typhoons in the summer.

———— 4. Cross it, and the day changes.

———— 5. The most popular overseas continent for North American travelers.

———— 6. An African coast that has cool ocean water temperatures.

———— 7. The country with the most time zones.

———— 8. An area a jet would cross if flying from Seattle to Japan.

———— 9. A continent that has winter in July and has a cyclone season.

———— 10. A place where prevailing winds typically come from the east.

Canda → Province
USA → states

GREENLAND

BEAUFORT SEA

BAFFIN BAY

Alaska Range

LABRADOR SEA

CANADA

HUDSON BAY

Provinces

Pacific Northwest

Lake Superior

St. Lawrence River

Rocky Mountains

Missouri River

Columbia River

Lake Huron

Cascade Range

Great Salt Lake

Lake Ontario

STATES

Appalachian Mountains

PACIFIC OCEAN

Sierra Nevada

Lake Michigan

Lake Erie

Lake Mead

Lake Powell

Mississippi River

ATLANTIC OCEAN

Grand Canyon

UNITED STATES

Colorado River

Rio Grande

→lake

GULF of CALIFORNIA

MEXICO

GULF of MEXICO

Everglades

Florida Keys

~islands

II

North America
Charm of the Familiar

Think you know North America? Then what U.S. city draws more visitors than any other? Where are the Thousand Islands? In what city is Disneyland located? Which region has the most thunderstorms yearly?

Maybe you knew the answers, maybe not. (The answers, in order: New York City; between upper New York State and southern Ontario; Anaheim; central Florida.) The important point is this: Many of your clients will have only the haziest of images about any destination beyond a few hundred miles of their home town. To make an effective sale, you'll have to bring those distant images into focus. And you, yourself, will need to know North America just about as well as you know your own backyard.

That yard probably extends farther than you think. Geographers define North America as everything from Canada to the Panama-Colombia border. That includes rarely-visited Greenland, the island-nations of the Caribbean, and many of the south-of-the-border countries, such as Mexico, Guatemala, El Salvador, Honduras, Nicaragua, Costa Rica, and Panama. (We'll treat these Caribbean and Latin American countries later, in Part III.) Greenland we'll say very little about, except that it's a self-governing territory of Denmark, its 839,999 square miles are mostly ice covered, it supports only 58,000 people, and it draws few tourists.

So, in this Part II of the text, we'll limit ourselves to Canada and the United States. And Hawaii is, of course, part of the United States, but it is treated toward the end of this book, in Part VI, Chapter 28. The reason: Hawaii is actually closer to Asia than to North America and certainly has much in common with the other islands of the Pacific (which are covered in Part VI).

Where the Regions Are

Take a look at a map of North America. Two states in the top-left corner of the U.S. make up the **Pacific Northwest: Washington** and **Oregon**. Above them, and separated from them by Canada, is **Alaska**. Below them are **California**, **Nevada**, **Utah**, **Arizona**, and **New Mexico**—often labeled the **Southwest**. (Occasionally, you'll hear of California, Nevada, Oregon, and Washington grouped as the **Far West**.)

The **Rocky Mountains** region is a buffer between the Pacific region and the middle of the United States. Though the precise states that make up the Rocky Mountain area are somewhat debatable—several of them qualify for inclusion under the Southwest and others as part of the Great Plains area—under this heading we include, from north to south, **Montana**, **Idaho**, **Wyoming**, and **Colorado**. **Texas**, the second largest state after Alaska, almost needs a category for itself, though it's often mentioned in

The United States spans six time zones.

the same breath with **Oklahoma**, which is just north of it. The flat agricultural area that stretches above Oklahoma is generally called the **Great Plains**. It's made up of, from north to south, **North Dakota**, **South Dakota**, **Nebraska**, and **Kansas**.

The **Midwest** encompasses many large states, including **Minnesota**, **Wisconsin**, **Michigan**, **Iowa**, **Illinois**, **Indiana**, **Missouri**, and **Ohio**. (Yes, many of these states are in the eastern half of the United States, but they still call themselves midwestern.) The **South** also covers a vast area. Its states are **Kentucky**, **Tennessee**, **North Carolina**, **Arkansas**, **Mississippi**, **Alabama**, **Georgia**, **South Carolina**, **Louisiana**, and **Florida**. **West Virginia** and **Virginia** are occasionally labeled southern; more frequently they're classified with the **Mid-Atlantic** states: **New York**, **New Jersey**, **Pennsylvania**, **Maryland**, and **Delaware**. And just between Maryland and Virginia is the **District of Columbia**, a "neutral" area that marks the nation's capital, **Washington, D.C.** Finally, **New England** nestles in the northeast corner of the United States. Its members are **Maine**, **Vermont**, **New Hampshire**, **Massachusetts**, **Connecticut**, and **Rhode Island**.

Canada consists of ten provinces and two territories (becoming three territories in 1999). We give more precise information about Canada in Chapter 6.

A Satellite View

Imagine you're in the space shuttle. You look down on North America. What do you see? A continent of sharp contrasts. From the flat plains of the Midwest to the worn peaks of the Appalachian Mountains or the barren deserts of the Southwest, the land offers crisp differences. Because these natural features (and other ones like lakes, rivers, and oceans) have such a strong impact on your client's travel plans, it's important to understand where and what they are.

Bodies of Water

Looking down from the space shuttle, you notice that the continent is flanked by two oceans: the **Atlantic Ocean** that lines the eastern shores, and the **Pacific Ocean** that laps against its western coast. Curving into Mexico and the U.S. southeastern border is the **Gulf of Mexico**; winds blowing over the Gulf help create the warm and often humid climate of that area. To the northeast, separating the United States from Canada, are the **Great Lakes: Lakes Superior**, **Michigan**, **Huron**, **Erie**, and **Ontario**. However, these lakes are primarily outlets for commerce rather than for tourism. Toward the western side of the continent is another noticeable body of water, the **Great Salt Lake**, and to the north are several huge lakes: **Great Bear**, **Great Slave**, and **Lake Winnipeg**. Dominating this northern region is huge **Hudson Bay**.

Look more closely, and you'll spot several major rivers. The **Mississippi River** divides the United States almost in half, starting up in Minnesota and traveling down through the Midwest and South to Louisiana, where it empties into the Gulf of Mexico. Even today, tourists can still take a riverboat trip past its historic riverfront towns. The **Missouri River** starts in Montana and passes through the Great Plains states, finally merging with the Mississippi River in Missouri. In the Southwest, the **Colorado River** winds from Colorado through Utah and forms part of the borders of Arizona, Nevada, and California; along the way, you'll see that it's been dammed, creating two lakes that are major recreation areas: **Lake Mead** in Nevada, and **Lake Powell** in Utah. The Colorado is also a popular rafting site for tourists. The **Rio Grande** marks off a large part of the country's southern border between Texas and Mexico. To the northwest, the **Columbia River** forms the border between Oregon and Washington. And, to the northeast, the St. Lawrence flows out of the Great Lakes toward the Atlantic.

Throughout North America, many smaller rivers and lakes add to the landscape. In New England and eastern Canada, numerous inlets dig into the coastline and are popular recreation centers. Swampy bayous cover much of Louisiana, as do those of the **Everglades** in Florida. And Florida's collection of islands off its southwest coast, the **Florida Keys**, is a major destination for tourists.

A unique way to cruise the Mississippi: the *R/B River Explorer*
Courtesy of RiverBarge Excursion Lines

Mountains

Three mountain ranges loom over the North American landscape. They have a major effect on climate, travel conditions, and skiing. The impressive scenery they offer is a major factor for tourists. The weathered **Appalachian Mountains**—prime camping and hiking areas—rise in Pennsylvania and continue southwesterly down through Maryland, West Virginia, Virginia, Tennessee, North Carolina, Kentucky, and end in northern Georgia. Other mountain ranges farther north, in New York, New England, Quebec, New Brunswick, and Newfoundland are popular summer tourist and winter skiing resorts. (Some geographers consider those northerly mountains an extension of the Appalachians.)

The **Rocky Mountains** run down the entire western length of North America, from Alaska to New Mexico, through Canada, Montana, Idaho, Wyoming, Colorado, Utah, and Arizona. One depression in the Rockies would be very noticeable from above: the cavernous **Grand Canyon** in Arizona. Stretching down the Pacific coast are two ranges (actually "tributaries" of the Rockies): the **Cascade Mountains** in Washington and Oregon, and the **Sierra Nevadas**, running most of the length of California. Like the Rockies, they both present great skiing and hiking opportunities. The Cascades continue northward through Canada into Alaska, where they become the **Alaska Range**. Between the Rockies and Appalachian Mountains are the flat lands of the Great Plains and Midwest.

Climate

As a rule (and there are many exceptions), the northern portion of the contiguous United States and the southern portion of Canada have warm or even hot summers, but cold snowy winters; whereas the southern region is mild to hot year round. Because of this, southern portions of the continent tend to be all-year destinations, whereas tourism in the north is largely limited to the summer. Of course, skiers do head north in the winter, and October is prime foliage season there.

Alaskan and Canadian winters can be brutal. However, late spring, summer, and early fall are surprisingly mild; even winter isn't as bitter in southern Canadian cities as clients might imagine.

Rainfall and humidity patterns vary widely across the continent. Rain is frequent in the Pacific Northwest and, often in the form of thundershowers, in the South and Southeast. The American Southwest is dry and desert-like, with rain

Four state capitals carry the names of United States presidents: Lincoln, Madison, Jackson, and Jefferson City.

coming mostly in the winter months. Hurricanes are most likely along the Gulf and Atlantic coasts in the summer and fall.

Tourism Patterns

North American tourism patterns are probably familiar to you. In brief, summer is high season for most of Canada and the United States. (This high season extends from the last weekend of May to the first weekend of September.) The one exception is the desert resorts in California, Arizona, and Nevada. These areas, where summer temperatures can be scorching, have their low season during June, July, and August.

Fall and spring are off-seasons for tourism in most places. On the other hand, many travelers with flexible schedules (for example, retirees) profit from the lower rates and the cool (but not yet cold) temperatures that prevail. So, too, do conventions, which seem to flourish during this time. Easter, however, is a springtime high period, especially in Washington, D.C., Florida, and to some extent, California; students and families often travel during the week before or after this holiday. October's fall foliage season is also a high period in many northern forested areas.

Winter is a very low period for Canadian and U.S. tourism, except at ski resorts and at certain warm-weather places (for example, desert resorts). Special winter events, too, can draw crowds to cold-weather locations. For instance, Quebec City's Winter Carnival and New York City's pre-Christmas shopping opportunities serve as magnets for tourists.

North American Distances

What is most striking to Europeans visiting North America? How big it really is. Even North Americans underestimate their continent's size. Why? The answers are many: The states are so familiar, airplane travel has compressed journey time greatly, states and countries are commonly seen as being parts of large blocks (for example, Ohio and Minnesota seem close to each other because they're both in the Midwest).

There's a flip side to this. Since cities like **New York**, **Boston**, **Philadelphia**, **Baltimore**, and **Washington**, **D.C.**, have strong identities, your clients may be sur-

The only place on United States soil where you drive on the left is the U.S. Virgin Islands.

"Bonhomme Carnaval" and snow sculpture at Quebec Winter Carnival
Photo by Camirand; Courtesy of Carnaval de Quebec

prised to find how close they are to one another. (Theoretically, you could drive through them all in one day.) In fact, though the northeast is populous, many of its states are tiny and the area is actually quite compact. On the other hand, the western states are so vast and uncrowded that distances between major cities are considerable. (For instance, even though **Los Angeles** and **Portland** are in adjacent states, they are more than 1,000 miles apart; conversely, **Providence** and **Boston**, also in adjacent states, are only 50 miles from each other.)

For all the continent's size, however, air service is so good between urban centers that travel distances will seem short to your clients. And within states, commuter airlines shrink those distances even more. On busy routes, fares can be very reasonable—even cross country. However, if a route isn't greatly traveled, even if it's a short distance, prices can be high. Keep in mind that air travel isn't a cure-all for distance: Service between small towns can be limited or nonexistent.

America's love of cars is well-known, and many clients will want to drive to their destination, especially in the compact northeast. The network of highways is generally excellent, and so, too, are most state and rural roads. Out west, though, the wide open spaces truly are wide; direct major routes between secondary destinations aren't always possible to find.

Getting around within a city is another matter. Urban transportation in the United States often leaves something to be desired. (Not so for Canada, which has great city transportation systems.) Your recommendations to clients will vary according to the situation: a car rental for Los Angeles, taxis for New York City, the streetcars and subways for San Francisco.

Train travel in Europe is often the mode of choice. Not so in the United States. Although **Amtrak** offers some major routes (with high-speed service between Washington, D.C., and Boston), the train system in the United States is geared more to commerce than to commuters. Trains here aren't nearly as fast, nor the routes as diversified, as those in Europe. That's one reason why motorcoach tours and intercity buses, usually operated by **Greyhound**, are the ground transportation of choice for many travelers in the U.S. Still, there *are* good rail routes throughout the country; special fares are commonplace; and train travel remains one of the great, romantic, scenic means of travel. You can book complete lodging-transportation packages through Amtrak Vacations. Remember, too, that Canada's **VIA Rail** system is very good.

Cruises have become a common means of seeing North America. Among the most popular itineraries: New England and the St. Lawrence River, Alaska's Inside Passage, and the Mississippi, along with its many tributaries.

A number of "private" train experiences are offered across America, especially in Alaska.

Some Miscellaneous Considerations

Here are a few items that may prove useful when dealing with people traveling within North America:

- The "hub and spoke" concept is important to North American air travel. Each airline has one or two cities where they have an especially large number of flights connecting. Among North America's busiest domestic hub cities, with the airlines that rely on them the most:

Atlanta (Delta)	Dallas (American and Delta)	Phoenix (America West)
Charlotte, NC (US Airways)	Denver (United)	Pittsburgh (US Airways)
Chicago (United)	Detroit (Northwest)	St. Louis (TWA)
Cincinnati (Delta)	Houston (Continental)	Salt Lake City (Delta)
Cleveland (Continental)	Minneapolis (Northwest)	Toronto (Air Canada)

For international departures, North American carriers concentrate on Los Angeles, San Francisco, Miami, and New York City as hubs, though many other cities can serve as departure points for travelers heading for foreign places. These cities serve as hubs to domestic coastal and near-coastal cities as well.

- Check with your clients to find out which frequent-flyer program they are members of. This is usually an important consideration when booking an air carrier, hotel, or car rental.

- Hotels in North America often have special reduced-rate packages with easy requirements, such as age, business, or membership in organizations. Ask your clients if they qualify.

- If you or your client is a AAA member, don't forget the free or low-cost maps and travel kits that are available; these materials are superb to help plan your clients' motoring trips.

- The costs of staying in any North American city can vary enormously. Big cities (for example, New York) tend to be expensive; smaller cities (especially in the South and Midwest) tend to be less so.

- Most hotels in North America belong to chains, and each chain tries to maintain a certain quality level among all its properties. Though there can be *great* variation within a chain (especially Hilton, Sheraton, Hyatt, and Holiday Inn), here is what level each chain generally represents:

Luxury	High End	Mid-Range	Budget
Four Seasons	Canadian Pacific	Clarion	Baymont
Peninsula	Crowne Plaza	Crown Sterling Suites	Best Western
Regent	Hilton International	Doubletree	Comfort Inns
Ritz-Carlton	Hyatt Regency	Embassy Suites	Days Inn
	Inter-Continental	Hilton	Econo Lodge
	Marriott	Holiday Inn	Hampton Inns
	Meridien	Hyatt	Howard Johnson
	Omni	Radisson	La Quinta
	Renaissance	Ramada	Quality Inn
	Sheraton Resorts	Sheraton	Red Roof
	Sofitel		Rodeway Inn
	Westin		Travelodge

Travel Trivia

North America's Most Scenic Drives

Pacific Coast Highway (California Highway 1, U.S. 101), California

Columbia Gorge Highway (U.S. 30), Oregon

Coastal Highway (U.S. 1), Maine

Going-to-the-Sun Road, Glacier National Park, Montana

Skyline Drive, Blue Ridge Parkway, Virginia

Million Dollar Highway (U.S. 550), Colorado

Oak Creek Canyon Drive (U.S. 89), Arizona

Highway 7, Arkansas

The Cabot Trail, Nova Scotia

Route 89, Vermont

Icefields Parkway, Alberta

Source: Rand McNally Road Atlas *and others*

Creative Activity

Listed below are seven possible vacation trips through North America. Try to think of *one or more persons you know* who might enjoy taking each trip. Write down his/her name for each vacation and give several reasons why you think it would appeal to them. If necessary, browse through Chapters 1 through 7 for additional information to guide you.

1. A seven-day riverboat cruise up the Mississippi River

2. A visit to Winter Carnival in Quebec City

3. A weekend in Utah's Rocky Mountains

4. A week's stay in July at a New England hotel that faces the Atlantic

5. A nine-day escorted motorcoach tour of Boston, New York, Philadelphia, and Washington, D.C.

6. A raft trip down the Colorado River

7. A four-day stay in the Florida Keys

Travel Trivia
North America's Distinctive Foods and Drinks

Tortiere in Quebec
Espresso in Seattle
Beignets in New Orleans
Chili on spaghetti in Cincinnati
Key lime pie in Florida
Cheese steak in Philadelphia
Stone crabs and black beans in Miami

Sourdough in San Francisco
Sausages in Milwaukee
Deep dish pizza in Chicago
Enchiladas in Santa Fe
Chestnuts and pretzels in New York City
Quahogs, scrod, clam cakes, coffee cabs, chow mein,
    and chourico in Southeastern Massachusetts

CHAPTER 1

New England
The Cradle of Liberty

Everyone has heard stories of the Pilgrims stepping on Plymouth Rock, church lanterns signaling Paul Revere, and American Minutemen confronting Redcoats at Old North Bridge in Concord. Your clients have heard these stories, too. Mention New England to them, and their minds will swirl with images both historical and contemporary: whaling ships, monuments, museums, white-clapboard houses, and clambakes by the sea. These strong mental impressions will make it easy for you to sell New England to almost anyone.

There are many cities, states, and attractions in the compact northeast corner of the United States. Northernmost is **Maine**, a sparsely settled state of wild, stark beauty. To the southwest of Maine are **Vermont** and **New Hampshire**. (To keep these two straight, remember that Vermont is shaped like a V.) Both states are mountainous and wooded, with many charming towns dotting the landscape. South of Vermont and New Hampshire is **Massachusetts**, the most visited of the New England states. Finally, in New England's south are **Connecticut** and **Rhode Island**, America's smallest state.

How Travelers Get There

Your clients will probably already have decided how they intend to get to New England. If it's by car, they'll most likely enter through New York State or Canada, via a major interstate highway. If it's by air, they'll fly in on one of a half-dozen carriers that service the area. Cruise ships stop at New England cities on their way between New York City and Canada. Train service to New England is limited, but bus service is a good option to offer budget-minded clients.

Most travelers bound for New England fly into **Boston's Logan Airport** (BOS), but you may want to recommend **Providence**, Rhode Island (PVD); **Burlington**, Vermont (BTV); or **Hartford**, Connecticut (BDL), as alternatives. Why? Because Logan is a terribly congested airport, with poor access in and out, and Boston itself would be a difficult city to navigate on arrival day. Flying time to New England is about five to six hours from the West Coast and one hour from New York.

Weather Patterns

"If you don't like New England's weather, wait a minute." That's a common saying locals use to describe their wildly changeable climate (see Figure 1-1). Winters are cold and snowy, especially in the mountain areas and away from the coast. Crisp, blue-skied winter days can be glorious. Early spring can be dreary, but May is usually a beautiful month. Summer temperatures are generally around 70 or 80 degrees, though very hot, humid spells occur more than New Englanders would like. Fall is especially beautiful; the fall foliage in October is justly famous.

Overall, New England's precipitation is about the same all year long. Multiday storms are possible most of the year, except in summer, when rainfall tends to occur in short, intense downpours. Tourist season peaks in the summer months and again during fall foliage time, with a sharp drop-off, except for skiers, in the winter.

Getting Around

Boston cream pie is the official dessert of Massachusetts.

Boston's city transportation system—especially the "T" subway-train network—is extensive. Local transportation in other New England cities is acceptable but not extensive. To visit all New England, however, your clients would do best to use a car. (If they fly in, offer to book a car rental.) The highway network is superb and the quaint rural roads are numerous. Traffic jams are rare, except in and around Boston, where they can be monumental, or during summer weekends and holidays, when certain roads that access popular vacation places (for example, Cape Cod and New Hampshire) get congested.

Climate at a Glance
BOSTON, MASSACHUSETTS

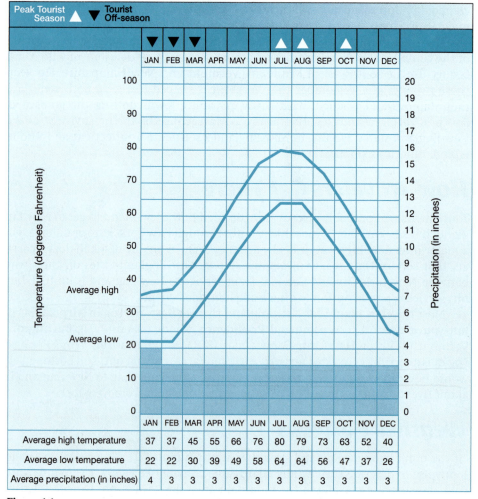

	JAN	FEB	MAR	APR	MAY	JUN	JUL	AUG	SEP	OCT	NOV	DEC
Average high temperature	37	37	45	55	66	76	80	79	73	63	52	40
Average low temperature	22	22	30	39	49	58	64	64	56	47	37	26
Average precipitation (in inches)	4	3	3	3	3	3	3	3	3	3	3	3

Figure 1-1

If your clients don't want to drive, you might suggest booking a New England motorcoach tour for them. Budget clients might be advised to use the region's excellent bus system; rail travel isn't a viable alternative, except in a few areas. Distances are so short that brief commuter flights are useful only for those in a real hurry and willing to pay for it. Ferry service from New Bedford, Falmouth, Hyannis, or Woods Hole to the offshore islands of **Martha's Vineyard** and **Nantucket** can make for a pleasant day's outing.

Important Places

Which places in New England should you recommend? It's a hard choice—there are so many. What follows are New England's most popular cities and attractions.

Boston

Boston is a graceful and historic city. Because its attractions are clustered in a compact area, your client can walk the well-marked, three-mile-long **Freedom Trail** and see most of the historic sites in a day. City tours are also an excellent way for clients to orient themselves to Boston. Cultural opportunities and fine dining experiences abound.

Among the sights you should advise your clients to visit are:

- **Boston Common**, the oldest park in the nation, and its adjoining Public Garden, with its unique "swan" boats.
- **The Old State House**, the seat of Massachusetts's government.
- **The Boston Tea Party Ship**, a full-sized replica of one of the ships involved in the well-known protest. A museum next door documents its history.
- Many **museums**, especially the **Museum of Fine Arts**, the **Museum of Science**, **Computer Museum**, **New England Aquarium**, and **JFK Library and Museum** (south of the city on Columbia Point).

The most scenic ferry stop on Martha's Vineyard is Oak Bluffs.

The Italian food in Boston's North End is superb.

Massachusetts State House, Boston, Massachusetts
Photo by C. J. Ghormley

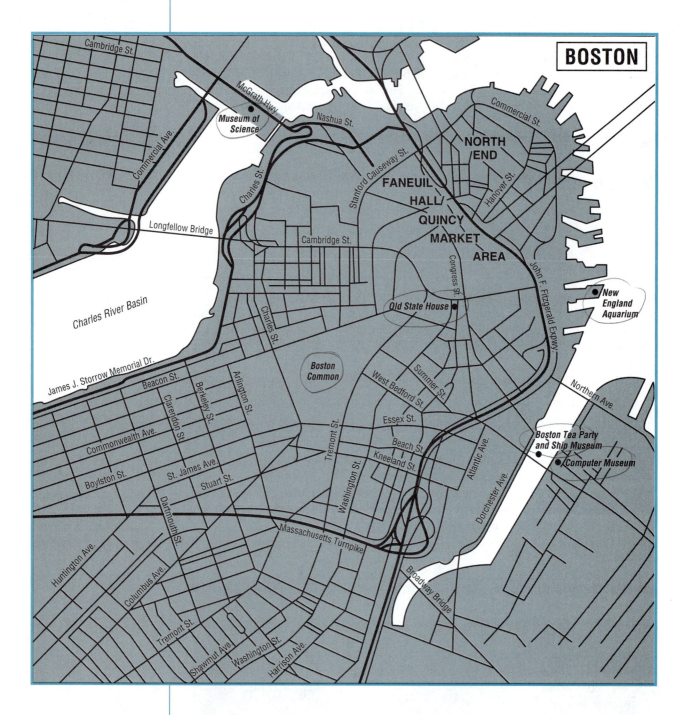

- **Faneuil Hall Marketplace** (also known as Quincy Market), a restored complex of shops, dining facilities, and historic buildings.
- **Cambridge**, home to Harvard University and its own fine museums.

  Among the **day trips** you may wish to recommend to your clients are:

- **Salem**, the infamous seat of Massachusetts's witchcraft trials and the location of Hawthorne's *The House of the Seven Gables*.
- **Lexington and Concord**, where the War of Independence began.
- **Plymouth**, with its universally known rock (it's a bit of a disappointment), replica of the Mayflower, and fascinating re-created settlement, Plimoth Plantation.

- **The Berkshires**, Massachusetts's western mountain range, with its breathtaking vistas, especially in fall foliage season, and its **Old Sturbridge Village**, which captures New England as it was centuries ago.
- **Cape Cod**, potentially a stayover option in itself, which boasts superb beaches and **Provincetown**, at the Cape's tip.

The most scenic road on Cape Cod is 6A.

Vermont, New Hampshire, and Maine

These three northern states share much in common: forested hills, country inns, small towns, and dramatic scenery. Many of New Hampshire's attractions are only a little more than an hour's drive from Boston and could be made into a day trip. Most of this state's sites lie in the **White Mountains**, along old Route 3. **The Old Man in the Mountain** rock formation is well-known; **Mt. Washington**, whose summit can be reached by a cog railway, is New England's highest mountain; and **Laconia** is every visitor's idea of a New England town. **Portsmouth**, New Hampshire's former capital and its only seaport, is filled with many quaint homes, shops, and taverns.

Minute Man Statue, Concord, Massachusetts
Photo by C. J. Ghormley

Vermont is even more picturesque than New Hampshire, perhaps because it's less industrialized than its neighbor. It's a state of pristine lakes, covered bridges, and excellent ski trails. Many cute little towns dot two major highways; **Barre** [BAA-ree] (once the source of most of the nation's granite), **Montpelier** (the capital), and Burlington are along Interstate 89; and **St. Johnsbury** (noted for maple syrup) is on Interstate 91.

Maine is more than three times larger than any of its neighbor states, yet most of its area is dense forest and uncultivated brush. Maine's rocky coastline is breathtaking. This is best seen at **Bar Harbor**, the gateway to **Acadia National Park** and to cruises into Canada. **Boothbay Harbor** is a major boating center. **Kennebunkport** is a charming summer resort that has attracted the likes of Booth Tarkington, Rachel Carson, and George Bush. **Kittery** is a well-visited shipbuilding center, and **Brunswick** has many historic buildings.

As for skiing, **Killington**, Vermont; **Sugarloaf**, Maine; **Mount Cranmore**, New Hampshire; and **Okemo**, Vermont, are highly praised. Other well-known ski resorts: **Mount Snow** and **Stowe**, Vermont, and **Waterville**, New Hampshire.

The Southern Coast

Many travelers make the mistake of treating this area as simply a road from New York to Cape Cod or Boston. Some of New England's finest attractions lie along its southern coast. From west to east, they are:

- **New Haven**, Connecticut, the home of Yale University and a very good museum.
- **Foxwoods Resort and Casino** in Ledyard, Connecticut, a Native American–owned casino that brings Vegas-like glitz to New England.
- **Mystic**, Connecticut, a seaport that looks much the same as it did in its whaling heyday.
- **Newport**, Rhode Island, a gem of an attraction that features nearly a dozen great cliff-side mansions that are open to the public. (Two of the most impressive: The Breakers and Marble House.) Here, too, are the **Tennis Hall of Fame** and **Touro Synagogue**, founded in 1763. It's about an hour and a half from Boston.
- **New Bedford**, Massachusetts, where Melville's *Moby Dick* is set, with its restored downtown area and remnants of a once-booming whaling industry.
- **Martha's Vineyard** and **Nantucket**, Massachusetts, charming islands accessed by ferry from New Bedford, or **Woods Hole** on Cape Cod.

Possible Itineraries

If your clients plan to hub out of Boston or another city, they'll need at least a week to fully sample New England. They may also decide to stay over in several towns and cities, with their whole itinerary taking as much as two weeks. An appropriate itinerary for you to design would start in Boston; have clients travel up a few days into New Hampshire, Maine, and Vermont; and then head down through the Berkshires and continue south to New Haven. The trip could continue along the south coast to Cape Cod, then back to Plymouth and Boston.

Lodging Options

Hotels and motels are plentiful in New England. Boston's luxury properties are expensive, as are those on Cape Cod; lodging in the summer outside Boston, though, can be reasonable. In fact, if clients intend to stay in only one or two cities and hub their way out to various attractions, a good option would be to lodge them in and around Providence, Rhode Island, or **Fall River**, Massachusetts, or any one of

The longest place name in the U.S. belongs to a Massachusetts lake: Chargoggagogmanchauggagoggchaubunagungamaugg, which means "You fish on your side of the lake, I'll fish on my side, and nobody fishes in the middle."

Stroll the Cliff Walk, a path that skirts the ocean and mansion lawns.

The Borden house in Fall River, Massachusetts, where Lizzy Borden (may have) murdered her parents, is now a B&B.

Boston's outlying towns. Each of these is at a major juncture of highways. A well-developed network of inns and bed-and-breakfasts exists throughout New England.

Allied Destinations

A trip to New England can be easily combined with a trip to the Mid-Atlantic region, especially to New York State and New York City (a little more than four hours driving time from Boston). One intriguing option for you to recommend to your client is to continue on to Canada: Montreal is only about 300 miles from Boston; and Halifax, Nova Scotia, is but a short cruise from Bar Harbor, Maine.

Factors That Motivate Visitors

Among the factors that will pique client interest and should be stressed are:

- It has a historic heritage and plenty of cultural and educational opportunities.
- Travel outside Boston and especially during the off-season is quite affordable.
- Scenery—both seaside and in the mountains—is impressive.
- Driving around is very easy, especially outside Boston.
- The region is very close to New York and Canada.
- Cruises afford an efficient way to see its coastal towns.
- The fine food of the area (especially the seafood) has a renowned reputation and is reasonable.

There are more people of French Canadian descent in the United States than there are French Canadians in Canada.

Rhode Island is only thirty-seven miles wide and forty-eight miles long, but it has 400 miles of shoreline.

Qualifying the Client
New England

FOR CLIENTS WHO WANT	APPEAL			REMARKS
	HIGH	MEDIUM	LOW	
Historical and Cultural Attractions	▲			Especially Boston area
Beaches and Water Sports		▲		Mostly summers
Skiing Opportunities	▲			Very good, but not alpine
Lots of Nightlife			▲	Boston, mostly
Family Activities		▲		Experiencing history
Familiar Cultural Experience	▲			Well-known landmarks
Exotic Cultural Experience			▲	Some ethnic neighborhoods
Safety and Low Crime		▲		Some crime in Boston
Bargain Travel		▲		Outside Boston and off-season
Impressive Scenery	▲			In mountains, along ocean
Peace and Quiet		▲		Especially northern areas
Shopping Opportunities	▲			Mill outlets for clothing
To Do Business		▲		Especially in and around Boston

Figure 1-2

- Excellent skiing facilities exist in Vermont, Massachusetts, and New Hampshire.
- The summer beaches and water-sport opportunities are quite good, especially along the southern coast and Cape Cod.
- The fall foliage season is beautiful. (Make sure to book clients early!)

Possible Misgivings

Even the most appealing destinations provoke a few misgivings. Here are some you're likely to encounter:

- "All that history and scenery will be boring." Suggest New England's beaches, ski trails, and the nightlife in Boston.
- "It's too expensive." Only Boston and a few other areas are costly. Lodge your clients off-season or in off-the-beaten-path cities, such as Providence, Fall River, New Bedford, or Boston's outlying towns. Bargains can also be easily had in New Hampshire, Vermont, and Maine (except during fall foliage season).
- "I don't like to drive." Concentrate the client's plans in Boston so that rapid transit can be used. Suggest an escorted tour or a cruise.
- "New Englanders aren't friendly." The old notion of the stoic Yankee is out of date. In fact, many of today's New Englanders are of Portuguese, Italian, African, Irish, or French-Canadian descent. They are usually warm and hospitable to visitors.
- "I once flew into Boston and the place was frantic!" Suggest Providence or other cities as alternatives.

Sales Strategies

The best way to sell-up New England is to suggest an expansion of the client's planned itinerary or to bring up the idea of a motorcoach tour or a New England/Canada cruise. Some of Boston's lower-cost hotels leave something to be desired; to recommend a top-class hotel, here, is advisable. A city tour of Boston and, especially, a car rental are obvious cross-sell opportunities. If an upscale client has limited time, and, especially if he or she doesn't want to drive, commuter airlines between New England's points of interest could yield substantial commissions. Winter ski packages and fall foliage tours of New England are perennial best sellers.

Boston food = seafood. Diff type. of seafood ber. of is population. (Portugal-spain)

One of the best collections of Titanic memorabilia is at the Marine Museum in Fall River, Massachusetts.

The Trapp Family, of *Sound of Music* fame, owns a ski lodge in Stowe, Vermont.

Creative Activity

You're a travel counselor at an agency that sells many trips to New England. Recently you saw a chart in an industry magazine that lists all the possible cross-sell items that could be offered to travelers. You want to create a list that you can consult whenever you send someone to New England. Check all the cross-sell items that you think could apply to a New England holiday.

- [x] air sightseeing excursion
- [ ] attraction admission
- [x] balloon ride
- [ ] barge cruise
- [x] bicycling tour
- [ ] boat cruise (limited)
- [ ] bon-voyage party
- [x] campground reservation
- [x] car rental
- [ ] car rental insurance
- [ ] city tour
- [ ] concert
- [ ] convention arrangements
- [ ] culinary classes
- [x] cultural event
- [ ] dine-around package
- [ ] dinner theater
- [ ] diving package
- [x] ferry transport
- [ ] fishing package
- [ ] gambling package
- [ ] glass-bottom boat tour
- [ ] golf package
- [x] helicopter tour

- [ ] hiking package
- [ ] honeymoon package
- [x] horseback riding package
- [x] hunting package
- [ ] insurance
- [ ] interpreter service
- [x] jeep rental
- [ ] kennel service
- [ ] limo service
- [ ] luau
- [ ] meal plan
- [ ] meet-and-greet service
- [ ] meeting arrangements
- [ ] motorhome rental
- [ ] nightclub show
- [ ] nightlife tour
- [ ] passport photo service
- [ ] post-cruise land package
- [ ] pre-cruise land package
- [ ] private car
- [ ] private guide
- [ ] pub-hopping tour
- [ ] raft adventure
- [ ] rail excursion

- [ ] rail pass
- [ ] resort package
- [ ] safari outing
- [ ] sailing package
- [ ] shopping tour
- [ ] shore excursion
- [x] ski package
- [ ] snorkel package
- [ ] spa enrollment
- [ ] sporting events ticket
- [ ] submarine ride
- [ ] tennis package
- [ ] theater ticket
- [ ] theme park admission
- [ ] tramway ride
- [ ] transfer service
- [ ] travel accessories
- [ ] traveler's checks
- [ ] video rental/sale
- [ ] walking tour
- [ ] wedding package
- [ ] welcome party
- [ ] yacht charter

Travel Trivia

Unusual American Cities and Towns

Bald Head, Maine	Toad Suck, Arkansas	Clam, Michigan
Happy Jack, Arizona	Cut and Shoot, Texas	Funk, Nebraska
Lollipop, Texas	Zzyzx, California	Black Gnat, Kentucky
Truth or Consequences, NM	Couch, Missouri	Colon, Missouri
Noodle, Texas	Porkee, Pennsylvania	Lithium, Missouri
Droop, West Virginia	Hygiene, Colorado	Broken Arrow, Oklahoma
Bat Cave, North Carolina	Asphalt, Kentucky	Tuna, Pennsylvania
Okay, Oklahoma	Walla Walla, Washington	Egg Harbor City, New Jersey

CHAPTER 2

New York and New Jersey
Broadway and Boardwalk

What does a traveler imagine when he or she thinks of New York City? Skyscrapers? Great museums? Nightlife until dawn? Crowding? Broadway theater? It'll be a complex vision, for sure.

There's plenty past "The Big Apple," too: **upstate New York**, the gambling along **Atlantic City**'s Boardwalk, the beaches of **Long Island**. Your clients will feel a powerful attraction to New York City, yet they may express weighty reservations about visiting it, and unclear ideas about what surrounds it. Good salesmanship, here, is a must.

First, a little geography: New York City is just off the Atlantic Ocean, between New England (Connecticut, specifically) and the Mid-Atlantic States. America's most populous city, New York comprises five divisions, or boroughs; when your clients say, "New York," though, they usually mean not the entire city, but the borough-island of **Manhattan**, where the business and tourist action is. The other four boroughs are largely residential and industrial.

New York, of course, also refers to the entire state New York City is in. New York State, which stretches several hundred miles northward and westward from New York City, has many attractions of its own, including: **West Point Military Academy**, the **Catskills** and the **Adirondack Mountains**, the **Finger Lakes**, and **Niagara Falls**. **Albany**, not New York City, is the state capital.

To New York City's south is the state of New Jersey. The fifty-mile-long **Jersey Shore** is famous for its beaches. **Atlantic City**, the best known of its beach cities and now famous for its gambling, is about a two-hour drive from Manhattan.

How Travelers Get There

A vast network of highways, rail lines, and air routes converge on New York City. Getting your clients there won't be a problem. Choosing which airport to fly them into might be a more difficult decision. **La Guardia** (LGA) is only eight miles from downtown Manhattan, but the route between them can be slow moving, especially around rush hour. **Kennedy International Airport** (JFK) is a good fifteen miles out, as is **Newark International** (EWR) in nearby New Jersey.

How your client will transfer from any of these airports to the city is even more complicated. Cabs and limousines (usually cars, not limos) are the favored means of transportation, but they're expensive, especially from Newark. Share-a-ride cabs can be had from La Guardia. Buses and minibuses also provide transfers from all three airports, and car rentals are an option, as well.

What should you recommend? Clients in a hurry or on a budget should, if possible, be flown into La Guardia, especially if they will not arrive during rush hour. (One problem: La Guardia does not easily accommodate jumbo jets; few long-haul flights land there.) Newark is perhaps the best choice for clients who won't be shocked by a hefty taxi fare or who want to avoid stop-and-go traffic. Because of traffic and distance, JFK is rarely the best choice, yet it receives more flights (especially from a long distance) than the other two, so you may have no choice but to book clients into this airport. For your clients who want to drive into and around New York City, a warning: City traffic is intense and parking fees astronomical.

Several smaller airports service New York City and the overall region. Atlantic City has a modest, but fast-growing airport; **Rochester** (ROC) serves the northern part of the state; and **Buffalo Niagara** (BUF) is often used by visitors to western New York State and Ontario, Canada. Many other New York State cities have medium-sized airports. Rail lines and highways enter New York State and New Jersey from every direction. They are heavily used. For example, more than 90 percent of all visitors to Atlantic City arrive by car or bus.

A reminder: New York City is a major cruise port, with ships leaving for (and coming from) Canada, New England, Bermuda, and occasionally Europe and the Caribbean.

Weather Patterns

New York City has nearly 150 buildings over 50 stories high.

New York State and New Jersey have typical northeast weather: warm to hot summers and cold winters. Late spring and fall are extremely pleasant. Humidity can be a factor at any time of the year, with rainstorms or snowstorms in the winter and sudden thundershowers in the summer. Upstate New York has colder winters than the city itself, often with considerable snow. New York City tends to be warmer than most cities, perhaps because all that concrete retains the heat. Precipitation can also wreak havoc in the city, causing traffic jams and making an available taxi almost impossible to find (see Figure 2-1).

As for tourist patterns, upstate New York and most of New Jersey peak in summer, but tourism drops off as the cold sets in. Atlantic City is packed on weekends. New York City has virtually no off-season, except perhaps in January and, to some extent, on weekends.

Getting Around

New York State and New Jersey have well-developed highway systems. Prepare your clients for the many tolls. The train and bus systems are also quite convenient and are popular with New York commuters. Several local boat cruises can be booked for your clients out of New York City. One of the most popular short cruises: a trip up the Hudson on the Day Line.

The best way to get around New York City is by taxi; they are plentiful, relatively inexpensive, and fast (sometimes too fast). The subway system is extensive and convenient (though it looks run-down). Contrary to what you may have heard, New York subways are relatively safe, especially during the day. Buses, for crosstown trips, are also an option. A multitude of cars for hire and limos swarm through the city; they are a good choice to book for your upscale clients. New York is also a very walkable city, though only in certain areas and at certain times. Tell your clients to check with hotel staff before setting out on foot for a destination within the city.

Clients can also get around by tour. Bus tours are usually excellent (guides are licensed by the city), and the boat tour that circles Manhattan is famous. The ferry rides to the Statue of Liberty, Ellis Island, and Staten Island afford wonderful, inexpensive views.

Climate at a Glance
NEW YORK, NEW YORK

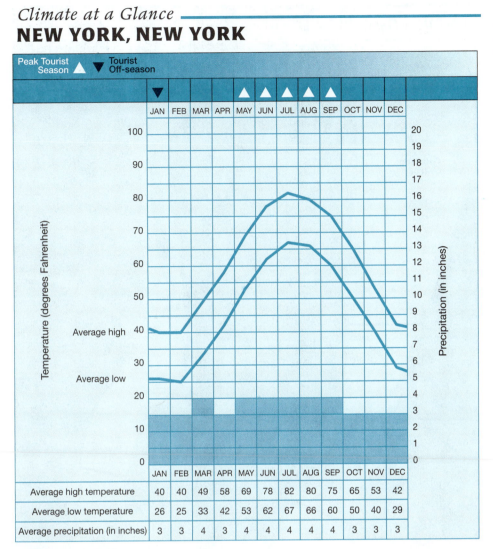

	JAN	FEB	MAR	APR	MAY	JUN	JUL	AUG	SEP	OCT	NOV	DEC
Average high temperature	40	40	49	58	69	78	82	80	75	65	53	42
Average low temperature	26	25	33	42	53	62	67	66	60	50	40	29
Average precipitation (in inches)	3	3	4	3	4	4	4	4	4	3	3	3

Figure 2-1

Important Places

This area's destinations can be lumped into two categories: New York City itself, and New York State and New Jersey. Some of the latter category's attractions may be done as day trips from New York City, though most clients who stay in Manhattan rarely take such day trips, except perhaps the Hudson River cruise.

New York City

New York City is extremely rich in attractions. Many, like **Chinatown** or the huge **St. John the Divine Cathedral**, are best visited as part of a city tour. Among the most popular attractions your clients may visit on their own are:

- **The Statue of Liberty**, perhaps the world's most famous statue, and **Ellis Island**, both accessed by a ferry from Battery Park.
- **The Empire State Building**, whose higher levels afford the best views of Manhattan. Another excellent vantage point is the **World Trade Center** in downtown Manhattan.

in the pasd th imigrations wan kept ther historical island

Three original stores—Macy's, Bloomingdale's, and FAO Schwarz—are worth a special visit.

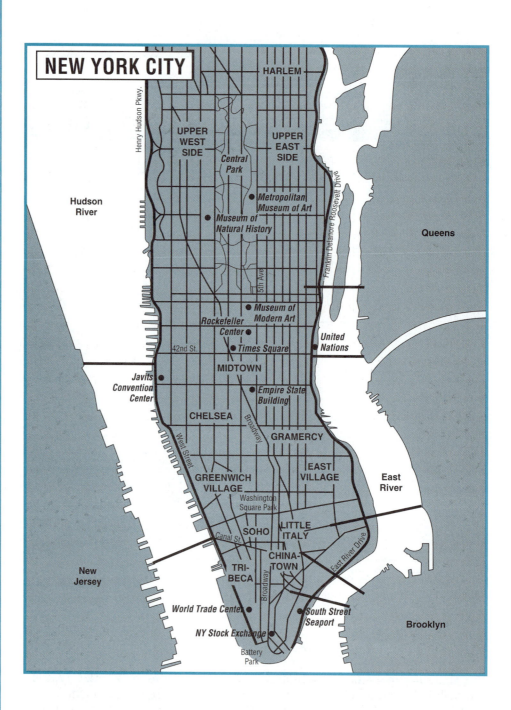

NEW YORK CITY

HARLEM

Henry Hudson Pkwy.

UPPER WEST SIDE

Central Park

UPPER EAST SIDE

Hudson River

Metropolitan Museum of Art

Museum of Natural History

Franklin Delamore Roosevelt Drive

Queens

5th Ave

Museum of Modern Art

Rockefeller Center

42nd St.

Times Square

United Nations

MIDTOWN

Javits Convention Center

Empire State Building

CHELSEA

GRAMERCY

Broadway

West Street

EAST VILLAGE

East River

GREENWICH VILLAGE

Washington Square Park

SOHO

LITTLE ITALY

Canal St.

CHINA-TOWN

East River Drive

New Jersey

TRI-BECA

Broadway

World Trade Center

South Street Seaport

Brooklyn

NY Stock Exchange

Battery Park

A fascinating tour of
Radio City Music Hall
is available.

- **The United Nations**, one of New York's most graceful structures and an important world forum.
- **Rockefeller Center**, a "city of tomorrow" designed in the 1930s, with its famous skating rink (a cafe in the summer), the **NBC Studio tour**, **Radio City Music Hall** (one of America's largest theaters), and nearby **St. Patrick's Cathedral**.
- **Superb museums**, most notably the **Metropolitan Museum of Art**, the **Museum of Modern Art** (MOMA), and the **Museum of Natural History**.
- **Well-known neighborhoods**, including **Greenwich Village**, **Chinatown**, **Little Italy**, **South Street Seaport** (a renovated riverside restaurant and shopping area), **Soho** (what Greenwich Village used to look like), neon-lit **Times Square** (still a bit tacky, but vastly improved), and **Central Park** (superb during the day, *not* advisable at night).

St. Patrick's Cathedral, New York City
Photo by C. J. Ghormley

- **Abundant nightlife opportunities**, most notably the wealth of Broadway and off-Broadway plays and musicals, and major sporting events.

New York State

Some clients will prefer to visit the rest of the state of New York. The following are the most popular with leisure travelers:

- **The Hudson River Valley**. Often called "America's Rhine," this picturesque route just north of New York City features many points of interest. Among them: **Tarrytown**, which captures the world of Washington Irving's "The Legend of Sleepy Hollow"; **West Point**, the U.S. military academy; and **Hyde Park**, best known for its Vanderbilt Mansion and the home of Franklin Roosevelt.
- **Long Island**. Stretching eastward from New York City and paralleling the southern New England coast, Long Island features excellent beaches, superb boating and fishing, many rental cottages, and mansion-dotted towns. It's more of a destination for New Yorkers, though, than for tourists from other regions.

Half-price theater tickets are available on the day of performance at Times Square.

Niagara Falls
Photo by George Bailey; Courtesy of Niagara Falls Parks Commission

- **The Catskills.** Northwest of Hyde Park is the Catskill Mountain area, long known for its old-time entertainment. Nearby is **Woodstock**, now an artists' community, which once hosted the legendary '60s rock concert. Northeast of the Catskills is the state's capital, Albany, with its huge, stark complex of government buildings.

- **The Upstate Lakes District.** Both **Lake Champlain** and **Lake George** are lined with resorts, hotels, old forts, and all manner of tourist attractions. In fact, things can get a little too touristy in both places. Here also are the Adirondack Mountains, which offer six million acres of campsites, chasms, fishing, unspoiled hiking trails, and fall foliage. **Lake Placid**, within the Adirondacks, is a noted ski resort area (and was host to the 1980 Winter Olympics). The very northwest part of the state borders Lake Ontario and the St. Lawrence River. Here can be found the **Thousand Islands**—with its many pleasing vistas, homes, and mansions—which is most often visited via half-day cruises out of the town of **Alexandria Bay**.

- **The Finger Lakes.** This region, in the west-central part of the state, will delight your photographer-clients with its waterfalls, wineries, scenic vistas, imposing gorges, and 600 miles of shoreline. Also nearby: **Corning**, with its well-known glass factory and museum; **Watkins Glen**, famous for its gorge and Grand Prix racing; and the Baseball Hall of Fame, in **Cooperstown**.

- **Niagara Falls.** Although near Buffalo, New York, Niagara Falls is covered in greater detail in Chapter 6 (Canada and Alaska). The New York State side of the Falls is not so dramatically beautiful as the Canadian side, nor is it where you would probably lodge your clients.

Atlantic City

The first thing to strike your clients about Atlantic City will be the familiar street names: Atlantic City inspired the board game Monopoly. The second thing to grab their attention: the intense strip of hotels, casinos, restaurants, amusements, shopping centers, and night spots that line the Boardwalk. Beyond that, there's not

Ausable Chasm, in upstate New York, is one of America's oldest private attractions.

Corning glassware can be purchased at discount at the factory store.

much else to see; the beach is impressive and the convention center vast, but the area away from the Boardwalk is poverty-ridden. Those clients who have spent time in Las Vegas may be a bit disappointed; Atlantic City isn't quite the attraction for high rollers and theme parks that Vegas is. Indeed, most people who go to Atlantic City do so as a brief getaway from the East Coast cities, to perhaps win a few dollars, and to take in some first-rate entertainment.

The entire Jersey Shore boasts broad beaches, popular night clubs, and much family entertainment, though it's not the beach resort area it was a hundred years ago. **Wildwood** is probably the best known town along the shore, with a half-dozen amusement areas and lively after-dark entertainment. **Asbury Park** is also well known as the place where many rock performers became famous. And a visit to **Cape May**, an astonishing collection of well-preserved Victorian buildings and homes, would be a delightful recommendation for you to make. Two other New Jersey options: **Camden**, with its impressive aquarium, and the ruggedly scenic **Delaware Water Gap National Recreation Area**, with its camping, hiking, and other outdoor activities.

In Flemington, New Jersey, is a $9 million, 52,000-square-foot model railroad set-up called "Northlandz."

Possible Itineraries

For a genuine New York City experience, your clients should be booked in Manhattan for five to seven days, though the city's high cost may make such a stay quite expensive. A three- or four-day stay could enable them to see New York's principal highlights at a more reasonable cost. Atlantic City probably warrants no more than two days. A motoring tour of upstate New York could be done in about a week, with one or two days at such attractions as Niagara Falls, Lake Champlain, the Finger Lakes, or Lake George.

Lodging Options

One thing your clients must know: Lodging in New York City is about twice as costly as what they would expect at the same level of value in most other U.S. cities (though weekend "bargain" packages are available). Rooms also tend to be small.

Among the most famous hotels in New York City are the Waldorf-Astoria, the Plaza, the St. Regis, and the Pierre.

The Plaza Hotel and Central Park, New York City
Photo by C. J. Ghormley

The most popular, pleasant, and safe lodging area in New York City is south and east of Central Park, though fine hotels are scattered throughout the midtown area. Hotels in the Times Square-Broadway theater district are plentiful; many new properties have been built there and many older ones renovated. Strangely, New York's downtown district—where the **Wall Street** stock exchanges, numerous corporate headquarters, and quite a few tourist attractions are located—offers few lodging choices, though that's likely to change.

Atlantic City is a comparative bargain. The glitzy, hulking properties along the Boardwalk can be expensive, but special three-day, two-night packages (especially on weekdays) are plentiful and can be a genuine bargain. You may also book your clients on many bargain tour packages that are available. And tell your clients to visit the **Taj Mahal** hotel; it's an attraction unto itself.

Accommodations across the rest of New Jersey and New York are generally reasonable, with the usual spectrum of hotels, motels, bed-and-breakfasts, and camping facilities.

Allied Destinations

All the following are within a day by land or an hour or two by air from the New York/New Jersey area: New England; Ontario and Quebec; Pennsylvania; Delaware; Maryland; Washington, D.C.; and parts of Virginia, West Virginia, and Ohio. Destinations in any of these areas are a logical extension of your client's stay. Remember, too, that New York City is a hub for cruises (especially to Bermuda, the Caribbean, and Canada) and for flights to Europe, Africa, and in a few cases, South America. Clients bound for these places may like the notion of a day or two in New York City as a way to break up a long trip.

Factors That Motivate Visitors

Those of your customers who wish to visit New York City will probably want to do so for the following reasons:

- There's a wealth of tourist attractions.
- There are numerous transportation options into and out of the city.
- The shopping is extraordinary; as one brochure puts it, "If you can't find it in New York, it doesn't exist."
- New York City is home to more corporations and hosts more conventions than any other U.S. city.
- No city has a greater variety of choices for fine dining and nightlife.
- Christmastime is festive.
- There's a constant stream of major sporting events.
- The cultural, artistic, and entertainment opportunities are plentiful.

Clients will have a separate set of expectations for the rest of the area. Among the features that may attract them are:

- Camping and skiing opportunities, especially in the Adirondacks, and the great natural beauty of upstate New York and parts of New Jersey.
- The convenient system of highways, making driving easy.
- The beaches and water sports, especially on Long Island, the Jersey Shore, and in the upstate Lakes District.
- Gambling in Atlantic City and Native American–run casinos.

The New York Stock Exchange has a fascinating exhibition tour on weekdays.

There are actually 1,865 islands in the Thousand Islands.

The River Cafe, in Brooklyn's riverfront area, affords a spectacular view of Manhattan's skyline.

Qualifying the Client
New York City

FOR CLIENTS WHO WANT	APPEAL			REMARKS
	HIGH	MEDIUM	LOW	
Historical and Cultural Attractions	▲			Superb museums
Beaches and Water Sports			▲	Mostly for locals; Long Island is good
Skiing Opportunities			▲	Catskills and Adirondacks
Lots of Nightlife	▲			Superb theater
Family Activities	▲			Famous tourist sites
Familiar Cultural Experience		▲		New York City *is* different
Exotic Cultural Experience		▲		New York City *is* different
Safety and Low Crime			▲	Not as bad as reputation
Bargain Travel			▲	Extremely expensive
Impressive Scenery			▲	Must go north of city
Peace and Quiet			▲	A noisy city
Shopping Opportunities	▲			For luxury items
To Do Business	▲			More corporate headquarters than in any other city

Figure 2-2

Possible Misgivings

New York and New Jersey are wonderful destinations. However, uninformed clients may have reservations about going there, especially to New York City. Don't automatically give in to their fears, though, and suggest another destination, for their desire to go to Manhattan may be just as strong. Here are a few examples of misgivings and how to handle them:

- "New York City is too expensive." You can't get around the truth of this statement, but there are ways to reduce the cost of a New York City holiday. Recommend a shorter stay than they may have intended, thus cutting lodging cost; seek out weekend bargain rates at moderately priced hotels; emphasize the low cost of transportation to, around, and from Manhattan; mention discount theater ticket prices; advise them to eat at coffee shops and delis rather than at full-blown (and full-priced) restaurants.

- "New York City is dangerous." New York City is less dangerous than several other U.S. cities, but your client may have a tough time believing this. Stress that you're lodging them in a safe area (and do so). Advise them to check with hotel personnel about when and where it's safe to walk around.

- "New Yorkers are rude." This is rarely true anymore. Many New Yorkers do have a rather colorful and direct way of dealing with life. Just tell your client that New York is a perpetually harried, hurried place, and people sometimes don't

The world's largest cathedral (St. John the Divine) and largest synagogue (Temple Emanuel) are both in New York City.

have time for niceties; it's no reflection on what they think of tourists. And tell clients to watch for that great majority of New Yorkers who are utterly thoughtful, cultured and kind.

- "Upstate New York sounds boring." The wealth of natural and manmade attractions is striking; even the most jaded can't help being impressed. If mentioning this doesn't work, maybe this is the kind of client who will flourish in New York City.

- "Atlantic City is only for gambling." The beach here and all along the coast is wonderful, the entertainment is excellent, nearby Cape May is an architectural wonder, and just watching gamblers can be an entertainment in itself.

Sales Strategies

An urban legend: If you were to stay in Times Square, within a few days you'd see someone you know.

Selling-up hotels in New York City and Atlantic City is an attractive strategy, since budget properties in both places can provoke complaints from your clients. Outside these cities, car rentals and bus or train travel are appropriate services to offer to clients not driving their own cars.

For New York City itself, offer to set up airport transfers via limousine services. Theater tickets, city tours, and boat cruises can be booked and sold to your clients in advance. Suggest FIT extensions into allied destinations if your client's vacation time permits. Remember that business clients may wish to extend their stay in New York City for leisure, perhaps with their families joining them. Be sure to bring this idea up if it seems appropriate. Also, cruisers might be offered a pre- or post-cruise package in New York City.

For clients who like tours, virtually every major tour operator offers a gamut of tours to Atlantic City, New York City, and upstate New York. Ski packages to upstate resorts are popular.

Travel Trivia

Where Fast Foods Were Invented

Hot dog: New York City
Sandwich: England
Submarine sandwich: Groton, Connecticut
Big Mac: Pittsburgh
Pizza: Greece, Italy

Fortune cookie: Los Angeles
Chop suey: San Francisco
Ice cream: China
Ice cream cone: St. Louis
Ice cream soda: Philadelphia

Source: The History Channel

Creative Activity

You're an executive with ACME Hotels, a chain of mid-priced lodging properties headquartered in Boston. The company, which targets families with children, has decided to expand into New York State and New Jersey. The corporation has asked you to propose five cities to locate these hotels in. What would your five recommendations be, and why?

LOCATION

1. New York City

2.

3.

4.

5.

REASONS

1. Key American tourist city. New York City has need for more hotels that are family affordable. Large population within car-driving distance.

2.

3.

4.

5.

Travel Trivia

Where the Brand-Name Museums and Tours Are

Corning Glass Center, Corning, NY
Ben & Jerry's, Waterbury, VT
Tupperware Museum, Kissimmee, FL
Goodyear World of Rubber, Akron, OH
Levi Strauss Museum, San Francisco, CA
Crayola Factory, Easton, PA
World of Coca-Cola, Atlanta, GA

Jack Daniel's Distillery, Lynchburg, TN
Louisville Slugger Museum & Factory, Louisville, KY
Anheuser-Busch Museum, St. Louis, MO
Boeing Aircraft, Everett, WA
Hershey's Chocolate World, Hershey, PA

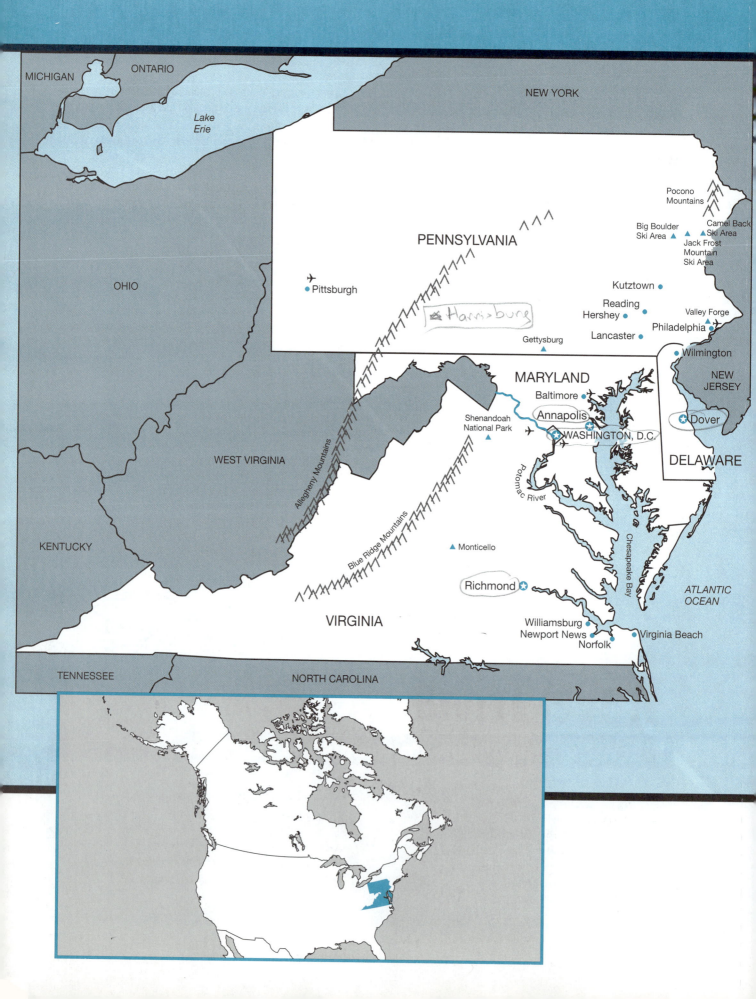

Wash. DC – is a very historical place.

CHAPTER **3**

Pennsylvania, Maryland, Virginia, and Washington, D.C.

The Mid-Atlantic Medley

The Mid-Atlantic is a symphony of sounds: the mute ringing of the Liberty Bell in **Philadelphia**, the emotional strains of "The Star Spangled Banner" written outside **Fort McHenry** near **Baltimore**, wheels rolling along the cobblestones of the first American settlement in **Jamestown**, or the old echoes of debate in **Washington, D.C.** The Mid-Atlantic region also embraces both New York and New Jersey (each covered in the previous chapter) and Delaware. So it's no wonder that this is one of the nation's most-visited tourist areas.

Pennsylvania is the northernmost of the states to be covered in this chapter. Stacked south of it are Delaware, Maryland, Washington, D.C., and Virginia. In Pennsylvania, the **Pocono Mountains** resorts are in the northeast part of the state; in the very southeastern corner, on the eastern border, is Philadelphia; and just west of this major city are the Amish of the **Pennsylvania Dutch country**. **Pittsburgh**, in the state's southwest, also has some interesting sights.

South of Pennsylvania Dutch country is Baltimore, located on the west coast of **Chesapeake Bay**, just across from the eastern peninsula where the rest of Maryland and Delaware are. A short drive south of Baltimore, on the **Potomac River**, is the nation's capital, Washington, D.C. Most of the attractions that will interest your clients in Virginia are found in the **Tidewater Virginia** region, the southeastern portion of that state: the colonial villages of **Williamsburg**, **Yorktown**, and **Jamestown**; **Virginia Beach**; and harbor communities such as **Newport News** and **Norfolk**. The beautiful **Shenandoah National Park** begins in northern Virginia and runs southwesterly through the state.

How Travelers Get There

Access to this busy, highly populated region is diversified and convenient. For air travelers, the major gateway into Philadelphia and much of Pennsylvania is **Philadelphia International Airport** (PHL). Western Pennsylvania's gateway is **Pittsburgh International Airport** (PIT). Flights to Baltimore land at **Baltimore-Washington International Airport** (BWI), which can also serve as a gateway to Washington, D.C. The nation's capital is also directly serviced by both **Ronald Reagan National Airport** (DCA), which is almost downtown, and **Dulles Airport** (IAD), which is about forty-five minutes away in Virginia. Most of these cities are, by air, about five hours from the West Coast, and an hour from New York City.

There's also an extensive network of highways into the region for clients who'll be either driving themselves or taking the bus, a good option for the budget-minded. Train service to Philadelphia, Baltimore, or Washington, D.C., is very good, too, though limited for the rest of the area.

Weather Patterns

The climates of Philadelphia and Baltimore are similar: hot and muggy summers, with average high temperatures of around 80 or 90 degrees, and cold, snowy winters, with average low temperatures of around 30 degrees. Spring and fall are very pleasant. The Poconos are a little cooler, with cold and snowy winters. Summer is the main tourist season.

Washington, D.C., is renowned for its beautiful, temperate springs when the cherry blossoms bloom (and student tours are everywhere). Summers are also well known, but for being muggy and hot. These are by far Washington's two busiest tourist seasons (though tourism begins to drop off as early as August). Falls are pleasant, with some rain, and winters get chilly and a bit snowy (see Figure 3-1). Southeast Virginia has mild summers and fairly mild winters. September to May are the best times for clients to visit here; summers are the most crowded. Fall is a

Climate at a Glance
WASHINGTON, D.C.

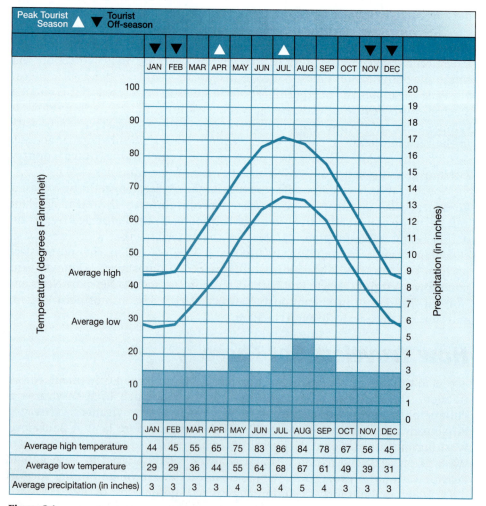

	JAN	FEB	MAR	APR	MAY	JUN	JUL	AUG	SEP	OCT	NOV	DEC
Average high temperature	44	45	55	65	75	83	86	84	78	67	56	45
Average low temperature	29	29	36	44	55	64	68	67	61	49	39	31
Average precipitation (in inches)	3	3	3	3	4	3	4	5	4	3	3	3

Figure 3-1

particularly spectacular time for clients to see the changing foliage of Shenandoah National Park.

Getting Around

Most of the region's major cities are so close to one another that it's not usually necessary to recommend that your clients fly within the region. But if they do fly, there are many airports, as well as major carriers and commuter airlines serving them. Train and bus connections are good. However, driving is probably the best way for your clients to get around. Prepare them for the heavy traffic in the congested Mid-Atlantic corridor.

Once within a tourist center, however, it's another story. The cities are large, and hectic urban driving conditions almost always prevail. Philadelphia is crowded, with limited parking and expensive taxis; however, there's a good subway and bus system, or your clients may enjoy a horse-drawn carriage ride. Washington, D.C., has limited parking, and streets become one-way during rush hour. Taxis are inexpensive; there's an excellent subway system and very good buses. Most major sights are fairly close to one another. As in Philadelphia, city tours are an excellent way for clients to get around. Escorted tours through the Pennsylvania Dutch country are very popular. And you should remind clients that vehicles aren't allowed in Colonial Williamsburg.

Important Places

The historic sites of Philadelphia, Washington, D.C., the Williamsburg area, and Baltimore are this region's most popular. In addition, there are the lovely natural attractions of the Pennsylvania Dutch country, the Poconos, and Shenandoah National Park.

Philadelphia

If the entire region embodies American liberty, Philadelphia is its historic heart. The first capital of the United States, Philadelphia is a city of 1.6 million residents, where Franklin, Washington, Jefferson, and many other notable figures lived, worked, and founded a nation. Among the many attractions you should recommend to your clients are:

- **Independence National Historical Park**, which comprises most of the city's famous sights. These include **Independence Hall**, where the Declaration of Independence was signed and the Constitution drafted; **Congress Hall**, where the first U.S. Congress met; and the **Liberty Bell**, which is housed in a glass pavilion, by Independence Hall. Other park attractions: **Betsy Ross's House** (where legend says she made the first U.S. flag); **Christ Church** (the house of worship for Benjamin Franklin and George Washington); and **Franklin Court** (the grounds of Franklin's home).

- **The U.S. Mint**, where tourists can see money being made.

- **Philadelphia Zoo**, the nation's oldest zoo.

- **Valley Forge State Park**, just outside town, the famous site of George Washington and his troop's encampment.

- **Great museums**, including the **Franklin Institute Science Museum**, with its hands-on exhibits, a planetarium, and Franklin artifacts; the **Rodin Museum**, with the largest collection of artwork by Rodin outside France; the excellent collection of the **Philadelphia Museum of Art**; and one of the most unusual, rich,

The tradition in Philadelphia is to throw a penny on Benjamin Franklin's grave in the Christ Church graveyard.

Independence Hall, Philadelphia, Pennsylvania
Photo by C. J. Ghormley

During the Christmas season, visit Wanamaker's (department store) for the traditional light show and booming organ music under its famous bronze eagle.

and eccentrically displayed collections in the nation, the **Barnes Foundation**, housed in a mansion-like structure.

• North of Philadelphia is **Reading**, which many consider the discount outlet shopping center of North America.

Pennsylvania Dutch Country

The beautiful farmland of this area—about fifty miles west of Philadelphia—is home to the Amish and Mennonites, descendants of a strict German religious sect. (They weren't Dutch at all, but *Deutsch*.) The region's center is **Lancaster**, which features several farmers' markets with banquets of justly renowned homemade food. Among the other interesting towns is **Hershey**, famous for its chocolate world exhibit, eccentric streetlight posts (they're shaped like Hershey kisses!), and an enjoyable theme park.

A half-day trip from this area is **Gettysburg National Battlefield**, where Abraham Lincoln delivered his famous address in 1863 commemorating the decisive Civil War battle that took place here.

The Pocono Mountains

Only two hours north of Philadelphia, this mountain resort area is popular in the summer (especially among honeymooners) and also in winter for skiing. The best of its ski resorts: **Big Boulder**, **Camel Back**, and **Jack Frost Mountain**. Nearby is the **Delaware Water Gap National Recreation Area** (which extends in from New Jersey).

Pittsburgh

This city, majestically located at the confluence of three rivers, was once picked as America's most "livable" city. There's a great symphony; the **Allegheny Observatory**, one of the world's best; excellent Renaissance art in the **Frick Museum**; and the **Carnegie Institute**, a world-renowned center for culture.

Baltimore

Baltimore has many treasures of its own. With around a million residents, it has a symphony, fine museums—like the **Museum of Art** (with its post-Impressionist collection) and the huge **National Aquarium**—and many renovated historical buildings.

Among the other points of interest here that your clients might enjoy are:

- **Fort McHenry National Monument**, where Francis Scott Key watched the battle that inspired him to write the "Star Spangled Banner."
- **The Baltimore City Life Museums**, a collection of six unusual and unique museums.
- **The U.S. Frigate Constellation**, the oldest warship in the U.S. Navy.
- **Harborplace**, erected over Baltimore's old dock area, with nearly 200 restaurants, cafés, and shops.

Recommend to your clients a day trip to **Annapolis**; it's just thirty miles away. The state capital boasts many restored eighteenth-century buildings, among them the colonial State House. The **U.S. Naval Academy** is here, too.

Delaware

Delaware, a small state, contains several noteworthy attractions. **Winterthur Mansion and Gardens** in Wilmington is quite beautiful and worthy of a visit. Also of interest are the historical town of **Lewes**, the beach town of **Rehoboth**, and the restored sections of the state capital, **Dover**.

Washington, D.C.

The sights of the nation's capital are numerous and well known. But the city isn't always what everyone expects. Washington is a company town, and the business of the town is, of course, government. Among the many wonderful attractions are:

- **The White House**, home of the President. The White House Visitors Center distributes admission tickets and has exhibits.
- **The Mall**, a long, park-like rectangle where many of the city's famous monuments are located, including the inspirational **Vietnam Veterans Memorial** and the obelisk-like **Washington Monument**, the tallest structure in the city. Nearby are the stately **Lincoln Memorial** and the graceful **Jefferson Memorial**.

In early July, Kutztown hosts an extremely popular Pennsylvania Dutch Folk Festival.

Soft-shell crabs and crab cakes are Maryland delicacies.

Wilmington, Delaware, was once a Swedish colony. Fort Christina marks the site.

Through your congressman, you can book "private," VIP early-morning tours of the White House.

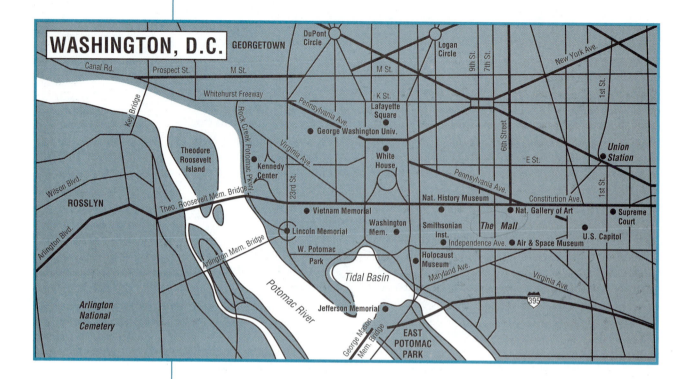

WASHINGTON, D.C.

- **The Smithsonian Institution**, the granddaddy of museums, also on the Mall. Actually, the Smithsonian is a fascinating collection of separate museum buildings, including the huge **National Air and Space Museum**, which displays such gems as the Wright brothers' airplane. Others include the **Museum of Natural History**, **National Museum of American History**, and the **Holocaust Museum**. The red sandstone "Castle" houses the Smithsonian Information Center, which gives an overview of the Institution.

- **The National Gallery of Art**, on the Mall as well, with a vast collection of artwork from around the world.

The Lincoln Memorial, Washington, D.C.
Photo by C. J. Ghormley

The U.S. Capitol Building, Washington, D.C.
Photo by C. J. Ghormley

- **The Washington National Cathedral**, the sixth largest cathedral in the world. One of its stained-glass windows commemorates the Apollo 11 flight and contains a piece of moon rock.
- **Arlington National Cemetery**, just outside town, the resting place of some of the most famous names in U.S. history, and the location of a memorial to the crew of the Space Shuttle Challenger and of the **Tomb of the Unknown Soldier**.
- **Capitol Hill**, where the seats of government are found. Your clients can tour the Capitol itself, where the Senate and House of Representatives meet; there's artwork throughout the halls, and the galleries are open to watch the legislative sessions. Clients can also watch the proceedings in the nearby **Supreme Court Building** from October through June.

Not far from the city, and a popular half-day trip, is Virginia's **Mount Vernon**, the plantation home of George Washington. And **Wolf Trap Farm Park**, the location of an internationally famous summer festival, is the first national park devoted to the performing arts.

Some "short-stop" D.C. attractions: the National Archives (with the Declaration of Independence and the Constitution), Ford's Theater (where Lincoln was shot) and, just across the street, Peterson House (where Lincoln died).

Tidewater Virginia

Located in a triangular area along the Chesapeake Bay, Tidewater is one of the most historic regions in the United States. The scenic **Colonial Parkway Drive** will take your clients through this beautiful area of colonial villages and plantations.

Williamsburg is the most popular site, a lovingly restored eighteenth-century town with period craftsmen, taverns, horse-drawn carts, and a standing militia. Its preserved structures include the second oldest college in the country, the **College of William and Mary**, with a building designed by famed architect Christopher Wren. Jamestown was the first permanent settlement in America; the **Jamestown Festival Park** harbors the three ships that brought John Smith's retinue across the ocean in 1607. Yorktown was where the final battle of the Revolutionary War took place. **Yorktown Battlefield** has tours and a museum.

The most impressive and best-known plantations in the region are located west of Williamsburg and along the James River's north shore. A large amusement theme park, **Busch Garden's "Old Country,"** is close by.

A day trip just south of the Tidewater area is to the harbor towns of **Newport News**, with its Mariner's Museum, and **Norfolk**, where NASA's Langley Research Center offers fascinating aeronautical artifacts. Just south is the popular summer resort of **Virginia Beach**, which could merit a longer stay.

Another day trip you could suggest to clients is **Richmond**, the state capital. Its attractions range from the Revolution—**St. John's Church** is where Patrick Henry cried out, "Give me liberty, or give me death"—to the Civil War, since the city was the capital of the Confederacy. Thomas Jefferson's mansion home, **Monticello**, is nearby.

Thomas Jefferson designed Richmond's capitol building; he based it on a Roman temple in France.

Shenandoah National Park

This park—in Virginia but only seventy-five miles from Washington, D.C.—lies between the Blue Ridge Mountains to the east and the Shenandoah River to the west. The Appalachian Trail runs through the park, as does the beautiful 105-mile-long **Skyline Drive**. It's most crowded in the fall, when the forest colors are stunning. The famed **Luray Caverns**, with their remarkable stalactites and stalagmites, are close by.

Possible Itineraries

For first-time tourists, nine days through historic Philadelphia, Washington, D.C., and Tidewater Virginia would permit a sampling of the area's attractions. For return visitors, several side trips would be worthwhile, including excursions into Pennsylvania Dutch Country, Baltimore, or the Virginia harbor towns. Short trips to the resorts of the Poconos or Virginia Beach would also be good suggestions. For clients who just want to see Washington, D.C., five days or so would be enough to visit most of the major sights.

Lodging Options

As befits such popular tourist centers as these, your clients will have a wide range of accommodations to consider, from grand luxury hotels to budget motels. In Philadelphia, most hotels are around Rittenhouse Square and Logan Circle. In Baltimore, they're between the Civic Center and Center Plaza. In Washington, D.C., hotels are clustered north of the Kennedy Center and Lafayette Square; around Union Station; and along the Potomac, south of National Airport. For political buffs, two hotels stand out: the **Willard Inter-Continental** is where, legend has it, the art of lobbying began; and, of course, there's the **Watergate**. The **Hay-Adams Hotel** offers views of the White House across Lafayette Square. From

The Rittenhouse Hotel on Rittenhouse Square is one of Philadelphia's finest.

Capitol Hill to the White House, your clients might find older, less expensive hotels. Many hotels and campgrounds are just outside the Tidewater Virginia area. In Williamsburg, the **Williamsburg Inn** is elegant and beautifully restored. Most hotels in Virginia Beach are along Boardwalk. Shenandoah National Park has a few lodges and many campgrounds.

This area also offers a wide selection of alternative lodging. Washington, D.C., contains some bed-and-breakfasts. In the Pennsylvania Dutch Country, your clients might enjoy staying in a Mennonite farm house. And guest houses in the Tidewater Virginia area are popular.

Allied Destinations

The Mid-Atlantic States are strategically located for clients wishing to extend their trip to other areas. Pennsylvania borders Ohio to the west and New York to the north, which in turn leads to New England through Connecticut and Massachusetts. Keep in mind also that New York and Washington are jumping-off points for flights to Europe, so the area could be a side trip for clients before such a long flight. Canada is separated from Pennsylvania by only Lake Erie. Virginia borders West Virginia, Kentucky, North Carolina, and Tennessee, opening a gateway to the South.

Factors That Motivate Visitors

Although American history colors every corner of the Mid-Atlantic states, it's important to understand *all* the reasons that could draw your clients to the region. These include:

- Historical buildings, monuments, and sites are everywhere.
- Low airfares, convenient ground transportation, and reasonable lodging make the area a good bargain.
- The area brims with superb cultural attractions: great museums, symphonies, arts festivals, and the unique lifestyle of the Pennsylvania Dutch.
- Virginia, especially, has a mild climate all year long.
- The scenery is impressive, especially in Shenandoah National Park.
- There are very good winter and summer resorts.
- Skiing opportunities abound, especially at the Virginia resorts of Homestead and Wintergreen, or the Pocono ski areas at Jack Frost and Big Boulder.
- The area is accessible: Cities and attractions are fairly close together and are near many other parts of the United States.

Possible Misgivings

As strong as the appeal of this area will be to many of your clients, others will have concerns that you'll have to address:

- "Washington, D.C., is so hot and muggy." It is, but only in the summer; and all buildings are air-conditioned. Spring and fall are particularly beautiful.
- "Except for its historic buildings, Philadelphia is dull." In fact, the city has a world-class orchestra, great museums, and a lively nightlife. This objection might also be raised about Washington, D.C., and more justifiably: The capital's nightlife is largely limited to dining, museums, and concerts.
- "There's not much to see in Baltimore." Besides being home to some important historical sites, the city is a great jumping-off point to Washington, D.C., and Philadelphia.

- "Tidewater Virginia is restored buildings and nothing more." Nearby are the harbor communities, Virginia Beach resorts, an amusement park, and the state capital of Richmond.
- "There's a lot of crime in Washington, D.C." As in any large city, clients should use caution. However, the tourist areas are very safe during the day and relatively so at night.

Sixty-one percent of tourists in Washington, D.C., say they go for "cultural reasons."

Sales Strategies

The region presents you with some special opportunities to sell-up and cross-sell your client's trip. City tours of Washington, D.C., and Philadelphia are popular and excellent ways to see those cities. Don't forget car rentals for those clients who prefer to drive. Booking an escorted tour of the Pennsylvania Dutch Country will facilitate visiting the area for your clients; for a special tour of this part of the country, you might even suggest setting up a personalized guide. Escorted tours of the Tidewater Virginia area can help tie those communities together. And keep in mind that many of the cities covered in this chapter are extremely close to one another, so you could easily extend a client's vacation by adding an additional destination to their already-planned trip.

Qualifying the Client
Washington, D.C.

FOR CLIENTS WHO WANT	APPEAL			REMARKS
	HIGH	MEDIUM	LOW	
Historical and Cultural Attractions	▲			Extremely high appeal
Beaches and Water Sports			▲	Must leave city
Skiing Opportunities			▲	Must leave city
Lots of Nightlife		▲		Good restaurants
Family Activities	▲			A must for students
Familiar Cultural Experience	▲			Well-known sites
Exotic Cultural Experience			▲	
Safety and Low Crime		▲		Crime mostly outside tourist areas
Bargain Travel		▲		
Impressive Scenery		▲		Impressive parks
Peace and Quiet		▲		Quiet at night
Shopping Opportunities			▲	
To Do Business	▲			Government-related

Figure 3-2

Creative Activity

You're about to participate in an unusual scavenger hunt. The object: to take your Polaroid photo next to seven attractions (described in clues) that are scattered throughout the Mid-Atlantic region. The clues will be given to all contestants at noon on the steps of the U.S. Capitol. The first person back to the steps with all seven photos will be declared the winner. (Their outing must be by car.) Using the following clues, try to name the attractions. You may have to consult other chapters or other reference tools to arrive at the answers.

YOUR PHOTO NEXT TO: **WHERE IS IT?**

A bright kiss

A famous Thinker

Old pointy things

Discounted Levi's

A cluster of stars

Midshipmen

The building that sank Nixon

How long do you think it would take to win the contest? Consult an atlas or a AAA road map, if you need to, and plot out a routing for the most efficient path from place to place.

Travel Trivia

American Cities with Dubious Names

Panic, Pennsylvania	Hell, Michigan	Odd, West Virginia
Bad Axe, Michigan	Chunky, Mississippi	Eek, Alaska
Gross, Kansas	War, West Virginia	Pitts, Georgia
Boring, Maryland	Last Chance, Colorado	Roachtown, Illinois
Crummies, Kentucky	Looneyville, West Virginia	Terror Bay, Alaska
Girdle Tree, Maryland	Muck City, Alabama	Tightwad, Missouri
Belcher, New York	Hemlock, Ohio	Goodno, Florida

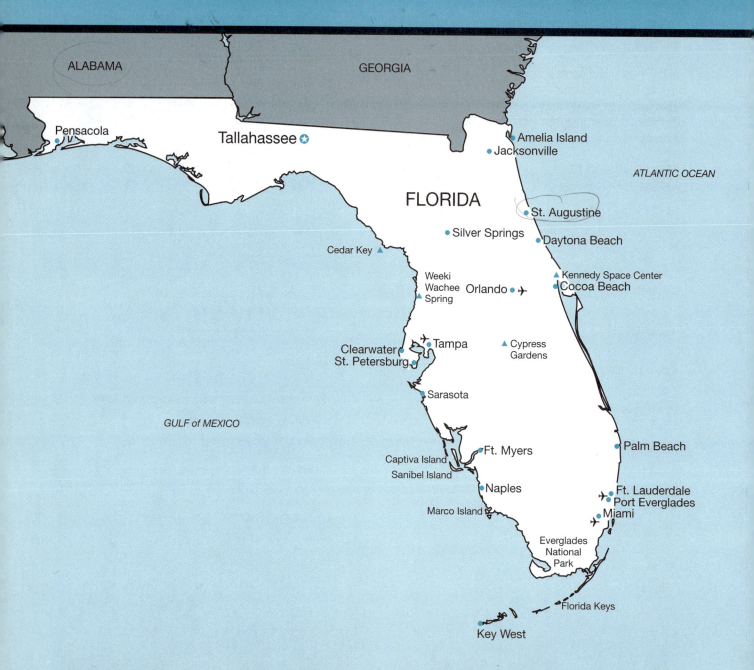

ALABAMA

GEORGIA

ATLANTIC OCEAN

Pensacola

Tallahassee ✪

FLORIDA

Amelia Island
Jacksonville

St. Augustine

Silver Springs

Daytona Beach

Cedar Key ▲

Weeki
Wachee ▲
Spring

Orlando ● ✈

Kennedy Space Center ▲
Cocoa Beach

Tampa ✈

Cypress ▲
Gardens

Clearwater
St. Petersburg

Sarasota

GULF of MEXICO

Ft. Myers

Captiva Island
Sanibel Island

Naples

Marco Island

Palm Beach

Ft. Lauderdale ✈
Port Everglades

Miami ✈

Everglades
National
Park

Florida Keys

Key West

CHAPTER **4**

Florida
Where the Mouse Roars

Orlando wasn't much more than a sleepy little citrus town until a mouse showed up. *The* Mouse. Mickey himself. Walt Disney, creator of Mickey and much, much more, had long regretted not having bought up more land in Anaheim, California. Though Disneyland prospered there, its expansion was limited by the other entrepreneurs who surrounded the Magic Kingdom with hotels, motels, restaurants, and minor attractions. This time it would be different, Disney decided. His corporation bought up vast swaths of land, planned out extensive services, even envisioned an entire "city of tomorrow" where employees would live in futuristic happiness.

Most of Disney's dream—somewhat altered, but just as grandiose—has come true. Many other attractions also have sprung up around the Disney property. The result: The Orlando area has become one of the most popular vacation spots in the United States. And Florida, long a magnet for vacationers, has become the most visited state of all.

It's almost certain, then, that many of your clients will bring up Florida as a potential vacation destination. You'll have to be well-acquainted with what it offers. And what it offers goes well beyond Orlando.

Florida is a flat peninsula, sticking southward into tropical waters: The Gulf of Mexico is on the west, the Atlantic Ocean on the east. Florida's east coast has been a resort destination for a century. From north to south are the cities of **Jacksonville**, **St. Augustine**, **Daytona Beach**, **Cocoa Beach**, **Palm Beach**, **Ft. Lauderdale**, and **Miami**, to name a few. Extending southwestward are the **Florida Keys**, a string of bridge-connected, water-flanked islands that ends at **Key West**.

Florida's west coast, more recently developed as a destination, boasts several first-rate beach resorts, most especially around the tri-city area of **St. Petersburg**, **Clearwater**, and **Tampa**. The **Pensacola** area, in Florida's northwestern "Panhandle" corner, is also a major resort destination, especially for those of your clients who'll be driving from Louisiana, Mississippi, and Alabama. It boasts some of the most beautiful beaches in North America. And, of course, almost dead-center in the Florida peninsula: **Orlando**.

How Travelers Get There

Florida—especially Orlando—is a family destination, and loading up the car with kids and baggage is an efficient way to get there. Most of your profits, then, will come from booking hotel space and, when possible, attraction admissions. Several extensive, low-cost air-shuttle services (usually packaged with hotels, admissions, and car rentals) are available to Orlando; this is the preferred choice of most of your clients, if they live a good distance from Florida. Many airlines fly to Florida's other major cities, too. Its busiest airports are **Miami** (MIA), **Orlando** (MCO), **Tampa** (TPA), and **Ft. Lauderdale** (FLL). Flying time to Florida is about three hours from New York City, four from Chicago, and four-and-a-half from California. Florida's airports (except perhaps Miami) are models of efficiency.

Several convenient train and bus routes lead into scenic Florida as well. An off-beat choice: Amtrak auto trains that will carry the family car—and family—from Lorten, Virginia (just south of Washington, D.C.), to Sanford, Florida, north of Orlando.

Weather Patterns

Florida has extraordinary weather, especially in the winter, when daytime temperatures hover around 70 or 80 degrees with only occasional rain. Days and certainly nights can be a bit nippy; humidity can also make things uncomfortable, even at this cooler time of the year. Tell your clients to bring sweaters just in case (see Figure 4-1). Summers are very hot and humid, with frequent brief—but intense—

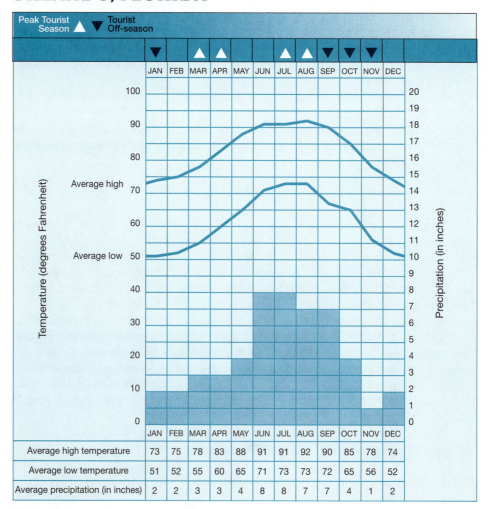

Climate at a Glance _____
ORLANDO, FLORIDA

	JAN	FEB	MAR	APR	MAY	JUN	JUL	AUG	SEP	OCT	NOV	DEC
Average high temperature	73	75	78	83	88	91	91	92	90	85	78	74
Average low temperature	51	52	55	60	65	71	73	73	72	65	56	52
Average precipitation (in inches)	2	2	3	3	4	8	8	7	7	4	1	2

Figure 4-1

The highest spot in Florida is only a few hundred feet high.

thunderstorms (and an occasional hurricane) from June through September. You might remind your summer-traveling clients, however, that breezes temper the heat, especially along the coast.

Since people who live in colder climates visit Florida in the winter, and families visit in the out-of-school summer period, there's no real tourist off-season in Florida, though the number of vacationers does drop off a bit in June, and between Labor Day and Thanksgiving. Advise most of your clients to avoid holiday periods, if at all possible, because of the crowds. Winter holidays, when students swarm to Florida, are especially frantic in beach cities.

Getting Around

It's virtually certain that you'll recommend a car rental to your clients. A car will be needed, whether they intend to tour around Florida or hub out from Orlando or Miami. Car rental prices are extremely low in Florida. Bus travel is an option for your clients on a budget. One conceivable way a client could avoid a car rental or bus travel would be to stay in **Walt Disney World** (where there's a monorail and shuttles to take people from place to place) or in a single resort city and never leave, which can be an attractive option for some.

It's possible to fly your clients between Orlando and Miami, or between several Florida cities and Key West. Several cruise lines call on Key West as a Caribbean cruise port-of-call. Remember to recommend the **Conch Train** to your clients visiting Key West; it will take them on an interesting hour-and-a-half trip around this quaint island-town.

Important Places

Florida is best understood when divided into four principal tourist areas: Orlando, the Atlantic Coast Cities, the Miami-Florida Keys area, and the West Coast. Each appeals to a somewhat different kind of client, as we'll see later.

Orlando

Your client will find three distinct clusters of attractions in the Orlando area: Walt Disney World, non-Disney attractions in the Orlando region, and attractions that can be visited as day trips from Orlando proper.

Walt Disney World clearly dominates the area. Within its enormous boundaries—it's about the same size as San Francisco—are hotel clusters, shopping villages, camping grounds, animal sanctuaries, sports complexes, a learning center (The Disney Institute), and water parks. Four Disney attractions, though, will probably monopolize your clients' attention:

- **The Magic Kingdom**, an ultimate theme park, usually tops any client's list. It's very similar to California's Disneyland, though it covers much more acreage.
- **EPCOT Center** is, in effect, a permanent world's fair, with both national and corporate pavilions—all of them providing spellbinding entertainment. This—along with the nighttime entertainment area, Downtown Disney—is the most adult of Orlando's attractions.
- **The Disney-MGM Studios Theme Park** is a diverting look at how movies are made; it includes many buildings that are reproductions of Hollywood landmarks.
- **Disney's Animal Kingdom** is a 500-acre cross between a zoo and a theme park. It stresses what we must do to preserve endangered species.

Outside Disney's vast empire are several other independent attractions, both major and minor. The most impressive: **Sea World**, the world's largest marine

The busiest days at the Magic Kingdom and EPCOT are Monday through Wednesday; at the Disney-MGM Studios, Wednesday through Friday.

A Saturn V rocket at Kennedy Space Center
Photo by H. Fukushima

To avoid theme park lines: Arrive at morning opening time, walk to the far end of the park, and work your way back to the entrance.

park, and **Universal Studios** (which has a character very distinct from the Disney-MGM Studio Tour and requires two days to see).

Other attractions lie within about a two-hour drive from Orlando. To the east, near **Cocoa Beach**, is the **Kennedy Space Center** (also called SpacePort USA), the home of America's space program. Bus tours will take your clients on a tour of the facility; its excellent museum traces the history of man's exploration of the cosmos. To Orlando's south is the 233-acre **Cypress Gardens**, one of America's oldest theme parks; it boasts impressive gardens, water-ski shows, and amusement rides. And to Orlando's west in Tampa is **Busch Gardens**, an extensive attraction that melds a zoolike wild animal preserve with an amusement park. Other attractions within range of Orlando: **Silver Springs** and its glass-bottomed boats, **Bok Tower** and its restful gardens, and **Weeki Wachee Spring**.

The Atlantic Coast Cities

In the late 1800s, several entrepreneurs decided to run railroad lines down from the U.S. northeast and develop Florida into a resort vacation and retirement mecca. Their plan worked. A sun-bleached string of towns and cities sprang up along the coastal routes; they still draw millions of visitors each year. Among those that your clients may ask about are, from north to south:

Baseball fans can root for their favorite teams in Florida during Spring Training.

- **Jacksonville**, with its many cultural activities, sports events, nearby beaches, and, to the north, the offshore resort of **Amelia Island**.
- **St. Augustine**, the oldest city in the United States, with its old Spanish fort (the Castillo) and ancient restored streets.
- **Daytona Beach**, the home of Daytona International Speedway, and one of the college vacation crowds' favorite haunts.

On many of Florida's Atlantic beaches, you're permitted to drive on the beach itself.

- **Cocoa Beach**, a smallish city with reasonable seaside lodging just a few miles from the Kennedy Space Center. Close by is **Port Canaveral**, from which some cruises depart.

- **Palm Beach**, an upscale beach city with outstanding architecture, most especially the old mansions along Ocean Boulevard. The city has an unusual ordinance: no fast food restaurants, movie theaters, neon signs, or car dealerships are allowed within city limits.

- **Ft. Lauderdale**, with its miles of prime sand, 3,000 eating establishments, and 40,000 registered boats. Nearby **Port Everglades** is a major departure point for cruises.

The Miami/Florida Keys Area

Miami has long been known for everything that is good and bad: On the plus side are the fabulous restaurants, fascinating architecture, rich cultural diversity, cruise opportunities, and picture-perfect beaches of **Key Biscayne** and **Miami**

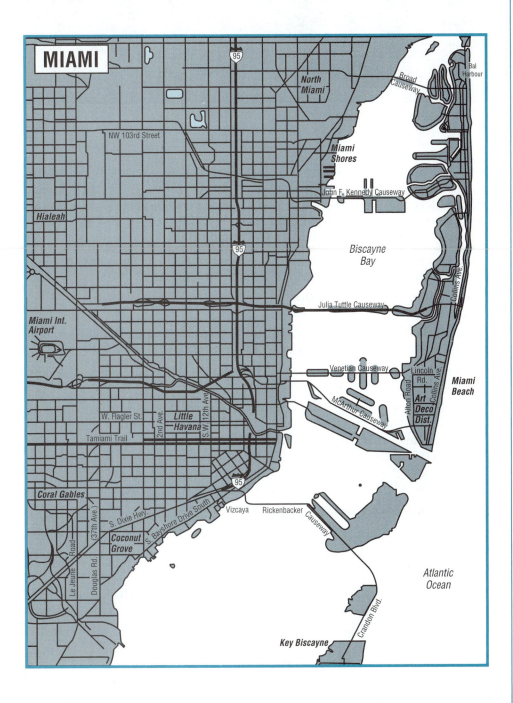

Miami Museum of Science, Miami
Courtesy of Miami Museum of Science

A rather unusual attraction in Miami: Monkey Jungle, where the visitors are in cages and the monkeys are outside.

In Key Largo, there's an underwater hotel where the bellhops wear scuba gear.

Beach (a separate city from Miami); negative factors include crime, racial and ethnic unrest, and the locals' occasional tendency toward rudeness. Though your clients will be sensitive to Miami's well-publicized problems, they'll also be aware that it has undergone an intriguing renaissance.

You should counsel your clients to see the following:

- **Vizcaya Palace**, a baronial home that's near Miami's famous artistic community, **Coconut Grove**, and the upscale **Coral Gables**.
- **The South Beach Art Deco District**, a vibrant strip of old renovated buildings that features trendy seaside eateries.
- **Little Havana**, a colorful and festive enclave of Cuban restaurants and shops.
- Several museums, including the **Museum of Science**.
- **Everglades National Park**, the swampy habitat of alligators, weird birds, and tourist air-boats that's about an hour from Miami.
- **The Florida Keys**, a destination unto itself, with its 180-mile-long string of thirty-two islands, forty-two bridges, and awesome seascapes that stretch out to the magical town of Key West. A drive from Miami to Key West, with stops, can easily take a half-day, so you should perhaps suggest lodging in Key West for them.

Florida's West Coast

Many interesting beach cities dot the Gulf of Mexico rim of Florida, yet Florida's west coast remains less well-known than its Atlantic side. Those places you're likely to tell your clients about are:

- **Ft. Myers**, a major port of sailing for your clients who love to fish.
- **The Resort Islands—Sanibel** and **Captiva** (off Ft. Myers) and **Marco** (off Naples)—with their fine fishing, seashell-laden beaches, and many upscale hotels and condos.
- **Sarasota**, home of the **Ringling Circus Museum**.

- **Clearwater**, the west coast's prime beach community, only a short distance from the fast-growing, progressive metropolises of St. Petersburg (with several interesting museums) and Tampa (with its Busch Gardens).
- **Cedar Key**, a quintessential fishing village that's now also an artists' colony.
- **The Florida Panhandle**, which faces southerly onto the Gulf and is in Florida's northwest corner. Here can be found numerous beaches (some noisy and crowded, others pristine and preserved), fishing resorts, old Spanish-themed Pensacola, and Florida's capital **Tallahassee** (which is inland).

Possible Itineraries

Probably the most popular itinerary you can offer to clients (especially families) requires about six or seven full days in Orlando, with three or four days in Walt Disney World and the rest spent visiting nearby attractions. To simply lodge your clients within Walt Disney World and have them limit themselves to its attractions is a possible strategy, especially for shorter trips. They would miss, however, the fascinations that lie outside Disney World's perimeter. For clients who want to see everything in and around Orlando and have the time to do it, recommend about ten days.

An Atlantic-coast itinerary would require about a week, with clients driving from Jacksonville to Miami and stopping along the way. Miami and the Keys merit six or seven days, as would a trip along Florida's west coast.

Some clients will want to see all of Florida in a week. Explain to them that it's almost impossible. Suggest that they stay in Orlando or Miami and hub out. If they want to see the highlights of Florida, it might be possible to stay in Orlando for three days, drive up to St. Augustine, and down to Cocoa Beach for two days. From there, they could drive down to Miami and the Keys for four days, and up to the Clearwater-Tampa area for two. This results in an eleven-to-twelve-day trip, but a *very* hectic one.

Remember that Miami and Ft. Lauderdale are major jump-off points for cruises and flights to South America and the Caribbean. Indeed, a short stay in Miami can be a welcomed add-on to your clients' Caribbean plans. Orlando land package–Bahamian (or Caribbean) cruise combinations—usually out of Port Canaveral and some on Disney-owned ships—are also very popular with families.

Lodging Options

Lodging in Florida is comparatively inexpensive, especially in the Orlando area. Your clients may wish to stay right on the Walt Disney World grounds; there's everything from expensive to budget-priced, and most Disney hotels are theme-oriented. Many very fine hotels—and a few awful ones—are located a few miles from the Magic Kingdom. Some of the best are in the **Main Gate** area, and many are along **International Drive**. The best strategy: Carefully study your reference guides and stick with well-known chains.

Miami has many downtown hotels (frequented by business clients and conventioneers), but most of your clients will want to stay on the long island of seaside property that is Miami Beach. For your upscale clients, recommend the super-deluxe properties in the Key Biscayne, Coral Gables, central Miami Beach, and **Bal Harbour** areas. (The central Miami Beach district features three of America's most famous properties: the **Doral Ocean Beach Resort**, **the Fontainebleau Hilton**, and **Eden Roc**.) Clients seeking moderate lodging should be booked in the "art deco district" and North Miami Beach "Motel Row." Be careful: The quality of lodging in both these budget areas varies enormously. Throughout Florida are also many condominiums, several spas, and resorts. One of the most famous: **The Breakers**, in Palm Beach, is considered by some to be the most striking hotel in Florida.

An unexpected treat in St. Petersburg: The Salvador Dali Museum.

Over 90 percent of visitors to Florida have visited the state before.

The most popular Disney park is the Magic Kingdom at Walt Disney World.

Allied Destinations

The most obvious add-on to a trip to Florida is a voyage into the Caribbean by either ship or plane. A stay in Florida's Panhandle and, for that matter, all of Florida, is easily combined with a New Orleans vacation. So, too, are any vacations spent in the southern states, especially in the Savannah, Georgia, area. Remember that air service from Miami to South America and Europe is considerable. A short stay in Miami might be a way to break up a trip to these two major tourist areas.

Factors That Motivate Visitors

Florida boasts a wealth of client-motivating factors, including:

- It has a year-round tropical climate
- A low-cost vacation is feasible.
- It's easily accessible by car, train, or plane.
- Many bargain air-hotel-car-rental packages are available.
- There's an astonishing concentration of family attractions in the Orlando area.
- Deep-sea fishing and other sport opportunities abound.
- Florida is an air and cruise gateway to Latin America and the Caribbean. Its principal cruise ports are Miami, Port Everglades (Fort Lauderdale), Port Canaveral, and Tampa.
- It's a major destination for students on Spring Break.
- Miami has great cultural diversity.
- A well-developed highway system crisscrosses Florida.
- Superior beach resorts are found along both the Atlantic and Gulf coasts.

Possible Misgivings

As popular as Florida is, your clients may offer certain objections to a trip there:

- "It's only for families and kids." Recommend any destination outside Orlando. Remind the client that even in Orlando, EPCOT can be entertaining for adult visitors.
- "It's too hot and humid." Recommend a late fall, winter, or early spring visit.
- "There's no cultural opportunities." Miami appeals to culture-seekers, and Key West has many historical assets. Orlando's EPCOT is a pop-cultural experience. It is true that Florida, as a cultural destination, is not on a par with, say, Europe.
- "I've been to Florida, and the people aren't very friendly." This can be true, especially in Miami. But most Floridians are friendly and even engagingly upbeat.
- "Miami is crime-ridden." There's a bit of truth to this, but most areas—especially the upscale ones—are quite insulated from Miami's problems. Warn clients to avoid driving off the tourist-beaten path and to remain alert and cautious when driving between the airport and their Miami lodging.

Sales Strategies

Comprehensive packages are probably the best way to draw maximum commissions from an Orlando vacation: You can sell air, hotel, ground transportation, admissions, and maybe some meals—all at once. You should always try to sell-up lodging almost anywhere in Florida; even deluxe properties can be reasonable. Always offer to book

Florida is the number one family destination in North America. (California is number two.)

Florida has the second longest coastline in America. (Alaska has the longest.)

Florida is a major destination for Canadians and Brazilians.

Case Study

Bart Beavis, fifty years old and recently divorced, is an outgoing individual who lives in Anaheim, California. He wants to get away for his two-week vacation and is interested in Florida. He loves fishing, water sports, and sightseeing; a few of his buddies who live in Florida may join him for these activities. He's not a fan of idling on the beach, though, and he hates hot, humid, or stormy weather. He's prepared to spend a good sum of money on his trip.

Circle the answer that best suits your client's needs:

1. When would you suggest that he go?

   September   June

   Early May   Late August

   Why?

2. What should you probably *not* sell to this client to expand his FIT?

   A side trip to Nashville   A stopover in New Orleans

   A cruise   A side trip to Jamaica

   Why?

3. What would be best to cross-sell to this client?

   A yacht charter   A train tour of all of Florida

   A Magic Kingdom package   An alligator hunt

   Why?

4. Of the following cities, which one should you *not* consider as a lodging spot for the client?

   Ft. Lauderdale   Key West

   Ft. Myers   Orlando

   Why?

Creative Activity

Travel and Leisure magazine once conducted an on-line poll to determine which cities, places, and attractions were "worth revisiting." The winner: Washington, D.C. (i.e., 40 percent said that Washington, D.C. merited a second trip). Why do you think those polled felt the way they did? Write your answer below.

Now, consider the following places. Do you think they merit a second visit? Again, write your reason in the blank provided.

PLACE **YES OR NO?** **WHY OR WHY NOT?**

1. The Florida Keys

2. Orlando

3. The Kennedy Space Center

4. Miami

What three places in the United States and/or Canada, other than the ones above, do you think *most* merit a return visit? Again, explain why.

PLACE

1.

2.

3.

Travel Trivia

Top Ten U.S. Water Parks

1. Wet 'n Wild, Orlando, FL
2. Typhoon Lagoon, Orlando, FL
3. Blizzard Beach, Orlando, FL
4. Schlitterbahn, New Braunfels, TX
5. Raging Waters, San Dimas, CA
6. Six Flags Wet 'n Wild, Arlington, TX
7. White Water, Marietta, GA
8. Water Country USA, Williamsburg, VA
9. Wild Rivers, Irvine, CA
10. Wet 'n Wild, Las Vegas, NV

Travel Trivia

Where Fast Food Chains Began

Burger King: Miami
Kentucky Fried Chicken: Salt Lake City
Nathan's: New York City
Pizza Hut: Wichita, Kansas
Domino's: Detroit
McDonald's: San Bernardino, California

Source: The History Channel

CHAPTER 5

California and Arizona

Glamour and Grandeur

It all depends on which of your clients you ask. Say the name "California," and the first thing some will think of is the glitz of **Hollywood** or the free-spirited sophistication of **San Francisco**. Others will conjure up the images of magnificent natural wonders like awesome **Yosemite National Park**, the rolling **Wine Country**, or the majestic **redwoods**.

California should be divided geographically into two areas, North and South, each with a distinct character. Southern California is largely desert and industrial, with **Los Angeles**, bordering the **Pacific Ocean** off its west coast, as its heart. The L.A. metropolitan area sprawls far south, through **Anaheim** (and **Disneyland**) in **Orange County**, down to lovely **San Diego**. Just north of L.A. is the San Fernando Valley, home of **Burbank**, where many of the movie studios are found.

Northern California is more mountainous and forested. Its centerpiece is the port of San Francisco. Just south of the city are the beautiful towns of **Monterey** and **Carmel**, and to its north is the Wine Country of the **Napa Valley** and **Sonoma County**. Yosemite National Park is southeast of San Francisco, near the Nevada border. Northeast of San Francisco, incidentally, is the state capital, **Sacramento**; it's not, however, much of a tourist center.

California is connected on the southeast to Arizona. Largely a desert (though there are mountains throughout its northern portion), Arizona has stunning scenery, notably in the area around the **Grand Canyon** and **Sedona**. In the center of the state, but a bit south, is **Phoenix**, Arizona's capital and cultural center. Off in the southeast corner is **Tucson** [TOO-sahn], a city heavily influenced by Native-American culture.

How Travelers Get There

L.A. is one of the most easily reached cities by air in the United States. Most flights land at **Los Angeles International Airport** (LAX); however, **Burbank Airport** (BUR) is convenient for clients who are staying in the San Fernando Valley or who prefer less crowded terminals. There's also **John Wayne Airport** (SNA) in Orange County (for those visiting Disneyland and other attractions in that area), and **Ontario Airport** (ONT), east of L.A. Clients can also land at **San Diego International Airport** (SAN).

Flights to northern California are also numerous. The major gateway is **San Francisco International Airport** (SFO). However, many flights land at **Oakland Airport** (OAK), and **San Jose** (SJC) as well.

Most Arizona-bound travelers will fly into **Sky Harbor International Airport** (PHX) in Phoenix, though there's also a busy airport at Tucson (TUS). Flying time to all these destinations from the East Coast is about five to six hours.

A leisurely and scenic way of reaching the area is by train. Amtrak has lines to both Los Angeles and San Francisco that can be accessed from many cities across the United States. One of the L.A. routes goes through Flagstaff. Cruises access San Diego and L.A. from Acapulco and, on repositioning cruises, from San Francisco, Alaska, and Hawaii. A rich complex of highways flows into Arizona and California from their neighboring states.

Weather Patterns

To describe the climates of California and Arizona is no easy task. The reason: Totally different climate conditions can exist within miles of each other. For example, a visitor to southern California can drive from Santa Monica Beach to inland San Bernardino and into the nearby mountains, passing from pleasant, breezy beach temperatures through hot desert air, and into snow—all in less than two hours.

Four general climate patterns exist in California and Arizona. **Coastal California**, which includes the beach areas, tends to have warm but dry summers and

To visit L.A.'s new Getty Center by car, you should make a parking reservation many weeks in advance.

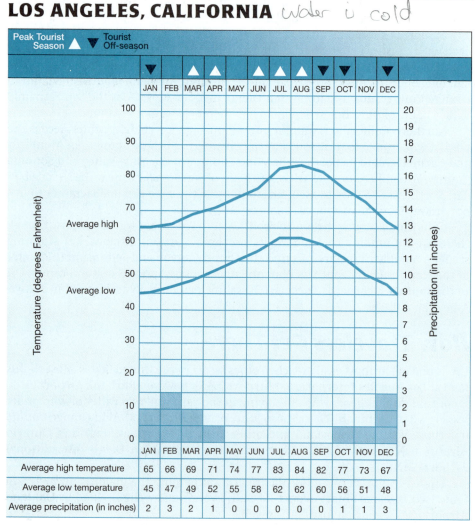

Climate at a Glance
LOS ANGELES, CALIFORNIA

	JAN	FEB	MAR	APR	MAY	JUN	JUL	AUG	SEP	OCT	NOV	DEC
Average high temperature	65	66	69	71	74	77	83	84	82	77	73	67
Average low temperature	45	47	49	52	55	58	62	62	60	56	51	48
Average precipitation (in inches)	2	3	2	1	0	0	0	0	0	1	1	3

Figure 5-1

pleasantly comfortable winters, with occasional rainstorms between November and March (see Figures 5-1 and 5-2). Fog along the immediate coast can occur anytime, though it happens less frequently in the fall (which may be California's most pleasant season). Nights are almost always cool. Of course, the farther north a traveler goes up the coast toward San Francisco and beyond, the chillier the year-round temperatures become. As Mark Twain put it: "The coldest winter I ever spent was a summer in San Francisco."

The second pattern occurs in California's **valleys and near-coastal areas** (for example, Anaheim). The climate is somewhat like coastal California, but with temperatures that run 10 to 15 degrees warmer and with fog only rarely. The third pattern marks the vast, flat **deserts** of California and Arizona. Summer, early fall, and late spring feature extremely sunny, torridly hot, and bone-dry weather. Winter is much more pleasant, with warmth, sunshine, and only occasional rain (see Figure 5-3). **High-elevation areas** (for example, the Grand Canyon and California mountain resorts) represent the last pattern: cold, snowy winters with warm daytime sun (even if there's snow on the ground) and pleasantly cool to warm summers.

Remember: California's ocean temperatures are chilly. As for tourist patterns, California enjoys major tourism year-round, with a slight thinning of crowds in the fall. The desert and ski resorts have their high seasons in the winter; rates plunge during the summer.

It snows in Los Angeles two or three times per century.

Climate at a Glance
SAN FRANCISCO, CALIFORNIA Earthquakes

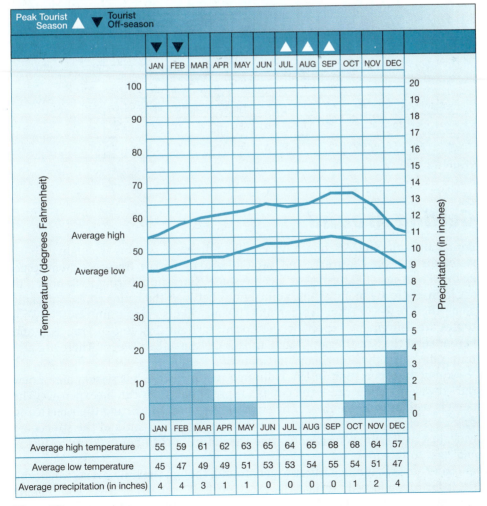

	JAN	FEB	MAR	APR	MAY	JUN	JUL	AUG	SEP	OCT	NOV	DEC
Average high temperature	55	59	61	62	63	65	64	65	68	68	64	57
Average low temperature	45	47	49	49	51	53	53	54	55	54	51	47
Average precipitation (in inches)	4	4	3	1	1	0	0	0	0	1	2	4

Figure 5-2

Climate at a Glance
PHOENIX, ARIZONA

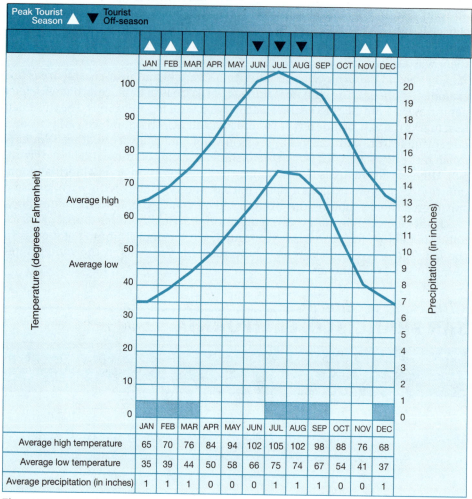

Peak Tourist Season ▲	▼ Tourist Off-season											
	▲	▲	▲			▼	▼	▼			▲	▲
	JAN	FEB	MAR	APR	MAY	JUN	JUL	AUG	SEP	OCT	NOV	DEC
Average high temperature	65	70	76	84	94	102	105	102	98	88	76	68
Average low temperature	35	39	44	50	58	66	75	74	67	54	41	37
Average precipitation (in inches)	1	1	1	0	0	0	1	1	1	0	0	1

Figure 5-3

Getting Around

Both California and Arizona have excellent freeway systems (though in both states, distances can be great). And, yes, California's massive freeway system—especially in southern California—suffers awesome congestion during rush hours. In addition, there are many airline connections between the major cities, especially along the L.A.-to-San Francisco corridor. If your clients enjoy train travel, several routes are convenient, especially the **Coast Starlight** (L.A. to San Francisco and beyond) and the **San Diegan** (from San Luis Obispo to San Diego). There are also train rides through California Wine Country.

Public transportation in L.A. is limited to a mediocre bus system and a new rail-subway system. Because the city is so spread out, taxis can be expensive. The best choices for your clients are the popular city tours, or gritting their teeth and driving themselves. The highways, however, are well laid out and the streets are wide. Just make sure your clients avoid them during rush hours (7 A.M. to 10 A.M. and 3 P.M. to 7 P.M.).

San Francisco is much easier to get around, though the hilly streets can be difficult for cars and pedestrians. The excellent BART subway will get your clients around the Bay Area. And, of course, there are the famous and fun cable cars.

Study a map before driving on L.A. freeways; many roads aren't marked by direction, but by only a city name (like "405 to San Diego").

To get to the Grand Canyon from Flagstaff, your clients can either drive themselves on a beautiful (but slow) route or take a bus from the city's bus depot. One-day air excursions to the Grand Canyon from Los Angeles can be booked. Phoenix is also spread out; book a car rental for your client or recommend the adequate bus system.

Important Places

California and Arizona have a wealth of attractions. Here are the principal ones:

Los Angeles

Los Angeles is the heart of any trip to southern California and a magnet for forty million visitors yearly. A sprawling city of extremes, L.A. is a city your clients will probably either love or avoid like the plague. As befits the second-largest city in the United States, the Los Angeles area brims with first-rate attractions: theme parks, museums, beaches, nightlife, theater, and its own brand of glitz. Among the most popular attractions are:

- **Disneyland**, the granddaddy of theme parks, which is actually in Anaheim, about a half hour from Los Angeles itself. Clients could easily spend two days here, especially if they have children. This is a definite must-see.

- **Other theme parks**, like the **Universal Studios Tour** (another must), **Knott's Berry Farm**, **Six Flags Magic Mountain**, and tours of **NBC Studios**.

- **Mann's Chinese Theater**, where movie stars' footprints are enshrined in cement. Nearby is the **Walk of Fame**, where starlike plaques honoring the famous are embedded in the sidewalk.

- **Beverly Hills**, with its posh Rodeo Drive and mansions (which can be viewed via a "Stars' homes" tour).

- **Excellent museums**, like the **L.A. County Museum of Art**, the offbeat **Museum of Contemporary Art**, and the new **Getty Center**, perhaps the world's wealthiest museum.

Disneyland is least crowded on weekdays in October and February (except during Presidents' week).

"Real" studio tours at Warner Bros. and Paramount are available.

Farmer's Market is a favorite among locals for food and shopping.

The *Queen Mary*, Long Beach, California
Photo by C. J. Ghormley

- **The Queen Mary**, in nearby Long Beach, permanently docked as a hotel and tourist attraction. Nearby: a good number of waterfront restaurants, hotels, shops, secondary attractions, and the world-class **Aquarium of the Pacific**.
- **The Venice Boardwalk**, with its assortment of beach-side eccentrics (and those who come to see them). Two more trendy places to look, shop, and stroll: **Santa Monica**'s **Third Street Promenade** and **CityWalk**, which adjoins Universal Studios.

Various **day trips** can be taken from Los Angeles, many of which can be extended into longer stays. Some of your clients might enjoy:

- **Catalina Island**, twenty-six miles across the sea from L.A., exactly as the song said. There are beautiful coves, mountains, hiking, buffalo herds, and boat and bus tours.
- **Big Bear** and **Lake Arrowhead**, popular and pretty water-and-ski resorts, in the nearby **San Bernardino Mountains**.

A little farther out from L.A. and reachable within an easy day's drive are some places that could make nice, short overnight stops of their own:

- **Palm Springs**, a fashionable desert resort. It's not as posh as it once was, but the nearby **Palm Desert** and **Rancho Mirage** resort complexes are luxurious. During colleges' spring break, it's a zoo. A major nearby attraction is an aerial tramway that takes visitors to the top of lofty Mt. San Jacinto.
- **Joshua Tree National Monument**, not far north of Palm Springs. This is one of the unsung treasures of California, with spectacular rock formations and great hiking.
- **Santa Barbara**, with missions, boutiques, great ocean views, good small museums, and lovely gardens.
- **Sequoia and Kings Canyon National Parks**, with their famed towering redwood trees. These parks are about equidistant from San Francisco and Los Angeles.

San Diego

Only a couple of hours from Los Angeles, San Diego has about one million residents. Though close enough for a long, tiring day trip from L.A., this beautiful city—with its revitalized downtown core—should be seen on its own. Among its popular attractions are:

- **San Diego Zoo**, one of the world's greatest zoos. Most of the animals are kept in natural habitat surroundings, not cages. The zoo is actually just one part of **Balboa Park**, the city's centerpiece, with lakes, gardens, and many museums.
- **Wild Animal Park**, a large animal preserve with tours.
- **Sea World**, one of the world's great marine-life amusement parks.
- **Tijuana**, the Mexican city about twenty minutes away, across the border from San Diego. It's dirty and impoverished, but bargain hunters still love to go there.

San Francisco

As Los Angeles is to southern California, so, too, is San Francisco the hub of northern California. San Francisco, a city of nearly 700,000, has wonderful restaurants, cutting-edge nightlife, and excellent symphony and opera.

Among the attractions your clients may enjoy are:

- **Fisherman's Wharf**, a lively waterfront open-air market, with stalls selling that day's catch and the smells of sourdough bread permeating the air. This crowded district has excellent restaurants and interesting shops.

A movie crew filming a 1912 western brought buffalo to Catalina. When the shoot was finished, the buffalo were left to fend for themselves.

Some consider The Golden Door in Escondido (near San Diego) to be America's finest spa.

San Franciscans dislike their city being called "Frisco."

- **Ghirardelli Square**, a busy, fun shopping center right near the Wharf. Several similar shopping complexes are also in the area.
- **Golden Gate Park**, a wonderful, huge recreation area with many lakes, several museums, and the beautiful **Japanese Tea Garden**.
- **Alcatraz**, the famed old prison that the National Parks Service maintains as a tourist attraction.
- **Chinatown**, where there are the largest number of Chinese in any area outside of China. It gets crowded, but your clients will surely enjoy walking among the pagoda-like buildings, checking out the import shops, and eating.
- A few other attractions: the oddly shaped **Coit Tower**, crooked **Lombard Street**, and the **North Beach** restaurant area.

Several areas outside San Francisco can be recommended as **day trips** to your clients:

- **Monterey** and **Carmel**, to the south. These gorgeous towns have beautiful scenery, famous golf courses, and a lovely old mission. Monterey's aquarium is outstanding. The renowned **17 Mile Drive** is a must-see.
- **Muir Woods National Monument**, to the north of San Francisco. This stunning park features walks among spectacular redwoods. On the way, your client could stop at **Sausalito**, a quaint waterfront town just across the Bay from San Francisco. Getting there offers a good opportunity to cross the **Golden Gate Bridge**, a world-famous landmark.
- **Hearst San Simeon State Historic Park**, the famous ornate castle. It's a long day trip from San Francisco, at the southerly end of the scenic **Big Sur** Coastal Road.

The most scenic cable car route is the Powell-Hyde line.

Your ski-loving clients might want to know about **Lake Tahoe**, a popular resort on the Nevada border, just across from Reno, Nevada. It's about a four-hour drive from San Francisco. The Tahoe area contains a number of world-class ski resorts, including: Heavenly Valley, Alpine Meadows, and Squaw Valley. To the south of the Lake (nearer Yosemite) is the Mammoth Mountain/June Mountain ski area.

The Wine Country

Only an hour's drive north of San Francisco, Napa Valley and Sonoma County—the two biggest wine-producing regions in the United States—are commonly visited for several days on their own. The wineries have fascinating architecture; redwood forests and lovely little shops are all along the way. They can be visited by car, train, or boat. The town of **Calistoga** is famous for its mineral springs and spas, which have attracted visitors since the nineteenth century.

Yosemite National Park

Yosemite is one of the most beautiful locales in the world, with such justly renowned spectacles as Half Dome and El Capitan. If your clients are near the area, they must visit here.

Phoenix

This fast-growing desert city (it's Arizona's capital) is surrounded by hulking mountains and is steeped in Native-American history. The city has several mega-resorts and all manner of dude ranches. Phoenix is also a baseball mecca from late February to early April, when major league teams train there.

Its most popular attractions include:

- **The adjoining town of Scottsdale**, with impressive upscale art galleries, resort hotels, golf courses, and shops specializing in Native-American crafts.
- **Architectural centers**, notably **Taliesin West** (the fascinating school created by Frank Lloyd Wright) and the **Cosanti Foundation** (the strangely wonderful, futuristic workshop of Paolo Soleri). Tours of both are available.

Eat in one of the several country-and-western restaurants on the outskirts of Phoenix. A western delicacy: rattlesnake (which tastes like chicken).

The Golden Gate Bridge, San Francisco, California
Photo by C. J. Ghormley

An attractive day trip you can suggest to clients is to the town of Sedona, famed for its astonishing red cliffs; Sedona can be accessed by driving along the scenic Verde River valley or from Flagstaff, as part of a shorter, half-day trip through spectacular Oak Creek Canyon. Not far from Sedona is Montezuma Castle, the 800-year-old ruin of an ancient North American civilization, situated in the side of a cliff. In addition, your clients may enjoy the long trip to **Lake Havasu**, most famous as the site of the relocated **London Bridge**. (There's nothing weirder than seeing this structure in the middle of the desert.)

Grand Canyon National Park   *north part of Arizona*

This is possibly the most famous natural landmark in the United States. It's breathtaking. The South Rim, which offers the best views, is the most popular area for your clients to visit, and it's jam-packed in the summer. The canyon's depths can be seen by hiking, riding on a mule, flying in a helicopter or plane, or rafting on the Colorado River.

Hotel accommodations in the park are limited, so you should probably lodge your clients in Flagstaff (about ninety miles away). From here, you can suggest other places to visit, including the **Painted Desert** and **Petrified Forest National Park** (east of Flagstaff) and **Monument Valley** (northeast) with its ancient Native-American ruins and familiar vistas. (Monument Valley appeared repeatedly in western movies.)

Meteor Crater, outside Winslow, is where a giant meteor crashed into the ground 22,000 years ago.

Tucson

The city is extremely popular in the winter for its dude ranches, resorts, and the controversial, ecologically sealed community, **Biosphere 2**. **Old Tucson Studios**, where many Westerns were shot, is just west of town. Several Tucson museums showcase Native-American art. The city is also near **Saguaro National Monument**, with its giant cacti. About 100 miles southeast of Tucson is **Tombstone**. Here your clients can experience the Old West as it must have been, complete with the legendary **OK Corral**, **Boot Hill**, and the **Bird Cage Theater**.

Possible Itineraries

Where should first-time tourists to California go? Probably to either L.A. or San Francisco and their surrounding areas. There's enough to do close by each city to warrant a stay of five to seven days. Clients often want to drive the coastal road between the two cities, but it's a long distance that's better done in two days, with a stop perhaps at Hearst Castle. Return visitors may prefer to get out of the urban centers and discover the riches of the state, exploring the southern California coastal communities or the desert for a week, or driving through the Wine Country and forest land of the north. A five-day trip to Yosemite or the Grand Canyon and their surrounding areas are worthwhile trips of their own. Or a relaxing three to five days in Phoenix might let your clients get away from it all.

Lodging Options

California offers an abundance of lodging choices. In Los Angeles, there's no real lodging center; there are, though, hotel clusters around the L.A. Airport, Beverly Hills, Universal Studios, **Marina del Rey**, **Century City**, **West Hollywood**, downtown (more appropriate for some business clients), and Disneyland in Anaheim. The **Beverly Hills Hotel**, with its famous bungalows, is where legendary movie stars have resided; L.A.'s secluded **Hotel Bel-Air** is frequently rated as one of America's best lodgings. The San Diego area also has some excellent hotels, especially the **Hotel Del Coronado**, an astonishing bit of wooden Victorian whimsy; and Santa Barbara's **Four Seasons Biltmore** is a landmark.

At San Luis Obispo's Madonna Inn, each room has a different theme. (The Cave Man room is the most popular.)

In San Francisco, hotels tend to be based at Nob Hill, Union Square, Fisherman's Wharf, and on either side of Market Street. There are at least a half-dozen world-class hotels here (including the **Ritz-Carlton**, the **Fairmont**, and the **Mark Hopkins Inter-Continental**), as well as many lesser-known gems. Yosemite has a wide range of accommodations, from hotel rooms to tents and cabins; the **Ahwahnee Hotel** is rustic, yet elegant, and a national landmark. For a change of pace, bed-and-breakfasts are popular in California, especially in Wine Country.

Some Arizona resorts in the north close in the winter, whereas those in the south may close during summer months. Most hotels are open all year, though, but may drastically lower their rates off-season. Lodging in the Phoenix area is clustered downtown, and north of the city near the Metrocenter, as well as throughout Scottsdale. Frank Lloyd Wright designed the luxurious **Arizona Biltmore resort**. In Scottsdale is the **Phoenician**, a glitzy resort carved out of the side of a mountain. Dude ranches offer an intriguing lodging option, especially for clients who are horse lovers. Tucson has a surprisingly rich collection of upscale resorts (such as the **Canyon Ranch**) and ranches.

Allied Destinations

California is a good jumping-off point for the Pacific Northwest states of Oregon and Washington. It also borders Nevada and is a short flight to Las Vegas. California is a common stop for long flights to Hawaii; you might suggest a couple of days to break up a client's trip. Both California and Arizona border Mexico, with many cruise ships heading southward to Baja, Mexico, and beyond. Remember, too, that Arizona is next to Colorado, New Mexico, and Utah (with its many national parks).

Factors That Motivate Visitors

Among the diverse reasons that motivate travelers to southern California are:

One of the most bizarre attractions in America: Winchester Mystery House in San Jose, California. This rambling Victorian mansion has—among other things—stairs leading nowhere and windows that open onto other rooms.

- It has superb weather year-round.
- They want to see the "movie capital," Hollywood. (They also hope to bump into a movie star; good luck to them.)
- There's wonderful outdoor recreation available all year.

Buttes at Monument Valley, Arizona
Photo by C. J. Ghormley

- L.A. is a departure point for cruises to Mexico and the Panama Canal.
- The area brims with natural wonders.
- L.A. is a convenient way to break up a trip to trans-Pacific destinations.
- There's plenty to do at night in the major cities.
- Some of the finest theme parks are here.

Northern California will appeal to your clients for altogether different reasons. They might prefer visiting here because:

- San Francisco is sophisticated yet has a small-town, European feel.
- There's the natural splendor of mountains and redwood forests.
- The Monterey-Carmel area has renowned golf courses.
- The climate is temperate.
- San Francisco has exciting nightlife and great restaurants.
- The Wine Country is a unique, almost European attraction.
- Northern California has world-class skiing; there are several less-extensive ski resorts northeast of L.A., too.

Arizona, too, has its own appeal:

- The Grand Canyon is a unique spectacle.
- There are several interesting resorts and ranches.
- It boasts an Old-West and Native-American ambience.

The San Francisco telephone book lists restaurants by fifty-seven nationality groups.

Qualifying the Client
Southern California

FOR CLIENTS WHO WANT	APPEAL			REMARKS
	HIGH	MEDIUM	LOW	
Historical and Cultural Attractions		▲		L.A. and San Diego museums
Beaches and Water Sports	▲			Water is cool
Skiing Opportunities			▲	Some in San Bernardino Mts.
Lots of Nightlife		▲		Mostly L.A.
Family Activities	▲			Especially theme parks
Familiar Cultural Experience	▲			A little different yet still U.S.
Exotic Cultural Experience		▲		Offbeat lifestyles and Hispanic influence
Safety and Low Crime		▲		Tourist areas safe
Bargain Travel		▲		
Impressive Scenery	▲			Mts., desert, and ocean
Peace and Quiet		▲		Only in desert and mountain towns
Shopping Opportunities		▲		Just about everything
To Do Business	▲			Key to the Pacific Rim

Figure 5-4

Possible Misgivings

Some parts of California will set off warning bells for a few of your clients. Arizona might raise some questions for others. Among client concerns you'll have to address are:

- "People are bizarre in Los Angeles." Mention to your client that the city is a melting pot of people and cultures. It's diverse, open, free-spirited, and friendly.
- "Driving in L.A. frightens me, and there's no public transportation." City tours are very popular. Driving at times other than rush hour is usually easy. And there are buses and a growing rail system.
- "Los Angeles is so smoggy." Tell your client that the late fall to early spring is much better than summertime. Coastal areas are also far less smoggy. L.A. smog is 50 percent less than it was two decades ago.
- "All there is in southern California is L.A." A short drive out of the city, and your client will be in the desert, mountains, San Diego, or Santa Barbara . . . just for starters.
- "San Francisco is sort of depraved and radical." Like all stereotypes, this one holds little water. Yes, San Francisco is a somewhat counter-culture city, but the diversity actually helps make it a more interesting place.
- "Arizona's too hot." Suggest that clients go in the winter, when it's more pleasant in the south. In the summer, send them to Arizona's northern regions.
- "There's nothing to do in Arizona." Phoenix is a very cultured city, but it takes energy to find that culture. Tucson and Tombstone are quite unique attractions.
- "The Grand Canyon is crowded." Suggest that the client try touring the North Rim, rather than the South Rim, or that he or she go off-season.

San Francisco's Lombard Street is the world's crookedest.

Sales Strategies

California and Arizona offer many ways to fully sell a trip to your client. A car rental is an obvious recommendation. L.A. city tours are very popular, since the city is so spread out. City tours are also a good idea in San Francisco. You might suggest that clients extend their trip in southern California to include the Grand Canyon or Mexico (including a cruise), or even Las Vegas. For a memorable way of arriving, your clients might enjoy a train trip in a sleeping car. A popular winter activity is a whale-watching cruise: The most common ports for you to book clients out of are San Diego and Monterey. And around the Christmas holiday, the lavish, glorious **Bracebridge Dinner** is a long-standing pageant at the Ahwahnee Hotel in Yosemite; it must be booked far in advance by lottery.

For your clients going to Arizona, a river-rafting trip down the Colorado River through the Grand Canyon is spectacular. You might also book a helicopter or plane trip through the canyon. Arizona is a popular resort state, and selling-up a client to a resort hotel could make this quiet state a great deal of fun.

Cruises to Mexico or repositioning cruises along California's coast are quite popular. Small-ship cruises and railway excursions can be sold to clients wanting to tour Wine Country in an unusual way.

There's an exact reproduction of Shakespeare's Globe Theater in San Diego's Balboa Park.

Creative Activity

You're driving down a lonely desert road outside of Palm Springs. Your car inexplicably stalls. Suddenly, a flying saucer lands next to you. A four-foot-tall green alien exits the craft and, in perfect English, says, "Human being! I wish to visit five interesting things in California and Arizona. No more, no less! What must I see? They must please me, or I will disintegrate you!" List your five responses below:

YOUR SUGGESTION

1.

2.

3.

4.

5.

YOUR REASON

1.

2.

3.

4.

5.

Travel Trivia

Western Attractions

Roy Rogers/Dale Evans Museum, Victorville, CA
Autry Museum of Western Heritage,
    Los Angeles, CA
Ponderosa Ranch, Incline Village, NV
Buffalo Bill Historical Center, Cody, WY
Old Tucson Studios, Tucson, AZ

George Ranch Historical Park, Richmond, TX
Will Rogers Memorial, Claremore, OK
Boot Hill Museum, Dodge City, KS
Old Cowtown Museum, Wichita, KS
Wanuskewin Heritage Park, Saskatoon, SK

CHAPTER 6

Canada and Alaska

The Great White North

The French philosopher Voltaire once called Canada "20 million acres of snow." Americans once labeled the United States purchase of Alaska, at 2.5 cents an acre, a "folly." Follies, indeed. These two areas are keys to the wealth of the North American continent and popular destinations for tourists from everywhere.

Why does this chapter lump a U.S. state and an entire country together? The reason is geographic. Alaska and Canada form a physical cap to North America. The entire area has a certain similarity of climate, topography, and history. Tourists also often get to Alaska via Canada. Don't conclude, though, that the whole region is a simple extension of U.S. culture: Canada has its own cultural identity, and Alaskans pride themselves on their distinct way of thinking.

In the far northwest of the North American continent (and only a few miles from Russia, to which it once belonged), Alaska is the largest U.S. state. Its total population, though, is only about 600,000; **Anchorage**, its largest city, has only about 250,000 residents.

For Your Information . . .

Canada   FYI

CAPITAL: Ottawa

AREA (SQUARE MILES): 3,852,000

TIME ZONES: GMT −8 to −3:30

DRIVE ON: Right

POPULATION: 29,700,000

RELIGIONS: Roman Catholic and Protestant

LANGUAGES: English and French

CURRENCY: 1 Canadian dollar = 100 cents

ELECTRICITY: 110 volts, 60 cycles AC

CAPSULE HISTORY: Cabot arrives, 1497; Cartier claims it for France, 1534; British defeat French, 1763; confederation, 1867; railroad spans Canada, 1885; St. Lawrence Seaway begun, 1954; first constitution enacted, 1981–1982.

For reference sources, tourist bureaus, and suggested lengths of stay, see the Appendices.

Canada is the world's second biggest nation in size (slightly less than four million square miles), with ten provinces and two territories. But like Alaska, Canada is sparsely settled; its population is about twenty-five million, not much more than that of the state of California (which is one-twenty-fourth the area). Most Canadians, for reasons of climate and commerce, live along their country's southern border; nearly five million reside in only two cities, **Toronto** and **Montreal**. Canada can be divided into six principal regions of tourism, from west to east: **The Yukon**, **British Columbia**, **the Canadian Rockies**, **Ontario**, **Quebec**, and the **Atlantic Provinces**. Canada's vast Northwest Territories and extensive plains provinces (Saskatchewan and Manitoba) are places of great natural beauty and a few significant cities (such as Winnipeg), but they're not prime destinations for tourists.

How Travelers Get There

Churchill, in northern Manitoba, is perhaps the world's best area for viewing polar bears.

To drive into Canada is relatively simple: Much of eastern Canada is within a day's drive of New England and New York; western Canada is similarly close to Washington, Oregon, Idaho, and Montana. Your clients can drive into Alaska via the Alaskan Highway, which ties into roads in British Columbia and Canada's Yukon Territory, which borders eastern Alaska. Ferries and cruise ships are also a prime way of accessing Alaska: On the West Coast, boats sail from Seattle to several spots in British Columbia and Alaska; on the East Coast, the *Prince of Fundy* sails from Bar Harbor, Maine, to **Yarmouth**, **Nova Scotia**.

Air service is extremely convenient. **Air Canada** (AC) and **Canadian Air** (CP) both offer connections from U.S. cities into Canada, as do several U.S. carriers. The four main Canadian gateways are **Vancouver** (YVR), **Edmonton** (YEG), Toronto (YYZ), and Montreal; if you book your clients to Montreal, fly them into **Dorval** (YUL), not **Mirabel** (YMX), which is primarily an international airport and is some distance from the city. As for Alaska, convenient service exists from many points in the United States to Anchorage (ANC) and **Juneau** (JNU), the state capital. **Alaska Airlines** (AS) is the state's well-known carrier. Train service into Canada is quite good, especially on the East Coast: Niagara Falls, Toronto, and Montreal are served by trains that depart from Washington, D.C., New York City, Chicago, and Boston.

Weather Patterns

Canada and Alaska have cold climates. Winters are snowy and freezing, especially in the interior. But there are a few surprises. Coastal British Columbia, though wet, has very little snow or real cold in the winter. Your clients may encounter hot days in July and August in Toronto, Montreal, and even in **Fairbanks**, in Alaska's interior (see Figures 6-1, 6-2, and 6-3). Rainfall is moderate throughout the year, except in coastal British Columbia and in the Alaskan **Panhandle**, where Juneau is located; here rainfall, as in the U.S. Pacific Northwest, can be plentiful, especially in the late summer and during the fall.

In certain very northern areas of Alaska and Canada, during a few days in summer, the sun never sets.

As for tourist seasons, the summer, as you would expect, is the most crowded. Temperatures are warm, sunshine is more common, and daylight lasts for long stretches each day. The number of tourists, especially in Canada, increases sharply around the last week of June and tapers off around Labor Day. For this reason, it would be a good planning strategy to send your clients in May, June, or September, since the weather can still be quite pleasant, yet the attractions are uncrowded.

Getting Around

To drive through Canada and Alaska can be an enjoyable experience, since intercity traffic is rarely a bother. If your client wants to stray very far northward from the major highway systems, though, it's a different story: Roads can leave something to be desired. (A few fine routes do stretch northward here and there.) To get

Climate at a Glance
ANCHORAGE, ALASKA

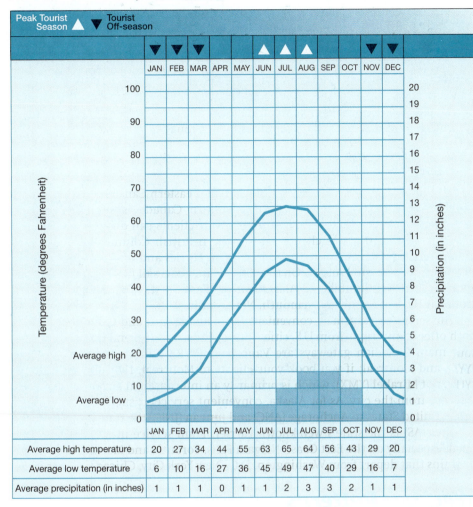

	JAN	FEB	MAR	APR	MAY	JUN	JUL	AUG	SEP	OCT	NOV	DEC
Average high temperature	20	27	34	44	55	63	65	64	56	43	29	20
Average low temperature	6	10	16	27	36	45	49	47	40	29	16	7
Average precipitation (in inches)	1	1	1	0	1	1	2	3	3	2	1	1

Figure 6-1

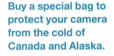

Buy a special bag to protect your camera from the cold of Canada and Alaska.

to the north country, air taxis, helicopters, and seaplanes are more commonly used, though service isn't always timely (often because of weather). Of course, regular jet routes interconnect all the major southern cities of Canada and Alaska.

Two forms of transportation are especially useful in this region: trains and cruise ships. Canada's railroad system, **VIA Rail**, is a model of efficiency, and the now-seasonal Trans-Canada route is very popular. (In a way, the Vancouver to Toronto and Montreal portion of the trip is an attraction in itself.) Rocky Mountaineer Railtours operates between Vancouver and Jasper/Calgary. It follows an even more scenic route than VIA Rail's and does so during the daylight hours (not necessarily true with VIA Rail). Train service within Alaska, especially between Anchorage and Fairbanks, is also quite convenient. Alaska now has something called the "Alaska Pass": For one fee, a client can have unlimited travel on certain ferries, buses, and trains.

Cruises along the St. Lawrence River and beyond (between Montreal and New York City) are gaining in popularity. But your clients will be best informed about the Alaska cruises: multi-day round-trip excursions from Vancouver into the Alaskan **Inside Passage**, or beyond, one-way, into the **Gulf Coast** region to the Anchorage area. To see the glaciers, snow-capped peaks, dense forests, and animal life along the way can be an overwhelming experience. Be sure to be well acquainted with the brochures of companies that offer these cruises. Larger ships offer more entertainment options for clients. On the other hand, smaller vessels are able to get into

VANCOUVER, BRITISH COLUMBIA

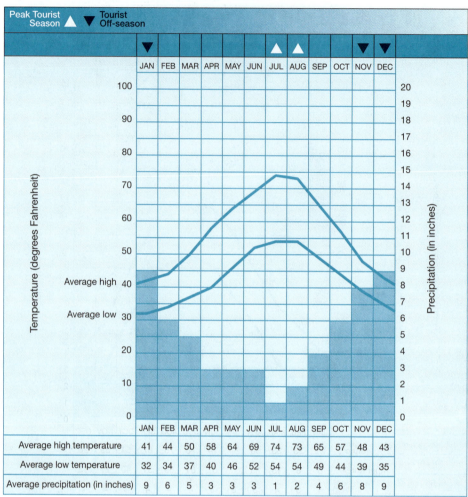

	JAN	FEB	MAR	APR	MAY	JUN	JUL	AUG	SEP	OCT	NOV	DEC
Average high temperature	41	44	50	58	64	69	74	73	65	57	48	43
Average low temperature	32	34	37	40	46	52	54	54	49	44	39	35
Average precipitation (in inches)	9	6	5	3	3	3	1	2	4	6	8	9

Figure 6-2

There are plenty of mosquitoes and biting flies in northern, less-populated areas: Take insect repellent.

narrower (and often more scenic) inlets and call on less-visited ports. A cruise can also be done in reverse, starting in Anchorage and ending in Vancouver. Your clients can even take plane or helicopter trips directly from their moored ship. Note: Anchorage has three ports: Whittier, Seward, and the city of Anchorage, itself.

Local transportation, especially in Canada, tends to be exemplary. Subways, buses, streetcars, and taxis serve most Canadian cities, with inexpensive fares and clean, modern comfort. Another interesting transportation service to sell is a helicopter tour of the Canadian Rockies: Vacationers are set down on glaciers, alpine meadows, and mountain summits. Motorcoach tours of both Canada and Alaska are also extremely popular.

Important Places

As we mentioned in the introduction, tourists tend to visit only certain parts of Alaska and Canada. The highlights are as follows:

Alaska

Alaska appeals to a particular type of client: someone who loves natural beauty, can afford what could turn out to be a rather expensive trip, and doesn't mind a

The Inside Passage can be visited by cruise ships or ferries.

Climate at a Glance
MONTREAL, QUEBEC

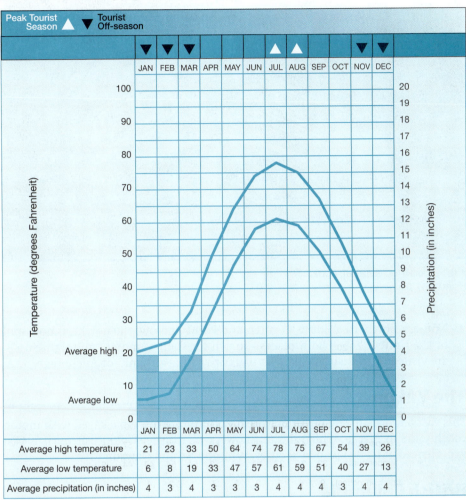

				JAN	FEB	MAR	APR	MAY	JUN	JUL	AUG	SEP	OCT	NOV	DEC
Average high temperature				21	23	33	50	64	74	78	75	67	54	39	26
Average low temperature				6	8	19	33	47	57	61	59	51	40	27	13
Average precipitation (in inches)				4	3	4	3	3	3	4	4	4	3	4	4

Figure 6-3

possibly slow-paced but certainly dramatic adventure. Among the highlights of any trip to Alaska are:

- **An Inside Passage Cruise**, with its striking views and stops at **Sitka** (with its remnants of Russian influence), picturesque Juneau (at the base of towering mountains), **Glacier Bay** (where clients may see icebergs tumbling into the water from glaciers), **Skagway** (a key town in Alaska's gold-rush era), and **Ketchikan** (a center of Native-American culture).

- A day trip from Juneau or Sitka to dramatic **Mendenhall Glacier**.

- **Anchorage**, Alaska's largest city (40 percent of all Alaskans live there), and close to major glaciers (the Portage Glacier is best known), parks, and a zoo where Alaskan wildlife is featured.

- **The 356-mile Anchorage-Fairbanks Alaska Railroad Trip**, which crosses several awe-inspiring national parks, most notably **Denali** [den-AH-lee] **National Park**, a home to grizzlies and the location of Mt. McKinley, North America's tallest peak. This journey is often combined with a cruise.

- **Fairbanks**, a gold-rush frontier town that features stern-wheeler trips, old gold camps, and the **Alaskaland Theme Park**.

Glaciers are often bluish, rather than white.

A tribal house in Ketchikan, Alaska
Photo by C. J. Ghormley

- **Nome**, a northern gold-rush center, and **Point Barrow**, the northernmost spot in the United States. Both places—known for their summer "midnight sun"—are visited by tourists via plane as day trips from Fairbanks or Anchorage.

The Yukon

This vast territory to the north of British Columbia is often packaged with motor-coach tours to Alaska, which lies to the west. Its frontier Gold Rush spirit is best experienced at its two principal cities, **Whitehorse** and **Dawson City**.

British Columbia

This western province is a prime destination for West Coast residents of the United States and Canada. Its mist-shrouded mountains and graceful bays make it one of North America's most pleasant places to visit. Its highlights include:

- **Vancouver**. Like many Canadian cities, Vancouver is an urban wonder, with neat homes, tree-lined streets, and flowering gardens. Late spring and summer would be the best times for your client to go. Among its attractions: the restored **Gastown** area, **Chinatown**, the huge and beautiful grounds and zoo of **Stanley Park**, and nearby **Grouse Mountain**. Vancouver has many wonderful dining and shopping opportunities.

- **Victoria**. British Columbia's capital, on Vancouver Island, is a city of legendary beauty. Its most astonishing attraction: **Butchart Gardens**, a 200-acre private park carved out of an old limestone quarry. To reach Vancouver Island, your clients can take a ferry from Tsawwassen (about thirty miles from Vancouver), from Port Angeles, Washington, or from Seattle, Washington. Even more swift are large catamaran ships that sail between Victoria and Vancouver.

> Near Grouse Mountain is the Capilano Suspension Bridge, a swinging 400-foot-long bridge that spans a deep chasm. It looks as if it's right out of an Indiana Jones movie.

The Canadian Rockies

Every bit as scenic as the Alps, the Canadian Rockies are a magnet for both winter and summer visitors. Most of its attractions are to be found along the western boundary of the province of Alberta. You'll probably want to start your clients from either Calgary or Edmonton. Each summer, Calgary hosts a renowned rodeo, the **Calgary Stampede**, though a long stay in Calgary probably isn't warranted at other times of the year. Edmonton is quite famous for its shopping mall (one of the largest in the world), several good museums, and an excellent polar wildlife zoo. To the west of these two gateway cities are the following attractions (which are connected by the scenic Icefields Parkway):

- **Banff National Park and Lake Louise**, considered by some to be among the most picturesque places on earth, and a prime ski destination.
- **Jasper**, just northwest of Banff, Lake Louise, and Calgary (and due west of Edmonton), a gateway to several overwhelming glaciers, ice fields, and national parks. Jasper is also the departure point for helicopter trips into the Canadian Rockies, both in Alberta and into nearby British Columbia.

Ontario

Ontario is often confused with **Ottawa**. Ontario is a large eastern province, and Ottawa is Canada's capital (which happens to be on Ontario's easternmost border).

To further complicate things, Ontario is also the name of a large airport east of Los Angeles. On occasion, travelers have been sent to this airport, instead of to Ottawa.

Ontario is fast becoming a major tourist destination. Among its many features are:

- **Toronto** is a culture-filled metropolis that designer Buckminster Fuller once called "the only modern city that works." Its restaurants and theater life are rich and diversified. The **Casa Loma** castle and lofty **C.N. Tower** are essential attractions to visit. The **Sky Dome** baseball stadium and **Eaton Shopping Center** are attractions that will also appeal to many of your clients.
- **Niagara Falls** is one of North America's best-known attractions and now the site of a huge casino. The only really full views of the two major Niagara cascades are from the Canadian side, not the United States side. The parkland that lines both sides of the Niagara River is also beautifully maintained, though the areas just inland from it are touristy. Many small attractions, such as the **Scenic Tunnels** and the **Maid of the Mist** boat ride, should be recommended. For the more

The short ferry ride to Toronto Island affords relaxing beauty and unparalleled views of Toronto.

Mountains reflected in Lake Louise, Alberta
Photo by C. J. Ghormley

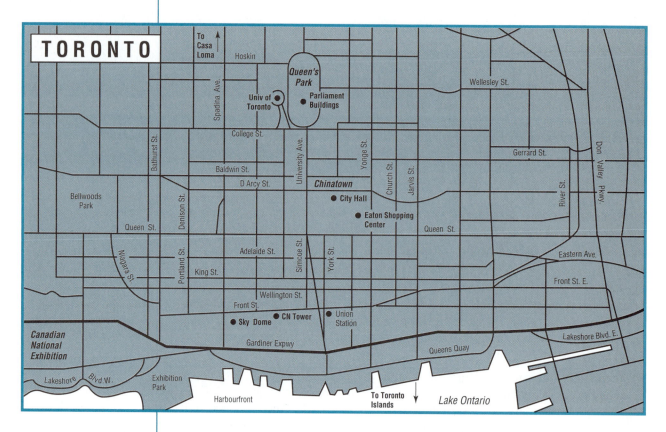

adventurous, a high-powered jet boat now challenges the river downstream from the falls. Niagara can also be a day trip from Toronto or Buffalo.

- **The Thousand Islands**, dotting the area where the St. Lawrence River flows out of Lake Ontario, are well worth visiting via cruises from **Gananoque** [gan-ah-NAH-kway], **Rockport**, and **Kingston** (where there's also a famous fort). (On the New York side, the access port is Alexandria Bay.)

- **Ottawa**, Canada's splendid capital, has much charm, several dramatic museums, and stately **Parliament** buildings. (There's a changing of the guard there every morning in the summer.) Ottawa is often bypassed by tourists, but you would do well to sidetrack your clients there for a day or two. (It can also be a day trip from Montreal.)

Quebec

Here's another easy mistake to make: Quebec is a province, **Quebec City** is its capital and quaintest place, and **Montreal** is its largest and most cosmopolitan city. Canada is a country of many heritages, but the English and the French predominate. And as you probably know, Quebec is the bastion of French influence (though French-Canadian communities can be found in many other Canadian regions). Many residents of the U.S. northeast know what other Americans do not: that a trip to Quebec is the next best thing to a trip to Europe. The areas you're most likely to send your clients to are:

- **Montreal** has remarkable churches (especially Notre Dame), a restored "Old Montreal" district, and hundreds of great eateries. A major casino is located here (as well as at several other Quebec locations). Several day trips from Montreal are possible, usually to Ottawa, the **Laurentian Mountains** (which have good winter skiing), and Quebec City.

- **Quebec City** can be a Montreal day trip, but your clients would probably appreciate it if you lodged them here. Quebec City is what sixteenth-century French towns must have been like; its ambience invariably charms clients.

French-Canadians are generally patient with Americans who try out their high-school French.

Roadside homemade-bread stands are a delight on the road eastward from Quebec City.

Horse carriages, Montreal
Photo by C. J. Ghormley

- **Gaspe**, with its rolling hills, Breton-like villages, and quaint little shops, is a frequent trip extension from Quebec City.

The Atlantic Provinces

The easternmost provinces of Canada have long associated themselves with their seafaring traditions. They're all uncrowded and scenic, appealing to clients who want to get away from it all. The Atlantic provinces include the following:

- **New Brunswick**, which resembles Maine in many ways. Its most famous cities are the port city of **St. John**; **Fredericton**, the provincial capital; and **Moncton**, famous for several natural oddities that are nearby, including the "Reversing Falls," "Magnetic Hill" (where things seem to roll *up* inclines), and the awesome tides of the **Bay of Fundy** (which are more commonly viewed in Nova Scotia).

- **Nova Scotia**, the focal point of Canada's fishing industry, and a province significant in both history and literature. Its best known attractions: the **Cabot Trail**, a scenic drive along Nova Scotia's northernmost point; **Halifax**, the provincial capital; and **Peggy's Cove**, a picture-perfect fishing village not far from Halifax.

- **Prince Edward Island**, also called PEI, Canada's smallest province. The island can be toured in a day, with stops at fishing villages, rolling beaches, and the **Anne of Green Gables Home**.

- **Newfoundland**, a genuinely rustic area of Canada, with many picturesque spots, friendly villages, and ruins of settlements. The mainland portion of Newfoundland is called **Labrador**, an excellent site for whale-watching. **L'Anse Aux Meadows National Park** is home to the only validated Viking settlement in North America.

The Bluenose II schooner, based in Halifax, is pictured on the Canadian dime.

Possible Itineraries

Your clients can visit many Canadian and Alaskan areas by simply day-tripping from key cities. Among the most popular multi-day itineraries would be a week to ten days in the Rockies, starting in Calgary and traveling northward, overnighting at Banff and Lake Louise, and then continuing through scenic roads up to Jasper (for possible side trips to Edmonton, various ice fields, and perhaps a helicopter excursion into the Rockies). Another popular one-to-two-week itinerary: Niagara Falls to Toronto, the Thousand Islands, up to Ottawa or to Montreal, and finishing in Quebec City.

Lodging Options

Alaska has many hotels and motels, but they can be expensive (as are many things in Alaska). This is one more reason why cruises are an excellent option to recommend. Among the famous hotels are Juneau's **Alaskan Hotel** (whose bar is a tourist attraction in itself) and the **Alyeska Prince** (in Alyeska Resort, south of Anchorage). Canada has a full range of lodging choices, from luxury hotels to camping grounds. Most U.S. chains have properties there; **Canadian Pacific** and **Four Seasons** (both Canadian companies) offer at least one elegant property in each major city. Your clients might be very pleased if you book them in one or more of the castle-like hotels that the railroads built across Canada in the early 1900s. The most famous (and all of them are landmarks): **The Empress** (Victoria), **The Banff Springs Hotel**, **The Chateau Laurier** (Ottawa), and **The Chateau Frontenac** (Quebec City). Other hotels you could suggest are the **Ritz-Carlton Kempinski** (Montreal), the **King Edward** (Toronto), and the **Pan Pacific** (at Vancouver's Canada Place cruise port).

Niagara Falls bears special attention. Lodge your clients on the Canadian side, preferably in one of several hotels that offer falls-view rooms. Make sure to specifically book these view rooms, for that will at least partly make up for the exorbitant summer prices that almost all Niagara Falls properties charge. (There are real bargains off-season, though.)

Allied Destinations

The interesting destinations that can be combined with a trip to Alaska or Canada don't usually occur to clients. It's your job to suggest a few; your suggestions may lead to an expanded, more enjoyable, and (for the agency) more profitable itinerary.

Alaska lends itself to combinations with the Pacific Northwest, British Columbia, the Yukon, and the Canadian Rockies. Remember, too, that Alaskan airports are occasionally stopovers for flights bound for the Orient from the United States or Canada. Your client may want to break up a trip with a brief stayover. On the East Coast, Quebec and the Atlantic Provinces can be consolidated with a stay in New England or New York. Ontario is close to New York, Pennsylvania, Ohio, and Michigan. Both Toronto and Montreal are occasionally stopover points on the way to Europe from West Coast or Midwest points of origin. Again, a brief stay might be an appropriate recommendation.

Factors That Motivate Visitors

Canada and Alaska have a specialized touristic appeal. Here are some of the reasons for going there:

- The area's natural beauty is stunning, especially in the Rockies, along the shore, and into the wilderness.
- Toronto, Montreal, Quebec City, and Vancouver are especially safe, clean, historic, beautiful, and lively.
- The area is "foreign" (especially Quebec) yet familiar, comparatively near and generally English-speaking.
- The people are friendly and welcome visitors.
- The winter sports, fishing, and camping opportunities are plentiful.
- Canada is, in many respects, a travel bargain.
- Wildlife, especially in Alaska, is relatively easy to observe.

Afternoon "High Tea," a long-standing British tradition, is making a comeback in certain Canadian hotels.

The Bay of Fundy recorded the greatest tide change in history: seventy feet.

- Transportation in the southern portions of the area is convenient.
- Cruise possibilities are numerous.

Possible Misgivings

The appeal of Canada and Alaska does have its limitations. Among your clients' concerns that you may have to address are:

- "What is there to see up there?" This will be the most common client objection you'll hear. Paint a clear picture of whatever attractions you think will appeal to the client: majestic scenery, sophisticated cities, uncrowded roads, natural wonders, great winter sports, and so on.
- "It's boring, isn't it?" Toronto, Montreal, and to a lesser extent, Anchorage, Vancouver, and Quebec City are energetic, lively, good-sized cities. The Calgary Stampede may also appeal to excitement-seekers.
- "Isn't it expensive?" Alaska can be expensive, but stressing the all-inclusive nature of a tour or cruise may be the right sales approach. Canada is, in almost all places, a real travel bargain. For budget-minded clients, suggest spring or fall travel.
- "Isn't there turmoil in Quebec?" The separatist movement, for now, remains dormant. Canada is a relatively safe and peaceful country, where locals are especially friendly to foreign visitors.
- "I'd love to see Niagara Falls, but isn't it a tourist zoo?" July is truly hectic, but things slow down a bit in August. Suggest late spring or early autumn instead. Or lodge clients in Toronto, with Niagara as a day trip.

Watch a ship or boat go through a lock. Ottawa has several small locks; bigger ones can be found near Montreal, Niagara Falls, and several places in Ontario.

Qualifying the Client
Alaska

FOR CLIENTS WHO WANT	APPEAL			REMARKS
	HIGH	MEDIUM	LOW	
Historical and Cultural Attractions		▲		Native American and Russian
Beaches and Water Sports			▲	Great fishing, though
Skiing Opportunities		▲		Mostly cross-country
Lots of Nightlife			▲	Anchorage and on cruises
Family Activities			▲	
Familiar Cultural Experience	▲			
Exotic Cultural Experience			▲	Native culture especially
Safety and Low Crime	▲			
Bargain Travel			▲	Alaska is expensive
Impressive Scenery	▲			Greatest strength
Peace and Quiet	▲			
Shopping Opportunities		▲		
To Do Business			▲	Natural resources and tourism industries

Figure 6-4

Qualifying the Client
Eastern Canada

FOR CLIENTS WHO WANT	APPEAL			REMARKS
	HIGH	MEDIUM	LOW	
Historical and Cultural Attractions		▲		
Beaches and Water Sports			▲	Summer lakeside resorts
Skiing Opportunities		▲		North of Montreal
Lots of Nightlife		▲		Mostly Montreal and Toronto
Family Activities		▲		
Familiar Cultural Experience		▲		Enough like U.S.
Exotic Cultural Experience		▲		Especially Quebec Province
Safety and Low Crime	▲			
Bargain Travel		▲		U.S. dollar buys much here
Impressive Scenery	▲			
Peace and Quiet		▲		Outside Toronto, Montreal, Quebec City
Shopping Opportunities		▲		Crafts in countryside
To Do Business		▲		Especially Toronto and Montreal

Figure 6-5

Sales Strategies

Several obvious recommendations can create a fine opportunity to increase your potential profits from a client trip to Canada or Alaska. Among them are cruises, escorted tours, train trips, and ski packages. Among the most popular ski destinations: Whistler (near Vancouver), Mt. Tremblant (north of Montreal), and the Banff area. Clients who wish to stay in Niagara Falls should be sold-up to a falls-view room. Niagara Falls is also a long-standing honeymoon destination, though that reputation has become somewhat tarnished because of the place's touristy feel and the rising popularity of tropical honeymoon destinations. To clients who do want to honeymoon in Niagara, you might suggest a suite.

Few clients can resist the stunning natural grandeur of the Canadian Rockies and Alaska. To reinforce the appeal, consider lending clients videos of these areas. A moving picture will be worth ten thousand of our words. You should also take into consideration how special events can attract tourists even in supposedly off-seasons. Examples: Niagara Falls' **Festival of Lights** (November-December), Quebec City's **Winter Carnival** (February), and Anchorage's **Iditarod Sled Dog Race** (March).

For any destination in the area, mention the many potential allied destinations and stopovers that are possible. And for clients bound for Alaska or the Rocky Mountains, suggest excursions via helicopter or air taxi; both can be booked in advance.

The first person to go over Niagara Falls in a barrel was a woman, Annie Taylor.

Creative Activity

Train travel has long been important to tourism in both Alaska and Canada. The president of the Railroad Buffs of America comes to you to help plan a 21-day Anchorage-to-Halifax rail journey, using a private train with sleeper cars. This trip will be unique; no regular train service on this long route is sold to the public.

The club wishes to make only five stops between Anchorage and Halifax. What should they be and why? (Note: The train can go up to sixty miles per hour. Also, Vancouver to Toronto takes three days on a train.)

1st stop: Reason:

2nd stop: Reason:

3rd stop: Reason:

4th stop: Reason:

5th stop: Reason:

Travel Trivia

Top Ten Motorcoach Attractions

1. Niagara Falls
2. Fall foliage
3. Washington, D.C.'s monuments
4. Yellowstone National Park
5. The Smithsonian museums
6. Mount Rushmore
7. Walt Disney World
8. Cape Cod
9. Opryland, Nashville
10. Grand Canyon

Source: National Motorcoach Network survey

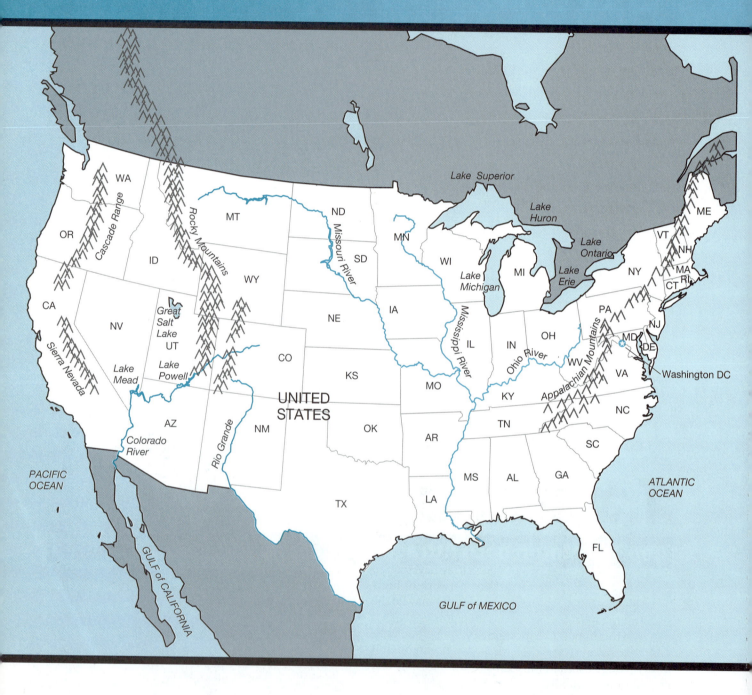

CHAPTER 7

North American Potpourri

Pretend you're a foreign tourist. What would be the best place to visit in North America? A city? An entire state? A man-made attraction? A natural wonder? The point is this: North America is a continent of vastly diverse attractions. And each of your clients will have different tastes and opinions about what to see. There's something for just about everyone.

In the preceding chapters, you've read about major tourist centers in the United States and Canada. However, dozens of other locations may appeal to your clients. Indeed, this chapter treats many of America's most popular cities, including New Orleans, Chicago, Atlanta, Santa Fe, Seattle, and Las Vegas.

What follows isn't a compendium of *every* popular tourist attraction. Some, though wonderful, simply won't be places you'll be called on to book often. Others are visited mainly by business clients, or by tourists who live nearby and who know the area well enough that they won't come to you for help.

There's a lot of information to digest in this chapter. Read it slowly and carefully. Highlight as many important points as possible. Follow along on the chapter-opening map.

Forty percent of Nevada's population have jobs related to the tourist industry.

The South

In many ways, it's unfair to gather all the southern states not covered in previous chapters into one collection, but we can make some generalizations about the South. Its many major cities have convenient air service, and an excellent network of highways crisscrosses the area. In fact, driving may be the best way for your clients to see the region.

The South's climate is generally temperate, especially along the coasts of the **Atlantic Ocean** or **Gulf of Mexico**. Summers can be uncomfortably hot and humid; winters are chilly at worst but pleasant. Spring can be a particularly beautiful time throughout the region—the magnolia blooms are legendary. Fall is very nice as well, but hurricanes and rain may occasionally interfere with your client's trip.

The South has many forests, rivers, and hills, especially where the southern **Appalachian Mountains** are prominent. Hiking, camping, and fishing are

popular activities. The South is, in general, a rural land of quiet small towns; however, there are several sophisticated cities. Elegance, pride, and a strong sense of history—these are what the South is all about.

Important Places

The commercial, transportation, and convention gateway to the South is **Atlanta**, Georgia (ATL). Many other cities have large airports, including Charlotte, North Carolina (CLT), and New Orleans, Louisiana (MSY).

Among the most popular areas in the South are the following, listed clockwise by state, starting with Georgia:

- **Atlanta, Georgia**. This growing, affluent, and cosmopolitan city has impressive cultural venues for symphony, ballet, and theater; the fascinatingly designed **High Museum of Art**; the many Olympic sports facilities; the best upscale shopping in the South (at Phipps Plaza); lovely magnolia tree-lined streets; the **Six Flags Over Georgia** theme park; and **Stone Mountain Park**, with its plantation, riverboat, small museums, and huge mountain carving of Confederate leaders. At **the Martin Luther King, Jr., National Historic Site**, you can still attend services at the church where Dr. King preached.

- **Savannah, Georgia**. A beautifully restored and preserved city, Savannah has retained much of the charming heritage of the Old South. There are several museums and countless buildings in a two-mile national landmark district that predates the Civil War. **River Street**, in the historic area, has upscale shopping and fine hotels.

- **Macon, Georgia**. This small city was spared any damage from the Civil War and, therefore, has a superb historical district.

- **The Alabama Space and Rocket Center**. This is one of the largest space museums in the country, and is located in **Huntsville**. Alabama is noted for its grand old homes and wide spectrum of outdoor recreational activities.

- **Natchez, Mississippi**. This city boasts hundreds of antebellum mansions, as does the resort port city of **Biloxi**.

- **Vicksburg, Mississippi**. Vicksburg is famous for its military park commemorating the famous Civil War battle.

- **New Orleans, Louisiana**. One of the world's most unique cities, it flaunts a strange, heady mixture of elegance, raucousness, great Dixieland jazz, and internationally renowned cuisine. The **French Quarter** is where the city really jumps, **Jackson Square** is the Quarter's focal point, and **Preservation Hall** is a center for music. A world-class aquarium is located here, and day and multi-day riverboat cruises are very popular. There are also tours of the surrounding bayou swamps and old, graceful plantations. The Tuesday before Ash Wednesday is when the spectacular, wild **Mardi Gras** festival is held.

- **Hot Springs National Park, Arkansas**. This famous Ouachita [wah-SHEE-tah] Mountains resort has long been a favorite of vacationers. The Ozark Mountains, in northern Arkansas, has equally dramatic spas and scenery.

- **Nashville, Tennessee**. Nashville proudly calls itself "Music City, USA," home of country music. Here's where your clients will find that great showcase for country-western music, the **Grand Ole Opry**, the immense **Opryland Hotel**, **Opry Mills** (an entertainment and shopping mall), and a first-rate **Country Music Hall of Fame**. Andrew Jackson's home, the **Hermitage**, is nearby, and an almost exact reproduction of Athens's Parthenon sits in a lovely Nashville park.

- **Memphis, Tennessee**. Like Nashville, this city is best known for its contributions to America's musical heritage. **Beale Street** boasts an active nightlife and many "blues" cafés. **Graceland**, the legendary home of Elvis Presley, features

Underground Atlanta is a subterranean shopping, entertainment, and dining area on the original nineteenth-century site of the city.

Try a _beignet_ at the Cafe Du Monde in New Orleans.

Ducks parade twice a day in the lobby of the Peabody Hotel in Memphis.

two of Elvis's private jets, a collection of his cars, his outrageously decorated mansion, and his burial site.

- **Pigeon Forge**, **Tennessee**. This town is home to the **Dollywood Theme Park** and a spectacular yearly "Winterfest" of lights. It's just north of the **Great Smoky Mountains**, one of the most visited national parks in the United States.
- **Mammoth Caves National Park, Kentucky**. With its 300 miles of massive underground caves, this attraction certainly makes an impression. Kentucky's two key cities, **Lexington** and **Louisville** (home of the Kentucky Derby) are gracious and charming.
- **Harpers Ferry, West Virginia**. This historic city is where John Brown made his ill-fated attempt to arm a slave rebellion. To its west are among the South's most beautiful outdoor recreation areas.
- **Cape Hatteras National Seashore, North Carolina**. Cape Hatteras features remarkable scenery and excellent beaches. The Wright brothers made the first airplane flight from nearby **Kitty Hawk**.
- **Hilton Head Island, South Carolina**. With twelve miles of superb beaches, wind-swept scenery, and countless opportunities for water sports, Hilton Head is one of the most popular resorts in the country. Like another resort in this state, **Myrtle Beach**, it's a mecca for golfers and tennis players.
- **Charleston, South Carolina**. Charleston is one of the most elegant and charming cities in the United States; the Battery is a historical district of beautiful antebellum houses. **Fort Sumter**, where the first shots of the Civil War were fired, is off the coast. Spectacular plantations and gardens lie just down the road; the most famous are **Magnolia Plantation** and **Middleton Place**.

Sales Considerations

The Southern United States appeals strongly to travelers looking for music-themed experiences, water sports, historic sites, and a still genteel way of life. The many offshore islands that stretch from Virginia through the Carolinas and down the coast of Georgia provide remarkable settings for a number of outstanding resorts.

Clients visiting certain regions of the South may find them convenient jumping-off points to other vacation spots. West Virginia and Virginia are gateways to Washington, D.C., Philadelphia, New York City, and beyond. Louisville is not far down river from Cincinnati; in fact, Kentucky borders not only Ohio, but Indiana and Illinois as well. Louisiana is an excellent extension of a trip to Texas. And any of the coastal states (especially Florida) could lead to a Caribbean holiday. Atlanta is fast becoming a major destination for business travelers, so popular hotels should be booked ahead of time. All hotels should be booked far in advance for clients interested in visiting New Orleans during Mardi Gras. Several river- and sea-going cruise ships call New Orleans their home port.

Remember: the South's great charm, strong tradition of preserving history, splendid outdoor recreation areas, and vital urban centers can each attract a different kind of client.

Texas and Oklahoma

These states are an anomaly. Together or separately, they could be considered part of the Great Plains, the Southwest, or even the South. Because these two states are so closely related, for tourism purposes it's best to look at them together.

Both states are quite hilly, though **Texas** has long stretches of desert in its southwestern region. The Gulf Coast on the southeast of Texas offers popular resort recreation areas. The climate in these two states is quite hot in the summer, with chilly winters; spring and fall are generally pleasant. Temperatures in

Paducah, Kentucky, is famous for its quilts.

The airport at Charlotte, North Carolina, has rocking chairs.

Greenbrier, a luxury resort in West Virginia, has a once-secret government base buried beneath it.

Oklahoma are usually cooler. The eastern portion of both states tends to be rainier than the west, which is arid.

Texas is easily reached via major gateways in **Dallas-Fort Worth** (DFW) and **Houston** (IAH), with other airports in smaller markets. **Oklahoma City** (OKC) is the main air route into Oklahoma. A few major interstates crisscross Texas, but because of the state's size, driving distances are long, and many areas don't have easy access. However, three important cities, Houston, **San Antonio**, and **Austin**, are reasonably close to one another.

Important Places

Both states are renowned for their strong cowboy traditions. Texas, the second largest state in the union, offers many attractions, the most popular of which are in Dallas, Houston, and San Antonio. These attractions include:

Six flags have flown over Texas (thus the amusement park chain name). Whose flags? The United States, Mexico, Spain, France, Texas, and the Confederacy.

- **Dallas**. A cosmopolitan and sophisticated commercial center, Dallas offers good museums, the popular **Six Flags Over Texas** theme park (in nearby Arlington), and a wonderful **Texas State Fair** in October. Its sister city, Ft. Worth, has some excellent Western art museums. Dallas will, sadly, forever be linked with the death of President Kennedy; and the **John F. Kennedy Memorial** commemorates the tragedy. The **Texas School Book Depository** now houses a museum.

- **Austin**. The capital of Texas. Austin is famous for its (not just country) music clubs and is the self-proclaimed bat capital of the world. (At sunset, a million and a half bats set out for their evening hunting.)

- **San Antonio**. This very popular city harbors the centerpiece of Texas's struggle for independence: the **Alamo**. The **Paseo del Rio** is a lovely river walk through downtown. There's also a **Sea World** and **Six Flags Fiesta Texas**, a large amusement theme park.

"Tex-Mex" cuisine is much spicier than Mexican food found elsewhere.

- **Houston**. The fourth largest city in the United States, Houston is home to the **Lyndon B. Johnson Space Center**, NASA's training facility for astronauts and tracking center for space flights. **Astroworld** is a popular theme park, and next to it is the world's first indoor stadium, the **Astrodome**.

- **Padre Island**. Actually two separate islands, Padre is made up of a pristine national seashore area and clusters of rapidly developing resort areas. Padre Island is 115 miles long and stretches from Corpus Christi to Port Isabel.
- **The National Cowboy Hall of Fame and the Western Heritage Center**. Both of these **Oklahoma City**, Oklahoma, sites have excellent collections of mementos of the Old West.

Sales Considerations

Texas is a logical gateway for clients interested in a trip to Mexico. In addition, Houston is within a day's drive of New Orleans. Easily packaged with a trip to the Southwest, the region is particularly well-suited for clients who like Western history and the rugged outdoors. But don't be fooled: Dallas and Houston are both major urban centers, with sophisticated lodging (Dallas's Mansion on Turtle Creek is a legend). An interesting place for your clients to stay is at a ranch outside either of these cities.

A car rental is almost essential to get around the Dallas-Ft. Worth area.

The Midwest

The Midwest is what the region is best known as, but to some of your clients this may seem like a misnomer. At the area's eastern end, **Ohio** could almost be considered a part of the East. **Missouri** was a part of the South during the Civil War. Even the area's westernmost boundary barely reaches the center of the country. Perhaps a tourist might be more comfortable calling the region the Prairie States, but even that doesn't fully apply to much of the territory. And so, the Midwest it is.

Without question, the centerpiece of the Midwest is **Chicago**, Illinois, the third largest city in the nation. Not only is it the major gateway to the region, but its **O'Hare International Airport** (ORD) is one of the busiest in the United States. (Chicago's **Midway Airport** [MDW] is an alternative.) However, there are many other large Midwestern urban centers set within rich farmland and beautiful forests. Parts of **Minnesota**, **Wisconsin**, and **Michigan** are a bit hilly, offering some winter skiing possibilities for clients, but for the most part the Midwest is flat.

It's very easy to fly into the Midwest, with major terminals not only in Chicago but also in **Detroit**, Michigan (DTW); **Milwaukee**, Wisconsin (MKE); **Cleveland**,

Ohio (CLE); **Cincinnati**, Ohio (CVG); **St. Louis**, Missouri (STL); and **Minneapolis-St. Paul**, Minnesota (MSP). The highway network is excellent for car or bus travel; however, since the region is so very large, distances might make that prohibitive. Chicago is also the major hub of train travel in the country.

The Midwest can be hot in the summer and somewhat humid; winters can get quite cold and snowy. Spring is rainy and usually chilly. Fall is beautiful, especially when the leaves change.

An important note: Though such states as Minnesota and Michigan have beautiful and popular recreation areas, they depend mainly on local Midwesterners for their tourism. Scenic as they are, they're not likely to be destinations you will book as often as others.

Important Places

Beginning with Illinois in the center, and going clockwise from Missouri at seven o'clock, the most popular attractions in the Midwest include:

- **Chicago, Illinois**. This huge, cultured city is the Midwest's focal point. There's a world-class symphony, the renowned **Lyric Opera**, the **Goodman Theater** repertory, and **Second City** comedy—all centerpieces of its strong theater community. Moreover, the city has superb museums. The most notable: the **Museum of Science and Industry**, one of the world's finest, with hands-on exhibits, an indoor farm, an underground coal mine, and a German U-2 submarine among its huge collection; the **Art Institute**, with its famous French Impressionist wing; the **Field Museum of Natural History**, and the **Shedd Aquarium**.

    The city also offers such attractions as the **Brookfield Zoo** (the first natural-habitat zoo in the country), the **Marriott's Great America** theme park, great shopping on the **Magnificent Mile** along North Michigan Avenue, and excellent ethnic cuisine.

- **Lincoln Country**. This is the region in Illinois where Abraham Lincoln lived. It includes **New Salem**, where Lincoln grew up and made his famous long walk to return a book, and **Springfield**, the state capital and Lincoln's home.

- **Hannibal, Missouri**. This charming town is Mark Twain's birthplace and boyhood home.

- **Branson, Missouri**. This small town attracts millions of visitors a year with its dozens of music-related (especially country-western) entertainment venues. It's nestled in one of the most scenic areas of the Ozark Mountains. Visitors usually fly in to Springfield, Missouri, then drive to Branson.

- **The Amana Colonies, Iowa**. This is a communal society of seven small towns founded by a strict European religious sect. There are good cultural museums, and excellent local food and crafts are available.

- **Minneapolis-St. Paul, Minnesota**. The twin-city area is justly proud of its excellent symphonies, opera, and theater, especially the famed **Guthrie Theater**. Also here are a great zoo, and such museums as the **Minnesota Institute of the Arts** and the **Science Museum of Minnesota**. St. Paul celebrates a famous "Winter Carnival" each February.

- **The Wisconsin Dells**. An hour north of the state capital of Madison and northwest of Milwaukee, this extremely popular recreation area has the Wisconsin River running through scenic cliffs. Other impressive Wisconsin recreational areas include **Lake Geneva** and the **Door Peninsula**.

- **Mackinac Island**. A charming and famous Michigan resort, the island has retained an Old World feel. No automobiles are allowed here; clients get around in horse-drawn carriages or on bicycles. The ornate **Grand Hotel** is wonderful; its 660-foot porch is legendary.

- **The Henry Ford Museum and Greenfield Village, in Dearborn, Michigan**. Some of the country's most famous edifices have been brought here intact, including

---

Try deep-dish pizza where it was invented: Chicago. Pizzeria Uno, Pizzeria Due, Gino's East, and Lou Malnati's make the best.

The most popular act in Branson is violinist Shoji Tabuchi.

The Mall of America, with its 400 stores covering an area greater than seventy-eight football fields, is in nearby Bloomington.

Fudge and antiques are Mackinac Island specialties.

Skyscrapers on Michigan Avenue, Chicago, Illinois
Photo by C. J. Ghormley

those of Edison, Webster, the Wright brothers, and Ford himself. This unique indoor-and-outdoor facility also includes a great collection of classic cars.

- **The Professional Football Hall of Fame, in Canton, Ohio**. This museum honors football's greats. Also in Ohio, just north of **Cincinnati**, is **King's Island**, the nation's most visited seasonal amusement park. And **Cleveland**, Ohio, on a beautiful lakeside location, is home to the immensely popular **Rock and Roll Hall of Fame**.

- **Indianapolis Speedway, Indiana**. Every Memorial Day, the famous Indianapolis 500 auto race is held here. A museum traces the history of racing.

Sales Considerations

The Midwest is a strategic spot from which to start a driving trip to Canada. You can book space on ferries that take your client's car across the Great Lakes, saving a tremendous amount of driving time. Because it is so spread out, different areas of the Midwest also lead into trips to the East, the South, and the Great Plains. Chicago

Branson is one of America's most popular motorcoach tour destinations.

is a major business and convention destination, and some clients may want to extend their visits or even bring their families along. The Midwest can be a particularly good area for clients who seek a mix of rural vacation and urban culture.

The Great Plains

The Great Plains states are rocky in the north but flatten out toward the south. Winters are cold and snowy, and summers are hot. The farther north your clients go, the lower the temperatures get. The interstate highway network is good but limited; and because there are fairly long distances between urban centers, driving should perhaps be recommended only to clients who want to enjoy the rural scenery. There are no gigantic cities in the region, though **Omaha**, Nebraska (OMA); **Wichita**, Kansas (ICT); and **Kansas City**, Missouri (MCI), are of respectable size and interest. They are the main gateways into the area.

Important Places

The Great Plains region offers some famous attractions. Some of the most recognizable, from north to south, are:

- **Theodore Roosevelt National Park, North Dakota**. The park's Badlands offers a beautiful rocky landscape and such wildlife as buffalo and bighorn sheep. North Dakota is home to many other impressive recreation areas, wildlife preserves, and state parks.

- **Mount Rushmore National Memorial, just outside Rapid City, South Dakota**. One of the country's most familiar tourist sites, Mount Rushmore is where huge busts of four former presidents have been carved out of the mountainside. Nearby are three other attractions: Wind Cave National Park, Jewel Cave National Monument, and Badlands National Monument. To the north is Deadwood, a preserved Old Western town that features gambling. And to the southwest another huge carving is being created: The Crazy Horse Monument.

Mount Rushmore's sculptor originally intended to carve the four presidents' full bodies, not just their heads.

- **Boys Town, in Omaha, Nebraska.** Father Flanagan's home for homeless boys offers tours.
- **Fort Robinson State Park, Nebraska.** This remote park is one of the most interesting on the Great Plains. The site of an old cavalry post, it's strategic to several lovely recreation areas and to intriguing prehistoric fossil beds.
- **Dodge City, Kansas.** The famous Western town, now restored, features the Boot Hill Museum, Boot Hill Cemetery, and historic areas like Front Street and the Long Branch Saloon. Another reconstructed cowboy town is **Wichita Cowtown**.

Sales Considerations

The Great Plains are wedged between the Midwest and the Rocky Mountain States, and offer a good gateway to Canada. There's a pioneer history and spirit here, which may appeal to certain clients, especially Old West buffs. Anyone flying to the Great Plains should consider a car rental, since it's the best way to travel the great distances.

The Rocky Mountain States

Its name clearly defines the region's topography: rocky. From the northern border of the United States, this massive mountain range twists down through the Rocky Mountain States. Areas of **Montana** and **Wyoming** also contain huge grasslands that spill over from the Great Plains. With its truly wide-open spaces, the area offers some of the most magnificent scenery and distant horizons in the country. The winters get quite cold and snowy, especially in the north; but summers are warm and pleasant. Surprisingly, eastern Wyoming and Montana, as well as southwestern **Colorado**, can get quite hot in the summer.

Denver, Colorado, serves as the main entrance into the area for air travelers. Clients fly into **Denver International Airport** (DIA). Driving, though presenting

Arbor Day Farm is an attraction and hotel in Nebraska City, where Arbor Day was founded.

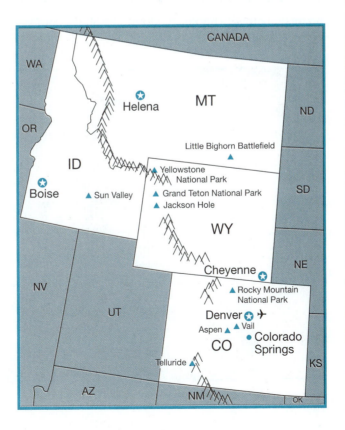

your clients with dramatic scenery, can be difficult, especially in the winter when many mountain roads may be closed. Even under good conditions, interstate highway connections are few and distances long.

Important Places

The natural wonders of this area represent many of the top attractions, which include (going from south to north and then turning west to **Idaho**):

Know someone high up in military ranks? They may be able to get you a tour of the "secret" NORAD base within Cheyenne Mountain, near Colorado Springs.

- **Denver, Colorado**. With spectacular mountains as a backdrop, Denver has an interesting combination of modernity and its Old West past. There are fine museums and excellent skiing. **Rocky Mountain National Park** is seventy miles northwest of Denver, and the **U.S. Air Force Academy** is sixty-five miles to the south in **Colorado Springs**.

- **The ski resorts of Colorado**. One of the prime skiing areas in the country, Colorado has dozens of popular slopes, including **Aspen**, **Vail**, and **Telluride**.

- **Yellowstone Park and Grand Teton National Park**, **in northwestern Wyoming**. Together, these two parks provide some of the most breathtaking scenery to be found anywhere in the world. Yellowstone, whose most famous site is **Old Faithful** geyser, was the nation's first national park. Within the park are some fine lodges where you can book your clients.

- **Jackson Hole**, **Wyoming**. Just south of the Grand Tetons, Jackson Hole is one of the country's top ski resorts. Here, too, is the **Snake River**, which offers many fishing and rafting opportunities.

- **Little Bighorn Battlefield National Monument, Montana** (formerly known as Custer Battlefield). The famous battle took place here.

- **Sun Valley, Idaho**. In a region known for winter sports, Sun Valley was one of the nation's first great ski resorts.

Sales Considerations

Because many of the Rocky Mountain States could easily be considered parts of either the Great Plains or the Southwest, they clearly are excellent places for your

Air Force Academy, Colorado Springs, Colorado
Photo by C. J. Ghormley

clients to visit in conjunction with those areas. The great mountain ranges here will particularly appeal to clients who ski or appreciate dramatic scenery.

Between 1978 and 1992, twelve people were injured by bears in Yellowstone, fifty-six by buffalo.

The Pacific Northwest

Oregon and **Washington**, two of the best-loved states in the country, are notable for their lush farmland, rugged coastline, lofty mountains, high waterfalls, and charming towns. The region's coastal strip is especially rainy, particularly from late summer through early spring. The climate is temperate near the coast, but colder in the eastern mountains. **Seattle**, Washington (SEA), and **Portland**, Oregon (PDX), are the major cities here; they're also the major air gateways for clients. Driving along the coast is actually the preferred mode of travel in the region, but venturing to the picturesque outer areas of the states can be more challenging, since the highway network is limited.

Important Places

This region covers only two states, but the overall beauty of the area is impressive. Its highlights include:

- **Seattle, Washington**. This cosmopolitan, beautiful city rests on Puget Sound. The **Space Needle** tower is the city's most recognizable landmark. Other attractions include: the Museum of Flight (perhaps the Pacific Northwest's finest museum), Pike Place Market, Pioneer Square (a restored historic district), and, to the northwest, **Olympia National Park**. It's also just a few hours drive or ferry ride to either **Vancouver Island** or the city of **Vancouver** in British Columbia, Canada.

- **Mount St. Helens, in Washington**. The volcano that erupted in 1980 is now a national, starkly troubling, monument. Another volcano, **Mount Ranier**, is a glacier-coated site (and a National Park).

- **The Oregon Coast**. This area offers a breathtaking drive along the Pacific Ocean. A leisurely trip would take your clients past dunes, rugged cliffs, national forests, and lovely towns.

Oregon's Crater Lake is America's deepest lake.

- **Portland**. Oregon's largest city has a restored old town and many impressive rose gardens. Nearby is the road along the **Columbia River Gorge**, with its towering cliffs and ribbonlike waterfalls. Many believe that this is one of America's most beautiful drives. Along the Gorge, on the Washington State side, is **Maryhill**, where a chateau-like museum boasts a surprisingly rich collection of paintings and Rodin sculptures.

Sales Considerations

The Pacific Northwest combines naturally with a trip to western Canada. The region is also an excellent jumping-off point for cruises to Alaska. In addition, Oregon borders California to the south, and the Rocky Mountain States and their superb skiing opportunities lie directly to the east. (There's some skiing in Oregon and Washington, too.) River-rafting tours are very popular in the Pacific Northwest; it would be a good idea to arrange one of these for clients who love the outdoors. Small cruise ships ply the area's waters.

The Southwest

The Southwest is noted for its deserts and arid climate. However, its range of conditions is wider than this. **Utah** is extremely mountainous, as is the western portion of **New Mexico**. Summers get blisteringly hot in the desert area, whereas the mountains are cold and snowy in the winter. The major air terminals in these states are **Las Vegas**, Nevada (LAS); **Salt Lake City**, Utah (SLC); and **Albuquerque**, New Mexico (ABQ). It's common to drive from Albuquerque to **Santa Fe**, New Mexico, but most other sites are far apart and require long driving times.

Important Places

The most popular places for tourists in the Southwest tend to be in California and Arizona. However, the remaining states in the region offer some superb attractions. Among them are:

- **Las Vegas, Nevada**. This city—a desert-situated spectacle of neon and non-stop activity—is one of the unique tourist draws in the country. With numerous

The ten largest hotels in America are in Las Vegas

The Luxor Hotel, Las Vegas, Nevada
Photo by C. J. Ghormley

casino-hotels lining the "Strip" and "Downtown" areas, Vegas is a magnet for gamblers. Excellent showrooms feature top entertainment stars. Dining is relatively inexpensive and some of the city's buffets are legendary. Now with the construction of theme parks and huge, dramatic hotels, Las Vegas has become a family entertainment center, too. Several mega-hotels on the Strip are attractions unto themselves: Treasure Island, the Luxor (a pyramid-shaped structure), New York-New York (with a scaled-down Manhattan skyline), the Las Vegas Hilton (home of Star Trek: The Experience), the Venetian (complete with gondolas), the Bellagio (boasting a huge water show and an impressive art collection), Paris (with its own Eiffel Tower), and Caesar's Palace (with the Forum Shops, an astonishing Roman street-like indoor shopping center adjoining it). A four-block section of Fremont Street (in the older Downtown area) is now covered with a "roof" that contains 2.1 million light bulbs for an hourly sound-and-light show. Rising above Las Vegas is the 100-story Stratosphere Tower. **Lake Mead National Recreation Area**, the **Valley of Fire**, **Hoover Dam**, and even winter snow skiing are close by.

- **Reno, Nevada.** This little brother to Las Vegas also offers gambling and shows, though on a smaller scale. Reno is near the resort area of **Lake Tahoe**. Other growing gambling centers are **Laughlin**, Nevada, which caters to an older, budget-seeking clientele, and **Primm** (at the California-Nevada border), which targets budget-minded families.

- **Virginia City, Nevada.** Museums, mine tours, and mansions are attractions in this old mining town, where visitors stroll the wooden boardwalk street full of shops and saloons.

- **Utah's National Parkland.** Some of the country's most spectacular national parks are in this state: **Zion**, **Bryce Canyon**, **Arches**, **Canyonland**, and **Capitol Reef**.

- **Salt Lake City, Utah.** The capital of Utah, Salt Lake City is the heart of the Mormon religion. It's a point of great interest for those of the faith. Tours of the famous **Mormon Tabernacle** are available. Remind clients to visit the **Genealogical Library**, whose resources are open to visitors of all faiths. Superb ski resorts—including **Snowbird**, **Park City**, **Deer Valley**, and **Alta**—are close by.

The chance of winning in casinos located away from the Strip is greater than on the Strip.

The Ponderosa Ranch, seen at the beginning of the old TV series "Bonanza," is an attraction near Lake Tahoe.

Many hotel rooms in Santa Fe come equipped with distinctive, funnel-like fireplaces.

- **Santa Fe, New Mexico**. This absolutely charming capital city is famous as an arts and crafts center. Native-American crafts are available everywhere; the city's dining facilities—birthplace of "Southwestern cuisine"—are first rate. From July to August, the city hosts the internationally acclaimed **Santa Fe Music Festival**. Clients must fly into Albuquerque, then drive or bus to Santa Fe.
- **Taos, New Mexico**. This artists' colony is also one of the most popular ski resorts in the country. In addition, **Taos Pueblo** is a classic Pueblo village.
- **Carlsbad Caverns, New Mexico**. Its underground rooms (one of them could accommodate eleven football fields) and twenty-one miles of rocky passages carved out of the rock are renowned.

Sales Considerations

Among the best buffets in Las Vegas: Rio (off the Strip), Stratosphere, and Main Street Station (downtown).

The Southwest region is easily combined with a trip to Mexico or the Rocky Mountain States. In addition, New Mexico and Texas border each other, and California is a gateway to the Pacific Northwest. The Southwest is of particular interest to those fascinated by Native-American culture. Ski lovers will be drawn here as well. Keep in mind that Nevada's gambling cities are extremely popular for weekend trips (hotel rates are much lower on weekdays), and many special packages are available. If your clients want to attend the Santa Fe Music Festival, be sure to book accommodations well in advance.

Travel Trivia

Museums with the Greatest Collections of Picasso Paintings

Metropolitan Museum of Art, New Ylork
Centre Georges Pompidou, Paris
The Hermitage, St. Petersburg, Russia
The Kunstmuseum, Basel, Switzerland
Musee Picasso, Paris
Museu Picasso, Barcelona
Museum of Modern Art, New York
National Gallery, Prague, Czech Republic
National Gallery of Art, Washington
Philadelphia Museum of Art, Philadelphia

Source: Smart Money *magazine*

Creative Activity #1

Jurassic Park is a reality! Scientists have actually found a way to clone dinosaurs. But the investor who bankrolled the research wants to open the park, not on an island off the coast of Costa Rica, but somewhere in the United States or Canada.

And he has hired you to recommend where it should be located! You are given the following guidelines:

- It must be in a place remote enough that if the dinosaurs escape, they're unlikely to get very far or do any harm before being captured.

- Yet they must be close enough to lodging, transportation hubs, etc., to guarantee a considerable number of visitors. No tourists will be housed at the park. They will have to drive, bus, or sail in from somewhere else.

- Climate, terrain, accessibility to foreign tourists, etc., should all also be considered.

What's your recommendation? Give your reasons why:

Travel Trivia

The Ten Itchiest Cities in the U.S.

1. Denver, CO
2. Cheyenne, WY
3. Flagstaff, AZ
4. Duluth, MN
5. Bismarck, ND
6. Great Falls, MT
7. Albuquerque, NM
8. Cedar City, UT
9. Billings, MT
10. Grand Junction, CO

Source: Lanacane Dry Itchy Skin Index

Creative Activity #2

You're a documentary filmmaker. You're currently scripting a one-hour special for The Discovery Channel, called "North America's 'Personality' Cities." You intend to choose ten cities that have unusual character and distinctiveness. Your first five choices are San Francisco, New York City, Miami, Los Angeles, and Orlando. What would the other five be? Give reasons for your choices.

City

1.

2.

3.

4.

5.

Reason

1.

2.

3.

4.

5.

Pulling It All Together: The Matching Game

Directions: Below is a list of places and attractions, some which we have covered and some which we haven't. There are all manner of connections among them. With your group, you have exactly ten minutes to come up with as many connections as possible. (Items may be used more than once.) Write your answers below. Note: There are at least twenty possible connections. E.g., The CN Tower and the Space Needle—both are tall towers.

Mt. Rushmore	Padre Island	West Point
Greenfield	Clearwater	High
Hudson	Washington, D.C.	Hilton Head
Yellowstone	CN Tower	Columbia
Aspen	Juneau	Santa Fe
San Diego	Hermitage	Sturbridge
Dulles	Williamsburg	Mt. Vernon
Space Needle	Shenandoah	Branson
San Simeon	Barnes Foundation	Stowe
Huntsville	Vizcaya	Logan
Orlando	Annapolis	Port Everglades
Valley Forge	Mackinac	Mammoth
Carlsbad	Cape Kennedy	Ottawa
Monticello	Vancouver	Stone Mountain

summer

ATLANTIC OCEAN

UNITED STATES

Baja Penninsula

GULF of MEXICO

MEXICO

GULF of CALIFORNIA

Sierra Madre Ranges

Acapulco

GUATEMALA

EL SALVADOR

COSTA RICA

PANAMA

Canal

BELIZE

HONDURAS

NICARAGUA

Lake Nicaragua

CARIBBEAN SEA

Lake Maracaibo

VENEZUELA

COLOMBIA

GUYANA

SURINAME

FRENCH GUIANA

PACIFIC OCEAN

Galapagos Islands

ECUADOR

Amazon River

there are birds with blue feathers. giant tortoise (p.149)

Andes

PERU

Lake Titicaca

BOLIVIA

BRAZIL

Easter Island

25,000 miles

Gigantic curved heads are there

Atacama Desert

PARAGUAY

Mountains

Rio de Janeiro

CHILE

URUGUAY

Buenos Aires

ARGENTINA

WINTER

Strait of Magellan

Falkland Islands

III

Latin America and the Caribbean
Rhythms of Culture

Examine this sentence carefully: *Mexico is South America's most popular destination, Costa Rica is that continent's hottest new place to visit, and Bermuda is perhaps the Caribbean's most gracious destination.*

Find any mistakes? There are three major ones:

Mexico is *not* in South America; it's in North America. Costa Rica isn't in South America either; it's a Central American country. And Bermuda, though generally lumped together with the Caribbean islands, is actually in the Atlantic—at about the same latitude as Charleston, South Carolina.

For many of us, Latin America and the Caribbean are lesser-known, complex neighbors. To be able to successfully sell this area, you'll have to bring its assets into better focus. Once you've done that, you'll realize that there's so much to sell: from ancient cultures to magnificent beach resorts; from jungles, islands, and mountains to cosmopolitan cities. The nations we cover in this chapter can be as beckoning as the pulse of the tango or the beat of a steel drum band.

Where the Countries Are

Mexico is the nation just south of the U.S. border. Continuing south (and connecting Mexico to the continent of South America) is the cluster of nations making up Central America. From north to south, they're **Belize**, **Guatemala**, **Honduras**, **El Salvador**, **Nicaragua**, **Costa Rica**, and **Panama**. Then comes South America. Except for **Bolivia** and **Paraguay**, both of which are landlocked in the center of the continent, South America's countries are located almost in a circle along the coast: **Brazil** is by far the largest country in South America (indeed, slightly larger than the contiguous United States), occupying nearly half the continent as it protrudes to the east; continuing clockwise, we have **Uruguay**, **Argentina**, **Chile**, **Peru**, **Ecuador**, **Colombia**, **Venezuela**, and the **Guianas** (**Guyana**, **Suriname**, and **French Guiana**).

The geography gets more difficult when we examine the Caribbean islands. In Chapter 9, we'll fully sort out the Caribbean picture for you. For now, you should remember that the Bahamas and Bermuda are not officially part of the Caribbean islands. They're actually north of the Caribbean Sea, in the Atlantic. (They are, however, all generally viewed as part of the same sales market by the travel industry.)

A Satellite View

From above, Latin America's landscape would seem amazingly diverse. Two of the world's great natural wonders predominate: the Amazon River and the Andes mountain range. Their impact on the region, as you'll see, is profound. Many lakes also dot the land, wide grasslands sprout up, rivers crisscross the countryside, even a bleak desert area edges the continent's west coast. And, of course, there are thousands of islands, some floating isolated in the Caribbean Sea, others seemingly broken off from the South and Central American mainland.

Bodies of Water

If you were in a space shuttle, you'd first notice the vast waters surrounding Central and South America: the **Pacific Ocean** to the west and the **Atlantic** to the east. The **Gulf of Mexico** is bordered by Mexico to its west and the U.S. to its north. Southeast of the Gulf is the **Caribbean Sea**, which opens onto the Atlantic Ocean.

Another gulf, though much smaller than the Gulf of Mexico, also stands out from your vantage point: Splitting the mainland of Mexico from its western **Baja Peninsula** is the **Gulf of California**.

Your eye will likely next be drawn to one of the major rivers in the world, the **Amazon**. This mighty river runs from west to east almost across the entire breadth of northern South America, finally emptying into the Atlantic. A great many tributaries flow into the Amazon, creating the massive Amazon Basin, which affects much of the continent's (and, for that matter, the world's) weather. It's here in the north that you can see South America's lush, tropical jungles. A few other major rivers are noteworthy. In the south, the **Rio Parana** and **Rio Uruguay** connect to the major estuary, **Rio de la Plata**, which in turn flows into the Atlantic. In the north, Venezuela's **Orinoco River** empties into the Atlantic, just east of the Caribbean.

A few good-sized lakes interrupt the landscape. In Central America is **Lake Nicaragua**. As your glance moves down to northern parts of South America, there's **Lake Maracaibo**. And finally, at the western bend of the continent is **Lake**

The Gulf of California is also called the Sea of Cortes.

A fjord glacier in Chile
Photo by C. J. Ghormley

Giant tortoise, Galapagos Islands
Photo by William and Marie Rourke

Titicaca, a popular resort area between Peru and Bolivia. Farther south, just east of the Andes, is the **Lake District** of Argentina; this is a major resort region.

Also in the south, just to the west of the continent's tip, the coastline breaks up into a mass of islands (separated at its tip by the **Strait of Magellan**). Far west (2,300 miles, actually) is **Easter Island**, a fascinating destination. Two other island groupings catch your eye: the **Galapagos Islands** (a popular expedition site), off the northwest coast; and the **Falkland Islands**, off the coast to the southeast.

One final feature is highly significant. Splitting the isthmus connecting Mexico and South America is the man-made **Panama Canal**.

Mountains

From your satellite view, there's only one major mountain range of any note. But what a range: the **Andes**, beginning in the northwest corner of South America and following the western coast down to the very southern tip. These mountains greatly influence life in the western part of the continent. Even a few popular ski resorts can be found in their southern reaches. One other range is apparent: In Mexico, two branches of the **Sierra Madres** parallel the east and west coasts and finally join south of Mexico City.

The Andes is the longest mountain range in the world (4,500 miles).

Climate

As a rule, the weather in much of Latin America and the Caribbean is hot and humid, with frequent summer afternoon cloudbursts (though winters in the south can get chilly). The Amazon Basin is extremely hot, humid, and rainy year-round. Mexico is also hot, but the central plateau area tends to be more temperate and dry. Mountain temperatures, of course, are colder. And on the west coast of South America, from the northern border of Chile southward for about 600 miles, is the **Atacama**, perhaps the driest desert in the world.

Ocean temperatures on the east coast are quite warm, though waters off the west coast can be cold, since the prevailing currents carry water up from the

Antarctic. Even the Galapagos Islands, which lie virtually on the equator, are surrounded by surprisingly cool ocean waters.

One other point must be made concerning the area's weather. Much of the region lies south of the equator, which bisects the northern part of South America. As a result, most of the continent has seasons that are opposite to those of the Northern Hemisphere: Summer is December through February, and winter (which tends to be the rainiest season) is June through August.

Tourism Patterns

Of all the Latin American countries, Mexico attracts more visitors than any other: About five million visit annually. But, as a group, the Caribbean islands are even more popular. The Bahamas and Puerto Rico draw nearly three million annually. The Dominican Republic, Jamaica, the U.S. Virgin Islands, and St. Martin post equally impressive figures.

In South America, Brazil is by far the most popular destination, with some two million people visiting yearly. Argentina and Uruguay aren't far behind. Peru, with several world-class attractions, has huge tourist possibilities and will certainly be seeing major growth in the future.

Latin American Distances

Because many of your clients think of the region only in terms of its highly popular cities, such as **Rio de Janeiro**, **Buenos Aires**, and **Acapulco**, Latin America may seem far smaller than it is. In truth, it spills over two continents and covers an area several times greater than that of the United States.

All the major cities have very good airline connections, which helps shrink the distances. In addition, most of the smaller cities within each country can be reached by air, since virtually every country has its own national airline. Cruises are one efficient way to see Mexican and Caribbean beach resorts; ships also stop

Boat excursion on the Amazon River
Photo by William and Marie Rourke

In a 1493 decree, the Pope decided which parts of South America should belong to Spain and which to Portugal.

at many ports in Central and South America. A number of Caribbean and Mexican cruise patterns exist; we'll review them in Chapters 8 and 9. As for South America, three itineraries seem to predominate. The first would start in Florida or a Caribbean island such as Barbados or Puerto Rico, sail past French Guiana, then up the Amazon River. The second would begin from the same area, but bypass the Amazon and continue down to Rio de Janeiro, Sao Paulo, or Montevideo. A third would be most ambitious, entirely circling the continent.

There are other ways of getting around, but not all are efficient or comfortable; even when they are, the great distances to be covered may make them prohibitive.

Train service, for instance, is inconsistent, though there are a few fine networks. Buses are for the more adventurous. In a few instances (usually between islands or through the river-crowded jungles), smaller boats and ships are the most useful way of getting around. They're slow, of course, but the scenery can be very beautiful—and your clients may have no other choice.

Driving is always an alternative, too; plenty of rental cars are available. However, again, except for a few short distances over rather well-maintained roads (including the Pan-American Highway), this is a less likely recommendation. Major cities are *very* crowded, and in rural areas roads often are not in good shape; moreover, heavy rains commonly wash out the roads in some areas.

Remember, too, that the climate plays an important role in travel. Tropical rains, hurricanes, or snow in the Andes can dramatically affect your clients' plans.

Some Miscellaneous Considerations

Latin America has a very distinct culture. Some important factors for you to keep in mind are:

- Your clients will likely be aware that Spanish is the national language in virtually all these countries. (It's called Latin America because Spanish was derived from ancient Latin.) A few exceptions exist: Brazilians speak Portuguese; Belize's and Guyana's national language is English; Dutch is the official language of Suriname; and French Guianaians speak French. The Caribbean is an even greater potpourri of languages, and all have been somewhat altered by African and Indian influences. However, English is widely spoken in the major cities and by most travel personnel.

- Some areas in Latin America are off-limits to photography. Make certain your clients are discreet when taking pictures (especially of government buildings) and when talking about politics.

- Inflation is a major problem in many Latin American nations. One way to offset this is by booking packages early, thus locking in prices.

- Political turmoil can flare up in most any of these countries, turning an attractive destination into a dubious one. Keep up on the news and consult travel advisories.

- People living in South America consider themselves Americans, just as people from the United States do. They can get offended when this is ignored. Remind your clients to be sensitive about equating Americans only with U.S. citizens.

- The use of space and time in South America is different from that in North America. Tell your clients not to be surprised if a South American stands very close to them during a conversation. Though your clients should strive to be on time for an appointment, they shouldn't get offended if someone they are supposed to meet is late; time is very elastic here.

- In some South American countries, such as Chile and Bolivia, it's an insult not to hold eye contact with the person to whom you're talking. Be sure your clients (especially business clients) know this.

- Crime is, unfortunately, a problem in some Latin American and Caribbean countries. Simple precautions and common sense will avert most predicaments.
- Many clients mistakenly believe that all of the Caribbean and Latin America is a bargain. Not true. Argentina, Venezuela, and several Caribbean islands (for example, St. Martin) are somewhat pricey. On the other hand, Brazil, Peru, Colombia, and Jamaica *are* bargains.

Travel Trivia

Hotel Pools with the Best Views

Copacabanca Palace Hotel, Rio de Janeiro
Hotel du Cap-Eden-Roc, Cap d'Antibes, France
Hotel Cipriani, Venice, Italy
Arizona Biltmore, Phoenix
Beverly Hills Hotel, Beverly Hills

Hollywood Roosevelt, Los Angeles
Biltmore Hotel, Coral Gables, FLoirda
The Raleigh, Miami Beach
Crane Beach Hotel, Barbados

Source: Travel & Leisure *magazine*

Creative Activity

NAME _____ DATE _____

You work for a tour wholesaler that specializes in independent tours to Latin America. Anticipate five possible objections—either real or imaginary—that a client might have to going to Latin America and meet them with the information that might overcome each objection.

CLIENT OBJECTION

Example: I don't know Spanish. I'll have trouble being understood.

1.

2.

3.

4.

5.

OVERCOME OBJECTION WITH . . .

English is widely spoken in major cities and by most travel personnel.

1.

2.

3.

4.

5.

Travel Trivia

The World's Top Ten Cruise Destinations

1. Caribbean
2. Mediterranean
3. Alaska
4. Europe
5. Bahamas

6. Trans-Canal
7. Mexico
8. Bermuda
9. South America
10. Trans-Atlantic

Source: Cruise Lines International Association

CA
San Diego
Mexicali
Tijuana
Ensenada

ARIZONA
NEW MEXICO

OKLAHOMA
ARKANSAS

MS
ALABAMA

FL

Nogales
El Paso
Ciudad Juarez

TEXAS

LOUISIANA

Baja Peninsula

Chihuahua

Copper Canyon

Nuevo Laredo

GULF of CALIFORNIA

Loreto

Los Mochis

MEXICO

GULF of MEXICO

La Paz
San José del Cabo
Cabo San Lucas

Mazatlán

Tampico

Colonial Region

Progreso
Cancun

Mérida

Puerto Vallarta
Guadalajara

Cozumel Island

PACIFIC OCEAN

Mex. Riviera

Manzanillo

Mexico City

Yucatan Peninsula

Cuernavaca
Taxco

CARIBBEAN SEA

Ixtapa
Zihuatanejo

Veracruz

BELIZE

Acapulco
Oaxaca

oldest resort

Huatulco

newest government built.

GUATEMALA
HONDURAS

EL SALVADOR

NICARAGUA

CHAPTER 8

Mexico
Tropical Fiesta

Sure, every tourist has heard stories of how you can eat, drink, and dance all night at Mexico's beach cities, then take a siesta all day under the hot tropical sun. But there's much more to Mexico than that. Mexico, for example, is rich with historical attractions and archaeological sites. There *are* some drawbacks, though. The biggest problem: Poverty is widespread. Indeed, this may be the greatest misgiving your clients have about a trip to Mexico.

First, some geography. Mexico is quite large—about a quarter the size of the United States—and it's not all palm-lined beaches. Mexico is a land of diverse landscapes: craggy canyons and cliffs; vast and arid deserts; dense tropical rain forests; and broad, high plateaus. Mexico is sandwiched on the north by the United States and on the south by Guatemala and Belize. To the west are the warm waters of the Gulf of California and the Pacific, and to the east are the even warmer waters of the Gulf of Mexico and the Caribbean Sea.

For Your Information . . .

Mexico   FYI

CAPITAL: Mexico City

AREA (SQUARE MILES): 761,600

TIME ZONES: GMT: –6 to –8

DRIVE ON: Right

POPULATION: 92,700,000

RELIGION: Roman Catholic

LANGUAGE: Spanish

CURRENCY: 1 peso = 100 centavos

ELECTRICITY: 120 volts, 60 cycles AC

CAPSULE HISTORY: Mayas, Toltecs, and Aztecs rule, pre-1519; Cortes conquers, 1519–1521; Mexicans overthrow Spaniards, 1821; war with U.S., 1846–1848; French invade and rule, 1861–1867; Juarez is president, 1855 and 1867; Civil War, 1920; major oil deposits discovered, 1975; political unrest, 1996.

For reference sources, tourist bureaus, and suggested lengths of stay, see the Appendices.

It's useful to divide the country into five major tourist areas. The **Baja** [BAH-hah] **Peninsula** stretches southward from California for nearly 700 miles. On the northern part of Baja, just across the California border, is **Tijuana** [tee-yah-WAH-nah], a city that's usually seen in a day trip from San Diego, California. Toward the southernmost tip are several small resort cities: **La Paz**, **Cabo San Lucas**, and **San José del Cabo** (as a group, they're often called **Los Cabos**). To Baja's east and south is a second major destination, the **Mexican Riviera**: a string of resort cities that lines Mexico's long western coast.

The **Yucatan Peninsula**, which curves out from Mexico's east coast, is a third key destination and is often considered part of the Caribbean. **Cancun** [kan-KOON] is its chief resort. The Yucatan is also the location of many of Mexico's most dramatic ruins. Northwest of the peninsula are **Veracruz**, **Tampico**, and other port cities that your clients are less likely to visit, except perhaps as a cruise stopover. But not all of Mexico's attractions are along the beach. **The Copper Canyon**, in Mexico's north-central area, is a fourth major destination. And the fifth is Mexico's **colonial region**, which includes **Guadalajara**, **Cuernavaca**, **Taxco**, and **Mexico City**, the nation's capital.

The meteor that helped kill off the dinosaurs probably hit the earth at the tip of the Yucatan Peninsula.

How Travelers Get There

Mexicana (MX), the country's national carrier, flies out of several North American gateways, as does **Aeromexico** (AM). Quite a few U.S. and Canadian carriers fly into Mexico; clients commonly feel that service will be more reliable on these airlines than on Mexico's own. Unlike many countries, there's no real hub to the Mexican air system. There are enough connections that you can just fly your clients into the cities they wish to visit. Among the principal airports: Mexico City (MEX), **Acapulco** (ACA), and Cancun (CUN).

To take a train, bus, or car into Mexico is usually inadvisable. Its trains and buses leave something to be desired for the average client and driving can be perilous. (If you get into an accident or break a traffic law in Mexico, you might be detained indefinitely in jail.) Cruises, usually out of Los Angeles, are an extremely popular way to see Ensenada, Cabo San Lucas, and/or the Mexican Riviera. Mexico's Gulf-Caribbean east-coast ports—especially Cozumel and Cancun—serve as occasional ports of call for ships (usually on Western Caribbean cruise itineraries). Note: Access to Cancun is via the port of Playa del Carmen.

Weather Patterns

Most people imagine all of Mexico to be hot and humid. Not so. Mexico City, for example, sits on a high plateau. The city can certainly be warm in the summer (though rainy), but it's quite cool in the winter, with an average daytime high around 60 degrees in December. And at almost any time of the year, Mexico City is cool at night. The beach cities are indeed hot and humid in the summer and early autumn, with frequent afternoon downpours and an occasional hurricane. (As you can guess, this is the season for travel bargains.) But winter, the high tourist season for Mexico, is pleasantly warm and dry (see Figures 8-1 and 8-2). The only exceptions: the smaller resorts along the Baja and on the Gulf of California, where winter air and water temperatures can be a bit chilly.

In central Mexico, near Morelia, millions of Monarch butterflies congregate each winter.

Getting Around

It's best to fly from place to place in Mexico. But there are a few exceptions: The Copper Canyon train ride is a first-rate trip to book for your client through a reputable wholesaler. And several tour companies operate a comfortable-enough motorcoach trip between the major beach resort of Acapulco and Mexico City, with stops at interesting towns in between.

Climate at a Glance
MAZATLAN, MEXICO

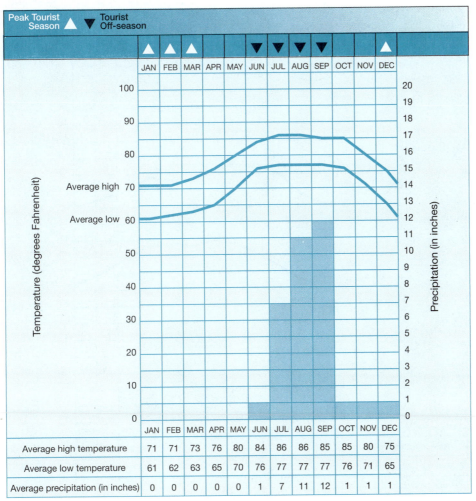

Peak Tourist Season ▲	▼ Tourist Off-season											
	▲	▲	▲			▼	▼	▼	▼		▲
	JAN	FEB	MAR	APR	MAY	JUN	JUL	AUG	SEP	OCT	NOV	DEC
Average high temperature	71	71	73	76	80	84	86	86	85	85	80	75
Average low temperature	61	62	63	65	70	76	77	77	77	76	71	65
Average precipitation (in inches)	0	0	0	0	0	1	7	11	12	1	1	1

Figure 8-1

Getting around each Mexican city is relatively easy. There's a major subway in Mexico City, though taxis, as in all cities in this country, can be an inexpensive way of getting around. Beware: As with most things in Mexico, the fare should perhaps be negotiated in advance, especially if the taxi has no meter.

Important Places

Carefully probe your clients' likes and dislikes. This will guide you in tailoring their Mexican vacation to their preferences. A list of those destinations you're most likely to sell to them follows.

The Baja Peninsula

If your clients intend to travel from San Diego to Tijuana, prepare them for the run-down environment they'll encounter as soon as they cross the border. (They should park their cars on the U.S. side and walk or taxi into town.) Tijuana, though, isn't a seriously dangerous place, except perhaps at night. Why would your clients go? To bargain at the thousand little shops, to engage in the nightlife, and to say they've been to Mexico—if only for a few hours. **Ensenada**, a beach and college "party" town down the coast, is a frequent weekend getaway

Almost all the taxis in Mexico City are Volkswagen "bugs."

Climate at a Glance
MEXICO CITY, MEXICO

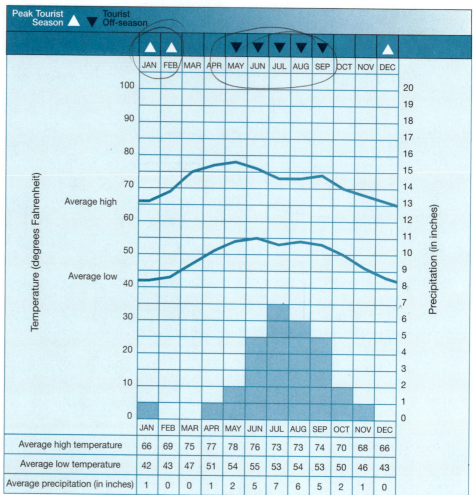

	JAN	FEB	MAR	APR	MAY	JUN	JUL	AUG	SEP	OCT	NOV	DEC
Average high temperature	66	69	75	77	78	76	73	73	74	70	68	66
Average low temperature	42	43	47	51	54	55	53	54	53	50	46	43
Average precipitation (in inches)	1	0	0	1	2	5	7	6	5	2	1	0

Figure 8-2

from southern California, either by car or by three- or four-day cruises out of Los Angeles.

The area between Ensenada and the tip of Baja can be an arduous drive. Fly your clients instead either to **Loreto**, a quiet but growing resort, or to the **Los Cabos** area, where they can visit and swim in several beautiful coves. The big attractions here are the superb deep-sea fishing and the many resorts that dot the twenty-two-mile "corridor" between San Jose and San Lucas.

The Mexican Riviera

Mexico has an astonishing 6,000 miles of warm, tropical coastline. Its most famous resorts, except for one, are along the Pacific coast. From north to south, they are:

- **Mazatlan**. This middle-priced resort has a large harbor that can easily accommodate major cruise ships. It's most famous as a fishing paradise, but it also offers quite a few nonwater activities, including jungle tours, bullfights, shopping, an aquarium, rodeos, and well-known Mardi Gras festivities. A ferry crosses daily from Mazatlan to La Paz, on the Baja Peninsula.

- **Puerto Vallarta**. Puerto Vallarta [vah-YAR-tah] is more active than Mazatlan, with many fine hotels, a market, and superb beaches. Tours into the mountainous interior jungle are popular here, too.

A twelve-foot, 988-pound marlin was caught off Mazatlan.

- **Manzanillo**. The beach is small and the lodging choices limited. So why sell Manzanillo? Because one of the world's most elaborate and romantic resort hotels is located here: **Las Hadas**. Deep-sea fishing is also excellent at Manzanillo.

- **Ixtapa** [is-TAH-pah]. A quieter and more exclusive beach resort than either Mazatlan or Puerto Vallarta, Ixtapa is a destination of great beauty. It's especially attractive to clients because of the nearby picturesque fishing village of **Zihuatanejo** [zee-WAT-ah-nay-hoh], the location of the area's airport, several good hotels, some shopping, and a few beaches.

- **Acapulco**. This is the grand old resort of Mexico; it's been popular for many decades and has recovered from damages suffered in a 1997 hurricane. A wall of large hotels lines Acapulco's many beaches; numerous night spots, countless restaurants, and several moonlight cruises are available. And, of course, there are the famous cliff divers. The city has been spruced up, though beggars and pickpockets still patrol the streets and beaches. If Mexico is a fiesta, Acapulco is its brash featured act.

- **Huatulco** [wah-TOOL-koh]. This, Mexico's newest government-planned beach resort, faces a string of nine secluded bays and ten miles of beach. Snorkeling is a prime activity.

The Yucatan Peninsula

Few destinations combine beaches and history so tantalizingly as does the Yucatan Peninsula. Its chief city is Merida, but most travelers never see this bustling inland urban center. They usually arrive directly at Cancun. Among the peninsula's attractions are:

- **Cancun**, a vast governmentally planned seaside resort, boasts glorious beaches, dozens of first-rate hotels, many lively restaurants and night spots, a wildlife reserve, and clean prosperity. Cancun is strategically located: By air, it's only a few hours from Dallas and Miami, less than four from New York, and about five from Los Angeles.

- **Cozumel Island**, not far off the coast from Cancun, also offers quite a few resort hotels, though the ambience is a bit more low-key. Cozumel is a haven for divers and snorkelers. It is reached by air, ferry, or cruise ship.

Pyramid at Chichen Itza
Photo by C. J. Ghormley

Las Hadas hotel was made famous by the 1979 movie, *10*.

Some of Cancun's best restaurants aren't in the tourist area, but in the town where locals live.

Climbing a pyramid is popular, but the toughest part is coming *down*.

- **The archaeological ruins** that dot the Yucatan are often seen via bus day trips from Cancun. As dramatic as any in the world, they include **Chichen Itza** (with its well-known ball court and ancient observatory), **Uxmal** [oos-MAHL] (with an astonishingly steep pyramid), and **Tulum** (one of the only major Mexican ruins to overlook the Caribbean Sea). Among the ruins that are increasingly popular to visit: Kabah, Sayil, Labna, Coba, and Dzibil Chaltun.

The Copper Canyon

Almost as dramatic as Arizona's Grand Canyon or Kauai's Waimea, the Copper Canyon stretches through north-central Mexico. A train ride (which you should book for your clients only through well-known wholesalers) starts in Chihuahua, in the north, and finishes in Los Mochis, on the Gulf of California. The multi-day Copper Canyon tours take passengers through dramatic scenery and make stops in various villages and towns along the way. Chihuahua is less than an hour's flight south from El Paso, Texas; Los Mochis is across the Gulf of California from La Paz and a relatively short flight from Mazatlan. In other words, you can easily combine the Copper Canyon trip with stays at Baja and Mexican Riviera resorts.

The Colonial Region

Mexico was long a Spanish colony and briefly a French one; remnants of this colonial past mark many of Mexico's inland cities, most of which lie on the country's somewhat cooler central plateau. Among the cities your clients are likely to visit are:

- **Guadalajara**, a city of lovely flowering parks, graceful European architecture, and one of Latin America's largest zoos.
- **Cuernavaca**, a charming town inhabited by many retired Americans. It has several interesting buildings, including Cortes's palace. It's an easy day trip from Mexico City.
- **Taxco** [TAHS-ko], the "Silver City," often visited by clients traveling by motorcoach between Mexico City and Acapulco.

Copper Canyon train ride
Photo by William and Marie Rourke

Oaxaca's Camino Real
is a converted
convent.

- **Oaxaca** [wah-HAH-kah], the most southerly of Mexican colonial cities, best known as a center for arts and crafts. It has an impressive church (Santo Domingo), a fascinating museum, and several nearby ruins (especially **Monte Alban**).

Mexico City

Only a few sights remain of Mexico City's colonial past; earthquakes, traffic congestion, exploding population, and smog have seen to that. Yet Mexico City has a European-like cosmopolitan air that's unique in the country. And it does have many famous, first-rate attractions, including:

- **The National Museum of Anthropology**, one of the world's great museums, with its dazzling collection of Olmec, Mayan, and Aztec artifacts.
- **The Zocalo**, a huge town square bordered by the city's dramatic cathedral and governor's palace.
- **The Floating Gardens of Xochimilco** [soh-shee-MEEL-koh], a charming attraction that your clients can boat through. Popular with locals, it's all that's left of the system of canals that criss-crossed Mexico City in ancient times.

Several day trips from Mexico City are popular, but the one day trip you must recommend is to the Toltec **Pyramids of Teotihuacan**—a major archaeological site about an hour away. America's first planned city, it housed 200,000 people in 500 A.D., and covered an area larger than imperial Rome.

The Border Towns

Many tourists envision Mexico through her border towns: Tijuana, **Mexicali**, **Nogales** (south of Tucson, Arizona), **Ciudad Juarez** (across from El Paso, Texas), and **Nuevo Laredo** (next to Laredo, Texas). Though these dusty, bustling places have their interesting points, they're hardly representative of the rest of Mexico.

Possible Itineraries

Booking a trip for a client to any Mexican destination almost always requires the use of a wholesaler; the package is usually a bargain, and Mexican hotels are more likely to honor a reservation made through a large tour company than through an individual agency. So your itineraries will usually be shaped by a prearranged tour package. Mexico City, the Copper Canyon, or the inland colonial cities are almost always combined with a single beach resort in a four-to-nine-day itinerary. You can

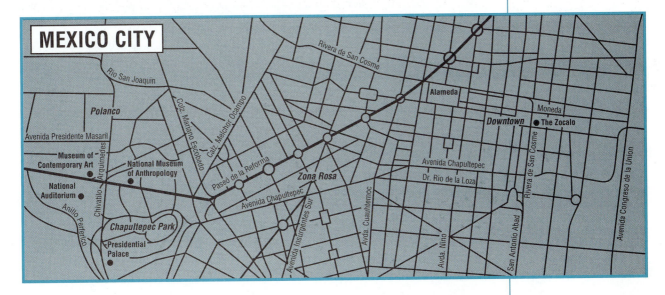

Nun's Quadrangle at Uxmal
Photo by William and Marie Rourke

also package together two beach resorts, though it would be good to set up a contrast, say, Acapulco with Ixtapa or Cabo San Lucas. As for an all-beach itinerary, a client will likely prefer to stay at one place for anywhere from a weekend to a week.

Lodging Options

Lodging in Mexico ranges from superdeluxe properties to budget hotels. To ensure clean, satisfying lodging for your clients, recommend first-class and deluxe hotels whenever possible. Mid-priced chains include: **Calinda**, **Fiesta Inn**, **Posada Real**, and **Hoteles Mision**. A step above these are **Fiesta Americana** hotels. Deluxe chains include **El Presidente**, **Krystal**, **Camino Real**, **Maeva Resorts** (all-inclusives), **Quinta Real** (all-suites), and **Melia**, along with many U.S. and Canadian hotel groups. Indeed, such hotels as Las Hadas (Manzanillo) and the **Las Brisas** or **Princess** hotels (Acapulco) are world-famous and may already be familiar to your clients. Remember: Modified American plans (MAPs), where the client must take breakfast and one other meal daily at the hotel, are typical in Mexican hotels during high season.

Three other lodging options are open to your clients. **Club Med** has all-inclusive properties in many Mexican beach cities. Cruise ships offer lodging that moves from one resort port to another. And condos or private homes are a useful option for some.

Two romantic getaways in Zihuatanejo: Villa del Sol (a hideaway on Playa La Ropa) and **La Casa Que Cantor** (terraced down a cliff with views of the bay).

Allied Destinations

Mexico's east coast resorts combine readily with vacations in the Caribbean, Texas, New Orleans, and Florida. Central and west coast destinations often precede or follow stays in California, Arizona, New Mexico, and Texas. Mexico can also be a stop-off point for journeys into Central and South America, or even from the U.S. East Coast to New Zealand and Australia.

Cultural Patterns

Though it borders the United States, Mexico presents unique cultural experiences to most clients. Business clients, especially, should be made aware of false assumptions that may stand in the way of good relationships.

- The custom of "mañana" (putting off a task until tomorrow) persists. Don't let your clients confuse this with laziness. Time is perceived differently here; the pace is slower, more relaxed.
- You might inform your clients that a popular time to do business is often during a long lunch. Business is commonly brought up after an extended period of socializing.
- If a client visits the home of a local, it's customary to bring a small gift.
- Mexicans give starting times for parties that are rarely observed. If a party is to start at 7 P.M., few will arrive before 8:30 P.M. This is especially true at beach resort cities.
- Almost anything is negotiable in Mexico, especially souvenir purchases. Don't be intimidated; what may seem like impatience, anger, or obstinacy in the seller is simply part of the "game." Counter with a price that's 50 percent of the original quote and work from there.

Each year, on the evening of December 23, Oaxaca celebrates "The Night of the Radishes."

Factors That Motivate Visitors

A wide spectrum of reasons motivates a traveler to visit Mexico:

- The beaches are, in most places, glorious.
- All manner of water-sport options are available.
- Mexico is a shopping and lodging bargain, especially off-season.
- Archaeological treasures are everywhere. (In fact, one estimate claims that the jungle still covers 90 percent of all ancient Mayan and Aztec sites.)
- Air and cruise transportation into and around Mexico is convenient, plentiful, and relatively inexpensive.
- Superdeluxe resorts in Mexico are a bargain compared to similar properties across the world, especially in the summer off-season.
- The foreign, exotic culture of Mexico is less than five hours away from most U.S. locations.
- The winter weather is warm, dry, and inviting.

On Isla Mujeres (off Cancun), there's a cave where divers can actually pet sharks; the water's content makes the fish groggy and therefore unthreatening.

Possible Misgivings

Mexico elicits both positive and negative reactions in potential travelers. Among the objections you may hear are:

- "I'll get sick." For possible intestinal problems—"Montezuma's Revenge" is genuine—consult your doctor about medication to take along. (Several over-the-counter remedies are also highly effective.) And, of course, avoid drinking the water. Even brushing your teeth with tap water or having ice cubes in your drink may create problems. Coffee, tea, canned soft drinks, and bottled wine or beer are generally safe. Never eat uncooked meats, fish, or vegetables.

- "I don't speak Spanish." Many people in major cities and at tourist facilities speak English.

- "Mexico is poverty-ridden." Poverty and its symptoms—crime, corruption, street-begging and unsanitary conditions—do plague many Mexican cities. Suggest Cancun, which is largely free of such problems. Self-contained mega-resorts such as the Acapulco Princess or Club Meds also can insulate clients from most of the poverty.

- "The food disagrees with me." Mexican food has great diversity. Tell your clients that familiar American-style food is available in many places. Mention also that nonspicy food is usually available in many locations, especially in the Yucatan.

- "The only time I can afford a Mexican vacation is when it's hot and rainy." Late spring or early autumn is a good compromise: Rain isn't as frequent, the weather may not yet be very hot, and low or shoulder-season rates may still be in effect.

Sales Strategies

Cruises, all-inclusive resorts, Copper Canyon packages, and high-season hotel MAPs maximize the potential profit you'll receive from selling a Mexican vacation. Independent and escorted tours also offer efficient ways to profit from as many components of your clients' holiday as possible. You can also sell them diving, fishing, or day-trip excursions in advance. Because most clients are somewhat leery of budget or even moderate-class hotels in Mexico, the possibility to sell them superior or luxury accommodations is strong.

Qualifying the Client
Cancun

FOR CLIENTS WHO WANT	APPEAL			REMARKS
	HIGH	MEDIUM	LOW	
Historical and Cultural Attractions	▲			Ruins are nearby
Beaches and Water Sports	▲			Warm, clear water
Skiing Opportunities			▲	None
Lots of Nightlife	▲			In hotels
Family Activities		▲		
Familiar Cultural Experience		▲		
Exotic Cultural Experience	▲			
Safety and Low Crime	▲			One of safest Mexican destinations
Bargain Travel		▲		Expensive for Mexico
Impressive Scenery		▲		Primarily seascapes
Peace and Quiet		▲		Active, but not overwhelmingly so
Shopping Opportunities		▲		Crafts markets
To Do Business			▲	Low in Cancun, but high elsewhere in Mexico

Figure 8-3

Creative Activity

Mexico has decided to release a series of ten commemorative stamps that portray tourist-related places, landmarks, and activities for which the country is famous. If you were hired as a consultant, what ten things would you recommend be put on the stamps? Be prepared to say why.

1.

2.

3.

4.

5.

6.

7.

8.

9.

10.

Travel Trivia

Places with Unlikely Names

- Yucatan, Mexico—The response that natives gave to Spanish explorers who landed here; it means, "I don't understand you."
- Singapore—Means "city of the lion," even though there are not now (nor have there ever been) lions here.
- Cape of Good Hope—Near the southern tip of Africa, with intensely rough seas.
- Greenland—One of the coldest, snowiest places on earth.
- Iceland—Much less icy—and greener—than Greenland.
- Nome, Alaska—Miscopied from a map that indicated "Name?" at this spot.
- The Pacific—Called this by Magellan, who crossed at a time of no storms; of course, it has many dramatic ones.

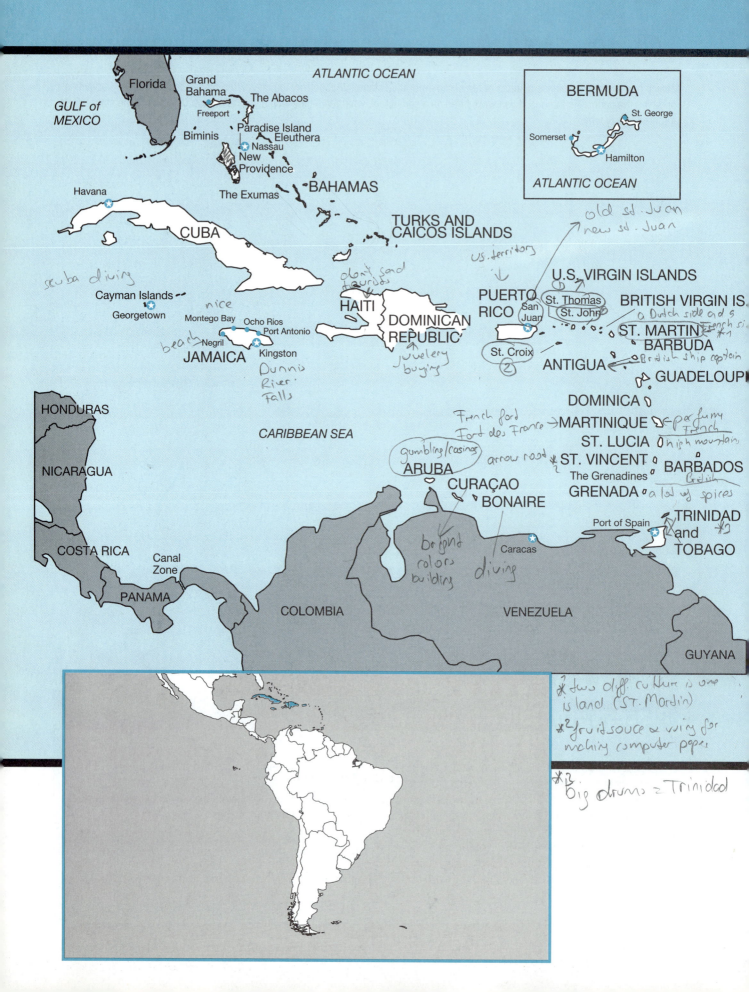

ATLANTIC OCEAN

GULF of MEXICO

Florida

Grand Bahama

The Abacos

Freeport

Biminis

Paradise Island
Eleuthera

Nassau

New Providence

BAHAMAS

The Exumas

Havana

CUBA

scuba diving

Cayman Islands

Georgetown

nice

Montego Bay

Ocho Rios
Port Antonio

beach

Negril

JAMAICA

Kingston

Dunns River Falls

TURKS AND CAICOS ISLANDS

don't send tourists

HAITI

DOMINICAN REPUBLIC

jewelery buying

US. territory

old sd. Juan
new sd. Juan

PUERTO RICO

San Juan

St. Croix

PERTO RICO

U.S. VIRGIN ISLANDS

St. Thomas

St. John

BRITISH VIRGIN IS.

a Dutch side and s

ST. MARTIN

French si

#1

BARBUDA

British ship captain

ANTIGUA

GUADELOUP

DOMINICA

BERMUDA

Somerset

St. George

Hamilton

ATLANTIC OCEAN

HONDURAS

NICARAGUA

CARIBBEAN SEA

French ford
Fort des France

MARTINIQUE

parfumy French

ST. LUCIA

high mountain

gambling/casinos

ARUBA

arrow road

#2

ST. VINCENT

The Grenadines

BARBADOS

British

COSTA RICA

Canal Zone

PANAMA

CURAÇAO

BONAIRE

beyond colors building

Caracas

diving

GRENADA

a lot of spices

Port of Spain

TRINIDAD and TOBAGO

#3

COLOMBIA

VENEZUELA

GUYANA

*two diff. cultures on one island (ST. Martin)

*2 fruit sauce & wing for making computer paper

*3 Big drums = Trinidad

CHAPTER 9

The Caribbean
A Sea of Nations

Let's face it, selling the Caribbean can be intimidating.

Dozens of islands arc across this vast tropical region. Remembering which is where isn't easy. Furthermore, each island may have its very own government, culture, value level, range of services and accommodations, topography, and language. To match a Caribbean destination to a client takes great skill and knowledge. In this chapter we sort out and organize information about the Caribbean so that you'll feel far more confident about your understanding of the area and your ability to sell it.

A good way to start is to divide the Caribbean into six destination groupings. The first two, **Bermuda** and the **Bahamas**, aren't even part of the Caribbean, though many think of them as such. Bermuda is way off in the Atlantic, at about the same latitude as Charleston, South Carolina; and the Bahamas is a string of 700 islands that stretches southeastward from Florida into the Atlantic (and not into the central **Caribbean Sea**, which is farther south). Geographers label the third cluster the **Greater Antilles** ("greater" because most of them are large). Just south and southeast of Florida, they are, from left to right on the map: **Cuba** (only now developing tourism); the **Caymans**; **Jamaica**; **Haiti** and the **Dominican Republic** (which together make up one island, Hispaniola); and **Puerto Rico**.

The fourth set of islands forms a crescent on the Caribbean's eastern side, starting near Puerto Rico and curving gently southward toward the shores of Venezuela. Because of their comparatively small size, they're called the **Lesser Antilles**. Trying to memorize them all would be quite a chore, so we concentrate on those likely to be the most popular with your clients. They are, from north to south: the **Virgin Islands**, **St. Martin**, **Antigua**, **Guadeloupe**, **Martinique**, **Barbados**, and **Trinidad** and **Tobago**.

The fifth cluster of destinations is just northwest of Caracas, Venezuela: **Aruba**, **Bonaire**, and **Curaçao**, often called the ABC islands because of their first letters. The Caribbean destinations forming the sixth group aren't islands at all; they're the mainland cities that encircle the Caribbean, especially those of Mexico, Colombia, Venezuela, and Central America. These latter destinations we treat under their respective countries' chapters.

Two historical notes: The Caribbean islands were once called the West Indies, since early explorers thought that they had arrived in India. And the origin of the word *Antilles* is shrouded in mystery, though it's certainly French and probably means "land near the continent."

How Travelers Get There

You can get clients to the Caribbean islands through major U.S., Canadian, and Caribbean airlines; several small commuter airlines and seaplane companies; chartered boats and cruise ships. Cruise vessels have become the principal means of visiting the islands. They usually stop at several major ports, plus a few obscure, out-of-the-way ones. Four cruise itinerary patterns predominate: Short three- or four-day cruises into the Bahamas, almost always out of Florida; Eastern Caribbean or Western Caribbean seven-day sailings, again usually out of Florida; and seven-day Southern Caribbean cruises, often out of Puerto Rico, the U.S. Virgin Islands and, occasionally, from Barbados or Aruba. Longer sailings also exist, and Caribbean cruises are often the final (or initial) leg of a trans-Canal cruise. Bermuda sailings are in a separate category: usually about seven days long, they generally depart from and return to New York City.

Most airlines fly to the Caribbean from Miami, though many other mainland cities serve as a point of departure. If you fly your clients to the Caribbean, limit their trip to only a few islands (each of which might be serviced by the same airline). Otherwise, the air fares may turn out to be very high; inter-island flights can be quite expensive, especially when you are using more than one carrier or small local planes. If clients want to visit multiple islands, their best bet is a cruise.

Keep some extra local money for the airport departure taxes that are common at Caribbean airports.

Weather Patterns

The Caribbean is a year-round destination to sell. Winters are pleasant and dry, though Bermuda gets chilly, and the southernmost islands (such as Trinidad and the ABC islands) can still remain uncomfortably warm (see Figure 9-1 for one example). High tourist season extends from just before Christmas to around April, except for Bermuda, which attracts more people in the summer. Summers can be quite hot and humid most everywhere in the Caribbean, and even in northerly Bermuda, with fierce hurricanes tearing through the area mainly from July through September. For this reason, summer and fall are considered off-seasons, with hotel rates dropping as much as 60 percent. (Again, it's just the opposite for Bermuda.)

Trade winds are important to the Caribbean's climate. They generally blow, as in all tropical regions, from east to west, bringing some relief even on the hottest days. The winds along the southernmost islands (e.g., the ABCs) are especially strong. Those islands with mountains (just about all of them except Bermuda, the Bahamas, the Caymans, and the ABC islands, which are of coral, not volcanic origin—and therefore flat) tend to be drier on their western and, in some cases, northern shores.

The branches of divi-divi trees (on the ABC Islands) grow horizontally because of the strong winds.

Getting Around

The means of transportation on each island are quite informal: mopeds, jeeps, buses, and car rentals. Glass-bottom boats and even minisubmarines take tourists to view the underwater life off several islands. When reserving rental cars for your clients, remember to check if it's one of many islands where traffic flows on the left, not the right, since this might affect your clients' decision. (If it has a British heritage, it probably has left-side driving.) Remember, too, that tourists aren't allowed to rent cars in Bermuda; it's a way to control traffic.

Charter yachts are a popular way to get around the islands. The yacht-chartering capital of the Caribbean is the U.S. Virgin Islands, though some clients charter vessels out of Florida or other islands. Generally, there are two options: a **crewed** charter, in which the yachting company provides all staff to operate the boat; and a **bareboat** charter, on which the clients actually do the sailing.

Your clients should be made aware of several other things. First, Caribbean destinations aren't exactly into time and efficiency management. Their relaxed

Climate at a Glance
KINGSTON, JAMAICA

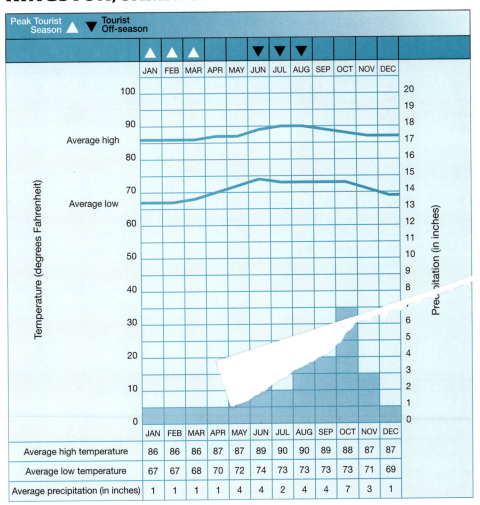

Peak Tourist Season ▲	▼ Tourist Off-season											
	▲	▲	▲			▼	▼	▼				
	JAN	FEB	MAR	APR	MAY	JUN	JUL	AUG	SEP	OCT	NOV	DEC
Average high temperature	86	86	86	87	87	89	90	90	89	88	87	87
Average low temperature	67	67	68	70	72	74	73	73	73	73	71	69
Average precipitation (in inches)	1	1	1	1	4	4	2	4	4	7	3	1

Figure 9-1

way of doing things can lead to lost reservations, especially for car rentals. Be sure to give your clients the confirmation number you were given (and maybe even a photocopy of the confirmation, if possible). Second, taxis are very expensive on certain islands; tell your clients to determine the approximate price before getting in. Third, mopeds are a great way of getting around, but your clients should beware: People who aren't used to them get into far too many accidents.

Important Places

Here's a thumbnail sketch of each major Caribbean and Caribbean-related island destination that you may sell. There's also a section on some of the minor destinations, in case your client brings them up.

Bermuda

Even though Bermuda isn't part of the Caribbean, it does share much with its southerly neighbors: fine beaches and resort hotels, gorgeous weather and the like. What makes Bermuda special, though, is how it differs from Caribbean destinations: its mixture of temperate and tropical climate (including all manner of vegetation), the surprising combination of formal and informal elements, the neat little houses with white coral roofs, the pink sand beaches and azure waters that look straight out of a campy 1950s painting.

Remember three things when discussing Bermuda with a client: The hotels are expensive (though less so in the winter); both the air and water are chilly in the winter, when the only bargains can be had; most visitors get around in taxis or on mopeds.

The capital of this English-speaking country is **Hamilton**. **St. George** and **Somerset** are historic towns. The island is dotted with several modest attractions, including a limestone cave, a lighthouse, and several churches. A politically stable island, Bermuda is ideal for clients who want a little formality and culture to go along with their beach vacation.

The Bahamas

Only fifty miles off Florida's southeast coast, the Bahamas are perfect for those clients who don't want to travel far for their Caribbean vacation or who are first-time travelers to the area. Though the Bahamian chain is composed of hundreds of islands, only twenty-two are inhabited and even fewer are tourist meccas.

The Bahamian destinations you're most likely to sell are:

- **Nassau**, on the island of New Providence, offers many opportunities to visit historical places, gamble, and shop (especially in and around its Straw Market). **Cable Beach**, ten minutes from Nassau, is a major beach development on New Providence Island; it boasts a famous, strikingly colored resort hotel, the **Crystal Palace**.

- **Paradise Island**, a complex of resort and gambling facilities, reached by ferry or taxi from Nassau. Paradise Island is sometimes called the Bahamian Riviera. The **Atlantis** mega-resort is an attraction in its own right.

- **Freeport**, on the quiet island of Grand Bahama, another shopping treat. Since Freeport has no beaches, to get some sun your clients will have to travel about five miles to **Lucaya Beach** and its world-class golf course.

- **Bimini** [BIM-uh-nee], made famous by author Ernest Hemingway, a legendary place for fishing.

The striking roofs of Bermuda houses help capture rainwater for home use.

At Ardastra Gardens, you can see the world's only performing flamingos.

A fourteenth-century European cloister was moved to Paradise Island in the 1920s.

NASSAU & PARADISE ISLAND

Atlantic Ocean

Colonial Beach

Cruise Docks

Nassau Harbour

Pirates Cove Drive

Causarina Drive

Paradise Beach Street

Atlantis Hotel

PARADISE ISLAND

Paradise Island Drive

Casino Drive

Harbour Road Drive

Cloisters

POTTER CAY

Straw Market

Bay Street

Paradise Island Bridge

NEW PROVIDENCE ISLAND

Shirley Street

East Bay Street

Sea Gardens

Blue Hill Road

Collins Avenue

Nassau

Mackey Street

Village Road

Montagu Bay

- **The Out Islands**, also called the **Family Islands**, lining the eastern Atlantic edge of the Bahamas. These relaxed and scenic islands are havens for yachting, sports-fishing, and diving enthusiasts. The principal ones are: **Eleuthera**, the **Abacos**, and the **Exumas**. A few of the smaller islands have been converted into "private" islands, where cruise ships anchor for the day.

The Caymans

Another legendary place (especially for your clients who are divers and snorkelers) is the Cayman Islands. It's a great destination, with some quaint (but expensive) restaurants and shops, dozens of water-sport opportunities, but virtually no scenery. (The Caymans are, in fact, large, flat coral reefs.) **Grand Cayman Island** and its capital, **Georgetown**, offer the most conventional diversions, including a Maritime and Treasure Museum that displays artifacts taken from the 325 shipwrecks that surround the island. Other Grand Cayman attractions: a Turtle Farm and Stingray City, where divers can swim with the ominous yet gentle creatures. North of Georgetown is **Seven Mile Beach**, where most resort hotels are located. **Cayman Brac** and especially **Little Cayman** are small tranquil islands that draw snorkelers, divers, and fishing enthusiasts by the droves.

Jamaica

Jamaica, an island of wide terrain variations that's due south of Cuba, certainly has a high client-recognition factor. That can be both good and bad. Its reggae music, jungle waterfalls, and sweeping beaches have made it a major Caribbean destination. But it also has well-known problems: Poverty, crime, drugs, and voodoo don't exactly endear it to some clients. Sending your clients to the right places in Jamaica is critical to their enjoyment. Here's some information that will help:

- **Negril** has become Jamaica's favorite beach. Once a hangout for counterculture types, it has become much more respectable and upscale. Nightlife here, though, is rather limited.
- **Montego Bay** is a major cruise port. Shopping and nightlife are good, the "Rose Hall" tour is fascinating, but the beaches are so-so. If you lodge a client here, it should be only as a base for excursions to the rest of the island, including to **Kingston**, the capital city.
- **Ocho Rios** is another cruise port, with pleasant beaches, several outstanding hotels, and a dramatic mountain backdrop. Nearby are the **Dunns River Falls**, Jamaica's most famous attraction. Here, a river cascades down a series of stone steps that your clients can climb.
- **Port Antonio**, a great beach area, has several minor attractions and one major one: the nearby **Rio Grande**, a river on which tourists can cruise on unusual bamboo rafts. (Tell your clients to take the shorter raft cruise; the three-hour cruise is a bit much.) Note: Several other Jamaican rivers feature bamboo raft cruises. Clients can get to Port Antonio from Kingston by car (a slow sixty-one-mile drive), hotel shuttle bus, or air.
- **Two hotel hints**: Jamaican lodging taxes are very high; many major all-inclusive resorts are here, including the well-known **Hedonism II** (part of a grouping called **SuperClubs**) and several **Sandals** (for couples only) resorts.

Puerto Rico

You've probably heard more and more travelers ask about Puerto Rico: It's relatively inexpensive, accommodations are first-rate, many Americans trace their roots to its soil, and, since it's American, there's no need to deal with immigration

Jamaica was the birthplace of reggae (and singer Bob Marley).

El Morro fortress, San Juan, Puerto Rico
Photo by C. J. Ghormley

and customs. Some crime and poverty does plague the island, though, and this may be an obstacle to selling this lush and culturally rich island.

Clients can be offered two options: to stay either in the bustling and historic **San Juan**, or at the resort beach complexes of **Palmas del Mar**, **Dorado**, and **Cerromar**. The most popular sightseeing attraction is El Yunque, a 28,000-acre rain forest. (It's a bit less impressive in the dry summer.) Nearby is **Luquillo Beach**, probably Puerto Rico's loveliest. **Old San Juan**'s historic ambience is worth experiencing, too, as is its adjoining **El Morro** fort. Many clients are drawn to Puerto Rico's gambling casinos.

is the only rainforest in the U.S.

The world's largest radio telescope (seen in movies such as Contact) can be visited at Arecibo.

Pusser's is a world-famous bar at Virgin Gorda.

Charlotte Amalie was the name of a Danish queen.

The Virgin Islands

One thing to know right away: There are *two* sets of Virgin Islands. **The British Virgin Islands**, sleepy little destinations, appeal primarily to yachters and divers, or to beach-loving clients who are seeking to really get away from it all. Two of its better-known islands are Tortola (a haven for yachters) and Virgin Gorda, which features one of the Caribbean's most remarkable attractions, a pile of seaside boulders called **The Baths**.

The U.S. Virgin Islands are just southwest of their British counterparts. Sailing, fishing, and diving are also major attractions here, but these islands are more lively than the British islands. The U.S. Virgin Islands are relatively clean and prosperous. These islands can also be accessed by boat from both the British Virgin Islands and San Juan, Puerto Rico.

Three principal islands make up the U.S. Virgin Islands. Each has its own character and can be used as a lodging point:

- **St. Thomas** is where you'll probably lodge most of your clients. It's the most developed of the three, with the city of **Charlotte Amalie** [ah-MALL-ya] providing most of the touristy attractions and extensive duty-free shopping. (St. Thomas is a convenient port of call for many cruise ships.)

- **St. Croix** [CROY] is quieter than St. Thomas, though it harbors several minor but appealing points of interest. It's also a popular cruise port.

The Baths, Virgin Gorda, B.V.I.
Photo by C. J. Ghormley

- **St. John** is the least developed of all. Its campgrounds (in a U.S. national park) are highly popular with clients who like that sort of thing. St. John has the most dramatic scenery, with dense rain forests, sharp reefs, and extinct volcanoes.

St. Martin

St. Martin (also spelled "St. Maarten") is perhaps the most unusual and satisfying of the Caribbean islands. Both France and the Netherlands govern it. The northern portion is French, and the southern, Dutch, but the island's informality leads to relaxed co-government over the entire island. The Dutch south is more commercialized, while the French north more relaxed, upscale, and scenic.

There's a little sightseeing to do in St. Martin's two principal towns, **Philipsburg** (Dutch) and **Marigot** (French). But mostly it'll be the food, shopping, and sun that will preoccupy your clients. Your clients can also get away by plane or boat to one of the several attractive (but quiet) nearby islands: **St. Kitts** (a lush, flowery place), **St. Bart's** (with its fine beaches, gourmet restaurants, and rolling hills), **St. Eustatius** (also called Statia, it has several historical points of interest and some good snorkeling areas), **Saba** (a picturesque blend of seascapes and cottage-dotted hills), and **Anguilla** (a favorite of many frequent Caribbean visitors for its fabulous beaches).

The town of Grand Case features some of the finest restaurants in the Caribbean.

Antigua

Pronounced "an-TEE-gah," not "an-TEE-gwah," this lush, tropical island and major cruise port claims that it has a beach for every day of the year: 365. Antigua, for its

A chain of jewelry stores, Little Switzerland, serves just about every island in the Bahamas and the Caribbean.

size, is well developed, with many good hotels and casinos, and one unique historic attraction: **Nelson's Dockyard** at English Harbor. In the eighteenth century, Antigua was home port to the British Caribbean naval fleet; Admiral Lord Nelson commanded it from English Harbor, which has been energetically restored by the Antiguans. Another attraction is sparsely settled **Barbuda**, a coral island thirty miles north of Antigua that boasts pink sand beaches reminiscent of those on Bermuda.

Your clients who like sailing, diving, and get-away-from-it-all beaches may like a stay on Antigua. Most likely, though, your clients will visit it as part of a cruise itinerary.

Guadeloupe and Martinique

Both these islands have much in common: French culture, volcanoes, deep green scenery, and so-so beaches. For clients who want French ambience to go along with their water activities, both islands will be intriguing.

The largest cities, **Pointe-A-Pitre** (Guadeloupe) and **Fort-De-France** (Martinique), are *not* where you want to lodge your clients. They are hectic and rather rundown towns. Major resort hotels aren't far away, though; and the all-inclusives are an excellent recommendation to make, especially since lodging and food can be quite expensive in the French West Indies. Two other islands in this area are for clients who want a quieter tone: **Dominica** (where the only descendants of the original Carib natives live) and **St. Lucia** [LOO-shah] (which has the best beaches of these four islands and a well-known sight: the twin mountain peaks of the **Pitons**).

Barbados

George Washington visited Barbados in 1751.

Most of the Caribbean islands you may sell have been tourist destinations for only a few decades. Not so Barbados. This most easterly of the Antilles ports has been attracting tourists for centuries. So it's not surprising that Barbados offers many small but fascinating historical attractions (including several plantations), as well as the usual great beaches, water-sport opportunities, small golf courses, and an underground wonder, the **Harrison Caves**.

Lodge your clients on the island's warm west "Platinum Coast" shore; the east can be windy and rainy. Which clients will most like Barbados? Those who want the calm, prosperous ambience of a very British, surprisingly formal island. Indeed, Barbados is quite reminiscent of Bermuda, but on a smaller scale.

Trinidad and Tobago

Trinidad and Venezuela to the south are involved in oil exporting. This is where steel drums originated.

Mention these islands and your clients are sure to have visions of steel drum bands, calypso music, and limbo competitions. Among the Caribbean islands, Trinidad is one of the liveliest and most prosperous, with a broad selection of international cuisine, entertainment, and shopping. Nearby Tobago, on the other hand, is a quiet, fantasy-like desert island, accessed by ferry or flight. If you fly your clients from the mainland to Trinidad, you can do a round-trip Trinidad-Tobago flight for them at no extra charge. Tobago has only a few, small hotels and almost no nightlife.

The locals in Trinidad seem more friendly to tourists than most, perhaps because poverty is less of a problem here. (But there is occasional unrest.) The principal city, **Port of Spain**, is filled with architectural surprises; walking around the town can occupy some of your clients' time. However, the rest of Trinidad is best explored by car; offer to book a car rental for your clients so they can go out exploring from their hotel on their own. You should also book hotel space well in advance; Trinidad doesn't have that many lodging options (though the situation is improving). Most of Trinidad's hotels are up in the hills, rather than on the island's only adequate beaches.

The ABC Islands

Aruba, Bonaire, and Curaçao [koor-a-SOW] are the ABC Islands that lie just north of Venezuela. Two things about these tidy little islands are surprising: They're very dry and desertlike, rather than lush; and they combine Dutch and Hispanic influences in a most unusual cultural blend. Aruba is best known for its fine beaches and casino-resort hotels, Bonaire for its superb dining and diving, and Curaçao for its fine dining, extensive shopping, and Grotto of Hato caves (its beaches are only so-so.)

Lodging choices are good in Aruba and Curaçao, but limited in Bonaire. Casinos are on all three; the ABCs are quite popular among gamblers. Many flights connect the mainland to Aruba; fewer are available to Curaçao and Bonaire. Inter-island flights and ferries are also available.

The Portuguese gave Curaçao its name because sailors were cured of scurvy there.

Curaçao buildings, seen from a ship's deck
Photo by C. J. Ghormley

Miscellaneous Islands

A few of the lesser Caribbean destinations have not been covered, since it's less likely that a client will ask about them. Still, you never know what a client may ask about. Here's a list that will prepare you:

Amber jewelry is a specialty in the Dominican Republic.

- **The Dominican Republic** occupies the eastern side of the large island of Hispaniola. It has perhaps the best variety of historical sites in the Caribbean and has many golf courses.

- **Haiti**, on the western side of Hispaniola, is poorer and politically more unstable than the Dominican Republic. Its blend of French and African cultures, though, may intrigue some of your clients. Haiti has become the folk-art capital of the Caribbean.

- **Grenada** [grah-NAY-dah] (not to be confused with Granada, a city in Spain) received unfavorable press coverage during the U.S. invasion of 1983. This sleepy little island has been slow to come back, though it has excellent beaches and a wide variety of water-sport activities. It's just north of Trinidad and Tobago, in the southern portion of the Lesser Antilles. Its nickname: The Spice Island.

- **Montserrat** was once a pleasant, offbeat destination to visit. However, a 1997 volcanic eruption has devastated the island.

- **St. Vincent and the Grenadines** are a collection of more than 100 islands 100 miles west of Barbados. These casually formal destinations have great beaches, snorkeling, yachting, and a broad variety of volcanic landscapes.

- **The Turks and Caicos Islands** are, geographically, a southeasterly extension of the Bahamas (but under a different government). They have some of the same features of the Bahamas, but without the crowds. They're ideal for any client who seeks an isolated getaway or superb diving and yachting opportunities.

Possible Itineraries

Since many clients visit the Caribbean as part of a cruise, their itineraries will be predetermined. If you fly a client to a specific island, it's always nice to combine his or her stay with a side excursion to another island. Remember, though, that air or sea connections between islands aren't always convenient. Concentrate on islands that are easily combinable, yet contrasting: St. Martin with, say, Anguilla; Barbados with St. Vincent; or Antigua with Barbuda.

Lodging Options

When booking a client to the Caribbean, remember several things. First, good rooms are hard to get during high season; if your client is a last-minute type, suggest a cruise (if space is still available). Second, sell-up the client to the highest classification possible; budget lodging in most of the Caribbean is dicey. Third, always propose all-inclusive packages, such as Hedonism II (on Jamaica) or Club Med (on many of the islands). The quality is relatively dependable, the activities endless, the beaches good, and the price (especially on some of the islands where food is costly) a bargain. Virtually every Caribbean island has at least one all-inclusive resort. Jamaica and the Dominican Republic have the most.

Three very luxurious resorts: Jumby Bay (Antigua), La Samanna (St. Martin), and Caneel Bay (St. John, U.S. Virgin Islands).

Most international hotel chains also have presences here; **Sandals** is a Jamaica-based couples-only resort chain that has properties on several other islands. Other chains that have properties throughout the Caribbean are the **Divi**, **Wyndham**, **Sonesta**, **Rex**, and **Ramada** hotel chains. The **Atlantis** mega-resort is the largest in the Caribbean.

Allied Destinations

The Caribbean islands are a natural extension of a visit to Miami, New Orleans, Houston, Mexico, or South America. You can also sell an Orlando-islands cruise combination; at least one cruise line has an official arrangement with the Disney properties and acts as an extension of the Magic Kingdom experience itself—ideal for families wishing to cruise the region. You can set up an interesting "triangle" construction for a client flying along the U.S. East Coast; for example, a client traveling from Miami to New York could stop over in Bermuda. And, of course, any of the islands are natural allied destinations for one another, as long as the air or sea connections are convenient.

Cultural Patterns

The relaxed pace of the islands is renowned. This will present an especially unusual environment to your business clients.

- Though informality marks most of the Caribbean, some of the islands have a reputation for having a genteel, conservative side as well. For example, your clients shouldn't wear clothes that are too casual wherever they go; a few restaurants and night spots may even require a jacket and tie for men and dresses or skirts for women.

- For your clients interested in experiencing the local lifestyle closely, perhaps even staying with a family, you might suggest they consider either the **People to People** program in the Bahamas or the **Meet the People** program in Jamaica.

- A number of colorful festivals occur throughout the year in the Caribbean. The three most famous: the Bahamian **Junkanoo** (a Mardi Gras-like celebration on December 26 and January 1, but often beyond that), Trinidad's **Carnival** (just before Ash Wednesday), and Jamaica's **Reggae Sunsplash** (a musical festival in August).

Factors That Motivate Visitors

To kindle interest in a Caribbean vacation is generally easy. A client would be drawn to the area for many reasons, including:

- A tropical island stay beguiles almost anyone.
- The area features a wide variety of cultural experiences.
- No area in the world has more cruise options.
- The diving, fishing, and yachting possibilities are virtually endless.
- Many all-inclusive resorts dot the islands, as do several superdeluxe hotels.
- The weather is almost always warm and pleasant.
- Several of the islands offer a great deal of nightlife and gambling opportunities.
- Shopping and lodging bargains are possible, especially in the off-season.

Possible Misgivings about the Caribbean

As easy as the Caribbean is to sell, some clients will have concerns you'll need to address:

- "The islands are unsafe." Political unrest and petty crime plague some of the islands, but in most destinations, serious problems arise only once in a while. Clients worried about this should be steered to more stable islands, such as Bermuda or the Bahamas.

Most experts believe Columbus first landed in the New World at San Salvador island in the Bahamas.

Paradise Island's original name was Hog Island.

About 50 percent of all people who take a cruise each year do so in the Caribbean.

Qualifying the Client
The Caribbean

FOR CLIENTS WHO WANT	Antiqua	ABC Islands	Bahamas	Barabados	Bermuda	British Virgin Islands	Cayman Islands	Dominican Republic	Guadeloupe	Haiti	Jamaica	Martinique	Puerto Rico	St. Lucia	St. Martin	Trinidad	U.S. Virgin Islands
Cultural Attractions	▲	▲	▲	▲	✪	▲		✪	▲	✪	✪	▲	✪		▲	✪	
Lots of Nightlife		▲	✪		✪			▲			✪	✪		✪		✪	▲
Familiar Cultural Experience			▲				▲						▲				✪
Safety and Low Crime	▲	▲	▲	✪	✪	▲	▲								▲		▲
Impressive Scenery	▲			▲	✪	▲		▲	✪		✪	▲	▲	✪	▲		▲
Peace and Quiet	▲	▲	▲	▲		✪	▲		▲					▲	▲		▲
Shopping Opportunities		✪	✪	▲	✪			▲		▲	▲	▲	✪	▲		✪	▲	✪
Gambling	▲	✪	✪					▲	▲	▲		▲	▲		▲		
Sailing	✪		✪		✪							▲		▲	▲		✪
Diving	✪	▲	✪	✪	▲	✪	✪		▲	▲	▲	▲		✪	✪	▲	✪
Fishing	▲	▲	✪	▲	▲	▲	✪	✪	✪	▲	✪	▲	✪	▲	▲	▲	✪
Friendly locals	✪	✪	▲	✪	▲	▲								▲	▲	✪	▲
Cleanliness	▲	▲	▲	✪	✪	▲	✪								✪		▲
Golfing		✪	▲		✪			✪			✪		✪				▲
Hiking		▲						▲	✪		✪	✪	▲	✪		▲	▲
To Do Business		▲	✪		▲		✪				▲		✪			✪	▲

▲ = BETTER THAN AVERAGE ✪ = EXCELLENT

Figure 9-2
Source: Miseyko Consultants

- "What about hurricanes?" For clients with this concern, suggest the winter months or cruises; ships usually reroute their itinerary in response to a hurricane's predicted path.
- "Lying on a beach bores me." Recommend cruises or all-inclusive resort lodging. Suggest such islands as the Bahamas, Bermuda, Jamaica, Puerto Rico, and Trinidad, which are more lively than most.
- "Do they speak English?" About a third of the islands in this area are English speaking. French, Spanish, and Dutch are spoken on other islands, but people involved in tourism usually speak English.
- "Aren't the islands rather dirty?" Poverty and squalor do plague a few of the islands, especially those with a Spanish or French heritage. The situation is bet-

Case Study

Vickie and Larry Minkoff, who live in Bozeman, Montana, want to go to the Caribbean to celebrate their tenth wedding anniversary. They want to get completely away from it all, though Vickie wouldn't mind at least two nights on a second island with plenty of nightlife. (They have a week off from work.) They both are experienced divers.

Circle the answer that best suits your clients' needs:

1. Which is the island you should probably recommend as their principal, get-away-from-it-all destination?

   Nassau   Trinidad

   Little Cayman   Jamaica

   Why?

2. Based on your recommendation above, what relatively nearby island could serve as the lively second destination?

   Cuba   Tobago

   Jamaica   Dominican Republic

   Why?

3. Which of the following should you offer to sell to these clients?

   A cruise   A four-day car rental

   A week at Club Med   Upgraded accommodations

   Why?

4. Which would be the most likely month for *bad* weather?

   March   September

   May   November

   Why?

Creative Activity

Slogans are a key to promoting destinations. For example:

Korea: More Than Seoul!

Mexico: Something Old, Something New

New Orleans: Come Join the Parade

Invent a clever and evocative slogan that could help sell each of the following islands:

ISLAND	SLOGAN
1. Bermuda	1.
2. The Bahamas	2.
3. St. Martin	3.
4. Aruba	4.
5. The Caymans	5.
6. Puerto Rico	6.
7. Grenada	7.
8. Trinidad	8.
9. Martinique	9.
10. Jamaica	10.

Travel Trivia

Ten Top Honeymoon Destinations

1. Hawaii
2. Jamaica
3. Orlando
4. Cancun
5. Aruba

6. Florida
7. Las Vegas
8. The Bahamas
9. U.S. Virgin Islands
10. Gatlinburg, TN

Source: Bride's *magazine*

VENEZUELA
GUYANA
SURINAME
FRENCH GUIANA
COLOMBIA
ATLANTIC OCEAN

is a city both in Portugal & Brazil.

Equator
Rio Negro
ECUADOR
Manaus
Santarém
Belem
Amazon River
Fortaleza

three color of water
"The wedding of water"

you can cruise to Amazon

Recife

PERU

BRAZIL

region

Salvador

about 25 years old. *african influence*
a lot of churches
⭐ Brasilia *build high.*

BOLIVIA

SOUTH
PACIFIC
OCEAN

CHILE
PARAGUAY

tourist attraction
Rio de Janeiro ✈
Sao Paulo ✈
Guaruja ● Santos
busiest capital

Iguazu Falls

Otavalo
the biggest Indian market in the world.

ATLANTIC OCEAN

ARGENTINA

URUGUAY

CHAPTER 10

Brazil
Where Everything Sizzles

What do clients imagine about Brazil? The blistering temperatures along the **Amazon River**? The frenetic Carnival atmosphere of **Rio de Janeiro**? Such sizzling images come easily to mind, but they're only part of the picture.

One thing is certain: Brazil is a huge country. Larger than the contiguous United States, it covers almost half of the South American continent. For all its rich diversity, however, it's unlikely that your clients will ever venture out to see most of what's here; much of it is inaccessible. But what they *will* discover is dazzling: lush rain forests (so dense in places that sunlight can't even reach the ground); some of the world's greatest beaches (on 4,603 miles of coastline, more than one-and-a-half times the distance from New York to Los Angeles), and cosmopolitan, ultramodern cities.

Brazil is shaped a little like a triangle, with the base at the top. The northern region's largely jungle landscape is dominated by the Amazon, arguably the

For Your Information . . .

Brazil   FYI

CAPITAL: Brasilia

AREA (SQUARE MILES): 3,286,344

TIME ZONES: GMT −5 to −3

DRIVE ON: Right

POPULATION: 161,100,000

RELIGION: Roman Catholic

LANGUAGE: Portuguese

CURRENCY: 1 real = 100 centavos

ELECTRICITY: 110 or 220 volts, 60 cycles AC

CAPSULE HISTORY: Claimed by Portuguese, 1500; Dutch invade Brazil, 1630, and driven out, 1654; Portuguese royal family lives here, 1808–1821; independence and monarchy, 1822; republic proclaimed, 1889; revolution, 1930, Vargas becomes dictator; Vargas overthrown, 1945; capital moved from Rio to Brasilia, 1960.

For reference sources, tourist bureaus, and suggested lengths of stay, see the Appendices.

longest river in the world. **Belem** is at the Amazon's mouth; **Manaus** [mah-NAWS] is located in the interior, just upriver on the Amazon's major tributary, **Rio Negro** [NAY-groh]. Northeastern Brazil has a strong African influence, centered in the city of **Salvador**, located in Bahia province. The southeast is the cultural, commercial, and industrial heart of the country: the joyous spirit of Rio de Janeiro and the international business of **Sao Paulo**, one of the largest cities in the world. At Brazil's southern tip is where most of its agriculture and coffee-growing is found. And finally, the central and western regions are largely lush wilderness; however the capital, **Brasilia** is here, in the center. Though a modern city, it's unlikely that it will attract many of your clients.

The national language is Portuguese. Though your clients shouldn't think that it's identical to Spanish, those who do speak Spanish should be able to get along fairly well (especially when reading signs, menus, and the like). English, however, is widely spoken in the major cities.

Brasilia is laid out in the shape of an airplane.

How Travelers Get There

There's easy access into Brazil. The national airlines are **Varig** (RG) and **VASP Airlines** (VP), but several other foreign and domestic carriers also serve the country. Galeao International Airport (GIG) in Rio is the main gateway into the country, with flying time from New York eight hours, from Los Angeles twelve hours, and from Miami seven hours. There are also two major terminals in Sao Paulo: Guarulhos International Airport (GRU) and **Viracopos International Airport** (VCP). In addition, Brazil has extensive airline service throughout the country, with airports at most major destinations (including Manaus, by the Amazon). Another way that your clients may reach the Amazon or Rio is via a cruise out of Miami, San Juan, Barbados, or even New York City.

Weather Patterns

Brazil experiences three climate patterns. The Amazon Basin, which includes Belem and Manaus, has a year-round temperature range of 80 to 90 degrees, with high humidity and rain most of the year. (The period from June through November is less rainy.) The plateau area (where Iguazu Falls is located) is even hotter, but there's less rain and humidity, and nights can be cool. There's almost no rainfall here from May through September. The coastal region (e.g., Rio) is a little bit cooler (mid-70s to 80s), with sea breezes to offset the humidity. Rain comes here from October through May, but showers can occur anytime. Reminder: In most of Brazil, the seasons are opposite those in North America.

Getting Around

There's extensive airline service within Brazil. Internal air transportation can be costly, but low-cost flight-coupon programs are available. Buses going outside urban areas are less expensive, but probably not up to the standards your clients expect. Driving is no picnic either: Cities are very crowded, streets can be confusing, breakneck speed is the rule among drivers, and, outside the cities, heavy rains can wash out roads. Trains are very limited, except for a popular run between Rio and Sao Paulo.

In a country with extensive waterways and a long Atlantic coastline, ships and boats often represent an alternative means of travel. The most famous water journey is up the Amazon, all the way to Manaus. Many cruise lines include this adventurous trip as part of their South American itineraries.

In the major cities, there are good, inexpensive buses, but they can get very crowded. Taxis are a good way to get around, but remember that drivers go very fast. Because of a fluctuating economy, you should remind clients to check the

Climate at a Glance
RIO DE JANEIRO, BRAZIL

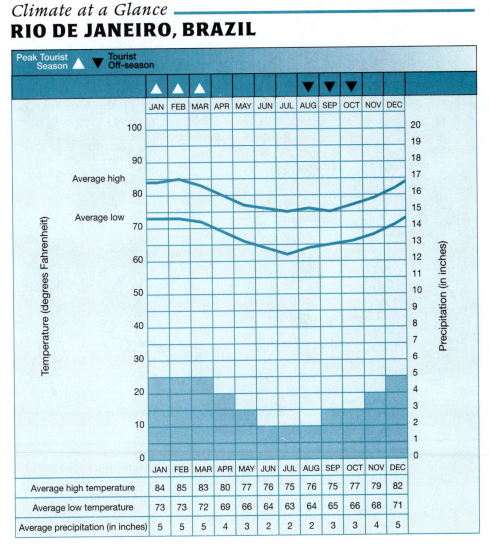

	JAN	FEB	MAR	APR	MAY	JUN	JUL	AUG	SEP	OCT	NOV	DEC
Average high temperature	84	85	83	80	77	76	75	76	75	77	79	82
Average low temperature	73	73	72	69	66	64	63	64	65	66	68	71
Average precipitation (in inches)	5	5	5	4	3	2	2	2	3	3	4	5

Figure 10-1

meter prices before getting in a cab. (The prices may be reasonable, but they may not be what's listed.)

Important Places

Brazil is the fifth largest country in the world and the sixth most populous. Most of your clients, however, will center their trips in three areas: around Rio de Janeiro, along the Amazon, and in the Salvador region.

Rio de Janeiro

Rio is one of the world's great cities. If it were only for the stunning scenery—beautiful mountains and lush jungles surrounding the city, and superb beaches and the glistening **Atlantic Ocean** at its doorstep—Rio would be famous. But Rio offers more. This is a cosmopolitan city with rich culture, wonderful cuisine, and a frenetic nightlife, all wrapped in a casual, yet elegant charm. Rio, though, is far from perfect: The city is very crowded; it has slums, plenty of petty crime, and, like all of Brazil, an unpredictable economy. Among the most popular Rio attractions that you can suggest to your clients are:

The Feirarte, a great open-air market, is held on Sundays in the Ipanema area of Rio.

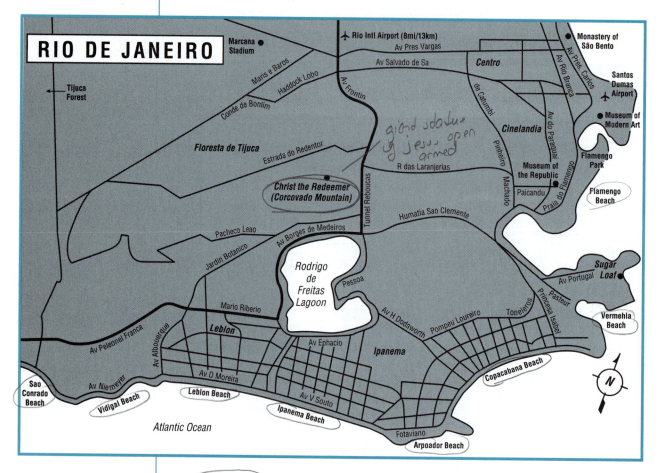

RIO DE JANEIRO

Handwritten note on map: giant statue of Jesus open armed

- **Sugar Loaf,** the oddly shaped mountain that's the city's landmark. The summit offers beautiful views and is reached by cable car. Tell clients to try to go on a weekday; weekends are crowded and the waiting line for the cable car is long.
- **The Monastery of Sao Bento,** a beautiful and peaceful religious complex.
- **Floresta de Tijuca,** a lush, tropical forest just outside the city.
- **World-renowned beaches,** most notably **Copacabana** (the biggest and most popular) and the trendy **Ipanema**. Other well-liked beaches: **Sao Conrado, Leblon,** and **Gavea.**
- **Cinelandia,** where the city's nightlife sparkles.
- **Excellent museums,** many of which can be found in Flamengo Park, including the Museum of Modern Art.
- **Quinta de Boa Vista,** a huge park featuring the National Museum and a zoo.
- **Corcovado Mountain,** serving as the base for the city's other famous landmark, the 120-foot-high, open-armed statue of Christ the Redeemer. The views from here are also astounding.
- **Carnival,** a spectacular festival starting the Saturday before Ash Wednesday and ending the following Wednesday evening. If your clients are in the area at the time, this should not be missed. The city virtually shuts down; no one seems to go to bed; and anything goes.

Several **day trips** from Rio de Janeiro would surely add to your client's visit to the area:

- **Sao Paulo,** one of the world's largest cities. The commercial center of Brazil, Sao Paulo has world-class international restaurants and shopping, some of South America's best museums, and a good nightlife. (Unfortunately, it also has considerable traffic and pollution problems.) The **Sacred Art Museum** has

Never leave your valuables unattended on the beach.

Handwritten margin note: Manaus = three colors of water. The wedding of the waters.

Sugar Loaf Mountain, Rio de Janeiro
Photo by C. J. Ghormley

the largest collection of religious art outside the Vatican, while the **MASP** museum boasts a huge collection of Impressionist paintings. The zoo's great menagerie of jungle animals shouldn't be missed, especially by clients not planning to see the Amazon. Your clients shouldn't carry valuables or go walking at night (taxis should be taken instead), since street robberies, sadly, happen far too often.

- **Guaruja** [gwah-ruh-ZHAH], an elegant beach town, actually a day trip from Sao Paulo. **Casa Grande** is one of the world's great resorts.
- **Costa Verde**, the beautiful coastal area between Rio and **Santos** (the coastal village just south of Sao Paulo). The beaches here are much quieter than those in Rio.
- **Iguazu Falls** (also spelled Iguacu), a breathtaking attraction on Brazil's border. To get there from Rio, you should book clients on the necessary short flight. Nearly 300 falls here cover 2.6 miles and they span an area much higher and

Soccer is a Brazilian passion. Attend a soccer match in one of Sao Paulo's or Rio's huge stadiums.

Iguazu Falls
Photo by C. J. Ghormley

wider than Niagara Falls. (For clients who are movie buffs, this is where the film *The Mission* was made.) January through March is peak season, but it's also the hottest, steamiest time of year. August through October may be best for visiting Iguazu.

The Amazon

A trip up the Amazon promises one of the world's legendary tourist adventures. The river is about 4,000 miles long and up to 200 miles wide. The dense jungles and lush rain forests are home to wildlife seen nowhere else on the globe, with fishing villages and small islands dotting its length. There are also a few major cities along the way:

- **Manaus**, deep in Brazil's hot interior, is a crowded city. Surprisingly, many Victorian buildings remain from the city's early boom days. Today, the city is a free port with popular duty-free shopping; it's also a launch point for Amazon River boat trips to jungle lodges and for hunting expeditions. Manaus is also an inland stop for cruise ships.

  The sites of Manaus include the **Teatro do Amazonas**, an ornate opera house built in 1892, where many of history's great opera singers and actors have performed; **Mercado Municipal**, a marketplace of fascinating design; interesting museums and zoos; and **Salvador Lake**, just outside town, a nature preserve with a remarkable array of wildlife. **The Wedding of the Waters**, twelve miles from town, is where the Amazon, the Rio Solimoes, and the Rio Negro meet. Each has water of a different color and the colliding swirls of separate hues provide a thoroughly unique attraction. Half-day boat excursions can be taken from Manaus to visit this area.

- **Belem**, at the mouth of the Amazon, is home to a huge open-air market, **Ver-O-Peso**, which features all manner of items for sale. Lush parks and interesting old buildings decorate the city. The **Goledi Anthropology Museum and Zoo** has intriguing collections. You might also want to suggest a boat excursion to the ranches on the vast nearby island of **Ilha de Marajo**.

- **Santarem** is a quiet city about halfway between Manaus and Belem. Although not offering anywhere near the attractions of those two cities, it's less crowded, less developed, and quite charming. A bit of trivia: This city was originally settled by people from South Carolina and Tennessee. Several other Brazilian towns (including Americana, outside Sao Paulo) were founded by nineteenth-century U.S. expatriates.

Salvador

Salvador, the capital of the **Bahia** district, is a Baroque city with a strong African heritage. This coastal city, with perhaps the finest climate in the country, has excellent beaches, old neighborhoods with winding streets, fine museums, and 365 churches. The city is built on two levels into a cliff, connected by the Lacerdo Elevator. The views are gorgeous, the locals are extremely friendly, and the unique African-European cuisine is great. And like Rio, the city holds a festive Carnival for the four days before Ash Wednesday. Its most interesting sites include:

Colonial building, Salvador
Photo by C. J. Ghormley

Salvador once belonged to the Dutch.

- Many churches, the finest of which are the **Cathedral**, a wonderful 400-year-old structure; the ornate **Church of St. Francis**, with a remarkable gold-leaf interior; and **Church of Our Lord of the Good Ending**, whose congregation often wear the traditional clothes of the faith.
- **The Mercado Modelo**, with good buys on silver, rosewood, and fabric souvenirs.
- Superb beaches, the best of which are **Itapoa** and **Piata**.

   There are a few interesting **day trips** from Salvador:

- **Excursions** to the numerous islands off the coast. **Itaparica** is probably the best known; it's quiet, lovely, and virtually undeveloped.
- **Recife**, reachable from Salvador in a day, but probably requiring an overnight stay. This city of 1.2 million has been compared to Venice because of its canals and bridges, though unlike Venice, there is also normal vehicle traffic. There are many classical churches, an old fort, an eighteenth-century prison that's been turned into a shopping center, and great beaches. The lovely artist colony of **Olinda** is nearby. Farther north is **Fortaleza**, a beach area that has grown in popularity.

Possible Itineraries

For first-time visitors, Rio de Janeiro is a must-see. The surrounding area, including Sao Paulo, would be a logical, almost necessary addition. If your clients have the time, you might suggest a flight into Manaus for a day or two. In all, six to eight days could suffice. Return travelers might enjoy visiting the exotic Bahia region around Salvador for three or four days, as well as taking a couple of days to experience Iguazu Falls. Clients returning to Brazil, or those specifically interested in the area, could spend up to six days taking a cruise up the Amazon.

Lodging Options

Hotels in Brazil run the gamut from deluxe to budget; but the lower down the ladder your clients go, the greater the chance for disappointment. (Of course, during Carnival, everything is expensive.) The major luxury chains include **Othon**, and hotels represented by **Leading Hotels of the World**. **Luxor** is a popular first-class chain. A few North American companies are also present in Brazil.

   In Rio de Janeiro, the largest hotel grouping is along Copacabana Beach, with other clusters on Ipanema Beach and upscale Gavea Beach. Lodging is expensive by South American standards, but less so than many other top resort areas around the world. The turn-of-the-century, deluxe **Copacabana Palace Hotel** is internationally renowned. If clients stay in Sao Paulo, most hotels are in the western part of the city. The nearby **Casa Grande** in Guaruja is one of the world's finest resorts. In Manaus, you should sell-up your clients into the best-class hotels. For clients staying in Salvador, you can save them some money by lodging them in hotels off the beach, since most of the finest beaches in the area, notably Itapoa and Piata, are out of town.

   An interesting alternative for lodging in Rio: furnished apartments, called *apartotels,* that have complete hotel services. There are also ranches in many areas of the country, as well as jungle lodges.

Rio is a noisy city. A beach-front or interior room will shield you from the constant din.

Allied Destinations

Taking up half of South America, Brazil is the ideal connection to the other countries on that continent. To the north, it borders French Guiana, Suriname, Guyana, Venezuela, and Colombia. Peru and Bolivia are to its west. And to the south are Paraguay, Argentina, and Uruguay. In fact, the only South American countries it doesn't border are Chile and Ecuador. Brazil is also close to Central

America and the Caribbean. A cruise, especially, would be an excellent way to extend a trip between those areas.

Cultural Patterns

Brazil is an adventurous, lively country. Understanding the customs here will go a long way toward making your clients' experiences, business and otherwise, even more rewarding:

- Brazilians are physically and emotionally open. Shaking hands, embracing, and so on, are the rule.
- Warn clients that the "O.K." sign in North America—made with the thumb and forefinger—is an obscenity in Brazil.
- Brazilians have an extremely lax attitude toward time. Your clients should nonetheless be punctual for business appointments, even if they turn out to be the only ones there on time.
- To be invited to a Brazilian's home is an honor. Guests shouldn't plan to drop by for a brief visit; rather, they should be prepared to stay for many hours. It's also customary to arrive a little late. In addition, some small gift should be brought along. (An important note here, especially concerning flowers: Purple, in Brazil, is the color of death.) Tell your clients that Brazilians are very conscious of keeping their hands on the table when dining.

Since 1900, nearly ninety indigenous groups in Brazil have become extinct.

Factors That Motivate Visitors

Among the reasons that will motivate your clients to visit Brazil are:

- Rio de Janeiro and Sao Paulo promise excitement, fun, fine dining, and much nightlife.
- There are great beaches throughout the country.
- Considering what its great cities offer, Brazil is a relative bargain.
- The locals are extremely open and friendly.
- The Amazon is adventurous and unique.
- There's great cuisine.
- The history and culture of Brazil are fascinating.
- Rio's Carnival is world renowned. Salvador's is almost as impressive.

Possible Misgivings About Brazil

The culture of Brazil offers up a very foreign experience. The concerns that you'll have to address include:

- "There's malaria, cholera, and other diseases in the Amazon." Most of the worst areas are closed off to travelers. Your clients should check with a doctor before coming here, get shots, and, if necessary, bring medication.
- "They speak Portuguese." Portuguese is somewhat similar to Spanish. More important, English is widely spoken in the major cities and by travel professionals.
- "I'm afraid to drink the water." Bottled soft drinks can be purchased everywhere. And Brazilian beer is excellent.
- "I won't like Brazilian food." Brazil is a mix of cultures. There is wonderful international cuisine. A special treat: Churruscaria restaurants that serve up barbecued meats, carved at your client's table.

Qualifying the Client
Brazil

FOR CLIENTS WHO WANT	APPEAL			REMARKS
	HIGH	MEDIUM	LOW	
Historical and Cultural Attractions		▲		Especially Rio
Beaches and Water Sports	▲			Legendary beaches
Skiing Opportunities			▲	None
Lots of Nightlife		▲		Especially Rio
Family Activities		▲		
Familiar Cultural Experience		▲		
Exotic Cultural Experience	▲			
Safety and Low Crime			▲	Petty theft common
Bargain Travel		▲		Air/hotel packages excellent
Impressive Scenery	▲			Seascapes and jungle
Peace and Quiet		▲		Cities noisy, but outlying areas not
Shopping Opportunities		▲		Semiprecious stones, rosewood, leather
To Do Business		▲		In large cities

Figure 10-2

- "The government and economy are unstable." This is true, though this doesn't necessarily impact tourism.
- "There's a lot of street crime." Unfortunately, this is true. Common-sense precautions should be taken, such as leaving valuables in the hotel, dressing casually, keeping wallets protected, and not walking outside at night.

Sales Strategies

The unique qualities of Brazil lend themselves to special ways for you to sell-up and cross-sell a trip there. Because of the economic uncertainty and sometimes high inflation, selling an escorted tour package or cruise will lock prices in early, as well as help ease clients' fears about traveling alone in such an exotic country. At the very least, booking city tours can be helpful, since driving in Brazilian cities is not recommended. (For that matter, driving *anywhere* in Brazil is not recommended.) Since intercity bus and train service is limited, you'll probably want to set up airplane flights between cities. Accommodations in lower-rated hotels can be risky, so you'll be doing clients a favor by booking upgraded lodging for them. For clients visiting the Amazon, a boat excursion is a must; a special excursion to the Wedding of the Waters would be a worthwhile addition. If clients are going to Iguazu Falls, a local helicopter tour is exciting.

Creative Activity

At EPCOT, in Orlando, many nations maintain pavilions that reflect their heritage and culture. For example, Morocco has reproduced a bazaar; Mexico a Mayan pyramid (with a ride inside); France a cafe-lined street. If you were a pavilion designer for the Walt Disney Company (which owns EPCOT), what concept would you propose if Brazil decided to set up a pavilion? Describe or even draw it below.

Travel Trivia

Places Famous for Pre-Lenten Carnivals

Rio de Janeiro, Brazil
New Orleans
Venice, Italy
Nassau, Bahamas
Salvador, Brazil
Oruro, Bolivia

Caracas, Venezuela
Beuel, Germany
Trinidad
Nice, France
Martinique
Corrientes, Argentina

CARIBBEAN SEA

GUATEMALA
BELIZE
HONDURAS
Guatemala City
Tegucigalpa
EL SALVADOR
NICARAGUA
Managua
Lake Nicaragua
Canal
Zone
COSTA RICA
San Jose
Panama
PANAMA

Caracas
Lake Maracaibo
Orinoco River
VENEZUELA
Georgetown
Paramaribo
FRENCH GUIANA
Cayenne
Bogota
GUYANA
COLOMBIA
SURINAME

Quito
ECUADOR

Galapagos
Islands

Andes
Amazon River

PERU
Lima

BRAZIL

Lake Titicaca
BOLIVIA
La Paz

PACIFIC OCEAN

Mountains

PARAGUAY

Easter Island
Asuncion

Rio Uruguay

CHILE
URUGUAY
Santiago
Montevideo
Buenos Aires
Rio de la Plata
ATLANTIC OCEAN

ARGENTINA

Falkland Islands

STRAIT of
MAGELLAN

South Georgia

CHAPTER 11

Latin American Potpourri

Too often when a North American client thinks of heading south, he or she will consider only certain well-known destinations: Rio, the Mexican beach resorts, the principal islands of the Caribbean. Yet Central and South America boast many first-rate but not well-known attractions, many off the beaten tourist track.

There's a waterfall nearly three times the height of the Empire State Building and another almost as wide as the Grand Canyon. There's the world's second biggest coral reef, huge mysterious drawings on a vast plain, an island covered with oversized stone heads, and an abandoned city at 8,000 feet in the Andes.

Do you know the names of these places? If not, you soon will. And you'll be able to use your knowledge to enhance the trip for any client bound for Latin America.

Central America

The Central American isthmus, which connects Mexico to the South American continent, will probably be low on the priority list of most clients. Though the land itself can be quite lovely and the weather tropical, the historical and cultural attractions are relatively undeveloped. More important: Some of the area's countries have been torn by enough intermittent wars and anti-American sentiments to keep tourists away.

For those clients who wish to visit Central America, air connections are their best bet to and throughout the area. Car rentals are available and occasionally offer a good way to see the countryside; however, driving can be difficult in some places and dangerous in others. Bus service is widespread, but not recommended. Cruises may stop here as well, especially in **Panama**. Indeed, cruises that pass from the Pacific to the Atlantic through the canal have become quite popular.

Spanish is the national language in all Central American countries (except **Belize**, where English is the official language). English, however, is commonly spoken by travel personnel.

Pyramid at Tikal, Guatemala
Photo by C. J. Ghormley

Important Places

Here are some of the countries, from north to south, you should know about:

Guatemala.   Guatemala has had political instability. Its rich Mayan culture is its major attraction, particularly in the town of **Tikal** [tee-KAHL], which has excellent ruins and artifacts. Otherwise, most Guatemalan ruins remain covered with earth and vines. **Guatemala City**, the capital, has some fine museums that explain Mayan civilization.

Belize.   Formerly British Honduras, Belize [beh-LEEZ] is a tiny, politically stable country on the Caribbean coast, with many Mayan ruins, a lush landscape, and some of the best dive spots in the world. Belize has the world's second largest coral reef. At the reef's northern end is **Ambergris Cay**, with fine beaches, good fishing, and great diving. In the reef's middle are the **Turneffe Islands**, which feature what some consider the world's best dive site, the Blue Hole. The country strives to ensure that all new development is environmentally sensitive, most especially at its nature reserves.

Honduras.   Honduras has a poor economy and has been affected by fighting in neighboring countries, some of which occasionally spills over its borders. Its capital, **Tegucigalpa**, is quite pretty. The town of **Copan** is renowned for its Mayan ruins. The Bay Islands off Honduras offer good diving sites, including one where you can actually dive with dolphins.

El Salvador.   El Salvador, sadly, has been strife-ridden for many years. This scenic, mountainous country has much to offer, though. There are fine beaches, Mayan ruins are everywhere, and the capital of **San Salvador** is beautiful.

Nicaragua.   Nicaragua has also suffered, on occasion, from war and crime. For the literature lovers among your clients, the **Mosquito Coast** (the setting for the novel of the same name) lies on this country's Caribbean shore. Mayan ruins, abandoned gold mines, beach activities, and an old pirate's settlement are among its attractions.

Costa Rica.   Costa Rica is the success story of Central America: It's stable, prosperous, and has decent tourist facilities. In the country's central highlands is the capital city of **San Jose**, which contains some interesting museums and churches, a lovely National Theater, and plenty of shopping. The climate here is pleasant. There are also interesting tours through the countryside and jungle: Costa Rica has a wealth of national parks and rain forest reserves, which makes it an appealing destination for ecotourists. The most famous of these is **Monteverde Cloud Forest Reserve**. Cruise ships call on the ports of **Limon** and **Puerto Caldera**, usually on Panama Canal itineraries. Offshore sports-fishing in Costa Rica is especially attractive.

Panama.   Panama varies between pro- and anti-American sentiment, between substantial tourism and no tourism at all. Politics greatly affect tourism here. The most impressive attraction is **Panama City**, the capital, near the **Panama Canal**. This city—with a history strongly influenced by the Spanish, Indians, and pirates—is a popular cruise stop. Panama City boasts interesting Spanish colonial structures, old churches, and colorful plazas. **Balboa** is the American district: There's not much history to be found here, but it's safe and comfortable. Off Panama's Pacific coast is pretty **Taboga** island; off its Caribbean side are the **San Blas** islands, a haven for Indian culture.

The Pacific Ocean is at the Panama Canal's *eastern* end.

Sales Considerations

The area lends itself to cruises, particularly along Costa Rica, through Panama, or to some of the nearby islands. Book only the finest hotels in Central America. Tourists seriously interested in the local culture, those on cruises to South America or the Caribbean, or clients who have relatives or ancestors from here will likely be the ones to whom you will sell the area. Clients who love fishing, secluded beaches, and diving are rapidly "discovering" Central America; its safer destinations can make for an appealing recommendation for those who've seen the more traditional ocean-oriented spots. Note: A few fine resorts have just opened or are under development in Central America.

Costa Rica means "rich coast," based on the hope that there was much gold there. (There wasn't.)

Colombia

The legendary El Dorado, stocked with golden riches, was reputedly in this region. It has never been found. But with three Andes ranges, broad beaches, miles of coffee plantations, and an Amazon jungle, **Colombia** has a wealth of another kind. Unfortunately, the country's long history with crime may discourage your clients from sampling its attractions.

For clients who are interested, **Avianca** (AV) is the national airline, flying into the capital of **Bogota** (BOG), which is deep in an Andean valley. Major airports are also in the Caribbean port city of **Barranquilla** (BAQ) and the resort town of **Cartagena** (CTG), once a walled fortress. Good airline connections crisscross the

country, along with so-so rail service, crowded buses, and poor driving conditions. The national language is Spanish.

Bogota's residents live in a cool, springlike, almost unchanging climate. The El Dorado tradition lives on here in the huge collection of the city's famous **Gold Museum**. A half-day trip from the city is **Zipaquira**, with its "Salt Cathedral" carved out of rock 450 feet below the ground. Astonishingly large, it can hold 10,000 people. **San Agustin Park** is a 150-square-mile archaeological reserve dotted with stone monoliths. **Leticia**, accessible only by air or boat, is a gateway to Amazon adventure cruises. San Andres island, about 300 miles north of Colombia, was the base of English pirate Captain Henry Morgan.

Venezuela

Caracas, **Venezuela**'s capital, lies in a northern Andean valley. Venezuela's other major geographic feature is the **Orinoco River**, which flows through the grassy plains (the *llanos*), into the Atlantic. **Simon Bolivar Airport** (CCS) in Caracas will be your client's gateway into the country, though cruise ships also come to the nearby port of **La Guaira**. **Merida** is the Venezuelan air gateway to the Andes, where travelers can ride the world's highest cable car. There's good airline and bus service, but no train service to speak of. Though your clients can easily rent a car, driving is difficult. *Por puestos* (taxis that pick up and drop off passengers along their routes, like a minibus) are a popular way of getting around. Spanish is the national language.

The climate in Venezuela is very steady; in Caracas, for example, daytime temperatures average in the upper 70s year-round. Jungle areas are hotter and Andes destinations cooler. Venezuela has a dry season from December to early May, with moderate and occasional rainfall the rest of the year.

Important Places

Venezuela has a number of interesting destinations. The sites that will probably most interest your clients are:

- **Caracas**, for the most part, is a handsome, modern city. It has retained a strong Spanish influence and has an active, international nightlife. **Mt. Avila** offers

Venezuela named its unit of currency, the bolivar, after Simon Bolivar.

great views of the city. The most notable among the city's churches is **Santa Teresa Basilica**. The birthplace and grave of Venezuela's national hero, Simon Bolivar (who helped free South America from Spain), is here. **Colonia Tovar**, an interesting German-like village, is nearby.

- **Angel Falls**, at 3,212 feet, is the world's loftiest waterfall. (That's nearly eighteen times higher than Niagara.) Located in the southeast jungle, near the town of Ciudad Bolivar and reached by plane, the area also has thousands of varieties of orchids.

- **Beach resorts** are found along the Caribbean coast. Two of the most popular are **Macuto**, not far from Caracas, and the immensely popular **Margarita Island** (in the Caribbean, just east of the ABC islands).

Angel Falls, which plummets from "Devil Mountain," was discovered by and named after an American, Jimmy Angel.

Sales Considerations

Venezuela is particularly convenient as an extension of a client's trip to the Caribbean. It's a frequent stop on Southern Caribbean cruise itineraries. The government is a moderately stable democracy, which might strongly appeal to those of your clients who are concerned about the political climate in Latin America. Because of Venezuela's wealth, tourist services tend to be first-rate: Offer an air tour to Angel Falls; the drama of this attraction appeals to clients who seek off-the-beaten-path experiences.

The Guianas

These three very small countries—Guyana, Suriname, and French Guiana—huddle together on the Atlantic coast. Few first-rate attractions are here, so it's unlikely that many of your clients will visit, except perhaps those who love rugged exploring. The Guianas are largely jungle, with many rivers (especially in Guyana) and savannahs. Guyana has a national carrier, **Guyana Airways** (GY), which flies into the capital of **Georgetown** (GEO); Suriname's national airline, **Suriname Airways** (PY), lands in **Paramaribo** (PBM), the capital. Other airlines service the region as well. The gateway into French Guiana is its capital, **Cayenne** (CAY). These three countries' ports are occasionally stops on Caribbean or South American cruise itineraries. Train, bus,

and boat are the easiest ways to get around; there are also some air connections. Rental cars are available, but driving conditions aren't good.

Each of these countries has its own national language: English in Guyana, Dutch in Suriname, and French (of course) in French Guiana. The climate is tropical, with conditions steadily humid and hot (though nights from December through February can get chilly). July through November might be the best time for clients to visit here. May and June also have pleasant temperatures, but this is the rainiest season.

Important Places

- **Guyana**, sadly, is best remembered for the tragic Jonestown massacre in 1978. There are, however, excellent trout and ocean fishing opportunities, and some interesting sites—notably in Georgetown. There's also **Kaieteur Falls**, which cascades down from a height of 740 feet.

- **Suriname** has a strong mix of cultures and religions, including Hindu, Moslem, and Catholic. In Paramaribo, a fairly sophisticated city, there are many interesting churches, marketplaces, and colonial buildings. Jungle excursions into Suriname's nature parks and reserves will appeal to your ecotourists. Note: Suriname has occasional civil unrest.

- **French Guiana** is the least developed country of the three. Its most noted attraction: a tour of the notorious penal colony, **Devil's Island**, which is offshore from **Kourou**. This is where the French soldier Alfred Dreyfus was unjustly imprisoned at the turn of the twentieth century. Devil's Island is a frequent stop for cruise ships heading to or from South America. On the mainland, jungle and river excursions are possibilities. But since poverty, heat, and crime are ever-present problems, such trips are suitable only for the hardiest of adventure travelers.

Sales Considerations

Since these are such challenging destinations, you should advise clients to visit the Guianas via a cruise or a well-established tour operator.

The world's tallest wooden structure is Georgetown Cathedral.

French Guiana is the launch site for France's aerospace program.

Ecuador

Located in the northwest corner of South America, Ecuador borders the Pacific Ocean. The Andes mountain range shapes much of the country's geography. The climate stays fairly steady all year, though different areas vary greatly. The highlands—which include the capital, **Quito**, (often called the City of Eternal Spring)—tend to have cool temperatures. The west coast—where the largest city of **Guayaquil** is located—is much warmer, with highs in the 90s. Ecuador has a rainy season from January to April; the rest of the year it is very dry.

The national airline of Ecuador, **Ecuatoriana** (EU), provides service to **Mariscal Sucre International Airport** (UIO) in Quito and **Simon Bolivar Airport** (GYE) in Guayaquil, as do a few other carriers. Cruises dock at Guayaquil. Within the country, there's good airline service. To get to the **Galapagos Islands**, clients can fly to either **Baltra** or **San Cristobal** or take a boat there. Train service is limited in Ecuador, but there's a complicated series of connections between Quito and Guayaquil; the winding route through mountain passes is spectacular. Buses are very crowded; and though car rentals are widely available, road conditions aren't good. Taxis are a good way to navigate cities. Spanish is the national language.

On Ecuador's Trans-Andean railroad, passengers are allowed to ride on the train's rooftops.

Important Places

Though Guayaquil is Ecuador's largest city, its attractions are limited to some interesting Spanish buildings and a few cultural museums. Ecuador has two major destinations: Quito and the Galapagos Islands.

Surrounded by immense mountains, Quito has a natural setting that few country capitals can match. A strong Spanish architectural influence marks the city. Quito boasts some fine museums specializing in pre-Columbian art, and a great many churches. The city's historical district, "Old Quito," is quite interesting. A beautiful day drive will take your clients to **Mt. Cotopaxi**, a national park. A half-day trip that clients might enjoy is fifteen miles north to the **equator**, which is marked with a monument; some interesting ruins are along the way. Farther to the north and south lie a string of colorful towns, each with a popular marketplace (**Otavalo** is the best known).

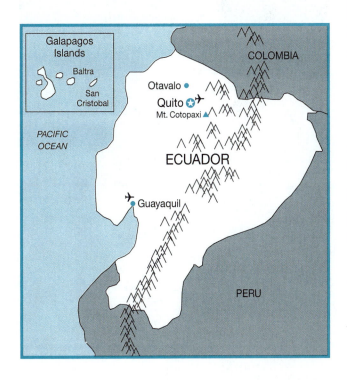

The Galapagos Islands possess some of the world's most remarkable wildlife. (Here can be found giant tortoises believed to be the world's oldest living animals.) Charles Darwin did much of his research for his theories on evolution here. The cindery islands are of volcanic origin and a few active ones still exist. The Ecuadoran government sets a strict limit on the number of visitors to the Galapagos, so trips and tours should be booked well in advance.

Sales Considerations

Ecuador is less developed than some of the more popular sites in South America. However, it's also less crowded and is relatively stable; this might be just what some of your clients want. The Galapagos Islands greatly appeal to nature lovers and you could easily book an excursion for them; in fact, for some, it could even be a separate trip.

Peru

In terms of the number of visitors, Peru is somewhat behind many Latin American countries as a destination, yet few countries can boast as many well-known, first-rate attractions as can Peru. Most tourists land first in **Lima** (LIM) or, via cruise ship, in the port city of **Callao**. They encounter a nation of dramatic contrasts: the warm, dry Pacific coast; the mighty Andes just inland (which can get quite cold during the June-to-September, south-of-the-equator winter); and the hilly, rainy jungles of the eastern lowlands, where the Amazon finds its source.

Important Places

Lima, which was the center of Spain's New World government, retains much of its colonial architecture, especially at its **Plaza de Armas**. Lima brims with fine muse-

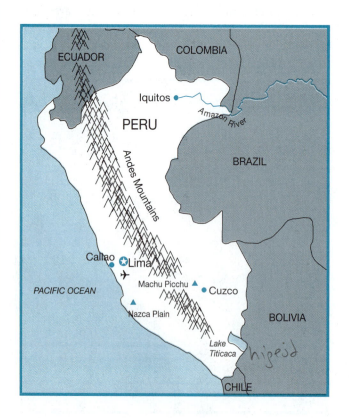

Machu Picchu, Peru
Photo by C. J. Ghormley

[handwritten notes: very high up in th Andes mountain. Incas — Peru (built machu Picchu) Mayan — Mexic]

ums and several ornate churches (most notable is the Church of St. Francis, which has a vast system of catacombs beneath it). Nearby are Pachacamac, an Incan ruin; Miraflores, a charming beach town; and the **Nazca Plain**, whose huge mysterious designs drawn on the ground have intrigued archaeologists and tourists for decades. Only visible from the air, the drawings of animals, people, and geometric shapes are best seen via local charter plane expeditions that you can book in advance.

Cuzco, the former capital of the Incan empire, is another of Peru's well-known attractions. About 400 miles southeast of Lima, it features ancient ruins, colonial mansions, several museums, and a Renaissance-style cathedral. Not far is **Pucara**, an ancient Incan fortress. But Pucara pales in comparison to Peru's most remarkable attraction, **Machu Picchu**. Perched high in a dramatic Andes setting and hidden until it was discovered in 1911 by former U.S. Senator Hiram Bingham, Machu Picchu boasts more than 200 Incan temples, terraces, and residences. Most tourists visit it via a special morning train from Cuzco, returning in the late afternoon.

Iquitos, a city in northeast Peru (on the Amazon), is the jump-off point for "Green Hell" boat tours into the jungle, up the Amazon River.

Sales Considerations

What draws visitors to Peru? The country's felicitous climate, accessible location, startling scenery, budget prices, and high-recognition attractions make it one of Latin America's easiest "sells." It's frequently sold as an add-on destination to such bordering countries as Ecuador, Colombia, Brazil, Bolivia, and Chile. Many escorted tour packages are available to this "soft" adventure country.

There *are* problems related to a trip to Peru. As with many Latin American destinations, poverty leads to petty crime, terrorism, and health concerns—even in Lima and Cuzco. These problems, as well as inflation and limited hotel space, make booking packaged tours an advisable sales strategy. Since budget hotels leave much to be desired, upselling to luxury-class accommodations is an attractive option. Travelers to the region should discuss with their physicians possible treatments for preventing or minimizing altitude sickness.

Soroche is what Peruvian locals call altitude sickness.

The map shows Bolivia bordered by Brazil, Peru, Paraguay, Argentina, and Chile, with the Andes Mountains, Lake Titicaca, Copacabana, La Paz, and Tiahuanaco labeled. The Pacific Ocean is to the west. Handwritten annotations read: "highest lake in the world," "the highest city," "the capital of Ecuador 'QUITO' is the 2nd highest city in the world."

Bolivia

Bolivia's Aymara Indians were the first to cultivate the potato.

Located in the center of the continent, Bolivia is one of the two landlocked countries in South America. (The other is Paraguay.) It's dominated by the Andes and is at extremely high altitudes; in fact, the thin air might be difficult for most of your clients until they adjust. **La Paz**, the world's highest capital city, is in the far west-central portion of the country, not far from **Lake Titicaca**, which Bolivia shares with Peru.

Clients can reach Bolivia by air, landing at **El Alto Airport** (LPB) in La Paz. **LAB** (LB) is the national carrier, though other airlines service the country. The railway network is extensive, but trains are slow. There are air connections between major cities as well. Because of the high altitudes, the climate in Bolivia is cooler than in the rest of South America; June through August, especially, is extremely chilly. The regions deepest in the mountains get quite cold. Spanish is the national language.

Important Places

The two main sites for tourists in Bolivia are around La Paz and Lake Titicaca. Here are some of the most popular attractions:

- **La Paz** is a modern, fairly sophisticated city. The main boulevard and hotel area, **El Prado**, provides fascinating markets of all kinds, including a legal "black market." The city also has many fine cultural museums.
- Forty miles from La Paz is **Tiahuanaco**, with its famed ancient stone ruins and the unusual rock formations of the **Valley of the Sun**. The drive to the **Chacaltaya** ski run (the world's highest, at 18,000 feet) is breathtakingly stunning, but its steep and winding curves should be recommended only for the fearless.
- **Lake Titicaca** is shared by both Bolivia and Peru, though it's most commonly accessed from Bolivia. It's the highest navigable lake in the world. **Copacabana** is a popular, lively resort on its southwestern shore.

Sales Considerations

Bolivia is a beautiful country, but quite challenging. It should particularly be recommended to your more adventurous clients. It's very well suited as an extension of a trip to Peru, since Lake Titicaca covers parts of both countries. Bolivia has begun to exploit its appeal to ecotourists. Many specialized tour companies are developing and selling adventure tours that appeal to hikers, campers, and lovers of nature. If you have clients who fall into this category, think of Bolivia. Note: Because so much of Bolivia is at high altitudes, warn your clients that they may need some time to adjust.

Paraguay

Paraguay, just east of the Andes, is the second of two landlocked countries on the continent. The country is one of the safest on the continent for tourists. The capital city, **Asuncion** (ASU), is the gateway into Paraguay; buses are the most common means of getting around. The climate is hot from September to April, with rain possible at any time of the year. It's also fairly humid and rainy. From May through August, the temperature finally cools down to the 70s during the day. The national language here, too, is Spanish.

The Mennonite sect, which is best known for its presence in Pennsylvania Dutch country, also settled in Paraguay and Mexico's Copper Canyon.

Important Places

Though it's not likely that many of your clients will request travel to Paraguay, it offers some pleasing attractions for those who do visit:

- **Asuncion** is a charming city. There's an odd, small-town feel here, with trees and gardens everywhere. The city's slow pace is especially evident during a three-hour siesta at midday. There are some churches, parks, and museums. A particularly charming train ride leads to the botanical garden and zoo. For cruise lovers, the Paraguay River connects Asuncion to Buenos Aires, Argentina.
- **The Golden Triangle** is the eastern farmland area of Paraguay. Your clients will find small, old villages throughout the Golden Triangle.

Sales Considerations

Paraguay is most noted for its comparative safety; it might be a good destination for clients concerned with crime and political unrest. Since it's often missed on the larger "sampler" tours of South America's high points, Paraguay is a good

recommendation to make to travelers who are returning to this southerly continent for a second visit. You may pre-book a jungle safari trip, often as part of a more general escorted tour package. Because of holiday festivities, it's not advisable to book clients during December and January. May through September (their winter) probably offers the most pleasant weather and the fewest crowds.

Uruguay

Tucked between Brazil and Argentina, **Uruguay** is one of the most European countries of South America and, along with Paraguay, one of the safest. For this reason, it's one of South America's most visited nations. Its capital, **Montevideo** (MVD), on the southern coast, is where most of your clients will arrive, either by air or by cruise. Ninety miles east is the superb **Punta del Este**, the most famous beach resort on Uruguay's 200-mile-long "Riviera of South America."

Uruguay has a very comfortable, temperate climate. Its lengthy summer lasts from November until March. July is the coldest month, with daytime temperatures in the 50s. Rental cars are widely available here and your clients might enjoy driving around the countryside. (Montevideo's traffic, though, can be insane.) There's also a good bus system here. Spanish is the national language.

Important Places

Though small, Uruguay has some particularly interesting sites that your clients might enjoy:

Montevideo is well-known for its cuisine.

- **Montevideo** is a friendly and spacious town. Many of its attractions surround the **Plaza Independencia**, including the mosaics and marble of the **Palacio Legislativo** and the beautiful **Teatro Solis**. There are also very good parks, markets, and museums. The nearby resort town of **Carrasco** has excellent beaches and grand old mansions. And a half hour away is **Tablada**, often called "The Town of the Gauchos."

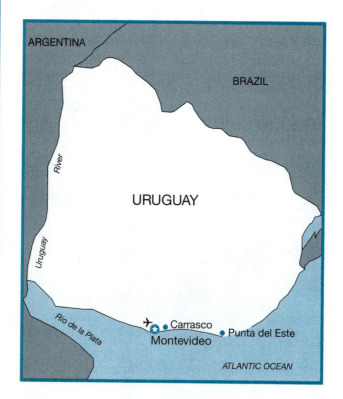

- **The "Riviera"** runs east from Montevideo. Punta del Este is an especially popular resort. Trendy and lively, it offers gambling and has many nightclubs. Excellent fishing is nearby.

Sales Considerations

Uruguay is a good choice for clients interested in exotic nature, for gamblers, and for clients who want to visit a South American country largely free of crime and political turmoil. It is also a wonderful add-on to a visit to Brazil and/or Argentina. Booking a stay in Punta del Este could be much appreciated by your sun-seeking clients who might love "discovering" a new resort destination. Day air trips from Montevideo to Buenos Aires or to Iguazu Falls are potential cross-sell opportunities.

Your clients may find Uruguay's blend of cultures rather intriguing. (Uruguay, like Argentina, has many people of Italian and German descent.) This—and the availability of fine meats from Uruguay's ranches—makes for an especially diversified cuisine.

Argentina

Argentina, South America's second largest country and a magnet for tourism, is about one-third the size of the United States. The country shares its western border

The Tango originated in Argentina at the end of the nineteenth century.

Over one-third of all Argentineans are of Italian descent.

with Chile; the Andes serve as a border between the two. Its major city and capital is **Buenos Aires**. The popular beach resort, **Mar del Plata**, is south of Buenos Aires. The Lake District, which has been compared to Switzerland, is in the western part of the country, near the Andes.

There's a strong European influence here, where a local is almost as likely to have an Italian name as an Hispanic one. English is widely spoken in the major cities, though Spanish is the national language. Buenos Aires is the gateway into Argentina for flights, at **Ezeiza-Eze Airport** (EZE), and for cruises. (Flying time from New York is nine hours; from Los Angeles it's fourteen hours.) **Aerolineas Argentinas** (AR) is Argentina's large national carrier, though many other airlines serve the country. Within Argentina, there's very good air service. (If your clients plan to travel around the country, you should be aware of an excellent unlimited air package offered by the national airline; however, it must be purchased in North America.) There are also good bus and railroad networks. Rental cars are widely available, but distances can be long and challenging in some areas, and city traffic is hectic. The weather in Buenos Aires is wonderful: The summer months of December through February hit the mid-80s and descend to the mid-60s at night. Winter (June through August) is cooler but still pleasant (see Figure 11-1).

Climate at a Glance
BUENOS AIRES, ARGENTINA

	JAN	FEB	MAR	APR	MAY	JUN	JUL	AUG	SEP	OCT	NOV	DEC
Average high temperature	85	83	79	72	64	57	57	60	64	69	76	82
Average low temperature	63	63	60	53	47	42	42	43	46	50	56	61
Average precipitation (in inches)	3	3	4	4	3	2	2	2	3	3	3	4

Figure 11-1

Important Places

No visitor to Argentina should miss a stay in **Buenos Aires**, one of the world's major cities, with lively, active nightlife. Considered by some to be a South American Paris (some of the buildings even have gray mansard roofs), sprawling Buenos Aires is very cosmopolitan and has wonderful cuisine, top fashion, good museums, many parks and wide boulevards. The city is also fairly safe for tourists. Notable attractions are:

- **Plaza de Mayo**, the political heart of the city, with colonial buildings, the center of government, and churches.
- **Colon Theater**, a world-class opera house that has hosted the likes of Toscanini, Nijinski, and Baryshnikov. Many other cultural events are presented here, too.
- **Diverse neighborhoods**, such as **San Telmo**, the old colonial section with cobblestone streets, tango nightclubs, and markets. Another fun neighborhood for your clients to visit is **La Boca**, the Italian district, noted for its fine art galleries, alfresco dining opportunities, and lively restaurants. And **Calle Florida** is a popular tourist shopping area.
- **Lujan**, a half-day trip from the city. This town is a center of religious activity to which a famous pilgrimage is made every December.

On Calle Florida is a replica of Big Ben's tower, given to Buenos Aires by the city of London.

If your clients will be spending more than just a few days in Argentina, you might want to recommend some of the country's other destinations, including:

- **Mar del Plata**, about 250 miles south of Buenos Aires, with five miles of great beaches. There's excellent shopping, hundreds of hotels, and a huge casino.
- **Iguazu Falls**, probably the widest waterfall in the world. The falls are shared by Argentina, Brazil, and Paraguay, but are usually visited from Brazil.
- **The Lake District**, often compared to Switzerland. The town of **Bariloche**, just south of Lake Nahuel Huapi, is a popular resort year-round; summer offers great fishing; whereas winter (from June through October) provides excellent skiing. Other major ski resorts are **Las Lenas** and **Chapelco. Nahuel Huapi National Park** is a beautiful, immense natural wonder.

Gaucho ranches feature barbecued meals and horseback riding on the *pampas* (broad, grassy plains).

Bariloche, in the Lake District of Argentina
Photo by C. J. Ghormley

Sales Considerations

Argentina will appeal to clients who want a European flavor to their Latin American experience. It's safer than many other South American destinations, a consideration for some clients (though many political atrocities have happened here and may be known to your clients). Selling-up a client to a nicer hotel in Buenos Aires or any of the resort areas might get a note of appreciation. If clients are planning to travel around the country, offer them the Aerolineas Argentinas air package. Argentineans are lovers of sports of all kinds; sports packages are therefore an attractive cross-sell for Argentina-bound clients. One note: Argentina is not a bargain destination; Buenos Aires is, in fact, Latin America's most expensive city.

Chile

This pencil-thin country—at one point, it's only fifty-six miles wide—snakes down the west coast of South America to the tip of the continent. Chile is separated from Argentina by the Andes. Most of the sites your clients will be interested in visiting are in the central plains of the country. The area is flanked by bone-dry desert to the north, whereas the south (split by the Strait of Magellan and reaching almost to Antarctica) breaks up into little islands and fjordlike inlets. Chile's capital, **Santiago**, is located almost directly in the center of the country. Northwest of it is the major port of **Valparaiso** and the popular beach resort, **Vina del Mar**. A bit farther north is **Portillo**, a major ski resort. Another of Chile's most famous sites is actually more than 2,000 miles west of the mainland: **Easter Island**, with its mysterious, giant statues.

LAN-Chile (LA) and **Ladeco** (UC) are the national airlines and fly into the gateway of Santiago (SCL). Valparaiso is the port of entry for cruises. Air service and trains (basically limited to the southern part of the country) connect the major cities. Chile has an excellent bus system. Rental cars are widely available, though some of the conditions off the Pan-American Highway can be quite difficult. Spanish is the national language.

The weather in Santiago from November through March (summer) is pleasant and dry, but it can get hot. Winter will get chilly, dropping as low as the 30s at night. Vina del Mar's climate tends to be milder throughout the year. On Easter Island, the weather is temperate, ranging between 60 and 80 degrees.

Important Places

Santiago, surrounded by the Andes, offers beautiful scenery, lovely colonial architecture, and many modern structures. The city has good museums and an excellent planetarium. The most interesting sites include:

- **Plaza de Armas**, where many of the finest colonial buildings are found, including the huge cathedral and the National Historical Museum.
- **San Francisco Church and Colonial Art Museum**, a fascinating complex.
- **Fantisilandia**, a popular amusement park.

In addition to Santiago, Chile provides tourists with other wonderful places to visit, including:

- **Vina del Mar**, a very expensive, fashionable beach resort.
- **Portillo**, one of the world's finest ski resorts, open at full operation from June through September and on a more limited basis the rest of the year. A lively ski carnival takes place here in August (which, of course, is in the middle of winter!). Two other Chilean ski resorts are Valle Nevado and Chillan.

Chile is 2,650 miles long and has no rivers of any size.

Case Study

German and Leah Ruiz are a couple in their late thirties. Though they were both born in the United States, German's grandparents are from Venezuela and he has relatives there whom he's never met. They plan to take a ten-day trip; six days will be spent in Venezuela and the remaining time they will spend in Buenos Aires. They don't have to worry about an itinerary in Venezuela; the relatives will take care of that. Buenos Aires is another matter, and that's where they'll need some help.

Circle the answer that best suits your clients' needs:

1. They want to experience the famed Buenos Aires nightlife. Where would you suggest they go?

   La Boca   Plaza de Mayo

   San Telmo   Portillo

   Why?

2. They're willing to spend a day to see some natural wonder. What's the nearest site you can recommend?

   Angel Falls   Iguazu Falls

   The Amazon   The Sea of Tranquility

   Why?

3. Which of the following services would be most appropriate for you to book for the Ruizs?

   An Aerolineas Argentinas air pass   A city tour

   An Amazon cruise   A ski package

   Why?

4. They decide that they want to drive down the coast for a couple of days and spend some time at a beach resort. Which would you suggest?

   Mar del Plata   Punta del Este

   Vina del Mar   Villa D'Este

   Why?

Creative Activity

A new *Star Wars* movie is in the works. Here's the plot: Luke Skywalker, now an old man, must find a successor to carry on the Jedi tradition. At the same time he is pursued by the evil clone of Darth Vader. First, Skywalker goes to a planet of mountains and ice. Then he travels to a hot, jungle planet. He leaves its lowlands, crosses a parched desert, and climbs to a mysterious ruined city in the cliffs, where a Yoda-like creature gives him many clues. But his pursuers catch up to him here. They chase him behind vast waterfalls and corner him in a fjord.

What? Did you think we'd give away the ending?! Anyway, you're the producer for this movie. You must find the necessary locations to shoot the scenes described. You decide, Why not shoot the entire film in Latin America? It will save money, and it has all the scenery needed.

In which Latin American place would you put up cast and crew for each location, assuming that you could take them by train or bus to and from the location each day? (Don't worry about the routing from base to location.) Assume flights are available to all places—no need to look up schedules.

SETTING	PLACE?
1. Mountains and ice	1.
2. Jungle	2.
3. Desert	3.
4. City in the cliffs	4.
5. Waterfalls	5.
6. Fjord	6.

What might be your flight itinerary for this shoot, assuming it starts and ends in Los Angeles?

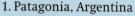

Travel Trivia

Top Ten Whale-Watching Areas

1. Patagonia, Argentina
2. Southern Ocean Whale Sanctuary, Antarctica
3. Bay of Samana, Dominican Republic
4. Campbell River, BC
5. Cape Cod, MA
6. Baja California
7. Kaikoura, New Zealand
8. Cape Town to Cape Agulhas, South Africa
9. Shikoku, Japan
10. Lofoten Islands, Norway

Source: World Wildlife Fund

Pulling It All Together: The Matching Game

Directions: Below is a list of cities, attractions, etc., some which we have covered, some which we haven't. There are all manner of connections among them. With your group, you have exactly ten minutes to come up with as many connections as possible. (Items may be used more than once.) Place your answers below. Note: There are at least twenty possible connections.

E.g., Sugar Loaf and Corcovado—both are mountains

Dunns River	Bogota	Bariloche
Galapagos	Vina del Mar	Iguazu
Machu Picchu	Las Hadas	Sierra Madres
Las Brisas	Asuncion	Sugar Loaf
Angel	Corcovado	French Guiana
Copacabana	Andes	Easter
Plaza de Mayo	Chichen Itza	Cayman
Copan	Mar del Plata	Haiti
Portillo	Bonaire	Zocalo

Tour de France ≈ Armstrong

A new bridge bw. sweden& Denmark

Great Britain ≈ Scotland - Wales, N. Ireland, England

Denmark - Iceland - sweden - Finland - Norway ≈ scandiva

BARENTS SEA

Tiger woods

Scotland
(North g Er)
St. Andrews
golf courser in England
place

NORWEGIAN SEA

SWEDEN

FINLAND

Helsinki

ICELAND

Reykjavik

NORWAY

Oslo

Stockholm

BALTIC SEA

ESTONIA

Baltic Nations

COMMONWEALTH OF INDEPENDENT STATES
(formerly Soviet Union)

LATVIA

LITHUANIA

Moscow

GREAT BRITAIN

NORTH SEA

religion diff.

NORTHERN IRELAND

SCOTLAND

DENMARK

Copenhagen

IRELAND

Dublin

IRISH SEA

ENGLAND

NETHERLANDS

POLAND

Warsaw

BELARUS

becoming now popula
g busines burism

WALES

London

Amsterdam

GERMANY

Berlin

Brussels

Bonn

Warsaw

UKRAINE

BELGIUM

LUXEMBOURG

English Channel

Paris

Munich

CZECH REPUBLIC

SLOVAKIA

Chunnel

SWITZERLAND

Geneva

Salzburg

AUSTRIA

HUNGARY

MOLDOVA

ATLANTIC OCEAN

FRANCE

ITALY

SLOVENIA

CROATIA

ROMANIA

Bucharest

Nice

BOSNIA

Belgrade

BLACK SEA

Iberion

ANDORRA

Barcelona

Corsica

ADRIATIC SEA

SERBIA

BULGARIA

GEORGIA

SPAIN

Rome

MACEDONIA

Ankara

ARMENIA

PORTUGAL

Madrid

Sardinia

TYRRHENIAN SEA

IONIAN SEA

ALBANIA

GREECE

TURKEY

Lisbon

Sicily

Athens

AEGEAN SEA

Benelux
Low Countries
Belgium
N. Land.
Luxembourg

TUNISIA

MALTA

CYPRUS

SYRIA

IRAQ

Crete

LEBANON

MOROCCO

ALGERIA

MEDITERRANEAN SEA

ISRAEL

JORDAN

LIBYA

EGYPT

SAUDI ARABIA

Iberian = Portugal, Spain

Alp = Switzerland, N. Italy, Austria, S. Germany, E. France

Baden Baden = S. Germany.

Danube = Germany, Yugoslavia, into Black Sea

? like Las Vegas (a resort)

Rhine = Switzerland - Germany, Netherlands → North Sea

→ famous for Wein

Europe
Continental Flair

Pyrenees

Pyrenese mountain seperates France & Spain.

If a traveler decides to leave the North American continent for a trip, it will in all probability be to visit Europe. Indeed, Europe is a magnet for tourists from all countries. Among the top ten destinations for world travelers, seven are European. Celebrated historical monuments, sun-baked beaches, sparkling ski resorts, landmark hotels, gourmet restaurants, intriguing cultures and people—Europe has all of these. A host of jets crisscrosses the Atlantic, so it's easy to get there. And once your clients arrive in Europe, they'll find an efficient network of railroads, highways, buses, motorcoach tours, and subways to get around. This broad array of services will offer you, the travel professional, countless opportunities for cross-selling and selling-up.

Where the Countries Are

Over forty countries splash across the terrain of Europe; many of them have their own language and way of life. Don't be intimidated. Their locations can be mastered easily, especially when you sort them into logical geographical groupings.

Look at the map. Across the north are the **Scandinavian countries**: **Iceland**, **Norway**, **Sweden**, **Denmark**, and **Finland**. (Greenland, a seldom-visited destination to the west of Iceland, is considered part of North America.) On the Baltic Sea, just beneath the Scandinavian Peninsula, are the **Baltic Nations** of **Estonia**, **Latvia**, and **Lithuania**. In the northwest are the **British Isles**, which consist of **Great Britain** and **Ireland** (which isn't really British at all).

In western Europe are **France** and the **Benelux countries** (**Belgium**, the **Netherlands**, and **Luxembourg**), as well as the **Iberian Peninsula**, which features **Portugal** and **Spain**. Spain is also sometimes included as part of the **Mediterranean countries**, which curve along the northern shore of this legendary sea. Among them are **Italy**, **Greece**, and **Turkey** (which spills over from Asia).

The Eastern European countries, which have swung their doors wide open to tourism, are: **Poland**, the **Czech Republic**, the **Slovak Republic**, **Hungary**, **Romania**, **Bulgaria**, and **Albania**. The former nation of **Yugoslavia** is also among these, but it has broken down into a series of smaller countries: **Slovenia**, **Croatia**, **Bosnia and Herzegovina**, **Macedonia**, and what remains of the original Yugoslavia (also called **Serbia**). Conflicts among these countries could alter their boundaries further. In the far eastern portion of Europe is **Russia** and its co-nations in the **Commonwealth of Independent States** (formerly the Soviet Union), which stretches well into Asia. And in the middle of Europe are the nations of **Alpine Europe**: Germany, **Switzerland**, and **Austria**.

That's about all you need remember now. We mention Europe's smaller countries and principalities as allied destinations in the chapters that follow. Meanwhile, practice filling in a blank European map to master where each country is situated.

A Satellite View

If you were looking down from space, it would be impossible to tell one European country from another. Borders, after all, aren't painted across the face of the earth. But things like mountains, oceans, lakes, and rivers have long defined Europe's national boundaries. And these geographic features affect your clients' travel plans in major ways.

Bodies of Water

The first thing you'd see from a satellite would be the broad blue expanse of the **Atlantic Ocean**, which lies along Europe's western shore. In the north, the **Baltic Sea** separates Scandinavia from Russia and the Baltic States; and the **North Sea** cuts off Great Britain from the Benelux countries, Germany, and Scandinavia. From space, the narrow blue line that separates Great Britain from France, the **English Channel**, wouldn't seem very significant, but it has been a critical body of water for centuries and is crossed by numerous ferries, hovercraft, and the new Channel Tunnel or "Chunnel." And, of course, you'll easily make out the **Mediterranean Sea**, that long, azure feature that splits Europe from Africa. In several places, it stretches long fingers into Europe, including those of the **Adriatic** and **Ionian** seas (between Italy, Greece, Croatia, and Albania) and the **Aegean Sea** (between Greece and Turkey). The Mediterranean is peppered with islands, many of which are potential beach or cruise destinations to sell to your clients. Finally,

Cruising on the Rhine River, Germany
Photo by C. J. Ghormley

Europe is the smallest continent after Australia.

the blue oval to the east is the **Black Sea**, a major resort for Eastern European and Russian tourists.

If you have keen eyes, you could also spot a few major rivers crisscrossing Europe. The **Danube**, celebrated in literature and music, snakes its way eastward out of Germany through Eastern Europe and empties into the Black Sea. Down through Europe's middle is the **Rhine**, a river that finds its source in Switzerland and flows northward through Germany and the Netherlands, and eventually into the North Sea. Both rivers offer major cruise opportunities to your clients.

You may even be able to spot the **lakes** of northern Italy and of Switzerland, the **fjords** of western Norway, and the **lochs** of northern Scotland. Many man-made waterways course through the continent, too: Barge rides on canals are a popular, upscale option for clients to consider.

Mountains

It's critical to know where the mountains of Europe are; they have a significant impact on the weather, travel times, and facilities your clients will encounter. The most obvious are the **Alps**, the thick, lofty mountains that ripple across Switzerland, Austria, southern Germany, eastern France, and northern Italy. The **Pyrenees**, massive ridges that separate Spain from France, are important, too. Medium-sized mountains and hills are in many other areas; only Denmark, Poland, Hungary, and the Benelux countries are relatively flat.

Climate

Europe's weather varies immensely according to latitude, altitude, and season. The Alpine mountain areas tend to be cold in winter and cool in summer. Skiers will favor the winter, of course, but it will probably be best to sell these areas to others as summer destinations. (Late spring or early fall, though, can be glorious and uncrowded.) Northern France, the Benelux countries, Eastern Europe, much of Germany, and the Alpine lowlands are similar to America's Pacific Northwest: cool to cold in winter, with much dampness and cloudiness; cool to warm in the spring or fall. The Mediterranean rim is an all-year destination, though summers can get very hot; winters are mild, but cold weather is not unheard of here. Mediterranean water temperatures are chilly in the winter months.

Precipitation also varies greatly. As you'd expect from what you learned in the introductory chapters, Europe's west coasts are wet; this is especially true of Norway's fjord area, Scotland's and Ireland's west coasts, northwestern Portugal, and the eastern shore of the Adriatic. There are also some very dry areas, especially southeastern and central Spain and the area northeast of the Black Sea. Rainfall in the rest of Europe tends to be like that of the northeastern United States: humid and showery in the summer; rainy, snowy, or cloudy in the winter, with brief, welcome spells of crisp sunshine.

Tourism Patterns

France is, by far, the giant among European countries in tourism. Spain, Italy, the United Kingdom (Great Britain and Northern Ireland), and Poland form a second tier of success. The Scandinavian nations lie behind in numbers, but not in amount spent: Tourists tend to spend more, proportionally, in these countries.

One other important pattern: Europeans tend to take very long summer vacations, usually from mid-July to late August. And they generally head south to Spain, the French Riviera, Italy, and Greece. As a result, northern European capitals seem

There are about 40,000 ski runs in the Alps.

Mont St Michel, France
Photo by Karen Fukushima

empty at this time. Hotel room availability in central and northern Europe is therefore surprisingly good in late summer.

European Distances

Because Europe brims with so many countries, it seems enormous. Yet the United States is almost the same size as Europe. A better comparison would be to think of each nation of Europe as a geographic equivalent of a U.S. state.

Remember, too, that certain cities in totally separate countries can, in reality, be very close to each other; for example, Brussels, the capital of Belgium, is only about a half-day drive or train ride from Paris; Paris is a mere one-hour flight from London; and Munich, Germany, is quite close to Salzburg, Austria.

Once Europe's compactness sinks in, however, it's easy to mistakenly think that traveling times within Europe are always short. Not so. Some nations—like Germany, Belgium, and the Netherlands—do have complex and modern highway systems; it would be appropriate for you to book a rental car for your clients to drive around in these countries. On the other hand, Spain, Portugal, Greece, Ireland, Scotland, most of Scandinavia, and Eastern Europe have a more limited network of highways. People there depend on slow rural roads. As a result, to drive from the Italian Riviera to Rome would take your clients at least two days—even though the distance is about the same as from Boston to Washington, D.C., which (because of the U.S. interstate system) is only about an eight-hour drive.

Trains can be a direct and swift alternative for your clients, but not always. Europe's high-speed trains are a wonder: They'll whoosh from Paris to Geneva in only three-and-a-half hours and at speeds approaching 200 miles an hour. On the other hand, Lisbon to Madrid (a distance equal to that of Paris to Geneva) takes a full ten hours by train. Old tracks, curving routes, and awkward train connections can make some rail trips long and slow. For most of your clients, this wouldn't be acceptable. (On the other hand, a leisurely trip might be exactly what some of your clients want.) Several luxurious train excursions exist in Europe, including the most legendary of all: the Orient Express. Its principal route is London to Venice, but there are many alternative itineraries.

The most famous high-speed trains are: Eurostar (Transchunnel), ICE (Germany), TGV (France), X2000 (Sweden), AVE (Spain), and Pendolino (Italy).

The Temple of Athena at Delphi, Greece
Photo by William and Marie Rourke

Cruises are an important alternative. Major cruise areas are: the Eastern Mediterranean (including Greece, Turkey, and sometimes Israel and Egypt); the Western Mediterranean (Italy, France, and Spain); a route between Barcelona, Spain, along Portugal and France, and on to Great Britain; a Britain-Ireland itinerary; and several routings that call on ports in France, Germany, Scandinavia, the Baltics, and Russia. Many European cruises are seven days in length, with shorter ones in the Greek Islands and occasional longer ones throughout. In addition to cruise ships, Europe's waterways also feature barges and ferries (which are often huge and offer overnight accommodations).

And what of aircraft? Of course they provide rapid European connections, though sometimes high-speed trains are just as fast. Short European flights can also be surprisingly expensive, although current deregulation has brought some fares down dramatically. Air travel, however, doesn't provide those features that make train travel and motoring attractive to your clients: the scenery along the way, travel unaffected by snow or fog (especially true for trains), and the option to stop and see some magnificent castle or fairy-tale town. One offbeat option: short or multi-day balloon trips, most often staged in France and Italy, but also available in Switzerland, Austria, and Turkey.

Some Miscellaneous Considerations

Europe requires certain bits of knowledge to fine-tune your sale of that appealing continent. Here are a few considerations:

- Many hotels are old, have small rooms, and feature only single-sized beds. Always check standard agency reference books before making reservations for your client, and make sure the lodging matches what he or she wants.
- **Eurail passes** are handy (though not quite the bargain they used to be) and a critical item to cross-sell to a client. These passes often cover airport transfers and ferries, too. Keep a current Eurail guide on hand to refer to for rates, countries covered, services offered, and the like. Recommend the first-class version, since second-class cars can be crowded, uncomfortable, or both.

Russia, Azerbaijan, and the United States have one thing in common: They're all split into two pieces by another country.

Eurail passes (and many single-country and regional passes) can be purchased only in North America.

According to the European Travel Commission, the number one objection to visiting Europe is its cost, followed by "the time it takes getting there."

- If your client will travel extensively in only one country, recommend a single-country or regional train pass. Some countries even offer rail-with-car-rental-and-hotel packages.

- Seeing Europe by car appeals to clients who are used to driving when they take North American vacations. It offers much more routing, scheduling, and sight-seeing flexibility than trains. The same applies to camper rentals, which have become an increasingly popular way of motoring through Europe. One warning, though: European driving—with its very high-speed highways, twisting secondary roads, narrow city streets, limited parking, many tolls, and high gas prices—can challenge the best driver. Also, if your client rents a car in central or northern Europe, he may be told when he picks up his car that he cannot drive it in southern Europe, or that his insurance will not cover him in the south. Inquire in advance if these conditions will apply.

- Ask your clients which they would prefer: a North American airline or a foreign carrier. Most countries in Europe have their own airlines with regular service to major U.S. and Canadian gateways and are partners in the frequent-flyer programs of North American carriers—a major consideration for clients.

- Foreign carriers often offer fly-drive packages at substantially discounted rates.

- Always check on current passport and visa requirements. These are things clients need to know about well in advance of their departure.

- Most major European cities are quite expensive, with Paris, Milan, Venice, London, and the Scandinavian capitals among the most costly in the world. Portugal, Ireland, Greece, Turkey, and some places in Eastern Europe are still relative bargains.

- In the following chapters, under "Lodging Options," you'll be reading about hotel chains that have major presences in Europe, such as CIGA, Forte, Meridien, and such U.S. companies as Sheraton, Best Western, Hyatt, and Hilton. Be aware that there are many hotels that are part of no official chain, but *are* represented by reservation organizations. For example, some of Europe's (and the world's) most exclusive hotels are booked via **Leading Hotels of the World** and **Preferred Hotels**. Even some hotels that *are* part of major chains can also be affiliated with these two organizations for the prestige it brings. A service the represents a broader range of hotel values in Europe is **Utell**.

- Europe has strived to become a more unified political and economic unit, though progress toward this goal has been slower than expected. It has become easier for tourists to cross borders; eventually intra-Europe flight costs will drop, and more multi-country high-speed train lines will be built. Europe intends to have a single currency (the euro), standardized electrical outlets, uniform value-added taxes (VAT: taxes on all goods and services), and passport-free travel. But long-standing traditions have made these tourism-facilitating breakthroughs a bit slow to achieve.

CHAPTER 12

Great Britain and Ireland
Foreign, Yet Familiar

For a client who hasn't yet been to Europe, Great Britain and Ireland may be perfect for a first visit. Far across the Atlantic, they're distant and different enough to be intriguing, yet their language and familiar culture offer security.

So how do England, Great Britain, and the United Kingdom differ? The *United Kingdom* is made up of four quasi-independent countries. Three of them constitute the island of *Great Britain:* **England**, the largest (about the size of New York State), is to the southeast (the term *England is* sometimes used—incorrectly—for all of Great Britain); **Wales** is southwest; and **Scotland** is to the north. The fourth is **Northern Ireland**, across the Irish Sea on the northeast corner of Ireland. (We'll use the term *Great Britain,* since we're focusing on England, Scotland, and Wales.) **Ireland** is distinct from Northern Ireland. It's a separate country from the United Kingdom and feels very strongly about its independence.

Nearly the size of Oregon, Great Britain has two centers of tourism. **London**, a world to itself, is a base for day trips; and **Edinburgh** [ED-in-boh-roh] is the heart of Scottish touring. Ireland has no real hub; visitors travel from town to town.

How Travelers Get There

There's extensive service to London on domestic and foreign carriers. Though most of your clients will fly to **Heathrow Airport** (LHR), **Gatwick** (LGW)—which is farther out—also handles traffic. **Stansted Airport** (STN), 30 miles north of London, has become a third option for domestic flights. All three offer rail service into the city. Visitors heading directly to Scotland will want to fly into **Prestwick** (PIK)—near **Glasgow**—or even to **Manchester** (MAN), which lies halfway between London and Scotland. Edinburgh airport mainly gets domestic flights. Travel time to London from New York is six-and-one-half hours; from Chicago it's seven-and-one-half hours, with most flights nonstop. Los Angeles to London takes about ten-and-one-half hours. The domestic airlines are **British Airways** (BA), **Virgin Atlantic** (VS), and for domestic flights and to the Continent, **British Midland** (BD).

A hovercraft crosses the English Channel from Dover to France, and there are many ferries from other towns. The **Channel High Railway Tunnel** (or "Chunnel") connects **Folkestone** (west of **Dover**) to **Calais**, France, and permits clients to travel from Paris to London (or vice versa) via the high-speed Eurostar train in a little under three hours.

Even though **Dublin** (DUB) is Ireland's capital and has a major airport, the country's principal airport is **Shannon** (SNN), outside **Limerick**. **Aer Lingus** (EI) is the major carrier from Boston and New York into Shannon, but service is also provided

For Your Information . . .

Great Britain and Ireland — FYI

CAPITALS: Great Britain: London
Ireland: Dublin

AREAS (SQUARE MILES): Great Britain: 94,500
Ireland: 27,000

TIME ZONES: GMT + −0

DRIVE ON: Left

POPULATIONS: Great Britain: 58,100,000
Ireland: 3,600,000

RELIGIONS: Great Britain: Protestant
Ireland: Roman Catholic

LANGUAGE: English

CURRENCIES: Great Britain: 1 pound = 100 pence
Ireland: 1 Irish pound = 100 pence

ELECTRICITY: 220 volts, 50 cycles AC

CAPSULE HISTORY: **Great Britain**: Rome invades, first century B.C.; Angles and Saxons invade, fifth century; England united, eleventh century; Normans invade, 1066; Magna Carta signed, 1215; Church of England breaks from Pope, sixteenth century; formation of Parliament, eighteenth century; World War I, 1914; World War II, 1939; first woman prime minister, 1979; greater autonomy given to Scotland and Wales, 1997.
Ireland: St. Patrick introduces Christianity, 432; Norsemen defeated, 1014; becomes separate republic, 1921.

For reference sources, tourist bureaus, and suggested lengths of stay, see the Appendices.

by many other air carriers. Flights are just over six hours; and some continue on to Dublin, which takes approximately another thirty-five minutes.

Cruises to Great Britain and Ireland from Spain, France, Germany, and other countries are numerous. Britain has three embarkation ports: **Southampton**, **Tilbury**, and **Tower** (in London itself). One cruise line offers regularly scheduled sailings from New York City to Southampton; and ships on repositioning or round-the-world cruises also access the British Isles from New York City or Florida.

Your upscale clients may wish to experience the supersonic transport (SST) **Concorde** from New York to London. It takes less than four hours to make the crossing.

Weather Patterns

Because of the warming influence of the Gulf Stream, Great Britain's generally moderate climate is similar to Oregon (even though it's almost at the latitude of southern Alaska.) The famous London fog is a memory of the past; it was actually smog, and it has been brought under control. English summers hover around 70 degrees. Clients, though, should be made aware that conditions change often between sunshine and rain. Winters are sharp, in the 40s, and wet, with occasional snow (see Figure 12-1). Most of your clients, however, will want to visit from mid-April to mid-October; the peak tourist season extends from June to September. Scotland is cooler and rainier than England in winter, but summers are about the same. The best time for your clients to see Great Britain may be spring or fall, when the weather is still good enough and crowds are somewhat thinner. Further,

The British Open golf tournament, held in mid-July, is usually played in Scotland at St. Andrews or Gleneagles.

Climate at a Glance
LONDON, ENGLAND

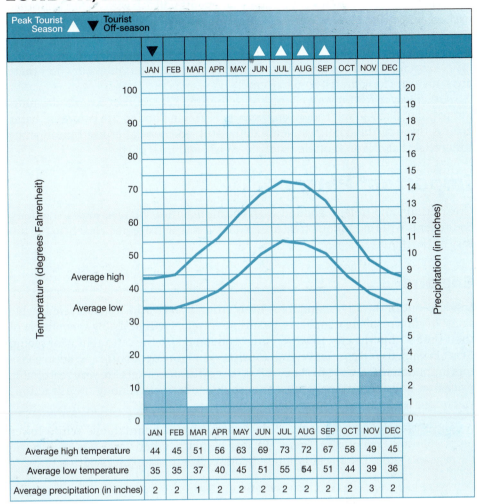

	JAN	FEB	MAR	APR	MAY	JUN	JUL	AUG	SEP	OCT	NOV	DEC
Average high temperature	44	45	51	56	63	69	73	72	67	58	49	45
Average low temperature	35	35	37	40	45	51	55	54	51	44	39	36
Average precipitation (in inches)	2	2	1	2	2	2	2	2	2	2	3	2

Figure 12-1

the period just after New Year's is particularly slow; it's one of the only times to get bargains in London.

Ireland's weather is similar to Great Britain's, but runs slightly cooler, cloudier, and wetter. As a result, the tourist season is a bit shorter: May to September. Summers are in the 60s, with frequent rain showers and fog (but long periods of daylight). Winters have more misty, rainy, or overcast days. It's hard to avoid precipitation here, but this is why the land is such a deep green. Ireland isn't called the Emerald Isle for nothing.

Getting Around

Many airlines and flights connect the area's major cities. And the excellent British Rail runs between towns throughout Great Britain, as do many buses. (Some high-speed trains cover distances in half the time a car would.) Tourists can also reach Ireland by ferry; and once there, CIE, the government-run transportation service, provides numerous trains and buses.

London, despite its size, is easy for tourists to navigate. The Underground sub-way (or Tube) goes almost everywhere. And your clients can use two of the great

BritRail passes for unlimited train travel in Britain can be bought only in North America. The Eurail pass does *not* cover Britain (but does cover Ireland).

transportation icons: the red double-decker buses and the black, lumpy taxis. London is also a very walkable city.

What about driving? It's a question your clients will ask with either unbridled excitement or white-knuckled fear. Rental cars are widely available, but mastering the art of tooling down the wrong side of the road is, without question, one of life's challenges. Actually, though, driving down a quiet country road can be a joy—except for the odd intersections called roundabouts—but in major cities there are saner ways for a tourist to get around.

Other ways exist for your clients to see the area. City tours and multi-day tours are popular. Boats along the **River Thames** [TEMZ] in London are common, barge cruises through the countryside are delightful, and several cruise lines operate itineraries that call on Scottish, English, Welsh, and Irish ports.

Important Places

Great Britain and Ireland abound with charming cities, villages, and attractions. Your clients will find unique treasures, even a few which are tied closely to the history of North America.

England

London—one of the largest and most lively cities in the world—offers a remarkable range of culture, history, and arts. First-time travelers will probably spend most of their time within the city. However, since London is also the central hub for seeing Great Britain, day trips offer veteran tourists even more opportunities. Return visitors to London will always find new plays to see (theater tickets are very reasonably priced), as well as unexplored museums, shops, and streets. Among the attractions you might recommend to your clients are:

The Tower of London, home of the Crown Jewels, the infamous White Tower prison, and armouries. There are lots of tourists here and lots of historic pageantry, too. The Tower is, after all, one of Britain's top tourist attractions.

Purchase visitor discount transit passes at Tube stations in London. They save money and allow you to bypass the long lines waiting to buy tickets.

Luxurious Apsley House, once home of the first Duke of Wellington, is now open to visitors.

You can tour the interior of famous Tower Bridge.

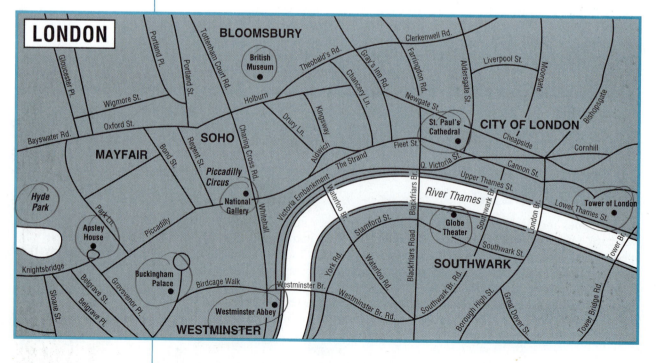

- **St. Paul's Cathedral**, the largest church in London, designed by Christopher Wren. In its Whispering Gallery, a word whispered to the wall can be heard clearly on the other side, over 100 feet away.
- **The British Museum**, a legendary collection of such items as the Rosetta Stone, the Elgin Marbles, and the Magna Carta.
- **Buckingham Palace's Changing of the Guard**, perhaps what tourists think of most when they think of London. Parts of the palace are occasionally open to tourists.
- **Westminster Abbey**, housing, under its magnificent Gothic architecture, the burial places of many of Great Britain's royalty, historical figures, and literary giants.
- **Several well-known shopping districts and stores**, including **Harrods** and **Selfridges** (two famous department stores), Oxford Street, Regent Street, and Covent Garden.

An exact reproduction of Shakespeare's Globe Theatre has been built in London near its original site.

Parliament's Clock Tower, Churchill's statue, and a London double-decker
Photo by C. J. Ghormley

You should advise your clients to take the following **day trips** from London (many of which you can book yourself, especially through Brit Rail):

- **Stonehenge**, the strange, mystical circle of stones, a close drive to **Salisbury** (with its beautiful cathedral).
- **Stratford-upon-Avon**, a charming town that's Shakespeare's birthplace and home of the **Royal Shakespeare Company**.
- **Hampton Court Palace**, the expansive estate of Henry VIII, with its famous garden maze.
- **Windsor Castle**, home to Britain's monarchs for nearly a thousand years and newly restored after a devastating fire.
- **Greenwich**, just down river from London, site of the **National Maritime Museum**, the **Old Royal Observatory**, and the clipper ship **Cutty Sark**.
- **Bath**, a lovely city of Georgian architecture and Roman baths.
- **Canterbury**, with its magnificent cathedral that's the centerpiece of the Church of England and the subject of Chaucer's famous work, *The Canterbury Tales*. Minutes away are the **White Cliffs of Dover**.

Scotland

Edinburgh, a regal-looking city and the capital of Scotland, has a medieval ambience. It's a port city located on the **Firth of Forth** and is a good jumping-off point for the area. Among the attractions you might suggest to your clients are:

- **Edinburgh Castle**, looks the way a traveler imagines a castle should look, looming high above the city and built out of the rock it sits on.
- **The Palace of Holyroodhouse** is the residence of Queen Elizabeth II when she is in the city; it retains an infamous association with Mary, Queen of Scots.
- **The Royal Mile** connects Edinburgh Castle and Holyroodhouse. It's the oldest and most historic area of the city.

You should advise your clients to take the following **day trips**:

Edinburgh Castle, Scotland
Photo by Karen Fukushima

Attending an Evensong service at a British cathedral can be a moving experience.

The Edinburgh International Festival, the world's largest arts festival, is held in late August.

- **The Trossachs**, the area of Scotland's most beautiful moors and lochs (lakes), are a long drive and deserve more than one day.
- **Glasgow** is an industrial town, but with excellent theater, fine arts, and the superb **Burrell Collection** museum. It's near famous **Loch Lomond** and is surrounded by very pretty countryside.
- **The Glasgow-Edinburgh area** is considered a virtual shrine for your golfer-clients. There are seven championship courses, including the Old Course at **St. Andrews**, and **Gleneagles**.
- **Loch Ness** is well-known for its often sighted but never-found monster.

Wales

Though perhaps not as well known as other parts of Britain, Wales nonetheless contains sights worth seeing. It's a land of mountains and castles, with a strong Celtic influence. In fact, many residents of northern Wales speak Welsh as their first language. Among the attractions in Wales:

- **Snowdonia National Park.** Steam trains climb to the summit of **Mount Snowdon** for spectacular views of northern Wales. Also in the park is **Blaenau Ffestiniog**, a slate quarry center where visitors can take tours of the underground mines.
- **Caernarfon.** The town is still partially encircled by its walls and is dominated by the huge castle where Charles was invested as Prince of Wales. Other impressive castles in northern Wales include Conwy (with a landmark suspension bridge nearby) and Harlech (built high on a rocky crag).
- **Portmeirion.** This extraordinary Italian-style village overlooking the sea was the setting for the 1960's TV series *The Prisoner*. It's now a hotel and is also famous for Portmeirion china.
- **The Wye Valley.** In this valley on the English border are many semi-ruined castles and churches, including the well-known Tintern Abbey. Hay-on-Wye is a

> The village with the longest place name in the world is in northern Wales: Llanfairpwllgwyngyllgogerychwyrndrobwllllantysiliogogogoch, known locally as Llanfair P.G.

Portmeirion, Wales
Photo by Karen Fukushima

book-lovers dream; most of the town is made up of second-hand book stores. At its annual literary festivals, world-famous authors give readings.

- **Cardiff**. The capital of Wales, Cardiff boasts a whimsically restored castle and the **Welsh Folk Museum** at **St. Fagans**. Buildings from all over Wales were reassembled here, providing a living history of the country.

Ireland

Since there's no true center of Ireland, your clients will most likely want to travel about this entire compact country. So consider cross-selling them a tour or a car rental. Among the towns and attractions you might recommend to your clients are:

- **Dublin**, the capital of Ireland, has a stormy and vibrant past. It offers a rich collection of medieval history, modern arts, and pubs. Among its attractions:
  - **St. Patrick's Cathedral** contains many monuments and plaques.
  - The vaulted crypt of **Christ Church**.
  - **Dublin Castle** (which dates some of its sections to the Celts) is where English rule in Ireland was based.
  - **Trinity College** boasts a collection of old book treasures.
  - **The National Museum** holds one of the world's great gold collections, dating from as far back as the Bronze Age.
- **Bundoran**, a popular resort, is located on **Donegal Bay**. Nearby is picturesque **Glenveigh National Park**.
- **Galway**, a beautiful and charming town on **Galway Bay**, is best visited by taking a relaxed walking tour. Just outside town are the spectacular **Cliffs of Moher**.
- **Limerick** is the first stop in Ireland after arriving at Shannon airport. Historic, ancient architecture is everywhere, including **St. Mary's Church**.
- **Killarney** is renowned for its magnificent scenery of lakes, forests, and mountains. Nearby are **Bourne Vincent Memorial Park**, a national park; **Gap of Dunloe**, a stunning gorge; and the **Ring of Kerry**—a scenic drive past cliffs, mountains, lakes, and villages.
- **Cork** has extensive arts and cultural activities, including choral and drama festivals, ballet, and opera.
- **Blarney** is the town—only six miles from Cork—that's famous for its **Blarney Stone**, which is said to give the gift of eloquence to anyone who kisses it.
- **Waterford** is best known for its world-famous **Waterford crystal factory**.

Remember, too, that Northern Ireland, despite its deep political problems, still manages to attract many travelers. Visitors to Scotland or to Ireland often sidetrack for a few days to see Northern Ireland's scenic countryside or to play on its many golf courses.

Possible Itineraries

You should advise first-time visitors to spend about a week in London, including time for day trips through the area. More experienced clients will still probably want to spend some time there before (or after) exploring the English countryside and Scotland. Ireland could stand on its own for a full week. If your clients want to visit the entire area of Great Britain and Ireland, you should sell them a stay of at least two weeks.

Lodging Options

Some of the most famous (and expensive) hotels in the world are in London's West End: **Claridge's**, the **Dorchester**, the **Berkeley**, the **Connaught**, the **Ritz**, and the

The Giants Causeway, a natural formation of volcanic columns in the sea, is fascinating.

The Wimbledon tennis tournament is held in late June and early July.

Savoy. For your less well-heeled clients, there are many interesting alternatives in London and throughout Great Britain. These include popular bed-and-breakfasts and flats (apartments). Bed-and-breakfasts exist all over the country, as does lodging in manors and castles. Your clients may also like trying the **Farm Holidays**, which permit them to stay on a working farm.

If hotels remain the lodging of choice, there are other wonderful places to choose from, such as the very-English **Brown's** in London and the **Caledonian** in Edinburgh (though both, again, are costly). Among the most popular chains in Great Britain: **Forte**, **Swallow**, and **Thistle**. American chains such as **Hilton**, **Sheraton**, **Radisson**, and **Ramada International** are also present.

Ireland offers its own wide range of accommodations; in general, your client can stay there for less than he or she can in Great Britain. There are still, of course, many first-class hotels, like Dublin's **Shelbourne** and **Burlington**. And a big, deluxe chain is **Jurys**. However, like Great Britain, Ireland can present your clients with wonderful alternative housing. Notable among these that you can recommend are the spectacular **Ashford Castle** near Galway and **Dromoland Castle** near Limerick, both of which offer stunning grounds. Other castles and manors can be found through the Irish Tourist Bureau. Again, check your reference books for bed-and-breakfasts, farmhouses, and cottages.

Allied Destinations

Great Britain and Ireland are an ideal starting point for a visit to the rest of Europe. France, especially, is an easy connection. And just across the North Sea are Copenhagen and the rest of Scandinavia. Your clients can get to all these places via air, ferry, cruise, and now (through the Chunnel), by train.

London's Heathrow is the world's busiest international airport.

Cultural Patterns

Your clients—whether they fly over for business or pleasure—shouldn't confuse comfortable, familiar conditions with the reality that they're still foreign visitors. Here are a few tips:

- Business appointments must be booked well in advance.
- Honorary titles are *always* used, even among friends.
- Food words are often different from those used in North America. *Pudding* can refer to dessert in general. *Beer* is generally bitter, dark, and tepid. (What North Americans call beer is known as *lager*.) *Crisps* are potato chips; while *chips* are french fries.
- Don't talk shop over drinks and dinner unless a Brit does it first.
- Make sure your clients understand the importance of being generally reserved and subdued. Politeness is still the standard here.
- The peoples of Great Britain and Ireland are proud of their respective histories, and your clients would do well to show an interest in these countries' pasts as well as current events.
- Promptness is important. Make sure your clients keep on time.
- Inform your clients that, when visiting the home of a local, it's not necessary to bring a gift; however, it's considered a thoughtful gesture. Any gift should be presented to the lady of the house.
- Be sure that your clients are aware that Scotland, Wales, and Northern Ireland are *not* England; they are all distinct regions of the United Kingdom.
- Clearly, it's impossible and inappropriate to stereotype how people in each of these countries will act in every instance. There are, however, generalizations: Tell your clients that Scotland tends to be more open, independent, and

When shopping, ask the salesperson about refunds on the VAT (a tax on all goods and services). Many stores participate in a service that mails you a check or credits your credit card account for the VAT on purchases over a certain amount.

fun-loving than England. Your clients should be careful about discussing religion and politics in Northern Ireland, where it's an extremely sensitive subject. And Ireland is generally a friendly, exuberant land.

Factors That Motivate Visitors

Your clients might want to visit the area because of the cultural ties and ease of language; however, there might be other reasons, too. Understanding all of their reasons is essential in setting up a memorable trip. Among their reasons might be:

- There are more airline connections from North America to London than to any other international city.
- Convenient public transportation and cruise options make the countries easy to get around.
- Picturesque villages are just about everywhere.
- A diverse span of accommodations and price levels are available.
- London is a major center for cultural attractions and the theater.
- Ireland is particularly inexpensive and can be the choice of budget-minded clients.
- Scotland, Wales, and Ireland are well-known for their lush scenery.
- Many clients have retained a close family association to Ireland and Great Britain and want to trace their roots there.

Qualifying the Client
London

FOR CLIENTS WHO WANT	APPEAL			REMARKS
	HIGH	MEDIUM	LOW	
Historical and Cultural Attractions	▲			London's chief asset
Beaches and Water Sports			▲	So-so beaches to south
Skiing Opportunities			▲	None
Lots of Nightlife	▲			Especially theater
Family Activities		▲		Mostly sightseeing
Familiar Cultural Experience		▲		Foreign, but English-speaking
Exotic Cultural Experience		▲		
Safety and Low Crime		▲		Some clients fear terrorism
Bargain Travel		▲		Some hotels are a bargain
Impressive Scenery		▲		Especially the countryside
Peace and Quiet			▲	Some parts quiet
Shopping Opportunities	▲			Antiques, china, woolens, legendary department stores
To Do Business	▲			Many U.S. businesses are British-owned, and vice versa

Figure 12-2

Case Study

Don and Karen Robinson are a couple in their late thirties, living in Toronto. They were in London thirteen years ago, when they were first married; now, however, they have a twelve-year-old son and are planning to return to the area. They would like to see some new sights, but don't want their child to miss out on anything. They have great curiosity and love theater, but Karen is not very adventurous in traveling. They can take off five work days.

Circle the answer that best suits your clients' needs:

1. How many days total would you recommend for their trip?

   Three   Five   Eight   Ten

   Why?

2. On what area would you ʒ Ɡest they concentrate?

   London and environs   London and Scotland

   London and Ireland   Wales and Northern Ireland

   Why?

3. Which of the following would you *not* recommend?

   A trip to Stonehenge   A BritRail pass

   A barge cruise   A city tour

   Why?

4. Which of the following tips would the family find most helpful?

   Pack extra sun screen.   Buy travel passes at Tube stations.

   Avoid political troubles in Ireland.   Rent a car to help get around London.

   Why?

Creative Activity

You've been hired to be a London city Blue Guide. Blue Guides are considered to be among the world's most knowledgeable tour guides. You're in the early research phase of your job—you haven't given a city tour yet. Using reference books (refer to the Appendices for suggestions), answer the following questions regarding sights you'll have to be informed about.

1. Who designed St. Paul's Cathedral?

2. Where is the Rosetta Stone?

3. What is Piccadilly Circus?

4. Where is London Bridge?

5. Whose statue is in Trafalgar Square?

6. What is the London subway popularly called?

7. In front of which London palace does the Changing of the Guard take place?

8. Who lives at 10 Downing Street?

9. Where was Anne Boleyn beheaded?

10. Which river flows through London?

11. Where is Chaucer buried?

12. What is Harrod's?

13. In which palace, begun by Cardinal Wolsey, is there a famous maze?

14. When during the year does the Wimbledon tennis tournament take place?

15. Where are England's crown jewels kept?

Your research sources:

CHAPTER 13

France
The Movable Feast

Ernest Hemingway, in a bit of memorable phrasing, called **Paris** "a movable feast." The same can be said for all of France. Whether it's because of food, culture, language, or history, your clients will surely bring back with them strong, fond memories of their feast-like visit to this rich country.

Paris is the focal point of any trip to France. However, you'll have to get your clients beyond the city for them to acquire a full appreciation of this country. Indeed, its eight richly diverse regions could each merit a separate vacation.

France is the largest country completely within Europe; it's about the size of Indiana, Illinois, Iowa, and Missouri combined. Cosmopolitan, unique Paris sits in the north-center of the country. Heading west (and counterclockwise) are the beaches of **Normandy**, with their seaside towns, war memorials, and medieval architecture. Below Normandy and Paris are the magnificent châteaux (castles) of

For Your Information . . .

France   FYI

CAPITAL: Paris

AREA (SQUARE MILES): 212,841

TIME ZONE: GMT +1

DRIVE ON: Right

POPULATION: 58,300,000

RELIGION: Roman Catholic

LANGUAGE: French

CURRENCY: 1 franc = 100 centimes

ELECTRICITY: 220 volts, 50 cycles AC

CAPSULE HISTORY: J. Caesar conquers Gaul, 57–52 B.C.; becomes distinct country, 843; Louis XIV reigns, 1643–1715; revolution, 1789; Napoleon becomes emperor, 1804; Louis XVIII begins reign, 1815; second revolution, 1848; second empire, 1852; Germany invades, 1940; France liberated, 1944; DeGaulle begins rule, 1946; DeGaulle loses election after violent demonstrations and strikes, 1969.

For reference sources, tourist bureaus, and suggested lengths of stay, see the Appendices.

the **Loire** [LWAHR] **River Valley**. South of the Loire region is the **Aquitaine** district, with its legendary wines, Roman ruins, and prehistoric sites. Along France's border with Spain are the **Pyrenees**, a place of scenery, shrines, and skiing.

Stretching along France's Mediterranean coast are the chic beaches of the **French Riviera**, also known as the **Côte d'Azur**. To the north are the fashionable ski resorts of the **French Alps**. Then, stretching northward toward Paris is France's **Eastern Wine Country**, including the **Champagne** and **Burgundy** districts. To the southwest, off the coast, lies the French island of **Corsica**.

English is commonly spoken by those in the tourist trade here; however, though many citizens of this country have a strong command of English, they are *passionately* partial to speaking their own language.

How Travelers Get There

Among airlines, Air France is the world's largest purchaser of caviar.

Paris is serviced by many flights, on both domestic and foreign carriers, including the national airline, **Air France** (AF). Two major airports serve the city: **Charles de Gaulle** (CDG) and **Orly** (ORY). In addition, flights from New York to the Riviera land in **Nice** at the **Nice-Côte d'Azur Airport** (NCE). There's also **Satolas Airport** (LYS) in **Lyon** (a gateway to the Eastern Wine Country and the Alps).

Flying time to Paris from New York is seven hours; from Miami and Chicago, it's eight-and-a-half hours; and from Los Angeles, it's ten-and-a-half hours. Flights to the Riviera take ninety minutes longer. Travelers can get from London to Paris via a brief air flight, on the trans-Channel hovercraft or ferries, or through the Channel tunnel. Cruise ships regularly call at ports on the Riviera, along the Atlantic Coast and in northern France.

Your affluent clients and corporate heads may wish to save time and enjoy the experience of flying on the supersonic transport **Concorde** into Paris. The SST takes just under four hours and leaves only from the U.S. East Coast.

Weather Patterns

By and large, the climate of France is temperate. Paris has weather similar to London, though slightly warmer, ranging from the mid-70s in summer to near 40 in winter. Temperatures do vary, however, in certain regions of the country. The Riviera's climate is somewhat similar to that of Los Angeles: summers in the 80s and winters in the 50s. In the Alps, winters are cold with snow—but then, that's exactly what skiers want (see Figures 13-1 and 13-2).

Who hasn't heard of April in Paris? It's famous. And rainy, which most of your clients will be surprised to learn. September is a better month for your clients to visit; the weather's usually nice, and crowds are smaller. The main tourist season is June to September, peaking in July. But be sure to tell your clients that Parisians go on vacation in August (making for better lodging availability). The city empties, and the Riviera gets packed.

Getting Around

In Paris, it's against the law to honk your car horn except in an emergency; blink the headlights instead.

France has some of the finest transportation systems in the world. The **TGV** is a premier rail system with 200 mile-per-hour trains. For your clients who prefer to do their own driving, France has many good highways. Rental cars are easily available. And for flying within the country, **Air-Inter** is the national domestic airline.

What the TGV is to France, the **Metro** is to Paris. One of the world's great subways, the Metro is simple to use: Each station has a map and pushing a destination button lights up the best route. Paris buses are cheap but slow; the huge tour buses, though, give first-rate city tours. Taxis are a bit expensive and drivers can be selective about where they'll go. If your clients decide to drive in the city,

Climate at a Glance
NICE, FRANCE

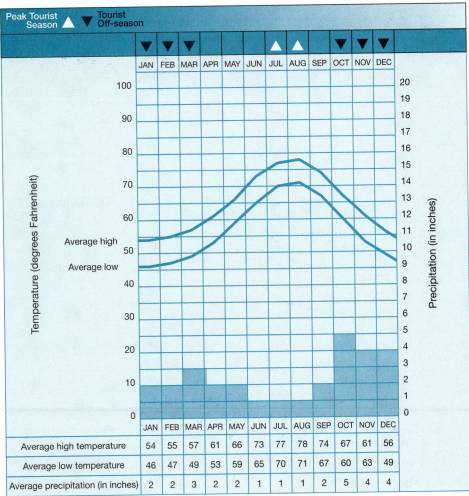

	JAN	FEB	MAR	APR	MAY	JUN	JUL	AUG	SEP	OCT	NOV	DEC
Average high temperature	54	55	57	61	66	73	77	78	74	67	61	56
Average low temperature	46	47	49	53	59	65	70	71	67	60	63	49
Average precipitation (in inches)	2	2	3	2	2	1	1	1	2	5	4	4

Figure 13-1

tell them they'll be dealing with aggressive drivers, non-existent lanes, and expensive parking.

France offers adventurous travel alternatives for you to sell to your clients. Balloon trips over farmland and châteaux are quite memorable. Barges—with cabins on board for tourists—cruise down the Loire and through the wine country. **River Seine** tours are a wonderful way to see Paris.

Important Places

Though Paris will most likely come to your client's mind first when thinking of France, the country offers many other regions, all of which should be considered when planning a trip to the country.

Paris

The French are fiercely proud of their culture and nowhere more so than in Paris. From history to arts, from architecture to haute cuisine and fashion, Paris has earned its reputation. The capital and largest city in France, the "City of Lights"

Paris's Musée Rodin has virtually all of the great master's works, including *The Thinker.*

Climate at a Glance
PARIS, FRANCE

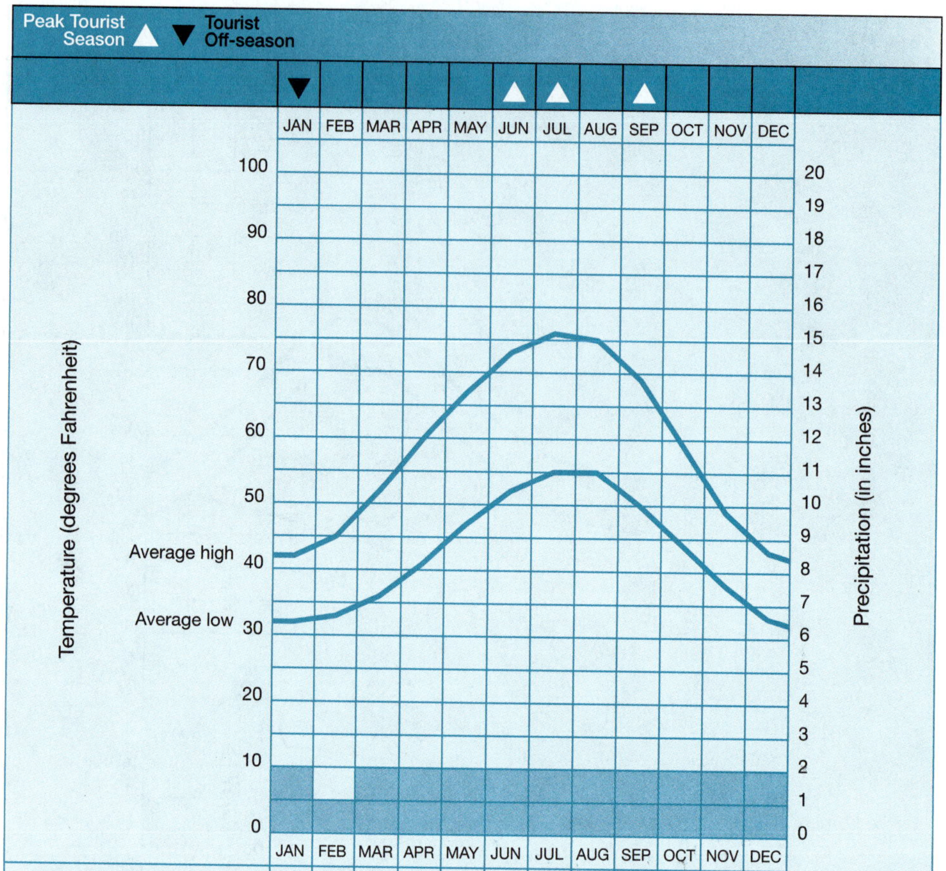

Peak Tourist Season ▲ ▼ Tourist Off-season													
	▼					▲	▲		▲				
	JAN	FEB	MAR	APR	MAY	JUN	JUL	AUG	SEP	OCT	NOV	DEC	
Average high temperature	42	45	52	60	67	73	76	75	69	59	49	43	
Average low temperature	32	33	36	41	47	52	55	55	50	44	38	33	
Average precipitation (in inches)	2	1	2	2	2	2	2	2	2	2	2	2	

Figure 13-2

is also the nation's business center and perhaps the most romantic city in the world.

The list of Paris attractions is lengthy. Among those you might recommend to your clients are:

- **The Eiffel Tower**, maybe the most famous icon of any city in the world. Built for the 1889 World's Fair, it rises high above the Seine and offers panoramic views.
- **Notre Dame**, the Gothic cathedral on the Île de la Cité, guarded by its stone gargoyles (best viewed by climbing up the staircase in one of the towers). Tell your clients to visit the nearby **Sainte-Chapelle** cathedral, whose stained-glass windows are renowned.
- **The Arc de Triomphe**, commemorating Napoleon's victories. The top offers a grand vista over Paris, especially down the **Champs-Elysées** boulevard to the **Place de la Concorde**.
- **The Paris Opera**, the ornate setting for *The Phantom of the Opera*.
- **The Louvre**, perhaps the greatest museum in the world. It houses such masterpieces as the *Mona Lisa*, *Winged Victory*, *Whistler's Mother*, and the *Venus de Milo*. A

Tours are offered of the sewers of Paris.

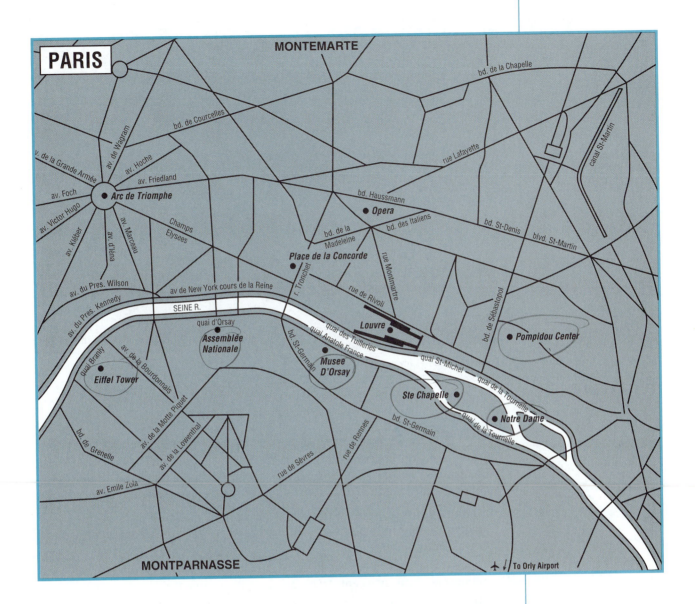

PARIS

MONTEMARTE

MONTPARNASSE

To Orly Airport

half-dozen other great museums exist in Paris: the **Centre Georges Pompidou**, with its modern art and bold exterior; and the **Musée d'Orsay**, a converted railway station with impressionist works, are musts.

You should counsel your clients to take the following **day trips** from Paris:

- **Versailles** [ver-SIGH], a sprawling, opulent palace with spectacular grounds.
- **Chartres**, one of the world's great medieval cathedrals, with its stained-glass windows.
- **Fontainebleau**, the home of Napoleon, Marie-Antoinette, and many others, with its beautiful gardens.
- **Reims**, at the northern tip of the wine country. Its Gothic cathedral is where most French kings were crowned.
- **Giverny**, with its gardens made famous by the painter Monet. (His home is here, too.)
- **Disneyland Paris**, east of Paris on the main route to Brussels, Belgium.
- **The Loire Valley**, best seen as a separate visit.

The foundations of the original Louvre Palace can be viewed in the Sully Wing.

Detail of the Eiffel Tower, Paris
Photo by C. J. Ghormley

Normandy

The area along the English Channel will forever be a monument to the World War II D-Day landing. Beyond that, Normandy is a place of green farmland and medieval architecture. Among the attractions you might suggest your clients visit are:

- **Omaha Beach**, the site of the Allied invasion, is made up of what were originally three separate beaches. It is often seen along with **Arromanches** and its invasion museum.
- **Rouen**, the "City of 100 Steeples," is famed for medieval architecture. Indeed, many of its fifteenth-century homes are still occupied.
- **Deauville** [doh-VEEL], a restored seaside resort, is to northern France what St. Tropez is to the southern Riviera. It has a mile-long boardwalk.
- **Honfleur** is an oft-painted, highly picturesque fishing port.
- **Bayeux** [bye-YOO] boasts a Gothic cathedral. The remarkable tapestry of the same name, housed in an adjacent museum, depicts the Battle of Hastings.
- **Mont-St.-Michel** is a stunning fortified abbey from the eleventh century—perched, like a spired silhouette, on a rock cut off from the mainland at high tide. Mont-St.-Michel also borders the peninsula of **Brittany**, with its many castles and strange, prehistoric monuments.

Across the English Channel is the British abbey, Mount St. Michael, which was modeled after Mont-St.-Michel.

The Loire Valley

Spread throughout the Loire River area are more than 100 majestic châteaux. The heart of the area is the charming town of **Tours**. Some châteaux offer *son et lumiere* (sound and light) shows at night. The sites you might recommend to your clients include:

Most Loire Valley châteaux close between noon and 2 P.M., as do many other French attractions.

- **The châteaux.** Among the most famous: **Amboise, Chambord, Blois, Villandry,** and **Azay-le-Rideau.** If your clients are rushing through the valley and have time to see only one château, suggest that they stop at the awesome **Chenonceaux.**

The chateau of Chenonceaux, on the Loire River
Photo by C. J. Ghormley

- **Saumur**, famous for its National Riding School, many wine cellars, and, of all things, a Mushroom Museum.

The Aquitaine Region

The Aquitaine (also called Perigord) is one of France's most diversified tourist centers. It's famous for its vineyards, Roman ruins, prehistoric cave paintings, and bastides (quaint towns built on hillsides). Recommend the following:

- **Bordeaux** [bor-DOE], a sophisticated port city of parks, salons, bistros, casinos, and beaches. (wine)
- **St.-Emilion area**, in the heart of Bordeaux's wine country. The medieval town of St.-Emilion, itself, is one of the most charming in all of France.
- **The Medoc**, another of the major wine regions, known for some of France's top vintages. More formal than St.-Emilion, many of the estates have extremely grand châteaux.

You should advise your clients to take the following **day trips** from the Aquitaine region:

- **The Dordogne** [door-DOI-ing] **River Valley**, with its prehistoric cave paintings. The most famous, at **Lascaux**, are now closed to the public, but an exact reproduction can be visited nearby.
- **Biarritz**, a lovely beach town near the Spanish border on the **Bay of Biscay**. It's one of Europe's few surfing venues.

The Pyrenees

In the lofty mountains that separate France from Spain are several ski resorts. The shrine of **Lourdes** is a mecca for Catholic pilgrims seeking cures and is one of the most visited sites in France. As with the Aquitaine, a number of bastides dot the hillsides. The city of **Toulouse**, called the "rose city," boasts Europe's largest Romanesque church. And Carcassonne is a huge, hulking medieval fortress of a

The French wine industry dates back to around 600 B.C.

Carcassonne
Photo by C. J. Ghormley

town—the largest in all of Europe. Within its walls is an impressive **Castle of the Counts**.

The French Riviera

The Mediterranean-hugging Riviera offers an unusual blend of features. Its stunning beaches, wonderful weather, superb dining, and many art galleries have long enticed the jet-setting elite. It's also the most popular spot for the French, themselves, during their July and August holidays. Towns and attractions of the Côte d'Azur that you might recommend to your clients include:

Except for a few private sandy beaches that visitors have to pay to use, the Riviera's beaches are quite pebbly.

- **Nice** [NEES], the largest city on the Riviera, is crowded but still charming. Fine museums are around Nice, including the **Musée National Marc Chagall**, **Musée Matisse**, and **Museum of Modern and Contemporary Art**.

- **Cannes** is famous for its international movie festival, beaches, and boardwalk. With casinos and nightclubs, it's trendy and perhaps a bit noisier than other Riviera towns.

- **St.-Tropez** is very chic, but beginning to get crowded and just a bit aged. The twentieth-century artwork housed in the **Musée de l'Annonciade** is excellent.

- **Cap d'Antibes** [CAHP dahn-TEEB] is for your clients who are looking for an especially luxurious seaside vacation. The nearby town has a **Picasso Museum**.

- **St.-Paul de Vence** and **Grasse** [GRAHS] lie in the hills above the Riviera. St.-Paul has many galleries, boutiques, fine restaurants, and the nearby **Maeght Foundation**, a world-class museum. Grasse is famous for its perfume factory.

You should advise your clients to take the following **day trips** from the French Riviera:

- **Marseilles** is 2,500 years old. This spirited city is quite attractive, though a bit scruffy on the edges. Many museums dot the city.

- **Monaco**, an independent principality close to the Italian border, is best known for its **Grand Casino**, and the **Monte Carlo Grand Prix** auto race held at the end of May. The road between Nice and Monaco goes through an area called the **Corniches**, a series of winding cliffside roads with spectacular sea views.

- The inland **Provence** [pro-VAHNS] **Region** features many spas, Roman structures, and **Avignon**—with its **Palace of the Popes** (where popes lived in the fourteenth century) and famous bridge.

The French Alps

Skiers love the Alps for their winter facilities, and admirers of scenery are likely to visit at any time of the year. Among the towns you might recommend to your clients are:

- **Chamonix** [shah-mo-NEE] (near **Mont Blanc**, one of Europe's highest mountains), a large, trendy resort town with spectacular views. There's also a casino.
- **Val d'Isere**, a charming village with fewer tourists. It's an ideal place for clients earnest about their skiing.
- **Grenoble**, the site of the 1968 Winter Olympics. Reachable from **Geneva**, Switzerland, it's one of the most picturesque towns in the Alps.
- Other world-class resorts, including Megeve, Tignes, and Albertville, site of the 1992 Olympics.
- Several charming cities, including Annecy (the Flower City) and lakeside **Evian** (of the famous spa and bottled water).

The Eastern Wine Country

France's legendary wine country extends all the way from near Reims in the **Champagne District**, southeasterly through the **Alsace** region, and down through **Burgundy** into the Rhône River Valley. Among its major attractions, from south to north: ˢ) most expensive wine

- **Lyon**, France's second largest city and a center of business and gastronomy. Nearby is **Perouges**, one of Europe's best preserved medieval villages. business city
- **Dijon**, another place of fine cuisine and the heart of Burgundy. Between Dijon and **Beaune** (a medieval town) are numerous wineries.
- **The Alsace area**, with its melding of German and French ambience. Here is the fabled "Route du Vin," a 75-mile-long drive through vineyards and mountains.
- **The Champagne District**, another region of vineyards and wine cellars. It's anchored by the city of Reims.

Possible Itineraries

You should suggest that first-time visitors spend a week in Paris—with day trips to Versailles, Chartres, and perhaps the Loire Valley. Recommend that seasoned clients put aside two weeks to visit a broader area. Starting in Paris, they could travel to the Loire, then continue down through the Aquitaine region, perhaps ending up in the Riviera.

Each area of France can easily sustain a five- to seven-day stay. In the winter, France offers the skiing splendor of the Alps and, in the summer, the pleasant beaches of the Riviera.

Lodging Options

The French pride themselves in having the best: haute cuisine, haute couture, great novelists, trend-setting artists. France's hotels are no different. Your clients can find some of the world's best here. In Paris, many hotels are on the Right Bank,

The TGV covers the 250 miles between Lyon and Paris in two hours.

especially the areas just off the Champs-Elysées and near the Opera. Among them are the world-class **Ritz**, **George V**, **Bristol**, **Crillon**, and **Plaza Athenée**. On the Riviera, the **Negresco** in Nice is an official national monument. Clients in the French Alps can choose such renowned places as the **Royal Club Evian** resort in Evian-les-Bains, **L'Imperial Palace** in Annecy, and **Hôtel Mont Blanc** in Megeve. And—for clients seeking the out-of-the-ordinary—in Biarritz, there's the **Hôtel du Palais** (Napoleon III's former residence).

Lodging ranges from deluxe to four-star down to one-star. Alternatives to hotels are abundant. In Paris, for instance, apartments can be rented for your clients. In the countryside, farmhouses, castles, manors, and monasteries have been converted to upscale lodging facilities and have banded together into a network called **Relais et Châteaux**.

Many North American hotel chains serve France. Among the other major chains are the deluxe **Sofitel**, **Meridien**, **Concorde**, and **Forte**. At the other end of the budget are the more economy chains of **Hôtel Campanile** and **Timôtel**. **Primôtel** and **Hôtel Mercure**, two moderate chains, also have a major presence in France.

Allied Destinations

France borders Spain, Andorra, Italy, Switzerland, Germany, Belgium, and Luxembourg. The Netherlands is just around the corner and Great Britain is right across the English Channel. Although closely related to France, Monaco is a principality of its own. Your client's France itinerary can be expanded to include any of these countries.

Cultural Patterns

The French are proud of their country's cultural heritage. Make sure your clients understand that this isn't limited to artistic endeavors, but to all French customs. A business client, especially, wouldn't want to commit a *faux pas* (literally, a false step).

- The French prefer somewhat formal greetings. Tell your clients to use such titles as Monsieur, Madame, and Mademoiselle. And a quick, simple handshake is all they need give—nothing flamboyant. Once a French person knows someone, he or she may give the traditional *kiss by* the cheek. (The cheek isn't kissed, but the air next to it.)

- The French are proud of their language. Although many speak English, tell your clients not to assume that they will. Your clients should ask, *"Parlez-vous anglais?"* not "Do you speak English?"

- Be sure that your clients are careful in their use of the O.K. sign when conversing with the French. The thumb and index finger together means *zero* here, almost the opposite of what a client may be trying to convey.

- Gift-giving should be done carefully. A business gift should not be embossed with a corporate logo; a handwritten note should accompany it; and flowers must be in an uneven number (not thirteen, though). Gifts that are intellectual or artistic in nature make a great impression on the French.

- Tell your clients that the French admire promptness. On the other hand, the idea of standing in line is somewhat foreign to them.

Factors That Motivate Visitors

Many of your clients know of France by its reputation. However, it's important to think about the reasons the country truly intrigues them. Among their reasons:

Motorhomes are an increasingly popular way to visit the French countryside.

Be aware of pickpockets—which include young children—in Paris.

Lunch, not dinner, is the Parisian's main meal.

Qualifying the Client
Paris

FOR CLIENTS WHO WANT	APPEAL			REMARKS
	HIGH	MEDIUM	LOW	
Historical and Cultural Attractions	▲			Superb museums
Beaches and Water Sports			▲	Must go to the Riviera
Skiing Opportunities			▲	Must go to the Alps
Lots of Nightlife	▲			Nightclubs are expensive
Family Activities		▲		Mostly sightseeing and Disneyland Paris
Familiar Cultural Experience			▲	
Exotic Cultural Experience		▲		
Safety and Low Crime		▲		Petty crime
Bargain Travel			▲	In the countryside
Impressive Scenery		▲		Mostly in the countryside
Peace and Quiet			▲	Sidestreets quiet
Shopping Opportunities	▲			Especially luxury items
To Do Business		▲		Especially Paris, Lyon, and Marseilles

Figure 13-3

- It's romantic.
- The cultural and artistic attractions are seemingly endless.
- The cuisine and wines are legendary.
- There are many airline flights into Paris.
- Easy public transportation makes it simple to get around.
- Winter skiing, especially in the Alps, is readily available.
- The beaches are trendy.
- Picturesque villages dot the countryside.
- The casino in Monaco offers gambling in sophisticated surroundings.
- Clients want to see the cutting edge of fashion and arts.
- There's great shopping.

Possible Misgivings

No matter how graceful France might appear, clients will still have concerns you'll have to address:

- "The French are rude." Parisians—like many big-city residents—can seem abrupt, but they're usually polite if treated with respect. Locals in the countryside tend to be more friendly.

Best time to see the Louvre's treasures: Monday and Wednesday evenings.

Thousands of rabbits live in the grasses around the runways at Charles de Gaulle Airport.

- "All there is in France is Paris." There's also the wine country, Loire Valley châteaux, Normandy memorials and architecture, the Riviera, and the Alps.
- "They don't speak English and are intolerant of French that isn't flawless." Most people in any way connected to tourism speak English and prefer doing so to dealing with a foreigner's French.
- "The French dislike Americans." Maybe true once, but far less so today. In fact, U.S. culture has become trendy.
- "Traffic in Paris is terrible." Public transportation is excellent, and there are many wonderful city motorcoach tours.
- "France is expensive." It's true that Paris and the Riviera (in spring and summer) are among the most expensive places in the world. However, bargains can be found (especially off-season). Other areas of France are generally more reasonable.

Sales Strategies

The diversity of France will allow you many ways to sell-up and cross-sell. Balloon trips offer a spectacular way to see the country. Staying in a château would be memorable for your client. Renting a car to drive through the countryside or booking train travel lets your clients see more than just the well-known highlights. Barge cruises, too, are a unique way of getting around. City tours of Paris will make that sprawling city more manageable. A few extra days added on to a Paris trip will allow the client to visit the châteaux country or other regions. Cruises allow you to easily combine a client's trip to, say, the Riviera, with visits to Italy and Spain. And don't forget to suggest the Concorde to upscale vacationers or businesspersons in a hurry.

The Tour de France bicycle race takes place in July.

Travel Trivia

Where the Famous Paintings Are

The Mona Lisa (Da Vinci)—The Louvre, Paris
The Starry Night (Van Gogh)—Museum of Modern Art, New York City
The Last Judgement (Michelangelo)—The Sistine Chapel, Vatican City
Syndics of the Cloth Guild (Rembrandt)—Rijksmuseum, Amsterdam
Three Musicians (Picasso)—Museum of Modern Art, New York City
The Artist's Mother (Whistler)—The Louvre, Paris
The Blue Boy (Gainsborough)—The Huntington Library, Pasadena, California
Campbell's Soup Can (Warhol)—Museum of Modern Art, New York City
Luncheon on the Grass (Monet)—Musée D'Orsay, Paris
The Last Supper (Da Vinci)—Santa Maria Delle Grazie Church, Milan, Italy

CHAPTER 14

Italy
Pisa and Pizza

How often have you heard a child confuse **Pisa** and pizza? Well, that child grows up and one day becomes a client. Even as adults, people think of Italy in terms of ancient ruins and pasta. The country, however, is much more; indeed, it's one of the richest experiences in Europe you can offer clients. Just pizza? Hardly. It's a banquet.

Italy is about the size of Arizona and is easily recognized by its famous boot shape. The country is so full of attractions that there's really no center point to the country's tourism. It could, in fact, be said that there are four Italys: First, there's northern Italy, with its mix of mountains, lakes, and the **Italian Riviera**; then comes the Italy of great cities, including the art, history, fashion, and commerce of **Venice**, **Florence**, and **Milan**; next are **Rome** and its environs, the country's political and cultural center; finally, there's southern Italy, with the area that surrounds **Naples**, as well as the islands of mountainous **Sicily** and of resort-lined **Sardinia**.

For Your Information . . .

Italy   FYI

CAPITAL: Rome

AREA (SQUARE MILES): 119,690

TIME ZONE: GMT +1

DRIVE ON: Right

POPULATION: 57,200,000

RELIGION: Roman Catholic

LANGUAGE: Italian

CURRENCY: lira

ELECTRICITY: 220 volts, 50 cycles AC

CAPSULE HISTORY: Rome settled, about 800 B.C.; Roman Empire falls, 476–493; France, Austria, and Spain control parts of Italy, 1494–1815; Italy unified, 1861; Mussolini dictatorship, 1922–1943; free elections, 1946; many government changes and controversies since.

For reference sources, tourist bureaus, and suggested lengths of stay, see the Appendices.

How Travelers Get There

The major international gateways into Italy are Rome's **da Vinci Airport** (FCO) and Milan's **Malpensa Airport** (MXP). Venice, Pisa, Florence, and Naples all handle shorter flights.

Alitalia (AZ) is Italy's national airline; of course, the country is also served by North American carriers. Flying time to Rome from New York is eight hours; from Chicago, nine-and-a-half hours; and from Los Angeles, twelve hours. Cruises also stop at dozens of Italian mainland and island ports. Indeed, Venice and Rome's **Civitavecchia** [chee-vee-tah-VEK-ee-ah] are two of the Mediterranean's busiest ports. Clients can also drive into the country from the north, often via trans-Alpine tunnels.

Weather Patterns

Who hasn't heard of "sunny Italy"? It's a well-earned reputation, but Italy's climate is a little more complicated than that.

Italy has three climate patterns. The northern Alpine area has cold winters but mild, sometimes rainy summers. The region between Milan and Venice has hot, sunny summers, but winters are chilly and misty. The rest of Italy is like California, with dependably hot, dry summers. Winters are mild, with changeable, unpre-

Climate at a Glance ────────────
ROME, ITALY

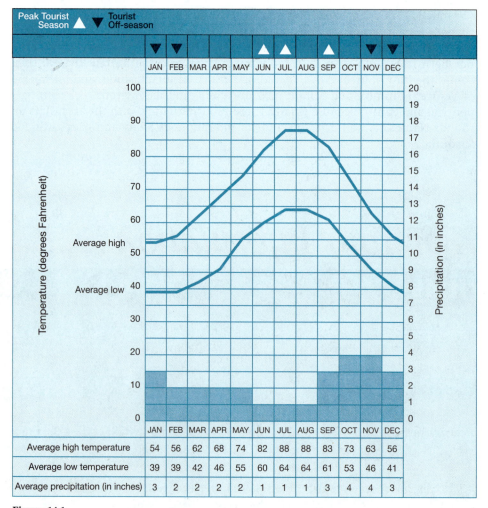

	JAN	FEB	MAR	APR	MAY	JUN	JUL	AUG	SEP	OCT	NOV	DEC
Average high temperature	54	56	62	68	74	82	88	88	83	73	63	56
Average low temperature	39	39	42	46	55	60	64	64	61	53	46	41
Average precipitation (in inches)	3	2	2	2	2	1	1	1	3	4	4	3

Figure 14-1

dictable weather. Occasionally in the summer and fall, a hot, humid wind (the *Sirocco*) blows from the south, while in the winter, a *fohn* wind from the north sometimes increases temperatures and lowers humidity in the Alps. Waters around Italy are pleasantly warm from May to October, but chilly the rest of the year.

June, July, and September are the busiest tourist months—with a small drop-off in major cities in August, when Italian tourists head for other countries or for the Riviera.

Getting Around

Italy's train system is inexpensive and fast, though efficiency is not its strong suit. The **Pendalino**, or **ETR**, is Italy's fastest train. Your clients can also fly between major cities—Alitalia and **ATI** are the main airlines. If clients prefer to drive, all major rental car companies are available; however, you should warn them that cities, especially Rome and Milan, are treacherous for "amateurs." Escorted city tours are the best bet. Taxis are fairly priced, but they can be expensive, and cab drivers have been known to play loose with the meters.

Eurail passes and Italy rail passes for unlimited train travel can be bought only in North America.

In Rome, the subway and bus system are very good, with many lines traveling beyond the city. Buses and trolleys are also good in Florence, but just so-so in Milan (which also has a subway).

A unique transportation system for your clients to experience, of course, is found in Venice. No cars are allowed in the city. (If you're driving into Venice, you must park in one of several huge garages on the city's perimeter.) Boats are the way to get around. The most famous, romantic, and expensive are gondolas. Water taxis are fast but also expensive. *Vaporetti* are slow water "buses," and *motoscafi* are express ones.

Important Places

Italy is a treasure-trove of diverse places for your clients to experience. Among its most popular cities and attractions are:

Rome

The Eternal City was originally built on seven hills along the **Tiber River**; its center today is on the river's left bank. Rome is the political, cultural, and religious heart of Italy. Among the attractions you might recommend to your clients are:

- **The Colosseum**, one of the most recognizable sites in the world. It's an ancient stadium where gladiators fought and Christians were martyred.
- **The Forum**, once the center of the Roman Empire and now a broad area of ruins.
- **The Spanish Steps**, a place where locals and tourists have gathered for centuries.
- **The Trevi Fountain**, of *Three Coins in the Fountain* fame. Throw a coin over your left shoulder and you'll return to Rome, says the legend.
- **The Pantheon**, renowned as a remarkably preserved domed Roman building.
- **Vatican City**, actually one of the smallest countries in the world. It's the site of **St. Peter's Basilica** and the overwhelming **Vatican Museum**. Michelangelo's *Creation* is painted on the **Sistine Chapel** ceiling, his *Last Judgement* on its wall.

The Forum is best viewed from Capitoline Hill.

Visitors to St. Peter's must not wear shorts.

Panthenon versus Pantheon.

Outside Rome are wonderful attractions. You should advise your clients to take the following **day trips**:

- **The Villa d'Este**, in **Tivoli**, is famed for its majestic, terraced water gardens and fountains. Nearby is **Hadrian's Villa**, a remarkable archaeological find.
- **Ostia Antica** contains the vast excavated ruins of an ancient port.
- **The Catacombs**—where early Christians secretly buried their dead—are located just outside town (there's a smaller version near the Via Veneto), as is the Roman Empire's principal road, the **Appian Way**.

underground cities

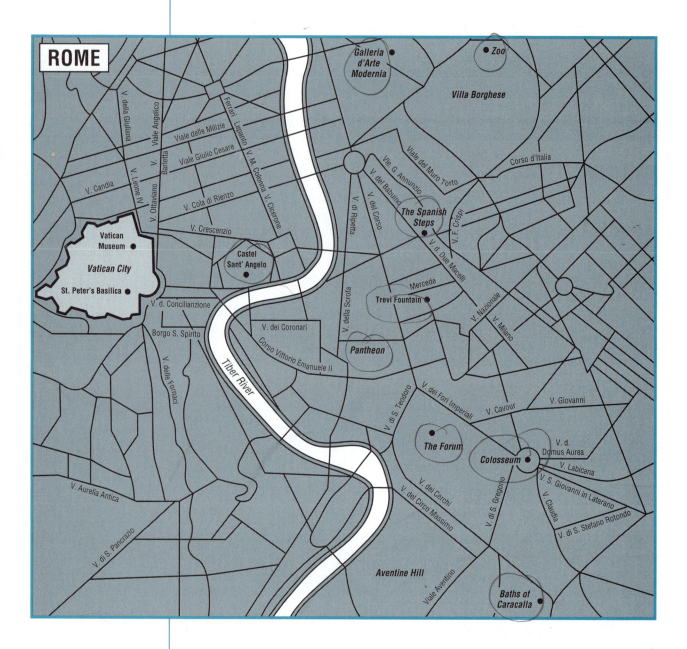

ROME

Galleria d'Arte Modernia

Zoo

Villa Borghese

V. della Giuliana

Viale Angelico

Ferrari Lepanto

Viale delle Milizie

V. M. Colonna

Viale Giulio Cesare

V. Cicerone

Corso d'Italia

Viale del Muro Torto

Vle. G. Annunzio

V. dei Babuino

V. del Corso

The Spanish Steps

V. Candia

V. Leone IV

V. Ottaviano

V. Barletta

V. Cola di Rienzo

V. di Ripetta

V. F. Crispi

V. Crescenzio

V. d. Due Macelli

Vatican Museum

Vatican City

Castel Sant' Angelo

V. della Scrofa

Mercede

Trevi Fountain

V. Nazionale

St. Peter's Basilica

V. Milano

V. d. Concilianzione

V. dei Coronari

Pantheon

Borgo S. Spirito

Corso Vittorio Emanuele II

V. delle Fornaci

Tiber River

V. di S. Teodoro

V. dei Fori Imperiali

V. Cavour

V. Giovanni

The Forum

V. d. Domus Aurea

Colosseum

V. Labicana

V. Aurelia Antica

V. dei Cerchi

V. del Circo Massimo

V. di S. Gregorio

V. S. Giovanni in Laterano

V. Claudia

V. di S. Stefano Rotondo

V. di S. Pancrazio

Aventine Hill

Viale Aventino

Baths of Caracalla

Venice

Venice could never happen again. One of the unique cities of the world, it was built on 118 islands connected by 160 canals and more than 400 bridges. Located on the Adriatic, the city is expensive, with polluted waters and crowds of tourists (over two million each year, for a city whose population is less than 80,000). Yet a walk through its back alleys opens up a quiet, romantic, fragile world of another time. Among the attractions you might recommend to your clients are:

The view from the tower at St. Mark's is best at sunset.

- **St. Mark's Square** is the city's busy gathering place. It's enclosed at one end by the fanciful **St. Mark's Basilica** and has numerous outdoor cafes, each with "dueling" orchestras.

- **The Doge's Palace**, near the basilica, reflects a Moorish architecture. One of the world's great collections of maps and globes is here.

- **The Bridge of Sighs** is the most famous of Venice's bridges. It's near the Grand Canal, the city's main waterway.

Arch of Constantine with the Colosseum in the background
Photo by C. J. Ghormley

- **The Lido**, a trendy, luxury beach resort, is on its own island across from the Grand Canal.

  You should advise your clients to take the following **day** or **half-day trips:**

- **Murano** is a touristy island where glass has been made for some 700 years. (The sales push to buy can be very aggressive.)
- **Burano** is the quaint island-capital of lace making.
- **Padua** is a town with charming medieval buildings.

Address an Italian by his or her first name only when invited to do so.

The Grand Canal, Venice
Photo by C. J. Ghormley

- **Verona** has noteworthy architecture and a renowned outdoor opera festival. "Juliet's balcony" is here as well. Verona can also be visited en route to Milan or the **Lake District**.

Florence — *one of the worlds universities in the world.*

A city of art and architecture, with a strong intellectual community, Florence is where the Renaissance began and flourished in the fifteenth century under the Medici family. It's located on the **Arno River** in the beautiful **Tuscany hills**. This international city remains, in many ways, a town of artisans and elegance. Among the many sites you could recommend to your clients are:

Duomo is an Italian term for any large cathedral.

- **The Duomo,** one of the most architecturally important cathedrals in the world. Started in 1256, it took 173 years to finish.
- **The Galleria delle'Academia**, with its very fine collection of Florentine art, best known for Michelangelo's *David*.
- **The Church of Santa Croce**, where Michelangelo is buried.
- **The Vecchio Palace**, an opulent "town hall" built by the Medicis.
- **The Ponte Vecchio**, the renowned bridge over the Arno, lined with gold and jewelry shops.
- **The Pitti Palace,** a lavish home of the Medicis, which is so large it houses several museums.
- **The Uffizi Gallery**, a Renaissance palace housing one of the premier collections of art in Italy.

Because of all the noise from mopeds, it's best *not* to have a room facing a busy street in Florence.

You should advise your clients to consider taking the following **day trips** from Florence:

- **Pisa** is world renowned, of course, for its leaning tower.
- **Fiesole** is a beautiful, old Etruscan village. Plays are still performed in the amphitheater, built in 80 B.C.
- **Siena** is a pretty Renaissance village in the hills of the Tuscany wine country.

The Italian Riviera

An extension of the French Riviera, the Italian Riviera offers stunning scenery along a mountainous coast. It's very crowded in the summer.

Portofino, an exclusive and high-priced resort town, is perhaps the most beautiful on Italy's Riviera. **Santa Margherita Ligure** and **San Remo** are popular beach resorts, as well. **Genoa**, a major Italian port, was the home of Christopher Columbus. It has many fine museums and Gothic architecture.

Christopher Columbus came from.

Milan

Milan is the financial, business, fashion, and publishing center of Italy. The city has a sophisticated cultural life and is the gateway to the Alps and Lake District. Among the attractions you might recommend to your clients are:

To see its intricate carvings, go up to the roof of Milan's Duomo.

- **The Church of St. Mary of Grace**, the location of da Vinci's *The Last Supper*.
- **The Duomo,** an intricate marble structure and one of the world's largest cathedrals. The square that fronts it is famous for its pigeons.
- **La Scala**, the world's most famous opera house. Its season runs from December to June.

[opera]

The Lake District

This Alpine region, near Switzerland, is one of magnificent scenery and charming villages. The many lakes and surrounding Alps are part of the same geologic development, which glaciers carved out millions of years ago. Among the towns you can recommend to your clients:

- **Como**, on Lake Como (one of two main lakes in the district), with wonderful architecture. Its structures include a 700-year-old palace and a Renaissance Gothic cathedral.
- **Stresa**, the largest town on the area's other major lake, Lake Maggiore, with extremely beautiful villas.
- **Bergamo**, a two-level city. Its main plaza is surrounded by stunning medieval buildings.

Not far from the lakes are the ski resorts of the Italian Alps. Among the favorites are beautiful **Cortina d'Ampezzo** and **Courmayeur**, the area's largest, with a very busy nightlife.

Aosta is off the tourist beaten path, but has a picture-perfect location.

Naples

Naples is crowded and a bit run-down. Though it may not be a place you would advise clients to visit, the region nearby offers fascinating attractions, including:

- **Mt. Vesuvius** and **Pompeii** had their histories intertwined in 79 A.D., when the volcano (now dormant, but potentially still active) erupted and buried the town. The ruins have since been excavated. A second nearby town, Herculaneum, was also buried. Like Pompeii, it has been uncovered and can be visited.
- **The Isle of Capri** is a trendy resort. Though there aren't many beaches, it's an area of charming villages and great vistas. Here, too, is the **Blue Grotto**, a watery cave of eerie azure light.
- **Sorrento** has long been one of the most beautiful, romantic, and famous resort areas in Italy. Unfortunately, it's becoming rather crowded, worn, and expensive.
- **Amalfi Drive**, along the peninsula of the **Amalfi Coast**, offers breathtaking views past cliffs, coves, and villages.

Sicily   Sisili

Located just off the toe of Italy's boot, this beautiful island is mountainous and dry. It's excellent for water sports and has very good beaches. In the winter, there's also some good skiing in the mountains. Among its attractions: **Mt. Etna**, a still-active volcano; **Taormina**, a charming and popular beach resort town; and **Palermo**, the seaport capital, with ancient buildings and Norman palaces.

Positano is a resort located on a pyramid high above the water on the Amalfi Coast.

Sardinia

About 100 miles off Italy's west coast, this sparsely populated island is known for its beaches and water sports, especially fishing. The beautiful countryside and picturesque villages hold remnants of many ages. Easily the most popular beach area on Sardinia is **Costa Smeralda** (the Emerald Coast), one of the trendiest luxury resorts in all of Europe.

Possible Itineraries

Advise first-time clients to visit Rome and the great cities of Italy, perhaps Venice and Florence. A week is the bare minimum. Seasoned travelers will probably want to explore the other areas of the country, as well as spend perhaps a bit more in-depth time in the major cities. A week concentrated in any one area, such as the Lake

Buy detailed guidebooks for each city. Many of Italy's attractions have poor signage and no guided tours.

Many attractions and most businesses, except restaurants, close between 1:00 P.M. and 3:30 P.M., but stay open as late as 8:00 P.M.

District or the region south of Rome, is just about right. Two weeks in Italy, however, would give your client ample opportunity to visit several major regions and cities.

Lodging Options

Your client will have a wide range of hotel chains to choose from in Italy. At the expensive end are such organizations as **CIGA** [CHEE-gah], **Atahotels**, **Starhotels**, and **Jolly Hotels** (some of whose hotels are more moderately priced than others). Many North American chains are also represented in Italy.

Hotels in Rome are concentrated around the railroad station, the Spanish Steps, and the Via Veneto (famed for its many sidewalk cafes). In Venice, most are along the Grand Canal and near St. Mark's Square. Hotels in Florence are mostly to the north, along or near the Arno River. On Sicily and Sardinia, most of the accommodations are on the northern parts of the islands.

Request rooms in the oldest part of the Danieli.

Italy has several famous, luxurious hotels. In Rome, there's the **Hotel Hassler** and the **Hotel Excelsior**, both with superb locations. Venice has several renowned hotels, including the **Cipriani**, **Danieli**, and **Gritti Palace**. Outside of Florence is the **Villa San Michele**, a former monastery with a facade designed by Michelangelo. On Sardinia, hidden in a cove, is the opulent **Cala di Volpe**.

Although lower-rated hotels may present your clients with unwelcome surprises, Italy does offer wonderful alternative lodging, notably the chance to stay in old villas. Though some are expensive, many are moderately priced.

Allied Destinations

Although most of the country is surrounded by water, Italy is bordered on the north by France, Switzerland, Austria, and Slovenia. The lovely French island of Corsica is just off the west coast and the island-nation of Malta is to the south. Moreover, located as it is at the southern tip of Europe, Italy is also a perfect jumping-off point to Africa, across the Mediterranean Sea. Nearby are Morocco, Algeria, Tunisia, Libya, and Egypt. Note that many Eastern Mediterranean cruises start out in Venice, while Western Mediterranean cruises often begin at Civitavecchia.

St. Peter's Basilica, Vatican City
Photo by C. J. Ghormley

Cultural Patterns

Italy has a rich, exuberant culture, and many of your clients will feel comfortable here. However, the traditions can be quite different from those to which most North Americans are accustomed. Business clients should pay close attention to the customs with which they come into contact.

- If your clients will be spending time in the south, let them know that the daily pace is slower here than in the north.
- Dinner can be a long, social event, but, generally, lunch is the day's biggest meal. Your clients shouldn't rush their meal, and they should try their best to eat everything placed before them.
- When doing business, wear your finest clothes. In Italy, great clothing is a badge of success.
- It's appropriate for a guest to bring a small gift to an Italian home. However, be sure your clients are aware that chrysanthemums are funeral flowers.
- The North American gesture for one (the index finger raised) means two in Italy, since the thumb is counted as one.
- Don't eat fruit (except grapes and cherries) or cheese with your hands. Use utensils.

Extra tips are expected for most service-related jobs. Waiters should be tipped a few lire in addition to the service charge on the bill.

Factors That Motivate Visitors

In as diverse a country as Italy, it's important to understand precisely what your clients' motives are for going there. Among their reasons might be:

- Some of the world's best-known ancient sites are here.
- The food is familiar and wonderful.
- The country serves as a center for Christian religious pilgrimages.
- The culture is rich with opera, art, architecture, and history.
- There's the opportunity for water sports in summer and skiing in winter.
- There's great shopping.
- Many Americans have their cultural roots in Italy.
- Some of the world's finest resorts are here.
- Italy is a major departure point for cruises.

Trattorias are less expensive for dining than *ristorantes* and offer very good food.

Possible Misgivings

For all Italy's attributes, your clients will have specific concerns about the country that you'll have to address:

- "Everything's so expensive." Italy is indeed expensive; pre-booked tours can help a client manage expenses.
- "It's so disorganized." Book clients on an escorted tour, where the tour management will deal with whatever problems may arise.
- "There's a lot of crime." Most are petty offenses. But crime does happen and normal precautions must be taken.
- "It's so hot." Spring or fall offers nice weather. Send your clients then, or at any time to Italy's northern regions.
- "Italy suffers from terrorism." It's unlikely that a client will be affected by the rare incidents. But if it's a concern, the client should at least be booked on an air carrier that inspires confidence.

Best time to see the Sistine Chapel: at opening (bypass the museum, go straight to the Chapel, then work your way back) or in February.

FOR CLIENTS WHO WANT	APPEAL			REMARKS
	HIGH	MEDIUM	LOW	
Historical and Cultural Attractions	▲			Cities are virtual museums
Beaches and Water Sports		▲		Especially Riviera and Sardinia
Skiing Opportunities	▲			Northern Alps
Lots of Nightlife		▲		Especially Rome
Family Activities		▲		Mostly sightseeing
Familiar Cultural Experience			▲	
Exotic Cultural Experience	▲			
Safety and Low Crime			▲	Petty crime frequent
Bargain Travel			▲	Venice especially costly
Impressive Scenery	▲			Especially countryside and the north
Peace and Quiet		▲		Countryside
Shopping Opportunities	▲			Designer items, glass, gold, jewelry, high fashion
To Do Business		▲		

Figure 14-2

- "The people are rude, and the men are aggressive." Your client should be booked in better hotels or on escorted tours.
- "Driving in cities is dangerous." Suggest that they take the fine public transportation.

Sales Strategies

Italy offers unique selling avenues for you in working with your clients. With city driving so treacherous, you might consider booking city tours for them in advance and offering train transportation to them. For that matter, with so many different attractions in Italy, escorted tours or day trips can be excellent ways to see the country. So, too, are cruises, which often call on Italy's less visited areas (for example Sicily and Sardinia) before continuing on to other countries.

If clients are staying at a beach resort or island, you might set up a boat tour for them along the coast. Lodging in villas ranges from inexpensive to costly, but all offer a way to help make Italy memorable. Hotels along Venice's Grand Canal or with views in Florence may be expensive, but recommend them anyway; their drama will cap off any client's trip.

The best buys in Italy are leather, jewelry, and textile goods.

CHAPTER 15

Spain and Portugal
Everything Under the Sun

Have you ever been faced with so many choices, you didn't know where to start? That's the problem with **Spain**. There are so many different cultures, climates, and topographies that you'll have to really know the country to recommend the right region to your clients.

The one constant: all the sunshine. Though the climate changes in Spain from area to area, it's almost always a case of good, better, best. And though the fact may not be well-known in North America, it is in Europe: Spain (along with Italy) is one of the top vacation destinations for European tourists.

Actually, there may be a logical place to start in Spain: right in the center of the map, at **Madrid**, the country's capital. If your client viewed Spain as if it were a clock, one o'clock would be **San Sebastian** (center of the **Basque** region). Moving around the country clockwise, there's the beach resort of **Costa Brava**, followed by charming **Barcelona**. Off the coast in the **Mediterranean Sea**, at three o'clock, are the **Balearic** [bah-lee-AIR-ik] **Islands** of **Majorca** [mah-YOR-kah] and **Ibiza**.

There are two more exquisite beach regions: the **Costa Blanca**, along Spain's southeastern coast, and the **Costa del Sol**, along the southern coast. Then comes the mountainous area that your clients most likely imagine when they think of Spain—the **Andalusian** region, the home of bullfighting and flamenco. Centered in **Seville**, this area also includes **Granada**.

Spain is about the size of Arizona and Utah together. It is also, in fact, only one part of what's known as the **Iberian Peninsula**; **Portugal** occupies the remainder. Bordering Spain on the west, Portugal is the size of Indiana. It, too, has its own beach resort area: the less-developed **Algarve** [all-GARVE-ah], on the southern coast. The capital of Portugal, **Lisbon**, rests up against the **Atlantic Ocean**. Several Spanish- and Portuguese-controlled islands lie far offshore in the Atlantic. The Portuguese **Azores**, 800 miles west of Lisbon, are gentle islands with a few spas and beach resorts. The **Madeira Islands**, also Portuguese, are farther south— 400 miles west of Morocco. And Spain's **Canary Islands** are southwest of the Madeiras.

In major tourist areas, English is spoken by many. Elsewhere, however, it's far less common; the national languages of Spanish (in Spain) and Portuguese (in Portugal) predominate.

For Your Information . . .

CAPITALS: Spain: Madrid
         Portugal: Lisbon

AREAS (SQUARE MILES): Spain: 197,897
                 Portugal: 35,387

TIME ZONE: Spain: GMT +1
         Portugal: GMT +0

DRIVE ON: Right

POPULATION: Spain: 39,700,000
           Portugal: 9,800,000

RELIGION: Roman Catholic

LANGUAGES: Spain: Spanish
           Portugal: Portuguese

CURRENCIES: Spain: 1 peseta = 100 centimos
            Portugal: 1 escudo = 100 centavos

ELECTRICITY: 220 volts, 50 cycles AC

CAPSULE HISTORY: **Spain**: Part of Roman Empire, 201 B.C.; barbarians invade, 412; Moslems invade, 711; last Moslems defeated, 1492; defeat by British of Spanish Armada, 1588; republic declared, 1931; civil war, 1936–1939; Franco rules, 1939–1975; parliamentary system takes effect, 1982.
Portugal: Independence from Spain, twelfth century; world power, 1433–1581; republic, 1910.

For reference sources, tourist bureaus, and suggested lengths of stay, see the Appendices.

How Travelers Get There

The major gateway into Spain is Madrid's **Barajas Airport** (MAD), served by several North American carriers and **Iberia** (IB), the Spanish national airline. Flights originate from New York and Boston (each of which takes six-and-a-half hours), Chicago and Miami (both of which take eight hours), and Los Angeles (which takes eleven hours). In addition, several carriers fly into **Malaga Airport** (AGP) on the Costa del Sol, and into **Barcelona Airport** (BCN).

Flights to **Portela Airport** (LIS) in Lisbon can also be booked on the Portuguese national airline, **TAP Air Portugal** (TP), and on a few North American carriers.

Tourists can also access the Iberian Peninsula from France via railroad and highways. Many ships end (or begin) their Western Mediterranean cruises in Barcelona. Several lines sail regularly from Great Britain, down Europe's Atlantic coast, to ports in Portugal and Spain.

Weather Patterns

A hot, dry wind, called the *leveche,* sometimes blows from Africa across southern Spain and Portugal.

Most of Spain is very warm and dry in the summer, but during the rest of the year, three separate patterns occur. In the north and northeast, winters are a bit rainy, with plenty of snow in the mountains. Central Spain (where Madrid is located) has chilly winters, with frequent showers. (After all, the rain in Spain stays mainly on the plain. . . .) The coastal areas and Balearic islands have a climate similar to

Climate at a Glance
MADRID, SPAIN

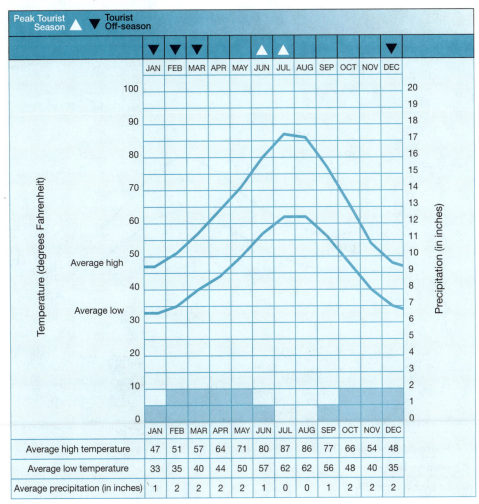

| Peak Tourist Season ▲ | Tourist Off-season ▼ | | | | | | | | | | |

	JAN	FEB	MAR	APR	MAY	JUN	JUL	AUG	SEP	OCT	NOV	DEC
Average high temperature	47	51	57	64	71	80	87	86	77	66	54	48
Average low temperature	33	35	40	44	50	57	62	62	56	48	40	35
Average precipitation (in inches)	1	2	2	2	2	1	0	0	1	2	2	2

Figure 15-1

southern California, with mild, occasionally rainy winters and hot, dry weather the rest of the year (when tourism is heaviest).

Portugal's climate has less temperature variation year round, with more rain in the winter than in Spain (especially as one goes farther north). Water temperatures along the Algarve are warmer than on Portugal's Atlantic Coast.

Getting Around

Spain is the second largest country in Europe (after France). Therefore, your clients may do better to fly from one area to the next, especially since the highway and railroad systems aren't quite as extensive or efficient as in some other European countries. Iberia and **Aviaco** (AO) have connections among thirty cities and offer economy plans that can be bought only in North America. The Spanish national railway uses good equipment only on the high-speed, long-distance **AVE** routes. Shorter runs can be slow and uncomfortable.

Trains in Portugal, however, are generally modern and comfortable. The many daily runs on the pretty ride from Lisbon to the Algarve can get crowded. There's also a connection between Lisbon and Madrid. Buses are quite comfortable in

Spain's unlimited rail passes are available only in North America.

Climate at a Glance
LISBON, PORTUGAL

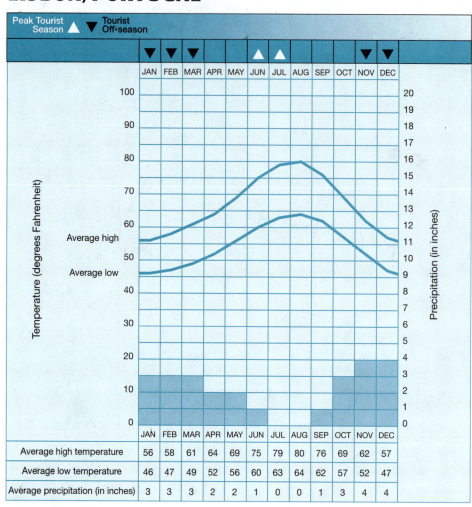

Peak Tourist Season ▲	▼ Tourist Off-season											
	▼	▼	▼			▲	▲			▼	▼	
	JAN	FEB	MAR	APR	MAY	JUN	JUL	AUG	SEP	OCT	NOV	DEC
Average high temperature	56	58	61	64	69	75	79	80	76	69	62	57
Average low temperature	46	47	49	52	56	60	63	64	62	57	52	47
Average precipitation (in inches)	3	3	3	2	2	1	0	0	1	3	4	4

Figure 15-2

Portugal. If your clients want to drive themselves, rental cars in both countries are widely available—though recommending a self-driving trip may not be prudent: Portugal and Spain have high accident and car break-in rates.

Cruises are a good way to see many of Spain's and Portugal's coastal and off-shore sites, usually in combination with other European countries. In addition to Barcelona and Lisbon, ships call on the Balearic Islands, **Valencia**, the Costa del Sol, the Madeiras, and the Canaries (the latter two often in combination with Morocco).

In Madrid, there's a good, inexpensive bus system and a fine Metro subway. Taxis are low priced, but warn your clients to steer clear of unlicensed cabs. Barcelona's buses and Metro are well run. Lisbon's subway, the Metropolitano, is good but not extensive. Taxis in Lisbon are reasonably priced.

Important Places

Each region of Spain is virtually a world of its own. And Portugal, though closely related, has its own unique charm and beauty. These countries offer a wealth of interesting cities and attractions.

Reservations should be made for the crowded Lisbon-to-Algarve train well in advance.

Over 3,000 feasts and festivals take place each year in Spain.

San Lorenzo de El Escorial, Spain
Photo by C. J. Ghormley

Madrid

The largest city in Spain and its capital, Madrid is the center of Castilian culture. Free enterprise, new personal freedoms, and burgeoning arts and industry have revitalized this beautiful and strong city. Among the attractions you might recommend to your clients are:

- **The Prado,** one of the world's premier and most influential museums. Its collection of Spanish art may be unrivaled.
- **The Plaza Mayor**, an imposing square in the city's Old Madrid section.
- **The Royal Palace**, once home to King Charles III, and today an art museum with one of the finest medieval arms exhibits in the world. A sound-and-light show takes place on summer nights.

You should advise your clients to take the following **day trips** from Madrid:

- **San Lorenzo de El Escorial**, an awesome monastery and palace. This sprawling, sixteenth-century edifice is thirty miles northwest of Madrid.
- **Ciudad Real**, the city and region south of Madrid, known as **La Mancha**. Here are the windmills that Cervantes's Don Quixote made famous.
- **Toledo**, a multi-cultured settlement of Spanish history. The beautiful town was the home of the painter El Greco. Its **Alcazar fortress** was where the legendary leader, El Cid, was reputedly stationed.
- **Segovia**, a town famous for its imposing castle and Roman aqueduct.

San Sebastian

Built on three hills, San Sebastian lies at the heart of the picturesque Basque region, near the French border. The area is known for excellent cuisine—the city even has its own gastronomic academy. San Sebastian has fine beaches, an elegant casino, and is a popular summer resort. It's an excellent base for exploring the Basque country. Among the **day trips** you should advise your clients to take are:

Most signs in Barcelona are in two languages: Catalan and Spanish.

- **Pamplona**, a charming, hilly village best known for the famous **"running of the bulls"** in July.
- **Bilbao**, a port city on the **Bay of Biscay**, with a Gothic cathedral and many museums. Most noteworthy: the new, architecturally daring **Guggenheim Museum**.
- **Guernica**, made famous by Picasso's painting, memorializing the town's devastation in the Spanish Civil War.

Barcelona *architecture, food, music, art*

The second largest city in Spain, Barcelona was once a major seaport. The harbor has been renewed, and the city today is also a thriving business center and the heart of the distinctive Catalonian culture. This is a city of diverse art museums, unusual architecture, fine music, and excellent food.

The attractions you might recommend to your clients are:

- **The Picasso** and **Miro Museums**, with collections that span the careers of each of these great artists.

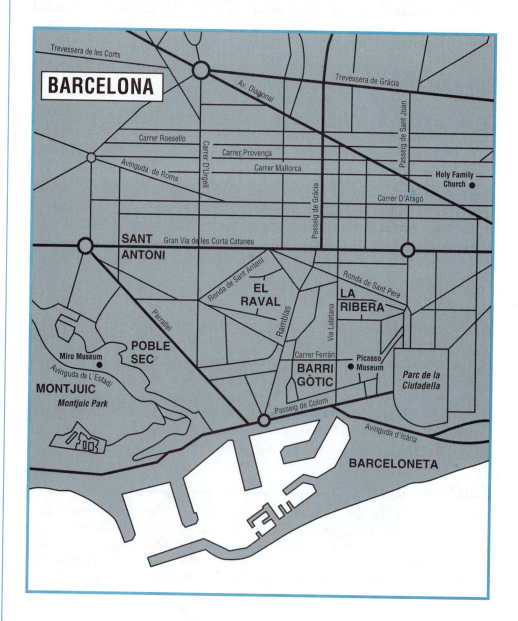

- **The Ramblas**, one of the great walking streets of Europe, with many little restaurants and shops.
- **Barri Gotic**, the old Gothic quarter, with fourteenth-century buildings and churches.
- **Montjuic Park**, with dramatic structures and gardens from the 1929 World's Fair and the 1992 Olympics.
- **The Holy Family Church**, a wonderfully bizarre edifice by architect Antonio Gaudi (who fashioned several other odd, striking buildings in Barcelona).

You should advise your clients to take the following **day trips** from Barcelona:

- **Montserrat** is the mountainous site of a monastery where pilgrims have come for 800 years. Housed here is a famous statue, the **Black Madonna**. *has volcano*
- **Andorra** is a charming, tiny country in the nearby Pyrenees, with great shopping buys.

Gaudi never created a blueprint for the Holy Family Church. He worked from a few rough sketches and simply instructed workers on what to build as they went along.

Holy Family Church, Barcelona, Spain
Photo by C. J. Ghormley

Costa Brava

Hire a car and driver to get around Costa Brava or Majorca; the roads can be treacherous. Rates are relatively reasonable.

Among the beaches of this popular resort that you can suggest to your clients are busy **Lloret de Mar**, the more isolated **Playa de Canyelles**, hectic **Tossa de Mar**, and luxurious **S'Agaro**. Other Costa Brava attractions include:

- **Ampurias** has excavation sites with rare Phoenician ruins. There's also an impressive archaeological museum.
- **Figueras** houses the **Dali Museum**, ingeniously converted from an old castle.

Balearic Islands

This group of islands is best known for the trendy and touristy resort island of Majorca. However, another island, Ibiza, is usually less crowded, more off-beat and relaxed, with a mix of jet-setters and artists. **Menorca** and **Formentera** are also in the Balearic group; their tourism is very low-key. Lodging is plentiful; there are twice as many hotel rooms in the Balearics as in all of Portugal.

Costa Blanca

Mayonnaise was invented on Menorca.

The second of the mainland beach resorts, Costa Blanca is to the south of Barcelona. At its center is the popular beach town of **Alicante**. The Costa Blanca is one of Spain's driest regions; it enjoys more than 3,000 hours of sunshine a year.

Costa del Sol

Located on the south coast, the Costa del Sol is one of the preeminent beach resorts in Europe. Highly developed with condominiums and high-rises, the area is known for having a very busy nightlife. Among the attractions you might recommend to your clients are:

- **Malaga**, the transportation center of the area, is **Picasso's birthplace** and home to the Malaga wine vineyards. There's also the **Museo de Bellas Artes**, with its diverse collection, including works by Picasso, El Greco, and Murillo.
- **Torremolinos** is the most popular (and crowded) beach town in the region.
- **Marbella**, the trendiest and most luxurious of the resorts, has been able to keep much of its old-world architecture.
- **Nerja** became famous in 1975 when two children discovered its underground prehistoric caves.

Not far from Costa del Sol are Granada and Seville. Your clients can visit them as day trips, but these cities are more commonly seen as part of a trip to Andalusia.

Andalusia

This mountainous region is the land of flamenco dancing, bullfighting, and lavish Moorish palaces. Among the cities and attractions you might recommend to your clients are: *Has a lot of moor influence (kind of a religion)*

- **Granada** is where your clients will find one of Spain's great structures, the **Alhambra**, a spectacular fortress and palace graced by flowing gardens.
- **Cordoba** is home to **La Mezquita**, a magnificent Moorish mosque so huge that a cathedral was later built inside it.
- **Seville** has a fifteenth-century cathedral that is the world's largest Gothic structure. The **Reales Alcazar** is a fortress remodeled to look like the Alhambra.

Lisbon

The capital of Portugal has an ancient history—possibly going back to the time of Ulysses, whom legend says founded the city. However, Lisbon is also in many ways relatively new. In 1755, an earthquake devastated much of the town, and it's since then that it was rebuilt. Lisbon is an easygoing place, gentle and less expensive than Madrid. Among the attractions you might recommend to your clients are:

- **The Alfama** and the **Barrio Alto**, famous for their cobbled streets and ancient medieval buildings. **The Baixa**, below them, is Lisbon's main shopping district.
- **Belem**, a riverside district that features the landmark **Tower of Belem** and the white marble **Jeronimos Monastery**, a striking building whose sea-inspired architecture is unique to Portugal.
- **St. George's Castle**, a huge structure atop the city, with ten towers and beautiful gardens.
- **Estoril**, a major seaside resort about fifteen minutes from Lisbon.

Monument to the Discoveries, Belem, Portugal
Photo by William and Marie Rourke

Though small, Portugal's seafaring tradition enabled it to have a worldwide empire.

You should also advise your clients to take a day trip to picturesque **Sintra**, in the middle of the Serra de Sintra mountains. Here, your clients will find the **National Palace** and the sprawling **Peña Palace**, with its extravagant 500-acre gardens.

The Algarve

The beaches of this south-coast resort area are quainter and quieter than those of Spain, though tourism to the region is escalating fast. Surrounded by high cliffs, the region is one of the most popular in Portugal. Its air gateway is the town of **Faro** (FAO). Among the towns your clients might enjoy are:

- **Lagos**, a walled seaside village with a rich history. It has wonderful beaches that are getting a little touristy.
- **Sagres**, a historical navigation center. Vasco da Gama, Magellan, and Diaz all studied here.
- **Portimao** has fine beaches. It has an active fishing trade and is fairly crowded.
- **Albufeira**, perhaps the busiest of the resorts. It's faster paced and has more of a nightlife.

Possible Itineraries

Your counseling skills will come in handy when planning trips to Spain and Portugal, since clients will face a wealth of choices. First-time visitors might enjoy a week that starts in Madrid before heading down to Seville and Granada or, instead, over to Barcelona. A few days could be added for one of the adjacent beach resorts. Return travelers could easily spend two weeks exploring: adding Portugal to a trip to Madrid, Seville, and the Costa del Sol; or, including the Basque country with a trip to Madrid, Barcelona, and the Costa Brava. Furthermore, any beach resort or Balearic Island would make a wonderful one-week visit, often as part of a cruise.

Lodging Options

Spain offers a wide range of accommodations for your clients; however, the lower-rated hotels might be less plush than what your clients are seeking. Many of the deluxe hotels are costly, but very special.

Madrid's most famous lodging is the **Hotel Ritz**, an extraordinary Edwardian-style property. In Seville, there's the classically elegant **Alfonso XIII**. Arguably the most opulent hotel in the country is **Hostal de la Gavina**, high on a cliff in S'Agaro on the Costa Brava. Giving it a run for its money is the grand **Hotel Hacienda**, with a stunning view of the coast, 600 feet up on Ibiza. In Barcelona is another elegant **Ritz**, as well as the old-world luxury of **Avenida Palace**.

The following chains offer the most lodging options in Spain: **Melia** (upscale), **Sol**, **NH**, and **Tryp**. Several North American and international hotel chains are also represented.

Alternative accommodations that your clients might find interesting are the **paradores**, converted castles and monasteries that are fairly priced. The top among these are **Parador Nacional San Francisco** in Granada, located actually inside the Alhambra; **Parador Nacional Gibralfaro** in Costa del Sol, which is small and has a breathtaking view of the Mediterranean; and the **Parador Nacional Almagro**, on the way from Madrid to Seville, in Almagro.

Most of the world's major chains have a few properties in Portugal. The country has a surprising number of opulent, five-star hotels; Lisbon's best known is the **Ritz**. An excellent alternative type of lodging here are the **pousadas**—inexpensive, government-sponsored inns, many of which are castles.

In Lisbon, the Feast of St. Anthony revelry on the night of June 12 and all day June 13 is as festive as New Year's Eve.

There are more people of Portuguese descent in Southern New England than there are in Lisbon.

Allied Destinations

At the very southern tip of Spain is British-controlled Gibraltar (and its famous rock), and across the Strait of Gibraltar is Morocco. Sandwiched between northern Spain and southern France is the tiny country of Andorra, which is a wonderful place for your clients to do some duty-free shopping.

Cultural Patterns

Though Western nations, Spain and Portugal present unique cultural challenges. Business clients, especially, should be sensitive to a few unique customs:

- Tell your clients that an invitation to a Spanish home is often made out of courtesy and shouldn't be accepted until one's host insists.
- Your clients should bring a small gift when visiting a Spanish home. Also inform them that they may receive a gift in return and that it should be opened on the spot.
- Your clients should be aware that many businesses close from 1:30 P.M. to 4:30 P.M. in Spain for siesta; in Portugal, they close from noon to 3 P.M.
- Dinner is served very late in Spain, where restaurants often do not open until 9 P.M. and don't fill until 11 P.M.
- Let your clients know that one's appearance is given meaningful attention in Spain and shouldn't be taken lightly; they should dress carefully and well for business occasions.
- After a meal, make sure your clients know to place their utensils together on their plate. To do otherwise would suggest that they weren't satisfied.
- Punctuality is not high among Spanish and Portuguese virtues. Yet the Portuguese *do* expect people to arrive on time for meetings (even if they start late).

> Nightlife is important in Spain. Take in some musical and dance performance, such as the flamenco.

Factors That Motivate Visitors

Among the reasons a client might be eager to visit Spain and Portugal are:

- The weather is sunny and beautiful.
- The countryside can be inexpensive, with great bargains for shopping and lodging. Portugal is even a greater bargain than Spain.
- The locals are extremely friendly.
- Both countries are easily accessible from North America.
- Water sports, beach activities, and cruise opportunities are readily available.
- The food is wonderful (though different from the Hispanic foods North Americans are accustomed to).
- There's rich cultural and artistic diversity to be found.

Possible Misgivings

Of course, as with any country, there will be concerns that your clients have about Spain and Portugal. Among the concerns you'll have to address are:

- "It's much too hot in summer." Northern Spain is cooler than the rest of the Iberian Peninsula. The heat elsewhere tends to be dry.
- "It's crowded in the summer." The beach resorts are indeed crowded in the peak seasons. Suggest that clients visit at a different time, find a less famous beach, or try another area of the country.

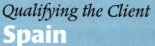

FOR CLIENTS WHO WANT	APPEAL			REMARKS
	HIGH	MEDIUM	LOW	
Historical and Cultural Attractions	▲			World-class museums
Beaches and Water Sports	▲			Both southern and eastern shores and islands
Skiing Opportunities		▲		Northern mountains
Lots of Nightlife		▲		Especially Madrid and Barcelona
Family Activities			▲	
Familiar Cultural Experience			▲	
Exotic Cultural Experience	▲			
Safety and Low Crime		▲		Much petty crime
Bargain Travel		▲		
Impressive Scenery	▲			Seascapes and countryside
Peace and Quiet		▲		Countryside
Shopping Opportunities		▲		Leather, lace, pottery
To Do Business		▲		

Figure 15-3

- "The Basque separatist groups commit terrorist acts." The few incidents that occur make the news. The chance of a client's being affected is slim.
- "It's expensive." Madrid and Barcelona—once bargains—have become pricey. However, many secondary Spanish cities and most of Portugal are less expensive.
- "There's a great deal of petty crime there." Unfortunately, there's crime in most big cities of the world. Normal precautions will reduce risk.

Sales Strategies

Lower-rated hotels can be unpleasant, so more highly regarded lodgings can make the difference between a successful and an unsuccessful trip. Deluxe hotels in Spain are expensive, but luxurious and special. Paradores can make a client's visit memorable. Because of the size of Spain, especially, tours can be appropriate. On the Costa Brava or Majorca, chauffeured cars are a much safer way of getting around the dangerous, winding roads. Motor boats or cruises along the coast and to the islands are also an enjoyable way of seeing the country.

Spain was once considered the wealthiest and most powerful country in the world.

CHAPTER 16

Germany
Romantic Roads

Germany is a culture-rich land of fairy-tale sights. Whether driving the Romantic Road or cruising the **Rhine River**, clients will find charming hamlets, delicate or imposing castles, and, in at least one city, people who—on occasion—still dress in medieval clothing. But you will, without question, have clients who resist going to Germany. This is a country that stirs up passions.

Once a single country, Germany was divided into two separate governments after World War II. It has now been reunified. German, of course, is the national language, though many Germans do have a good command of basic English.

When most of your clients think of Germany, the area they probably envision is **Bavaria**, in the south; with **Munich** as its center, this is the land of Alpine terrain, oom-pah bands, beer halls, and mountain skiing. Meandering north from

For Your Information . . .

Germany   FYI

CAPITAL: Berlin

AREA (SQUARE MILES): 137,787

TIME ZONE: GMT +1

DRIVE ON: Right

POPULATION: 81,900,000

RELIGIONS: Protestant, Roman Catholic

LANGUAGE: German

CURRENCY: 1 deutsche mark = 100 pfennigs

ELECTRICITY: 220 volts, 50 cycles AC

CAPSULE HISTORY: Germanic tribe, the Franks, controls Europe, 800 A.D.; Treaty of Verdun (843) and of Mersen (870) set German boundaries; Reformation, 1547; country divided by war, 1618–1648; Frederick rules Prussia, 1740–1786; Bismark dominates, 1862–1890; Germany reunified, 1871; World War I, 1914–1918; Hitler, chancellor, 1933; Holocaust begins, 1938; World War II, 1939–1945; Germany divided, 1945; communist influence reduced, 1989; reunification, 1990.

For reference sources, tourist bureaus, and suggested lengths of stay, see the Appendices.

Bavaria is the **Romantic Road**, so named because of its enchanting medieval villages. Running down the west side of Germany is the legendary **Rhineland**, with its stunning scenery along the Rhine river. This leads into the **Black Forest**, found in the southwest corner.

Cutting east to west across the country's center are the rolling hills and magical palaces of **Castle Road**. Nearby, in the middle of Germany, is **Frankfurt**. The flat, northern part of the country is less visited by foreign tourists; some clients may go to **Hamburg**, but it's mainly a business center. And **Berlin**, once divided, is regaining its status as Germany's preeminent city.

How Travelers Get There

You can take a shower at Frankfurt Airport's Terminal 1.

The major gateway into Germany is **Frankfurt Airport** (FRA). **Munich Airport** (MUC) and **Dusseldorf Airport** (DUS) are also used heavily. Secondary airports are in Berlin, Hamburg, and **Stuttgart**.

The national airline of Germany is **Lufthansa** (LH) and the country is also well serviced by North American carriers. Flying time from New York is seven-and-a-half hours; from Chicago, it's eight-and-a-half hours; and from Los Angeles, ten-and-a-half hours.

Hamburg (with several interesting attractions of its own) is an important port of arrival and departure for cruises to the British Isles, Scandinavia and the Baltics, and other European destinations. **Passau** is a launch point for Danube cruises into Eastern Europe.

Weather Patterns

Summer days are very pleasant, with temperatures in the 70s, but nights can drop to the 50s; temperatures in Bavaria can run even cooler. Winters are cold and often overcast or foggy, with rain and (especially in Bavaria) snow. Indeed, when the sun comes out, it seems as if every German heads outdoors. The fall and spring will be chilly but, in general, quite lovely and less crowded. Summers are the peak tourist season, whereas winters see a drop off in tourism. One exception: The Alpine area gets very busy in the winter with skiers. (See Figure 16-1.)

Getting Around

Germanrail Tourist Cards and Eurail passes can be bought only in North America.

Germany's rail system is one of the world's finest—so good that it often beats traveling between cities by air, though most major cities have excellent airport connections. Your clients can even get off their plane and get on a train, since rail terminals are located at several airports. The **autobahn** is a wonderful way to travel through Germany. On some of its stretches, speed limits are nonexistent or only "suggested." Major car rentals are widely available. Tourists who plan to buy a German car can order it before leaving North America and then drive the vehicle around Germany once they arrive.

On the autobahn, stay in the slower right-hand lanes—unless you're prepared to hurtle along at breakneck speeds.

Cruises down the Rhine have been popular for nearly a century. Cruises down the Elbe (from Hamburg to Dresden and on into the Czech Republic) provide a creative way to sightsee in eastern Germany.

In Munich, the U-Bahn is a very good subway system that connects with the S-Bahn local trains. There's also a well-run bus system. Taxis tend to be a little expensive. Berlin is usually reached by air, car, or train.

Important Places

Though most of your clients will think of Germany in terms of Bavaria, the country's many regions are diverse in their attractions.

Climate at a Glance
FRANKFURT, GERMANY

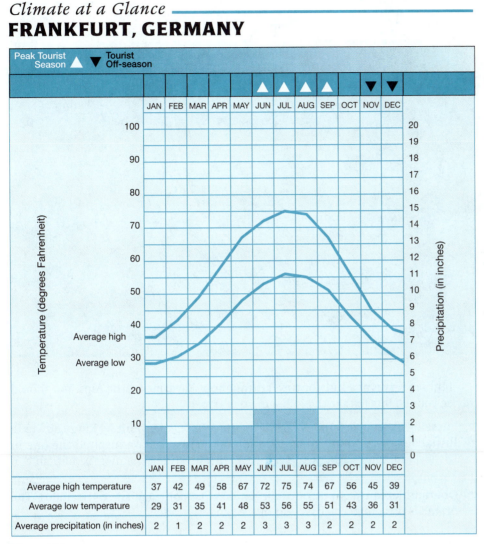

| Peak Tourist Season ▲ | | Tourist Off-season ▼ |

	JAN	FEB	MAR	APR	MAY	JUN	JUL	AUG	SEP	OCT	NOV	DEC
						▲	▲	▲	▲		▼	▼
Average high temperature	37	42	49	58	67	72	75	74	67	56	45	39
Average low temperature	29	31	35	41	48	53	56	55	51	43	36	31
Average precipitation (in inches)	2	1	2	2	2	3	3	3	2	2	2	2

Figure 16-1

Bavaria

This is what most of your clients will think of as Germany. Surrounded by the **Alps**, it's a robust area, with picturesque castles and medieval villages. The heart of Bavaria is the region's capital, Munich.

Like the rest of Bavaria, Munich is a lusty place, with beer halls, cabarets, and a lively nightlife, especially during the renowned Oktoberfest celebration. It's also, however, a sophisticated city with world-class opera and symphonies, high fashion, excellent museums, and important centers of learning. This 800-year-old riverfront city will appeal to almost all of your clients. Among the attractions you might recommend to your clients are:

- **The Marienplatz**, the heart of Munich, a town square with its famous glocken-spiel clock.
- **The Deutsches Museum**, the world's largest science and technology museum.
- **The Hofbrauhaus**, a renowned huge, lively beer hall.
- **Hellabrunn Zoo**, Europe's largest.
- **Nymphenburg Palace**, a seventeenth-century castle, with vast gardens and a museum. Located just outside town, it also houses a china factory.

Street names change often in Munich, and these names can be very long. Always carry a street map with you.

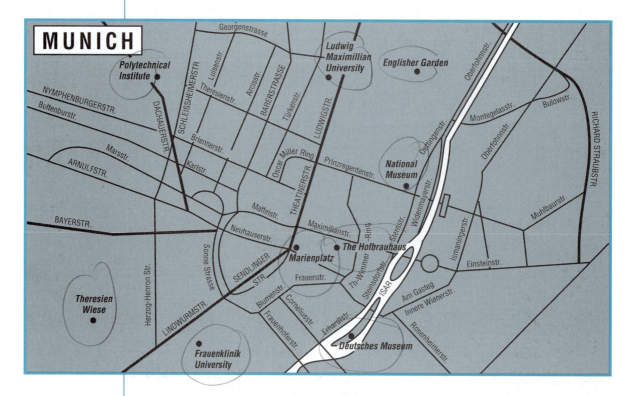

Munich serves as a hub for travel throughout Bavaria and the Alps. You should advise your clients to take the following **day trips:**

- **Fussen** [FEW-sen] is famous for the spectacular castles built by King Ludwig II. Just about every country has a castle that claims to have inspired the one in Disneyland, but **Neuschwanstein** [NOYSH-vahn-stine], the most remarkable of Fussen's castles, is *the* one.

- **Oberammergau** has put on its legendary passion play since the 1600s. The drama is presented the first year of every new decade.

In the seventeenth century, the villagers of Oberammergau vowed to stage the play every decade to give thanks for being spared during the Black Plague.

Neuschwanstein Castle
Photo by C. J. Ghormley

- **Dachau** is a stirring and disturbing memorial to the victims of Nazi concentration camps.
- **Garmisch-Partenkirchen** was the site of the 1936 Winter Olympics. It's a modern, yet charming, town—beautiful in summer, and a premier Alpine ski resort in the winter.

The Romantic Road

Beginning in the town of Fussen, in the heart of Bavaria, and winding north nearly 200 miles to **Wurzburg**, the Romantic Road is a string of medieval cities and ruins from the days of the Romans. Suggest that your clients visit it by car or on a motorcoach tour. Among the attractions you might recommend are:

- **Fussen**, with its remarkable collection of nearby castles.
- **Nordlingen**, a town where, on market day, the villagers often still dress in period clothes from the Middle Ages.
- **Dinkelsbuhl**, a walled city with fanciful houses.
- **Rothenburg**, perhaps the finest preserved medieval village in all of Europe.

The Castle Road

Stretching west to east, from **Mannheim** to **Nurnberg**, the Castle Road is a path of castles and fortresses dating to medieval times. It's also a fine wine district. The route can be driven or taken as part of a cruise along the **Neckar River**. More commonly, this area is visited as part of a shorter version, from Mannheim to **Heilbronn**. Among the towns you might recommend to your clients are:

- **Heidelberg**, home to one of the world's great universities. Its medieval castles and churches are the setting of the operetta *The Student Prince*.
- **Rothenburg**, the well-preserved medieval town.
- **Nurnberg (Nuremberg)**, remembered as the site of the World War II war-crimes trials. It's also famous for its gingerbread, toymaking, medieval structures, and massive Christmas Market in December.

In Rothenburg's oldest structures, tourists regularly bump their heads on overhead beams and door overhangs. The reason: People were much shorter when Rothenburg was built.

The medieval town of Rothenburg
Photo by C. J. Ghormley

Bridge across the Neckar River and Heidelberg Castle
Photo by C. J. Ghormley

Although not precisely on the Castle Road, you should also counsel your clients to take a day trip to **Worms**, a historical town associated with Attila the Hun and Martin Luther. It has the oldest synagogue in Germany and is the center for Liebfraumilch wine.

The Rhineland

The 825-mile Rhine is one of Europe's oldest trade routes. The Rhineland proper is generally considered to stretch from **Mainz** to **Koblenz**, though some feel it goes all the way up to **Cologne**. Winding its way past charming villages, castles high on cliffs, and vineyards, this river passes through the region from which many German legends spring. The Rhineland can be seen by train or car, but perhaps the most popular way of visiting this scenic area is on a cruise. Most cruises are run by **K-D River Cruises** and range from a half-day to three-to-six days (the latter covering more of the river). Among the towns you might mention to your clients are:

- **Cologne**, with its renowned twelfth-century Gothic cathedral and beautiful stained glass windows. (Its exterior was recently cleaned.)
- **Rudesheim**, a charming but touristy wine center.
- **Bonn**, the capital of the former West Germany and the birthplace of Beethoven.
- **Dusseldorf**, a fashionable city with an active nightlife and good shopping.

You might also want to suggest that your clients take a day trip to Frankfurt, the main air gateway to Germany. Although not a major tourist stop, Goethe's house is here, as are a few nice museums, a good opera company, and Gothic buildings.

The Black Forest

This beautiful region is rich with mountains, deep valleys, cool lakes, and dense forests. Beginning south of Frankfurt and continuing down to the thoroughly charming town of **Freiburg**, the area is particularly noted for spas, cuckoo clocks, and ski resorts. Among the towns you might recommend to your clients are:

Binoculars are essential for a Rhine cruise.

Lake Constance is also called Bodensee.

- **Stuttgart**, with its art and automobile museums, ballet and opera companies, and the nearby **Mercedes-Benz car factory**.
- **Baden-Baden**, one of the world's oldest, most famous, and trendiest spas, with an elegant casino. (When a city has the word *baden* in its name, it means that it has a spa.)
- **Furtwangen**, with its unique clock museum.

Berlin

This city sits in Germany's northeast corner, in the middle of what was East Germany. It's an active center of culture with a world-class orchestra, noted theaters, and fine museums. Among the attractions you might recommend to your clients are:

- **The Wall** (for what little is left of it), the infamous thirty-mile structure that once prevented East Berliners from going to West Berlin.
- **The Reichstag**, the original, ornate German parliament, now with interesting historical displays.
- **Charlottenburg Palace**, a grand, opulent structure built in the late seventeenth century.
- **East Berlin** (which used to be a separate area) with its many worthwhile attractions. Sights include **Unter den Linden**, the soul of the city and its main boulevard, lined with linden trees and many historic buildings; the **Brandenburg Gate**; the renowned **German State Opera**; and an entire island of museums.
- **Sans Souci Palace**, a monument to fanciful and elaborate excesses of the Rococo architectural style. Located in nearby **Potsdam**, Sans Souci sits in a charming park.

Eastern Germany

This formerly Communist region has now opened itself wide to tourism. For the moment, Eastern Germany's roads, restaurants, and hotels aren't up to the overall standards of the rest of Germany; but it's catching up fast. In addition to Berlin, Eastern Germany features two other intriguing places:

- **Dresden** is a jewel of a city. Firebombed into near-oblivion during World War II, Dresden rose from the ashes and is largely rebuilt. Its palaces, art galleries, and opera are first rate.
- **Leipzig**'s musical heritage is legendary. This graceful city is most often associated with composer Johann Sebastian Bach.

Possible Itineraries

Because it borders so many countries, Germany is often included as part of a larger trip. You should advise first-time visitors either to spend at least five days exploring the Romantic Road to Bavaria or to take a few days on or along the Rhine. These locations can, of course, be combined for a longer stay.

Return travelers may like to explore areas they haven't seen yet, such as the Black Forest or the Castle Road. A trip to Berlin would also be fascinating. You should keep in mind, too, that Germany is a very rich country and can easily be visited in-depth for two weeks on its own.

Lodging Options

Germany can be a fairly expensive country to visit and hotels are a large part of that cost. Germany's luxury chain is **Kempinski Hotels**. For clients looking for something less costly, **Queens**, **Dorint**, and **Arabella Hotels** are available. **Steigenberger**

During a famous speech, John F. Kennedy once said "Ich bin ein Berliner." Unfortunately, this actually translates to "I am a jelly donut."

A small German-English dictionary is especially useful when ordering from a menu; remember to bring one along.

hotels range from first class to deluxe. Quite a few North American chains are present as well. A voucher program called **Wundercheck** can be presold to your clients and can help them save money on lodging.

In Munich, hotels are clustered south and east of the railroad station. The **Bayerischer Hof** is a deluxe hotel, once used by King Ludwig I, though not quite as grand as it once was. Munich's **Vier Jahreszeiten** is one of Europe's most luxurious hotels. (An equally distinguished Vier Jahreszeiten can be found in Hamburg.) In Berlin, many hotels (including the noted, luxurious **Bristol Kempinski**) are near the **Europa Center**.

Germany offers assorted lodging options to book for your clients. Many castles have been converted into hotels; they're beautiful but can be expensive (the **Schlosshotel Kronberg**, near Frankfurt, is a prime example). **Gast im Schloss** is an association of somewhat reasonable castles that you might want to look into. In addition, spas (especially in the Black Forest) are popular; **Brenners Parkhotel** in Baden-Baden is almost legendary. For your clients on a budget, *pensions* offer pleasant and inexpensive lodging.

Allied Destinations

Germany is centrally located in Europe, which is one reason it's often combined on a vacation with other countries, both by land and by sea. It borders Denmark, Poland, the Czech Republic, Austria, Switzerland, France, Luxembourg, Belgium, the Netherlands, and the North Sea. You could expand your clients' FITs by adding any of these places, though Switzerland and Austria, because of their similar cultures and proximity to Bavaria, are the most logical choices.

Cultural Patterns

Located in the heart of the continent, Germany represents a rich mixture of Western European traditions and Eastern European ways of thinking. With the major changes this area has undergone in recent years, it's particularly important that your business clients are sensitive to its cultural diversity:

- Your clients should know that Germans tend to be somewhat reserved. First names should be used only when one has been given permission or knows the person well; if uncertain, your client should follow the lead of the person to whom he or she is talking.

- Germans often hold strong opinions and will challenge others to defend their own. Make especially sure your business clients are prepared to address questions that may arise.

- Punctuality and thoughtfulness (for example, acknowledging a birthday) are very important to the Germans.

- Warn your clients that it's considered rude to talk while one's hands are in one's pockets.

- Prepare your business travelers for an unusual custom: To show their appreciation at the end of a meeting, Germans will often bang their fists on the table.

Factors That Motivate Visitors

Knowing what your clients want will help you plan their trip. Among their reasons for wanting to visit Germany might be:

- Bavaria's scenery is spectacular.
- Germany is very accessible, clean, and organized.
- The country is filled with cultural riches and architectural landmarks.

Munich's Oktoberfest begins in late September and runs through the first week of October.

The Kiel Canal in Germany, which connects the Baltic and North Seas, carries more traffic than any other canal in the world.

- The people are friendly.
- The food is wonderful and hearty.
- Hamburg is a major cruise port and the Rhine is an important cruise waterway.
- There are lively festivals.
- There are great winter sports, especially skiing.

Possible Misgivings

As spectacular as Germany is, some clients may feel reservations toward this destination. Among the concerns you'll have to address are:

- "It's expensive." Yes, but there are bargains; and certain areas, like the Romantic and Castle Roads, can be a bit less costly. All-inclusive tours help minimize unexpected costs.
- "The Nazis caused World War II and the Holocaust. Neo-Nazi sentiments still exist." Be very sensitive about this. Some clients, indeed, will *never* go to Germany. For those who might, but have some reservations, suggest visiting the Dachau Memorial. A new generation now leads the country and only a small (but vocal) few still harbor Nazi sentiments.
- "Germans are a cold people." In fact, the locals are quite friendly toward visitors.
- "They don't speak English." Germans are very well-educated and many people do, indeed, learn English as a second language.

Fasching, usually held in February or March, is the Munich version of wild Mardi Gras revelry.

Qualifying the Client
Germany

FOR CLIENTS WHO WANT	APPEAL			REMARKS
	HIGH	MEDIUM	LOW	
Historical and Cultural Attractions	▲			
Beaches and Water Sports		▲		Scenic lakes
Skiing Opportunities	▲			Bavarian Alps
Lots of Nightlife		▲		Mostly Munich
Family Activities		▲		Primarily sightseeing
Familiar Cultural Experience			▲	
Exotic Cultural Experience		▲		
Safety and Low Crime	▲			
Bargain Travel			▲	
Impressive Scenery	▲			Especially in south
Peace and Quiet		▲		Only in countryside
Shopping Opportunities		▲		Steins, cameras, cuckoo clocks, porcelain
To Do Business	▲			A major trade partner with the United States

Figure 16-2

- "It's so far from North America." Germany is almost as close as Paris or Rome; a trip can easily be combined with one of those cities.
- "The weather's bad and there are no sun resorts." The weather's nice in the summer. A Bavarian resort or spa may do just fine; otherwise, Germany may be the wrong place for this type of client.

Sales Strategies

Germany's strengths lend themselves to a great many ways for you to sell-up and cross-sell. Indeed, very few countries offer as many opportunities to do so. For instance, staying in a castle high above a forest, though expensive, would be magical. A cruise down the Elbe, Rhine, or Neckar may be the best way to see those regions. Spas have long been famous in Germany, though they're just now catching on with Americans. Because there's so much history spread out across the country, an escorted tour might be perfect for some clients. City tours (especially of Berlin) are a good suggestion. And don't forget the Wundercheck hotel program.

A rail pass, too, provides efficient travel among Germany's far-flung attractions. Car rentals, because of the autobahn system, will appeal to many clients. And "European Delivery" Mercedes and BMWs appeal to upscale clients. In fact, you can sometimes set up a deal with your local car dealership in which you receive a percentage of the commission.

CHAPTER 17

Greece and Turkey

An Odyssey of Culture

Homer's classic tale, *The Odyssey*, is perhaps the most famous adventure story ever told: It traces the travels of Odysseus among some of Western civilization's greatest cultural monuments. Your client can now take the same trip—with fewer obstacles. The land of the Odyssey—the Eastern Mediterranean from Greece and its islands to Turkey—remains as classic today as it was in the time of Homer.

Greece, which altogether is about the size of New York State, spreads over a broad area. Greece is not only made up of its mainland, but also of more than 1,400 islands. Turkey is even larger: It's nearly as big as Texas and Louisiana together. Most of your clients will be interested in visiting three areas: **Athens** and the region around it, the **Greek islands**, and western Turkey.

Northern Greece, with cities such as **Salonika** (also called **Thessalonika**) and **Meteora**, is interesting, but somewhat off the beaten path. **Istanbul**, Turkey, is a fascinating, unique city often visited on cruises. Other Turkish destinations are the ports of **Izmir** and **Kusadasi**, and the inland ruins. In both countries, English is spoken by those in the tourist trade.

Greece and European Turkey are often classified as part of a larger group called the **Balkans**. The Balkans include Bulgaria (treated in the next chapter), **Albania**, **Slovenia**, **Croatia**, **Bosnia and Herzegovina**, **Yugoslavia** (Serbia), and **Macedonia**.

How Travelers Get There

Olympic Airlines (OA) is Greece's national airline and flies into the country's main gateway in Athens at **Hellinikon Airport** (ATH). A few North American airlines have flights as well. Secondary airports operate on the islands of **Corfu**, **Mikonos**, and **Rhodes**. **Turkish Airlines** (TK) operates out of Europe into **Istanbul** (IST) and **Antalya** (AYT).

Almost all North American visitors to Greece, however, visit the Greek islands and Turkey via cruises—from Athens's port of **Piraeus** (the Mediterranean's number one cruise port) or Istanbul—most of which operate from May to October. During the other months, the seas can be very rough; cruise opportunities, therefore, are limited beyond the high summer season.

Weather Patterns

Greece is renowned for its wonderful, temperate weather (see Figure 17-1). Summers are hot and dry, in the upper 80s, whereas winters can drop into the mid-50s, with occasional rain and gusty winds. Coastal areas and the islands are

For Your Information . . .

Greece and Turkey

CAPITALS: Greece: Athens
Turkey: Ankara

AREAS (SQUARE MILES): Greece: 50,944
Turkey: 301,382

TIME ZONE: GMT +2

DRIVE ON: Right

POPULATION: Greece: 10,500,000
Turkey: 61,800,000

RELIGIONS: Greece: Greek Orthodox
Turkey: Islam

LANGUAGES: Greece: Greek
Turkey: Turkish

CURRENCIES: Greece: 1 drachma = 100 lepta
Turkey: 1 Turkish lira = 100 kurus

ELECTRICITY: 220 volts, 50 cycles AC

CAPSULE HISTORY: **Greece**: Ancient Greece reaches peak, fifth century B.C.; Roman colony from second century B.C.; Greece becomes Turkish (Byzantine Empire) province, 1460; wins independence, 1827; becomes kingdom, 1832; becomes republic, 1924; monarchy restored 1935; Italy and Germany invade, 1941; liberated, 1944; military rule, 1967–1974; new republic, 1975.

Turkey: Captured by Alexander the Great, fourth century B.C.; Romans establish Ephesus, first century B.C.; Constantine founds Constantinople, 330; Moslems begin converting country to Islam, 11th century; Ottoman Empire established, 15th century; becomes republic, 1923; economic and political problems, late 1970s; military rule, 1980–1983; returns to civilian rule, 1983.

For reference sources, tourist bureaus, and suggested lengths of stay, see the Appendices.

Sudden strong winds often occur in the seas southeast of Greece. (They're what blew Odysseus off course.)

cooled slightly by their proximity to the water. Northern Greece runs about ten degrees cooler than the south. Summer is the peak tourist season; spring and fall are good times for a client to visit. The climate is still lovely and the country is less crowded. Tourism drops off in the winter, when bargains are available (and the waters get chilly).

Turkey has almost the same weather patterns as Greece. Istanbul, like Salonika, has cool winters and warm summers, with some winter rain and occasional summer showers. Izmir is like Athens—with hot, dry summers and cool, more humid winters; spring and autumn are pleasant shoulder seasons.

Getting Around

Olympic Airlines connects most major cities in Greece. However, cruises are the most common form of transportation among the islands, and many cruise lines operate there. Inter-island ferries are also a way for clients to get from island to island. Most cruises and ferries leave the mainland from the port of Piraeus.

On the Greek mainland, the railroad system is extensive but not the best way for tourists to get around; English isn't commonly spoken, which can make trips difficult. There are, however, excellent trains from major European cities to Athens.

Buses are not recommended for anyone but seasoned travelers. That goes for Athens and Istanbul, as well, where a ride can be a crowded adventure. Taxis are

Climate at a Glance
ATHENS, GREECE

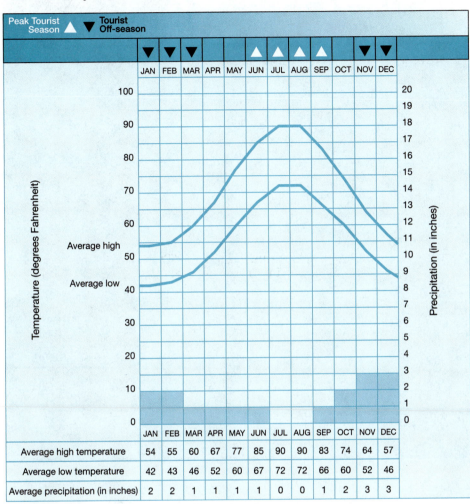

	JAN	FEB	MAR	APR	MAY	JUN	JUL	AUG	SEP	OCT	NOV	DEC
Average high temperature	54	55	60	67	77	85	90	90	83	74	64	57
Average low temperature	42	43	46	52	60	67	72	72	66	60	52	46
Average precipitation (in inches)	2	2	1	1	1	1	0	0	1	2	3	3

Figure 17-1

inexpensive and a good way to get around. Major car rentals are widely available; they're best for excursions beyond Athens. One small warning: Greece has among the highest traffic accident rates in Europe.

Most tourists get around Turkey via cruise ship or on escorted motorcoach tours to the interior. Turkish Airlines services the major cities. Buses and trains connect many cities in Turkey. And, as in Greece, car rentals (outside the major cities) and taxis (within them) are viable alternatives.

Important Places

Most of the best-known sights of Greece are located in the southern part of the country. On the mainland, there are the attractions of Athens and its environs and, for the seafaring, the magnificent Greek islands. For those venturing farther, Turkey offers many spots to visit.

Athens

Athens is the heart and soul of Western civilization. Philosophy, architecture, drama, and democratic government took root in the Athens of 2,500 years ago.

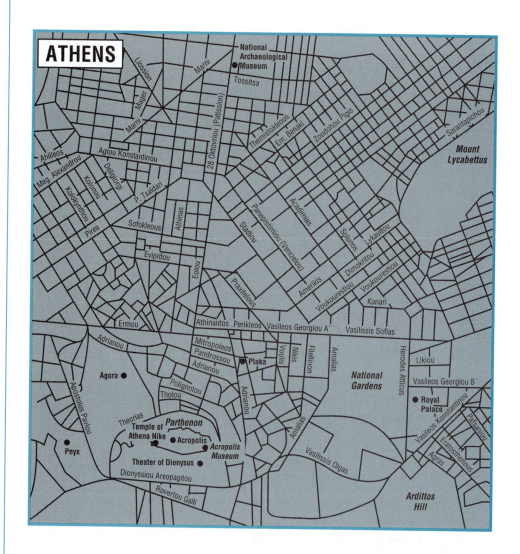

Unfortunately, it wasn't built with millions of inhabitants in mind; smog, poverty, and overcrowding are problems. However, the people of Athens are warm and friendly. And the pace of the city can be either relaxed or frenetic, according to the situation. Things can become almost like a nonstop party, especially when both locals and tourists dance late into the night to bouzouki music in the taverns.

Among the attractions you might recommend to your clients are:

- **The Acropolis** is one of the world's most magnificent, truly noble places. Towering over the city, this hill is covered with monuments and temples. At the top is its main temple, the **Parthenon**, many of whose treasures can be found in the **Acropolis Museum**. (The Parthenon has probably influenced more buildings in the Western world than any other.) Other sights of note: the **Temple of Athena Nike** and the **Theater of Dionysus**, the oldest Greek theater.

- **Pnyx**—just below the Acropolis—was the gathering place of ancient Athens, where issues were publicly decided. A sound-and-light show is held here at night.

- The **Agora** *market place* was the commercial center of ancient Athens. With fascinating ruins, the area is still active today. Even more active is the city's business and entertainment district, the **Plaka**.

- **The National Archaeological Museum** is a world-class museum, with a rich collection of Greek art and culture.

Athens is a hub for many memorable **day trips**. Among them are:

It can get hot when touring ruins; bring bottled water along.

The Acropolis, Athens, Greece
Photo by C. J. Ghormley

- **Delphi**, amid magnificent scenery, where the shrine of Delphi once housed a renowned oracle of the ancient world. There are also other temples and an amphitheater. The eleventh-century monastery, **Ossios Lukas**, is close by, as is the **Corinth Canal**, through which cruise ships pass.
- **Olympia**, where the well-preserved ruins of the first Olympic Games in 776 B.C. are found.
- **Epidaurus**, thought by many to be where modern theater was born. Its beautiful amphitheater, still used today, is renowned for its stunning acoustics.
- **Sounion**, with its **Temple of Poseidon** overlooking the rushing seas.
- **The Saronic Islands**, covered with fascinating ruins of fortresses and Doric temples, as well as beautiful forests.

The Greek Islands

Of the more than 1,400 islands, over 150 of them are inhabited. Most of the islands are off Greece's east coast in the **Aegean Sea**, although there is a scattered group to the west in the **Ionian Sea**. Most tend to be quite arid and none is really tropical-looking. They are most often visited on cruises or by ferry.

- **Crete**—the largest Greek island—is a mountainous place, with beautiful gorges, wonderful beaches, and caves to explore. The famous **King Minos's Palace**—the oldest European throne, which dates back 3,500 years—has been reconstructed in **Knossos**. There's also a good archaeological museum.
- **Mikonos** is a fashionable island with excellent beaches, abundant nightlife, and many churches. Bright, colorful, with whitewashed houses, it looks the way your clients most likely envision Greece to be.
- **Delos** is usually reached through Mikonos. Once a sacred island, Delos is small but filled with ruins and grand temples honoring Apollo (believed by the ancients to have been born here).
- **Santorini** (sometimes known as **Thira**) is one of the most dramatically beautiful places on earth. The island is formed by the blown-out cone of a huge

Most ancient Greek buildings and statues were originally painted in bright colors.

Delos may have more ruins per square inch than any other place in the world.

Riding donkeys in Santorini, Greece
Photo by William and Marie Rourke

volcano, with blue water within and bleached white buildings lining the slopes of what remains of the volcano's rim. Santorini is thought to possibly be what remains of the "lost continent" of Atlantis; there are several noteworthy excavation sites.

- **Corfu**, off Greece's west coast, is another trendy resort. Because it's more lush than Greece's other, drier islands, many call it the most beautiful spot in Greece. It has great beaches, a lively nightlife, and a semiformal casino. There are churches, a palace, and a very good museum.

- **Rhodes** lies off the coast of Turkey. At Lindos is a unique amalgam of Greek, Byzantine, European, and Turkish ruins. There are excellent beaches, a busy nightlife, and a casino. One of the Seven Wonders of the World, the Colossus of Rhodes (a giant statue, whose legs straddled the harbor), stood here before being felled by an earthquake.

The Balkans

Over the past decade, there has been great strife in this part of the world, with conflict between various ethnic and religious groups.

- **Albania**. Long a "mystery" country (it intentionally cut itself off politically from both East and West), Albania has begun, tentatively, to court tourism. Its assets: Adriatic beach towns, Greco-Roman ruins, and the capital city of **Tirana**.

- **The former Yugoslavia**. How sad that Yugoslavia—rich in attractions—has broken up into a series of countries at each other's throats. If any kind of long-lasting calm comes to this land, however, the potential for tourism should be great. **Slovenia** is the most peaceful nation in the group, yet nearby strife has limited tourism. That's unfortunate, since Slovenia has Alpine scenery, fine beaches, distinguished architecture, and bargain prices.

- **Croatia** has suffered from the region's turmoil. Its **Dubrovnik**, a medieval port on the Adriatic Sea, has been restored and is regaining tourist appeal. **Bosnia and Herzegovina** has been torn by war. Its capital, **Sarajevo**—once a historic

Dubrovnik is famous for its red tile roofs.

gem of a town and a major ski center—has been severely damaged. **Yugoslavia** (dominated by Serbians) has also been much involved in the fighting. Its capital, **Belgrade**, lies on the Danube and is famous for its museums, cafes and cabarets. **Macedonia** is considered by some an independent nation, by others as part of Yugoslavia.

Turkey

Although not likely to be a stop for first-time visitors to Greece, Turkey—the land of the dancers known as whirling dervishes—has some wonderful sites for seasoned travelers to explore. A small part of Turkey occupies a small portion of Europe, but most of the country is in Asia. The two sections are separated by the Straits of Bosporus. Among the destinations you might recommend to your clients are:

- **Istanbul**, the capital of the old Byzantine Empire, was once called Constantinople. Sultans' palaces, minarets and two important mosques—the **Blue Mosque** and the much older **Haya Sophia**—dot the city. Istanbul is an active city with bazaars and a busy nightlife. **Topkapi Palace** is renowned for its spectacular jewels, Moslem relics, and countless (mostly empty) chambers.

- **The Turquoise Coast**, with its white sands and forests of pine, spans the Aegean and Mediterranean Seas. It can be accessed by air (via Izmir or Antalya), charter yacht or cruise ship (the principal ports: Izmir and Kusadasi). Among the Turquoise Coast's most visited seaside cities—often near ancient ruins—are **Bodrum**, **Marmaris**, and Antalya. The most important ruins, however, are at **Ephesus** (mentioned in the Christian bible), about thirty miles south of Izmir and about the same distance north of Kusadasi. There's no better place to experience what ancient cities must have been like.

- **Inland Turkey**, including **Pamukkale**, with its hot springs and the white calcium terraces that look like "cotton castles"; **Cappadocia** [kap-ah-DOE-shah], a place of hundreds of cave churches and dwellings; and **Ankara** [ANN-kah-rah], the nation's capital.

Istanbul's vast Covered Bazaar may be the world's oldest indoor shopping center.

Above Ephesus is a site where legend says Mary, the mother of Jesus, spent her last years.

Haya Sophia, Istanbul, Turkey
Photo by C. J. Ghormley

Possible Itineraries

Because of the length of time needed to get to Greece from North America, combined with the slow pace of cruising between islands, your clients should ideally plan an extended visit.

However, if time is a constraint, first-time visitors can center a week-long trip around Athens and its environs. But to go to Greece and not experience its islands would be unfortunate. Nine days should be a minimum and twelve would be ideal. Travelers could see Istanbul and Kusadasi on a Greek Island cruise, but to see Turkey in-depth, visitors should take a week, starting in Istanbul, heading south to Pamukkale, then west to Ephesus, returning back to Istanbul. Return visitors would probably want to find new islands, explore old ones in greater depth, or take the occasion to see more of Turkey, including Ankara, Cappadocia, and Antalya.

Turkey is three percent in Europe and 97 percent in Asia.

Lodging Options

Greece's more upscale hotel chains include **Astir**, **Divanis**, and **Chandris**. Several North American companies have properties in Greece as well.

For your clients who are looking for a special hotel, the deluxe **Athens Hilton** provides a striking view of the Acropolis; the **Grande Bretagne**, built in 1826, retains its old-world elegance and is just blocks from the Acropolis, as is the luxurious **Athenaeum Inter-Continental**. Many hotels on the islands are reasonably priced.

Some of your clients may prefer an alternative type of accommodation. There are beautiful villas throughout Greece, but they aren't bargains, and many have maintenance problems. Other lodging includes bed-and-breakfasts and spas.

In Turkey, such international chains as **Hilton** and **Mercure** predominate. Istanbul's better hotels cluster around Taksim Square (including the **Hilton**, with its fine view) and along the Bosporus. The **Ciragan Palace Hotel** was once a sultan's palace.

Allied Destinations

Since Greece and Turkey are so far from North America, your clients may choose to add on other nearby countries to their trip. Italy is a good add-on as it's right across the Ionian Sea. Because the Middle East is just on the other side of the Mediterranean Sea, a trip to Israel or Egypt is a common add-on as well. Remember that you can break up a trip to Greece or Turkey from North America (especially the West Coast) by routing your clients through many spots in Europe, including those in the northern areas.

Cultural Patterns

Many of your clients may be apprehensive about a trip because of the image they have of Greece and Turkey. And your business clients may have serious concerns about what will be expected of them in their daily contacts:

Greece and Turkey are strong rivals. Be careful about discussing the countries while visiting either one.

- Put your clients at ease by informing them that both Greeks and Turks are extremely hospitable to visitors. Clients should be aware that handshaking is very important.

- Your clients should know that many businesses close at midday.

- Warn your clients that a small nod of the head upward means *no*, not *yes*, to Greeks and Turks.

- For those of your clients invited to visit a Greek home, tell them to bring a small gift as a token of appreciation. Also, if their host insists that they try a particular food, they should do so.

- Advise your clients to be careful about overpraising any item they see when visiting a Greek home. Their host may feel obligated to present it as a gift.
- Tell your clients going to Turkey, especially those on business, that it's important they deal with the person who has the most authority. This isn't snobbery; it's the way Turkish society is set up.

Factors That Motivate Visitors

To assume that tourists want to visit the area only because of its cultural history would be shortsighted. Among their many reasons might be:

- The culture and history of the region forms the basis for Western culture.
- It's one of the world's finest destinations for sunshine.
- Greece and Turkey are comparatively inexpensive countries to visit.
- Greek food is delicious.
- Many water sports and cruise options are available.
- The people are extremely friendly.
- There are many shopping bargains.
- When its more unstable nations settle down and the infrastructure improves, the Balkans' assets should be a powerful draw for tourism.

Angora (as in cats and sweaters) is derived from the word "Ankara."

Qualifying the Client
The Greek Islands

FOR CLIENTS WHO WANT	APPEAL			REMARKS
	HIGH	MEDIUM	LOW	
Historical and Cultural Attractions		▲		Some ruins, but not major reason
Beaches and Water Sports	▲			
Skiing Opportunities			▲	None
Lots of Nightlife		▲		On larger islands
Family Activities			▲	
Familiar Cultural Experience			▲	
Exotic Cultural Experience	▲			
Safety and Low Crime		▲		
Bargain Travel		▲		
Impressive Scenery	▲			But not tropical or lush
Peace and Quiet		▲		On smaller islands
Shopping Opportunities		▲		Pottery, jewelry, leather
To Do Business			▲	

Figure 17-2

Possible Misgivings

The rewards of visiting these countries are considerable. However, they may not be for every client. Among the concerns you'll have to address are:

- "I don't like long flights." You can book Greece or Turkey as part of a package to include other nearby countries, breaking up the length of travel.

- "The area is dirty, and there's so much poverty." Some of the Greek islands are quite upscale; you can recommend them to clients who have such misgivings.

- "There's terrorism there." The chances of being affected in Greece and Turkey are very small; on the islands, the odds are even less. The rest of the Balkans, however, are a different story. . . .

- "It's so hot." The climate is temperate and dry almost the entire year. Humid heat is rare. Spring and fall are beautiful.

- "There's nothing to do there except see ruins." The nightlife can be quite intense for clients looking for excitement.

Sales Strategies

Eurail passes and Greek rail passes can be bought only in North America.

You should strongly recommend that clients visiting Greece take a cruise to the country's islands. And for a special way of getting from island to island, you can suggest that clients go by yacht: A private one is expensive, but others will take up to thirty people and are more reasonable. Cruises calling on Istanbul and Kusadasi are also popular. City tours in Athens are a good way to see the town, because public transportation isn't great. For seeing remote areas of the country, rental cars and trains are always available. (Though, again, trains are not the best mode of transportation in Greece.) Escorted tours are a very good suggestion, too. Greek and Turkish budget hotels can leave something to be desired. Sell your clients up to better accommodations. Clients might be interested in villas for lodging. The Balkans should be recommended only to clients who *really* want something off the beaten path and don't worry about the conventional comforts or sudden political conflicts.

Travel Trivia

Top Ten Ruins

Ephesus, Turkey
Angkor Wat, Cambodia
Machu Picchu, Peru
Mayan Ruins, Guatemala, Mexico, Belize
Luxor, Egypt

Petra, Jordan
Rome's ruins
Wye River Valley, Wales
Fatehpur Sikri, India
Lindos, Greece

Source: America Online's Travel Center

CHAPTER **18**

European Potpourri

Collectors of countries—that's what clients bound for Europe often are. They forget that a single country can consume weeks of sightseeing. But, true, it sometimes is a matter of simple efficiency: A visit to Germany is readily combined with one to **Austria** and **Switzerland**; a trip to France can be easily sidetracked to **Belgium**; the **Netherlands** lends itself logically to a side trip to **Denmark** and on to the **Scandinavian countries** or to the **Baltics**.

Travel statistics bear this out. Six of the "lesser" European nations—Austria, Switzerland, Belgium, the Netherlands, Denmark and **Sweden**—are among the top twenty world destinations. It's unlikely that your clients will walk into your agency wanting to go exclusively to a single one of these places (unless they're skiers). But it's probable that a tourist will consider adding at least one of these countries to his or her itinerary. You can lose nothing by suggesting additional countries, and you can gain substantial new commissions if the client likes the idea.

Belgium

One of the three Benelux nations, Belgium could be a robust addition to your client's European itinerary. Its capital, **Brussels**, is only about two hours northeast of Paris by train or five by car. It's easy to get around this nation, not only because it's relatively small and flat, but also because a superb system of highways, trains, bus routes, canals, and small rural roads crisscrosses it. Your clients who prefer driving will find Belgium a good choice.

Sabena (SN) is Belgium's national air carrier, but many other airlines fly into Brussels (BRU). (In fact, Brussels is a prime gateway to Europe.) Eurostar trains run between Brussels and London via the Chunnel in a little over three hours. The climate is mild, with cool days in winter (snow is infrequent) and mildly warm summers. You should prepare your clients for the area's tendency toward fog, drizzle, and rain. French and Flemish are spoken here, but English is also commonly understood in key tourist cities.

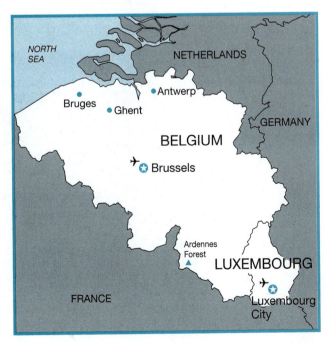

Important Places

You can lodge your clients in Brussels and have them use it as a base of operations for visiting all of Belgium. Brussels bills itself as a "living museum," and it's certainly that: Medieval structures are everywhere. But modern buildings have shoved their way into this fast-paced city. Your clients should be warned that Brussels is, therefore, not the uniformly quaint city they may imagine. To discover that quaintness, you should recommend that they visit some of Belgium's outlying towns.

Be sure to advise your clients to see the following attractions:

- **The Grand Place**, reputed to be Europe's most beautiful town square and the model for Munich's Marienplatz.
- **Several museums**, especially the **Museum of Old Masters** and the **Museum of Modern Art**.
- **Erasmus House**, a classic sixteenth-century home and garden.
- **City tours** of Brussels, a particularly appropriate cross-sell, since the city features dozens of small, fascinating attractions that clients might miss on their own.

To really see Belgium, it's essential that your clients take **day trips** out of Brussels. You should recommend the following attractions and pre-book them if you can:

- **Bruges** [BROOJ], one of Europe's best-preserved medieval cities, often called "the Venice of the North" because of its many canals.
- **Ghent**, a picturesque city of flowers, gardens, and bridges.
- **Antwerp**, well known as an outlet for diamonds, but also graced by many museums, galleries, and churches.
- **The Ardennes Forest**, with its handsome vistas and Battle of the Bulge memorials.

On certain feast days, the entire Grand Place is covered with flowers.

A great way to see Bruges is by boat.

The Grand Place, Brussels, Belgium
Photo by C. J. Ghormley

Sales Considerations

Belgium is a logical extension of a vacation in France or the Netherlands and should probably be sold as such. It's especially appropriate for people who like tours. It's also a shopper's paradise: its chocolates, linen, ceramics, and precious stones are well known. Since Brussels is a major destination for European government officials and business executives, its hotels tend to fill up—especially on weekdays. Book lodging, therefore, well in advance and recommend tours, both escorted and independent, as a way to obtain preblocked hotel space.

The Netherlands

Another Benelux country, the Netherlands (also called **Holland**) conjures a ready image of tulips, windmills, dikes, and canals. Holland is indeed a congenial destination, though its climate is often damp and its days gloomy.

Getting clients to **Amsterdam** (AMS), the center point of Dutch culture, will be easy. The national carriers, **KLM** (KL) and **Martinair** (MP), have frequent and convenient service, as do many other airlines. In fact, Amsterdam is one of Europe's major gateways. Most Dutch attractions are within a day's trip from Amsterdam—accessed by convenient rail and bus service, as well as by a well-developed highway system. The locals speak Dutch, though knowledge of English is widespread. A bit of trivia: The Dutch buy more books and bicycles per capita than any other people in the world.

Important Places

You should book your clients into a hotel in Amsterdam; it'll be their base for almost all of their sightseeing in the Netherlands. Amsterdam is the must-see city

of this country. Recommend a city tour or boat cruise to your clients, and tell them about the following:

- **The Rijksmuseum**, with its magnificent collection of Dutch masters.
- **Anne Frank House**, where the famed young diarist hid from the Nazis for two years.
- **Van Gogh Museum**, with the world's finest collection of works by the noted Dutch artist.
- **Rembrandt House**, where the artist lived and worked for two decades.

Convince your clients to venture out into the countryside to get a good feel for the country. They should visit:

- **Delft**, the world-famous pottery and tile center.
- **Haarlem**, a well-preserved old city, and the vast, nearby Keukenhof tulip fields, which bloom in April and May.
- **Zaanse Schans**, with its concentration of working windmills.
- **The Northern Hamlet Route**, which features many small, delightful towns.
- **The Hague**, a splendid city (and home of the **World Court**) that boasts one of Europe's best-known attractions, the **Madurodam**, a city fashioned in miniature.

The number one weekend getaway for the Dutch is the beautiful city of Maastricht, a culinary and shopping magnet.

Sales Considerations

Virtually every type of client will find the Netherlands appealing, except perhaps those exclusively drawn to beach resorts. One possible sales objection: Holland has a well-founded reputation for permissiveness. Drugs, prostitution, and pornography are all tolerated and in many places legal. Yet, the Dutch are a peaceful people. It's unlikely that your clients will find trouble unless they go looking for it. Two other points: The Netherlands has an unusually extensive system of camping facilities, and diamonds are a shopping specialty.

Switzerland

Central and small, Switzerland boasts no real tourist hub city (like, say, Great Britain's London). Gingerbread hamlets, crisp lakes, and dazzling vistas dot this entire mountainous Alpine country. You might be able to get a handle on Switzerland by dividing it up into its three linguistic areas: the German-speaking north, central and east; the French-influenced west; and the Italian-inspired south.

The Swiss are known for their efficiency; transportation to, within, and from Switzerland operates with clock-like precision. **Swissair** (SR) and **Balair** (BB) are the national carriers; both **Geneva** (GVA) and **Zurich** (ZRH) are major gateways for many airlines. Not even Alpine cliffs interfere with the country's superb rail and highway system; giant tunnels bore through wherever appropriate. Your client may be surprised to know that, except for its high mountain areas, Switzerland has a pleasant climate. Summers can even be quite hot (especially in the south) but without the humidity that makes other destinations uncomfortable. The *Foehn* wind also sometimes brings unseasonably warm and dry weather to Switzerland's mountain valleys; it may occur in any season.

Important Places

Though small in size, Switzerland has distinct regions. It's important to understand their differences in planning your client's trip.

- **Northern and eastern Switzerland** is anchored by **Zurich**, Switzerland's largest city and its financial center. Not far away is one of Europe's most visited natural attractions, tumultuous **Rhine Falls**. Also in northern Switzerland—on

the Rhine, near both the French and German borders—is **Basel**, with its many first-rate museums, an excellent zoo, and spectacular winter carnival. **St. Gallen** is a picturesque Alpine city that is often a stopover between Zurich and Innsbruck, Austria.

- **Central Switzerland**, just southwest of Zurich, is often called the **Interlaken District**. The city of **Interlaken**, itself, would perfectly satisfy the expectations of what your clients think of a Swiss town: cute chalets, imposing clocks, and views of the Jungfrau Mountains. **Bern**, the country's charming capital, is to the west; and **Lucerne**, a medieval walled city, is close by.

In a little town thirty miles south of Zurich is a huge surprise: The ornate church monastery at Einsiedeln.

Chillon Castle at Lake Geneva, Switzerland
Photo by C. J. Ghormley

- **Western Switzerland** will feel more French to your clients. Most of the attractions you'd want to recommend border **Lake Geneva**, including: **Lausanne**, **Chillon** [shee-ON] (with its famous dank castle), **Montreux** (the site of many music festivals) and **Geneva**, itself (whose most recognizable feature is the **Jet d'Eau** fountain, a geyser in the lake).
- **Zermatt** highlights the part of Switzerland that borders Italy to the south. Located at the foot of the well-known **Matterhorn** mountain, this town is quaint and car-free. Farther to the east, but still along the border, is the **Lake District**, which more fully captures the Italian influence on Switzerland. Chief lake cities are **Lugano** and **Locarno**.

There's usually enough snow on the Matterhorn to ski in summer.

Sales Considerations

With its ski areas, palm-lined southern lakes, cute villages, and cities filled with culture, Switzerland is a genuinely easy country to sell. Your sports-enthusiast clients especially will relish the thought of a trip to Switzerland—which offers many opportunities for boating, hiking, and, of course, skiing. The prime Swiss ski resorts to see are:

- **Zermatt**, a massive winter-sport development.
- **St. Moritz**, a pricey resort in Switzerland's southeast, and beautiful **Arosa**, which is nearby.
- **Gstaad**, a resort beautifully set in a valley in southwestern Switzerland.

Switzerland doesn't charge VAT taxes on car rentals. To start and end your client's European motoring vacation in Switzerland can save hundreds of dollars. For those who prefer trains, the **Glacier Express**—which slices through some of Europe's most spectacular countryside between Zermatt and St. Moritz—is a must. And for lovers of service and luxury, Switzerland's hotels are a strong selling point. Two legendary properties: Zurich's **Dolder Grand** and **Baur au Lac**.

There are major United Nations facilities in Geneva, yet Switzerland is not a member of the U.N.

Austria

Though small (it's about the size of the state of Maine), **Austria** ranks as a first-rate tourist destination. About 70 percent of its surface is mountainous, making it a prime ski destination. Its strategic position—bordering Germany, Switzerland, and Italy—makes it easily combinable with these major destinations. Its cultural legacy is rich, especially in music. Try to think of Austria without imagining the strains of Mozart, Strauss, and Haydn. You probably can't.

You can transport your clients to Austria with ease. **Austrian Airlines** (OS), **Lauda Air** (NG), and other carriers connect into Austria's two principal cities, **Vienna** (VIE) and **Salzburg** (SZG). Rail transportation into and within the country is good. The climate your client will find on arrival will perhaps be better than expected. Late spring, summer, and early fall are temperate—with occasional hot and dry *Foehn* winds in south-facing valleys. Winters are very cold and snowy in the high Alpine regions, but other areas are surprisingly mild. Austria is a German-speaking country, though your clients will find that most locals know some English.

Important Places

Austria boasts intriguing attractions, but three top the list: Vienna (*Wien* in German), Salzburg, and the **Alpine Ski Resorts**.

Vienna, Austria's capital, is a jewel-box of a city. Located in Austria's northeast corner on the legendary **Danube River**, it's filled with elegant castles, graceful fountains, quaint cafes, huge museums, and world-class hotels. (Its magnificent **Sacher Hotel** is famous for its tortes.) Yet imposing as it is, Vienna is a comfortable, civil city. Among its must-sees are:

- **The Hofburg Palace**, whose boys' choir is world famous.
- **St. Stephen's Cathedral**, whose soaring Gothic spire is a Vienna landmark.
- **The Spanish Riding School**, with its renowned white Lipizzaner stallions. (They perform there only in the spring and fall.)
- **The Schonbrunn**, a palace often called the Versailles of Austria.
- **The National Library**, whose main hall is a baroque architectural wonder.

Salzburg, near the German border (and not all that far from Munich), is a destination you should surely recommend. Though Mozart moved from Salzburg at the age of twenty-five, his spirit still breathes through this picture-perfect city. Its attractions include:

- **Mozart's Birthplace**, the apartment where he composed his earliest works.
- **Hellbrunn Palace**, a wonderfully eccentric place with "surprise" fountains that will spritz your clients when they least expect it.
- **Mirabell Palace**, with its vast marble decorations and gardens.
- **Day excursions**, most especially to **Werfen**, with its twenty-five miles of dramatic ice-lined caves; to **Hallstatt**, where visitors dress as miners and ride a tunnel train; and into the countryside on an ever-popular *Sound of Music* tour.

The Austrian Alps, with their superb skiing, are also celebrated summer destinations. Key resorts are at **Innsbruck**, **Kitzbuhel**, **Lech**, **St. Anton Am Arlberg**, and **Zurs**. This mountainous region is often called the **Tyrol**.

Sales Considerations

Austria is ideally combined with trips to its bordering countries; its powerful appeal makes it an ideal way to expand an FIT. If you're selling a European tour or a Danube cruise, you should highlight Vienna as a key stop along the way. Skiers should also be urged to extend their trips with visits to Vienna and Salzburg; both cities are lively cultural attractions, even in the dead of winter.

Austria appeals strongly to clients who seek safety, comfort, and well-organized facilities. Lovers of music, art, food, and winter sports will be especially drawn

Vienna's many coffeehouses are the legacy of a seventeenth-century occupation by the Turks.

to Austria. Some clients, however, may remember its close relationship to Nazi Germany in World War II and for this reason find Austria an unappealing destination.

Scandinavia

Held together by a common cultural heritage, the five countries of Scandinavia spread broadly across northern Europe. Norway, Sweden, and Finland compose the Scandinavian Peninsula, a fan of land that stretches from the North Sea on the west to Russia on the east. Denmark, a peninsula and series of islands that stretch northward from the Continent, and Iceland, way out in the North Atlantic, round out this nation-grouping. Most tourists who visit Scandinavia are from Germany; Scandinavia, however, is becoming a more popular destination for North Americans.

Scandinavia is cold most of the year. In summer the weather is generally pleasant, real heat is a rarity, and daylight lasts from very early to very late. Precipitation isn't excessive, except on Norway's west coast, which is rainy and snowy. Your clients may be surprised to know that Iceland, despite its name, isn't impossibly cold. (On the other hand, Greenland, with its optimistic name, is downright glacial.)

Several national carriers service Scandinavia, including **Icelandic Air** (FI), **SAS** (SK), and **Finnair** (AY); many other carriers go there, too. Internal transportation is excellent, with a wonderful system of trains, ferries, steamships, cruise ships, buses, and subways. The one weak link: Except for certain areas, Scandinavia's

roads tend to be rural and marked with hard-to-decipher signs. Offering a car rental should not be your first strategy.

Important Places

Here are Scandinavia's nations, and what each has to offer:

Denmark. Denmark, Scandinavia's most popular tourist destination, is a friendly little country; it's impossible to visualize it without thinking of Hans Christian Andersen's fairy tales. It was also once an immensely prosperous nation; all that wealth brought fine castles, rich artistic achievements, enlightened government, and the ability to create the ultimate open-faced sandwich.

Copenhagen, the capital, is the focal point of travel; city tours and day-trip excursions are excellent services to cross-sell. Make sure to tell your clients about Copenhagen's **Little Mermaid** statue and **Tivoli Gardens**, which served as a major early influence on Disney's amusement park plans.

Norway. Norway is an outdoorsy nation with few real urban centers. **Oslo**, its cozy capital, features a **Viking Ship Museum**, the **Kon-Tiki Museum**, and a park of unusual sculptures (**Vigeland**). You must offer to cross-sell Norway's prime attraction: a cruise through the **fjord** area. Fjords are steeply cliffed inlets from the sea; they are majestic and humbling. Most local fjord cruises depart from the city of **Bergen**, which can be accessed via a scenic train ride from Oslo. So they won't be too disappointed, remind clients that it is rainy along Norway's western fjord coast. Winter-sports enthusiasts also enjoy Norway. The Olympic center at **Lillehammer** is especially popular.

Sweden. Sweden is a friendly, modern country; and **Stockholm**, its capital, is cosmopolitan and charming. Advise your clients to visit the **Royal Palace**, the **Old Town** district, and the **Wasa Ship** (a seventeenth-century galleon that was hauled up from the bottom of Stockholm harbor). Recommend a day trip to **Uppsala**, a historic university town only about an hour north of Stockholm.

Finland. Finland and its capital, **Helsinki**, are often thought of as merely a stopover to Russia and the Baltics. That's unfortunate. For Finland, though a little stuffy, has a lot to offer your clients. The **Lakeland** area, to Helsinki's north, is truly picturesque. Your more adventurous clients might be drawn to **Lapland**, Finland's northern wilderness. (Lapland also extends across Sweden.) Helsinki itself has many interesting attractions; again, a city tour is an excellent option.

Iceland. Volcanoes, geysers, earthquakes, boiling cauldrons—that's not what most clients will expect, but that's exactly what they'll find in Iceland. Indeed, all this geothermal drama constitutes Iceland's prime tourist attraction. **Reykjavik**, the capital, has many appealing, though modest, architectural points of interest.

Sales Considerations

Your clients' lack of knowledge about Scandinavia will provide the major resistance factor to your selling this area. Counter it by citing some of the foregoing information. Another objection may be the costliness of visiting Scandinavia; budget-minded clients can visit these countries, but their choices will be limited. However, even moderate lodging is usually clean and comfortable. And hotel rates are surprisingly reasonable in summer, when business travel in Scandinavia drops and many residents head south for their holidays. Clients may also worry about the language barrier, especially if they've seen or heard any of the Scandinavian languages, which are often quite incomprehensible to Americans. But most Scandinavians know at least some English and love to practice it. Emphasize the clean, safe, friendly, and orderly nature of these countries. Suggest a fjord sailing, or the more extensive cruises that call on Scandinavia (usually out of Copenhagen, Hamburg, or London). And remember that many Scandinavian airlines route their flights to the rest of Europe and to the Middle East through their capital cities; a brief stopover can be easily arranged.

Legoland, a theme park made mostly of Lego toy bricks, is in Billund, about five hours by train from Copenhagen.

Helsinki has a large church carved entirely into a huge rock.

The most northerly capital in the world is Iceland's Reykjavik.

Eastern Europe

To lump together the many Eastern European nations is probably unfair; each does have a distinct character. These former communist countries were long closed to outsiders. But most of the nations involved are now doing an excellent job of serving tourists.

Several national airlines service Eastern Europe, as do some North American and Western European carriers. Remind clients that the Eastern European countries are quite a long distance from North America and often involve connecting flights.

Once your clients get there, they'll find it a bit difficult to get around on their own, since few locals speak English and major highways are rare. Escorted tours are, therefore, about the best way to sightsee. A Danube cruise, which starts in Vienna and continues through much of Eastern Europe, is an inspired way to visit the area's great capitals.

We can divide Eastern Europe into two groups. The northern group includes Poland, the Czech Republic, the Slovak Republic (or Slovakia), Hungary, and Romania. These nations are hilly, with cool-to-cold winters and mild summers (though areas of Romania can get hot). The southern tier of countries has a climate and topography more akin to Greece. They are **Bulgaria** and the Balkan countries (which were covered in the previous chapter).

Important Places

Poland.   A rapidly changing country, Poland has taken on greater tourist importance of late. Suggest that your clients include the following cities on their itineraries:

- **Warsaw**, the capital, with more than thirty museums, many coffee houses, casinos, and a restored old-town section.
- **Cracow**, a beautiful medieval town, 200 miles south of Warsaw. Near Cracow is **Auschwitz**, the former Nazi concentration camp that is now a museum.
- **Poznan**, with its sixteenth-century town hall and old market square.

The Wieliczka Salt Mine, near Cracow, is filled with religious and historical carvings.

The Czech Republic. This western portion of the former nation of Czechoslovakia has become a magnet for tourists visiting Eastern Europe. Its scenery, spas, villages, ski areas, and hundreds of castles provide it with a wide appeal. You should include the following on your clients' itineraries:

- **Prague** [PRAHG], the capital, a city of elegant architecture, parks, and shopping.
- **Cesky Krumlov** and **Tabor**, both ancient, atmospheric medieval towns.
- **Brno**, with its mixture of ancient and modern attractions.

To the Czech Republic's east is the now-separate nation of Slovakia. A less prosperous country, the Slovak Republic has potential, with its appealing villages, castles, mountains, and a splendid capital, **Bratislava**.

Hungary. A country rich in historical and cultural attractions, Hungary has become Eastern Europe's most popular tourist destination. It's a romantic country, with legendary food, lovely musical performances, many hot-spring spas, and

Czechoslovakia broke apart and became the Czech Republic and Slovakia in 1993.

Parliament, Budapest, Hungary
Photo by C. J. Ghormley

hundreds of historical structures. A hydrofoil links Budapest to Vienna. Among its chief destinations are:

- **Budapest**, a graceful city and the seat of Hungary's government. Almost all the rest of Hungary can be a day trip from Budapest.
- **The Danube Bend**, a short trip north of Budapest, with its pleasant scenery. The Danube, itself, bisects Budapest, creating two sections: Buda, all hilly and historical; and Pest, a center of business and commerce.
- **Lake Balaton**, a resort-lined lake offering all manner of water sports.
- **Pecs**, a southern city blessed with an unusual blend of Turkish and European architecture.

Romania.   Romania, a mountainous nation that borders the Black Sea, is also making an effort to attract tourists. Its facilities still leave something to be desired, but this will soon change. Your clients may be interested in the following:

- **Bucharest**, the capital, a somewhat rundown city of huge palaces.
- **Brasov**, a medieval town at the foot of the Carpathian Mountains. A day trip away is Transylvania's Bran Castle—the home of a Count Dracula who, though not a vampire, contributed to the legend through his merciless rule and violent cruelty.
- **The Black Sea Coast**, with its nearly 200 miles of coastline and flourishing resorts. Its key city is **Constanta**, a well-known cruise port.

Bulgaria.   One of the smaller Eastern European countries, pleasant Bulgaria has the most ancient history of any Eastern European nation. Its best-known attractions include:

- **Sofia**, the capital, with its Moorish and Byzantine influences. Near Sofia are many spas and monasteries, most especially the **Rila Monastery**, with more than 1,000 frescoes painted on its exterior walls.
- **The Black Sea Coast**, with some 200 miles of sandy beaches and so many resort hotels that it's often called The Second Riviera.

Sales Considerations

Your adventurous clients will find Eastern Europe an appealing destination, but others will be a bit reluctant about going behind what was once the Iron Curtain. These countries are hardly the foreboding presences they once were and, for the most part and unless things change, they have become extremely gracious to tourists. Still, you should sell Eastern Europe to those clients who have already seen the major attractions of the rest of Europe, who are seeking bargain travel, or who may be drawn to this area for ancestral reasons. Recommend an escorted tour or a Danube River cruise; they're efficient and fear-dampening options. Skiers and spa enthusiasts who seek more offbeat destinations may find Eastern Europe appealing. You'll find that clients who normally resist tours will gladly book one to any of these countries. Certainly offer to book their hotel rooms well in advance; Eastern Europe has a serious lodging shortage.

The CIS and the Baltics

Like Yugoslavia, the Soviet Union politically has "come apart" in the post–Cold War era. Unlike Yugoslavia, the process—in all but a few places and instances—has been a relatively peaceful one, marred primarily by economic awkwardness as these fifteen new countries transform their controlled, communist systems into more free-wheeling ones. Still, keep up on the news; the situation could change abruptly.

Romanian is the only Latin-based language spoken in Eastern Europe.

A number of airlines serve these nations, most notably Russia's **Aeroflot** (SU) and **Transaero** (UN). Cruise ships call on Russia's St. Petersburg and the ports of the Baltic States.

Russia is the biggest and most important country, touristically. The Baltic States, huddled in the northwest, consist of Lithuania, Latvia, and Estonia. To their south are Belarus, the Ukraine, and Moldova. Another group—wedged on an isthmus between the Black and Caspian Seas—is composed of Georgia, Armenia, and Azerbaijan. A final group of new countries with tongue-twisting names flows eastward from the Caspian Sea: Turkmenistan, Uzbekistan, Kazakhstan, Kyrgyzstan, and Tajikistan. These latter five, all Moslem-influenced, belong more properly to Asia than to Europe. A final note: These countries—except for the Baltics—are part of a loose confederation called the **Commonwealth of Independent States** (CIS).

The world's biggest bell is at the Kremlin. It weighs 223 tons.

Important Places

Let's take a look at your clients' most likely destinations:

Russia.   This huge nation stretches across 7,000 miles and eleven time zones. The disintegration of the Soviet Union put a damper on Russian tourism, but the many attractions that grace this area will surely reinvigorate travel. Its two most popular cities to visit:

- **Moscow**, the capital, with its **Tretyakov Museum**, **Red Square**, and its most important attraction, the Kremlin, which contains government buildings and ornate churches. Two very different places—the Bolshoi Ballet and the Moscow Circus—are prime attractions. The **Cathedral of Christ the Savior**, which was destroyed in 1931, has been rebuilt.

Moscow's subways are surprisingly ornate, with marble and chandeliers.

- **St. Petersburg**, an elegant, Western Europe–like city and cruise port that boasts one of the world's great museums (the Hermitage) and Russia's own version of the Tower of London (the **Peter and Paul Fortress**). Several huge "summer" palaces outside St. Petersburg are well worth the visit.

St. Petersburg used to be called Leningrad.

Other CIS Nations.   Which CIS places are your more adventurous clients most likely to be interested in? Here are a few:

- **The Ukraine**, a country of great agricultural wealth, featuring two interesting cities: **Kiev** boasts many fine monasteries and churches, most notably

St. Sophia's was patterned on the church of the same name in Istanbul.

St. Sophia's. And **Yalta**, on the Black Sea, is a resort town of surprising sophistication.

- **Georgia**, which has suffered much political infighting. Its cities of **Batumi**, **Sukhumi**, and **Tbilisi** used to be quite popular and could become so again.
- **Azerbaijan**'s capital of **Baku**, a Caspian seaside resort that was also popular before strife began in the region.
- **Uzbekistan**'s cities of **Bukhara**, **Samarkand**, and **Tashkent**. All three were important economic and religious centers and located on the legendary "Silk Road" that connected Europe with China. As a result, fine architecture and good museums are everywhere.

The Baltics. The first three nations to break from the Soviet Union—Lithuania, Latvia, and Estonia—have energetically begun to court tourism. The ports of **Riga** (Latvia) and **Tallinn** (Estonia) have become major cruise ports of call. To accommodate land-bound clients, these three nations have begun to develop a "Via Baltica" road system that begins in Warsaw, Poland, and works its way northward through inland **Vilnius** (Lithuania), then on to Riga and Tallinn.

Sales Considerations

The Baltics and Russia continue to be very attractive destinations for those who want something a little different in their European vacations. Tours and cruises will appeal to most of your clients. Be alert for political instability in all these countries. And warn clients that many American "necessities" are in short supply and that crime is a problem in the former Soviet Union (one more reason to sell them on an escorted tour).

Little Countries

Ever wonder how a week-long European tour could visit nine countries? The answer is simple: Europe is peppered with little countries (some of which are principalities that are under the protection of some larger country). Little countries make excellent day trips or places to pass through on a voyage from one major destination to another. Most emphasize their duty-free shopping opportunities. Weave a few of these nations into your client's itinerary and you'll be placing your knowledge where it belongs: in sales. Here's a thumbnail sketch of each:

- **Andorra**—ruggedly perched on the border between France and Spain—offers wonderful scenery, good-sized ski resorts, quaint villages, and great duty-free shopping. It's most often visited as a day trip from Barcelona, Spain.
- **Cyprus**, an island-republic in the far eastern portion of the Mediterranean, has lost some tourism because of internal strife between its two ethnic groups, the Greeks and the Turks. It's an air connection point between Europe and the Middle East, and a stop for several cruise lines. Among its attractions: the walled capital of Nicosia, the Crusader castle at Kyrenia, many beaches, and the availability of water sports.
- **Gibraltar** has a high recognition factor among clients, though they may never have thought of visiting it. This British-influenced island is three miles long and less than a mile wide. Its caves, beaches, ruins, and monkeys (yes, monkeys) are its principal attractions. Gibraltar can be ferried to from southern Spain or Tangier, Morocco.
- **Liechtenstein**, a sixty-one-square-mile patch of land on the Swiss-Austrian border, has much of the same appeal of its two neighboring countries: a prince's castle, hamlets, vistas, mountain paths, and chalets. It's only a half-hour train ride from Zurich, Switzerland. Innsbruck, Austria, is also relatively close.

The world's busiest McDonald's is on Moscow's Pushkin Square.

Because of an incomplete peace treaty, Liechtenstein is still at war with Prussia, a nation that no longer exists.

Case Study

Mr. and Mrs. Navratilova—a wealthy retired couple in their seventies—have seen much of the world. They've just returned from an Alaskan cruise, which they much enjoyed. They want to return to Europe, though Mr. Navratilova complains he hates seeing things twice. They have already visited France, Great Britain, Scandinavia, the Alpine countries, Italy, and Greece.

Circle the answer that best suits your clients' needs:

1. What area would you probably recommend to them?

   Austria in depth   Eastern Europe

   The Greek Islands   The little countries

   Why?

2. What primary means of transportation would you recommend?

   A Danube cruise   A railroad journey

   A rental car   Flying from city to city

   Why?

3. What allied destination would probably *not* be appropriate to combine with your recommendation?

   Poland   Italy

   Austria in depth   Russia

   Why?

4. What value level of lodging would you consider selling them?

   Budget   First-class

   Tourist-class   Superior

   Why?

Creative Activity

You've been a tour conductor for years, taking groups of Americans across Europe. You're very proud of your knowledge of European history and culture; many tour passengers on your motorcoach have commented on how you make the past come alive.

It's your day off. You live in Brussels and decide to sort through the cluttered attic of your recently deceased aunt, Marie-Louise Wells. Marie-Louise was the granddaughter of the famous British author and thinker, H.G. Wells.

But what's this in a dusty, dark corner? A weird contraption with a brass plate, that says . . . this is a time machine! Could it be that what Wells wrote about is real?! There's a note attached from your aunt. It tells you that, indeed, this time machine works. You can visit any person or place in the past. Though the machine's *time* range is unlimited, its distance is not. The farthest away, geographically, you can go from Brussels is 2,000 miles. You must also return to Brussels after each single "time trip."

You decide, on your first excursion, to visit six famous people and places from the past. Your first trip will be to visit Mozart, in Salzburg. What will the other five be? (You may need to use an atlas to calculate distances.)

PERSON	PLACE	REASON
1. Mozart	Salzburg	To see a young musical genius at work.
2.		
3.		
4.		
5.		
6.		

Travel Trivia

Signs Encountered by Travelers

Fur coats made for ladies from their own skin. (Sweden)

When passenger of foot heave in sight, toot the horn. Trumpet him melodiously at first, but if he still obstacles your passage, then tootle him with vigor. (Japan)

Our wine leaves you nothing to hope for. (Switzerland)

We take your bags and send them in all directions. (Denmark)

Swimming is forbidden in absence of the Saviour. (France)

Please do not feed the animals. If you have any suitable food, give it to the guard on duty. (Hungary)

Ladies may have a fit upstairs. (Hong Kong)

Please leave your values at the front desk. (France)

Pulling It All Together: The Matching Game

Directions: Below is a list of cities, attractions, etc., some of which we have covered, some of which we haven't. There are all manner of connections among them. With a group of fellow students, you have exactly ten minutes to come up with as many connections as possible. (Items may be used more than once.) Write your answers below. Note: There are at least twenty possible connections. E.g., Andorra and Gibraltar—both are small nations.

Hofburg Palace	Rothenburg	British Museum
Red Square	Turkey	Prado
Lillehammer	Yalta	Venice
Delft	Salzburg	Wasa
Malta	Madurodam	Ardennes
Istanbul	Santorini	Carcassonne
Courmayeur	Kitzbuhel	Bruges
Chillon	Grand Place	Hermitage
Andorra	Legoland	Albufeira
St. Peter's	Sherwood	Russia
Kiev	Parthenon	St. Moritz
Schonbrunn	Blarney	Waterford
Liechtenstein	Marienplatz	Gibraltar

ATLANTIC
OCEAN

Azores

Madeira
Islands

Canary
Islands

PORTUGAL SPAIN

ITALY ALBANIA BULGARIA

GREECE TURKEY

C.I.S.

CASPIAN
SEA

AFGHANISTAN

Strait of Gibraltar

MALTA MEDITERRANEAN SEA

CYPRUS LEBANON SYRIA

ISRAEL IRAQ IRAN

Atlas Mountains

MOROCCO TUNISIA

ALGERIA LIBYA

Sahara Desert

WESTERN
SAHARA

Cape
Verde

MAURITANIA MALI

Gambia River

SENEGAL

GAMBIA

GUINEA
BISSAU

SIERRA
LEONE

LIBERIA

Niger River

GUINEA

IVORY
COAST

Lake
Volta

GHANA

NIGER

BURKINA
FASO

BENIN

TOGO

NIGERIA

Lake
Chad

CHAD

CENTRAL
AFRICAN
REPUBLIC

CAMEROON

Sao Tome & Principe

EQUATORIAL
GUINEA

GABON

Cabinda

Congo River

CONGO

DEMOCRATIC
REPUBLIC
OF THE
CONGO

ANGOLA

NAMIBIA

BOTSWANA

Kalahari
Desert

SOUTH
AFRICA

EGYPT

Lake
Nassar

Nile

River

SUDAN

UGANDA

Lake
Albert

RWANDA

BURUNDI

Lake
Tanganyika

TANZANIA

MALAWI

ZAMBIA

Victoria
Falls

Lake
Malawi

Zambezi River

ZIMBABWE

JORDAN

Suez
Canal

Sinai
Peninsula

Jordan River

Gulf of Suez

RED
SEA

ERITREA

ETHIOPIA

Lake
Victoria

Lake
Turkana

KENYA

Mt. Kilimanjaro

Persian Gulf

SAUDI
ARABIA

BAHRAIN QATAR

UNITED
ARAB
EMIRATES

KUWAIT

PAKISTAN

OMAN

ARABIAN
SEA

YEMEN

DJIBOUTI

SOMALIA

INDIAN
OCEAN

EQUATOR

Seychelles

Comoro
Islands

MOZAMBIQUE

MADAGASCAR

Mauritius

Reunion

SWAZILAND

LESOTHO

INDIAN
OCEAN

ATLANTIC
OCEAN

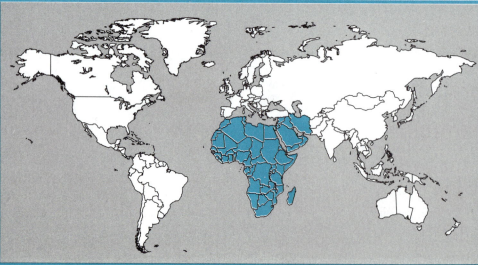

PART

V

Africa and the Middle East

Savannahs and Sand

Africa and the Middle East: the birthplaces of human culture, yet perhaps the earth's last unexplored touristic frontier. Just about everyone has wished to visit the homelands of the Bible and the Koran, to travel back in time to the palaces and pyramids of ancient pharaohs, to trek across the ever-shifting dunes of the Sahara, to witness the awesome spectacle of vast, migrating herds, even to pay a quiet visit to a family of mountain gorillas.

But few travelers ever get to Africa and the Middle East. Indeed, only about 100,000 Americans and Canadians travel to Africa each year; in contrast, six million make the voyage to Europe yearly. It takes stamina and spirit to pursue these destinations, but they are destinations that return their levy tenfold. Clients who venture here bring home powerful, eternal memories of these genuinely exotic places.

Where the Countries Are

It might seem odd to misplace a continent as large as Africa (the world's second largest), but it's possible that many of your clients don't exactly know Africa's position on the globe. It seems so distant. In fact, it's directly south of Europe, across the Mediterranean Sea. Indeed, some of the countries in northern Africa can be visited as day trips from Spain, Italy, or Greece. And what of the Middle East? Though often in the headlines, this region's location may also be obscure to many of your clients. But it's no mystery: It's to the northeast of Africa and, officially, is part of Asia.

Africa and the Middle East theoretically offer many countries that you could sell. Some, however, are developing nations and offer meager tourist facilities. Others, because of political tensions, won't be attractive possibilities. Some are simply too small and don't offer enough attractions to interest your clients. As a result, in this chapter, we concentrate on only those countries with which you'll most likely be dealing.

Remember, too, that things change quickly in Africa and the Middle East: Today's tourist hot spot can become passe at the first sign of political upheaval; other, sleepy little countries can suddenly begin courting tourism with a vengeance.

The many African nations can be grouped into seven sections. The first, North Africa, is a region of deserts, oases, and Islamic culture. The countries you're most likely to sell are, roughly from west to east: **Morocco**, **Mali**, **Algeria**, **Tunisia**, **Egypt** (which is sometimes grouped with the Middle East), and **Ethiopia**. The second

341

region is just northeast of Egypt: the Middle East. Leisure clients are most likely to inquire about **Israel** (and the now self-governing Palestinian territories), **Jordan**, and **Turkey** (covered in Chapter 17). Certain clients may have business that will take them to **Saudi Arabia**, **Bahrain**, **Kuwait**, and the **United Arab Emirates**—among others. Moslem clients may also, for religious reasons, be very interested in a trip to Saudi Arabia, to visit the holy city of **Mecca**.

A third touristic region is the massive peninsula of West Africa. Highly influenced by French culture, these countries include **Senegal**, **The Gambia**, **Sierra Leone**, **Liberia**, the **Ivory Coast**, **Ghana**, **Togo**, **Benin**, and **Nigeria**. The fourth area, located just to the east of these nations, is often thought of as the Central Safari Belt. Its most visited countries: **Cameroon**, the **Democratic Republic of the Congo** (formerly Zaire), **Rwanda**, **Tanzania**, **Kenya**, and **Uganda**. A fifth magnet for tourism is the more southerly Victoria Falls region, flanked by **Zambia** and **Zimbabwe**.

A sixth prime destination is southern Africa. **South Africa** dominates its tourism, but **Namibia**, **Botswana**, and the small nations of **Lesotho** and **Swaziland** are also becoming popular. The seventh and final category isn't an area at all. It comprises the many islands that lie off the shores of Africa. The best known are southeast of Africa, in the Indian Ocean, and include the **Seychelles**, **Madagascar**, and **Mauritius**. The others are northwest of Africa and can be stop-off points on flights between Europe and North America: the **Azores**, the **Canary Islands**, the **Madeira Islands**, and the **Cape Verde Islands**.

A Satellite View

From space, Africa would be a distinctive-looking continent. What would be its most prominent feature? Probably the **Sahara Desert**, which covers most of the continent's northern third. In addition, the **Kalahari Desert** takes up much of southern Africa. And most of the Middle East is desert as well, notably the **Sinai** region. Though too many Tarzan movies may lead your clients to think of the remainder of Africa as jungle, much of the rest of the continent is actually grassy savannah and veldt, with rivers and a few large lakes here and there. Furthermore, most of Africa is flat coastal and plateau regions, though some major mountains

The Sphinx, Giza, Egypt
Photo by William and Marie Rourke

rise up in the northwest and along the continent's eastern side. And the equator splits the continent almost directly across its center.

The features of Africa and the Middle East are a major part of what makes this land so adventurous and exotic. Those same features dramatically shape the conditions your clients will face when they venture here.

Bodies of Water

Two oceans lie on either side of Africa: the **Atlantic Ocean** on the west and the **Indian Ocean** on the east. Along the northern boundary is the **Mediterranean Sea**, and dividing the continent in the northeast from the Middle East (which is connected to Europe and Asia) is the **Red Sea**.

Two lake-like bodies of water, the **Black Sea** and the **Caspian Sea**, form partial boundaries between the Middle East and Europe. The **Persian Gulf** juts into the center of the Middle East and flows directly into the **Arabian Sea**, which in turn divides the region from western Asia. In the area separating the Middle East from Africa, you'll also notice the **Suez Canal**, which connects the Mediterranean with the **Gulf of Suez**.

Much of the region is desert, but there's quite a network of rivers. Indeed, some of the most famous rivers in the world flow here. Emptying into the Mediterranean is the mighty **Nile River**, which dominates northeastern Africa. The **Jordan River** courses through the western part of the Middle East. (It runs into the **Dead Sea**, a popular resort area.) Several major rivers flow off the west coast of Africa into the Atlantic, including the **Congo** and **Gambia** rivers. A major rain forest surrounds the Congo River basin. And the **Niger River** runs through northwestern Africa. Emptying at the east coast is the **Zambezi River**, which begins in central Africa and flows southward, then eastward, tumbling at mid-point over the mighty **Victoria Falls**. Victoria Falls is often visited in conjunction with stays in Zambia, Zimbabwe, or Botswana.

Africa and the Middle East have few lakes, but **Lake Victoria** is quite large and stands out in eastern Africa. Below it are a couple of long, thin lakes: **Lake Tanganyika** and **Lake Malawi**. In the north, just south of the Sahara, is **Lake Chad**. And in the south, the impressive Victoria Falls is a major tourist destination. One warning: Water in Africa is generally for viewing, not swimming. As picturesque and even pure as the water may seem, bacteria and who knows what other unaccustomed creatures usually lurk there. They may be harmless to locals (who often are resistant), but not to tourists. Ocean water is usually safe, but pollution and sharks can, in some places, be a danger.

Mountains

If you were to traverse Africa and the Middle East, it would become clear that they're not as mountainous as, say, Europe or Asia. Though much of Africa is very hilly or has plateaus, only two major ranges interrupt its surface: the **Atlas Mountains** in the northwest corner and the many mountains (most are volcanoes) of the eastern regions. Indeed, lofty **Mt. Kilimanjaro**, the highest mountain in Africa, rises more than 19,000 feet above sea level. One other prominent feature stands out: the **Great Rift Valley**, which begins in the Middle East and continues down to east-central Africa.

Climate

To fully describe the climate of Africa and the Middle East is a challenge. First of all, since the equator bisects Africa, the region has two seasonal patterns. North of the equator, the seasons are those that your clients are used to: Winter is in December, January, and February; and summer is in June, July, and August. South

The Black and Caspian seas are both almost entirely surrounded by land and therefore could technically be called lakes.

Mt. Kilimanjaro, Tanzania
Photo by William and Marie Rourke

Djibouti is the hottest inhabited place in the world. Aswan, Egypt, is the driest.

of the equator, winter starts in June, summer in December. What about temperatures? Winters in the desert areas of northern Africa and the Middle East, as well as in southern Africa, are warm to cool, with chilly temperatures especially at night. Summers in the north can be broiling, though southern Africa's summers are relatively pleasant. As you get closer to the equator, however, temperatures tend to be warmer year-round, with only minor temperature fluctuations between summer and winter.

But altitude is a component of this, too. The plateau and mountainous areas of southern and eastern Africa tend to be cooler, in general, than land closer to sea level. (There are even snow-capped African mountains on or near the equator.) The Atlas Mountain region can also be quite cold in the winter, hence the ski resorts there. And what of rain? Northern Africa tends to be dry year-round—as is Namibia, on the southwestern coast. On the other hand, the coastal areas of western and central Africa are very rainy (here are the rain forests and jungles). The rest of Africa has moderate rainfall patterns. One final point: Rainy seasons vary widely from place to place in Africa. Certain countries near the equator, like Kenya, even have two distinct rainy seasons.

Tourism Patterns

The Middle East attracts many more visitors than Africa. Jordan, surprisingly, leads with about two million tourists yearly, but few of them come from North America (unless it's part of a side trip from Israel). Egypt, Saudi Arabia, and Israel all attract more than a million tourists each year. South Africa and Kenya trail the Middle Eastern countries; each draws about three-quarters of a million tourists a year.

Political turmoil or a well-publicized crime against tourists in the Middle East or Africa usually impacts tourism intensely—not only in the immediate area of unrest, but thousands of miles away. For example, the 1990 crisis in Kuwait caused a 50 percent drop in tourism in Cairo, which is over 800 miles away. Even Morocco suffered a major downturn, though it was thousands of miles distant from the Middle Eastern turmoil.

A giraffe in Tanzania
Photo by C. J. Ghormley

African and Middle Eastern Distances

Africa and the Middle East span a vast distance. Africa alone is larger than South America and Europe combined. That, by itself, is enough to make point-to-point travel a major undertaking. Adding to the challenge is that, overall, the transportation networks found here aren't among the world's finest. This is still a developing region, and even the most progressive of the nations discussed in this section haven't reached the standards to which most of your clients are accustomed. Finally, the politically delicate climate in many of the countries here may necessitate roundabout travel plans. (Some governments, for instance, don't allow visitors to enter directly into their country from another rival nation; you'll have to reroute your clients through a third, neutral country. Be sure to check government advisories on this.)

In short, traveling through Africa and the Middle East is adventurous. Traveling times can be easily miscalculated: A short, direct road may be washed out or in poor condition. A simple flight between countries can become a circus of connections. In Africa and the Middle East, anything can change on a moment's notice.

Most public transportation (specifically, buses and trains) should be viewed by your clients with healthy skepticism. The systems can be uncomfortably crowded; in many cases English won't be spoken. Taxis are a better bet, but the fares can be quite slippery. Advise clients to consult with the hotel about local practice. Rental cars are widely available. However, a car rental can present challenges, especially because road conditions are so uncertain; some areas might not even be safe to drive through or are poorly marked. Zimbabwe, Namibia, and South Africa, especially, are the only places where car rentals are an acceptable option. A popular way for tourists to get around is by hiring a car and driver for the day, perhaps through their hotel's concierge, or to set things up via a reputable tour operator.

Traveling to Africa and the Middle East, though, is becoming easier. Most itineraries must be built via European gateways. A few nonstop jets do fly from North American cities. For example, Senegal is only a six-and-a-half-hour overnight flight from New York City.

Perhaps the best recommendation for most of your clients is an escorted tour. Africa and the Middle East lend themselves ideally to such a mode of transportation, and even clients who are independent spirits may greatly appreciate how much easier their trips are when someone else is responsible for creating their travel plans. And what about airlines? Service is fairly good between major cities; however, scheduling can be uncertain. And though the region is large, many of the individual nations aren't; thus, airplane flights may be unnecessary at best and a waste at worst.

Trains are a viable way of getting around in Egypt and South Africa. Indeed, South Africa's "Blue Train" is legendary. Cruises are even more reliable. Three cruise areas dominate: the region that includes Morocco, Tunisia, and the Atlantic islands (often out of Spain); a routing that features Kenya and the Indian Ocean islands, often in combination with South Africa or, occasionally, India; and the highly popular Nile cruises.

One last thing to remember when setting up schedules to get your clients around the area: The weather can play an important part in transportation. Rainy seasons can wash out roads, hurricanes brush along Africa's eastern coast, and desert dust storms can make traveling difficult or dangerous.

<aside>About one-tenth of the world's population lives in Africa.</aside>

Some Miscellaneous Considerations

Clients usually have a clear notion of only the most obvious destinations in this part of the world—the pyramids, for example, or Jerusalem. It will be necessary, therefore, for you to offer them as much travel-planning guidance as possible before they leave on their adventure. The situations you should be most aware of are:

- Health conditions here are far below the standards to which your clients are accustomed. Be absolutely certain that clients visit their physician before leaving on their trip.

- By North American standards, Africa and the Middle East are a bargain. Costs in Israel and certain Middle Eastern countries are somewhat higher.

- Crime and theft are a definite problem in some countries, decidedly not in others. The normal precautions should be taken. Begging, often by little children, is aggressive and common.

- AIDS has reached epidemic proportions in Africa (but not the Middle East). Unsafe sex here is a potentially deadly mistake.

- Some of your clients may hear of wonderful exchange rates on the local black markets and decide to take advantage of the prices. You should advise them that it would be wise to reconsider: Many of the nations here look down with grave severity on the practice. Indeed, the person offering that terrific exchange rate may be an undercover police officer.

- Similarly, your clients should be warned that drug usage in many of these countries is a terribly serious crime.

- These destinations are informal. But make sure that your clients don't dress too casually, especially when visiting temples and mosques—follow the rules for head coverings. Shorts or sleeveless dresses are a no-no.

- Bargaining at shops is usually lively and expected. But not always. Tell your clients to double-check the local customs with hotel personnel when they arrive in an area.

- Africa and the Middle East can be very hot; insects are everywhere; malaria is a problem, especially in West Africa. Advise your clients to bring sunscreen and insect repellent—as well as to update their inoculations.

- Outbreaks of lawlessness or political fighting sporadically occur across much of the continent. Keep abreast of travel advisories.

- Taking photographs is one of the great pleasures for many travelers. In many of these nations, however, certain sites may be off-limits (such as some government buildings or a special place of worship). Remind your clients to ask about any restrictions when they reach their destination or to consult a tour operator in advance.

- When booking a safari, ask about how many vehicles are used per voyage. A safari should have at least two vehicles, in case one breaks down, or should have a two-way radio to call another for help.

- Tell clients to reconfirm their next flight, if practical, immediately on arrival, and in person, *not* by phone.

- Advise them to arrive for flights very early so they'll be at the front when boarding occurs. (Seat reservations are often ignored.)

- The hotel chains with the largest presence in Africa and the Middle East are Hilton, Sheraton, and Inter-Continental.

Creative Activity

NAME _____ DATE _____

You won the state lottery! You can now indulge in your lifelong fantasy: to visit all seven touristic regions of Africa during a month-long trip. You have to plan your packing. What ten special items do you think you'll need to bring, other than essentials (for example, don't list shirts, a toothbrush, and so on), for this African holiday?

ITEM

REASON

1. binoculars

1. To see distant animals at wildlife reserves.

2.

2.

3.

3.

4.

4.

5.

5.

6.

6.

7.

7.

8.

8.

9.

9.

10.

10.

Travel Trivia

What They Said

"Everything in Africa bites, but the safari bug is worst of all." —Brian Jackman

"In the winter, Venice is like an abandoned theater. The play is finished, but the echoes remain." —Arbit Blatas

"Russia is the only country in the world you can be homesick for while you're still in it." —John Updike

"Prague is like a vertical Venice—steps everywhere." —Penelope Gilliat

"Whether you go to Heaven or Hell, you still have to change in Atlanta." —old saying

"I'm leaving because the weather's too good. I hate London when it's not raining." —Groucho Marx

"Rome was a poem pressed into service as a city." —Anatole Broyard

"He who rides the sea of the Nile must have sails woven of patience." —William Golding

MEDITERRANEAN SEA

main cruise port

more commercial

a resort in Israel
Eliat

Mersa Matruh ▲
Alexandria
Port Said
ISRAEL
JORDAN

Suez Canal

Sinai
Desert

Pyramids

Giza ✈ Cairo
Sakkara ▲
Memphis ▲

Eliat

Luxor ≈ Valley the Kings

GULF of SUEZ

Mt. Horeb ▲
▲ St. Catherine's Monastery

SAUDI
ARABIA

College is free there
80% have diplome (College)

Hurghada ▲

GULF of AQABA

Nile River

EGYPT

LIBYA

Valley of
the Kings ▲
Karnak ▲
Luxor

RED
SEA

Esna
Edfu

✈
Aswan
Philae Island

Lake Nassar

Temple of Abu Simbel ▲

SUDAN

CHAPTER 19

Egypt
Riddles in the Sand

It's perhaps the most famous riddle of all time: the riddle of the Sphinx. "What is it," the Sphinx asked passersby, "that walks on four legs in the morning, two legs during the daytime, and three legs at night?" If travelers couldn't answer the question, the Sphinx would slaughter them.

The Sphinx was a mythical creature, and the only Sphinx left in Egypt is a stone statue, anyway. Fortunately, it doesn't ask tourists questions. But riddles do remain. How were Egypt's great monuments built? Why were they built? What was ancient Egypt really like? These are the riddles that continue to draw tourists today.

Egypt is located in the northeast corner of the African continent. It's a large country—about the size of California, Nevada, and Arizona combined. Yet most of the population lives in the narrow, fertile **Nile River Valley**. Depending on how you measure, the Nile may be the world's longest river. (The Amazon is the other possibility.) It flows south to north through the eastern portion of the country and empties into the **Mediterranean Sea**. The capital of Egypt, **Cairo**, is on the Nile, in northern Egypt. Indeed, most of the destinations that your clients will likely be interested in—**Luxor**, in the center of the country, and **Aswan**, in the south—are on the Nile. (If you fly between cities, you'll see an astonishing sight: a blue and green ribbon of a river, cutting through the tan, dusty surface of Egypt.)

Western Egypt, which makes up the bulk of the country, is desert and largely uninhabited. The nation's eastern border is marked by the **Red Sea**, which (with the **Gulf of Suez** to the west and the **Gulf of Aqaba** to the east) helps form the border of the **Sinai** (**Peninsula**) desert. The famous **Suez Canal** lies to the north, between the Gulf of Suez and the Mediterranean. Arabic is the national language, but English is widely spoken by tourist personnel.

The answer, incidentally, to the Sphinx's riddle: "Man." For it's man who crawls on all fours during infancy, stands upright through the prime of life, and uses a cane in old age. The rest of Egypt's riddles are left to your clients to ponder on their own, during a fascinating journey to this faraway land.

The "Lower" Nile is in the north of Egypt, and the "Upper" Nile in the south.

How Travelers Get There

The national airline is **Egyptair** (MS), though other North American and foreign carriers fly into the main gateway at **Cairo International Airport** (CAI) as well. Flying times from North America to here are long, often with connections: twelve hours from New York, fifteen hours from Chicago, and nearly nineteen hours from Los Angeles.

For Your Information . . .

Egypt

FYI

CAPITAL: Cairo

AREA (SQUARE MILES): 386,101

TIME ZONE: GMT +2

DRIVE ON: Right

POPULATION: 63,300,000

RELIGION: Islam

LANGUAGE: Arabic

CURRENCY: 1 Egyptian pound = 100 piastres

ELECTRICITY: 220 volts, 50 cycles AC

CAPSULE HISTORY: Upper and Lower Kingdoms united, 4000 B.C.; "Golden Age," sixteenth to thirteenth century B.C.; Alexander conquers Egypt, 332 B.C.; Rome takes over, 30 B.C.; Islam introduced, 641; Turks take over, 1517; Napoleonic occupation, 1798–1801; Suez Canal, 1869; British occupy, 1882; independence, 1922; monarchy ends, 1953; various Israeli-Egyptian wars, 1956–1973; fundamentalist unrest and acts of terrorism, 1993–1998.

For reference sources, tourist bureaus, and suggested lengths of stay, see the Appendices.

Tolls paid by cruise ships and freighters going through the Suez Canal are a major source of income for Egypt.

Your clients may also reach Egypt following a stopover visit in Europe; it takes five hours to fly into the country from Paris, for example. It's also possible that you may book clients on a Mediterranean cruise; Egypt is a frequent cruise stop on Eastern Mediterranean cruise itineraries, usually out of Athens (Piraeus) or Istanbul. The main port in Egypt is **Alexandria**, in the center of the nation's northern coast. A secondary port is **Port Said** [sah-EED], on the Suez Canal.

Weather Patterns

Most tourists spend their time in Egypt at destinations along the Nile, whose climate is far more comfortable than that of the Western and Sinai deserts. The temperatures in Cairo, for example, during winter (the main tourist season) will reach only the 70s and cool down to as low as the upper 40s at night (see Figure 19-1). Late fall can be pleasant as well, reaching 80 degrees or more. Your clients should avoid visiting during the summer, however, unless they're willing to put up with intense heat and air pollution in order to take advantage of bargain rates; the average summer highs are in the mid-90s and dry (and it gets even hotter in southern Egypt). In addition, March through May is usually uncomfortable—not only because of shifting temperatures, but also because of shifting sand; lung-searing winds (called the *Khamsin*) can occur during this time. Rain, though, is unlikely to dampen your clients' visit; for it rains, on the average, only one day a month in Cairo and a little more than that along the northern coast, where Alexandria is located.

Getting Around

The most popular way for tourists to get to their Egyptian destinations is on a Nile cruise. Sometimes they may also travel by airplane; there are good connections between the major cities. Egypt also has adequate train and bus service. If your clients do decide to go by rail, you should recommend that they take first class

Climate at a Glance
CAIRO, EGYPT

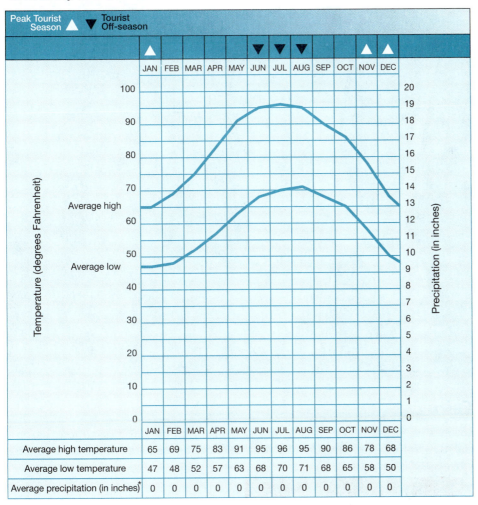

	JAN	FEB	MAR	APR	MAY	JUN	JUL	AUG	SEP	OCT	NOV	DEC
Average high temperature	65	69	75	83	91	95	96	95	90	86	78	68
Average low temperature	47	48	52	57	63	68	70	71	68	65	58	50
Average precipitation (in inches)*	0	0	0	0	0	0	0	0	0	0	0	0

* Occasional rain, but never totaling more than 1/2-inch in any given month.

Figure 19-1

only; second class can be very uncomfortable. Likewise, you shouldn't suggest that they travel via the crowded buses that cross the country. (Those bus routes used predominately by tourists are okay.) And remind clients that donkeys, horses, and, yes, camels are commonly used for getting around in certain areas (especially around the pyramids). Escorted tours are a popular alternative.

Within Cairo, taxis are an inexpensive way to see the city. However, tell your clients that meters are often ignored; the cost of the ride should be firmly set at the beginning (and that often depends on the age, condition, and make of the vehicle!). Rental cars are widely available, but driving can be a nightmare of crowded streets and lonely desert roads. You might recommend, however, that your clients hire a driver for the day; car rental companies and hotels can get one for you. The jam-packed city buses should be avoided. There's an adequate subway system, and your clients can also travel through the city by boat, along the Nile.

Important Places

Most of your clients will spend their trip to Egypt traveling along the Nile. There are several popular destinations.

The Pyramids were the tallest structures in the world until the Eiffel Tower was built in 1889.

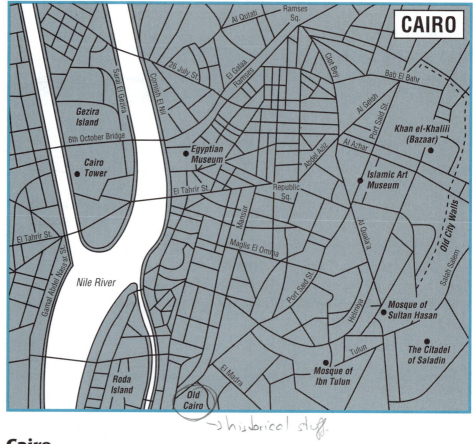

Handwritten notes (left margin):
On Nile River
El zamalic.
most rich people live there

Cairo Tower
you can see the older new Cairo & you can see the pyramids,

Handwritten (on map): Old Cairo → historical stuff.

Cairo

Located on the Nile, Cairo is a bustling, historic city (Africa's largest, by far). Clients should be prepared for the squalor of certain sections of the area. Among Cairo's attractions are:

- **The Egyptian Antiquities Museum**, near the Ramses Hilton Hotel, with perhaps the world's greatest collection of ancient Egyptian artifacts, including the mummies of most of the great pharaohs and the dazzling collection of King Tutankhamen. Tell your clients to get there early and to go directly to King Tut's room on the second floor.

- **Great mosques**, the most notable of which are the ancient **Mosque of Ibn Tulun**, the renowned **Mosque of El-Azhar** (close to the old bazaar), and the colossal **Sultan Hasan Mosque**.

- **The Citadel of Saladin**, a walled fort built atop a hill in the twelfth century. Within it is the legendary Alabaster Mosque, the citadel's central attraction.

- **Cairo Tower**, affording an excellent view of old Cairo, new Cairo, and the pyramids (on a rare, clear day).

- **The Museum of Islamic Art**, perhaps the finest exhibit of its kind in the world.

- **The Coptic Quarter**, with its old, narrow streets, ancient Christian churches, and a museum. (The Coptic Church is an ancient Christian sect.)

- **The Three Great Pyramids and the Sphinx**—among the most renowned attractions anywhere—located in the town of Giza, just west of Cairo. The pyramids were one of the Seven Wonders of the Ancient World, and they're the only one of the original wonders still in existence. The most famous of the pyramids is **Cheops.** Be sure to recommend to your clients the dramatic sound-and-light show, given on certain nights in English. Early morning visits are good, too, since the heat is less and the crowds still thin.

Sidebar:

Many people expect small tips, called *baksheesh,* **for favors that they've done; this includes letting their photographs be taken. Even museum guards may ask.**

When setting up a camel ride, negotiate the price first and wait until the end to pay and tip. The same applies for trips in *feluccas* **(small sail boats) and taxis.**

The Step Pyramid at Sakkara
Photo by C. J. Ghormley

A day trip from Cairo you could suggest is to **Sakkara**. There are remarkable underground tombs and fourteen pyramids, including the **Step Pyramid**, the world's oldest intact stone structure. Nearby is **Memphis**, which in ancient days was the capital of Egypt; brooding monuments and a huge statue of Ramses II are the attractions that remain from this city, now largely gone.

Luxor

Up river (south) from Cairo, Luxor features some of the most remarkable ruins in all of Egypt. In ancient days, this city was known as Thebes. It's in the **Valley of the Kings**—across the river from Luxor—that **King Tut's** tomb was discovered. Other ancient pharaohs were buried here as well. Their tombs are now empty, but the astonishing wall decorations remain. The area boasts two of the world's finest temple complexes: the **Temple of Luxor** and the nearby **Temple of Karnak**.

Aswan → Dam

Farther up river from Luxor, Aswan today is most recognized as home to one of the world's biggest structures—the **Aswan High Dam**. Your clients should visit the **Temple of Kalabsha**, which was relocated by German archaeologists to its present site. The outstanding temples on **Philae Island** provide the backdrop to a superb sound-and-light show. A number of excellent temples can be reached from Aswan; the best known is the towering **Temple of Abu Simbel**, where the figure of **Ramses II** is cut into a bluff. (The entire temple was cut into pieces—its original site was flooded when the Aswan Dam was built—and reassembled at its present location.)

Nile Cruises

Though cruises can be taken in either direction (or both), it's most efficient for travelers to fly south and then cruise north; the current is faster. For your clients with plenty of time, the week-long voyage from Aswan to Cairo is unforgettable. More common, however, is the shorter five-day trip between Aswan and Luxor. Here, the cruise ship will stop at such sites as **Esna** (with the **Temple of Khnum**)

Even on the finest Nile cruise ships, stomach disorders are common.

and **Edfu** (with the superbly preserved **Temple of Horus**). They'll also get a real feeling for everyday Egyptian life. Hotels operate most cruise ships; the cruise will include a cabin and most meals.

Though these are the main destinations in Egypt, other areas might please your clients, including:

- **The Sinai Desert**, where many Biblical sites are found, including **Mt. Horeb**, which some believe to be Mt. Sinai, where Moses received the tablets of the Ten Commandments. **St. Catherine's Monastery**, at the presumed site of the Burning Bush, is nearby. *When Moses received the 10 testamen.*

- **Alexandria**, Egypt's main cruise port. Though attractions are limited, there are some fine museums, several palaces, and some ancient ruins; the **Catacombs of Kom el-Shukafa** is especially interesting.

- **Resorts**, most notably **Mersa Matruh** (on the Mediterranean, west of Alexandria), **Sharm El Sheikh** (at the southern tip of the Sinai Peninsula), and **Hurghada** (on the Red Sea), a fine snorkeling and diving site.

In ancient times, Alexandria's library was considered the world's best.

The Sphinx at Memphis
Photo by C. J. Ghormley

PART V   Africa and the Middle East

Columns at Luxor
Photo by William and Marie Rourke

Possible Itineraries

Deciding on the length of stay in Egypt depends not only on the destinations to be visited, but also on the mode of transportation. If your clients take a Nile cruise for even a part of their trip, it will clearly take longer than flying around the country. A good suggestion would be ten days for first-time visitors; they would start in the area around Cairo and then fly to Aswan, where a boat can be picked up for a short cruise down river to Luxor, and return by air to Cairo. Experienced travelers may wish to take excursions to some of the lesser-known sites, visit the Sinai Desert, take a longer cruise, or even spend some time at one of Egypt's fine resorts.

Lodging Options

Budget accommodations in Egypt can provide your clients with unwelcome surprises. Very good lodging is fairly reasonably priced and should be recommended. Some fine first-class chains serve the country, the most popular of which are

Oberoi, Meridien, and Sonesta. In addition, Inter-Continental offers deluxe lodging. Perhaps the best hotel in Cairo is the Marriott, with a converted palace at its center. There's also a wide selection of North American chains in Egypt, especially in Cairo. Most Cairo bars and nightclubs are in the hotels. Few good hotels can be found outside Cairo, Alexandria, and Luxor.

Most of Cairo's lodging clusters around the Egyptian Antiquities Museum and along the Nile River. Quite a few hotels are also at the airport. If your clients plan to spend much time exploring the Great Pyramids and the Sphinx, you might recommend accommodations in Giza, where there are several hotels and resorts. (The most famous: the Mena House Oberoi.) For those clients taking a Nile cruise, the ships act as hotels; travelers stay on board at night.

Allied Destinations

It's not uncommon for a visit to Egypt to be combined with a trip to its neighbor, Israel. The country is also bordered by Saudi Arabia (across the Red Sea), Sudan, and Libya. Because of the great distance to Egypt from North America, your clients might prefer to break up the flight by stopping over in Europe for a few days before continuing. The country can also be seen as part of a Mediterranean cruise.

Cultural Patterns

Egypt's culture is different from what your clients are likely to be used to at home. This is most important to your business clients.

- Tell your clients that the use of titles (for example, doctor, professor) is important when addressing people in Egypt. And dress is fairly formal and conservative.

- Parties, dinners, and other gatherings often don't start until 10 P.M. If your client is staging the social gathering, tell him or her to have nonalcoholic beverages available.

- Building trust is important to Egyptians. As a result, your clients should be prepared to engage in extended conversation and coffee before starting a meeting. Even shopkeepers will offer a coffee or a cola.

- It's quite acceptable to ask an Egyptian about his or her opinion. However, to ask for personal facts is rarely done, except among close friends.

- If your clients are invited to someone's home, it's polite to bring a gift and good manners to leave some food on their plates. (It's a sign of abundance.)

- If your clients exchange an item (such as food or a gift) with another person, tell them never to use their left hand alone, which is considered ill-mannered and dirty.

- Remind your clients that many businesses close on Friday, the Moslem day of rest. Work weeks begin on Saturday and run through Thursday. Some places close completely (or early) on Sunday.

The most famous bazaar to see in Cairo is the Khan El Khalili.

Factors That Motivate Visitors

For clients who want to visit so distant a destination as Egypt, certain reasons must be prompting their decision, including:

- It has a unique and rich cultural history.
- Costs within the country are relatively inexpensive, and shopping is a bargain.
- The locals are friendly.
- It appeals to clients who like cruises. Nile cruises are appealing to clients who usually reject water travel because of seasickness; the Nile is quite calm.
- The weather is warm and pleasant during the winter.

Possible Misgivings

A trip to Egypt would likely be a unique experience for most of your clients. Among the concerns—some genuine, some unfounded—you'll have to address are:

- "Hasn't there been crime and terrorism directed against tourists?" Serious but sporadic incidents by fundamentalists have occurred and have dramatically impacted tourism, but, overall, Egypt is an astonishingly crime-free country.

- "The hostilities in the Middle East worry me." Egypt and Israel are no longer fighting with each other, and the Middle Eastern wars are taking place in other countries.

- "I've been told that the water is very bad." Drink bottled liquids instead, and be careful with fresh fruits and vegetables.

- "There's widespread disease there." Check with a physician before making the trip and get any necessary shots.

- "It's blisteringly hot." Avoid Egypt during the summer. Visit the country in the winter or late fall, when the weather is usually lovely.

- "The country is dirty and crowded." Book your clients into a first-class or deluxe hotel. Or set them up with an upscale packaged tour. Cairo's traffic, smog, and crowds are real, though; clients worried about this should perhaps stay only briefly in Cairo and move on to other Egyptian areas.

Qualifying the Client
Egypt

FOR CLIENTS WHO WANT	APPEAL			REMARKS
	HIGH	MEDIUM	LOW	
Historical and Cultural Attractions	▲			Legendary sights
Beaches and Water Sports		▲		Seacoast resorts; Red Sea diving
Skiing Opportunities			▲	None
Lots of Nightlife		▲		In Cairo, especially in hotels
Family Activities		▲		Primarily sightseeing
Familiar Cultural Experience			▲	
Exotic Cultural Experience	▲			
Safety and Low Crime			▲	Safer than most tourists think
Bargain Travel		▲		After airfare, can be inexpensive
Impressive Scenery		▲		The Nile and desert
Peace and Quiet			▲	Cairo very noisy; rest of country is quieter
Shopping Opportunities		▲		Pottery, handicrafts, false antiquities, cotton items
To Do Business			▲	Must understand the culture

Figure 19-2

- "Aren't there aggressive salespeople and beggars everywhere?" Much of this is a sort of game that locals play to make a meager living. Everyday Egyptians are among the friendliest, most hospitable, and helpful people in the world.

Sales Strategies

What's the most obvious way to sell-up a trip to Egypt? By booking a memory-of-a-lifetime Nile cruise for your clients. You might also suggest an escorted tour for clients who feel a certain hesitancy about their visit. Because the flight to Egypt from North America is so long, you could recommend stopovers in Europe to break up the traveling. A trip to Egypt goes well with a visit to Israel or Kenya; you might suggest that your clients extend their trip a few days and travel there. Further, because many budget hotels can be unpleasant, your clients will appreciate it if you book them into first-class hotels. Cruises are a grand way to maximize profits from a client's trip.

Travel Trivia

The Seven Wonders of the Ancient World

The Pyramids (Giza, Egypt)
The Hanging Gardens of Babylon (near Baghdad, Iraq)
The Statue of Zeus at Olympia (Greece)
The Temple of Diana at Ephesus (Turkey)
The Mausoleum (Helicarnassus, Turkey)
The Colossus (Rhodes)
The Pharos Lighthouse (Alexandria, Egypt)

Creative Activity

You're employed in the planning department of the Egyptian Ministry of Tourism. Tourism is a huge source of income to your country. Your government is always prepared to spend money if it can improve the safe flow of tourists across your nation and to cities in other countries.

A new idea is now floating around in higher circles: Build a bullet train—similar to Japan's, or France's TGV—that can go up to 200 miles an hour. Your job: to prepare a position paper on the pros and cons of the idea, as well as where *two* rail lines should go. (There's only money for two, each up to 500 miles long.) Fill in the outline below as a preparation for your final report to the Ministry; use an atlas for reference.

THE TWO LINES WOULD GO BETWEEN:

1. _____ and _____

2. _____ and _____

Reasons that such rail lines might be a good idea:

1.

2.

3.

Reasons why the idea might not work:

1.

2.

3.

[handwritten: rainy season = Jan, Feb, Nov. Dec. Winter]

Israel
Of Milk and Honey

I f Greece is the cultural heart of Western civilization, then Israel, it can be argued, is its soul. Not only is this remarkable land the homeland of the Jewish religion, it holds a preeminent place among Christians—as the site of Jesus' birth, death, and (for adherents to the faith) resurrection. Moreover, Israel is one of the holiest spots to those of the Islamic faith; for it's from here, Moslems believe, that Mohammed ascended to heaven. Perhaps what makes Israel so emotionally unique is that it's where spiritual belief anchors itself to solid reality: The cities and sites where biblical events occurred and people lived are *right here*.

Israel (along with the newly self-governing Palestinian territories) is a nation of great contrasts and diversity, not only of religion and cultural history but even of topography; isolated and desertlike, it has been transformed into a flowering landscape. The fragile beauty and majesty of this country, praised in the Bible's poetic prose, continue to enchant visitors today.

For Your Information . . .

Israel   FYI

CAPITAL: **Jerusalem**

AREA (SQUARE MILES): **8,302 (+2,239)**

TIME ZONE: **GMT +2**

DRIVE ON: **Right**

POPULATION: **5,700,000**

RELIGIONS: **Judaism, Islam**

LANGUAGES: **Hebrew, Arabic**

CURRENCY: **1 shekel = 100 agorot**

ELECTRICITY: **220 volts, 50 cycles AC**

CAPSULE HISTORY: Hebrew kingdom, 1000 B.C.; Rome takes control and rules 400 years, 63 B.C.; numerous invasions until 634–640 A.D., when Arabs take control; Crusaders arrive, 1099; Turks control, 1516–1917; Britain governs it and Jordan as "Palestine," 1923–1948; Jewish state founded, 1948; wars with Egypt, 1956–1973; war with Lebanon, 1982–1983; Israeli Palestinian peace agreements, 1993–   .

For reference sources, tourist bureaus, and suggested lengths of stay, see the Appendices.

Israel is about the size of New Jersey. Bordered by the Mediterranean Sea on its west and surrounded by Egypt, Jordan, Syria, and Lebanon, the southern two-thirds of the country consists primarily of the **Negev Desert**. The capital, **Jerusalem**, is located in the north-central portion of Israel. Indeed, virtually all the major cities and tourist destinations are found in the north. **Bethlehem** is just southwest of Jerusalem. And a bit farther south is the historic site of **Masada**, near the major resort area of the **Dead Sea**. **Tel Aviv**, the second largest city and a modern center of commerce and culture, is on the central coast; many government offices and foreign embassies are here.

To the north, on the coast, is **Haifa**, Israel's primary seaport. Southeast of Haifa are the biblical sites of **Nazareth** and the **Sea of Galilee** (Lake Tiberias). The major city in the south of Israel is the port of **Eilat**, today a growing resort destination, by the **Gulf of Aqaba** and the **Red Sea**. The **Jordan River** marks much of Israel's eastern boundary with the nation of **Jordan**.

The 1993 peace accords between Israel and the Palestinians gave self-governing status to parts of several regions taken over by Israel in previous wars. (See dotted areas on map.) The final form the governing will take, what areas it will extend to, and how it will impact tourism still remains in flux within the three occupied territories: the **Gaza Strip**, **West Bank**, and **Golan Heights**. Israel, western Jordan and the Palestinian areas are often collectively referred to by Christians as the **Holy Land**.

Hebrew is the national language of Israel, but Arabic is an official language as well; English is widely spoken throughout the country.

How Travelers Get There

The air gateway into Israel is **Ben Gurion International Airport** (TLV), which serves both Tel Aviv and Jerusalem. **El Al Israel** (LY) is the national airline and is considered one of the safest in the world; the security checks it employs are so extensive that a very early arrival for a flight is a must. Several North American carriers and many European airlines service Israel. Flying times, often involving connections in Europe, are ten-and-a-half hours from New York, fifteen hours from Chicago, fourteen-and-a-half hours from Miami, and eighteen hours from the West Coast. Many cruise ships on Eastern Mediterranean itineraries call on Haifa or **Ashdod**, Israel's chief ports.

Weather Patterns

Sharav **winds can bring very hot, dry weather in the late spring or early fall.**

Israel has two distinct climates. The Negev Desert, in the south, is hot—it's likely that only a few of your clients will want to spend time visiting there. In the north, the weather is pleasant year-round—though spring and fall are the best seasons to have your clients visit. (See Figure 20-1). Summer can be hot and dry, with highs averaging in the upper 80s (dropping down almost 20 degrees at night). Summer rain is a rarity. The winter (which is somewhat a tourist off-season) gets cool and rainy. Average highs reach only the upper 50s (again, there's a big drop at night to as low as the 30s). Winter rainstorms are heavy but infrequent. Some areas, like Jerusalem and Bethlehem, can even get snow. So all those Christmas cards that show biblical landmarks dusted with snow are more accurate than you might have thought!

Getting Around

The bus system is quite good and fairly inexpensive in Israel, both within cities and between them. Air service connects the major cities, but this is such a small country that it's not really necessary for clients to fly, unless they're pressed for time. The train network is limited. Your clients might wish to rent a car. The roads are well maintained, and rentals are extensively available. To get around within cities, taxis are another good means of transportation. As an alternative way for going between

Climate at a Glance
JERUSALEM, ISRAEL

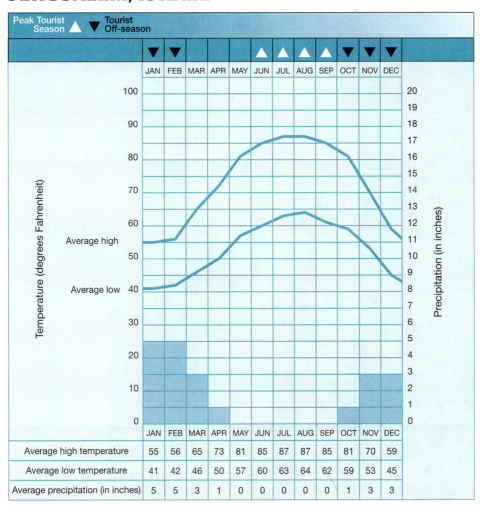

Figure 20-1

	JAN	FEB	MAR	APR	MAY	JUN	JUL	AUG	SEP	OCT	NOV	DEC
Average high temperature	55	56	65	73	81	85	87	87	85	81	70	59
Average low temperature	41	42	46	50	57	60	63	64	62	59	53	45
Average precipitation (in inches)	5	5	3	1	0	0	0	0	0	1	3	3

cities, your clients may want to try *sherut* taxis, which are larger than the regular cabs and take more passengers. Tours, both in cities and over the whole country, are popular for North American clients.

Important Places

Following is a list of the destinations that are most popular in Israel.

Jerusalem

This is perhaps the world's holiest city, home to some of the most sacred sights of the Jewish, Christian, and Islamic faiths. Jerusalem is located in the Judean hills. Its attractions are sprinkled throughout the city; they can be categorized into two groups: those within the **Old City** and those outside. The Old City is a walled area, reached via several ancient gates (the most notable is the **Damascus Gate**); it's divided into Jewish, Christian, Moslem, and Armenian quarters, and is filled with historical and religious structures, narrow streets, and bustling markets. Among the many locations to visit in the Old City are:

- **The Wailing Wall**, one of the most sacred sites in the world to Jews. It's all that remains of King Solomon's legendary Second Temple.

There are 1,072 synagogues, sixty-five churches, and fifty-nine mosques in Jerusalem.

The Dome of the Rock, Jerusalem
Photo by C. J. Ghormley

- **The Church of the Holy Sepulchre,** one of the most deeply sacred sites to Christians. The general location of Christ's crucifixion, burial, and resurrection is believed to be here.

- **The Dome of the Rock,** sacred to Moslems, the third of Jerusalem's most holy places. It's from here that Mohammed is believed to have risen to heaven. This site is also holiest to Jews, as the Dome was built on the Temple Mount.

- **Via Dolorosa,** where Jesus' last walk took place on his way to the crucifixion.

Outside the Old City, the popular sites of Jerusalem include:

- **Mount Moriah,** the location where Abraham prepared to sacrifice his son, Isaac, according to God's wishes.

- **The Dead Sea Scrolls,** held in the Shrine of the Book in the **Israel Museum**. The museum also contains works by Picasso, van Gogh, and Rodin. An instructive and inspirational museum is the **Museum of the Holocaust**.

- **The Mount of Olives,** with the Garden of Gethsemane and what is believed to be the tomb of Mary, Jesus' mother.

Much of Israel's early biblical history isn't all that precise. The traditional religious sites may or may not be accurate; after so many centuries, no one really knows.

- **The Garden Tomb**, considered by many to be Jesus' actual place of burial.
- **Mount Zion**, the tomb of King David, as well as where the room of the Last Supper is thought to be. A new addition is the Chamber of the Holocaust.

Among the superb **day trips** from Jerusalem that you should recommend to your clients are:

- **Bethlehem**, thought to be the birthplace of Jesus and also where King David was born. The **Church of the Nativity** supposedly sits on the place Jesus was born.
- **Jericho** (on the West Bank), considered the oldest city in the world, where Joshua fought the well-known battle. Northeast of Jerusalem on the Jordan River, it's now a favorite winter resort and scheduled to be under Palestinian self-government. Among the nearby attractions are Qumran (where the Dead Sea Scrolls were found), Herod's Winter Palace, and the Mount of Temptation.
- **The Dead Sea**, southeast of Jerusalem, the most popular resort area in the country. This is the lowest point on earth, and its waters are far saltier than those of the Great Salt Lake.
- **Masada**, one of the world's great archaeological sites. This is where nearly 1,000 Jewish Zealots are purported to have barricaded themselves against the Romans in 73 A.D., ultimately choosing mass-suicide to enslavement. Be sure to tell your clients to visit **King Herod's Palace**.

There are no fish in the Dead Sea.

Tel Aviv

This cosmopolitan city is the major center of commerce and culture in Israel. Located on the Mediterranean coast, the area in 1900 was nothing but sand dunes. Now, there's a lively nightlife, many sidewalk cafes, and excellent shopping. Among its most interesting sites are:

- **Very good museums**, most notably the **Tel Aviv Museum** and the **Museum of the Diaspora** (for a compelling history of the Jews).
- **The Israeli Philharmonic**, a very fine symphony orchestra that your clients should try to hear during its season.
- **Independence Hall**, where David Ben Gurion declared Israeli independence in 1948.
- **Dizengoff Square**, with sophisticated shopping and cafes. Another interesting visit for your clients would be to the ancient adjacent town of **Jaffa**, which dates from the time of King Solomon. This old port, with its cobblestone streets, is now an artists' colony.

Haifa

Haifa is the country's major cruise port. It has some interesting temples, particularly the **Bahai Shrine**, the center of the Bahai faith. Biblical **Mount Carmel** offers panoramic views; at the base of the mountain is **Elijah's Cave**.

Nazareth and the Sea of Galilee

These unique destinations can easily be reached in a day trip from Haifa. Nazareth is the city where Jesus grew up and is sacred to Christians. The **Church of the Annunciation** is, according to legend, on the spot where an angel told Mary that she was to be the mother of Christ. Jesus preached at the nearby Sea of Galilee and it's where Christians believe he performed miracles. The Jordan River flows from the Sea of Galilee, a major recreational area. Health resorts are also here, notably Tiberias Hot Springs and Hammat Gader.

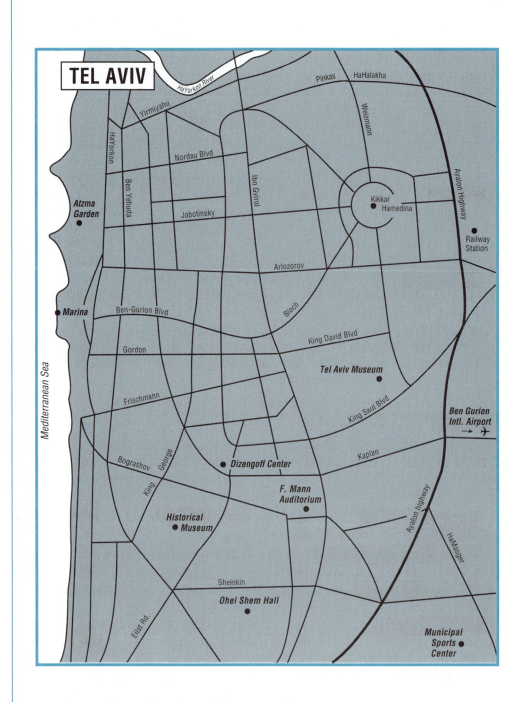

If your clients visit Tiberias, you should be sure to recommend that at mealtime they try the town's famous St. Peter's Fish.

Resorts

Besides the areas of the Dead Sea, Israel boasts some other popular resorts. On the Mediterranean coast, among the trendiest and most deluxe resorts are **Netanya** and **Herzliya**, located between Tel Aviv and Haifa. At the southern tip of the country, on the Red Sea, Eilat offers excellent skin-diving, snorkeling, and especially beautiful coral reefs.

Possible Itineraries

Seven days in Israel should be considered a minimum visit. After landing in Tel Aviv and spending a day or two there, your clients can head to Jerusalem for three

The Sea of Galilee
Photo by C. J. Ghormley

or four days and then explore the environs—including Bethlehem. They then can head up to Nazareth and the Sea of Galilee, over to Haifa, and then down the coast back to Tel Aviv for a couple of days. Return visitors or those wishing to explore more of the area outside Jerusalem can head into the Negev (and down to Eilat), and add some resort stops at the Mediterranean or Dead seas. It would be easy for a tourist to fill up two weeks in Israel.

Lodging Options

Atlas is an upscale Israeli chain, while **Moriah** rates as first class. Moderate hotels in Israel can be quite good, which should help you plan FITs for your budget-minded clients. **Isrotel** has a large presence in Eilat. There are also many North American chains represented in Israel; indeed, the **Hyatt Regency Jerusalem** may be the nation's best hotel.

In Jerusalem, the largest clusters of hotels are around the Convention Center and Independence Park, west of the Old City. One of the most famous hotels in town is the **King David**, offering great charm and elegance. Tel Aviv hotels are packed along the coast, south of the Atzma ut botanic gardens. For alternative lodging, you might suggest an all-inclusive resort or a health spa. Many kibbutzes (collective farms) also offer accommodations for visitors. The Israeli Tourist Bureau can help you arrange such accommodations for your clients, if this interests them.

Allied Destinations

Israel is an ideal gateway to the entire Middle East, bordering (as it does) Jordan, Saudi Arabia, Lebanon, Syria, and Egypt. European destinations are logical extensions of a trip to or from Israel. Indeed, most clients from North America who visit Israel stop off somewhere in Europe or North Africa.

Cultural Patterns

It's important that your clients visiting Israel, especially those traveling on business, understand the customs of the land.

It's against the law in certain hotels and restaurants to smoke during the Sabbath, from sundown Friday until nighttime Saturday.

Many businesses close on the Sabbath.

- Inform your clients that *shalom* has at least three meanings: hello, goodbye, and peace.

- Israeli society is quite informal. Some examples: Ties are worn only for important occasions; titles are rarely used; schedules aren't strictly adhered to. Your clients should feel comfortable in using an Israeli's first name soon after meeting him or her.

- Though Israelis are informal in their dealings, make sure your clients don't misunderstand this. For instance, Israelis expect precision in conversation, expect appointments to be met, and take few things for granted.

- Your clients should be aware that when an Israeli invites a guest to his or her home, this is not an offer made lightly or out of a sense of politeness. It's not necessary for your clients to bring a gift, but a book is appropriate.

Factors That Motivate Visitors

Among the reasons clients are inspired to visit Israel are:

All Jews throughout the world have the automatic right to be Israeli citizens.

- The country is important to many different religious faiths. It boasts places many of your clients have heard of from the time they were infants.

- The history, archaeology, and culture are fascinating.

- The climate is extremely good.

- There's great opportunity for outdoor activities, including diving.

Qualifying the Client
Israel

FOR CLIENTS WHO WANT	APPEAL			REMARKS
	HIGH	MEDIUM	LOW	
Historical and Cultural Attractions	▲			Sites appealing to Jews, Moslems, and Christians
Beaches and Water Sports		▲		Along Mediterranean
Skiing Opportunities			▲	Limited skiing in north
Lots of Nightlife			▲	Some in Tel Aviv and Jerusalem
Family Activities		▲		Primarily sightseeing
Familiar Cultural Experience			▲	
Exotic Cultural Experience	▲			
Safety and Low Crime			▲	Long history of strife; danger now seems low
Bargain Travel		▲		
Impressive Scenery		▲		
Peace and Quiet			▲	Jerusalem and Tel Aviv bustling
Shopping Opportunities		▲		Handicrafts, religious souvenirs
To Do Business		▲		Strong trade ties with U.S.

Figure 20-2

Case Study

Deborah and Jerry Levin have wanted to visit Israel for years. This spring, they've saved up and are finally going for seven days. The couple, in their early fifties, has never traveled much, and then mostly through the United States. They've been to Mexico and Canada a few times and went to Europe about five years ago. They've been reading all manner of history books and watching videos to get ready.

Circle the answer that best suits your clients' needs:

1. Which of the following services would be most appropriate for you to sell to the Levins?

   A Mediterranean cruise   A moderately priced hotel

   A two-day stopover in Europe   A stay at a seaside resort

   Why?

2. Which of the following places would *not* be a good idea to send the Levins to for a day trip from Jerusalem?

   Bethlehem   Jericho

   Luxor   Masada

   Why?

3. Which of the following tips would be the best one for you to tell to the Levins?

   Go in August.   Drink bottled beverages.

   Do your shopping on Saturday.   Dress is very informal.

   Why?

4. In addition to experiencing the history of Israel, the Levins would like to enjoy some of the modern-day culture. Where should you direct them?

   Tel Aviv   Eilat

   Haifa   Babylon

   Why?

Creative Activity

You're an American filmmaker who's been hired by the Israeli Department of Tourism to shoot a fifteen-second commercial for broadcast on U.S. television. You must start by creating a "shot" list of images that will go along with the music and narration that the Israelis have already decided upon.

Complete the list of shots below. (A few are already filled in.) Your images may be of people, places, or things.

SOUNDTRACK	IMAGES
Slow, romantic, full orchestrated music, with slight Middle Eastern allusions	1.
	2. Olive-treed garden
	3.
	4.
	5.
Music changes to peppy, intense, active beat	6.
	7. Cruise ship sailing into Haifa
	8.
Narration: "Israel: So much to see, so much to do, so much to relive."	9.
	10.
	11. Smiling children
	12.

Travel Trivia

Places with Dramatic Views

The Masada Plateau, Israel
Machu Picchu, Peru
The Pali Lookout, Oahu
St. Mark's Campanile, Venice
The Empire State Building, New York City
Mont Royal, Montreal
The 10th floor of the Samaritaine Dept. Store, Paris
Telegraph Hill, San Francisco
Westin Stamford Hotel (70th Floor), Singapore
Mulholland Drive, Los Angeles

Victoria Peak, Hong Kong
Pincio Hill, Rome
The Eiffel Tower, Paris
The Roof of St. Peter's, Vatican City
The Skylon Tower, Niagara Falls
Borobudur Tower, Indonesia
The Forum Hotel, Budapest
Corcorado Mountain, Brazil
Great Wall of China, Badaling

SUDAN

ETHIOPIA

Lake Turkana

UGANDA

KENYA

Rift

Valley

SOMALIA

▲ Samburu
National
Reserve

Lake Nakuru
National
Park

Aberdare
National Park

▲ Mt. Kenya

Equator

Lake
Victoria

▲ Hell's Gate

▲ Masai Mara National Reserve

✪ Nairobi

RWANDA

▲ Olorgesailie Prehistoric Site

ZAMBIA

▲ Serengeti
National
Park

▲ Amboseli
National
Park

▲ Tsavo
National
Park

● Malindi

Ngorogoro ▲
Crater

Arusha

Mt.
▲ Kilimanjaro

Mombasa

● Mkalama

Shimoni

TANZANIA

Zanzibar

● Dodoma

Dar es Salaam

Mafia Island

INDIAN OCEAN

ZIMBABWE

▲ Selous
Wildlife
Reserve

MALAWI

MOZAMBIQUE

Handwritten notes:

Egypt, Kenya
Tanzania on
save for tourist

moslem city
moslem architecture
Kenya: was a British
colony.

Cap idol, airport
on the ocean

CHAPTER **21**

Who might go to Kenya?
wild animals, national parks, reserves
birds migration,

Tunesia - is French

Kenya and Tanzania
The Lion Sleeps Tonight

A herd of antelopes race and leap across the high grass of a seemingly unending savannah, as giraffes, zebras, and elephants rest at nearby watering holes.
That one image defines both Kenya and Tanzania [tan-zah-NEE-ah]. These countries not only preserve their wildlife, they've made a mission out of it. Their
wildlife reserves and national parks attract considerable trade. That income has
fueled their drive to become among the greatest natural refuges for animals in the
world. The lions do indeed sleep here: in safety, in aloof majesty, and, unlike the
title of the famous song, during the day as often as at night.

Kenya is located on the east coast of central Africa. Ethiopia is to the north,
Somalia and the **Indian Ocean** are to the east. Uganda lies against Kenya's western
border and Tanzania fronts the southern border. About the size of Texas, Kenya is
bisected by the equator. Also splitting the country, but from north to south, is the
western region's **Rift Valley**, which continues south into Tanzania. **Nairobi**, the

A group of Masai people, Kenya
Photo by William and Marie Rourke

For Your Information . . .

Kenya and Tanzania

CAPITALS: Kenya: Nairobi
Tanzania: Dodoma

AREAS (SQUARE MILES): Kenya: 225,000
Tanzania: 364,899

TIME ZONE: GMT +3

DRIVE ON: Left

POPULATION: Kenya: 27,800,000
Tanzania: 30,800,000

RELIGIONS: Christianity, Islam

LANGUAGES: Swahili, English

CURRENCIES: Kenya:1 Kenya shilling = 100 cents
Tanzania: 1 Tanzanian shilling = 100 cents

ELECTRICITY: 200 volts, 50 cycles AC

CAPSULE HISTORY: **Kenya and Tanzania**: First occupied by bushmen; herdsmen arrive from the north, Bantu tribesmen from the west, early A.D.; Arab traders settle coastal area, pre-Middle Ages; Portuguese explore, late 1400s.
Kenya: British occupy, late 1800s; British protectorate, 1895; British Crown colony, 1920–1963; Mau Mau revolt, 1952–1955; independence, 1963.
Tanzania: Portuguese and Arabs create Sultanate of Zanzibar, through mid-1800s; Tanganyika becomes German protectorate, 1886; becomes British protectorate, 1920; gains independence, 1961; merges with Zanzibar to become Tanzania, 1964.

For reference sources, tourist bureaus, and suggested lengths of stay, see Appendices.

Don't even consider sneaking home ivory or wildlife items (such as skins). It's highly illegal and it encourages poaching.

capital, is in south-central Kenya; most of the country's wildlife reserves can be reached in a few hours from here by road or by air. **Mombasa**, in the very southeast, along the coast, is Kenya's main cruise seaport. Kenya also has nearly 400 miles of beaches along the warm waters of the Indian Ocean.

To Tanzania's north are Kenya and Uganda, and to the south are Zambia, Mozambique, and Malawi; across Lake Tanganyika to the west is the Democratic Republic of the Congo. Also to Tanzania's west are the small countries of Rwanda and Burundi. Like Kenya, Tanzania is bordered on the east by the Indian Ocean. **Dodoma**, in the center of the country, is the new capital. **Dar Es Salaam**, the former capital, is the major seaport and gateway.

There's a wide mix of cultures and tribes in Kenya and Tanzania. The national language is Swahili, though English is widely spoken.

How Travelers Get There

The main gateway into Kenya is Nairobi, at **Jomo Kenyatta International Airport** (NBO). Flying time from New York is thirteen-and-a-half hours. Many international airlines fly here, most notably European ones; since the flight from North America is so long, you might suggest a stopover in Europe. Kenya is a common cruise departure or return point for ships visiting the islands of Madagascar, Mauritius, and the Seychelles. Several European carriers land in Tanzania at **Kilimanjaro Airport** (JRO) or **Dar Es Salaam International Airport** (DAR). **Air Tanzania** (TC) services travelers within the country. It's also often accessed by land via Nairobi, Kenya.

Weather Patterns

The equator bisects Kenya; however, because of its generally high altitudes, the climate in much of the nation is cooler than your clients would expect in an equatorial country (see Figure 21-1). The desert-like northerly regions of Kenya tend to be drier and hotter than the southern highlands, though temperatures are fairly constant year-round. Nairobi, in the south, ranges from an average high in the 70s to an average low in the 50s; the north runs about ten degrees warmer. The only truly tropical climate is along the coast, where Mombasa is located. The main tourist season is November through February, but July through September is also popular. The Kenyan rain pattern is quite unusual. There are two rainy seasons: March through May (Kenyans call it "the long rains") and, again, October through early December (called "the short rains"). Tanzania's temperature is fairly steady year-round, in the 70s and 80s. Summer is the driest season, with most rain falling in the winter and spring. The mountain areas can get quite cold.

Getting Around

Since most of your clients will likely visit Kenya or Tanzania to see the wildlife, the most common way for them to travel is by minibus, four-wheel-drive vehicle, or

Climate at a Glance
NAIROBI, KENYA

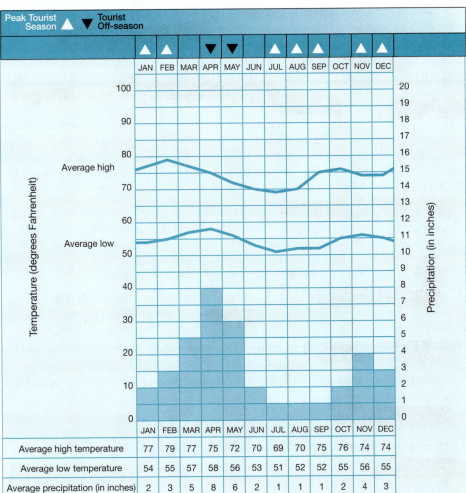

	JAN	FEB	MAR	APR	MAY	JUN	JUL	AUG	SEP	OCT	NOV	DEC
Average high temperature	77	79	77	75	72	70	69	70	75	76	74	74
Average low temperature	54	55	57	58	56	53	51	52	52	55	56	55
Average precipitation (in inches)	2	3	5	8	6	2	1	1	1	2	4	3

Figure 21-1

small plane—usually as part of an organized photo safari tour. If your clients do rent their own vehicles, let them know that driving in Kenya and Tanzania is on the left, that the roads are often narrow, and that unpredictable road conditions may make driving an unwise idea. There's a fairly good rail system here. Buses, however, are crowded and uncomfortable. In Nairobi, the taxi system is good: Your clients will have the choice of taking normal everyday cabs, or *matatus,* which pick up passengers and go to more than one destination. Finally, hot-air balloon trips over Kenya's sprawling grasslands have become increasingly popular, often as part of a safari.

Clients often ask what a safari is like. In brief, your clients will head out into the bush to lodges. The group will then set out from the lodges early in the morning along bumpy, dusty roads to spot the animals when they are most active. The vehicles sometimes leave the road to get to where the animals are; the vehicle roof opens—which permits tourists to view the animals from safety, yet at close range.

> **Safaris are no longer taken to kill animals, but to photograph them.**

Important Places

It's likely that most of your clients will want to visit Kenya in order to experience its remarkable wildlife. If so, they'll want to base their trip out of Nairobi.

Kenya

Nairobi, lying relatively near the equator, is a city of contrasts: at once sophisticated and primitive. A great many beautiful parks are here, along with a lovely forest preserve and an excellent aviary. The **Kenya National Museum** has a top collection of African arts and crafts, as well as a superb explanation of Kenya's prehistory. **Nairobi National Park** provides a wide range of animals in their natural habitat and a quick "sampler" of the safaris beyond. Day trips from Nairobi include the beautiful scenery of **Hell's Gate National Park**, as well as **Olorgesailie Prehistoric Site**, near **Lake Magadi**.

The national parks and reserves are beautiful year-round, especially when wildebeests and zebras are migrating. The Kenya Tourist Bureau can tell you when herds of a particular species will probably begin migrating. (That information will impress your clients!) About forty wildlife reserves exist in Kenya. The most popular of them are:

- **Masai Mara National Reserve**—perhaps the best of all—is the northern extension of the Greater Serengeti Plains and borders Tanzania in the southwest. A particularly wide range of animals gathers here, most notably zebra and wildebeest (both of which have renowned migrations through the region). **Lake Victoria**, the world's second largest freshwater lake, is nearby.

- **Aberdare National Park**, in the central highlands, is noted for its waterfalls, rain forests, and banyan trees. **Mt. Kenya**, the second highest mountain in Africa, is nearby.

- **Amboseli National Park** is on the Tanzanian border, southeast of Nairobi. In the early morning of a clear day, your clients will be able to look across its flat borderland and see Mt. Kilimanjaro. Elephants are found in especially large numbers in Amboseli.

- **Tsavo National Park** is in the southeast corner of Kenya, also on the Tanzanian border. It's Kenya's largest national park. Actually, Tsavo is closer to Mombasa than it is to Nairobi and may be more easily accessed from that coastal city.

- **The equator** is a popular destination itself. It's located a few hours north of Nairobi.

> **Lake Victoria has nothing to do with Victoria Falls, which is 800 miles to the southwest, on the Zambia-Zimbabwe border.**

Other destinations that may interest your clients visiting Kenya are:

- **Samburu National Reserve**, in the northern, dry bush country, has particularly exotic animals, such as the Beisa oryx, the blue-necked Somali ostrich, Grevy's zebra, and all manner of crocodile.
- **Lake Nakuru National Park** is a beautiful refuge for a variety of animals and especially for birds. It's located in southwestern Kenya, in the Rift Valley, northwest of Nairobi. It's most noted for its grand flock of pink flamingos.
- **Mombasa** is Kenya's main cruise port. Largely a Moslem city, it has a great many mosques. Your clients may especially enjoy the excellent crafts-shopping and some fine beaches nearby.
- **Coral reef beaches** are protected by the government. Easily accessible from Mombasa, there are some lovely towns here. **Malindi** and **Shimoni** are the most popular.

Tanzania

Arusha usually serves as the departure and return point for the multi-day safaris that visit Tanzania's many wildlife preserves. Swahili and English are the official languages.

The country's prime attractions lie mostly along the "Northern Crescent," which starts in Nairobi, Kenya:

- **Serengeti National Park** is one of the world's most famous and finest wildlife preserves. Located in the north, this 5,000-square-mile park is best known for its herds—especially wildebeests and zebras—that migrate during May and June, then again in September. Nearby is the renowned **Olduvai Gorge**, where Dr. Louis Leakey discovered some of the earliest-known fossils of man.
- **Other wildlife preserves** can be visited here as well. Among the best: the huge **Selous Wildlife Reserve**, noted for its elephants, and Lake Manyara National Park, a small reserve with spectacular pink flamingos. **Ngorongoro Crater**, ten miles across, shelters large herds of lions, zebras, elephants, and rhinos; clients can view them in the crater from four-wheel-drive vehicles.

A rhino at Ngorongoro Crater, Tanzania
Photo by C. J. Ghormley

- **Zanzibar**, a large and pretty island that once was an independent country, has fine, nearly empty beaches and interesting Arabic architecture, notably in Stone Town. (Wonderful beaches are also found at Dar Es Salaam and **Mafia Island**.)
- **Lake Victoria** is in an extremely scenic area. But it's just for viewing, not for swimming (too many bacteria).
- **Mount Kilimanjaro**, the highest mountain in Africa, is a stunning sight. Your more adventurous clients can hike to its snow-capped top in about five days, either on their own or, preferably, as part of a hiking group. September, October, January, and February are ideal for such hikes, since clouds often obscure the mountain at other times. (Best view, though, is from Kenya.)

Possible Itineraries

Unlike most destinations, Kenya and Tanzania may be different each time a visitor arrives—depending, of course, on which herds are migrating and which animals can be seen. Because each area of the country specializes in different species, you should recommend that your clients—especially first-time visitors—spend at least a week here. Starting in Nairobi, they could then visit Masai Mara and Aberdare, and then head up to Mt. Kenya and Samburu. For your clients who want to spend more time, you could suggest adding Amboseli and Tsavo, or direct them to Mombasa and the coral beach towns. Travelers to Tanzania use Arusha as a gateway to Serengeti National Park, Ngorongoro Crater, and Mt. Kilimanjaro. Extensions to this itinerary could include Selous Wildlife Reserve, or the beaches of Zanzibar (which also boasts historical sites) and Mafia Island.

Lodging Options

Several North American chains serve Kenya, including **Inter-Continental**. For a special experience, you could suggest that clients visiting Aberdare National Park stay

Treetops Lodge, Kenya
Photo by William and Marie Rourke

PART V   Africa and the Middle East

at nearby **Treetops Hotel** (a hotel whose fame may exceed its actual quality). Its lodging is raised on stilts, and your clients can watch the wild animals that come to drink water and lick salt. (You should try to book the more expensive rooms that overlook the watering hole.) Other renowned places for your clients to stay are the **Ark** lodging facility (similar to Treetops, but better) and the **Mt. Kenya Safari Club**, a lush, luxurious resort. Most hotels in Tanzania are in Arusha and the wildlife reserves. **Serena Lodges and Hotels** has properties in both Kenya and Tanzania. The **Lake Manyara Hotel** offers great views. Alternative accommodations include lodges and camping facilities, both of which can be found in the wildlife reserves.

Allied Destinations

If a trip to Kenya is to be extended, it most commonly would be to Tanzania, and vice versa. Most of the other countries in the region have political problems or limited tourist facilities which make these improbable add-ons. (However Ethiopia, Uganda, Malawi, and the Democratic Republic of Congo are beginning to attract visitors.) Two other major destinations, Israel and Egypt, are relatively nearby; your clients may want to include Kenya or Tanzania on a trip to either of these countries. Further, your clients may want to break up the long flight from North America with a stopover in Europe.

Qualifying the Client
Kenya and Tanzania

FOR CLIENTS WHO WANT	APPEAL			REMARKS
	HIGH	MEDIUM	LOW	
Historical and Cultural Attractions			▲	Wildlife, primarily
Beaches and Water Sports		▲		Impressive coral reefs
Skiing Opportunities			▲	None
Lots of Nightlife			▲	Some in Nairobi
Family Activities		▲		Children love safaris
Familiar Cultural Experience			▲	
Exotic Cultural Experience	▲			
Safety and Low Crime			▲	Recent incidents well-publicized
Bargain Travel			▲	Airfare and safaris can be expensive
Impressive Scenery	▲			A little of everything
Peace and Quiet		▲		Quietest on wildlife reserves, though animals can get noisy at night
Shopping Opportunities			▲	Local handicrafts
To Do Business			▲	

Figure 21-2

Cultural Patterns

It's likely that many of your clients visiting Kenya and Tanzania will be on an organized safari. Still, it's important that they understand the special traditions of the region. Moreover, you may also have business clients traveling there.

- In Kenya, pointing with an index finger is very insulting; tell your clients to use their whole hand. Remind clients not to use the left hand alone when passing or receiving an item. (This is true in Tanzania, as well.)
- Your clients should be prepared to give hearty handshakes on greeting a Kenyan. A "soft" handshake is considered effeminate. So, too, is the use of cologne by men, especially to those Kenyans who live outside urban centers.
- Tell your clients to bring a gift if they are visiting a home. And they should be aware that socializing is often done at the end of the meal rather than beforehand; they should follow their host's lead.

Factors That Motivate Visitors

It's easy to assume why your clients might want to visit Kenya and Tanzania. However, understanding all of their reasons will help you plan their trip. Among these reasons are:

- The wildlife is among the finest and most accessible in the world.
- Safaris are easily booked and provide safety in an adventurous environment.
- The culture is intriguing.
- Shopping choices are quite interesting.
- English is commonly spoken there.
- Tanzania has sites of historical interest.
- There are lovely beaches.
- There's warm, pleasant weather year-round.
- Mombasa is a prime cruise embarkation and debarkation port.

Possible Misgivings

Kenya and Tanzania are beautiful yet challenging countries. There'll be quite a few questions that you'll have to address when trying to sell this destination to clients:

- "It's so far." Break up the trip with European or Middle Eastern stops.
- "There's a great danger of disease." Kenya and Tanzania can be quite safe, so long as your clients check with a doctor before leaving North America and take necessary precautions.
- "African languages make it impossible to communicate." English is widely spoken in both countries.
- "The water and food can make you sick." Tell your clients to drink bottled liquids and make sure that food is properly prepared.
- "All there is to do there is go on a safari." There are also some very nice coral beaches off the east coast. However, if your clients don't like safaris, this may be the wrong destination for them, though hiking, shopping, and cultural exploration are all valid reasons to visit these countries.
- "It's so expensive to get there." It is expensive, but costs within the country are reasonable. An all-inclusive packaged tour can help keep prices under control.
- "It's dangerous." Crime does occur, often with a great deal of publicity. Check on any advisories. Book the client on an escorted safari with a reputable company.

Don't walk alone at night in Nairobi. Even walking in groups may be dangerous.

Case Study

Dr. Ernest Rollo and his wife, Anne, are a couple in their late sixties. They've always taken their annual vacation on their own. This year they want to go to Kenya, but are wary about traveling there alone, so they've decided to take a packaged tour. They've come to you to discuss which trip would be the best to take. They can go only in February.

Circle the answer that best suits your clients' needs:

1. They want to visit as many national parks as possible. Which of the following would you *not* suggest they go to?

   Amboseli   Aberdare

   Mombasa   Tsavo

   Why?

2. Which of the following tips would *not* be appropriate to pass along to the Rollos?

   You'll need to bring sweaters.   Zebra skins are great bargains.

   Exchange money only in a bank.   Drive on the left.

   Why?

3. Which of the following services would *not* be best for you to book?

   Business-class airfare   Accommodations in a lodge

   An Amazon cruise   A hot-air balloon trip

   Why?

4. The Rollos decide to extend their trip beyond just Kenya for a few days. What other nearby country might you suggest they visit?

   Tanzania   South Africa

   Morocco   Ivory Coast

   Why?

Creative Activity

Would the following famous persons like visiting Kenya and Tanzania? Why or why not? What specifically would appeal to them?

1. *Donald Trump* (multimillionaire):

2. *Madonna* (singer-actress):

3. *Homer Simpson* (cartoon character):

4. *Oprah Winfrey* (talk-show host):

5. *Tom Cruise* (actor):

6. *Your teacher:*

Travel Trivia

Cultural Surprises

In Kenya and Tanzania, the verbal "tch, tch" sound is considered an insult.

The American "okay" sign is obscene in Russia.

In Switzerland, asking for salt and pepper while dining is an insult to the cook.

The U.S. hitchhiking sign is obscene in Yugoslavia.

To drink ice water with a meal is a peculiarly American custom.

In France, a salad is served after the main course, not before.

In Japan, one should accept a gift with two hands.

In Moslem countries, to show the soles of one's shoes while seated is very rude behavior.

8 countries in Africa will be asked.

ATLANTIC OCEAN

Azores

Madeira Islands

Canary Islands

Strait of Gibraltar

BLACK SEA

CASPIAN SEA

MEDITERRANEAN SEA

Atlas Mountains

MOROCCO

TUNISIA

ALGERIA

LIBYA

EGYPT

Jordan River

JORDAN

Persian Gulf

BAHRAIN QATAR

Sahara

Desert

Lake Nassar

Gulf of Suez

SAUDI ARABIA

UNITED ARAB EMIRATES

OMAN

middle of nowhere MALI

WESTERN SAHARA

MAURITANIA

Gambia River

NIGER

CHAD

Nile River

RED SEA

ERITREA

YEMEN

ARABIAN SEA

hottest place in the world

SENEGAL

Niger River

SUDAN

GAMBIA

GUINEA BISSAU

BURKINA FASO

Lake Chad

SIERRA LEONE

IVORY COAST

GUINEA

NIGERIA

CENTRAL AFRICAN REPUBLIC

ETHIOPIA

INDIAN OCEAN

LIBERIA

Lake Volta

CAMEROON

UGANDA

Lake Turkana

SOMALIA

two British colony

GHANA

BENIN

TOGO

Congo River

Lake Albert

Lake Victoria

KENYA

EQUATOR

GABON

CONGO

RWANDA

BURUNDI

Mt. Kilimanjaro

highest mt. in Africa

Seychelles

DEMOCRATIC REPUBLIC OF THE CONGO

Lake Tanganyika

TANZANIA

Comoro Islands

MALAWI

ANGOLA

ZAMBIA

Lake Malawi

MOZAMBIQUE

Victoria Falls

Zambezi River

South America & Europe & Africa

imp. of suez canal.

* the first Africa slaves came to America from GAMBIA

ATLANTIC OCEAN

NAMIBIA

ZIMBABWE

BOTSWANA

Mauritius

MADAGASCAR

Reunion

"Rift Valley"

* Africa Queen based on the Congo River

Cold water

Kalahari Desert

SOUTH AFRICA

SWAZILAND

LESOTHO

INDIAN OCEAN

CHAPTER 22

African and Middle Eastern Potpourri

In describing the vast area that is Africa and the Middle East, writer John Gunther once said, "One travels like a golf ball, hopping from green to green." To Gunther, each "green" was a unique and far-flung tourist destination: sacred sites, archaeological wonders, towering waterfalls, great herds of exotic beasts. And such attractions aren't limited to Egypt, Kenya, Tanzania, and Israel. Africa and the Middle East constitute a huge region, one brimming with attractions. So, to make your selling of Africa as easy as possible, we divide this chapter into eight important regions of tourism.

Many of the emerging nations discussed in this section suffer from political and economic uncertainties. You should continually check government travel warnings on current situations and keep up on the news. Remember, too, to prepare your clients for the potential disorganization and lower levels of service that mark emerging countries such as these.

Morocco

North American travelers are finding out what Europeans have long known: Morocco is one of Africa's most exotic yet accessible destinations. Often visited as a southern side-trip from Spain, it's just a few miles across the Strait of Gibraltar. Most of its attraction-cities lie along the cool and dry Mediterranean coast, while inland are broad, hot deserts, and the **Atlas Mountains**. French and Arabic are the principal languages.

Important Places

- **Casablanca** (CAS) is Morocco's air gateway city. All the ambience made famous by the film of the same name—the dimly lit nightclubs, narrow streets, frenetic Casbah—is really here. Its **Great Mosque** is a noteworthy attraction, and two churches—**Sacred Heart Cathedral** and **Notre Dame of Lourdes**—are impressive. Several day-trip destinations are worthwhile: **Rabat**, the capital; and **Chellah**, the site of Roman ruins.

- **Tangier**, just across from Spain and Gibraltar, has long been a prime port of entry. As a result, cultures have mixed freely and Tangier has achieved

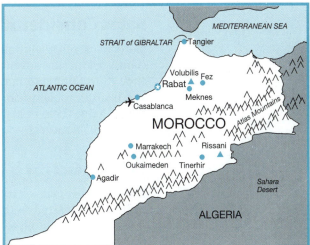

Walls of the Casbah, Tangier, Morocco
Photo by William and Marie Rourke

The world's oldest existing educational institution is a university in Fez. It was founded in 859 A.D.

renowned cuisine. The attractions are limited, but the **Sultan's Palace**, within the Casbah, warrants a visit.

- **Fez** is Morocco's oldest city and a major center of the Islamic religion. Its *medina* (Arabic for marketplace), **Qarawiyin Mosque**, and old walled city-section are usual stops for tourists. Two major day trips from Fez: **Meknes**, often called the "Versailles of Morocco"; and **Volubilis**, the site of some of the best Roman ruins in North Africa.

- **Marrakech**, Morocco's most popular tourist destination, is usually reached by train from Casablanca. Its most fanciful attraction is **Djemaa el Fna Square**—with its snake charmers, fortune tellers, food vendors, and close-by bazaar. Marrakech is also noted for its daily **Fantasia**—a feast of food, music, dance, and horse-mounted guards who (while firing their guns in the air) charge at your clients. Marrakech is also poised strategically between mountain and sea: **Oukaimeden**, an Atlas Mountain ski resort, is to the south; and **Agadir**, a beach resort, is to the southwest.

Sales Considerations

Morocco is relatively inexpensive, so it'll appeal to bargain hunters. It's sufficiently exotic for adventurous clients, yet geographically and culturally close enough to Europe to make it appealing to more timid travelers. Its street crime and health problems can be vexing to some clients; sell them up to high-quality hotels, lodge them in better areas, and book them on escorted tours to keep them from unpleasantness.

Northern Africa

This region—much of it covered by the **Sahara Desert**—exhibits a strong Arab influence. Bordered to the north by the **Mediterranean Sea**, a few of its destinations are close enough to Europe to be booked as day trips from there. And east of Northern Africa is the Middle East—technically a part of Asia.

[handwritten note: known for its casbah district. French]

Important Places

Northern Africa's destinations are among the most unusual on the continent. We've already discussed Egypt in its own chapter and Morocco in the previous section. We now cover the other countries.

Algeria. Algeria borders the Mediterranean at the northern tip of the continent. It's reached by several European carriers from the United States or Canada, as well as via **Air Algeria** (AH), the national airline, which flies in from Europe. Flights land at **Houari Boumedienne Airport** (ALG) outside **Algiers**, the capital, on the country's north coast.

Algeria's climate is best along the Mediterranean. Summers are dry and very warm, with average temperatures in the 80s, whereas winters can be chilly and rainy. The desert interior tends to be hotter and drier, and the Atlas Mountain area can get cool to cold. Algeria's national languages are Arabic and French. Among the most popular sites in Algeria are:

- **Algiers** is best known for its **Casbah** district *[handwritten: Islamic quater]* (made famous by Charles Boyer's movie line, "Come with me to the Casbah."); it's dirty, hilly, crowded, but historic. There's an excellent **Museum of Classical and Moslem Antiquities**, several noteworthy mosques, and the famed **Jardin d'Essai** gardens. Nearby are many Roman ruins.

- **Constantine**, and the Roman ruins that surround it, lie just east of Algiers, high on a rocky bluff. The **Ahmed Bey Palace** and the **Gustave Mercier Art Museum** are among the city's most noteworthy attractions.

- **Batna** is a gateway to vast Roman ruins in **Timgad**.

Algeria has experienced several acts of fundamentalist terrorism in recent years. Check the current political climate before recommending it.

Tunisia. Also on Africa's northern coast is Tunisia. Arabic and French are its national languages. With a long, winding coastline, much of the country is graced

The Coliseum at El Jem, Tunisia, rivals the one in Rome.

by a warm, breezy Mediterranean climate that's ideal for resorts; in fact, the first Club Med was built here. Winters can be rainy.

Tunis, the northern capital, occupies an area that, in ancient days, was the powerful city-state of Carthage. (You may remember from your history books how its general, Hannibal, nearly defeated the Roman Empire.) Today, Tunis boasts excellent ruins (including those of Carthage), the **National Museum**, the **Bardo Museum**, the **Medina**, and the **Great Mosque**. A visit to Tunisia often includes a visit to **Matmata**, an underground city where more than 10,000 people live. The southeastern island of **Djerba** has interesting ruins and beaches and is very popular among Europeans; **Hammamet**, in the north, is a modern beach resort.

Mali. Mali borders Algeria on the southwest. The national languages here are French and Bambara. Be sure to let your clients know that not much English is spoken in Mali. Tourist services here are somewhat unreliable.

Its most famous city is **Timbuktu**, once one of the world's most inaccessible areas. Timbuktu doesn't offer much to see—but, then, that's sort of the point. Your clients may enjoy going to **Mopti**, an island-city with good shopping, a graceful mosque, and the nearby cliff-dwelling Dogons, with their unique art and culture. There's an impressive mosque in the ancient city of **Djenné**; and **Bamako** (the capital) has lovely grottoes, a botanical garden, and extensive shopping. River trips up the Niger and desert safaris are popular among ambitious travelers.

Ethiopia. Bordering the east coast is Ethiopia, a mountainous, poverty-ridden country. It does feature some interesting mosques, tombs, palaces, and a good zoo in **Addis Ababa**, the capital. The ancient town of **Aksum** (a major religious site) features ruins, the country's crown jewels, and the **Palace of the Queen of Sheba**. A visit here could coincide with a trip to nearby Egypt or to Kenya.

Eritrea. Once controlled by Ethiopia and now independent, Eritrea has potential: Diving along its Red Sea coast is good and its capital, **Asmera**, feels like an Italian city. *Tourists may go bec. of Red Sea (diving)*

Sales Considerations

North Africa is strategically central to travel. The reason: It's just south of Europe (separated by only the Mediterranean), just west of the Middle East (indeed, Egypt can be considered a part of both regions), and the gateway to the rest of Africa. Escorted tours, especially desert safaris, are popular here, since they wrap lodging and travel into one efficient package. This is a destination, though, that appeals mostly to bargain-hunters, the adventurous (archaeologists, for instance), or lovers of desert culture. Its Mediterranean beaches offer your clients some excellent opportunities for a resort stay, usually among European tourists.

Haile Selassie, Ethiopia's emperor from 1931 to 1974, once visited Jamaica and made such an impression that many Jamaicans still revere him deeply.

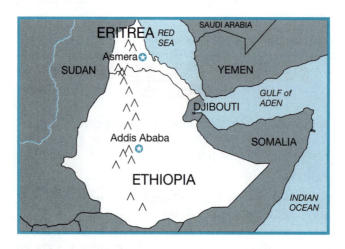

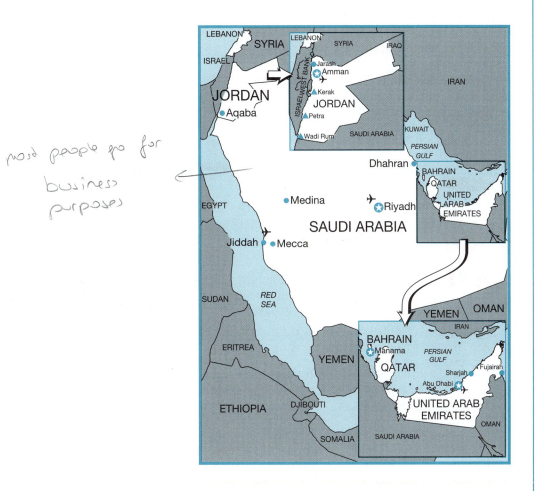

most people go for business purposes

The Middle East

The Middle East is one of the world's most newsworthy, volatile, and historically important regions. Though the political climate here fluctuates constantly, the area remains well visited, especially by business clients. (Tourists tend to gravitate toward Israel and Egypt.) The Middle East is bordered by Europe to the north, Africa on the west (in fact, Egypt—considered part of the Middle East—is actually on the African continent), and Asia on the east. The **Arabian Sea** lies just to the south.

Important Places

Religious sites and historical landmarks—that's what the Middle East is famous for. We've listed key nations in their order of importance to your clients.

Saudi Arabia.   Taking up the bulk of the Arabian Peninsula is Saudi Arabia. In a region known for its religious significance, the Islamic beliefs and laws in Saudi Arabia—the birthplace of Mohammed—are among the strictest. Jordan and the **Red Sea** are to its west, Iraq and the **Persian Gulf** to the east, and Yemen and Oman to the south. There's limited direct air service here via North American carriers; more direct service is available via **Saudia Airlines** (SV), the national carrier, and by several European airlines. The main gateway is in the capital, **Riyadh** (RUH), in the center of the country; your clients can also find international service on the western coast, in **Jiddah** (JED), which is also the major port.

The climate in Saudi Arabia varies immensely from place to place, but daytime heat is a near constant. Temperatures in Riyadh climb from a spring and fall average in the 90s to the 100s in the summer; winters are cooler. Be sure to warn your clients about sandstorms; they can happen in any season. The national language is Arabic.

Some major religious destinations exist here, especially for Islamic pilgrims. Remember that Saudi Arabia gets major business trade from Western countries.

Over two million Moslems visit Mecca each year.

- **Mecca**, Mohammed's birthplace, is the holiest city in the Islamic religion. This is a major pilgrimage destination—Moslems must visit it at least once in their lives as part of a voyage called the *haj*—but it is closed to non-Moslem tourists. Two of the most sacred sites are the gigantic **Holy Ka'aba Shrine** and a huge **Mosque**.
- **Medina**, where Mohammed is buried, is the second holiest city to Moslems. Like Mecca, only Moslem pilgrims may enter the city.
- **Riyadh**, sitting in the middle of the desert, is a modern capital city. There are palaces, museums, and an old-city area.
- **Jiddah** is an interesting mixture of modern and old. There's lovely scenery, a good marketplace, several palaces, an old-city quarter to walk around, and Red Sea beaches nearby. Snorkeling here is excellent.
- **Dhahran** is of note to business travelers; it's a major oil field area on the Persian Gulf east coast, with nearby oases and good beaches.

protect area for Americans you can wear shorts

Jordan. Jordan—a major destination for Middle Eastern and European travelers—is wedged between Israel, Syria, Iraq, and Saudi Arabia. Access is via **Royal Jordanian Air** (RJ) to **Amman** (AMM). Jordan's principal attractions are:

- **Amman**, Jordan's hilly capital, with a notable archaeological museum and an old **Roman amphitheater** still in use. Nearby are the ruins of the Temple of Hercules and many structures built by the Crusaders.
- **Excellent archaeological sites**, including astonishng **Petra**, with its second-century buildings carved out of a stone mountainside. Most impressive, too, are the ruins of an old fortress and castle at **Kerak**. Excellent Greco-Roman ruins exist at **Jarash**.

Petra was used as the Holy Grail's resting place in *Indiana Jones and the Last Crusade.*

- **Aqaba**, a port and resort in the southern desert, with many beaches on the Red Sea that offer good water-sports opportunities; **Wadi Rum** (a fort associated with Lawrence of Arabia) and its "Valley of the Moon" landscape is nearby. The **Dead Sea** is shared between Jordan and Israel and several resorts line its coast.

The United Arab Emirates. Sitting on the eastern tip of the Arabian Peninsula is the small country of the United Arab Emirates. Seven emirates (each led by an emir, an Islamic chief or commander) united to form this nation, which is extremely oil-rich. Like **Kuwait** to the north, it's mainly a business destination, but there are some historic buildings and small beach resorts for leisure travelers. **Gulf Air** (GF) serves the UAE and other nearby destinations.

Abu Dhabi, the capital, has ancient ruins, an archaeological museum, and a good open-air market. In addition, the city boasts a major Middle Eastern gateway at **Abu Dhabi International Airport** (AUH). Excellent beaches line the Persian Gulf at **Fujairah** and **Sharjah**.

Lebanon. Located north of Israel and west of Syria, Lebanon was once one of the most popular tourist destinations in the region, but decades of strife virtually eliminated visitors. That's now changing. Potential attractions are **Beirut**, the capital city once known as "the Paris of the Middle East"; **Tyre**, with the remains of the ancient Phoenician civilization; and **Byblos**, one of the oldest towns in the world.

Bahrain. Bahrain is a tiny, multi-island, oil-producing nation, just off the east coast of Saudi Arabia, in the Persian Gulf. Compared to many of its neighbors, the formerly British-dominated country is fairly sophisticated and has some active nightlife. **Bahrain Island**, where the capital city of **Manama** is located, has marketplaces, mosques, and interesting archaeological sites. Bahrain's shores have some good beaches.

Sales Considerations

Leisure clients may avoid this region because of its political situation or the torrid climate. The Middle East *will* attract those who travel for religious or business reasons. It's also a prime location for those deeply interested in archaeology. There are some good snorkeling, deep-sea-fishing, and beach-resort opportunities here, though services aren't always up to Western standards. If political tensions ease, Iraq, Iran, and Syria—because their lands were so important in antiquity—could become viable tourist destinations.

West Africa

This region—largely of French culture—lies in the most recognizable area of Africa: along the "crook" where the continent bends around the **Gulf of Guinea**.

Important Places

Though most of the nations in this coastal region are tiny, they offer many unique attractions.

Nigeria.   The densely populated country of Nigeria is the most visited of western African countries, though most travelers come for business reasons (Nigeria is an oil producer) or as tourists from places other than North America. Nigeria is often subject to political unrest.

Senegal.   Steeped in Moslem culture, Senegal is the most westerly country in Africa. **Air Afrique** (RK) offers limited service from North America to **Dakar** (DKR), the capital. There's also service by several European airlines. **Air Senegal** (DS), the national carrier, will fly your clients within the country.

Summers here are quite hot, and August is particularly rainy; Senegal's winters are very warm, with almost no rain. The official languages are French and several local dialects. Among the attractions you should be aware of are:

- **Dakar**, *very moslem.* a fairly sophisticated city on the central coast, was designed in a style reminiscent of Paris, with wide boulevards. Dakar is proud of its theater, ballet, and fine beaches. The **IFAN Museum** is known for its African culture and arts collection. Popular day trips include the historical harbor area of the **Island of Goree**, a place from which slaves were originally shipped out. Also, **Cape Verde**

capital of Senegal

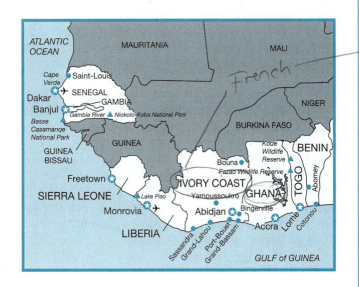

French → regions

(not to be confused with the Cape Verde islands, about 400 miles off the coast) profits from a rolling, volcanic landscape.

- **Saint-Louis**, the country's former capital, is a particularly beautiful fishing village.
- **Wildlife preserves** are favorite destinations here. Two of the best: **Niokolo-Koba National Park** and **Basse Casamance National Park**.
- **Cap Skirring** is a beach resort district not far from Basse Casamance National Park.

Ivory Coast.   Also known as Côte d'Ivoire, Ivory Coast lies along the southern coast of Africa's western arm. The influence of French culture is even stronger here than in Senegal and tourist services are better developed. There are limited flights from North America via Air Afrique (RK); a few European carriers also offer service from North America. The gateway is the capital of **Abidjan** (ABJ). The national carrier, **Air Ivoire** (VU), flies within the country. Ivory Coast has a hot climate almost year-round, though winters are largely rain-free. French and various local dialects are the national languages. Among the prime destinations:

- **Abidjan** is an active, fairly contemporary city; it's quite pretty and offers a zoo, palaces, a national museum, and gambling. It's often called "The Paris of Africa."
- **Luxurious (and expensive) resorts** can be found nearby in lovely **Grand-Bassam** (the country's former capital) and **Sassandra**.
- **Banana**, **pineapple**, and **coffee plantations** may be fun attractions for your clients. They can be visited not far from Abidjan in **Bingerville** and **Port-Bouet**.
- **Wildlife reserves** are located at such areas as **Grand-Lahou** and **Bouna**.
- **Our Lady of Peace** is a spectacular Roman Catholic cathedral; in fact, it's one of the largest in the world. Located in **Yamoussoukro**, this granite, glass, and marble structure cost more than $200 million and was paid for by the president of Ivory Coast, Felix Houphouet-Boigny.

Liberia.   Liberia began as a settlement of slaves freed from the United States. Its capital, **Monrovia** (founded in 1822), was named after U.S. President James Monroe. Liberia is frequently visited by African Americans. **Nigeria Airways** (WT), Air Afrique (RK), and European carriers fly here from North America into Monrovia (MLW), outside the capital. English is the official language; local dialects are also spoken.

Monrovia boasts a fine museum and cultural arts center. **Lake Piso** is in a beautiful area on the northwest coast. Liberia has recently suffered sporadic but serious political turmoil.

Sierra Leone.   On the west coast is the tiny nation of Sierra Leone. Settled by freed British slaves (English is one of its official languages), it is often visited along with Liberia; as such, it's a destination popular with your African-American clients.

The capital, **Freetown**, is in a beautiful, hilly area along the coast. A famous 500-year-old **cotton tree** stands near the fine **National Museum**, and several markets attract tourists. **Lumley Beach** is quite nice; in fact, the country features several deluxe resorts. Nearby are wildlife preserves.

The Gambia.   The Gambia runs from the **Atlantic Ocean** through a thin slice of Senegal, along the **Gambia River**. English and tribal languages are spoken here. The country is today best known as the starting point in Alex Haley's novel, *Roots;* it remains a popular destination of African Americans. This former British colony has good beaches and fishing. **Banjul**, its quiet capital, is a base for trips through the country and along the river.

Ghana.   Well known for its colorful festivals is Ghana, with its capital, **Accra**. Scenic beaches (but with rough waters), oceanside castles and forts, fishing,

NASA upgraded Banjul's airport to accommodate possible emergency landings by the space shuttle.

wildlife reserves, tribal ceremonies, and English-speaking locals—these are what account for Ghana's ever-increasing tourism.

Togo   The tiny nation of Togo is wedged along the southern coast of the western arm. The country is known for its beaches, casinos, and tribal rituals. Its main attractions, though, are probably the **Koue** and **Fazao Wildlife Reserves**, as well as the **Tchanga Wildlife Preserve**. (Strife and poverty have led to some of its animals being killed off.) The capital of Togo, **Lome**, has much nightlife and an open-air market. The spectacular **Akrowa Waterfalls** is a bit of a challenge to get to out of Lome.

Benin.   Formerly a French colony, Benin has begun to attract tourism. The country is generally visited out of **Cotonou**, where some modest lodging is available. Among the most popular day trips from Cotonou: **Ganvie**, a city of canals and houses on stilts; **Abomey**, with several ancient structures and offbeat shopping; and **Pendjari National Park**, with a nice collection of wildlife.

Sales Considerations

Though best known for wildlife safaris and the general friendliness of its people, West Africa presents some very good—and less crowded—sites for travelers to visit (though services are often below par). Beach resorts—some deluxe—dot the Gulf of Guinea. And your ambitious clients might want you to arrange a trip up the Gambia River. This is a popular destination for African Americans, and many of the nations here can be combined for an extended visit. Political unrest in certain countries is often a problem; make sure to check current advisories.

The Central Safari Belt

The central portion of the African continent can be divided into two sections: the Safari Belt and the Victoria Falls region. The Safari Belt, especially, is likely what many of your clients imagine when they think of Africa.

Important Places

Although Kenya (covered with Tanzania in an earlier chapter) is the most visited of the Safari-Belt countries, it's far from being the only area with spectacular herds. The countries that follow, in many ways, are just as awe-inspiring (though more adventurous). They're listed in order of importance to travelers.

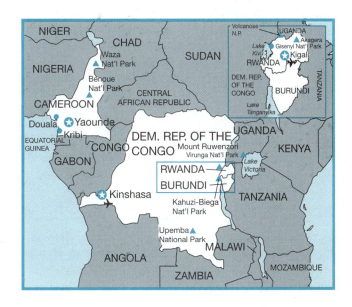

Rwanda. A tiny landlocked nation that has suffered intense political turmoil, Rwanda is just to the west of Tanzania. There's limited service by European carriers from North America to its capital at **Kigali Airport** (KGL). Temperatures here range in the 70s and 80s, with summer and fall the driest seasons—although **Volcanoes National Park**, one of the prime destinations, can get rain any day. The official languages are Kinyarwanda and French. Among Rwanda's main attractions are:

- **Volcanoes National Park** is best known for its spectacular array of mountain gorillas. Three of the gorilla families are so used to seeing humans that visitors on small tours can get near enough for a dramatic encounter. The hike to the gorillas' home, however, is arduous.
- **Gisenyi**, from which Volcanoes National Park is usually accessed, is a resort town on mountain-backdropped **Lake Kivu**.
- **Akagera National Park** is a huge park that offers an excellent variety of wildlife, amid numerous lakes.

Democratic Republic of the Congo (formerly Zaire, and not to be confused with the Republic of the Congo, its neighbor to the west). Almost directly in the center of the continent is the large country of the Democratic Republic of the Congo. Once also known as the Belgian Congo, this is a nation of great tribal diversity (and rivalries). The country is difficult to get around, there's sporadic unrest, and crime is common, so escorted tours are a good recommendation to make.

Virunga National Park is the Democratic Republic of the Congo's finest wildlife reserve, with mountain gorillas and scenery (notably the "Mountain of the Moons," **Mount Ruwenzori**). **Kahuzi-Biega National Park** has some lowland gorillas, and **Upemba** and **Kundelungu** national parks are also fairly interesting. The capital, **Kinshasa** (formerly called Leopoldville), offers a museum (the **Académie des Beaux Arts**), lovely gardens, churches, and a zoo. Nearby are the Zongo Falls and a pleasant botanic garden.

Cameroon. Though considered part of central Africa, Cameroon lies on the hilly western coast, not far from the French-influenced West African nations. Less crowded than most other wildlife-reserve countries, Cameroon has some first-rate destinations: **Waza National Park** is probably the most interesting, but **Benoue** and **Boubandjidah** national parks are good, too. The town of **Kribi** has excellent beaches and is about 125 miles south of Cameroon's largest city, **Douala**.

Sales Considerations

This region will appeal to your most hardy and adventurous clients: animal lovers, mountain climbers, and water-sports aficionados. Escorted safaris are obviously a popular item for you to sell. You could also extend your client's trip here to a visit to the Victoria Falls region. Remember that political turmoil, banditry, disease, and unpredictable tourist services can be potential problems for clients headed for the Safari Belt; as always, check for political advisories.

The Central Victoria Falls Region

South of the popular safari destinations of central Africa is another equally popular, but vastly different, area. The nations covered in this section are gloriously lush and highlighted by the awesome **Victoria Falls**.

Important Places

Its name tells most, but not all, of the story. Victoria Falls are one of the world's great natural sites. But this region offers many other beautiful attractions.

Zambia. Located almost directly in the center of Africa's southern leg is the landlocked country of Zambia, formerly Northern Rhodesia. European carriers

Victoria Falls is over a mile wide.

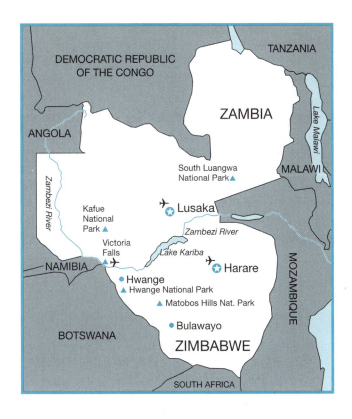

and **Zambia Airways** (QZ) will bring your clients here via flights from Europe. The gateway is at **Lusaka International Airport** (LUN), in the nation's capital. Zambia lies below the equator, so its seasons are opposite those of North America; it's also mostly plateau country, so temperatures are less tropical than you think. It's in the 80s from September to December, but the weather is usually in the 70s during all other months. Dry season extends from May to October. English and various tribal dialects are the national languages. Among the beautiful attractions in Zambia are:

- **Victoria Falls**, on the **Zambezi River**, is an awesome sight. Period. Your clients must not miss it—it's over twice the size of Niagara Falls—if they are anywhere near the area. (They'll usually stay overnight at nearby lodging.) The Zambian town closest to the falls is Livingstone; the **Livingstone Museum** houses memorabilia of Dr. Livingstone, as well as 300-year-old African maps.

- **Kafue National Park** is a huge area with elephants and more than 400 species of birds.

- **South Luangwa National Park**, in the Luangwa Valley, is perhaps one of Africa's most richly stocked animal preserves. It's best visited during dry season.

Zimbabwe.   Once known as Southern Rhodesia, Zimbabwe has had a delicate political situation for many years. Yet, located just south of Zambia, it offers many superbly beautiful destinations. There's limited service here from North America on European carriers, though more connecting flights leave from Europe directly. The main gateway is at **Harare Airport** (HRE) near its capital.

This below-the-equator country has seasons that are opposite those of North America. The climate is moderate: From November to February, temperatures may reach the 90s and there'll be rain. Otherwise, the weather is cool and dry, in the 60s and 70s during the day. The low-lying areas (like Victoria Falls, the Zambezi Valley, **Hwange**, and **Lake Kariba**) will be warmer. The official languages are English and tribal dialects. Among the top attractions in Zimbabwe are:

- **Victoria Falls**, as described earlier, is one of the most beautiful sights on the globe. Zimbabwe, in fact, offers a better vantage point of the Falls than does

Zambia (7/8 of the Falls are on the Zimbabwe side). Access is through **Victoria Falls Airport** (VFA).

- **Lake Kariba**, part of the Zambezi River system, offers water sports, houseboat rentals, and wildlife preserves.
- **Hwange National Park** is a wildlife reserve notable for its vast herds of elephants.
- **Matobos Hills National Park** offers fantastic rock formations, a rhino sanctuary, bushmen cave paintings, and the stunning gravesite of financier-colonizer Cecil Rhodes. It's usually accessed out of **Bulawayo**.
- **Great Zimbabwe National Monument** features the most impressive African ruins outside of the Sahara. There are many theories about who built the vast stone structures—that's what makes this place so intriguing.

The ruins of Great Zimbabwe are 1,200 years old.

Sales Considerations

Victoria Falls is what brings tourists to Zambia or Zimbabwe; you might want to suggest that your clients extend a trip to include both countries. When clients visit the Falls, be sure to offer to book a "Flight of Angels" for them. This airplane view of the rushing waters is stunning. Though there are wild-animal reserves in the region, its main attraction is the spectacular scenery. But adventurers will surely have a great time here: Safaris, walking tours, river rafting on the Zambezi, and boat excursions are all popular. Remember to check advisories before booking clients to either country.

Southern Africa

Though the nation of **South Africa** dominates the region, quite a few other countries are here as well. Nestled into the very bottom of Africa, the area is bordered by both the Atlantic and Indian Oceans—it ends in the south at the famous, scenic, and often-visited **Cape of Good Hope**, where the two oceans meet.

Important Places

With the elimination of its racial apartheid policy, South Africa—one of the most physically beautiful and westernized nations of Africa—is regaining its popularity

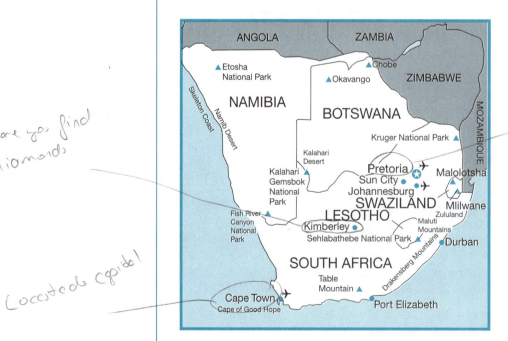

as a destination, as are the other countries that are within or near it (**Lesotho**, **Swaziland**, and **Botswana**). Political turmoil, however, has accompanied the process and has impeded the development of South Africa's tourism potential.

South Africa.   **South African Airways** (SA)—the national airline—flies to South Africa, Africa's southernmost country, as do several European carriers (for North American East Coast cities) and Asian carriers (an alternative for West Coast cities). Air gateways are **Pretoria** (PRV) (the administrative capital, located in the northeast), **Johannesburg** (JNB), and **Cape Town** (CPT) (the legislative capital, on the southwest coast). In addition, a few cruises start or disembark at Cape Town.

South Africa's subtropical, Southern-California-like climate is pleasant all year, though September to November (spring) is best. South Africa is south of the equator and its seasons are opposite those in North America. Most of the country is dry; indeed, the **Kalahari Desert** covers much of the northwest. The **Drakensberg Mountains** (lying southeast and east) and interior plateaus tend to have cooler temperatures and some rain, which falls from May to September. The official languages are Afrikaans and English. Among the remarkable attractions in South Africa are:

- **Johannesburg**, south of Pretoria, is an active city and the gold mining center. There are tours and a museum at Gold Reef City, as well as other nearby mines. You can suggest a long day trip to **Kimberley**, the diamond-mining center where tours of diamond mines are offered. (Kimberley and Johannesburg have somewhat of a problem with crime.) Johannesburg serves as a jump-off spot for trips to most of South Africa's major wildlife refuges.

- **Sun City**, a 90-minute drive northwest of Johannesburg, is sometimes known as the "Las Vegas of Africa." Its casinos, theme attractions, and resort hotels draw many visitors. Especially astonishing is the Lost City Resort with fake ruins, a 62-acre forest, simulated ocean waves, and the immense, ornate Palace Hotel.

- **Cape Town** lies at the edge of the Cape of Good Hope. It has fine museums, a couple of excellent botanical gardens, and good beaches. **Table Mountain**,

Buildings in Cape Town, South Africa
Photo by C. J. Ghormley

reached by cable car, provides grand vistas. There's an especially beautiful "Garden Route" drive from Cape Town to **Port Elizabeth** which has excellent beaches and vistas. Several "wine routes" lie east of Cape Town—it's estimated that the region has over 3,000 wineries.

- **Durban**, on the southeast coast, is a fashionable, upscale resort with spectacular beaches.
- **Kruger National Park**, in the northeast, is a massive, crowded wildlife reserve that matches those of Kenya for attracting foreign visitors. June through October are prime months for animal-watching here.
- **Zululand**, once a separate territory, provides five excellent wildlife reserves.
- **The Kalahari Gemsbok National Park**, quite remote, has a varied collection of animals. The desert boundaries cross over to **Namibia** and **Botswana**.
- **Sabi Sand** is perhaps the finest of South Africa's private wildlife refuges. Adjacent to Kruger National Park, it's also less crowded than many of the public preserves. Luxurious safari lodges are available and animal-viewing is from open vehicles.

The best time to take a safari here is in the winter, when more animals gather.

Lesotho.   Lesotho is surrounded by South Africa. Beautiful mountains crisscross this tiny country, notably the **Maluti Mountains** (which offer ski facilities). **Sehlabathebe National Park** is quite impressive.

Swaziland.   Like Lesotho, Swaziland is a small, independent, picturesque country. **Mlilwane** and **Malolotsha** are the best of its wildlife reserves.

Namibia   Lying along the Atlantic and bordering South Africa to the northwest is Namibia. It is becoming a popular safari destination: **Etosha National Park** is a beautiful park and wildlife preserve, as is **Fish River Canyon National Park**. The **Namib Desert** landscape and wildlife are magnificent. **Skeleton Coast**, nestled in the north between the ocean and desert, is the historical site of many sunken ships and moon-like landscapes.

Botswana.   Sandwiched between Namibia and Zimbabwe, Botswana has some of the finest and most uncrowded wildlife preserves in Africa. Two parks in the north are especially well known: **Chobe National Park** and **Moremi Wildlife**

In a safari jeep
Photo by C. J. Ghormley

Reserve. The latter occupies a portion of the **Okavango Delta**, one of the greatest homes for wildlife in the world. Northern Botswana is relatively near Victoria Falls, too; a visit to Botswana's reserves is often combined with a trip to the Falls. Botswana has the oldest democracy and perhaps the most stable government in Africa and is especially concerned with preserving its wildlife.

The Okavango is one of the world's only inland deltas.

Sales Considerations

Southern Africa will appeal to those who admire beautiful scenery, bargains, good weather, and safaris. There are also some world-class beach resorts and good skiing (though lodging tends to be simple, not luxurious). Gold and diamond mining tours are a popular attraction. (But diamonds here are no less expensive than elsewhere.) Reservations, especially at or near the wildlife reserves, need to be booked very far in advance. The Blue Train is legendary and offers a unique way to see the region. Rovos Rail operates vintage trains from Cape Town to Victoria Falls.

The African Islands

4th largest island in the world.

Off the southeast coast of Africa, in the Indian Ocean, are a number of islands that draw tourists; the largest of these, by far, is **Madagascar**, but others offer finer, more developed attractions. Indeed, **Mauritius** is one of the world's more popular island destinations. There are also some islands off the northwest coast, most notably the **Canary Islands**.

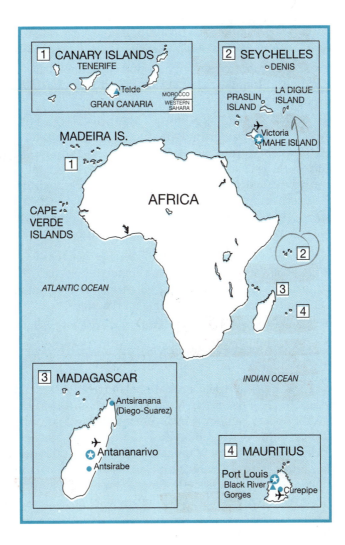

Important Places

The islands that surround Africa are largely neglected by tourists from North America. Part of the reason is that they're simply not well-known. These islands can be wonderful destinations for your clients, and they're growing in popularity. We've ordered them in their importance to travelers.

The Seychelles [say-SHELLS].   1,000 miles east of Kenya and lying northeast of Madagascar, the Seychelles is actually made up of nearly 100 tiny islands. There's limited service from North America by European carriers; **Air Seychelles** (HM), the national carrier, also flies from Europe, South Africa, and Singapore. The gateway is near the capital of **Victoria** at **Mahe Island Airport** (SEZ). There's air service among the country's various islands.

The Seychelles' climate is generally warm and balmy, and its look is absolutely distinctive among tropical islands: unusually shaped granite boulders line many areas. Being south of the equator, its seasons are opposite those in North America. Creole English and French are the national languages in this British-influenced country. Among its finest sights are:

- **Mahe Island** [ma-HAY]—the most populous—has great beaches, beautiful gardens, and a lovely mountainous national park. Mahe offers especially superb snorkeling and diving. Suggest a car rental, for the drive around the island is spectacular.

- **Praslin Island** [PRAH-LIN] has good facilities as well, to go with its wonderful scenery and beaches. Twenty-one miles from Mahe, it's reached by either boat or plane.

- **La Digue Island** [LAH-DIG], a half-hour boat ride from Praslin, has spectacular rock formations at Union Beach.

- **Animal sanctuaries** can be found throughout the Seychelles; the most notable are Bird Island (with its thick, colorful flocks) and Denis Island (famed for its tortoises).

Mauritius [moh-RIH-shus].   Mauritius lies east of Madagascar. **Air Mauritius** (MK), the national airline, flies here from Europe and Africa; and a few European airlines depart from their home countries, landing at **Plaisance Airport** (MRU), on the southeast coast. Spring and fall are lovely seasons here, with average temperatures in the 80s. June to August can get pretty chilly, whereas December until February is rainy. Once under British control, the dense population here is mixed, which is reflected by its official languages: English, French, Creole, and Hindi. Mauritius is a major getaway destination for European vacationers. It features some lovely attractions, including:

- **Port Louis**, the capital, is on the northwest coast. Fine museums, gardens, and an aquarium are located in Port Louis. There are some examples of interesting architecture and an enjoyable marketplace.

- **Beaches** and **coral reefs** abound. The resorts are low-key and relaxed.

- **The Black River Gorges** have beautiful views and gorgeous scenery.

- **Curepipe** is a fairly cosmopolitan town that offers excellent shopping.

Madagascar.   Madagascar, the fourth largest island in the world, is almost the size of Texas. It lies east of Mozambique, about 240 miles from the coast of southern Africa. Formerly under French control, Madagascar has a wide variety of assets: rain forests, semideserts, mountains, and excellent beaches. It's famous for its lemurs (primitive primates) and unique species of plant life. Attractions in the central capital, **Antananarivo**, include a palace, a zoo, and botanical gardens; **Ivato Airport** (TNR) is the main gateway. Not too far away is **Antsirabe**, which has interesting geothermal activity. **Antsiranana** (formerly Diego-Suarez) is on a very picturesque bay

The Seychelles is the only nation to have two natural World Heritage sites.

Eighty percent of Madagascar's plants are found nowhere else.

Case Study

Mike and Carolyn Robitaille have usually taken their vacations in Europe, but three years ago they decided to try something different: going to Africa on a safari in Kenya. The couple, in their early fifties, had a wonderful time. They loved the wildlife and everything about the trip was so well organized that it was much easier than they thought it would be. They've decided to go back to Africa.

Circle the answer that best suits your clients' needs:

1. Having gotten their feet wet, the Robitailles feel that it's time to get a little more adventurous. And as much as they enjoyed Kenya, they don't want to repeat the trip, preferring to see some different animals, if possible. Which country would you suggest?

   South Africa   Algeria

   Niger   Ivory Coast

   Why?

2. They decide not to limit their experiences in Africa merely to safaris and want to enjoy a different part of the continent's dramatic attractions as well. To what scenic area would you recommend they extend their trip?

   Tarzan's tree house   Iguazu Falls

   Victoria Falls   Lake Tanganyika

   Why?

3. The Robitailles decide that, after all, they do prefer a more relaxed, less adventurous trip; it's been a hard year. They'd still like to see some wildlife, but also miss the charms of Europe and wouldn't mind stretching out on the beach for a few days. Where would you suggest?

   Bahrain   Zambia

   Ethiopia   Senegal

   Why?

4. What services would be appropriate for you to book for the Robitailles?

   An escorted tour   A budget hotel

   A stopover in South America   First-class rail tickets to Mauritius

   Why?

Creative Activity

Ecotourism—tourism that is driven by a desire to see places in their natural state—has become a significant, profitable segment of the tour business. You are an itinerary planner for a tour company that has decided to sell a 15-day ecotour of Africa, starting and ending in Nairobi.

How would you construct the tour? Where would you go? Describe your tour below, remembering to set aside a day each time the group flies from one country to another. (Assume there are air connections between each place; no need to look them up.) And be *very* sensitive to what ecotourists might want to see:

DAY	CITY/PLACE OR COUNTRY	ACTIVITY
1.	Nairobi	Orientation meeting for group; reception dinner
2.		
3.		
4.		
5.		
6.		
7.		
8.		
9.		
10.		
11.		
12.		
13.		
14.		
15.	Nairobi	Free day; departure late day.

Pulling It All Together: The Matching Game

Directions: Below is a list of cities, attractions, etc., some of which we have covered, some which we haven't. There are all manner of connections among them. With a group of fellow students, you have exactly ten minutes to come up with as many connections as possible. (Items may be used more than once). Write your answers below. Note: There are at least twenty possible connections. E.g., Dakar and Nairobi—both are capital cities.

Lost City	Haifa	Sinai
Sultan Hasan	Alexandria	Zambezi
Dome of the Rock	Eilat	Mt. Kilimanjaro
Kalahari	Jomo Kenyatta	Okavango
Masai Mara	Dakar	Nile
The Ark	Mombasa	Sacred Heart
Zanzibar	Great Mosque	Ngorongoro
Ben Gurion	Serengeti	Hurghada
Ka'aba	Canary	Tel Aviv
Nairobi	Madagascar	Our Lady of Peace

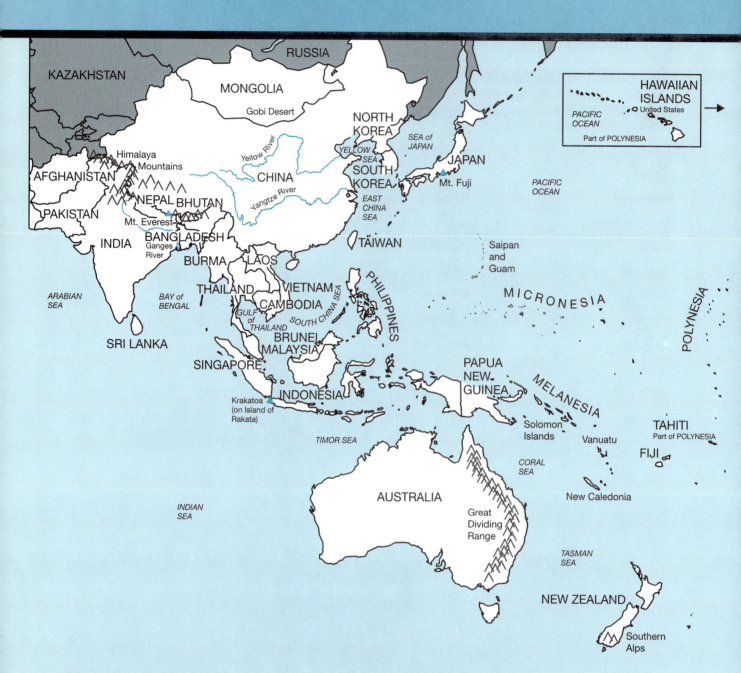

KAZAKHSTAN

RUSSIA

MONGOLIA

Gobi Desert

NORTH
KOREA

SEA of
JAPAN

JAPAN

Mt. Fuji

PACIFIC
OCEAN

Yellow River

CHINA

YELLOW
SEA

SOUTH
KOREA

Himalaya
Mountains

AFGHANISTAN

Yangtze River

EAST
CHINA
SEA

PAKISTAN

NEPAL

BHUTAN

Mt. Everest

BANGLADESH

TAIWAN

Saipan
and
Guam

INDIA

Ganges
River

BURMA

LAOS

MICRONESIA

POLYNESIA

ARABIAN
SEA

BAY of
BENGAL

THAILAND

VIETNAM

PHILIPPINES

GULF
of
THAILAND

CAMBODIA

SOUTH CHINA SEA

SRI LANKA

BRUNEI
MALAYSIA

SINGAPORE

PAPUA
NEW
GUINEA

MELANESIA

TAHITI
Part of POLYNESIA

Krakatoa
(on Island of
Rakata)

INDONESIA

Solomon
Islands

Vanuatu

FIJI

TIMOR SEA

CORAL
SEA

New Caledonia

INDIAN
SEA

AUSTRALIA

Great
Dividing
Range

TASMAN
SEA

NEW ZEALAND

Southern
Alps

HAWAIIAN
ISLANDS
United States

PACIFIC
OCEAN

Part of POLYNESIA

PACIFIC
OCEAN

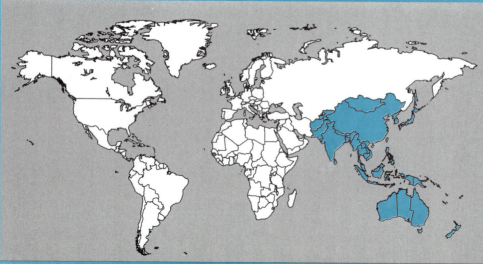

Asia and the Pacific
Rim of Mystery

In the great courts of Europe, word had spread about the fabulous riches—both cultural and physical—that existed off in the far, mysterious East. But no one truly knew what was there, until Marco Polo reached the Orient and returned with stories and treasures that dazzled the Europeans of his day.

Asia and the Pacific still offer treasured opportunities to those who visit the far rim of the Pacific. Yet 700 years after the great explorer made his journey, the Far East is still somewhat of an enigma, even though the nations of the Pacific Rim (as they have come to be called) have, in many ways, opened their doors wide to the world. For centuries, Europe has been a natural business partner to North America across the Atlantic: So too, now, are the lands on the other side of the Pacific. A Rip Van Winkle who went to sleep in the late-1950s would wake in culture shock. It's a very different world, indeed: Japanese cars, Korean VCRs, Australian movies—these all would have seemed impossible just a few decades ago.

With the growth in trade has come a major growth in travel. That Rip Van Winkle, were he one of your clients, would never have even given a thought to visiting Asia or the Pacific islands—not just because of closed cultures, but also because of the sheer physical logistics. However, with advent of long-distance jumbo jets, the Far East is not much more than a half-day away.

In days past, even crossing the international date line was a major event—a celebration. Today, a pilot merely informs the plane's passengers—assuming, of course, that they hear him through their mid-Pacific doze.

Where the Countries Are

Tourists and geographers don't always think alike. For instance, where exactly does Asia start and Africa and Europe end? Most geographers consider everything to the east of the Red Sea and the Ural Mountains to be Asia—and that includes the Middle East, Turkey, and the majority of Russia.

However, your clients will travel by their own rules and the Middle East is usually seen as part of a trip to Europe or Africa. Few tourists ever visit Russia in conjunction with a vacation to China; more likely, a Russian vacation is tied to a trip to Scandinavia. And Turkey is most commonly accessed as an extension of a Greek island cruise. As a result, we have covered many of Asia's forty or so countries in previous sections, in order to relate them to realistic client itineraries.

What's the most obvious place on a map of Asia? **China**, which physically dominates most of the continent. It dwarfs **Mongolia**, which borders it to the north, and **North** and **South Korea**, which take up the peninsula on its northeastern corner. (Communist North Korea is rarely visited by Westerners and therefore won't be covered in this section.)

Off China's east coast are a string of island-nations; from north to south: **Japan**, **Taiwan**, and the **Philippines**. Continuing south, the many islands of **Indonesia** lie just off the tip of Southeast Asia; though some of your clients will think of **Vietnam**, **Laos**, and **Cambodia** at the mention of this region, the only Southeast Asian nations here that attract a great deal of Western tourist trade are **Thailand**, **Malaysia**, and **Singapore**. (Part of Malaysia lies on Borneo, but the island has limited tourism.) Then, below China and to the west of Southeast Asia is the large area known as the Indian subcontinent. From west to east, it includes **India**, **Nepal**, and **Bhutan** (as well as less-visited Pakistan, Bangladesh, and Sri Lanka). **Myanmar**—better known by its traditional name, **Burma**—is to the east. Also in Asia are five newly independent nations of the former Soviet Union. **Azerbaijan** and **Uzbekistan** are the most important of these.

The islands of the Pacific may seem to many of your clients to be a great distance from Asia, but some of them are much closer to the continent of Asia or **Australia** than to the Americas: **Papua New Guinea** and **Fiji** (both parts of Melanesia) are relatively close to Australia and Indonesia; the **Micronesian** islands of **Saipan** and **Guam** are to the east of the Philippines. For this reason, visits to Asia can easily be combined with stopovers at Pacific islands. Though the tens of thousands of Pacific islands are clearly much too numerous to mention, the major ones are (from west to east): **New Zealand**, **Fiji**, **Tahiti** (one of the Polynesian islands), and the state of **Hawaii** (which is closest—about five hours—to the North American mainland).

A Satellite View

Looking down on Asia and the Pacific, it would be easy to distinguish the larger islands that float on the area's oceans and seas. The Asian continent is another matter; it blends into Europe and the Middle East (and, therefore, Africa as well).

Perhaps the most noticeable feature of the entire region is how flat much of it is. Most of western China is desert (notably the **Gobi Desert**), as is the western two-thirds of Australia. Much of Southeast Asia, too, is flat rain forest.

However, the exceptions to this flatness are dramatic and have an overwhelming impact on the region; to ignore the whole picture here would be folly. To properly plan trips for your clients to this region, it's essential that you fully understand the lay of the land.

Bodies of Water

As you would imagine, the Pacific Ocean is critical to this vast region. Moreover, the continent of Asia, being as large and geographically situated as it is, is ringed by an assortment of seas.

Beginning at the far west of the region, India is bordered on its west by the **Arabian Sea**, on its south by the **Indian Ocean**, and on its east by the **Bay of Bengal**. Farther east is the **Gulf of Thailand**, in the midst of Southeast Asia; the Gulf, in turn, flows into the **South China Sea**.

The **Sea of Japan** separates Russia and North and South Korea from Japan. The **Yellow Sea**—which forms a bay between northeast China and the Korean peninsula—empties into the **East China Sea**, which, in turn, merges into the South China Sea. Bordering all this region to the east is the vast **Pacific Ocean**.

The Pacific encompasses most of the South Sea islands. However, other major waters here bear note: the **Timor Sea** separates northern Australia from Indo-

In some places, the Indian Ocean is nearly five miles deep.

nesia; the **Coral Sea** lies northeast of the continent; and dividing southeast Australia and New Zealand is the **Tasman Sea**.

Asia, Australia, and the Pacific islands have only a few major rivers. The **Yellow** and **Yangtze** wind and twist their way through the center of China. They offer visitors a superb way of exploring the magnificent countryside. (There's also an important canal system in northeastern China that permits several popular excursions.) And the Ganges, which flows through the northeast of India, is perhaps the most sacred river on earth, for Hindu pilgrims immerse themselves in its waters to spiritually cleanse themselves.

Mountains

The 2000-mile-long **Himalaya Mountain range** is the loftiest range in the world. To put this in its proper perspective, Himalaya's **Mt. Everest** is the world's tallest mountain: It's 9,000 feet higher than the tallest mountain in North America, Mt. McKinley, and 7,000 feet higher than the tallest peak of the Andes. Of the world's fifty tallest mountains, virtually all are in the Himalaya. The challenging Himalaya are considered the finest trekking and mountain-climbing territory in

The correct term is Himalaya, not HImalayas.

Mt. Everest, seen from an airplane
Photo by William and Marie Rourke

the world; you'll be able to book excursions here for your adventurous clients. The Himalaya ripple through the top of Pakistan, northern India, Nepal, Bhutan, and the Tibet region of China, covering an area greater than all of Germany.

In addition, a spine of volcanic mountains runs down the length of much of Japan, the most famous of which is stately **Mt. Fuji**. There are also many mountains of volcanic origin in Indonesia (where the legendary **Krakatoa** erupted) and in Australia, with its **Great Dividing Range** down the east coast. The **Southern Alps** rise above New Zealand's South Island. Parts of western China are also somewhat mountainous—though it's unlikely any of your clients will visit there.

Climate

Since parts of Asia and the Pacific lie both north and south of the equator, two distinct patterns exist: North of the equator, seasons are the same as those in North America; south, they're the opposite. An important point to remember: Though many clients will think of this entire region as hot and humid, the extreme northern and southern areas have very cold weather. In addition, the Himalaya and other high regions are frigid. One more exception: Western China and western Australia have largely desert climates.

The Indian subcontinent, most of China, the islands of Japan and Taiwan (all of which lie north of the equator), and northern Australia (to the equator's south) have a subtropical climate. Summers in these areas are very warm and humid; winters are drier and more pleasant. A fully tropical climate can be found in those countries that flank the equator—most of Indonesia and all the South Sea islands—as well as in Southeast Asia, the Philippines, and Micronesia (north of the equator).

A final note: The region is famed for its monsoons, typhoons, and cyclones. Monsoons are long-standing summer rainstorms, usually associated with the Indian subcontinent and Southeast Asia. Typhoons are what hurricanes are called when they occur in the China Sea and west Pacific area. Cyclones (the generic name for hurricanes and typhoons) often whip along Australia's northeast coastal areas.

Tourism Patterns

Two words summarize the pattern of Pacific Rim tourism: *explosive growth*. It has not been unusual to see a doubling of the numbers of tourists in a matter of a year or two. China and Hong Kong are by far the most popular destinations in Asia. Singapore, Thailand, and Malaysia constitute a second tier of success; all of them have seen dramatic increases in inbound travelers. Japan, South Korea, India, and Australia aren't far behind, though high prices in Japan, turmoil in Korea, and poverty in India have blunted the kind of massive increases that other Pacific Rim countries have enjoyed. In addition to the leisure segment, business travel accounts for much movement across the Pacific between North America and the Far East.

What of the Pacific islands? The U.S. state of Hawaii, of course, is number one, but surprisingly, the Micronesian islands of Guam and Saipan are in second place (most of their tourists come from Japan, not North America). Fiji is the most successful destination in Melanesia, and Tahiti leads the Polynesian islands in tourism. Hawaii, Tahiti, and Fiji are all common stopover points on cross-Pacific travel itineraries, both on planes and on repositioning cruises.

Asian and Pacific Distances

For traveling through Asia, the mode of choice for most tourists is the escorted tour. This has as much to do with transportation conditions as it does with language. Country roads are often primitive and they can be washed out; city traffic may be impenetrable. Some trains are comfortable, but schedules aren't always adhered to. Buses—except those used on tours—are usually a challenge. An inde-

The Bullet Train, Japan
Photo by Brian Yokoyama

pendent flight itinerary is probably the best alternative to an escorted tour, but even flying can't always eliminate that major bugaboo for North Americans: Asian languages too often seem undecipherable to Westerners. It can make traveling on one's own a bit intimidating to your clients, especially if they get lost and can't read the signs. Even though many in these countries do speak English fairly well, the language is still a critical—and very real—obstacle. One way around the problem: cruises, which are fast becoming a popular option for visiting key Asian, Australian, New Zealand, and Pacific island port cities.

For your clients who are traveling on their own, distances in some Asian countries can be great—giant China and India being the obvious examples. However, in many Asian countries, the major destinations tend to be clustered in distinct, limited areas: In China, for instance, the sites your clients will be interested in visiting are almost entirely in the east.

The Pacific islands, on the other hand, don't pose that much of a problem. The inhabitants of many of the popular islands speak English; for many (Hawaii, Fiji, and Guam, among others), it's the official language. These islands are relatively small, so taxis, rental cars, and (perhaps) buses will do.

Certainly, roads on the smaller islands may be primitive, but again, distances are comparatively minor. The only modes of transportation of any great importance among the islands are airplanes that hop from one island to the next, ferries that weave their way among clusters of islands, and cruise ships that connect the islands.

Your clients will have to fly between sites in Australia that are far apart, unless they have a lot of time to spare. Australia is very big: It's about the size of the contiguous United States. Its attractions (except for a notable few) are along the east and west coasts. The majority of New Zealand's most popular attractions, too, tend to be conveniently clustered. Train and bus travel in both countries (as well as in Japan) is excellent. Trains and buses are less predictable elsewhere, though luxury trains travel through India, and between Singapore and Bangkok.

Some Miscellaneous Considerations

Asia and the Pacific are often thought of as exotic. It's likely that your clients will be looking to you for some sense of security before they leave. Among the suggestions you can give are:

Japan has the world's busiest rail system.

- Health conditions in some of these countries are far below the standard that your clients expect. Make certain that you check health advisories and that your clients visit their physician before leaving on their trip.

- Your clients will likely be aware that the cultures of the lands they'll be visiting are extremely different from their own. For a better sense of these differences, suggest they buy a book on the region they'll be visiting and read it on the flight over. They'll have a lot of time.

- Shopping in Asia, in Australia, and among the islands is of great allure to many tourists. The best prices on brand names can usually be found in Hong Kong, South Korea, and Singapore, while crafts are a bargain in almost all of these places.

- The engines of commerce are powerful in Asia. Nowhere in the world, these days, is business travel more important. The industrial nations of Asia, by the way, are often called "The Dragons." A few of them have suffered economic setbacks recently, but this helps tourism, since costs there may become more affordable to foreign travelers.

- Bargaining on prices is extremely common, indeed almost expected, in many of these countries—though not in Japan, Australia, and New Zealand. Tell your clients to check with hotel personnel about local customs, if they have questions.

- Even though many locals understand English, if your clients are having a difficult time communicating, suggest that they write out their questions. It's not uncommon for someone here to read English better than he or she speaks it.

- If your clients plan to take photographs in China and in Southeast Asia, make sure they check ahead of time that it's not prohibited in the area where they are.

- Some of the world's finest hotel chains are based in Asia: Among them are **Shangri-La**, **Regent**, **Peninsula**, **Mandarin**, and **Rihga**.

- The water in Asian lakes, ponds, and rivers (including the mystical Ganges) is often filled with microbes that North Americans have no resistance to. Swimming in Asian waters is generally a bad idea.

- Let your clients know that, in many of the regions here, they should expect only the most basic of comforts. Certainly Hawaii, Australia, New Zealand, and Japan offer great luxury and comfort.

- Uninformed clients often think of Asian nations as having the same general customs. Not so. Differences among Japanese, Chinese, Korean, Thai, and Philippine cultures are as pronounced as those among, say, French, British, Italian, and Greek cultures.

- Treks are becoming a popular form of adventure travel; several areas in China, India, Nepal, and Bhutan offer trekking tours, but know that only hardy clients who are prepared to walk for hours at high altitudes and to sleep in a tent should consider a trekking tour.

- Generally, costs in this vast region vary widely. For example, Japan is expensive, while China, Thailand, and Southeast Asia tend to be bargains.

Creative Activity

NAME _____ DATE _____

Based on the information in this chapter and in other sources, which ten separate Asia/Pacific destinations would you suggest to clients who are looking for each of the following? Be prepared to justify your recommendations.

1. Hiking:

2. Dry, warm climate:

3. A river cruise:

4. A rarely visited tropical country:

5. Diving:

6. An exotic cultural experience:

7. A bargain vacation:

8. Luxurious accommodations:

9. A stopover between Honolulu and Sydney:

10. A country that can be seen on a one-day visit:

Travel Trivia

The World's Ten Best Train Experiences

- India's Toy Train (Darjeeling–New Jaipalguri)
- The American-European Express (Chicago–New York City)
- South Africa's Blue Train (Johannesburg–Cape Town)
- The Trans-Siberian (Moscow–Khabarovsk)
- Switzerland's Glacier Express (St. Moritz–Zermatt)
- Britain's Settle-Carlisle (Settle–Carlisle)
- Peru's El Tren de Sierra (Lima–Oroyo)
- France's TGV (Paris–Lyon)
- India's Palace on Wheels (New Delhi round-trip)
- Australia's Indian-Pacific (Sydney–Perth)

Source: Los Angeles Times

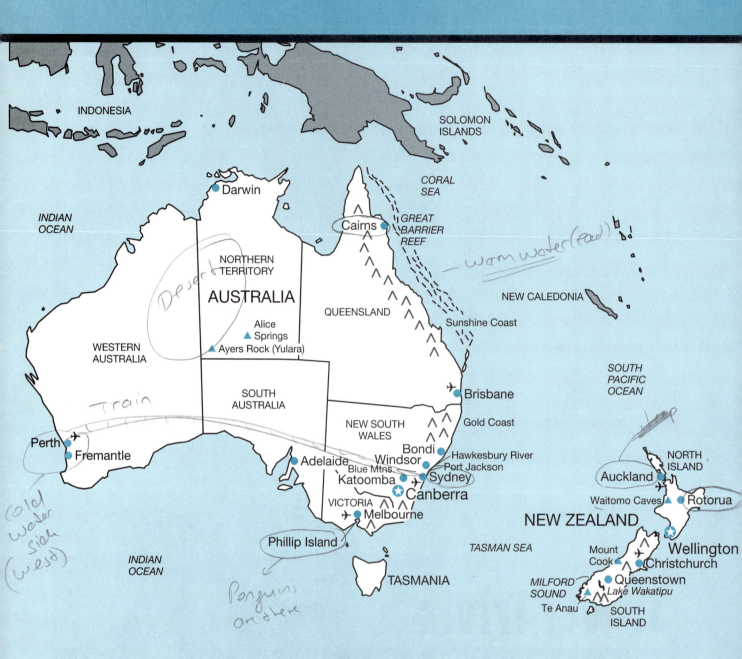

INDONESIA

SOLOMON
ISLANDS

*CORAL
SEA*

● Darwin

*INDIAN
OCEAN*

Cairns

*GREAT
BARRIER
REEF*

— *warm water (red)*

NORTHERN
TERRITORY

Desert

NEW CALEDONIA

AUSTRALIA

QUEENSLAND

*SOUTH
PACIFIC
OCEAN*

WESTERN
AUSTRALIA

Alice
▲ Springs
▲ Ayers Rock (Yulara)

Sunshine Coast

Train

SOUTH
AUSTRALIA

✈ ● Brisbane

NORTH
ISLAND

Perth ✈
● Fremantle

NEW SOUTH
WALES

Gold Coast

Auckland

● Adelaide

Bondi
Windsor
Blue Mtns. ✈
Katoomba Sydney

Hawkesbury River
Port Jackson

Waitomo Caves ▲ ● Rotorua

*Cold
Water
Side
(west)*

★ Canberra

NEW ZEALAND

VICTORIA

✈ ● Melbourne

TASMAN SEA

Mount
Cook ▲

✈ ★
● Wellington
● Christchurch

Phillip Island

*INDIAN
OCEAN*

*MILFORD
SOUND* ▲

● Queenstown
Lake Wakatipu

*Penguins
are here*

TASMANIA

Te Anau

SOUTH
ISLAND

CHAPTER 23

Australia and New Zealand

Where Things Are Jumping

It was the late-eighteenth century. European explorers were finally making serious excursions to the strange, distant lands of Australia and New Zealand. Other experiences had prepared them for much of what awaited them: fierce Maori [MAH-ree] warriors; the bleak, desertlike outback; the Alpine-like peaks of New Zealand. Similar things they had seen before.

But nothing could prepare them for the animals they found in this "Land Down Under": kangaroos who can leap a span of twenty-five feet; the koala, a bear-like little creature who lives in (and on) eucalyptus trees; and the platypus, a mammal with webbed feet and a duck-like bill who lays eggs. Indeed, the platypus is so weird that European zoologists at first thought it to be a patched-together hoax sprung on them by prankish sailors.

Visitors of today still find the fauna and flora of these two countries astonishing. That and the friendly reputation of their people are a powerful magnet for tourism. Indeed, Australia and New Zealand were two of the genuine travel industry success stories of the 1980s and still continue to draw more and more of your clients.

When you sell this area, remember that it's much more vast than your clients may imagine. The continent of Australia is about the size of the contiguous United States. (But its population is only eighteen million.) To its west is the Indian Ocean, to the east are the Coral and Tasman Seas, which in turn open onto the Pacific.

The principal cities on Australia's charming but less-visited western shore are **Perth** and nearby **Fremantle**. The nearer east coast is a more popular destination. Here are, from the northern state of **Queensland** to the southern state of **New South Wales**: the **Great Barrier Reef**, a 1,200-mile stretch of coral that is generally accessed from the city of **Cairns** (which Australians pronounce CANS); the **Sunshine Coast**, a beach resort area north of the key city of **Brisbane**; the **Gold Coast**, an even bigger Miami-like beach area that starts about 50 miles south of Brisbane; **Sydney**, Australia's largest and liveliest city; and **Canberra**, Australia's inland national capital. Along the southeastern coast are three popular destinations: **Melbourne**, **Adelaide**, and the island-state of **Tasmania**.

And what's in the middle? Several million square miles of bleak, desolate brush and desert, called the **Bush** and the **Outback**. Still, there are two Outback attractions your clients may ask about: **Alice Springs**, a frontier town that's a showcase for the culture and art of Australia's original dwellers, the aborigines [ab-uh-RIDGE-uh-neez]; and **Ayers Rock**, a massive red stone that's best seen in the crimson light of sunset. Even more remote (and less visited) is **Darwin**, a port on Australia's wet, tropical north coast.

For Your Information . . .

Australia and New Zealand   FYI

CAPITALS: Australia: Canberra
New Zealand: Wellington

AREAS (SQUARE MILES): Australia: 2,968,000
New Zealand: 103,736

TIME ZONES: Australia: GMT +8 to +10
New Zealand: GMT +12

DRIVE ON: Left

POPULATION: Australia: 18,100,000
New Zealand: 3,600,000

RELIGIONS: Protestant, Catholic

LANGUAGE: English

CURRENCIES: Australia: 1 Australian dollar = 100 cents
New Zealand: 1 New Zealand dollar = 100 cents

ELECTRICITY: Australia: 240 volts, 50 cycles AC
New Zealand: 220 volts, 50 cycles AC

CAPSULE HISTORY: **Australia**: Aborigine ancestors arrive, 30,000 B.C.; Dutch land here, 1606; British James Cook explores, leading to a British claim of possession, 1770; island remained a British penal colony until 1850s; gold discovered, 1851; Commonwealth declared, 1901; Australia Act severs many ties with Britain, 1986.

New Zealand: Maoris, a Polynesian group, arrived and settled, 1300s; discovered by Dutch, 1642; Britain annexes from Maoris, 1840; Maori wars, 1845–1870; gold rush, 1861; declared "nuclear-free" zone, 1984.

For reference sources, tourist bureaus, and suggested lengths of stay, see the Appendices.

The northernmost point of Australia is just south of the equator.

New Zealand, about 1,200 miles to Australia's southeast, may be a more difficult sell, since it doesn't elicit the strong mental pictures that Australia does. Yet it's very logical to sell it along with Australia. Its **North Island** has rolling green hills and considerable geothermal activity. **Auckland**, New Zealand's largest city, is here; as is **Rotorua**, a center of Maori culture and powerful, steaming geysers. **Wellington**, at the southernmost tip of North Island, is New Zealand's hilly and quaint capital. The **South Island** is dramatically mountainous and more frigid, with many fjord-like inlets. Its chief cities are **Christchurch** and **Queenstown**.

How Travelers Get There

Virtually everyone from North America who visits the "lands down under" arrives via jet. It's a long haul, though; from the West Coast, it's more than 7,000 miles. And if your client is flying from any point farther east, it'll be even longer. Most flights stop along the way to refuel in Hawaii, Fiji, or Tahiti. In fact, it's often possible to break up the long trip for your clients by having them stop over for a pleasant day or two at one of several South Pacific island destinations.

Almost all Australia-bound clients arrive through one of three gateway cities: Brisbane (BNE), Sydney (SYD), or Melbourne (MEL). Those heading to New Zealand usually land at Auckland (AKL) or Christchurch (CHC). And don't forget to tell clients that they'll be crossing the international date line (and therefore changing days) while airborne.

Several U.S. and Canadian carriers fly to the region. A client can also be booked on the countries' principal air carriers: **Qantas** (QF) and **Air New Zealand**

(NZ). Cruise ships sailing from North America on repositioning cruises often cross the Pacific and terminate in New Zealand or Australia, where they will begin to operate for the "Down Under" summer season.

Weather Patterns

Remember that the seasons in these Southern Hemisphere destinations are the opposite of those in North America: The coldest weather is in June, July, and August, while summer heat arrives in January and February (see Figures 23-1 and 23-2). New Zealand's North Island has cool and occasionally rainy winters (June to August), but warm and sometimes humid summers (January and February). The South Island is somewhat colder all year, especially in the mountains.

Australia has a warmer and generally drier climate than that of New Zealand. Cities such as Melbourne and Sydney have wonderful warm summers and mild, chilly-water winters—with relatively modest amounts of rain year-round. (Melbourne is a bit drier than Sydney.) Brisbane and Perth are even warmer, with more rain. Cairns and especially Darwin have a tropical climate (somewhat like Florida's or Mexico's coastal regions), with hot and rainy summers (January to March) and warm, dry winters. The climate of Australia's vast interior is Sahara-like.

Climate at a Glance _____
SYDNEY, AUSTRALIA

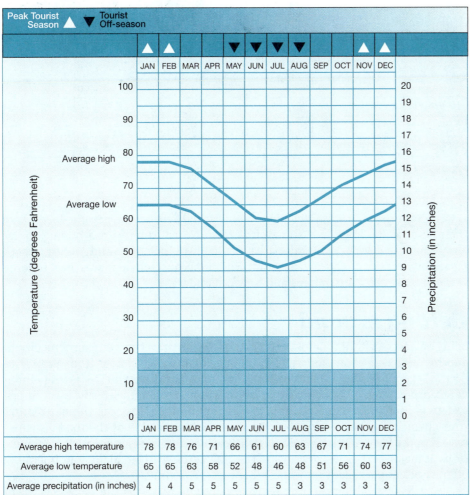

	JAN	FEB	MAR	APR	MAY	JUN	JUL	AUG	SEP	OCT	NOV	DEC
Average high temperature	78	78	76	71	66	61	60	63	67	71	74	77
Average low temperature	65	65	63	58	52	48	46	48	51	56	60	63
Average precipitation (in inches)	4	4	5	5	5	5	5	3	3	3	3	3

Figure 23-1

Climate at a Glance
WELLINGTON, NEW ZEALAND

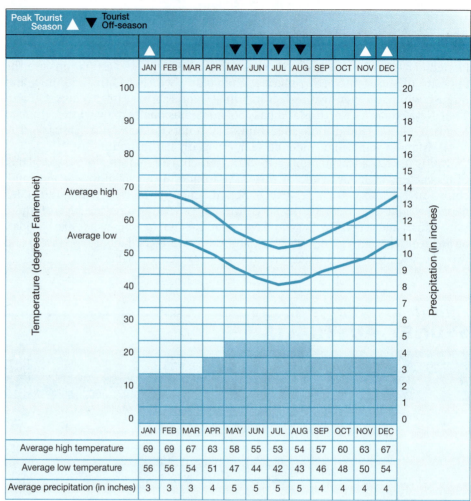

Peak Tourist Season ▲	▼ Tourist Off-season											
			▲			▼	▼	▼	▼			▲	▲

	JAN	FEB	MAR	APR	MAY	JUN	JUL	AUG	SEP	OCT	NOV	DEC
Average high temperature	69	69	67	63	58	55	53	54	57	60	63	67
Average low temperature	56	56	54	51	47	44	42	43	46	48	50	54
Average precipitation (in inches)	3	3	3	4	5	5	5	5	4	4	4	4

Figure 23-2

High tourist season is December, January, and February, when the locals take their summer holidays and snow birds from North America are hoping to get away from the cold. Bargain rates are most likely in June, July, and August, except in mountain resorts and Queensland, which (because of their weather) become winter getaways for Australians and New Zealanders.

Getting Around

Being so vast, Australia almost always requires air travel to get from one city to another. (It takes about four to five hours, for instance, to fly from Sydney to Perth.) Several airlines, such as **Ansett** (AN) and **Australian Air** (TN), provide internal transportation. Ground transportation is also excellent, with a well-developed system of motorcoach and rail routes. Car rentals are an option, though remind your clients that they'll have to drive on the left-hand side of the road (as is the case in most former British colonies). Several cruise lines service Australia, with stops at major port cities, or trips up the **Hawkesbury River.** Many tour operators offer excellent packages that you can book ahead of time.

New Zealand's internal transportation options are much the same as those of Australia. Since the country is relatively compact, however, visitors are more likely

The genuinely bizarre creatures down under make a zoo or animal park visit an essential activity.

to drive around, take buses, or ride the train from one city to the next, especially on the North Island. (The South Island perhaps warrants flights between its more far-flung points of interest.) Cruises also call at the major New Zealand ports, often continuing on to Australia.

One final note: Each country boasts a rather famous train ride. In Australia, it's the **Indian Pacific** route, from Sydney to Perth. And in New Zealand, it's the **Silver Fern**, between Wellington and Auckland.

Important Places

Unlike some countries, Australia and New Zealand have clear-cut centers of tourism. Here are those you're most likely to recommend to your clients.

Sydney

With nearly a quarter of Australia's population, Sydney is one of the world's most energetic, stylish, and progressive cities. Though enormous in area, Sydney has most of its tourist sites in a concentrated section near its fine harbor. Among the city's attractions are:

- **The Sydney Opera House**, an astonishing building with a design so unorthodox and original that it took years before anyone could figure out how to build it properly.
- **The Rocks**, the old, restored section of Sydney.
- **Kings Cross**, a nightclub, pub, and restaurant area that's Sydney's liveliest and rowdiest.
- **Harbor cruises** that afford a superb view of Sydney's lively waterfront area, hill-clinging skyline, and the landmark **Harbor Bridge**.
- **The Queen Victoria Building**, now converted into an attractive shopping center.
- **Several nearby beaches**, including **Bondi** [BON-dye] and **Port Jackson**.

Two short trips out of Sydney will bring you to Botany Bay, where Captain Cook's *Endeavour* anchored, and to any of several wild-animal parks, where you can see koalas and kangaroos up close. (Similar parks exist throughout Australia.) Three longer **day trips** can be recommended:

Sydney Opera House, Australia
Photo by C. J. Ghormley

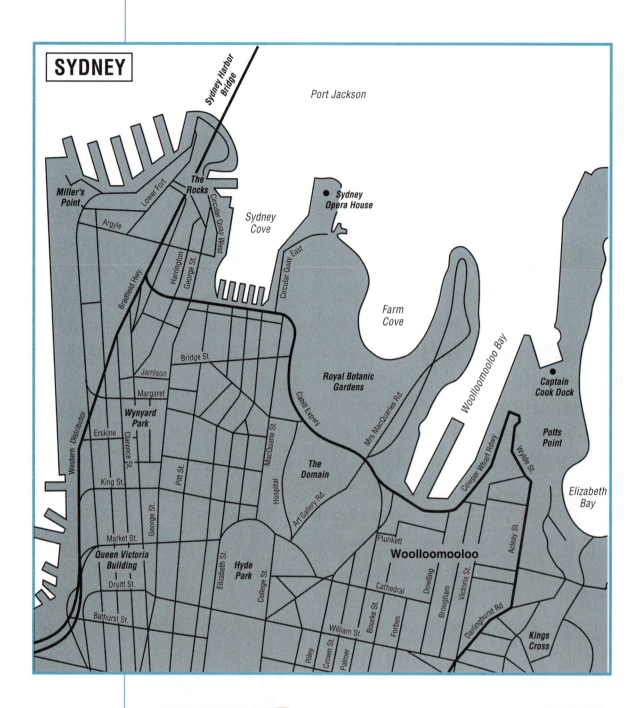

SYDNEY

Port Jackson

Sydney Harbor Bridge

Miller's Point

The Rocks

Lower Fort

Argyle

Sydney Cove

Sydney Opera House

Circular Quay West

Harrington

George St.

Circular Quay East

Farm Cove

Bradfield Hwy

Bridge St.

Jamison

Margaret

Royal Botanic Gardens

Cahill Expwy

Woolloomooloo Bay

Captain Cook Dock

Western Distributor

Wynyard Park

Erskine

Clarence St.

Pitt St.

MacQuarie St.

Mrs MacQuaries Rd.

Cowper Wharf Rdwy

Potts Point

King St.

George St.

Hospital

The Domain

Art Gallery Rd.

Wylde St.

Elizabeth Bay

Market St.

Elizabeth St.

Plunkett

Aclay St.

Queen Victoria Building

Druitt St.

Hyde Park

College St.

Woolloomooloo

Cathedral

Dowling

Victoria St.

Darlinghurst Rd

Bathurst St.

Brougham

William St.

Bourke St.

Forbes

Kings Cross

Riley

Crown St.

Palmer

The Blue Mountains got their name because of the blue haze given off by eucalyptus trees.

- **The Blue Mountains**, a scenic area that centers around the town of **Katoomba**, with its waterfall, railway (which travels steeply down into a valley), and sky way (a cable car that traverses between two cliffs).
- **Canberra**, Australia's sedate and isolated capital, which boasts some rather interesting modern architecture and a fountain jet, not unlike Geneva's.
- **Hawkesbury River Cruises**, available out of **Windsor** (a city north of Sydney). Ships take clients along the river's rugged gorges and into a national park. One- or two-day cruises are available.

Melbourne

Australia's second largest city—a melting pot of diverse ethnic groups—is as cosmopolitan as any of the nation's urban centers. It's well known for its quiet gardens, elegant stores, ever-present streetcars, sporting opportunities, and nearby ski resorts. Most hotels, restaurants, theaters, stores, and government buildings are within the city's "Golden Mile" district.

Just south off the coast from Melbourne is **Phillip Island**, one of Australia's most famous attractions. It's home to the "fairy" penguins—who, each day at dusk, march dutifully from the beach to their burrows. (The area is well-lit to ensure that your clients will see these creatures' waddling parade.) Warn clients, though, that at certain times the number of penguins dwindles, making for some disappointment. Farther offshore is the island-state of Tasmania, with its slow pace, mild climate, and deep green countryside.

Tasmania was a British penal colony whose nickname was "Devil's Island."

Queensland

Queensland is to Australia what California and Florida are to the United States: a region of palmy splendor, striking seascapes, and booming growth. Queensland is vast: It's much larger than any U.S. state. The state's principal points of tourism are, from north to south:

- **The Great Barrier Reef.** This 1,250-mile-long strip is made up of hundreds of offshore coral islands. Resort hotels anchor many of the larger islands; and the scuba diving, snorkeling, and marlin fishing here provide astonishing experiences. Cairns, at the Reef's northern end, is its principal gateway.

- **The Sunshine Coast.** This nearly forty-mile stretch of beaches, lakes, and mountains has a reputation of being less commercialized than its southerly competition. For clients who want relaxation or plenty of sporting opportunities, the Sunshine Coast is ideal.

- **Brisbane.** Queensland's capital is a lush, tropical paradise, with superb landscaping and several animal sanctuaries just outside the city.

- **The Gold Coast.** About an hour south of Brisbane, this beach resort area is Australia's most developed and crowded. It's somewhat reminiscent of Miami Beach, with many large hotels and resorts, as well as several family theme parks. (One well-known section is **Surfers Paradise.**) This is for the client who wants seaside hustle and bustle, not a get-away-from-it-all vacation.

The Outback

The vast, arid, near-empty center of Australia has an otherworldly quality that many visitors find absolutely intriguing. The art and culture of the aborigines, too, layer the region with even more mystery. Though vastly separate, two outback attractions (usually reached by plane) probably merit attention:

- **Alice Springs,** a frontier town with many art galleries, and surrounded by an almost surrealist landscape of red hills and hard, flat deserts.

- **Ayers** [AIRS] **Rock,** a massive stone outcropping that's best seen at sunset, when its reddish hue is most striking. It's a thousand feet high and six miles around and is a holy site for aboriginal people. Nearby is the tourist oasis of **Yulara,** with its unorthodox, tent-like structures.

Perth

This, Australia's largest west coast city, is a sunny amalgam of parks, hills, and friendliness. **Fremantle,** a nearby town, is famous for its yachting, restored buildings, and many art galleries. It's less likely, though, that your clients will ask to visit the Perth area, since it's a nearly ten-hour round trip from Australia's east coast. Still, Perth appeals to just about everyone who decides to see all of Australia.

Ayers Rock, Australia
Photo by C. J. Ghormley

(native population)
Moyiric culture

New Zealand's North Island

Your New Zealand-bound clients will certainly wish to see two cities: Auckland (New Zealand's largest city) and Wellington (its capital). Warn them, however, that both cities, though lovely, are relatively small and quiet—the kinds of places with many little points of interest (best seen via a city motorcoach tour).

Auckland's most notable sights are two waterfront theme attractions: **Kelly Tarlton's Antarctic Encounter** and **Underwater World**. Among the major attractions between these two cities are:

- **The Waitomo** [why-TOE-moe] **Caves**, where thousands of glowworms turn the ceiling of a deep grotto into a night-sky-like fantasy.
- **Rotorua** [roh-tuh-ROO-ah], a small city that boasts a number of features that make it a must-see. First, Rotorua is an important center of Maori native culture; its **Maori Arts and Crafts Institute** shows contemporary artists continuing the traditions of the country's first inhabitants. Second, Rotorua is the site of tremendous geothermal activity. Its thermal area boasts geysers, steam vents, and bubbling mud pots.
- **The Agrodome**, not far from Rotorua, an offbeat attraction where New Zealand's important sheep-raising industry is explained. It may sound boring, but it's not—your clients will love it when seventeen different kinds of "trained" sheep trot out to their appointed platforms on stage.

New Zealand's South Island   *more mountains*

Colder, larger, and more mountainous than its northern neighbor, the South Island claims several world-class attractions. Christchurch, with its graceful peaks, and Queenstown, a scenic mountain resort town that boasts a very active nightlife, are both essential stops on a South Island itinerary. So, too, are the following:

- **Mount Cook**, with its awe-inspiring glaciers, most frequently visited via ski planes.
- **Milford Sound**, a dramatic, carved sea inlet that's part of New Zealand's picturesque Fjordland National Park.

Several kiwi fruit farms in New Zealand are open to visitors and provide a fascinating glimpse of how these delicate fruits are grown.

Maori Lodge Hall, Rotorua, New Zealand
Photo by C. J. Ghormley

Other possibilities for your clients: a visit to the Te Anau [TAY AH-now] glow-worm caves, a cruise on Lake Wakatipu (near Queenstown), or white-water rafting on any of several South Island rivers.

Possible Itineraries

Because Australia and New Zealand are so distant from North America, clients, once they set out for this region, almost always wish to see as much there as possible. Typical is a minimum ten- to twelve-day itinerary that includes either New Zealand's North or South Islands and Australia's east coast, especially the areas around Sydney and Melbourne. Clients with the time for a more extended vacation or on a second, in-depth trip will certainly want to see both of New Zealand's major islands and either Australia's west coast (with a stop at Alice Springs and Ayers Rock) or the Queensland region. Finally, clients seeking a tropical stay or wishing to drive often limit their stay to Australia's east coast, with perhaps a day or two in Sydney and the rest of the time along the Great Barrier Reef and the beach areas north or south of Brisbane.

Lodging Options

North American chains have a strong presence here, as do such local companies as Australia's **Southern Pacific**, **Rydges**, and **Flag**. Both Australia and New Zealand have some deluxe properties (especially in Sydney and the Great Barrier Reef), but most of the accommodations in these countries tend to cluster at a mid-range, first-class level. Motels are popular; it's traditional here for motel rooms to have full kitchenettes, so this type of accommodation may appeal to families and the budget-minded. Home and farm stays can also be easily arranged—they're a wonderful option, since Australians and New Zealanders are among the world's friendliest people. Lists of farm and home-style accommodations are available from each country's tourist bureau.

Among the finest hotels: The Regent Sydney (which offers fine views of the harbor and Sydney Opera House), the Windsor (a historic landmark in Melbourne), and the Hayman Island Resort (on the Great Barrier Reef).

Allied Destinations

To advise your clients to visit any of the many Pacific islands that lie between North America and Australia or New Zealand is a wise and popular sales strategy.

But other options exist. Singapore, Malaysia, Indonesia, and several other less-visited countries lie just to the north of Australia. Even Japan, China, the Philippines, and the nations of Southeast Asia are potential add-on destinations, since your clients are already flying across the Pacific and may feel that they might just as well visit other transoceanic places if they have the time. Perhaps the most exotic option of them all: Antarctica. Several companies operate summer cruises from New Zealand to this bottom-of-the-world continent of ice.

Cultural Patterns

Clients may feel comparatively at home here. Yet Australia and New Zealand have their own customs:

- These are two friendly, very open nations and your clients should feel comfortable about using first names in greetings. However, a woman should still be allowed to offer her first name to a man before he assumes such an informality.

- Though these countries are easygoing in their ways, tell your clients that customs are more formal than a visitor might expect. Punctuality, for example, is important in both countries. And New Zealanders tend to be more formal than Australians; for instance, they're likely to be restrained with strangers at first meeting.

- Be sure your clients know that a gesture similar to the "thumbs up" sign is considered a profanity here.

- If your clients visit a home in New Zealand, they should be careful about praising any object too highly. They may find it presented to them as a gift.

- Tipping in restaurants is not common. As a visitor, you may wish to tip, but it's rarely expected.

- The food here was once considered bland. No longer. Foreign specialties have melded with post-British cuisine to create some wonderful eating treats. Two major specialties: oysters and lamb-based dishes.

- Nightlife in New Zealand often features Maori-Polynesian entertainment. Australian nightlife ranges from informal pubs to several nightspots that pay homage to Australia's colorful frontier history, as well as to aboriginal music. It's all very touristy, but then again, the locals somehow give it an unjaded, gee-whiz treatment. (Your clients will probably tire of sheep-shearing demonstrations, though, which are done in so many tourist places that they'll almost half-expect the flight attendants to do it on the plane home.)

Factors That Motivate Visitors

Client awareness of what Australia and New Zealand offer is growing daily. Among the features you should emphasize to make the sale are:

- Though distant and offbeat, Australia and New Zealand are culturally very accessible.
- The plants and animals are unlike those anywhere else in the world.
- The people are extremely friendly to tourists, have a wonderfully informal attitude, and speak English.
- Food and lodging are a bargain, especially if your clients stay in motor inns.
- The Queensland beaches are superb and especially uncrowded north of Brisbane, and the diving along the Great Barrier Reef is legendary.
- New Zealand and Australia rarely feel hectic or crowded, except perhaps in Sydney and along the Gold Coast.

Vegamite is a weird yeast spread that Australians slather on their bread. (Frankly, it tastes awful.)

- The Aborigine and Maori cultures are intriguing (though clients can experience this only in certain areas, such as Alice Springs and Rotorua, respectively).
- These countries bask in their most pleasant summer weather when many North Americans are shivering from winter's cold and are ready to get away for a warm-weather vacation.
- There's skiing in southeast Australia and in southern New Zealand, where many slopes are accessed only via helicopter.
- Both countries are extremely stable politically and have a relatively low crime rate.

The Great Barrier Reef is so big it's visible from the moon.

Possible Misgivings

Australia and New Zealand aren't for everyone. Here are some of the objections that may come up in a sale and how you might counter them:

- "It's too far." These countries are indeed a long flight from anywhere in North America. You could break up the trip, however, by adding a stop (generally at little or no additional air cost) at a Pacific island resort in each direction. East Coast clients could pause a day or two in Los Angeles or San Francisco.

Qualifying the Client
Australia and New Zealand

FOR CLIENTS WHO WANT	APPEAL			REMARKS
	HIGH	MEDIUM	LOW	
Historical and Cultural Attractions			▲	Some cities; Maori culture
Beaches and Water Sports	▲			In Queensland
Skiing Opportunities		▲		In southern mountains
Lots of Nightlife			▲	Sydney and Queenstown
Family Activities		▲		Children will find animals interesting; motor hotels plentiful
Familiar Cultural Experience		▲		
Exotic Cultural Experience		▲		Animals; Maori culture
Safety and Low Crime	▲			
Bargain Travel		▲		Flight expensive, but other costs reasonable
Impressive Scenery		▲		Bush and outback impressively bleak; mountains and seascapes
Peace and Quiet	▲			In countryside
Shopping Opportunities		▲		Opals, woolens, leather
To Do Business		▲		A common language facilitates business

Figure 23-3

Woolens are a relative bargain, but so are opals, which are mostly gathered and polished in Australia.

- "It's too expensive." Airfares can be hefty, but bargain rates appear in the off-season. Once there, clients can drive around, staying at motels or farmhouses.
- "We can't be away from work that long." If clients limit themselves to one area of Australia or New Zealand, a round trip can be done in nine days.
- "There's not all that much to see and do." You must explain the many wonders of this part of the world to offset your clients' preconceptions. You'll hear this objection, especially, about New Zealand, a nation that elicits a much hazier picture in clients' minds than Australia.
- "We'd like to bring our children, but they'll have nothing to do." Again, most people don't know about Australia's beaches, New Zealand's skiing, and so on. Further, children love animals and both countries have plenty of weird ones. The one legitimate objection for families: the cost of airfare.

Sales Strategies

Expand your clients' FIT by suggesting that as long as they'll be going to Australia, why not add New Zealand, Fiji, Tahiti, or Hawaii? It will require just a short lengthening of their trip. Suggest a larger rental car, especially if your clients expect to drive across Australia's vast stretches. Ski, cruise, and dive packages can all be sold in advance, as can city tours (especially appropriate in Sydney, Melbourne, and Auckland).

Travel Trivia

Top Ten Dream Destinations

1. Australia
2. Great Britain
3. France
4. Germany
5. Italy

6. Canada
7. Ireland
8. Mexico
9. Switzerland
10. Israel

Source: Louis Harris and Associates poll

Creative Activity

You're reading a magazine and see that Qantas is running a "Down Under Mystery Tour" contest. You're supposed to read the "Mystery Tour" description, guess each city or region where the tour will visit, fill out the contest blank, then wait to see if yours will be chosen from among the correct entries to receive an all-expenses-paid trip. Here's the description:

On the first few days you'll let a little steam off, have the wool pulled over your eyes, and see "stars" at noon. Two days later you'll pretend you're in Norway. Then it's across the water to someplace that everybody says is filled with cans. Next stop: a big reddish thing in the middle of nowhere. The next place is even stranger: it's for the birds, tuxedoed ones at that. We finish off with a drink on the Rocks.

PLACES THE TOUR WILL VISIT:

1.

2.

3.

4.

5.

6.

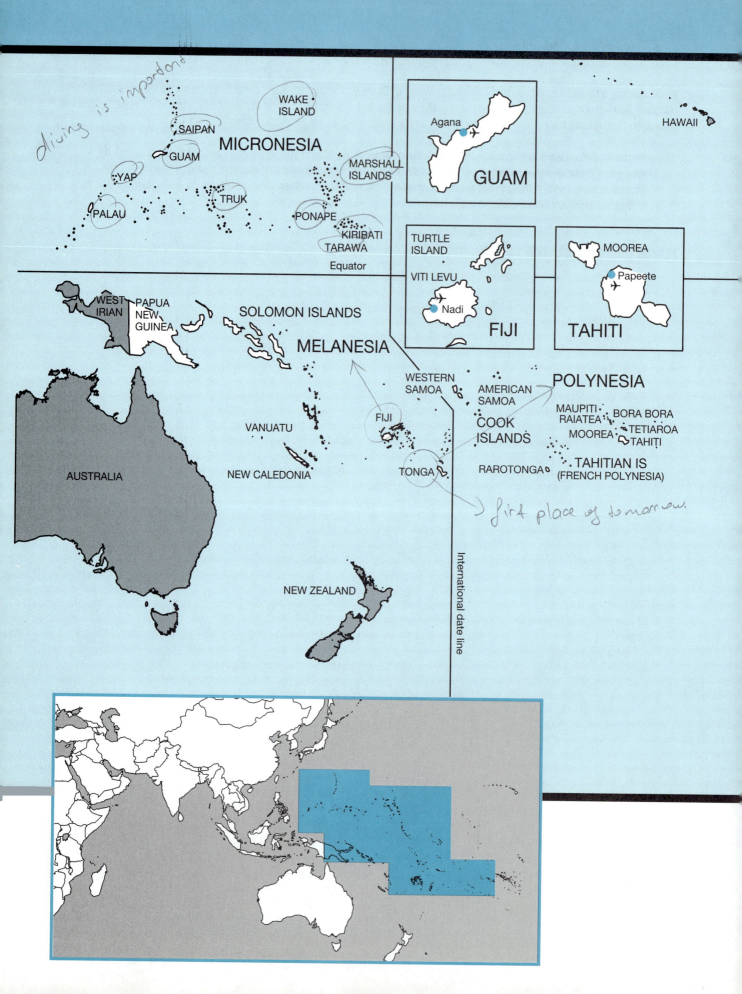

diving is important

MICRONESIA

WAKE ISLAND

SAIPAN

GUAM

YAP

TRUK

PALAU

PONAPE

MARSHALL ISLANDS

KIRIBATI
TARAWA

Equator

GUAM

Agana

FIJI

TURTLE ISLAND

VITI LEVU

Nadi

TAHITI

MOOREA

Papeete

HAWAII

WEST IRIAN

PAPUA NEW GUINEA

SOLOMON ISLANDS

MELANESIA

WESTERN SAMOA

AMERICAN SAMOA

POLYNESIA

COOK ISLANDS

MAUPITI
RAIATEA

BORA BORA

MOOREA

TETIAROA
TAHITI

VANUATU

FIJI

AUSTRALIA

NEW CALEDONIA

TONGA

RAROTONGA

TAHITIAN IS
(FRENCH POLYNESIA)

first place of tomorrow.

NEW ZEALAND

International date line

CHAPTER 24

The Pacific
Fantasy Islands

How many islands dot the Pacific? Thousands. In fact, tens of thousands. Either coral or volcanic in origin, spreading across vast stretches of ocean waters, these islands have been the subject of fantasy to the Western mind since 1519, when the explorer Magellan first passed through them. No, you'll not have to learn all of their names and locations. Probably the world's foremost geography experts would have trouble doing that. Only about a dozen or so have become significant tourist destinations. Some of these islands or island groupings are independent countries. Others are under various levels of administration by France, Great Britain, the United States, and others.

The islands of the Pacific can be loosely divided into three regions. (The whole area is sometimes called Oceania.) North and northeast of Australia are the islands of **Micronesia**. Tourism in Micronesia is limited, except for **Guam** and **Saipan** [sye-PAN], which appeal strongly to Japanese tourists. **Truk** [TRUCK], **Kiribati** [KIR-uh-bass], **Yap**, and **Palau** (also spelled "Belau") have an almost legendary appeal for divers.

Melanesia—so named for the natives' dark skin (*mela* means dark)—draws quite a few tourists from North America, though the islands of this group appeal most strongly to Australians and New Zealanders. **Fiji** [FEE-jee] is by far the most popular, but **Papua** [PAP-yuh-wah] **New Guinea** and **New Caledonia** also have their devotees.

Polynesia is perhaps the best known of the South Sea island groups. Legendary for its romantic scenery, soft climate, and graceful native lifestyle, it extends, technically, all the way to Hawaii on the north (covered in Chapter 28), to Easter Island on the east and to New Zealand on the west. We concentrate mostly on those dots of land to the immediate east of Melanesia—**Tahiti** and its nearby islands are the big draw here, but **Tonga**, **American Samoa**, **Western Samoa**, and the **Cook Islands** all have their admirers.

Two significant geographic lines cross the region. One is the **international date line**, which we spoke of in Part I of this book. It zigs and zags among the islands so that it crosses no major destination. (Otherwise, you could find yourself in another day just by crossing the street!) It does zag just to the east of Tonga. As a result, Tonga is technically the place where each new day starts. (That's why some Tongan stamps proclaim, "Tonga—Where Time Begins.") The other significant line is the **equator**. In this chapter, we treat mostly those destinations south of it (they're called the South Seas), but remember that quite a few Pacific islands spill out north of the equator, including Hawaii and almost the entire area that is Micronesia.

How Travelers Get There

Polynesia *Melanesia* *Micronesia*

Several major U.S. and Canadian airlines fly to these destinations from the North American West Coast and Hawaii, as do such foreign carriers as Qantas, Air New Zealand, Air France, and a number of Asian carriers. After clients fly on a major airline to the principal gateways—**Papeete**, Tahiti (PPT); **Nadi**, Fiji (NAN); and Guam (GUM)—they will have to hop aboard one of the dozens of local airlines to get to the less-visited islands. Some of these connections will be cited later; remember, though, that air service in the region is in a constant state of flux.

Several tour operators specialize in air-hotel packages to the South Pacific; they can often save your clients hundreds of dollars, while saving you booking and itinerary-planning time. Cruise ships visit the area (often on repositioning cruises) and all manner of ferries, yachts, and cargo ships unite the islands.

Weather Patterns

Since virtually every one of the Pacific islands lies within the tropics, the climate is relatively predictable: For Polynesia (except Hawaii) and Melanesia, May through October (their winter) is warm, fairly dry, and high tourist season, whereas November through April (their summer) is hotter, wetter, and sees a thinning of tourism. (Remember that Polynesia and Melanesia are in the Southern Hemisphere, so their seasons are precisely the reverse of North America's.) On the other hand, Micronesia—being largely north of the equator—has the best weather in *its* winter, from November through March, when temperatures are milder. Micronesian summers (July to October) are rainy and hurricanes are a threat in the summer and fall.

Ask about tipping early on. On many islands, it's not the practice.

Topography and location on the globe, though, can produce variations within these patterns. For example, clients who visit Papeete, Tahiti, in August can expect it to rain only about one day a week, but someone visiting Pago Pago, American Samoa, during that same month may experience rain just about every other day. To predict the leeward (and, therefore, drier) side of a mountainous island is not always as easy to do as in other parts of the world, since this region stretches across several opposite wind patterns. In general, though, the rule we learned in the book's opening section applies to these tropical islands: Western shores will tend to be drier and eastern shores will be rainier. For an example of a South Seas climate, see Figure 24-1.

Getting Around

Frequent flights and cruises connect the islands. On-island transportation is quite informal. Buses are usually a good option, since locals are often friendly and talkative. Mopeds and bicycles are a popular choice. Taxis are plentiful on the major islands and your clients can often rent a car or taxi with driver for a day's sightseeing at a reasonable cost. How about car rentals? Well, they're available on the major islands, but because of poor road conditions, a four-wheel-drive vehicle might be more practical. One thing to make clear to your clients: Don't expect the quality of service or efficiency of a vehicle to be anywhere near what they're used to in North America. Other options: helicopter rides, glass-bottom boats, and even riding on horseback.

Important Places

To bring some sense of order to this vast destination, we examine the principal islands according to their traditional cultural and geographic divisions: Polynesia, Melanesia, and Micronesia.

Climate at a Glance
PAPEETE, TAHITI

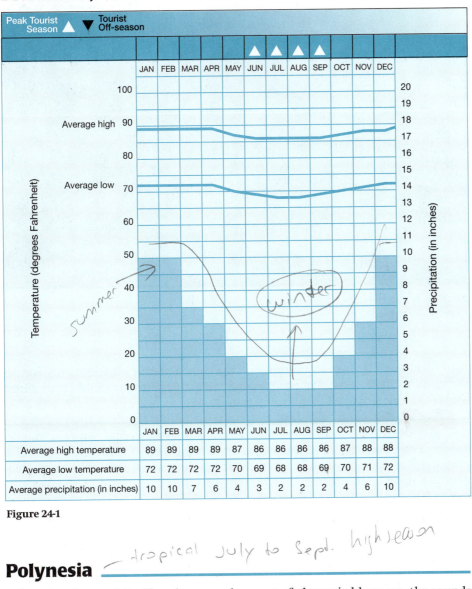

Figure 24-1

	JAN	FEB	MAR	APR	MAY	JUN	JUL	AUG	SEP	OCT	NOV	DEC
Average high temperature	89	89	89	89	87	86	86	86	86	87	88	88
Average low temperature	72	72	72	72	70	69	68	68	69	70	71	72
Average precipitation (in inches)	10	10	7	6	4	3	2	2	2	4	6	10

Polynesia *—tropical July to Sept. high season*

Polynesia—the word itself conjures up the scent of plumeria blossoms, the sounds of smiling voices, and the feel of warm, azure waters lapping at your feet. Five Polynesian island groups may appeal to your clients:

The Tahitian Islands.   The Tahitian Islands, also known as the Society Islands (an older term), comprise the western part of French Polynesia. Tahiti itself (with its capital, Papeete [pah-pee-AY-tee]) is the principal gateway to the region's 130 or so islands. Papeete is a bustling little city, with an open-air market and a small museum displaying the works of French artist Paul Gauguin, who lived here. An interesting law—no building can be higher than a coconut tree—keeps Papeete and the rest of Tahiti free of view-spoiling high-rises. There are many scenic areas on Tahiti itself, but even more dramatic scenery and the best tourist facilities are on the nearby island of **Moorea** and on **Bora Bora**, which is 143 miles northwest of Tahiti. **Raiatea** and **Maupiti** have fewer lodging options, but are excellent get-away-from-it-all islands. And little **Tetiaroa**—twenty miles north of Papeete—may be known to your clients: It's owned by actor Marlon Brando and has limited, exclusive accommodations. One warning: French Polynesia is one of the

On French islands, locals often speak only French. But unlike many of France's residents, islanders will happily tolerate a tourist's high-school French.

Bora Bora, French Polynesia
Photo by C. J. Ghormley

most expensive island destinations in the South Pacific. Recommend French Polynesia to clients who like water sports, all-inclusive resorts (which can blunt some of the high costs), and awesome scenery.

Tonga. Tonga has spectacular scenery—including several active volcanoes—and provides clients with just about every water-sport opportunity available. Boaters love Tonga for its comparative absence of reefs. Tonga, which is still a monarchy, is made up of several islands; Tongatapu, where the capital is located, provides most of the modest lodging choices and, by Polynesian standards, is somewhat crowded. To get your clients here, you'll probably have to route them through American Samoa, Western Samoa, Fiji, or Auckland.

American Samoa. Another mountainous (and picturesque) chain of islands, American Samoa has facilities even more limited than Tonga, but what is there feels more American than Polynesian. In other words, it's appropriate for clients who want to retain at least some of the feel and comfort of home. Deep-sea fishing is good here, as are hiking opportunities. Virtually all accommodations are in the town of Pago Pago [PONG-oh PONG-oh]. You can book clients to Pago Pago's airport from Fiji, Western Samoa, the Cook Islands, or even Hawaii.

Western Samoa. Western Samoa and its chief town, Apia, feel much more Polynesian than does American Samoa. Indeed, Western Samoa has the world's largest population of full-blooded Polynesians. Services, though, are limited; a growing influx of tourists may change that soon. For now, Western Samoa is still a bargain. Your clients can get here from Tahiti, Fiji, Tonga, American Samoa, or the Cook Islands.

The Cook Islands. Once sleepy and secluded, the Cook Islands are becoming more active, thanks to investment money from Australia and New Zealand. **Rarotonga** island has most of the hotels—several are deluxe—but most of the guests are from the lands down under. This would be an offbeat destination for some of your clients, especially those into snorkeling, diving, deep-sea fishing, or just beaching-it. They could be booked via Tahiti, Fiji, Western Samoa, or American Samoa.

Samoa was named after a sacred chicken.

Dancers, Moorea, French Polynesia
Photo by C. J. Ghormley

less expensive

Melanesia

Better known to Australians and New Zealanders (who are fairly close by), the islands of Melanesia are fast becoming destinations that appeal to North Americans. In some cases, they're destinations unto themselves, but more often they're stop-off points on the way to or from Australia and New Zealand. Two bits of trivia: Eighty percent of the Pacific's islander population lives in Melanesia; furthermore, nearly 1,200 distinct languages are spoken throughout Melanesia—fortunately, English is one of them and it's spoken on many of the islands.

The Fiji Islands. The Fiji Islands have become among the most important of South Sea destinations. The large island of **Viti Levu** has many fine tropical hotels—especially on the west coast around Nadi (where the airport is located) and along Viti Levu's southern coast, which has come to be known as the Coral Coast. Hotels dot other shores of Viti Levu, as well as those of other islands in the Fiji chain, including **Turtle Island**, a well-publicized, very expensive private resort. The rest of Fiji, though, is a comparative South Sea bargain and quite popular with divers, shoppers, and culture-seekers. (The islands' population is a not-always-harmonious blend of Polynesians, Indians, Chinese, and Europeans.)

Papua New Guinea. Papua New Guinea occupies the eastern half of the large island of New Guinea, which lies north of Australia (the western half is part of Indonesia). This tropical destination is especially interesting for its native culture: Until fairly recently some of its natives were Stone-Age headhunters. A few areas of the country are quite modern, with many conveniences, but most are thoroughly primitive. Papua New Guinea is an expensive destination, political and social turmoil is frequent, and crime can be a problem. Divers love its offshore areas and nature buffs appreciate its huge variety of orchids and birds. Air connections are generally made through several Australian east coast cities, though flights also arrive from Singapore and New Zealand.

New Caledonia. New Caledonia is famous for two things: its superb diving (one of the world's largest barrier reefs lies offshore) and its capital city, **Noumea.** Often called the "Paris of the Pacific," Noumea has a few elegant boutiques, some

Fijians are famous for their firewalking and intricate tattoos.

Villagers, Fiji
Photo by C. J. Ghormley

Bungee jumping originated on Vanuatu.

gourmet restaurants and not far outside town, a casino. Don't mislead your clients, though, into thinking that this is another French Riviera; New Caledonia seems elegant only in comparison to neighboring island destinations. Indeed, much of the island has a charming seediness about it. Yet like other French islands, New Caledonia can be a rather expensive destination. A short flight northeast of New Caledonia are the islands of Vanuatu, with their impressive scenery, good diving, and surprising array of good lodging.

Micronesia

Thousands of islands, but all of them isolated and small—that's the best way to describe Micronesia. The islands of Micronesia weren't exactly household words until World War II, when reports from Guam, Yap, Truk, and Saipan became commonplace. In the period following the war, nuclear testing took place here; one site, the island of Bikini (part of the seldom visited Marshall Islands), became permanently associated with a scanty form of bathing suit. Micronesia continues to be of military interest, but North American tourists are gradually finding out what Japanese tourists discovered decades ago: that these islands are truly appealing destinations.

Mosquitoes are ferocious and roaches are ubiquitous throughout the islands; bring repellent. Many hotels with open-air huts give clients special repellent incense coils to burn.

Guam. Part of a collection of islands geographically known as the Marianas, Guam is Micronesia's principal destination. The United States military's continued presence here helps assure air connections to Hawaii and many Western amenities. Water sports and dramatic scenery are its principal attractions. Most tourist facilities are around the capital, Agana, and on Tumon Bay, which is highly frequented by Japanese and Taiwanese tourists. Guam is also a gateway to most of the other Micronesian islands. Travelers who are into water sports, history (especially that of World War II), golf and other comforts typical of North America will find Guam appealing.

Saipan. Also part of the Marianas, Saipan is Micronesia's other well-developed tourist center. It, too, owes its success to its reputation as a Japanese honeymoon destination. More so than Guam, Saipan is mostly geared for Japanese, not United

States or Canadian, travelers. A strong point for most: It feels less military. Divers, windsurfers, golfers, and scenery lovers will find Saipan quite pleasing.

Truk. Politically part of the Federated States of Micronesia (which also includes **Ponape** [PO-nah-pay] and Yap) and geographically part of the Caroline Islands, Truk is a legendary destination for divers. Here, the United States bombed and crippled the World War II fleet of Japan; seventy wrecks lie on the bottom of Truk's forty-mile-wide lagoon harbor. Another diver's paradise in the Carolines (though accommodations are limited) is **Palau**, with its superb reef scuba diving opportunities and picture-perfect tropical island scenery.

Kiribati. These flat atoll islands—stretching across almost 2,000 miles of the Pacific—include the Gilbert and Phoenix island groups. Still relatively uncommercialized, Kiribati appeals to divers and others who want to get away from it all. Basic lodging is available on several islands, especially **Tarawa**, where the capital is located.

Possible Itineraries

There are two ways to consider the islands of the Pacific: as "pause-points" on the way to other destinations or as the endpoint of your clients' vacation. Polynesia and Melanesia can break up a trip to and from Australia and New Zealand. For example, you could fly your clients to Fiji, where they might stay two or three days before they continue on to, say, New Zealand. They could then pause for a few days in Tahiti or Hawaii on the way back. Similarly, Guam or Truk could be a several-day pause between the mainland or Hawaii and such countries as Japan, China, the Philippines, Singapore, or any of the other Southeast Asian countries. Unfortunately, the flight connections will be a little difficult to arrange.

What of those clients who want to visit only an island or combination of islands? It's best to keep them within one general island grouping. For example, a nine-day itinerary could include two flight days, four days on Moorea, and three days on Bora Bora. Another longer possibility would be to fly the clients to Fiji for a three-day stay, then connect them to two- or three-day stays in the islands to the east: Tonga, American Samoa, Western Samoa, or Rarotonga. Or you could hub them out to the west, to such Melanesian destinations as New Caledonia and Papua New Guinea. Divers might enjoy a nine- to fourteen-day itinerary to the Micronesian islands of Guam, Truk, and Palau, with a more lively stay in Hawaii along the way. Cruises provide efficient sail itineraries between or among island groupings.

New Caledonia means "New Scotland."

Lodging Options

The Pacific islands' range of accommodations is staggeringly wide. For example, on Moorea you can book your clients into a super-deluxe group of huts that sits on piers over a lagoon; at an all-inclusive resort; in simple, inexpensive bungalows; or allow them to bargain their own lodging in a local's hut. Among the Fiji islands, your clients can stay at the super-exclusive **Turtle Island Resort**, once featured on "Lifestyles of the Rich and Famous." Or you can book them into a New Guinean guest house run by the descendants of cannibals. For those seeking more conventional accommodations, many North American and international chains have properties throughout the Pacific.

A few warnings to give when you advise your clients: Even the most deluxe properties can be disorganized and messy; reservations can be lost (give clients a copy of the confirmation and pray); the locals sometimes don't speak English on French islands; bugs are everywhere in the tropics, including in the finest hotels; some of the less-visited islands don't have anything but the most basic of lodging—it's one more reason to depend on independent tour packages that select hotels carefully and place more clout behind your clients' reservations.

If you see little geckos (lizards) in your room, encourage the creatures to stay. They chase insects while avoiding humans.

Allied Destinations

Polynesia and Melanesia are easily combined with trips to Australia and New Zealand. Micronesia can be a stopover to the Philippines, Singapore, Malaysia, and all of mainland Asia. You can also combine several islands into one vacation package, including some South Sea destinations that few tourists visit and that we've not mentioned here. For information on such islands (including Nauru, Niue, the Solomons, Tuvalu, Vanuatu, Wallis, and Futuna), consult a more detailed agency reference book.

Cultural Patterns

Each of these many islands has its own unique customs of which your clients—vacationers and business travelers alike—should be aware. Among them are:

When shopping, don't try to bargain for items. Among most islanders it's considered inappropriate.

- Tell your clients that in Fiji, time is informal and that it may be permissible to arrive quite late. When visiting a home, your clients should remove their shoes before entering. The drink *kava* is often offered to guests; though it may taste harsh to North Americans, it would be considered rude to refuse it. (This also applies in Samoa.) When your clients talk with a Fiji resident, crossed arms is a sign of respect.

- Though it's not necessary for your clients to tip in French Polynesia, small gifts are often given.

- Tell your clients who visit Samoa that an elaborate greeting is considered very respectful. Be sure your clients know that it's rude for a person standing to sway while talking to a Samoan; indeed, almost all conversation is held while sitting.

- Completely give up the notion of punctuality or efficiency while in the islands; nothing there seems to work as it should. (Consider that at some small island airports, the air traffic controller is also the ticket taker and the skycap!)

- Your clients should know that, to Tahitians, shaking hands is very important. When visiting the home of a local, your clients should taste at least a little bit of everything offered and be prepared to eat with their fingers. And they should not praise any item in the home too highly; it may be presented as a gift.

Factors That Motivate Visitors

Among the motives that clients may have for traveling among the islands of the Pacific are:

- They seek the legendary beauty and romance of the islands.
- They want to break up a long trans-Pacific trip.
- The climate is spectacular.
- Water-sport, beach, and cruise opportunities are widely available.
- The cultural differences are fascinating.
- It's a good way to collect many off-the-beaten-path, get-away-from-it-all destinations without too many inconveniences.
- The food is fresh and generally wonderful.
- Bargains can be had for clients willing to put up with the barest of accommodations or with freighter transport.
- The scenery on the volcanic islands is dramatic.

Possible Misgivings

Perhaps you're in love with the South Pacific as a destination. Don't assume everyone else is. There are many potential objections to a South Seas vacation:

- "It's too expensive." This is a genuine concern; since most supplies are shipped to the islands, all costs are high, especially on French-governed islands. Suggest an off-season trip, when air costs are lower. Recommend one of the major islands, where a wide variety of services is available and air connections are easy. Suggest Fiji or Western Samoa, which are somewhat less expensive.
- "It's too far." The trip can indeed be long, with many potential connections if a lesser island is involved. Suggest a stopover in Hawaii to break up the initial long flight.
- "It seems too primitive for me." Suggest Fiji or Tahiti, where many conveniences are available.
- "I've heard of political unrest." On some islands, friction does sometimes occur between natives and the governing country or among different local factions. (This is especially true in Fiji.) Yet it seems that tourists are usually left alone here, even in revolutions. Still, check government advisories and give prudent, informed advice to clients.
- "There aren't enough cultural attractions." The people and their way of life *are* the culture here, especially in the non-U.S. territories. If this is the type of

In a poll of *Conde Nast Traveler* readers, the number-one factor that could spoil a tropical island vacation: A room overlooking a parking lot.

Qualifying the Client
Fiji

FOR CLIENTS WHO WANT	APPEAL			REMARKS
	HIGH	MEDIUM	LOW	
Historical and Cultural Attractions		▲		Melanesian culture
Beaches and Water Sports	▲			
Skiing Opportunities			▲	None
Lots of Nightlife		▲		In hotels
Family Activities		▲		Families will enjoy it, but airfare prohibitive
Familiar Cultural Experience			▲	
Exotic Cultural Experience	▲			
Safety and Low Crime		▲		Some unrest
Bargain Travel		▲		Many bargains; flights costly
Impressive Scenery	▲			Seascapes, volcanic mountains, jungle
Peace and Quiet	▲			Much quieter than Hawaii
Shopping Opportunities		▲		Carvings, jewelry
To Do Business			▲	

Figure 24-2

client who loves Europe but not island stays, though, you may have to counter with a destination other than the South Seas.

- "We didn't like Hawaii and we won't like this." Find out why the clients didn't like Hawaii. Was it the overt commercialism? If so, perhaps the South Seas are *exactly* what they're looking for.

Sales Strategies

Independent tour packages and cruises are a sterling way to assure maximum value and commission. The Club Meds of Moorea and Bora Bora are an all-inclusive bargain on these expensive islands. Dive packages and dive tours can often be booked in advance. Helicopter and even submarine rides are available on several islands. With a client who is worried about the quality of accommodations, sell-up to the best hotel possible and suggest an ocean-view room. For clients who dread long flights, suggest business or first class.

Creative Activity

In the Creative Activity for Chapter 21, you judged whether a group of celebrities would like to visit Kenya and Tanzania. This activity is the reverse of that. Below are eight Pacific island destinations. Try to think of a famous person who might enjoy each destination (you must have a different celebrity for each one). Be prepared to explain how you arrived at your solution.

DESTINATION	ISLAND	WHY
1. Moorea	1.	1.
2. Tetiaroa	2.	2.
3. Tonga	3.	3.
4. Pago Pago	4.	4.
5. Papua New Guinea	5.	5.
6. Fiji	6.	6.
7. New Caledonia	7.	7.
8. Truk	8.	8.

Travel Trivia

Top Ten Dive Sites for Serious Divers

1. Great Barrier Reef
2. Truk/Palau/Yap
3. Fiji/Tahiti
4. The Red Sea
5. Papua New Guinea
6. The Seychelles
7. The Channel Islands (California)
8. The Maldives
9. The Galapagos Islands
10. Cocos Island (Costa Rica)

Source: Beach Travel

CHINA

RUSSIA

NORTH
KOREA

SEA of
JAPAN

SOUTH
KOREA

Hokkaido

● Sapporo

Honshu

PACIFIC
OCEAN

Nikko
Nat.
Park ▲
● Nikko

JAPAN

✈ ★ Tokyo

Lake Hakone
Mt. Fuji ▲ ▲ ── Yokohama

Shugakuin ●
Hiroshima ● ✈ ● Kyoto
Osaka ● Nara ●

● Kamakura

→ 1ˢᵗ capital

Shikoku

Beppu ●
Nagasaki ▲ Kyushu

EAST
CHINA
SEA

CHAPTER **25**

Japan
Pearl of the Orient

Mitsubishi, Toyota, Sony—these are names that the whole world knows. Yet until the twentieth century, Japan—like some pearl hidden in a sleepy oyster—existed in almost complete isolation, a mystery to the world: small, unimpressive, largely unknown. Japan still is but a series of small islands in the shadow of that teeming behemoth, China. Yet a mere few decades after having faced defeat in World War II, Japan today powerfully influences world economics, business, and politics. It's a country of slow beauty and aggressive drive.

About the size of the state of Montana, Japan is bordered by the **Sea of Japan** to its west and the **Pacific Ocean** to the east. A spine of volcanic mountains runs along the western length of the country; indeed, most Japanese live along the country's eastern flank. One surprising fact: Japan is made up of not one, but more than 4,000 islands. Only four, however—**Hokkaido**, **Honshu**, **Shikoku**, and **Kyushu**—are populated to any great degree. And of those, it's Honshu, the largest, that dominates the country.

For Your Information . . .

Japan   FYI

CAPITAL: Tokyo

AREA (SQUARE MILES): 145,766

TIME ZONE: GMT +9

DRIVE ON: Left

POPULATION: 125,400,000

RELIGIONS: Buddhism, Shintoism

LANGUAGE: Japanese

CURRENCY: 1 yen = 100 sen

ELECTRICITY: 100 volts, 60 cycles AC

CAPSULE HISTORY: Contact with China, fifth century A.D.; first Shogun, 1185; Portuguese visit, 1542; U.S. Commodore Perry arrives, 1853; parliamentary system, 1889; Pearl Harbor attack, 1941; Japan surrenders, after two atom bombings, 1945; full sovereignty, 1952.

For reference sources, tourist bureaus, and suggested lengths of stay, see the Appendices.

On Honshu, **Tokyo**—the world's largest metropolitan area—lies near the center, on the east coast. **Kyoto** [kee-OH-toe], an ancient city of great charm, rests in the south-central region of the island, and the port of **Osaka** (a major business destination) is just to its southwest.

Although the national language of Japan is Japanese, many people (especially travel personnel) speak relatively good English and are eager to communicate.

How Travelers Get There

Tokyo is Japan's gateway. It has two major airports, though **Narita** (also known as **New Tokyo**) **International Airport** (NRT) is where most international flights land. **Haneda International Airport** (HND) mainly serves the major domestic cities, but it does handle limited international flights. If there's any way you can book your clients' flights into Haneda, it would be worth the effort: it's closer to the city. Narita, on the other hand, is forty-three miles to the northeast. But since it's likely that Narita is where most of your clients will arrive, strongly warn them against taking regular taxis into Tokyo: The fares are incredibly expensive. Limousine buses, cars (booked in advance), and an express train are the best alternatives and can cost much less than a taxi would. Osaka's **Kansai International Airport** (OSA) is another option for Japan-bound clients.

Nonstop service is available to Japan from North America. Several North American carriers fly there, as do many international airlines, especially those based in Asia. **Japan Air Lines** (JL) is the national carrier; and **All Nippon Airways**, also called **ANA** (NH), provides service as well. Flying time from Los Angeles is just over eleven hours; from New York, it's over thirteen hours. (It's common for travelers from the East Coast to stop over on the West Coast or in Hawaii.) Japan is also a cruise destination. A few cruises start in **Yokohama**, just south of Tokyo, while others stop off at various Japanese ports (especially **Nagasaki**) as part of a longer Asian itinerary.

Weather Patterns

In Japan, beer can be purchased from vending machines.

Japan's climate is temperate, though conditions are less than ideal; gray and drizzly days are all too common. (See Figure 25-1.) Summers are warm and humid, whereas winters are chilly. (Winter in Hokkaido and the northern portion of Honshu, however, is very cold.) Rain is common from March through October; only winter is relatively dry, with about five rainy (and occasionally snowy) days per month. Spring is a legendary time to visit Japan; the cherry blossoms are in bloom, the temperatures are pleasant, and the rainy season hasn't quite reached its full strength. September to November can also be pleasant. Temperatures average in the 60s to 70s during the day, and precipitation, especially in late fall, is less likely. (Typhoons bring heavy rains in early fall.)

A warning: Your clients should avoid traveling in Japan during major Japanese holiday periods, for accommodations and transportation get very crowded. The days before and after New Year's are one such vacation time; mid-August (the Obon Festival) is another. Finally, Golden Week, April 29 through the first week of May, is the third big holiday period. Tourism thins out a bit during winter, but rates—especially hotel costs—don't drop very much. There's no real budget season in Japan.

Getting Around

Japan Air Lines and All Nippon provide domestic flights between major cities. However, since most of the country's main tourist destinations are comparatively close to one another, air service may not be the most convenient mode of trans-

Climate at a Glance
TOKYO, JAPAN

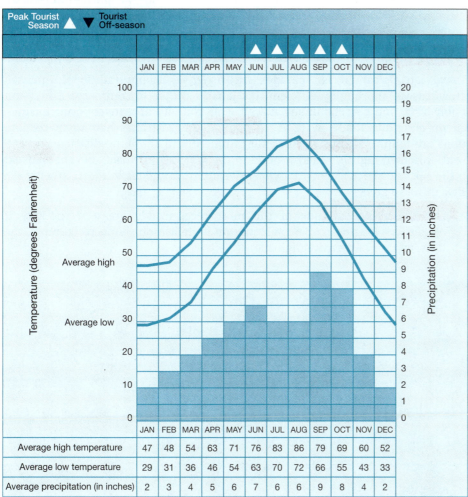

	JAN	FEB	MAR	APR	MAY	JUN	JUL	AUG	SEP	OCT	NOV	DEC
Average high temperature	47	48	54	63	71	76	83	86	79	69	60	52
Average low temperature	29	31	36	46	54	63	70	72	66	55	43	33
Average precipitation (in inches)	2	3	4	5	6	7	6	6	9	8	4	2

Figure 25-1

portation. That honor falls to the famed bullet trains (*shinkansen*), which hurtle down tracks at speeds up to 130 mph. You probably should book your clients on at least a part of the bullet train route between Tokyo and Osaka: The Hikari train offers near-express service, whereas the Kadama provides more stops (especially helpful for tourists who wish to see the sights en route). The **Japan Rail Pass** is a useful option for your clients who intend to spend a good length of time in Japan; it allows unlimited rail travel and can be bought only in North America. There also are regular service trains throughout the country, some of which are highly luxurious. (Note: A few trains are private and aren't covered by the Japan Rail Pass.)

Though rental cars are widely available, you should discourage your clients from driving. Because driving is on the left and most road signs are in Japanese, conditions can be extremely confusing. A better (though costly) alternative: a private car with driver or guide.

Tokyo and Osaka offer superb subways. The systems are frenetic, but not nearly as confusing as your clients might fear. (They're fairly well marked for Westerners.) Kyoto has a limited subway. Bus service in Japan is good and moderately priced. Do warn clients to avoid public transportation during rush hours. They may not take kindly to the kind of crowding that goes on.

During rush hours, Tokyo's subways have professional "pushers" who shove commuters into the packed cars.

Important Places

Japan has many unusual places for your clients to enjoy. Keep in mind that the country is also an especially important destination for business travelers.

Tokyo

Tokyo, Japan's capital, is a paradox: futuristic, yet deeply traditional; intensely crowded, yet thoroughly efficient. It's Japan's center of commerce, education, publishing, and entertainment as well. This is a city of districts: Your business clients should be made aware of the **Marunouchi** district, where many corporations are found; **Shinjuku** is an entertainment and shopping district; Western, youth-oriented nightlife can be found in the **Roppongi** district; and the **Akasaka** is the geisha district, a center for expensive nightlife and restaurants. Other major sites in Tokyo are:

- **The Ginza district**, one of the most recognizable areas of the city to Westerners. Its glittering neon shines on high-fashion shops, restaurants, theaters, and very expensive nightlife.

Japanese products aren't necessarily cheaper in Japan, but you'll probably find many items not yet available in North America.

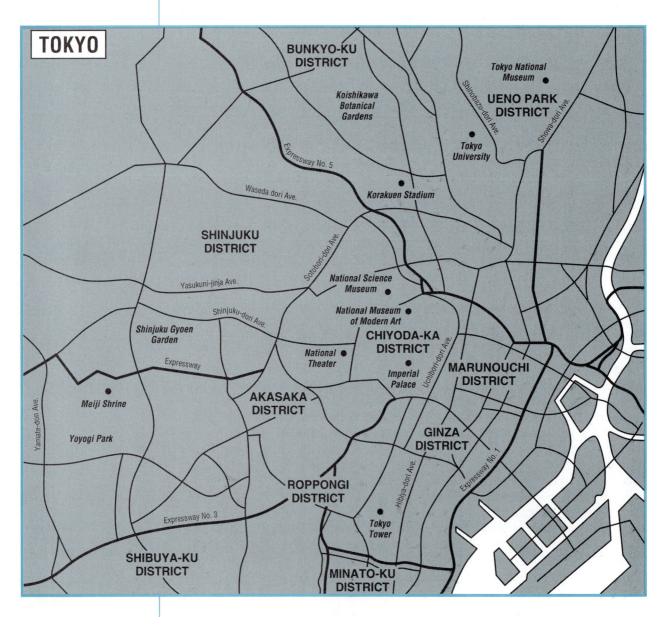

- **The Imperial Palace Plaza**, home of the emperor, in the center of the city. Though the palace itself is closed to tourists (except on special occasions), the sprawling grounds are open; they feature a moat, park, and museum.
- **Tokyo Tower**, over 1,000 feet high, offering the best view of the city (as long as it's clear, which it seldom is).
- **Temples and shrines**, the most popular of which include the **Meiji Shrine** and its sacred Shinto gardens, as well as the large, impressive **Asakusa Kannon Temple**.
- **The Ueno district**, where such museums as **Tokyo National Museum** and the **National Science Museum** are found. The **Ueno Zoo** is here as well. One problem for Westerners: Most of the signs are in Japanese only.
- **Tokyo Disneyland**, just outside the city. It's similar to its cousins in the United States, but there are a few differences—some cultural, some practical. ("Main Street USA" is covered with a canopy to keep out the rain.)

Your clients may wish to travel out of the city and take some **day trips**. Among the attractions you can recommend are:

- **Nikko**, considered by many the most beautiful place in Japan—it's two hours northwest of Tokyo by train, in a mountainous region. Its huge national park is spectacular, with glorious mountain views. The region features the intricately carved **Toshogu Shrine** (the "see no evil" monkey carvings are here) and its famed **Yomeimon Gate**, **Kegon Waterfall**, and **Futaarasan Shrine**.
- **The Kamakura-Hakone** region, an hour southwest of Tokyo, often visited on the way to Kyoto and Osaka. Kamakura, an ancient government seat, is home to the **Daibutsu**, the Great Buddha (a 500-ton statue more than 700 years old). **Lake Hakone** (also called Lake Ashi) provides a spectacular setting to view **Mt. Fuji**, the famous volcanic mountain. (That is, of course, if it's not shrouded in mist.)

Kyoto

Surrounded by hills, this ancient, historical city—for 1,000 years Japan's capital—is noted for its architecture, folk arts, and graceful beauty. Kyoto claims to have 2,000

Shoes should be removed before entering temples, homes, and rooms with straw *tatami* mats.

Lake Hakone
Photo by C. J. Ghormley

temples and shrines, not to mention many exquisite gardens. Indeed, there are so many small attractions that your clients should be urged to take a city tour or to buy a detailed guide book. Kyoto's popular sites include:

- **The Imperial Palace**, the ancient royal residence dating to the fourteenth century.
- **Heian Shrine**, a vermilion-hued structure featuring exquisite gardens.
- **Exotic temples**, the most famous of which are **Kinkakuji** (covered in gold leaf), **Ginkakuji** (the silver temple), **Daitokuji** (with beautiful gardens), **Kiyomizu** (for a superb view of the city), and the rock gardens of **Ryoanji**.

   The following **day-trip** destinations are usually reached from Kyoto:

- **Nara**, the capital of Japan 1,200 years ago, and the origin point of much of the country's art, religion, and government. It's only about a half hour from Osaka and Kyoto. Its most famous attraction is the **Todaiji Temple**, considered the largest wooden structure in the world: It houses a fifty-three-foot bronze

Japan's largest park is in Nara.

The Ginza, Tokyo
Photo by C. J. Ghormley

The Great Buddha, Kamakura
Photo by C. J. Ghormley

Buddha. **Kasuga Shrine** has a path lined with thousands of lanterns and a lofty pagoda. Legendary is Nara's 1,300-acre **Deer Park**, where the deer are so tame that they will nibble food right out of tourists' hands.

- **The Imperial Villas of Katsura** (to the southwest) and **Shugakuin** (to the northeast), impressive architectural and landscaping complexes for ancient royalty.
- **Hiroshima**, the first city ever to be devastated by a nuclear weapon. A very long day trip from Kyoto in southern Honshu, Hiroshima's **Peace Park** and other memorials are very moving.

Osaka

Though often bypassed by tourists in favor of nearby Kyoto, Osaka—one of the main commercial and industrial centers of Japan—has much to offer. Because of its successful history in world trade, this port city has had more contact with outside cultures than has most of the country. Excellent shopping can be found in large, underground complexes. Among Osaka's main attractions are:

Nara's deer are so aggressive that they'll poke into visitors' pockets and bags for food.

Osaka's corporate center is in the Nakanoshima district.

- **Osaka Castle**, a sixteenth-century structure that affords an excellent view of the city. A good museum is nearby.
- **Shitennoji Temple** (also called Teenoji), the oldest Buddhist monument in Japan. Another popular shrine is the nearly 1,000-year-old **Temmangu Shrine**.
- **The Minami and Umeda districts**, centers for entertainment, shopping, and restaurants.
- **Tennoji Park**, with a zoo, gardens, and art museum.
- **Performances of Kabuki** drama, **Noh** theater, and **Bunraku** puppet shows (all of which, frankly, can seem alien and boring to many North American clients).

Possible Itineraries

The Japanese tend to dress conservatively. When doing business, dress in dark, muted colors.

Japan is often visited as a business destination, but tourism is becoming increasingly important. The country is fairly compact, and most major attractions are centered on Honshu island, so your clients won't have all that much traveling to do. First-time visitors could spend about a week here: a couple of days in Tokyo, a day down to the Kamakura/Hakone area, and three or four days in Kyoto/Osaka/Nara. Return travelers may want to add visits to Nikko, Hiroshima, or the Imperial Villas. Some fine resorts are on the northern island of Hokkaido, including an excellent skiing facility in **Sapporo**, where the 1972 Winter Olympics were held, and in **Nagano**, where the 1998 Games took place. Kyushu island also has some popular hot springs, including those in the town of **Beppu**.

Lodging Options

Hailing taxis is not easy, especially late at night. Taxi stands are in many places, though, and the subway is a suitable alternative.

Hotel accommodations in Japan are among the best-run—and most wallet-thinning—in the world. To save your clients some money, you might look into voucher programs sponsored by tour operators: Participating hotels are usually in the first-class and tourist-class categories and offer substantial savings. Another possibility is a business-class hotel; these offer quite small and very basic accommodations that are popular among Japanese businessmen, though they wouldn't be appropriate for families. One other alternative: *ryokans,* or Japanese-style hotels, which offer soaking baths and thin futon mattresses. (They also have Western-style rooms and tend to assume that foreign visitors prefer such accommodations.) These can be booked through the Japan National Tourist Organization.

Tokyo's hotels are scattered throughout the city. But the best ones are clustered in two places: the area around the Imperial Palace and a section just west of the Shinjuku district.

Many major North American and other international chains serve Japan. The **Four Seasons at Chinzan-so** is particularly luxurious. Among the Japanese deluxe chains represented: **Okura**, **Akasaka**, and **New Otani**. Just a little below these in price are the **Palace**, **Miyako**, and **Rihga** chains. The **Dai-ichi** and **Prince** chains offer a range of accommodations. And for your clients watching costs, **Fujita Kanko** offers a more moderately priced (though far from cheap) option.

Allied Destinations

Japan is just across the Sea of Japan from the nations of South Korea and China. Both are potential add-on destinations. Russia is also adjacent; most major Russian destinations, however, are nearer Europe. The Philippines, Hong Kong, and the islands of Micronesia are often add-on destinations for Japan-bound clients. Southeast Asian countries such as Thailand, Malaysia, and Singapore aren't anywhere near as close to Japan as many of your clients might imagine; however, considering the distance that they've traveled to reach Japan from North America, it might be reasonable to recommend any of these nations to expand your client's FIT. And don't forget: Hawaii is a convenient way to break up a flight to or from Japan.

Cultural Patterns

Customs are of great importance in Japan. It's necessary that your business clients, or clients on holidays, understand them.

- The Japanese are very formal in their introductions. Tell clients that though handshaking is permissible, bowing is still the custom; moreover, they should bow as low as they are being bowed to in return. Titles are commonly used when addressing one another, and first names are used only among the closest of friends and family.

- One's position holds great meaning in Japan and business cards are widely exchanged; make sure your clients bring some along, even if only on vacation—they never know when a business contact will be made. (Bilingual cards are preferable and can usually be ordered through the hotels.)

- All dealings and relationships should be handled with restraint and reserve. And be sure that your clients treat the elderly with the utmost respect.

- The Japanese are astonishingly helpful to foreign visitors. If you get lost, try to find someone who knows a smattering of English. That person will then probably escort you to wherever you're bound.

- This helpfulness extends to stores. Don't be surprised by all the attention you'll get from sales personnel.

- Tell your clients to bring a small gift when arriving at a business meeting or visiting a Japanese home; these gifts should be wrapped in pastel-colored paper with no bows, and items that come in pairs (for example, pen and pencil sets) are often considered good luck. (By the way, warn your clients against over-complimenting an object in a Japanese home: It may be presented as a gift.)

- Though there's active nightlife in Japan, don't let your clients think it goes on until the wee hours. Because the subways don't run all night, restaurants and nightclubs close relatively early. And prepare clients for the cost.

- If receiving a gift, refuse once, modestly and calmly. Then accept it, using two hands.

- Be certain your clients know that punctuality is important, especially for business meetings.

- The Japanese don't like to say "no" if it can be avoided. Instead, they often answer "maybe" or "it is very difficult." This is an important distinction to understand, particularly if your clients are there on business, for they may misinterpret this to mean agreement with their position.

- Laughter is not always a sign of amusement; it may signify embarrassment.

- Although individualism is prized in North America, your clients should know that the welfare of the group predominates in Japan.

- It's considered rude to point with one finger; tell your clients to use the whole hand.

- Business is almost never discussed until the participants have socialized considerably—sometimes for days.

Factors That Motivate Visitors

It's important to understand why a client might want to visit Japan. This is a wonderful country, but it's not for everyone. Some reasons that clients give for wanting to visit Japan are:

Tipping in Japan is considered inappropriate, except perhaps if a taxi driver helps with baggage. Tips *are* sometimes automatically added to a bill as a service charge.

For buying electronic gadgets, visit the Akihabara district, which packs 1,000 shops into five square blocks.

There's an *indoor* ski facility near Tokyo.

- It's a very important business destination.
- Japan has a unique, exotic, and ancient culture.
- Some clients can trace their ancestry there.
- There's beautiful art and architecture.
- For an Asian nation, it's relatively Westernized and comfortable.
- Its level of service, efficiency, and creature comforts is astonishingly high.
- The countryside has great natural beauty.
- It's an absolute heaven for golfers, though they may find courses to be somewhat smaller and more expensive than those at home.
- Japan is an extremely safe place to visit.
- The Japanese are incredibly helpful to visitors. Tell your clients to not be surprised when a Japanese person goes very much out of the way to help them.
- A full schedule of nonstop flights makes connecting from North America convenient.

Possible Misgivings

For many people, Japan is a genuinely alien destination. Here are a few of the qualms some of your clients might have, and their counters:

Qualifying the Client
Japan

FOR CLIENTS WHO WANT	APPEAL			REMARKS
	HIGH	MEDIUM	LOW	
Historical and Cultural Attractions	▲			Mostly related to Japan's fascinating history
Beaches and Water Sports			▲	Some, but not frequented by foreigners
Skiing Opportunities			▲	Some, but less frequented by foreigners
Lots of Nightlife		▲		Tokyo and Osaka
Family Activities			▲	Cost discouraging
Familiar Cultural Experience			▲	
Exotic Cultural Experience	▲			
Safety and Low Crime	▲			One of world's lowest crime rates
Bargain Travel			▲	One of world's most expensive destinations
Impressive Scenery		▲		Outside cities
Peace and Quiet			▲	Only in the countryside
Shopping Opportunities		▲		Wide selection, but costly
To Do Business	▲			Must understand cultural diferences

Figure 25-2

Case Study

Jack Fujimoto has a small business in Seattle that's just starting out, but he's trying to land a major Japanese account. It's a stretch for his company, but he's decided to fly to Tokyo for three days. As long as he has to go over anyway, the forty-year-old executive and his wife, Grace, have decided to extend this trip into a personal vacation; they may not have another chance for a while. She will fly over with Jack, and they'll spend some extra days traveling around the country.

Circle the answer that best suits your clients' needs

1. What service would *not* be appropriate for you to offer the Fujimotos?

   A Japan Rail pass   An independent tour

   A business-class hotel   A stopover en route

   Why?

2. Which of the following tips should you pass along to them?

   Buy a Japan Rail pass when you get there.   Take a cab from Narita Airport into Tokyo.

   Be prepared to dine relatively early.   Always tip at least 10 percent.

   Why?

3. How many days would you recommend for their pleasure trip after business is over if they go only to Japan?

   Five   Twelve

   Nine   Four score

   Why?

4. The Fujimotos decide that, since they'll already be going as far as Japan, they might as well extend their trip three days to visit another country. They have to return to Tokyo for their flight home, so they don't want to travel too far away. Which of the following destinations would *not* be appropriate for them to visit?

   Thailand   South Korea

   Hong Kong   Taiwan

   Why?

Creative Activity

Since you're a travel professional, your friends often ask you for free advice. But this time the request is unusual: Your neighbors' daughter will be on her school's team in a statewide geography competition. She's been told that one of the destinations that will be focused on will be Japan, but that any other global destination may also come up. Can you help coach her?

You discover that she knows plenty about the world's cities and attractions, but not much about Japan. You give her a book on Japan to study. You also set up a little training exercise for her that you call "connections." You create a list of Japanese attractions and challenge her to come up with an equivalent somewhere else in the world. She must explain her choice. (You hope this will help her "connect" what she already knows about the rest of the world with what she is now learning about Japan.) You should also predict a possible answer for each, just in case she can't think of one.

JAPANESE PLACE/ATTRACTION	EQUIVALENT ELSEWHERE	WHY
E.g., The Imperial Palace	Buckingham Palace, London	Both homes to monarchs, rarely open to public.
1. Tokyo Tower		
2. Mt. Fuji		
3. The Ginza		
4. Hiroshima		
5. Osaka Castle		
6. Sapporo		
7. Tokyo Disneyland		
8. Yokohama		
9. Narita		
10. The *shinkansen*		

Travel Trivia

Top Ten Shopping Venues (Highest Rent per Square Foot)

1. Fifth Avenue, New York
2. The Ginza, Japan
3. East 57th Street, New York
4. Champs Élysées, Paris
5. Madison Avenue, New York
6. Rue du Rhode, Geneva
7. Rodeo Drive, Beverly Hills
8. Bond Street, London
9. Nathan Road, Hong Kong
10. Orchard Road, Singapore

CHAPTER 26

Singapore and Thailand
Crossroads of Asia

The great trader ships of yesteryear must certainly have been a sight, with their sails billowing in the wind. Bound for China and India from the South Pacific, they had but one direct route: through the Strait of Malacca, at the tip of the Malay Peninsula. Lying at the peninsula's southern end was the major port of **Singapore**, and just to the north was Siam. Today, Singapore remains one of the world's busiest ports; and Siam, now known as **Thailand** [TYE-land], has stayed— through wars, massive migration, and an unending onslaught of trade—a strong, independent nation. At the cornerstone of a continent, they both glory in their rich mix of cultures. And for both their past and present, they represent two of the world's most intriguing destinations for your clients.

Singapore, originally a British colony, is a unique island—it's both a city and a self-contained country. Thailand is approximately the size of Arizona and Utah combined. Its capital, **Bangkok**, lies slightly north of the **Gulf of Thailand**, just before the country thins out and winds its way down the peninsula. It's here that your clients will find two of the country's popular resorts: **Pattaya Beach** on the south coast and **Phuket** [poo-KET] **Island** just off the west. **Chiang Mai**, the second largest city, is in the hilly north.

Thailand's national language is Thai, though English is widely spoken, especially by travel personnel. In Singapore, because of the particularly diverse origins of its populace, there are actually several official languages: Malay, English (which is predominant in the business and travel industries), Mandarin Chinese, and Tamil.

How Travelers Get There

Two major gateways serve this region: Singapore and Bangkok. Singapore is accessed by the national airline, **Singapore Airlines** (SQ), which flies into **Changi International Airport** (SIN) (praised by many as the world's finest airport), as do other North American and international carriers. Flights from Los Angeles take nearly eighteen hours with connections, and New York is up to twenty-six hours away, again with connections. Singapore is also one of the world's busiest seaports and is a common embarkation and stopping point for cruises. In addition, although an island, Singapore is linked by causeway to the adjoining nation of Malaysia and can be reached from Malaysia by train. The national airline of Thailand is **Thai Airways International** (TG); it and other North American and international airlines land in Bangkok at **Don Muang International Airport** (BKK). Flying time, with connections, from Los Angeles is over twenty-one hours, and New York is twenty-nine hours away. Cruises call at Phuket.

For Your Information . . .

Singapore and Thailand

CAPITALS: Singapore: Singapore
Thailand: Bangkok

AREAS (SQUARE MILES): Singapore: 226.4
Thailand: 198,250

TIME ZONES: Singapore: GMT +8
Thailand: GMT +7

DRIVE ON: Left

POPULATION: Singapore: 3,400,000
Thailand: 58,700,000

RELIGIONS: Buddhism, Christianity, Islam, Taoism, Hinduism

LANGUAGES: Singapore: Malay, Chinese, Tamil, English
Thailand: Thai, Chinese

CURRENCIES: Singapore: 1 dollar = 100 cents
Thailand: 1 baht = 100 satangs

ELECTRICITY: 220 volts, 50 cycles AC

CAPSULE HISTORY: **Singapore**: Founded as separate entity by Sir Stamford Raffles, 1819; separate British Crown colony, 1946; independence, 1959; part of Malaysian federation, 1963; separate republic, 1965.
Thailand: Separate identity beginning sixth century A.D.; British dominate, 1824; absolute monarchy ends, 1932; Japan occupies, 1941–1945; many refugees migrate into Thailand, 1978.

For reference sources, tourist bureaus, and suggested lengths of stay, see the Appendices.

Weather Patterns

The temperatures of these two areas are quite similar (see Figures 26-1 and 26-2). Both are generally hot and muggy year-round, with little variation in temperature. Singapore, particularly, is stunningly consistent, since it's so near the equator: It averages a high in the upper 80s, down to the mid-70s twelve months a year. Though there's plenty of rain in every season, November to January are Singapore's wettest months. March and September are especially uncomfortable—cooling breezes are minimal or non-existent.

Unlike Singapore, Thailand has relatively little precipitation from November through April. May through October are the rainiest months. The hottest months of the year are March through August, with highs in the 90s and lows in the 70s. November through February is the coolest time, with temperatures somewhat lower—though it's still pretty warm (but nights can get chilly). Typhoons and monsoons can affect travel in the late summer and fall.

Tourism is fairly consistent year-round in Singapore, though the period from June through August draws more tourists than any other. The same situation prevails in Bangkok, though January and February there are off-seasons—a surprising fact, since Bangkok weather is at its best in the winter. (It's because Thais leave Bangkok for the southern beach cities at this time of year; as a result, tourism peaks at beach resorts such as Phuket in the winter, in complete reversal of the patterns for the rest of the country.)

Thailand is the only southeast Asian nation never to be colonized.

Climate at a Glance
BANGKOK, THAILAND

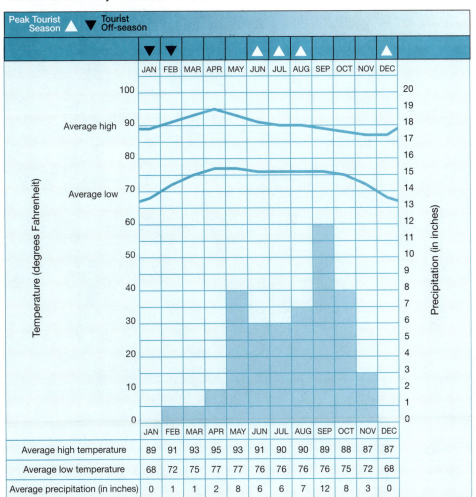

	JAN	FEB	MAR	APR	MAY	JUN	JUL	AUG	SEP	OCT	NOV	DEC
Average high temperature	89	91	93	95	93	91	90	90	89	88	87	87
Average low temperature	68	72	75	77	77	76	76	76	76	75	72	68
Average precipitation (in inches)	0	1	1	2	8	6	6	7	12	8	3	0

Figure 26-1

Getting Around

It's relatively easy to get around Singapore: Many taxis patrol the streets and they're reasonably priced. (Advise your clients that the main business district has a restricted area during early hours for vehicles with a minimum number of passengers; your clients who are there mainly for business should be sure to check the restrictions.) The bus system can be confusing. Three-wheeled "tri-shaws" can be an unusual way to travel; tell your clients to settle on a price first.

Thailand has a good bus system and fairly good trains. The roads are basically sound, but your clients should avoid them during the rainy season. In Bangkok, the hotel-run taxis are more expensive than private ones, but a little better. Because there are many canals through the city, river taxis can be a fun and inexpensive way to travel. The streets are crowded, so you should discourage your client from renting a car. Thailand's major cities are connected by air. And, of course, the two countries—and nations around and in-between—are interconnected by flights and cruises. A luxury train, the Eastern and Oriental Express, makes the 1,200-mile run between Bangkok and Singapore.

Bangkok's canals are called *klongs.*

Climate at a Glance
SINGAPORE

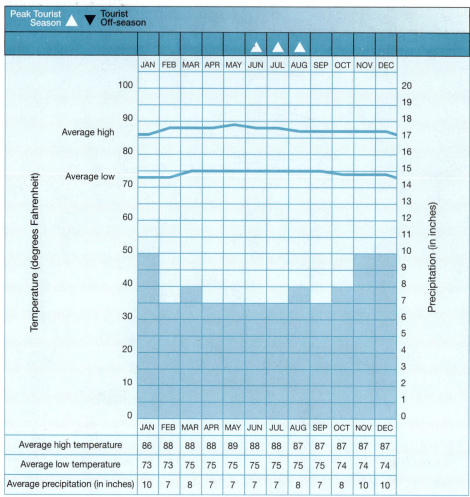

	JAN	FEB	MAR	APR	MAY	JUN	JUL	AUG	SEP	OCT	NOV	DEC
Average high temperature	86	88	88	88	89	88	88	87	87	87	87	87
Average low temperature	73	73	75	75	75	75	75	75	75	74	74	74
Average precipitation (in inches)	10	7	8	7	7	7	7	8	7	8	10	10

Figure 26-2

Important Places

Singapore and Thailand offer tourists a rich mix of cultures, superb scenery, and many ancient monuments. Tourism concentrates on the following areas.

Singapore ~~very clean country~~

> There are stiff penalties in Singapore for jaywalking and littering, and smoking is prohibited in many public places.

Singapore is a very contemporary city—and one of Asia's most prosperous. (It's also the second most densely populated country in the world, after Monaco.) It's one of the world's busiest ports and a major business destination. The nearly three-and-a-half million residents are largely of Chinese descent; yet there remains a strong British influence, left over from colonial days. Singapore boasts famous shopping, fine dining, active nightlife, and a well-scrubbed look. Among the most popular attractions are:

- **Haw Par Villa** (Tiger Balm Gardens), an odd attraction with grottoes, statues, amusement rides, and a superb view of the ocean. Other gardens you should recommend to your clients: the **Japanese Garden**, the **Chinese Garden**, and the **Mandai Orchid Garden**.

Tiger Balm Gardens, Singapore
Photo by C. J. Ghormley

- **Sri Mariamman Temple**, a particularly beautiful structure.
- **Chinatown, Little India,** and **Arab Street,** charming, fun, and interesting neighborhoods that offer excellent shopping and great food.
- **The National Museum,** which houses the renowned Aw jade collection.
- **The Singapore Zoological Gardens,** considered one of the world's finest zoos. It has a "Night Safari" so visitors can see nocturnal animals.
- **Jurong Bird Park,** a colorful and extremely large home to more than 3,000 birds from around the world.

Among the several **day trips** from Singapore that you might want to suggest to your clients are:

- **Kusu**, a popular island resort. Turtles are a major attraction here, notably at **Tua Pek Kong Temple.** (According to legend, the island itself was a turtle at one time.)
- **Sentosa,** another active island resort, located nearby, with many recreational activities and several major resort hotels. Here, too, is **Underwater World**, a $20 million oceanarium.
- **Malaysia,** just a short trip across the Strait of Malacca. A visit there includes the exotic capital—**Kuala Lumpur,** with its Moorish architecture—and the mosques of ancient **Malacca. Penang Island** is a lovely resort. **Johore Bahru** is the closest town in Malaysia to Singapore; a bazaar and Sultan's Palace are its prime attractions. (We examine Malaysia—a major destination in its own right—more fully in Chapter 29.)

Bangkok *is also very clean*

Bangkok is a chaotic, noisy, densely populated city, yet its spirit, friendliness, and heritage make it a top-class travel destination. The **National Museum** has an excellent and extensive collection of Oriental artifacts. However, what visitors notice

Cars in Singapore cost five to six times their original, overseas value. Two families sometimes share one car.

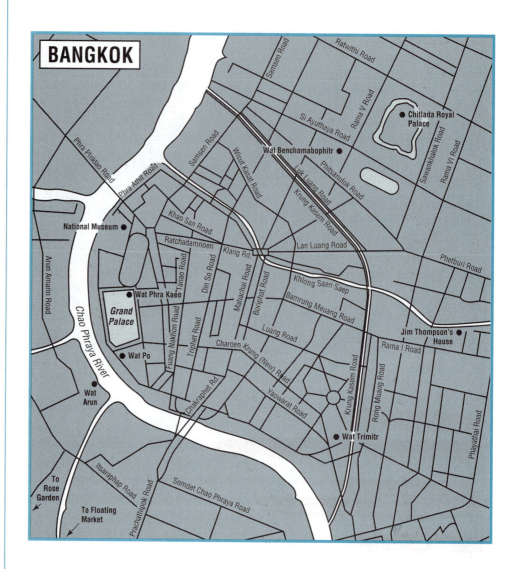

first are the temples. Hundreds of them embellish Bangkok's skyline. Among the most popular sites here are:

- **The Temples**, of course (called *wat* in Thai). The ones you should be sure to recommend to your clients are the soaring **Temple of the Dawn** (Wat Arun), from which your client can get a great city view; the **Temple of the Golden Buddha** (Wat Trimitr), with its five-ton, solid-gold carving; the **Temple of the Reclining Buddha** (Wat Po), with a 200-foot-long statue; and the beautiful **Marble Temple** (Wat Benchamabophitr).

- **Cruises** on the city's meandering river and canal waterways.

- **Jim Thompson's house**, the residence of an American silk merchant, which contains remarkably beautiful Asian artwork. While visiting Malaysia, Thompson mysteriously disappeared.

- **The Grand Palace**, the royal residence, once a walled fortress. Also a part of the complex is perhaps Bangkok's most famous site, the **Temple of the Emerald Buddha** (Wat Phra Kaeo).

- **The Pat Pong**, the city's notoriously wild nightclub, bar, and shopping district.

Not far from Bangkok lie some fascinating destinations for half-day trips. Those you should be most aware of are:

- **The Damnoen Saduak**, an aromatic floating market, about an hour southwest of Bangkok, in the province of Ratchaburi.

The Grand Palace, Bangkok
Photo by C. J. Ghormley

- **The Rose Garden Cultural Center**, less than a half hour west of the city, with its beautiful flowers, authentic dance performances, and array of outdoor activities. This is a comprehensive cultural experience that your clients will certainly enjoy.

Several good **day trips** from Bangkok should be recommended to your clients, including:

- **The Bridge on the River Kwai**, which many of your clients will recognize from the famed movie. It really does exist; it's in **Kanchanaburi**, west of Bangkok. Allied prisoners-of-war were forced to build the bridge during World War II in order for the Japanese to move their supplies into Burma (now called Myanmar).

- **Nakhon Pathom**, the biggest Buddhist monument in the country, which can be combined with the trip to the River Kwai bridge.

- **Ayutthaya**, the capital of Thailand before 1767. North of Bangkok and usually accessed by bus or a river cruise boat, it offers interesting archaeological sites, ruins, and museums.

River Kwai Bridge Week, held in late November–early December, features a sound and light show, exhibitions, and vintage train rides.

Palace grounds, Bangkok
Photo by C. J. Ghormley

- **Tropical resorts**, most notably the world-class Pattaya Beach—a somewhat polluted and unsavory, yet lively and, in most places, luxurious city that's a two-hour drive south of Bangkok; and Phuket—a lush, tropical island with particularly lovely scenery and towns. Phuket is about a one-hour flight south from Bangkok. It seems to be going the same way as Pattaya: Overdevelopment and pollution are becoming a problem. Less crowded is **Ko Samui**, on the east side of the peninsula.

- Beyond Phuket are a number of dramatic, rocky, uninhabited islands that clients can visit via a "long-tailed" boat. **Phang Nga Bay** is especially famous, with its gorges, caverns, and limestone pillars.

Chiang Mai

Located in the northwest corner of Thailand, about an hour's flight from Bangkok, this compact walled town is the second largest city in Thailand. It offers temples and museum art that are quite different from those of southern Thailand.

The **Po Ping Palace**, which has beautiful gardens, is the summer home of the royal family. Chiang Mai is also an excellent place for your clients to use as a base for trips through the nearby hills, national parks, teakwood forests, and tribal villages. Many modes of transportation are common: elephants, river rafts, and on-foot trekking. You should make sure, though, that your clients (or you) book with a reputable guide or tour company; otherwise, this beautiful but primitive area can be unpleasant at best and dangerous at worst. The cities of **Chiang Rai** and **Mae Hong Son**, though less known, are perhaps better starting places for treks into the wilderness.

Possible Itineraries

For clients interested in visiting Singapore and Thailand as their sole destination (rather than as part of a larger tour of Southeast Asia), you should suggest a minimum of ten days. Starting with two to three days in Singapore, they could then head up to Bangkok for a couple of days. A short jump to the north and to Chiang Mai would help round out the trip, as would a visit to one of Thailand's resorts, notably Phuket and the small offshore islands. Such a vacation could easily be extended, depending on how much your clients would like to more fully explore the sites and ruins around Bangkok. Return visitors might wish to spend more time on the beaches.

Lodging Options

Singapore boasts an extremely famous inn, **Raffles Hotel**, a place of English colonial gentility. The **Goodwood Park Hotel** is a Singapore national landmark. In addition to these two legendary hotels, Singapore boasts a number of world-class luxury hotels, including: the **Mandarin**, **Shangri-La**, and **Oriental**. Most hotels here are clustered in the Orchard Road area. The **Goodwood Group** is a deluxe chain in Singapore; **Le Meridien** offers deluxe accommodations, as well as more moderately priced units. Most North American chains are present in Singapore.

Among the first-class chains in Thailand are **Dusit Hotels** and Le Meridien. For your more budget-minded clients, you might look into the **Siam Lodge Group**, which is moderately priced. Most hotels in Bangkok—actually, there's a bit of a room shortage in this city—are centered on and east of the Chao Phraya River. Bangkok, like Singapore, features several hotels world-famous for their level of luxury and service: the **Oriental**, **Regent**, **Shangri-La**, **Sheraton**, and **Royal Orchid**. (There's another luxurious Regent in Chiang Mai. Phuket also has some super-deluxe lodging, especially the **Amanpuri Resort Hotel**. One interesting practice at many Thai hotels: Christmas Eve and New Year's Eve lodging requires a supplementary charge for a mandatory dinner-celebration at the hotel.

Allied Destinations

The most obvious allied destination for Singapore and Thailand: Malaysia, which is sandwiched between the two countries. Burma also borders them, as do Laos and Cambodia, though political turmoil makes it less likely that you'll have to book these countries. Nearby are the Philippines, Indonesia, and Borneo. For that matter, parts of China and India are a fairly short jet trip away. Thailand and Singapore are commonly reached as part of cruises of Southeast Asia.

Cultural Patterns

The customs of Thailand and Singapore will likely seem unfamiliar to most of your clients. Your business clients will especially want to understand the traditions of those with whom they will be dealing.

Tipping is uncommon in Singapore and Thailand (though it may be included on restaurant and hotel bills as a service charge).

The Singapore Sling cocktail was invented at the Raffles Hotel.

- When a client visits Thailand, tell him or her always to return a *wai* greeting (where one's hands are held together at the chest like a prayer and then a slight bow is given).
- Warn your clients that gestures in Thailand and Singapore carry meanings different from those in North America. For instance, they shouldn't point a finger or foot toward another person.
- Remember to remove your shoes before entering a temple. Female visitors should dress modestly and cover their heads when visiting religious attractions.
- Tell your clients not to pause on the doorsill of a house; this is where Thais believe a spirit lives. Guests shouldn't feel obligated to bring a gift when visiting. Moreover, they shouldn't overcompliment one of their host's possessions: It may later be presented to them.
- Never pat a Thai child (or for that matter, an adult) on the head.
- Both countries expect punctuality for meetings.

Factors That Motivate Visitors

Among the reasons that your clients might want to visit these countries are:

- The culture is intriguing.
- The food is superb.

Qualifying the Client
Thailand

FOR CLIENTS WHO WANT	APPEAL			REMARKS
	HIGH	MEDIUM	LOW	
Historical and Cultural Attractions	▲			Especially Buddhist temples
Beaches and Water Sports		▲		Excellent but less known outside of Asia
Skiing Opportunities			▲	None
Lots of Nightlife	▲			Lively and even notorious
Family Activities			▲	
Familiar Cultural Experience			▲	Western amenities, but exotic locale
Exotic Cultural Experience	▲			
Safety and Low Crime		▲		
Bargain Travel		▲		Especially outside Bangkok
Impressive Scenery		▲		Wide variety
Peace and Quiet		▲		Outside Bangkok
Shopping Opportunities	▲			Silks, precious stones, gold, antiques, wood items
To Do Business		▲		Singapore more so than Thailand

Figure 26-3

Food in Singapore, and especially in Thailand, can be very spicy.

Case Study

Karen Wise, age twenty-nine, will fly to Singapore in January on business. She hasn't had a real vacation in almost two years and has decided to stay in the area for eight days. She has money to spend and is interested in fairly active sightseeing. She's used to comfort, though, and doesn't particularly care to rough it.

Circle the answer that best suits your client's needs:

1. She wants to stay at a fine hotel while in Singapore, preferably one that's English colonial style. Which of the following might you recommend to her?

   Raffles   The Negresco

   The Victoria Princess   Underwater World

   Why?

2. What cultural suggestion would *not* be appropriate for you to give to her?

   Never point a finger at a Thai.   Try to return a *wai* greeting.

   Don't ever jaywalk.   It's polite to accept food from a stranger.

   Why?

3. Karen decides that because she's been working so hard, she'd like to kick back and relax for a few days in Phuket. Which of the following should you tell her?

   It will be high season.   Rent a car and do a day trip to Bangkok.

   Thai food is very mild.   Visit Jim Thompson's house.

   Why?

4. This business trip is a special one; Karen doesn't expect to get back to the area for quite a while. She'd like to see as much as possible. What destination could you suggest she add to her trip (from Singapore up to Thailand), without too much inconvenient flying?

   Burma   Malaysia

   Indonesia   Micronesia

   Why?

Creative Activity

You've taken tests on travel geography. Now is your chance to *make* a test. Pretend that you're a teacher and create a ten-question, multiple-choice quiz on Singapore and Thailand. Make sure your questions cover important information, use travel-related language, and are creative. Indicate the answers on a separate "answer key." (Your instructor may ask you to swap tests with another student.)

For example: Which of the following would *not* be an easy add-on destination to Singapore?

a) Thailand   b) Rwanda   c) Malaysia   d) Indonesia

1.

2.

3.

4.

5.

6.

7.

8.

9.

10.

Travel Trivia

Top Ten Airports

1. Singapore
2. Manchester
3. Melbourne
4. Amsterdam
5. Zurich

6. Cincinnati
7. Orlando
8. Montreal
9. Sydney
10. Calgary

Source: IATA survey

CHAPTER 27

China
Of Red and Gold

Two colors hold positions of great symbolic importance to the Chinese: red and gold. In ancient days, red signified good luck and gold was a color exclusive to the emperors. Today, these hues have taken on other meanings. Red is often used to refer to China's Communist regime, begun under Mao Tse-tung. And gold is the perfect color to symbolize the money now pouring into the vast, yet largely untapped, market that is China. And now that Hong Kong has become part of China, it is money, not an emperor, that rules.

China—or, more officially, the People's Republic of China—is a noteworthy land, but not merely for its history, culture, size, and population; it's remarkable, as well, that so important a nation is so poorly known to outsiders. China is the world's third largest country, slightly bigger than the United States (including Alaska and Hawaii); its population is more than one billion (four times greater than the U.S. population). One-quarter of all the people in the world live here.

China has only one time zone, though it spans six.

For Your Information . . .

China   FYI

CAPITAL: Beijing

AREA (SQUARE MILES): 3

TIME ZONE: GMT +9

DRIVE ON: Right

POPULATION: 1.2 billion

RELIGIONS: Buddhism, Confucianism, Taoism

LANGUAGE: Mandarin Chinese

CURRENCY: 1 yuan = 100 fen

ELECTRICITY: China: 220 volts, 50 cycles AC
Hong Kong: 200 volts, 50 cycles AC

CAPSULE HISTORY: Feudal states unite, 246–210 B.C.; arts flourish, 618–907; Mings rule, 1368–1644; Manchus invade and rule, 1644; Hong Kong ceded to Britain, 1841; Korea, Taiwan, and other areas ceded to Japan, 1895; Boxer rebellion, 1900; republic declared, 1912; communists take power, 1949; Red Guard revolts, 1966–1967; Mao dies, 1976; student revolt quelled, 1989; Hong Kong merges into China, 1997.

For reference sources, tourist bureaus, and suggested lengths of stay, see the Appendices.

Virtually the entire Chinese population lives in the arable eastern half of the country; the west is mountainous, sparsely populated, and extremely dry. Bordered on the east by **Russia**, **North Korea**, the **Yellow Sea**, the **East China Sea**, the **Pacific Ocean**, and the **South China Sea**, it's easiest to envision the major cities of China as if on the rim of a left-facing crescent. At the one o'clock position of the crescent, in northeast China not far from the coast, is **Beijing**, the capital. (It was formerly spelled "Peking.") Heading clockwise, **Shanghai**, the largest city and main port, is located at three o'clock. In the southeast is **Guangzhou** (also known as Canton), the city closest to **Hong Kong** and with the most contact with the West. **Macau** (sometimes spelled Macao), a Portuguese colony, is a close neighbor to Hong Kong. It is scheduled to be returned to China in 1999.

Guilin, considered by many the most beautiful area of China, is near the crescent's bottom. Out at the crescent's far tip, at about seven o'clock, is mountainous **Tibet** in the **Himalaya**. Considered to be the basis of the Shangri-La legend, Tibet is a popular tourist destination in China (though it's more often visited as part of a trip to Nepal and India; it's on the south-central border). And in the center of this Chinese crescent are the astonishing archaeological treasures of **Xian** [she-AHN], the ancient capital of China.

Many regional dialects are spoken in China, but the main languages are Mandarin and Cantonese. Your clients should not expect to find many people here who understand English, though some of the major tourist personnel may be helpful. This is one of the reasons escorted tours are almost always the mode of choice. English is spoken by almost everyone in Hong Kong.

How Travelers Get There

The two main Chinese gateways are the new **Chek Lap Kok Airport** (CLK) in **Hong Kong** and **Beijing International Airport** (PEK). There is some direct service to Beijing from North America by both domestic and international carriers, as well as by China's two national air carriers: **Air China** (CA) and **China Eastern Airlines** (MU). Both domestic and international carriers, including Hong Kong-based **Cathay Pacific** (CX), also serve Hong Kong. Your clients should be prepared for long flights, often with connections. Flying time to Hong Kong or Beijing is about thirteen hours from North America's West Coast and about nineteen hours from New York; it takes eleven hours from Honolulu, a frequent stopover for cross-Pacific trips. A flight from Hong Kong to Beijing takes two-and-a-half hours; from Tokyo, it's three-and-a-half hours.

Shanghai and Hong Kong are also very popular ports of call for either extended cruises or general boat arrivals from Japan. China can be reached via train from Russia (which borders China to the north). And your clients may access China from such countries as India, Nepal, or Pakistan.

Weather Patterns

The climate in much of China is similar to that of the United States, though the temperatures tend to be more extreme: hotter highs and colder lows. Generally, the north is colder and the south (except for Tibet, which can be extremely cold) is warmer, rainier, and more humid. Late fall to early spring can bring dust storms in the north, while monsoon rains sweep across the south coastal regions in late summer and early fall. Western China is very dry.

Beijing has a wide swing of temperatures, not only from season to season, but also from morning to night. From March to May and again from September to November, the highs average in the 80s; nights, however, can drop to as low as 20 degrees. Summer in Beijing can be very hot—as high as 100 degrees during the day—whereas winter ranges from the mid-50s to zero or below. A somewhat hot

Climate at a Glance
HONG KONG

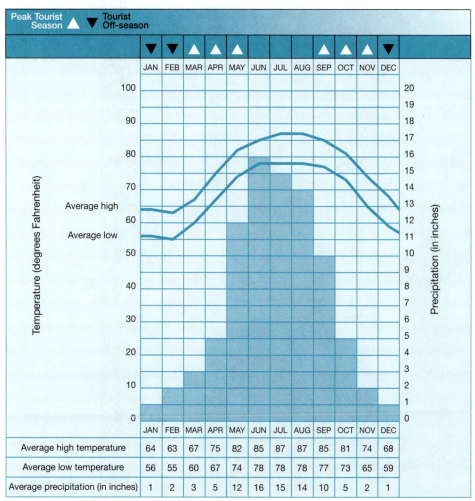

	JAN	FEB	MAR	APR	MAY	JUN	JUL	AUG	SEP	OCT	NOV	DEC	
	▼	▼	▲	▲	▲				▲	▲	▲	▼	

Peak Tourist Season ▲ ▼ Tourist Off-season

	JAN	FEB	MAR	APR	MAY	JUN	JUL	AUG	SEP	OCT	NOV	DEC
Average high temperature	64	63	67	75	82	85	87	87	85	81	74	68
Average low temperature	56	55	60	67	74	78	78	78	77	73	65	59
Average precipitation (in inches)	1	2	3	5	12	16	15	14	10	5	2	1

Figure 27-1

rainy season takes place from June through August, making spring and fall the best times for your clients to visit Beijing.

The climate in Hong Kong and Guangzhou is much steadier (see Figure 27-1). Late fall, winter, and early spring are particularly nice, with temperatures in the 60s to upper 70s. Summer can be brutal: From May to September there's plenty of rain, occasional hurricanes, high humidity, and daytime temperatures in the upper 80s to 90s.

As for tourism patterns, China generally sees a drop-off of tourism from early December to early April. Spring and fall are high season, with summer a slightly off-peak time.

Getting Around

China is huge. Since the transportation system isn't well set up for tourism, its great distances can seem even longer. The national airlines, Air China and China Eastern, can be a challenge if tickets aren't bought before leaving North America. The same holds for train travel. (The top class, "soft berth," is comfortable, but it's expensive.) Tourists can't rent a car (except in Hong Kong). You can book a driver

A pagoda-like structure in Guangzhou
Photo by C. J. Ghormley

Kublai Khan himself had much of the Grand Canal constructed.

with a car for your clients in advance, however; in fact, you can offer your clients a car, driver, and guide for a surprisingly reasonable price. Boat cruises are a popular way to travel along the **Yangtze**, **Li** [LEE], and **Yellow** rivers, as well as portions of the ancient **Grand Canal**.

Within cities, taxi service is good, but make sure your clients get their cab from a hotel, for long waits anywhere else are common. (This is why it's often a good idea for your clients to ask their driver to stay and keep the meter running on reaching their destination, even if it might cost quite a bit.) Buses are very crowded.

Hong Kong is a different matter. The subway system is useful and taxis are plentiful. Ferries are the easiest way to get around the harbor—the historic **Star Ferries** are renowned. Buses and double-deck trams are crowded, but counsel clients to take the cog railway up to **Victoria Peak** for the best view of the city. Rickshaws in Hong Kong are for tourists only and are very expensive. (Make sure your clients settle on a price first.) And renting a car is an option, though Hong Kong is so compact and crowded that renting a car isn't always a good idea.

Important Places

Many clients may have visions of the battles between students and the government in Beijing's **Tiananmen Square**; some clients may even avoid visiting the country out of protest. Those images are real, but in no way define what exists in China for a tourist. Whether or not to visit, of course, is always a client's personal choice. For those who do come here, though, China offers superb, exciting, and dramatic destinations.

Beijing

Beijing, the capital of China, is the country's economic and cultural center. It (like many of China's major cities) is extremely crowded; because many Chinese ride around on bicycles, though, that crowded feeling of some cities doesn't translate here. (The car traffic, though, *is* getting worse.) Your clients will find some good and diverse shopping in the city, especially in the **Liu Li Chang** district. Many lovely temples are scattered throughout Beijing, and the **zoo** here is noted for its pandas. But it's the grand and graceful structures of Beijing that clearly stand out. Among them are:

- **The Imperial Palace**, once known as the Forbidden City, the home of twenty-four of China's emperors. Commoners were not allowed inside (hence the "forbidden" city). One of the world's greatest attractions, this walled complex covers 250 acres and encloses 800 structures—each more dramatic than the last.

- **The Temple of Heaven**, a complex of structures whose pagoda-like Hall of **Prayer for Good Harvests** houses what may be China's most exquisite room.

- **Tiananmen Square**, the largest public square in the world. This infamous 100-acre plaza is the centerpiece of Beijing. Here Mao raised the flag of the People's Revolution. A giant portrait of him still looms over the place where students and soldiers clashed in 1989. The **Great Hall of the People**, site of the National People's Congress, sits on the western side of the square. Opposite it are the **Museum of Chinese History** and the **Museum of the Chinese Revolution**.

  Beijing offers several **half-day trips**, including:

- **The Great Wall**, a structure that's perhaps even more spectacular than your clients imagine. This architectural wonder is, from end to end, more than 2,800 miles long. That's greater than the distance from Boston to Los Angeles. However, because the ever-winding wall is full of twists and turns, it's actually about 10,000 miles long. The most popular site for tourists to visit this 2,300-year-old structure is at **Badaling**, forty-seven miles from Beijing. Remind clients that to walk along the wall's top is unforgettable—but also exhausting, for in Badaling it snakes up and down some rather steep hills. You might also suggest seeing the wall via helicopter tours, which you can book ahead of time.

- **The Ming Tombs**, at **Shin San Ling**, usually combined with a visit to Badaling. Thirteen emperors are buried in its cavernous, but now largely empty, halls.

- **The Summer Palace**, used for more than 1,000 years. The central palace and its extensive grounds are elegantly situated on a lake. One of the oddest sights here: a stone "boat" built with navy monies by an empress.

Shanghai

Shanghai is the largest city in China and its major port and commercial center. Because it was one of China's first international ports, Shanghai is one of the nation's most cosmopolitan cities. There are attractive gardens, such as the **Yu**

Legend says that construction workers who died on the job were buried in the wall.

Yuan (Mandarin's Garden), open markets, museums, a children's palace, the **Bund** (a European-like, water-skirting boulevard), a zoo with pandas, and the famous **Shanghai Acrobats**. Among the other sites are:

- **The Temple of the Jade Buddha**, a particularly beautiful structure. Another notable temple is the **Temple of Serenity**.
- **Longhua Park**, a charming area that houses the **Longhua Temple and Pagoda** and a well-known jade-carving factory.
- **The Museum of Art and History**, which contains one of the world's better collections of Chinese artwork.

A few day trips out from Shanghai may interest your clients. In fact, since many of these lie along the 1,000-year-old Grand Canal, your clients might enjoy visiting them via cruise. Among the most popular **day trips** are:

- **Suzhou**, a lovely city known for its great many gardens (the **Humble Administrator's Garden** is anything but humble), as well as numerous canals. Suzhou has also been renowned for silk since the Sung Dynasty. Your clients may also enjoy seeing **Yunyan Pagoda** at Tiger Hill.
- **Wuxi**, a city of gardens, canals, and pagodas.
- **Hangzhou**, an exceptionally pretty city. Its temples, canals, and lakes would make Hangzhou scenic, but the city's abundance of gardens are what really make it stand out.

The Yangtze River

In its upper stretches, the Yangtze is 10,000 feet above sea level.

This river of lore (called *Changjiang* in Chinese) is a popular cruise destination; your clients can pass among superb scenery along several parts of its 3,400-mile length. Though the river can be reached by a short flight from Shanghai to **Wuhan**, it's best to start farther west, at the historical city of **Chongqing** (also known as Chunking) and travel down river to the east, ending at Wuhan. The 118-

A boat on the water, China
Photo by C. J. Ghormley

mile stretch known as the **Three Gorges** is dramatic and spectacular, as the river wends its way through the mountains. Unfortunately, a new dam project will soon make the Three Gorges far less impressive and may sharply reduce tourism to this region.

Guangzhou

Because it's only eighty miles from Hong Kong, Guangzhou (better known to North Americans as Canton) has probably had the most contact with Westerners of any Chinese city. Guangzhou is a very active trading and commercial center. This is a frequent destination of business travelers; in fact, its Trade Fair attracts huge crowds from all over the world. (Check with Chinese travel authorities about the dates: Many business travelers will want to go at that time; everyone else will want to avoid it.) Wonderful shopping can be found in Guangzhou—as well as some fine temples, a museum of history, and an excellent zoo (of course, with pandas). **Guangzhou Cultural Park** offers many artistic and recreational activities. **Qingping Market** has a marvelous array of strange food.

Political regulations can change often. Always check with the China International Travel Service for the latest advisories before you leave.

Guilin

Guilin offers exceptional, strange beauty—many consider it to have the most spectacular scenery in China. Li River cruises, which generally last six hours, can take your clients past dreamlike rock formations: They look like something out of a Salvador Dali painting. Or, as one Chinese poet put it, "The fantastic peaks grow like a jasper forest, the blue waters ripple like silken gauze." Among Guilin's other attractions: **Reed Flute Cave** and the view from atop **Fubo Hill**.

Xian

Xian is the ancient capital of China. Until recently, that was its sole claim: enough to attract interest, but not enough to make it a major destination. Now, however, all that has changed. And it all begins with a legend.

An old epic poem extolled the riches of Qin Shi Huang Di, China's first emperor. It detailed the fabulous wealth he had buried with him, guarded by 7,000 soldiers. For centuries, this was viewed as a mere artistic and political myth. But no more. In the 1970s a farmer struck something by accident in the soil. It proved to be a life-sized **terra cotta statue of a soldier.** Hundreds upon hundreds of other statues of soldiers in full battle dress, horses, and wagons were excavated. Archaeologists suspect even more wonders are to be discovered in Xian (the Chinese are taking their time to be extremely careful); that which has already been found is now exhibited in a giant, roofed excavation. Other sites of interest in Xian include:

- **The Wild Goose Pagoda**, a very old, famous structure from the seventh century.
- **The Imperial Tomb of Qin Shi Huang Di**, with its stunning underground vaults and tombs.
- **Banpo Museum**, at the site of a 6,000-year-old prehistoric village.

Tibet

Once an independent country, Tibet is a very mountainous, underdeveloped area of China in the Himalaya. Make certain your clients are aware that the air is thin here: The average altitude is around 15,000 feet. The sites you should be most aware of are:

- **Lhasa**, the capital of Tibet, a major religious center. Nestled in a valley, Lhasa was once home of the Dalai Lama, who resided in the huge, nine-story **Potala**

Palace. The seventh-century **Jokhang Temple** is the holiest Buddhist temple in Tibet and attracts masses of pilgrims. **Drepung Monastery** is Tibet's largest and **Sera Monastery** is especially holy to a Tibetan religious sect. There are many open-air markets in this city.

- **Xigaze**, also known as Shigatse. **Tashilumpo Monastery** is particularly important to the Buddhist religion.

Hong Kong *Cantonese & English a their language.*

This port city returned to China in 1997. Hong Kong is a place of legendary shopping, where you can buy electronics, custom-tailored suits, gems—you name it and entrepreneurial Hong Kong will sell it to you, cut-rate. Hong Kong has two principal districts: **Hong Kong Island** and **Kowloon Peninsula** (which probably offers the best shopping). The predominant languages are Cantonese and English.

Among Hong Kong's attractions are:

- **Aberdeen**, a floating village on Hong Kong Island. People live here on junks, sampans, and fishing boats. There are also floating markets and restaurants.
- **Victoria Peak**, the best view of the city. Your clients can reach it via the "peak tram" cog railway.
- **Stanley**, an upscale district, with a popular open-air market.
- **The Hong Kong Museum of Art** and the **Hong Kong Museum of History**, containing interesting collections.
- **The Star Ferries**, boats that can carry your clients across the dramatic harbor. Other means of transportation exist here for this purpose, but the Star Ferries are too famous to be missed.

It's hard not to buy a custom-made suit before leaving Hong Kong. Measurements will be taken one day and the completed suit delivered to the hotel the next. Hong Kong's most famous tailor shop: Baron Kay's.

One Hong Kong experience that's a *must*: a meal aboard one of the huge floating restaurants (though they're certainly not the best restaurants in Hong Kong).

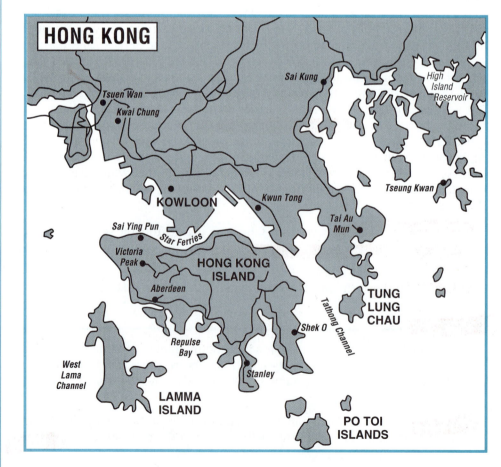

Hong Kong skyline
Photo by C. J. Ghormley

Two **day trips** from Hong Kong stand out:

- **Macau**, a quiet Portuguese colony that will be returned to Chinese rule in 1999. Macau presents a quieter alternative to the hustle and bustle of Hong Kong, though it's a bit run-down. Your clients will find several notable temples, especially the **Temple of Kun Iam**, with its lovely architecture and landscaping. **St. Paul's Church**—for a long time Macau was the only stronghold of Christianity in all of China—is worth a visit as well. Macau, which can be easily reached from Hong Kong by hydrofoil, is renowned as a gambling and horse racing center. The languages of Macau are Cantonese and Portuguese, but English is spoken by many.
- **The New Territories**, an outlying, surprisingly rural part of Hong Kong. One of the area's best-known attractions: the **Temple of 10,000 Buddhas**, in Shatlin.

Possible Itineraries

China is a long way from North America. Most tourists prefer to see as much as possible on a visit, presuming that they might not be back for a while. Nine- to fifteen-day trips are typical. The country can be seen starting with a couple of days in

Among the best buys in Hong Kong: silks, porcelain, jade, watches, and some electronics.

Shanghai and then on to the surrounding Grand Canal area of Suzhou for another two days. Heading north, your clients could stop in Beijing for three days before continuing to Xian for two more. Then on to a few days in Guilin, cruising along the Li River, before ending their stay at Guangzhou and Hong Kong for three days. (Hong Kong is an ideal final stop, since items may be bought at the end of this trip and not carried around for the trip's duration.)

Return visitors, or those who'd like to spend more time on their trip, may want to add a visit to Tibet, a cruise along the Yangtze River, and a stop in Macau. Trips to China are also often combined with a host of allied Asian destinations.

Lodging Options

Be aware that accommodations in most of China range from adequate (in smaller cities) to deluxe (especially **China World** and **Shangri-La** in Beijing, and the **Portman Shangri-La** in Shanghai). Hong Kong has dozens of outstanding hotels—many experts claim that there are more world-class facilities and better service in Hong Kong than anywhere else in the world. Among the most famous: the **Peninsula**, **Regent**, **Mandarin Oriental**, and **Grand Hyatt**.

North American and various international chains serve the country, providing first-class and deluxe accommodations.

In Beijing, hotels are found near the Imperial Palace, along Juanguomenwai, east of the city, and near the Beijing Worker's Stadium. For clients who will be staying in Hong Kong, try to book hotels in Kowloon, down by Victoria Harbor. Selling them up to a harbor river view will be worth it—the waterfront at night is an unforgettable sight. Hotels in other Chinese cities are often scattered about. It's best to try to book your client in a hotel close to each city's center.

Allied Destinations

More countries border China (fifteen) than any other nation in the world.

China is surrounded by many countries. In fact, it's so large that its allied destinations must be broken down into three separate locales. To the north are Russia and Mongolia (though most of Russia's main attractions are nearer Europe). In the northeast, your clients will find North Korea (rarely visited by Westerners) and South Korea—both of which are on the mainland—and Japan (across the Sea of Japan). And finally, there's the Indian subcontinent and Southeast Asia, with such nations as Pakistan, India, Nepal, Bhutan, Burma, Thailand, Singapore, and Malaysia. In addition, across the South China Sea are the Philippines and Taiwan (which for years claimed to harbor the legitimate government of China). For clients traveling between Taiwan and the People's Republic of China, be sure to check any government advisories on travel and custom restrictions.

Cultural Patterns

Hong Kong has always been a key business center. Now, all of China will take on that status. It has become increasingly important, therefore, to understand the cultural uniqueness of this land.

- Tell your clients that the use of full titles when addressing people is important. In addition, be sure your clients know that in a Chinese name, the family name is listed first. Bowing is common, though a handshake is also accepted.

- It's important that your clients understand that promptness is much-prized in China; it's even praiseworthy to be early.

- The Chinese don't call their country Red China or Communist China. Be sure to refer to it as the People's Republic (of China).

- Discussing business during a meal is considered improper by the Chinese. In addition, a client should be prepared to make a little speech after a more formal occasion, as an acknowledgment to his or her host.

- Be sure to tell your clients to use both hands when passing a gift or food. If one person in a business group is to receive a gift, all others within the group must also receive a gift.

- It's more likely that your clients will be invited to a home in Hong Kong than in the rest of the country, where government approval is often required. In either case, if they are, tell them to bring a small gift. And they should at least taste every dish served.

- Generosity is important to the Chinese. Also make certain your clients know to treat the elderly with respect.

- Social position is critical in China, and embarrassing situations are avoided, allowing one another to save face and retain self-respect. Tell your clients to avoid awkward situations.

- Chinese businessmen are generally cautious and slow in reaching decisions.

- White is the Chinese color for mourning and should be avoided in such things as gift wrappings.

Hong Kong has more Rolls Royces per capita than any other place in the world.

Some Chinese consider tipping to be demeaning (though this is changing). In Hong Kong, it's expected.

Qualifying the Client
Beijing

FOR CLIENTS WHO WANT	APPEAL			REMARKS
	HIGH	MEDIUM	LOW	
Historical and Cultural Attractions	▲			Especially Great Wall and Imperial Palace
Beaches and Water Sports			▲	Few facilities
Skiing Opportunities			▲	None
Lots of Nightlife			▲	Some in larger hotels
Family Activities		▲		Mostly sightseeing
Familiar Cultural Experience			▲	
Exotic Cultural Experience	▲			
Safety and Low Crime		▲		Sporadic unrest
Bargain Travel		▲		Packages are all-inclusive
Impressive Scenery		▲		In countryside
Peace and Quiet		▲		Crowded, yet calm
Shopping Opportunities		▲		Hong Kong much better
To Do Business	▲			China is a potentially huge market for the U.S.

Figure 27-2

Factors That Motivate Visitors

Among the factors that motivate a client to visit China are:

- There are remarkable archaeological treasures and sites.
- Chinese architecture and art are beautiful and impressive.
- China is viewed as a "soft adventure" destination by many North Americans.
- Hong Kong, Shanghai, Beijing, and Guangzhou are major business centers.
- The regional cuisines of China are superb and familiar.
- Many Americans can trace their ancestry here.
- Cruise ships increasingly call on Chinese ports.
- Hong Kong has legendary, world-class lodging.
- There's great shopping, especially in Hong Kong.

Possible Misgivings

Because this region is so far away, some of your clients might hesitate to visit. Some of their possible questions and your counters are:

- "China has a very repressive government." Events in the late 1980s brought China's politics into the forefront of the news. Though this might concern some tourists on an emotional level, it has had virtually no effect on traveling.
- "The country isn't set up for tourism and facilities are primitive." Conditions are less developed than in Europe, but China has been welcoming visitors for many years now and the situation is continually improving. A number of very good hotels have been built. Taking a fully inclusive escorted tour—by far the most popular choice—will go a long way toward making such a trip more convenient.
- "The Chinese don't like Americans." The Chinese people are very friendly and (though for generations unaccustomed to outsiders) warmly welcome visitors. They seem to have a special fascination with all things American.
- "I don't think I can take Chinese food every single day." Each region in China offers its own unique cuisine. It's possible to have five or six dishes at each meal, three times a day, for weeks, and never eat the same thing twice.
- "The language is undecipherable." Speaking English in Hong Kong is no problem at all. For those of your clients concerned about the rest of the region, you might suggest an escorted tour. Many Chinese guides are surprisingly fluent in English.

Sales Strategies

Because of travel restrictions and language problems, China is ideal for booking all-inclusive escorted group tours (including those that specialize in trekking expeditions). For your upscale clients, you can also book a custom-designed, personal tour—with driver and guide—for a reasonable price. You may also want to add a river cruise to your client's itinerary. You can enhance a visit to the Great Wall and Ming Tombs for your clients by booking a helicopter flight over the area. And because China is so distant from North America, you might suggest that clients extend their trip, either within China or to allied countries in the Far East, often via a cruise. Similarly, you could consider booking your clients at a stopover (for example, in Hawaii for travelers going west or in Europe for those flying east) to break up the long flight. Luxury lodging is especially attractive to travelers to this region.

Creative Activity

In the fifth century, B.C., Herodotus, the Greek historian, compiled a list of "Seven Wonders of the World" that every traveler should see. Among them: the pyramids, the Colossus of Rhodes, and the Hanging Gardens of Babylon. (Only the pyramids still exist.) The current government of China has decided that it, too, should now boast of its own seven wonders in all of its promotional materials. What would you think these seven should be? Be prepared to justify your suggestions.

1.

2.

3.

4.

5.

6.

7.

Travel Trivia

Signs, Brochures, and Memos Encountered by Travelers

Teeth extracted by the latest Methodists. (Hong Kong)
Visitors must complain at the office between 9 and 11 daily. (Greece)
Please bathe inside the tub. (Japan)
To move the cabin push button for washing floor. (Yugoslavia)
Ladies are requested not to have children in the bar. (Norway)
The flattening of underwear with pleasure is the job of the chambermaid. (Yugoslavia)
Not to perambulate the corridors in the hours of repose in the boots of ascension. (Austria)
A sports jacket may be worn to dinner, but no trousers. (France)
The lift is being fixed for the next day. During that time we regret that you will be unbearable. (Romania)

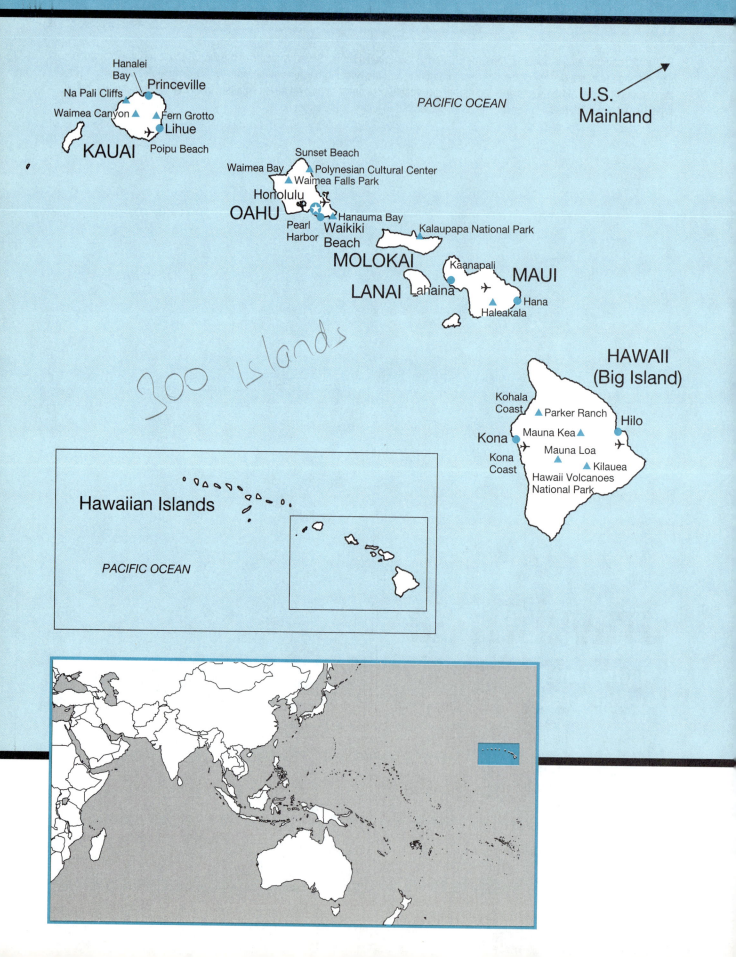

PACIFIC OCEAN

U.S. Mainland

Hanalei Bay
Princeville
Na Pali Cliffs
Waimea Canyon
Fern Grotto
Lihue
KAUAI
Poipu Beach

Sunset Beach
Waimea Bay
Polynesian Cultural Center
Waimea Falls Park
Honolulu
OAHU
Hanauma Bay
Pearl Harbor
Waikiki Beach
Kalaupapa National Park

MOLOKAI

LANAI
Lahaina

Kaanapali
MAUI
Hana
Haleakala

300 Islands

HAWAII (Big Island)

Kohala Coast
Parker Ranch
Hilo
Kona
Mauna Kea
Kona Coast
Mauna Loa
Kilauea
Hawaii Volcanoes National Park

Hawaiian Islands

PACIFIC OCEAN

CHAPTER 28

Hawaii
Paradise Found

It must have been an astonishing trip indeed: Around 700 A.D., hundreds of natives from the Marquesas Islands in the South Pacific set sail in great double-hulled canoes and crossed more than 2,000 miles of open ocean to arrive at what we now call the Hawaiian Islands. How did they know that the islands were there? Did they go back and forth many times, as legends insist? How did they relate with subsequent voyagers, who sailed in greater numbers from the Society Islands between the eleventh and fourteenth centuries?

No one really knows. But we do know that tens of thousands of tourists now cross that same Pacific each week to visit Hawaii—in jets, of course. And it's certain that you will send a great many people—some on FITs, others on prepackaged tours—to these sweet, gentle, and majestic islands.

Don't assume, as do many, that there are only one or two islands. In reality, 312 Hawaiian islands stretch in an arc of almost 1,500 miles in the middle of the Pacific. Only six, at the southernmost tip of the arc, are those you're likely to sell: **Kauai**, **Oahu**, **Molokai**, **Lanai** [lah-NAH-ee], **Maui**, and **Hawaii** (also called the Big Island). Each has its own personality: Kauai is the wettest and most tropical; Oahu is the bustling center of tourism and commerce; Molokai and Lanai are sleepy little islands off the typical tourist path; Maui is an island of great resorts and breathtaking beauty; and Hawaii, a rapidly developing destination, boasts active volcanoes and vast ranches.

How Travelers Get There

Dozens of American and foreign carriers service the islands. Several airlines permit a North American traveler to stop off at no charge in Hawaii on the way to and from such destinations as Hong Kong, Seoul, Auckland, and Sydney. (You can't book your clients on foreign carriers from the mainland to Hawaii—unless they are continuing on to the other side of the Pacific.) Most flights from the mainland to **Honolulu**, Oahu (HNL), are nonstop or direct with connections to the other islands. (It takes about five hours to get from the West Coast to Honolulu.) Some carriers operate nonstop flights from the mainland to the outer islands as well. Occasionally, cruise service exists from the mainland to Hawaii, especially when a cruise ship is repositioning itself, say, from Alaska to Asia.

Weather Patterns

Hawaii's climate barely varies all year (see Figure 28-1). The average high in August is 83 degrees and in January it's 77 degrees. Though it's generally humid, a strong east-to-west trade wind keeps the islands breezy and pleasant. It can get cool at night in the winter (in the mid-60s), and it's liable to shower at any time—though rain is much more likely in the winter, which is, ironically, one of the times when the number of tourists is at its highest. Summer, a time of minimal rain but greater heat, is also a busy tourist season. Hawaii is least crowded in the spring and especially in the fall. Advise your clients that if they have some leeway on departure dates, you can offer a better selection of accommodations and prices. Note: Hurricanes may occasionally reach Hawaii in late summer or early fall.

The weather does vary from place to place. The western, leeward side of each island tends to be dry (it's where you're most likely to lodge your clients), whereas the windward side and central mountainous areas have more frequent rain. Kauai's tourist areas, especially, are quite wet. And Mauna Kea Mountain, on the Big Island, is snow-capped much of the winter and has skiing (it's accessed by helicopter). So if your client is a real ski buff and loves the offbeat, here's a unique opportunity for you to recommend.

Honolulu has the lowest air pollution of any major U.S. city.

Climate at a Glance
HONOLULU, HAWAII

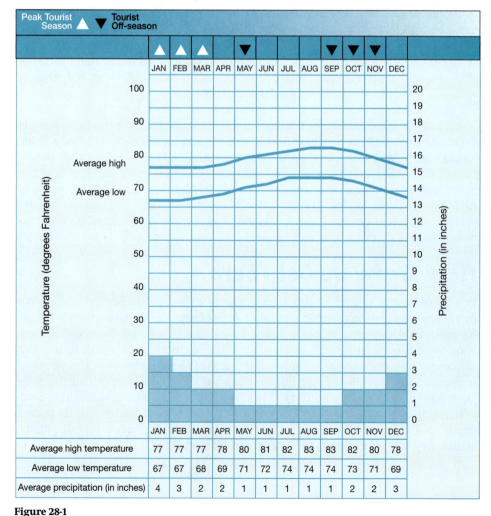

	JAN	FEB	MAR	APR	MAY	JUN	JUL	AUG	SEP	OCT	NOV	DEC
Average high temperature	77	77	77	78	80	81	82	83	83	82	80	78
Average low temperature	67	67	68	69	71	72	74	74	74	73	71	69
Average precipitation (in inches)	4	3	2	2	1	1	1	1	1	2	2	3

Figure 28-1

Getting Around

Several airlines provide inter-island flights; and swarms of small planes and helicopters fly tourists into the scenic but hard-to-get-to canyons of the Big Island, Maui, and, especially, Kauai. American Hawaii Line ships cruise from island to island as portable "hotels." Traveling by bus on Oahu is convenient, but for all other islands you should offer to book a rental car for your clients. Atlantis Submarines provide an unusual way to experience the waters off Oahu and Maui. All manner of rides on outrigger canoes, yachts, and rubber boats can be arranged by your clients on their arrival.

Important Places

Most of your clients will already know of **Waikiki Beach**, which lies to the southeast of Honolulu's center. But spending all one's time there is like visiting Las Vegas and thinking you've seen the United States. Each of the main Hawaiian islands offers a unique environment and wonderful experience.

Oahu

This is the most visited island, the most populated one, and a central transportation hub. Most tourists stay in Waikiki, though most business is carried on in nearby Honolulu, Hawaii's capital. The island's sparsely populated north shore is well-known for its surfing. And its windward northeastern beaches, though often cloudy or rainy, are spectacular and uncrowded; on a sunny day they make for a wonderful alternative to the tourist-packed sands of Waikiki. Among the principal attractions you might recommend to your clients are:

- **The Polynesian Cultural Center**, near the town of Laie, with its villages, crafts, and shows that try to convey Pacific Island life; the presentation is polished, exuberant, but somewhat touristy.
- **Hanauma Bay**, a paradise for even the novice snorkelers among your clients.
- **Pearl Harbor**, with its cruise to the USS Arizona Memorial and, soon, to the retired battleship USS *Missouri*.

Iolani Palace, Honolulu, Oahu
Photo by C. J. Ghormley

Quiet Kailua and Lanikai beaches, on Oahu's windward coast, are considered by some to be the best beaches anywhere.

Rent a car on Oahu for at least one day and drive around the island, perhaps pausing at the beaches on the north shore or the windward side.

The Elison Onizuka
Space Center at Kona
Airport houses a
museum on the space
program and a
memorial to the crew
of the Space Shuttle
Challenger.

- **The Bishop Museum**, with its displays on the geology and culture of Hawaii.
- **Waimea Bay** and **Sunset Beach**, two north shore areas, with occasionally massive waves and always expert surfers; nearby is pleasant **Waimea Falls Park**.

Maui

An often-visited island of condos and resorts, Maui features a broad stretch of wonderful beaches along its western coast. Most notable is the **Kaanapali** area, a planned development dotted with numerous resorts and hotels, anchored by **Lahaina**, an old whaling port. The island's northeast coast is tropical and spectacular. At the island's center is the dormant volcano, **Haleakala**. Among the attractions you might recommend to your clients are:

- **Lahaina**, a picturesque whaling village.
- **The road to Hana**, a winding, overwhelmingly beautiful drive past waterfalls, pools, and vine-covered trees.
- **Iao Valley State Monument**, a picturesque spot where a major ancient battle took place.
- **Haleakala**, where a drive to the top offers spectacular views, especially at dawn to see the sun rise. Haleakala is the world's largest dormant volcano.

Hawaii

Vast in size and with a wide variety of scenery, Hawaii (called the Big Island) is a good recommendation for almost any client (except those who seem chiefly attracted to Waikiki). The western **Kohala** and **Kona** coasts are rapidly developing resort areas. The island's largest city, **Hilo** (once a prime tourist destination), has somewhat lost its appeal and is now primarily a gateway to the volcanic area. For these reasons, the **Kona Airport** has become the choice (over Hilo's) for most tourists. Among the attractions you might recommend to your clients are:

The statue of King
Kamehameha was
once lost at sea off the
Falkland Islands, then
retrieved and erected
on the Big Island.

- **Hawaii Volcanoes National Park**, with its steaming craters, most notably that of active **Kilauea**. Have clients call ahead to find out if they can visit an active lava flow.
- **A drive from Hilo**, across the island's north shore, through the **Parker Ranch** area, and down through the moon-like lava field of Waikoloa.

Many of Hawaii's beaches are rocky. For this reason, the Big Island offers fewer water-sport opportunities than some of the other islands.

Kauai

"The Garden Isle" is lush, moist, and dramatic—precisely what clients picture a tropical island to be. The **Na Pali cliffs** loom majestically over the island's nearly inaccessible northwest coast; clients can see them only if they hike, boat, or fly there. Hotels are concentrated on the somewhat drier **Poipu Beach** area, in the area north and south of **Lihue** (where the airport is situated), and in the scenic **Princeville** area, on the north shore. Among the attractions you might recommend to your clients are:

- **The Fern Grotto**, with its beautiful fern-lined cliffs and cave. It can be accessed on a short boat cruise up the Wailua River. It's a popular site for weddings.
- **The Waimea Canyon**, a fourteen-mile-long, Grand Canyon–like spectacle that can be viewed from a road lookout, helicopter, or light plane.
- **Hanalei Bay**, a striking and serene area next to the resort city of Princeville.

Lava flow, The Big Island
Photo by C. J. Ghormley

Molokai and Lanai

With their small populations, few attractions, and limited lodging choices, these islands should be recommended only to clients who want to get away from it all or who are veteran Hawaii tourists who've seen most every other island. Molokai is famous for its **Kalaupapa National Park**, once the site of a famous leper colony and sometimes accessed by a mule trip down a series of cliffs. Lanai, through most of its history, was one big pineapple plantation; it's perhaps the only island where your clients can most easily mix with the locals. Several relaxed but upscale hotels have recently opened on Lanai.

Possible Itineraries

You should perhaps advise a first-time visitor to spend a week on one island or split between Oahu and an outer island. More experienced Hawaii travelers may bypass Oahu to see those islands they're unacquainted with. A three- or four-island itinerary via cruise ship is a popular option.

Lodging Options

Virtually every great hotel chain has numerous properties on the islands, though **Sheraton**, **Hyatt**, **Hilton**, **Outrigger**, **Castle**, and **Aston** predominate. Sheraton owns many older, historic properties. Hyatt fills its resorts with fine art. Hilton has most of the truly huge resorts. Outrigger features many budget properties. And both Castle and Aston have an unusually wide spectrum of properties, from budget to luxury.

Oahu has the most hotels, nearly all of which are concentrated along Waikiki Beach. Waikiki is a popular recommendation, especially for budget-minded travelers, since lodging is available at all price levels. Hotels and condos on the other islands tend to be somewhat more expensive, with few low-end properties. Maui's hotels are mostly clustered along its western coast, as are those of the Big Island. Kauai's are along its wet southern and eastern sides, since the somewhat drier

The world's highest sea cliffs are on Molokai.

Luaus are touristy but fun. Try the poi (a paste made from taro root).

Black sand beach, The Big Island
Photo by C. J. Ghormley

Mark Twain once sat
under the banyan
tree in the Moana
Surfrider's courtyard.

west coast is mostly cliffs. Molokai and Lanai have limited accommodations (though the Lanai properties are quite elegant).

Your clients may already know about certain Hawaiian properties, since several well-publicized hotels and resorts dot the islands. Oahu's list would be virtually endless, though the **Royal Hawaiian**, the **Moana Surfrider**, the **Halekulani**, and the **Kahala Hilton** are best known (and quite pricey). Two huge and extraordinary resort properties are located on the islands: the **Hyatt Regency** on Kauai and the **Hilton** in the Waikoloa area of the Big Island. The Big Island's **Mauna Lani Bay** and **Grand Wailea** have world-famous reputations for quality. The Big Island's **Kona Village** has upscale huts perched on stilts.

Allied Destinations

Since the Hawaiian islands are in the middle of the Pacific Ocean, no allied destinations are nearby. As we mentioned however, clients often go on from Hawaii to Korea, China, Japan, Singapore, Australia, or New Zealand. There's also the possibility to send them on to the South Pacific islands, including Tahiti and Fiji.

Cultural Patterns

Tell your clients that even though Hawaii is one of the United States, its way of life is much more relaxed; jackets and ties, for instance, are rarely worn. Also, clients shouldn't expect primitive, South Sea island conditions. Hawaii is a sophisticated, modern destination. Above everything, make certain that your clients don't refer to the mainland alone as the United States. Hawaii is also a part of the United States. Hawaiians are very sensitive about this.

Hawaiians are becoming increasingly proud of their own history, and this is showing up in hotel decor, accuracy of entertainment, and the like. Suggest to clients that they read James Michener's *Hawaii*—or rent the movie based on it—to find out more about island history and culture.

Factors That Motivate Visitors

Hawaii is a unique destination within the United States, and as such, there are unique reasons clients may want to go there:

- They want to visit an exotic and romantic tropical paradise, one that will still be relatively familiar, since it's part of the United States.
- Hawaii affords a wide selection of accommodations, flights, independent tours, and natural attractions.
- Hawaiian fly/lodge/drive packages, especially those on Oahu, are available at all price levels.
- Hawaii's climate is predictably warm and pleasant, even when it's cold and wintry on the mainland.
- Water sports and beach activities are readily available.
- The opportunities to practice other sports, such as hiking, tennis, golf, and horseback riding, are almost limitless.
- Clients have a choice of the intensely busy nightlife of Waikiki or the more relaxed possibilities of the outer islands.

Visitors who want to dive in Hawaii must either be certified divers or take courses available through resorts or independent dive operators.

Possible Misgivings

Though Hawaii is, in many ways, a magical destination, there may be things about it that raise questions in a client's mind:

- "There's not enough to do." This type of client should be steered to Waikiki, to an adventure tour or package, to a major outer island resort, to a cruise, or (perhaps) to an escorted tour, especially if he or she is older and has taken tours before.
- "Hawaii is too touristy." Keep this kind of client away from Waikiki and on the outer islands.
- "I've heard it's expensive." Waikiki's budget hotels and low-cost independent tour packages may appeal to this traveler.
- "There's nothing left of old Hawaii." Suggest stays on the island of Lanai or Molokai.
- "There's nothing cultural to see." Many small attractions underscore Hawaii's cultural heritage, but if your clients' idea of a great vacation is visiting Europe's museums and cathedrals, Hawaii may indeed not be appropriate for them.
- "I'm too old to hang out and sun on the beach or at a pool all day." This type of client may enjoy a packaged escorted tour that will take them sightseeing and keep them occupied. Oahu and the Big Island are especially appropriate for them.
- "Locals aren't friendly and there's a lot of crime." There's resentment and crime against tourists, but it's rarely encountered. A little prudence can lessen the chance of an unpleasant experience.

Oahu's shopping is especially good at the Ala Moana Center and Ward's Warehouse.

Qualifying the Client
Big Island of Hawaii

FOR CLIENTS WHO WANT	APPEAL			REMARKS
	HIGH	MEDIUM	LOW	
Historical and Cultural Attractions		▲		Polynesian culture
Beaches and Water Sports		▲		Many beaches rocky
Skiing Opportunities			▲	Downhill on Mauna Kea
Lots of Nightlife		▲		In hotels
Family Activities	▲			Especially resort hotels
Familiar Cultural Experience	▲			U.S. state
Exotic Cultural Experience		▲		Asian influences are strong
Safety and Low Crime		▲		Petty crime in certain areas
Bargain Travel		▲		Everything from budget to luxury
Impressive Scenery	▲			Mountains, rain forests, seascapes, volcanoes
Peace and Quiet	▲			One of the quieter islands
Shopping Opportunities			▲	Much better in Honolulu
To Do Business		▲		Key role between Asia and North America

Figure 28-2

- "Bugs are everywhere." As with any tropical destination, this is true. In rain-forest areas, the mosquitoes can be ferocious; tell your client to take insect repellent. Roaches are indeed numerous; an occasional sighting even in luxury hotels or rental cars can be expected.

Sales Strategies

Hawaii can be a bargain destination, but often a low-cost hotel or subcompact car can undermine that dream vacation in "Paradise" that your client has anticipated. Offer upgraded lodging; this is especially appropriate for Waikiki, where low-cost hotels may leave much to be desired. Ocean-view rooms are an upgrade that often appeals to clients. And if your clients are going to Oahu for the first time, why not mention the possibility of a second or third island stay? Since they've gone that far, they likely will be receptive to having a longer and more full Hawaiian experience. (Here, knowledge of the distinct character of each island is imperative for a multi-island stay, since clients may argue that "one island is the same as another.") Car rentals are extremely useful on all islands. Even Oahu warrants one for at least a day. Selling your client up to a convertible, jeep, or larger car may be an attractive strategy. And a multitude of cross-sell options (helicopter rides, dinner cruises, luaus, submarine rides, and so on) can often be booked and sold in advance.

Finally, remember that independent tours and inter-island cruises often enable you to secure bargains for your clients while deriving commissions from an entire package of services. There are escorted tours of the islands; such tours often appeal to seniors who prefer not to drive around or simply to bake on the beach.

Surfing conditions differ at each island, so surfers should consider a multi-island trip.

Creative Activity

You're a reservationist for a large, California-based, independent tour wholesaler to Hawaii. A caller has read an ad in the Sunday newspaper for a competitor's tour. The price is incredibly low: $399 per person, including air and six days in a hotel in Honolulu. The caller wants to know if you have something similar, since she's unfamiliar with the company in the ad, but knows yours well. She will be traveling with her husband and ten-year-old son. This will be their twelfth wedding anniversary.

You know you can't match it and for a good reason: this is a bare-bones, "cheapo" trip that would almost surely displease your client. The hotel might be in a poor location with no view, the available days might be at a bad time, etc.

What five possibilities might you suggest to the client to convince her that you could offer her a trip that would cost more, but would offer so many more pleasing features (and make more profit for your company via your up-selling and cross-selling)?

For example: We could offer you a hotel that's right on the beach and a room with an ocean view. Wouldn't that be much nicer? And it would only cost you $22 more per night.

1.

2.

3.

4.

5.

Travel Trivia

Surprising Facts About Hawaii

Hawaiians didn't invent the ukulele. The Portuguese brought it to them in the 1880s.
A new volcanic island is now forming underwater off the coast of the Big Island. It already has a name: Loihi.
Though the first Pacific islands were "discovered" by Europeans in the early 1500s, the Hawaiian chain wasn't reached by them until 1778.
Grass skirts aren't native to Hawaii. Micronesian immigrants brought them in the 1880s.
The majority of Hawaii's land is owned by the United States government and by the descendants of five missionary families.
The famous song, "Aloha Oe," was written by Hawaii's last reigning monarch, Queen Liliuokalani.

CHAPTER · **29**

Asia and the Pacific Potpourri

Japan, China, Australia, New Zealand, and somewhat beyond, Singapore and Thailand—these are the best-known destinations on the far side of the Pacific Rim. And between the palm-fringed shores of Asia and California float thousands of islands—many quite famous. But beyond that—well, it'll largely be unclear to most of your clients. They've heard of Krakatoa volcano, but where is it? In what country is Mt. Everest? And what, for heaven's sake, is a *yurt*?

We omit quite a few Asian countries from this chapter because they aren't major tourist destinations. The reasons are many: Warfare in some keeps travelers away; political turmoil is a major deterrent in others; and still others, like Vietnam, are opening up rapidly (Vietnam's war sites have become attractions and Ho Chi Minh City is an increasingly frequent stop on the more exotic cruise itineraries), but do not yet warrant their own sections. In addition, some countries, like North Korea and many of the Southeast Asia nations—Laos, for example, and Cambodia (also known as Kampuchea)—have governments with questionable human rights records and, therefore, limited tourist appeal. (Cambodia *is* taking efforts to reinstate tourism to the legendary **Angkor Wat** ruins.) Interestingly, there are also countries such as Brunei which, though having perfectly good relations with most countries, aren't especially interested in encouraging a tourist trade. But keep one important fact in mind: All this can change overnight. After all, the Berlin Wall came down, didn't it?

Mongolia

Mongolia's location—sandwiched between China and Russia—combined with its exotic history, makes this nation an intriguingly offbeat destination. Under Genghis Khan, Mongolia was once a world power. Today, the people of this nomadic, fairly primitive culture are more closely tied to Russia than to China.

Southern Mongolia is made up of the **Gobi Desert**; this arid, mountainous region is actually pretty, with much interesting wildlife. The rainier north is where most of the population lives. **Ulan Bator**, the capital, has many monasteries and quite a few museums. A good village for your clients to see the nomadic lifestyle at its best is **Khujhirt**; it is fairly

513

close to the historic town of **Karakorum**, the capital during the time of Genghis Khan, which also boasts a fine monastery. And it's here, as well, that your clients will spot *yurts,* the traditional wooden-framed tents that are transported by the nomads as they herd across the countryside.

South Korea

Separated from China by only North Korea, South Korea covers the southern strip of the Korean Peninsula; Japan is just across the **Sea of Japan** on the east, and the **Yellow Sea** borders Korea to the west. **Seoul** (SEL), the capital, located in the northwest, was host to the 1988 Summer Olympics and is the main air gateway. The national carrier, **Korean Air Lines** (KE), **Asiana** (OZ), and a few North American airlines fly here. Cruise ships, on occasion, will stop at **Pusan**, a major port on the southeast coast.

Most tourist destinations are toward the north, where the climate is humid. Spring and fall are pleasant in Korea, with temperatures in the upper 60s and chilly nights; these two seasons tend to be the driest times of the year. Summers are rainy—mid-July to mid-August is a mini-monsoon season—and the highs can soar into the 90s; winters, on the other hand, are cold, with temperatures often plummeting to the 20s or below. The official language is Korean, though English is quite common, especially in business.

The Korean language is closer to Finnish or Hungarian than to any Asiatic language.

Important Places

South Korean tourism, fueled by visitors who seek shopping bargains and business deals, has reached impressive levels. One place your clients will want to visit is the

capital city of Seoul [SOLE], historically surrounded by nine gates. This city is rich with temples and palaces; the cultural and shopping opportunities are excellent. Seoul's two most important designated national treasures are the **Namdaemun Gate** (the Great South Gate) and the **Tongdaemun Gate** (the Great East Gate): These grand, ornate structures are each adjacent to frenetic, popular marketplaces. (The **Itaewon district**, which includes underground complexes, is the city's major shopping area.)

Also make sure your clients visit the ancient **Changdok Palace**, noted for its huge and remarkable **Piwon** (or Secret Garden)—a seventy-eight-acre labyrinth of paths, ponds, and pavilions. Two other former palaces are converted to museums: **Toksu Palace** (the one-time royal residence, now housing modern art) and historic **Kyongbok Palace** (built 600 years ago by the first emperor of the Yi Dynasty). The National Museum is here, as is the **Kwanghwamun Gate**.

Interesting day trips and excursions include:

- **The Korean Folk Village**, in Suwon, a village museum where the ancient life in Korea is reenacted. Not far away is **Panmunjom**, where peace talks continue between North and South Korea; visitors are welcome to watch, and passes can be set up through the United Nations office in Seoul. Your clients can also visit nearby **Inchon**, a major port and the site of General Douglas MacArthur's landing.
- **Namhansansong Castle**, a spectacular fortress on Mt. Namhan. **Hyonchungsa** is a notable old temple in the area.
- **The Royal Tombs at Kumgoknung**, a majestic relic of the Yi Dynasty.

Other sites include:

- **Kyongju,** the old capital of Korea. Burial mounds, tombs, temples, and a National Museum are the attractions here.
- **Pusan,** South Korea's second largest city, with several good resorts close by. There's also a moving **U.N. Memorial Cemetery**.
- **Cheju Island**, off the southern coast, famed for its women pearl divers. The historical and revered Manjang-gul Cave and Samsonghyol Caves are important Korean sites. There are good beaches, major hotels, a casino, and excellent diving on the island. It's sometimes reached by a slow, ninety-mile ferry ride from Pusan.
- **Other resort areas**, like **Sokcho** and **Kangnung**, east of Seoul. Each area has popular beaches for the summer and offers nearby skiing during the winter.

Sales Considerations

South Korea is a convenient extension of a trip to Japan or China. Because of the unfamiliarity of the language, some clients would probably appreciate your booking them on an escorted tour. This country will appeal to clients who love Asian culture, ancient architecture, and bargain shopping. War veterans may also want to return to the site of their battles, under peaceful conditions. Korea offers beaches and skiing for your active clients. Business clients should be prepared for the brusque, no-nonsense approach of Koreans. Your clients may be aware of political unrest and the history of South Korea's conflicts with North Korea, but for the moment, neither unrest nor conflict is affecting tourism.

Taiwan

Until the mid-twentieth century, this 240-by-85-mile island was known as Formosa, which in Portuguese means "beautiful." The early settlers from Portugal knew what they were talking about; the island is a glorious one. For years, Taiwan's rulers claimed to represent the legitimate government of China. (It still

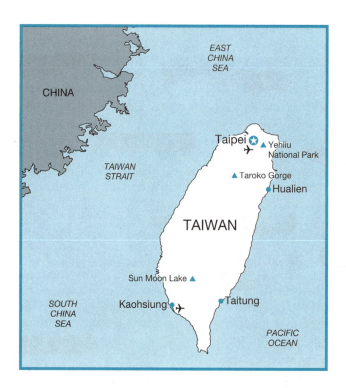

China considers Taiwan to be one of its provinces.

officially calls itself the Republic of China.) Its airline, for example, continues to be called **China Air** (CI)—not to be confused with mainland China's **Air China**. Taiwan's other carrier is **EVA Airlines** (BR). Taiwan is located off the southeast coast of China, slightly northeast of Hong Kong and just north of the Philippines. Your clients can reach **Taipei**, its capital and gateway in the north, via **Chiang Kai-shek International Airport** (TPE). There's also **Kaohsiung International Airport** (KHU) in the southwest, but it's less used. Taiwan is also serviced by a few North American airlines and several Asian carriers. The official language is Mandarin Chinese, but Taiwanese is also widely spoken, as is some Japanese. English is commonly used in business.

Most of Taiwan's tourist destinations are in the north. The weather there is humid; June through October are the nicest months, with temperatures in the 80s during the day. November through May is cooler, but also rainy. The south is drier and warmer, but there's not as much for your clients to see. The typhoon season here stretches from June to October. Mountain temperatures, of course, are chillier than in the lowlands.

Important Places

All your clients need do is gaze at its many shrines or travel through its lush countryside to discover Taiwan's beauty. One of its top attractions is **Taipei**—a busy, cosmopolitan capital. There's a wide selection of goods here and many excellent bargains for your clients who love to shop. The world-class **National Palace Museum** is a must-see; it has some 600,000 pieces of Chinese art, much of which was brought over from Beijing's Forbidden City when Taiwan's leaders fled the mainland. The classically styled **Martyrs Shrine** is designed after a hall in that same Forbidden City. The **Chiang Kai-shek Memorial Hall** honors the nation's late general and president; its huge complex features a tower more than twenty stories high. There are a great many temples in Taipei for your clients to visit; the most notable is the historic, 250-year-old **Lungshan Temple**. (A popular marketplace is nearby.)

Among the **day trips** you can recommend are:

- **Taroko Gorge**, a major destination, featuring an awesome twelve-mile drive on its eastern end, known as The Rainbow of Treasure Island. It's most commonly reached by a short flight from Taipei southeast to Hualien.
- **Yangmingshan** (Grass Mountain) **National Park**, noted for its scenic cherry and azalea trees. The trip here from Taipei passes by the Peitou Mineral Springs.
- **Yehliu National Park**, reached via an hour's drive to the east through lovely mountains and farmland. Yehliu's strange rocks and wonderful vistas make this a worthwhile half-day excursion.

One major destination, far away from the hub of Taipei, is **Sun Moon Lake**—created by a dam and offering rich green scenery. Beyond the natural beauty of the area, your clients will likely enjoy the **Shrine of Hsuan Chuang**, a site honoring the monk who helped spread Buddhism from India. **Wen-Wu** is a temple dedicated to Confucius, and **Filial Devotion Pagoda** is as charming as its name implies. Sun Moon Lake is accessed out of **Taitung**, a pretty town two hours away on the southeast coast.

Sales Considerations

Taiwan attracts visitors because of its scenery, graceful Chinese architecture, and bargain shopping. Since the island is so small, it's easy for your clients to sample Chinese cuisine and culture without having to tackle the vastness of China. Some clients may feel Taiwan to be a safer destination than mainland China. Taiwan makes a wonderful extension of most any trip to the Orient—particularly Japan, the Philippines, and South Korea, as well as China. Because of language problems, your clients may appreciate your booking them on an escorted tour or cruise.

The Philippines (manila)

Often capturing news headlines for its political turmoil, the Philippines is nonetheless an attractive destination to sell. Comprised of more than 7,000 islands, it's located off the southeast coast of China in the South China Sea and stretches from Taiwan in the north to Indonesia in the south. The main island here is **Luzon** in the north, where the capital of Manila is located. **Philippine Airlines** (PR), the national airline, services the country, as do several North American and international carriers and a few cruise lines. **Manila International Airport** (MNL) is the country's gateway; Manila also serves as a cruise port.

The climate is fairly steady year-round, with highs averaging in the upper 80s and dropping into the mid-70s at night. Winter tends to be a bit cooler and more pleasant; March through May are the hottest months. It's rainiest from June to October (when typhoons are most likely to hit). The official languages are Pilipino (based on Tagalog) and English.

Important Places

The Philippines provides your clients with historical attractions, scenic sites, and lovely beach resorts. Manila, on Luzon Island, is the political and industrial center of the Philippines. It's a place of contrasts, with millionaire communities hard by teeming slums. Most tourists stay in the Ermita District, near Luneta Park. Excellent shopping is available here. (The best known market is **Pistang Pilipino**.) Your clients can discover Manila's Spanish heritage at **Intramuros**, the old walled city, where battle-torn Fort Santiago—a former dungeon—is found. **Corregidor** is an island fortress across Manila Bay, with important World War II memorials. Manila has many fine churches. The pretty, nearby town of **Makati** features a good cultural center and quite a few museums.

Among the **day trips** you can recommend are:

- **Hidden Valley** harbors a lush rain forest. Your clients can also explore a dormant volcano close by.
- **Pagsanjan Falls** inspires visitors with its canyons, rapids, and craggy rock formations. The two-hour drive east of Manila will take your clients through coconut, sugar, and pineapple plantations.
- **Lake Taal** [TAH-AHL] is commonly viewed from Tagaytay Ridge, thirty miles south of Manila. Lake Taal offers a geographic oddity: At its center is a volcano which in turn contains another lake.

Other destinations in the Philippines include:

- **Baguio**, 150 miles north of Manila in the mountains, is often thought of as the summer resort center of the Philippines. (The climate is cooler here.) The **Banaue Rice Terraces** are an extremely popular, if challenging, attraction: Massive, awesome tiers cut into the mountainside.
- **The Visayas** are a cluster of islands in the middle section of the Philippines. Many old churches dot the Visayas, as do beaches and resort developments. The island of **Boracay** presents especially good water-sports possibilities.
- **Zamboanga** is on the southern island of **Mindanao**. Known as the City of Flowers, this beautiful, active port features hanging gardens, 300-year-old **Fort Pilar**, an impressive mosque, and nearby **Rio Hondo Village**, with homes built over water on stilts. Elsewhere on the island are good beaches, especially at **Davao**.

If placed end to end, the Banaue terraces would stretch halfway around the world.

"Jeaps" in Manila, The Philippines
Photo by C. J. Ghormley

Sales Considerations

This tropical island-nation appeals to clients who love scenic destinations, relaxing beaches, snorkeling, shopping, good value, and a mix of exotic cultures. World War II veterans may also want to return here. The Philippines provide good shopping opportunities for your clients. You can book them on escorted tours to get them around from island to island. And selling-up hotel accommodations will likely be appreciated, since budget lodging can leave much to be desired and luxury hotels are a relative bargain. The Philippines are close to Taiwan, Indonesia, Malaysia, Thailand, and China, creating potentially larger FIT combinations. Japan and Australia (though more distant) are also potential add-ons. Asian cruises often call on Manila. So far, political turbulence hasn't disrupted tourism in the Philippines, though there's always that possibility. Crime and tourist scams are occasionally a problem here.

Indonesia

Indonesia, with the fourth largest population in the world, boasts a land area about the size of Alaska and Oregon. Yet it stretches 3,000 miles—longer than the width of the United States. How can this be? Simply that Indonesia is made up of a spread-out arc of islands: 17,000 of them, stretching almost halfway up Peninsular Malaysia on the west and almost to Australia on the east. The largest of its islands, **Sumatra**, lies to the west; **Java**, a densely populated island and the location of the nation's capital, **Jakarta**, is a bit farther east; legendary **Bali** sits at the eastern tip of Java; and the jungles of **Borneo** are to the north. Jakarta (JKT) is the gateway into Indonesia (though cruises disembark at Bali), and it's reached via the national airline, **Garuda Indonesia** (GA).

Most of Indonesia's land mass lies below the equator, so its seasons—limited as they are—are opposite those in North America. The climate tends to be steamy all year. The driest months are June to early November (but it's still humid, and there'll be rain), with temperatures in the upper 80s. Inland temperatures run slightly cooler. Late November to March is extremely wet; the monsoon season is

Less than half of the Philippine islands have names; only around 900 are inhabited.

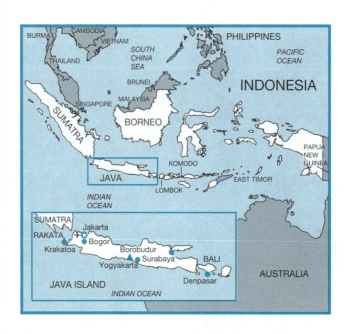

January and February. Bahasa Indonesia is the official language here, though many other dialects and languages are spoken. English is used by many Indonesians. Three interesting facts: Indonesia has the world's largest Islamic population, the second largest rain forest, and more active volcanoes than any other country.

Important Places

Indonesia is a mosaic of cultures. It's an ancient land: the prehistoric remains of Java Man were discovered here. Its attractions are varied and wonderful.

- **Bali** is one of the world's legendary leisure destinations and has often been called a paradise on earth: lush jungles, volcanic mountain peaks, exotic

Rice field, Bali, Indonesia
Photo by C. J. Ghormley

Hindu ceremonies, mystical temples, pristine beaches, and a culture that expects almost everyone to be an artist. **Denpasar** is the island's main business center—though most tourists stay at Bali's great resorts near the island's southern tip, which feature excellent snorkeling, surfing, and diving. Other resorts are at Sanur (east coast) and at Kuta (west coast). Bali is being heavily developed; you should tell clients it's no longer the "primitive" tropical place it was a few decades ago.

Bali's intricate, moat-surrounded **Pura Taman Ayun** is one of the oldest temples in Indonesia. **Pura Luhur** (Ancestors Temple) is a sacred shrine located on the edge of a cliff with stunning views. **Sengah** is a monkey forest, where the animals—considered sacred—wander about everywhere, including through the nearby village. The town of Ubud has quite a few art galleries and museums, the villages of Mas and Celuk specialize in native craft; and the **Bali Museum**, in Denpasar, features cultural arts.

- **Yogyakarta**, in the center of the island of Java, is a major cultural center. It's known for its batik factories, which are open to tourists. The **Palace of the Sultan** is a complex of elaborate, lavishly designed pavilions. You should strongly suggest that your clients take a trip to nearby **Borobudur** [bore-uh-buh-DUR] and its spectacular, immense, recently restored Buddhist temple that was built 1,200 years ago. The **Prambanan Temple** (Loro Jonggrang) is also impressive—and from June through October, a ballet depicting the famous Ramayana story is performed here on the nights of the full moon. (It's one of the two great Hindu epics, along with the Mahabharata.)

The temple of Borobudur was forgotten for 1,000 years and rediscovered by Sir Stamford Raffles (of Singapore's Raffles Hotel fame).

- **Jakarta**, Indonesia's busy and crowded capital, is located on the west end of Java. It has only a few sites of interest. The **National Museum** has some fine collections and your clients might have an enjoyable time visiting **Fatahillah Square** in the Dutch quarter. Batik factories can be visited. A little way out of town, in **Bogor**, a superb botanical garden has more than 50,000 species of plants and 10,000 species of trees.

- **Surabaya**, in east Java, is an area of many volcanoes. The town also operates a good zoo with famed Komodo dragons (huge lizards), which were often used in movies to portray dinosaurs.

- **Sumatra**, a beautiful island with excellent wildlife, is most famous for its Sumatran tigers. Attractions include the interesting **Sultan's Palace**, a native village built on stilts.

- **Krakatoa**, the legendary volcano, rises up on the island of **Rakata**—you can book excursions there. (By the way, there was a movie called *Krakatoa, East of Java*. Krakatoa is actually *west* of Java, but "East" apparently sounded better to Hollywood.)

When Krakatoa exploded in 1883, it created the loudest sound in recorded history.

Sales Considerations

Unless your client is going only to Bali, you might suggest setting up an escorted tour: Traveling around Indonesia can be challenging. And selling-up a client's lodging will likely be appreciated. This is a country that appeals to lovers of tropical splendor and to adventurers—you can set up rafting excursions in Sumatra or a side trip to Krakatoa. Indonesia will be popular among your clients interested in primitive cultures, the religions of the world, water sports, exotic food, shopping, and bargain travel. Ecotourists love it too: Here is the home of orangutans and Komodo dragons. Cruise ships stop at nearly a dozen different ports: **Lombok Island** (with its bargain shopping), Bali, and Semarang (for Borobudur) are the most popular. Cruises are also one of the easiest ways to get to see **Komodo Island** and its huge lizards.

Malaysia *tallest building in the world*

Malaysia's success at tourism has caught up to its neighbors, Singapore and Thailand. It could even surpass them as the prime destination in the area.

Malaysia is divided into two sections: The most populous region lies on a peninsula bordered by Thailand to the north and Singapore and Indonesia (across the Strait of Malacca) to the south; the more primitive jungle area sits atop the island of **Borneo**. **Kuala Lumpur** (KUL), the capital and air gateway, is near the west-central coast of Peninsular Malaysia. It's served by the national carrier, **Malaysian Airlines** (MH), as well as several North American and Asian airlines. (Because Singapore is so conveniently close to Malaysia, your clients may prefer to land there instead.) Malaysia is well situated for cruises: **George Town**, **Port Kelang**, and **Malacca** are its main ports.

Malaysia has a hot, tropical climate. Daytime highs average around 90 degrees, with evening lows in the 70s. It's humid all year, though October through January is rainiest, whereas March through June is the most pleasant period. Conditions on the peninsula are slightly cooler and drier than those on the island of Borneo. Malay is the national language, but English is widely spoken, especially in business.

Important Places

A lush country, Malaysia offers beautiful scenery, an austere but intriguing Islamic culture, and some wonderful beaches. Among the most popular destinations are:

- **Kuala Lumpur**, a beautiful city with Moorish architecture. Most notable are the **National Mosque**, the palace-like **railroad station**, and the new twin **Petronas Towers**, two of the world's tallest skyscrapers. The **Central Market** is a busy and entertaining place. Your clients may also enjoy the city's excellent **zoo** and **National Museum**. Outside the city are the **Batu Caves**, up nearly 300 steps to a Hindu shrine in an exotic grotto. And in the **Genting Highlands**, your clients may be surprised to find a resort and recreation area with a very busy casino.

- **Malacca**, three hours south of Kuala Lumpur. This historic port—it's Malaysia's oldest city—can be seen as a long day trip from Kuala Lumpur. A multicultured city settled at various times by the Chinese, Portuguese, Dutch, and English, Malacca's old quarter is called **Bandar Hillar**. **St. Paul's** and **St. Peter's** are interesting churches.

- **Penang Island**, a place of beaches and temples off the northwest coast. **Kek Lok Si** is a multitiered temple built into the hillside; thousands of tiny Buddha statues fill its pagoda. The **Snake Temple** is lovely—but perhaps not for your

Kuala Lumpur is commonly called "KL."

squeamish clients: poisonous, sacred snakes freely slither through the altar. (It feels like a place out of an Indiana Jones movie.) The gold and bejeweled **Waterfall Temple** is a popular site. **George Town** is the major city on the island, and its free port makes for excellent shopping. **Fort Cornwallis** marks the early British settlement, and the intricately carved **Khoo Kongsi** is a building many tourists enjoy.

- **The Cameron Highlands**, on the mainland, halfway between Penang and Kuala Lumpur. This recreation area offers waterfalls, tea plantations, and its famous butterflies. (There's even a butterfly farm.) The climate here is cooler than that of the lowlands.

- **Sarawak**, the northwest territory on Borneo. This is the legendary, ancient home of Dyak headhunters. **Kuching**, the capital, features a historical museum, some fine temples, and several mosques. A British dynasty was begun here by the White Rajah; his successor built a lovely palace, **Astana**.

- **Sabah**, the northeast territory on Borneo, a region for adventurous clients. The capital, **Kota Kinabalu**, has an impressive state mosque and good museum; the city can serve as a convenient hub for exploring the surrounding tribal area. **Mt. Kinabalu**, rising 13,500 feet, is a popular destination for climbers; its hilly national park is filled with exotic birds, flowers, and butterflies.

- **Tioman**, the principal island amidst a group of sixty-four volcanic islands off the eastern coast. With white coral beaches and crystal-clear waters, these islands are being discovered for their superb snorkeling opportunities and the spectacle of hundreds of turtles that swim to shore to lay their eggs.

Sales Considerations

Malaysia is well located for extending trips to Thailand, Singapore, and Indonesia. It's a country for clients who love scenery, beaches, shopping (especially batik and brassworks), and tribal culture. It also offers areas that are ideal for the adventurous among your clients. You would be wise to sell-up hotels rather than book clients in unpleasant, basic accommodations. Getting around the country can be a bother to some, so tours might be appropriate. And, again, Malaysia's proximity to many other nations encourages an expanded FIT, often via a cruise.

The British developed the resorts in the highlands to escape from the heat and humidity of the rest of Malaysia.

Burma (Myanmar)

Sandwiched between India, China, and Thailand, with the Bay of Bengal to the south, Burma—also known as Myanmar [mee-AHN-mahr]—was once a British colony and has retained much of its cultural heritage. The squalid capital of **Rangoon** (also called Yangon) features a gold-and-diamond-encrusted, bell-shaped complex—**Shwedagon Pagoda**—one of the most sacred Buddhist shrines. **Mandalay**, the former capital, has a strong cultural past; its **Kuthodaw Pagoda** houses more than 700 tiny pagodas.

Pagan—yet another former capital—is a beautiful, fascinating city with the ruins of 5,000 pagodas. This was the center of the powerful Pagan dynasty, until Kublai Khan overran it in the thirteenth century. **Inle Lake** is a growing resort area.

The high tourist season in Burma is from October through January, when the weather is most tolerable. The rest of the year tends to be hot and humid, but tourists will find fewer crowds and more available lodging at these times.

You should prepare clients for the adventurous nature of traveling to Burma—where lodging is hardly deluxe and there is much political and military turmoil in the hinterlands. One bit of trivia: The Burmese celebrate New Year's by throwing buckets of water on one another.

Most information and arrangements should be secured through **Tourist Myanmar**, the official agency for all Burmese travel. Burma is usually booked as a two- or three-day "extra" on a trip to the more popular destination—adjoining Thailand.

Bhutan

Slightly to the east of Nepal and separated from it only by a thin strip of India, lofty **Bhutan** [boo-TAN] is known as the Land of the Thunder Dragon. A country of unspoiled beauty, it has been open to outside tourists only since 1974; there continue to be strict limits placed on the number of tourists permitted yearly. The awesome **Himalaya** make Bhutan a major destination for treks and mountain climbing.

    Paro is Bhutan's largest city. An old temple, **Ta Dzong** (a *dzong* is a fortress-monastery), today houses the **National Museum**; though now in ruins, **Drukgyel Dzong** was once an impressive monastery; and **Kyichu Lhakhang** is an important temple. The capital of Bhutan, **Thimphu**, is the folk-cultural center, with many ancient structures and good crafts shopping. Nearby **Punakha** is a religious center nestled in a mountainous area; many temples can be found here, the most famous of which is **Punakha Dzong**, a major winter sanctuary for Buddhist monks. You

should be sure to recommend to your clients the drive between **Wangdiphodrang** and **Tongsa**: It's breathtaking.

Nepal

Imagine the most stunning and prodigious mountain range you can. It's likely that you (or your clients) will be imagining the Himalaya of Nepal. The northern region of this country is perhaps the prime trekking and mountain-climbing destination in the world: This is the land of **Mt. Everest**, the world's tallest peak. Special permits may be necessary for some of the excursions here, so be sure to check with the Ministry of Tourism. Southern Nepal is merely hilly and, thus, more populous. There has been unrest here, which may worry some of your clients, so check for government advisories.

Kathmandu is the capital, the main hub for treks, and a somewhat cosmopolitan city. Your clients may enjoy visiting its **Royal Palace** and **Durbar Square;** some impressive shrines are here as well. Adjacent to Kathmandu, **Swayambhunath Temple** offers superb views up a major stair climb—not to mention monkeys that roam freely. Also near Kathmandu is **Bhaktapur** (once known as Bhadgaon), a cultural arts center. It was built in 900 A.D. and has retained many temples, monasteries,

Edmund Hillary and Tenzing Norgay wre the first to climb to the top of Mt. Everest.

Durbar Square, Kathmandu, Nepal
Photo by C. J. Ghormley

a famous Golden Gate, and the Palace of Fifty-five Windows. Another town close by is **Patan**, an impressive and ancient center of religious art.

Pokhara has a resort area on nearby **Lake Phewa**; it's also the base for treks beginning on the Annapurna Range. In the lowlands, **Royal Chitwan National Park** is a popular wildlife preserve, with such rare animals as Royal Bengal tigers and one-horned rhinos. The warm weather and jungle scenery here lend themselves ideally to safaris and rafting excursions, which you can book in advance; **Tiger Tops** is the area's most famous base camp.

India

The seventh largest country in the world, **India** is one-third the size of the United States. It's also the world's second most populated nation, with 952 million people—more than three times that of the United States. The most populous area of India is the fertile plains around the sacred Ganges [GAN-jeez] River; this lies below the Himalaya, which anchor the northern border in spectacular fashion.

India is a beautiful, mystical land of splendor, exotic culture, and heart-rending poverty. It's located south of China, bordered on the west by the Arabian Sea and on the east by the Bay of Bengal [ben-GAHL]. The large island-nation of **Sri Lanka** (which used to be called Ceylon) rests off its southern tip.

New Delhi, the capital, anchors northern India; it's the main gateway, with flights arriving at **Indira Gandhi International Airport** (DEL). Near the northeast coast is **Calcutta** (CCU), India's largest city, major port, and commercial center; **Bombay** (BOM), on the west central coast, is another important port, and a fairly cosmopolitan city. The country is serviced from North America by **Air India** (AI), the national airline, as well as by North American and international carriers.

March through May is a dry and often uncomfortably hot period in India, whereas June through September is the notorious monsoon rain season. Your clients would probably be most comfortable visiting here from October to February: The climate in the south ranges from tropical daytime temperatures in the mid-80s to the mid-60s at night. The more mountainous north runs about twenty-five degrees cooler. The Himalaya, of course, can get quite cold. Of the sixteen official languages, Hindi is the national language, though English (an associate official tongue) is common in business and government; more than 1,500 recognized dialects are spoken across India.

India is second only to the United States in the length of its road systems.

Important Places

Some of the world's most historical cities and the Himalaya—these attract many clients to India. Among the principal destinations in India is **New Delhi**, which is actually made up of the old city of Delhi and a more modern development. Its seventeenth-century **Red Fort** was built under order of the Shah Jahan, who was responsible for creating the Taj Mahal; it houses the **Imperial Palace** and the **Hall of Private Audience**, with its ceiling of solid silver. This same shah also had built the beautiful, marble **Jama Masjid** mosque, the largest in India. (An antique market adjoins it.) Another religious building, **Lakshmi Narayan temple**, is one of the finest in the city. An impressively tall minaret, **Qutb Minar**, was built in the thirteenth century. **Humayun's Tomb** is a classical wonder, 450 years old. Another important tomb is the **Raj Ghat**, a memorial to Mahatma Gandhi; it's where his cremated remains lie.

Two excursions out of New Delhi that you should consider recommending are:

- **Agra**, home of the **Taj Mahal**—considered by many to be the world's most beautiful building. This exquisite memorial was built by Shah Jahan for his wife; some feel it's most impressive in moonlight. For clients who take the time to look beyond the Taj, Agra also has some other fine sights—including the complexes of **Agra Fort**, **Itmad-ud-Daulah** (often compared to the Taj Mahal, but on a much smaller scale) and **Fatehpur Sikri** (with palaces, mosques, and a beautiful mausoleum). From New Delhi, Agra is thirty minutes by plane or about three hours by car.

- **Jaipur**, called the Pink City for the color of stone used here. Forts and hills circle the city. The **Palace of the Winds** (Hawa Mahal) is, in fact, no more than a facade with nearly 1,000 windows. The **City Palace Museum** has a fine collection of crafts and the **Amber Palace**—Jaipur's principal attraction—impressively overlooks the city.

India's other major destinations are:

- **Varanasi**, also known as Benares. Pilgrims come here to cleanse themselves in the holy waters of the Ganges. Varanasi is the center of the Hindu religion in India; a great many sacred temples grace the city. Nearby is the town of **Sarnath**, a major Buddhist center; it's said that Buddha taught his first lesson here.

- **Calcutta**, the nation's commercial center and largest city. For all its importance, this major port city is painfully squalid. It's not a prime tourist destination, but there are some fine sites: the **Victoria Memorial**, which contains artifacts from the colonial days; **Eden Gardens**; the huge **India Museum**; the **Marble Palace Mansion** and its artwork; and **New Market**.

- **Madras**, on the southeast coast. The first British settlement was here, at **Fort St. George**. The city is also of major Christian and Hindu importance—with temples, palaces, and religious sites. Outside town are a number of ancient temples: The village of **Mahabalipuram** has a magnificent shrine, with its famous cave temples and sculptures cut out of rock (*rathas*).

- **Goa**, a somewhat different sort of Indian destination. A colony of Portugal until 1961, Goa is a tropical beach resort that has a very cosmopolitan feeling. The climate is extremely pleasant—even the monsoon season in Goa is relatively mild.

- **Bombay**, a fairly sophisticated industrial center. Sixth-century cave temples carved into rock can be found on **Elephanta Island**, reached by ferry. Your clients may enjoy exploring **Bombay Harbor** and **Chowpatty Beach** or shopping in Bombay's "Thieves' Market," the **Chor Bazaar**. The **Prince of Wales Museum** offers fine, diverse collections; and the **Hanging Gardens** at Malabar Hill are beautiful.

- **Ajanta and Ellora Caves**; these superb ruins lie about 200 miles to the northeast of Bombay. At Ellora, thirty-four impressive temples are cut out of the rock.

- **Udaipur**, a lovely city where palaces line a lake. The **City Palace Museum** is excellent. Other attractions include the ornate **Maharajah's Palace** and beautiful **Sahelion ki Bari** gardens. Just outside town are the **Jain Temples**, in the ancient ruins at **Nagda**.

- **The State of Jammu and Kashmir**, in the far north, lying among the Himalaya, a prime destination for treks. **Srinagar**, in the western region, is a resort area set in a beautiful valley. Once the Emperor's summer resort, it's the center of tourism in Kashmir and is a place of lakes, gardens, and mosques. The city of **Leh**, an access point to the region's monasteries, is particularly colorful and active.

Case Study

Sandra Durant, in her middle thirties, has a wanderlust spirit and enjoys going on adventurous trips by herself. This year, she has her sights set on about three weeks in Southeast Asia—Malaysia, Indonesia, perhaps the Philippines, and Singapore. Cost is important to her. The flight over is expensive enough, and she'll be looking for bargains along the way. But then, she's always felt that roughing it is the best way to see any country.

Circle the answer that best suits your client's needs:

1. Which of the following services could you recommend?

   First class air tickets   A side trip to Thailand

   An escorted safari   Deluxe hotel room

   Why?

2. Sandra plans to be on the go for most of her trip, but she wants to find one destination in the area where she can stop and spend a bit more time. Where might you suggest?

   Tahiti   Fiji

   Bali   Bora Bora

   Why?

3. Of the following sites, which would *not* be appropriate for you to recommend that Sandra visit?

   Borobudur   The Taj Mahal

   Taman Negara National Park   Banaue rice terraces

   Why?

4. Which of the following tips should you suggest?

   Lodging may be challenging.   Bring a sweater for the chilly nights.

   Convenient transportation is available.   There are major trekking opportunities throughout.

   Why?

Creative Activity

You work for ACME Cruise Lines, which has decided to inaugurate an 18-day cruise of Asia and the Pacific. The cruise, which will be targeted to culture-seeking clients, begins in Hong Kong at 7 P.M. Your job: to propose an itinerary that will call on at least four ports (you may end the cruise at any port). List the ports you've chosen, indicate what happens each day, and be prepared to justify your itinerary. Remember that the ship should not cruise a distance between ports that would take longer than three days. The ship is capable of speeds of 20 to 25 miles per hour. Note also that cruise lines usually like to have their ships leave in the early evening and arrive in the early morning so as to sail as much as possible at night. (If you can, give projected departure and arrival times.) You may have the ship stay at a port for several days or have it merely arrive at a port in the morning and leave that same evening. You may wish to study cruise line brochures to get a few ideas.

Day 1: Embark

Day 2

Day 3

Day 4

Day 5

Day 6

Day 7

Day 8

Day 9

Day 10

Day 11

Day 12

Day 13

Day 14

Day 15

Day 16

Day 17

Day 18

Travel Trivia

Questionable Cuisine

"Pork with Fresh Garbage" (Vietnam)
"As for the tripe served you at the Hotel Monopol, you will be singing its praises to your grandchildren as you lie on your deathbed." (Polish tourist brochure)
"Chopped up cow with a wire through it (shish-ke-bob)." (Athens hotel)
"Muscles of Marines/Lobster Thermos" (Cairo)
"Buttered Saucepans and Fried Hormones" (Japan)
"Sweat from the Trolley" (Europe)
"Dreaded Veal Cutlet with Potatoes in Cream" (Europe)
"Teppen Yaki—Before Your Cooked Right Eyes" (Japan)
"Goose Barnacles" (Spain)
"Toes with Butter and Jam" (Bali)

Pulling It All Together: The Matching Game

Directions: Below is a list of cities, attractions, etc., some of which we have covered, some which we haven't. There are all manner of connections among them. With a group of fellow students, you have exactly ten minutes to come up with as many connections as possible. (Items may be used more than once.) Write your answers below. Note: There are at least twenty possible connections. E.g., Dakar and Nairobi—both are capital cities.

Himalaya	Tahiti	Maldives
Lhasa	Katherine	Great Dividing Range
Japan	Queenstown	Yangtze
Wellington	Canberra	Nepal
Noumea	Vietnam	New Caledonia
Li	Coral	Southern
Darwin	Murray	Palace on Wheels
Brunei	Tonga	Alice Springs
Thailand	Silver Fern	Kuala Lumpur
Beijing	Micronesia	Gold Coast
Taroko	Phuket	Indian Pacific
Blue	Rotorua	Volcano
Truk Island	Shanghai	Western Samoa

APPENDIX **A**

Average Length of Stay – Leisure Clients

The following is a list of major cities and approximately how long the average tourist stays in each (including, perhaps, one day-trip) and assuming a leisurely pace. This will enable you to make the proper recommendation to your client. Remember that some may wish to fully explore that city's attractions. Although a city may require only one day to see, your client may need two nights' lodging in that city.

City	Number of Days	City	Number of Days	City	Number of Days
Acapulco	3–4	Helsinki	1–2	Paris	3–5
Amsterdam	2–3	Hong Kong	2–4	Philadelphia	1–2
Anchorage	1–2	Honolulu (Waikiki)	3–5	Phoenix	1–2
Athens	2–3	Houston	1–2	Portland, OR	1–2
Atlanta	1–2			Puerto Vallarta	2–3
Atlantic City	1–2	Istanbul	1–2		
Auckland	1–2	Jerusalem	2–4	Quebec City	1–2
				Quito	1–2
Baltimore	1–2	Kyoto	1–3		
Banff	1–2			Rio de Janeiro	2–4
Bangkok	2–3	Lancaster, PA	1–2	Rome	3–4
Barcelona	2–3	Las Vegas	2–3	Rotorua	1–2
Beijing	3–4	Lima	1–3		
Berlin	2–3	Lisbon	1–3	St. Petersburg (formerly Leningrad)	1–2
Bombay	1–3	London	3–5		
Boston	2–3	Los Angeles	3–5	Salt Lake City	1–2
Brisbane	2–3			Salzburg	1–2
Brussels	2–3	Madrid	2–3	San Antonio	1–2
Budapest	1–2	Marrakech	1–2	San Diego	2–3
Buenos Aires	1–2	Mazatlán	2–3	San Francisco	2–3
		Melbourne	1–2	Santa Fe	1–2
Cairo	1–2	Memphis	1–2	Savannah	1–2
Calgary	1–2	Mexico City	2–3	Seattle	1–2
Cancun	3–4	Miami	2–3	Seoul	2–3
Chicago	2–3	Milan	1–2	Stockholm	1–3
Christchurch	1–2	Montreal	2–3	Sydney	2–3
Copenhagen	2–3	Moscow	2–3		
Cuzco	1–2	Munich	2–3	Tampa/Clearwater	2–3
				Tangier	1–2
Dallas	1–2	Nairobi	1–3	Tokyo	2–3
Denver	1–2	Nashville	1–2	Toronto	1–2
Dublin	1–2	New Orleans	2–3		
		New York	3–5	Vancouver	1–2
Edinburgh	2–3	Newport, RI	1–2	Venice	2–3
Edmonton	1–2	Niagara Falls	1–2	Vienna	2–4
		Nice	2–3		
Fairbanks	1–2			Washington, D.C.	3–5
Florence	2–4	Orlando	3–5	Wellington, N.Z.	1–2
Frankfurt	1–2	Osaka	1–2	Williamsburg	1–2
		Oslo	1–2		
Geneva	1–2	Ottawa	1–2	Zurich	1–2
Guadalajara	1–2				

APPENDIX B

Tourist Bureaus

United States Tourist Offices

Alabama Bureau of Tourism and Travel
P.O. Box 4927
Montgomery, AL 36103-4927
www.touralabama.org

Alaska Division of Tourism
P.O. Box 110801
Juneau, AK 99811-0801
www.travelalaska.com

Arizona Office of Tourism
2702 N. Third St., Ste. 4015
Phoenix, AZ 85004
www.arizonaguide.com

Arkansas Dept. of Tourism
One Capitol Mail
Little Rock, AR 72201
www.1800natural.com

California Dept. of Tourism
801 K St., Ste. 1600
Sacramento, CA 95814
www.gocalif.ca.gov

Colorado Travel and Tourism Authority
P.O. Box 3524
Englewood, CO 80155
www.denver.org

Connecticut Dept. of Economic Development
505 Hudson St.
Hartford, CT 06106
www.state.ct.us/tourism.htm

Delaware Tourism Office
99 Kings Highway
Dover, DE 19901
www.state.de.us

Washington, D.C., Convention and Visitors Assn.
1212 New York Ave. NW, Ste. 600
Washington, DC 20005
www.washington.org

Visit Florida
661 E. Jefferson St., Ste. 300
Tallahassee, FL 32301
www.flausa.com

Georgia Dept. of Industry and Trade, Tourist Division
285 Peachtree Center Ave. NE
Atlanta, GA 30303-1232
www.gomm.com

Hawaii Visitors and Convention Bureau
2270 Kalakaua Ave., Ste. 801
Honolulu, HI 96815
www.visithawaii.org

Idaho Division of Tourism Development
700 W. State St.
Boise, ID 83720
www.idoc.state.id.us

Illinois Dept. of Commerce
100 W. Randolph St., Ste. 3-400
Chicago, IL 60601
www.enjoyillinois.com

Indiana Tourism Division
One N. Capitol, Ste. 700
Indianapolis, IN 46204
www.indianatourism.com

Iowa Dept. of Economic Development
200 E. Grand Ave.
Des Moines, IA 50309
www.state.ia.us

Kansas Dept. of Commerce Travel and Tourism Division
700 S.W. Harrison St., Ste. 1300
Topeka, KS 66603-3712
www.kansascommerce.com

Kentucky Dept. of Travel Development
P.O. Box 2011, Dept. M R
Frankfort, KY 40602
www.kentuckytourism.com

Louisiana Office of Tourism
P.O. Box 94291
Baton Rouge, LA 70804-9291
www.louisianatourism.com

Maine Office of Tourism
33 Stone St., 59 State House Station
Augusta, ME 04333-0059

Maryland Office of Tourism
217 E. Redwood St., 9th Fl.
Baltimore, MD 21202
www.mdisfun.org

Massachusetts Office of Travel
100 Cambridge St., Ste. 1305
Boston, MA 02202
www.mass-vacation.com

Travel Michigan
P.O. Box 30226
Lansing, MI 48909-7726
www.michigan.org

Minnesota Office of Tourism
500 Metro Square
121 Seventh Place E., Ste. 500
St. Paul, MN 55101
www.exploreminnesota.com

Mississippi Division of Tourism Development
P.O. Box 849
Jackson, MS 39205
www.mississippi.org

Missouri Division of Tourism
P.O. Box 1055
Jefferson City, MO 65102-1055
www.missouritourism.org

Montana Travel Promotion Division
P.O. Box 200533
Helena, MT 59620-0533
www.travel.mt.gov

Nebraska Travel and Tourism
P.O. Box 98509
Lincoln, NE 68509-4666
www.visitnebraska.org

Nevada Commission on Tourism
Capitol Complex, 5151 S. Carson St.
Carson City, NV 89710
www.travelnevada.com

New Hampshire Travel and Tourism
P.O. Box 1856
Concord, NH 03302-1856
www.visitnh.gov

New Jersey Travel and Tourism
20 W. State St., CN 826
Trenton, NJ 08625-0826
www.state.nj.us/travel

New Mexico Dept. of Tourism
491 Old Santa Fe Trail
Santa Fe, NM 87503
www.newmexico.org

New York State Dept. of Economic Development
One Commerce Plaza
Albany, NY 12245
www.iloveny.state.ny.us

North Carolina Tourism
301 N. Wilmington St.
Raleigh, NC 27601-2825
www.visitnc.com

North Dakota Dept. of Tourism
604 E Blvd Ave.
Bismarck, ND 58505
www.ndtourism.com

Ohio Division of Travel and Tourism
P.O. Box 1001
Columbus, OH 43216-1001
www.ohiotourism.com

Oklahoma Tourism and Recreation Dept.
P.O. Box 52002
Oklahoma City, OK 73152-2002
www.otrd.state.ok.us

Oregon Tourism Commission
775 Summer St. NE
Portland, OR 97310
www.traveloregon.com

Pennsylvania Office of Travel, Tourism, and Film
Forum Building, Room 404
Harrisburg, PA 17120
www.state.pa.us

Rhode Island Tourism
One W. Exchange St.
Providence, Rl 02903
www.visitrhodeisland.com

South Carolina Dept. of Parks, Recreation, and Tourism
1205 Pendelton St.
Columbia, SC 29202
www.travelsc.com

South Dakota Dept. of Tourism
711 E. Wells Ave.
Pierre, SD 57501-3369
www.state.sd.us

Tennessee Dept. of Tourism
320 Sixth Ave. N
Nashville, TN 37202
www.state.tn.us/tourdev

Texas Dept. of Economic Development Tourism Division
P.O. Box 12728
Austin, TX 78711-2728
www.traveltex.com

Utah Travel Council
Council Hall, Capitol Hill
Salt Lake City, UT 84114
www.utah.com

Vermont Dept. of Tourism and Marketing
134 State St.
Montpelier, VT 05601-1471
www.travel-vermont.com/tourism/
vermont.htm

Virginia Tourism Corp.
901 E. Byrd St.
Richmond, VA 23219
www.virginia.org

Washington State Tourism
P.O. Box 42500
Olympia, WA 98504
www.tourism.wa.gov

West Virginia Division of Tourism
2101 Washington St., E., Building 17
Charleston, WV 25305
www.state.wv.us/tourism/default.htm

Wisconsin Dept. of Tourism
P.O. Box 7976
Madison, Wl 53707
www.tourism.state.wi.us

Wyoming Division of Tourism
I-25 at College Drive
Cheyenne, WY 82002-0240
www.state.wy.us/commerce/tourism/
index.htm

Canadian Tourist Offices

Travel Alberta
999 Eighth St. SW, Ste. 500
Calgary, AB T2R 1J5

Tourism British Columbia
865 Hornby St., Ste. 802
Vancouver, BC V5Z 2G3

Travel Manitoba
155 Carlton St., 7th Fl.
Winnipeg, MB R3C 3H8

New Brunswick Dept. of Economic Development and Tourism
P.O. Box 6000
Fredericton, NB E3B 5H1

Newfoundland/Labrador Dept. of Tourism, Culture, and Recreation
P.O. Box 8700
St. John's, NF A1B 4J6

Northwest Territories Tourism
P.O. Box 1320
Yellowknife, NT X1Z 2L9

Nova Scotia Dept. of Economic Development and Tourism
P.O. Box 519
Halifax, NS B3J 2R7

Ontario Canada Tourism
Hearst Block, 900 Bay St., 4th Fl.
Toronto, ON M7A 2E1

Prince Edward Island Tourism
P.O. Box 940
Charlottetown, PE C1A 7M5

Tourisme Quebec
Tour de la Place-Victoria
Bureau 260, CP 125
Montreal, PQ H4Z 1C3

Tourism Saskatchewan
1900 Albert St., Ste. 500
Regina, SK S4P 4L9

Tourism Yukon
P.O. Box 2703
Whitehorse, YT Y1A 2C6

Foreign Tourist Offices

Anguilla Tourist Board
World Trade Center, Ste. 250
San Francisco, CA 94111

Antigua and Barbuda Dept. of Tourism
610 Fifth Ave., Ste. 311
New York, NY 10020
www.antigua-barbuda.org

Argentina National Tourist Council
12 W. 56th St.
New York, NY 10019

Aruba Tourism Authority
1000 Harbor Blvd.
Weehawken, NJ 07087
www.aruba.com

Australian Tourist Commission
2049 Century Park E., Ste. 1920
Los Angeles, CA 90067
www.australia.com

Austrian National Tourist Office
500 Fifth Ave., Ste. 800
New York, NY 10110
www.anto.com

Azerbaijan, Embassy of
927 15th St. NW, Ste. 700
Washington, DC 20005

Bahamas Tourist Office
150 E. 52nd St., 28th Fl.
New York, NY 10022
www.interknowledge.com/bahamas

Bahrain, Embassy of
3502 International Dr. NW
Washington, DC 20008

Bangladesh, Embassy of
2201 Wisconsin Ave. NW, Ste. 300
Washington, DC 20007

Barbados Tourism Authority
800 Second Ave.
New York, NY 10017
www.barbados.org

Belarus, Embassy of
1619 New Hampshire Ave. NW
Washington, DC 20009

Belgian Tourist Office
780 Third Ave., Ste. 1501
New York, NY 10017
www.visitbelgium.com

Belize Tourist Board
421 Seventh Ave., Ste. 1110
New York, NY 10001
www.turq.com/belize.html

Benin, Embassy of
2737 Cathedral Ave. NW
Washington, DC 20008

Bermuda Dept. of Tourism
310 Madison Ave., Ste. 201
New York, NY 10017-6083

Bhutan Travel Inc.
120 E. 56th St., Ste. 1130
New York, NY 10022

Bolivia, Embassy of
3014 Massachusetts Ave. NW
Washington, DC 20008

Bonaire, Tourism Corp. of
10 Rockefeller Plaza, Ste. 900
New York, NY 10020
www.bonaire.org

Bosnia and Herzegovina, Embassy of
1707 L St. NW, Ste. 760
Washington, DC 20036

Botswana, Embassy of
3400 International Dr., Ste. 7M
Washington, DC 20008

Brazilian Tourism Office
551 Fifth Ave., Ste. 590
New York, NY 10176

British Virgin Islands Tourist Board
370 Lexington Ave.
New York, NY 10017
www.bviwelcome.com

Brunei, Embassy of
2600 Virginia Ave. NW, Ste. 300
Washington, DC 20037

Bulgaria Tourist Information Center
c/o Balkan Tourist USA
20 E. 46th St., Ste. 1003
New York, NY 10017
www.visiteurope.com

Burundi, Embassy of
2233 Wisconsin Ave. NW, Ste. 212
Washington, DC 20007

Cambodia, Royal Embassy of
4500 16th St. NW
Washington, DC 20022

Cameroon, Embassy of
2349 Massachusetts Ave. NW
Washington, DC 20008

Canadian Tourism Commission
550 S. Hope St., 9th Fl.
Los Angeles, CA 90071

Cape Verde, Embassy of
3415 Massachusetts Ave. NW
Washington, DC 20007

Caribbean Tourism Organization
20 E. 46th St.
New York, NY 10017-2452
www.caribtourism.com

Cayman Islands Dept. of Tourism
6100 Blue Lagoon Dr., Ste. 150
Miami, FL 33126-2085

Chad, Embassy of
2002 R St. NW
Washington, DC 20009

Chile, Embassy of
1732 Massachusetts Ave. NW
Washington, DC 20036

China National Tourist Office
350 Fifth Ave., Ste. 6413
New York, NY 10118
www.cnta.com

Colombian Government Tourist Office
140 E. 57th St.
New York, NY 10022

Comoros Islands, Permanent Mission of
336 E. 45th St., 2nd Fl.
New York, NY 10017

Congo, Embassy of the Republic of
4891 Colorado Ave. NW
Washington, DC 20011

Congo, Embassy of the Democratic Republic of (formerly Zaire)
1800 New Hampshire Ave. NW
Washington, DC 20009

Costa Rica, Embassy of
2114 S St. NW
Washington, DC 20008
www.tourism-costarica.com

Cote D'Ivoire Tourist Office
2412 Massachusetts Ave. NW
Washington, DC 20008
www.afreenet.com/ivory

Croatia National Tourist Office
300 Lanidex Plz., 3rd Fl.
Parsippany, NJ 07054
www.networldinc.com

Cuban Interest Section
c/o Embassy of Switzerland
2630 16th St. NW
Washington, DC 20009

Curacao Tourist Board
475 Park Ave. S., Ste. 2000
New York, NY 10016
www.interknowledge.com/curacao

Cyprus Tourism Organization
13 E. 40th St.
New York, NY 10016
www.cyprustourism.org

Czech Tourist Authority
1109 Madison Ave.
New York, NY 10028
www.czech.cz/new_york

Danish Tourist Board
655 Third Ave., 18th Fl.
New York, NY 10017
www.goscandinavia.com

Djibouti, Embassy of
1156 15th St. NW, Ste. 515
Washington, DC 20005

Dominica Tourist Office
10 E. 21st St., Ste. 600
New York, NY 10010

Dominican Republic Consulate General Tourism Division
1501 Broadway, Ste. 410
New York, NY 10036
www.dr1.com

Ecuador, Embassy of
2535 15th St. NW
Washington, DC 20009

Egyptian Tourist Authority
630 Fifth Ave., Ste. 1706
New York, NY 10111

El Salvador, Embassy of
2308 California St. NW
Washington, DC 20008

Equatorial Guinea, Embassy of
1511 K St. NW, Ste. 405
Washington, DC 20005

Eritrea, Embassy of
1708 New Hampshire Ave. NW
Washington, DC 20009

Estonia, Embassy of
2131 Massachusetts Ave. NW
Washington, DC 20008

Ethiopia, Embassy of
2134 Kalorama Rd. NW
Washington, DC 20008

Fiji Visitors Bureau
5777 W. Century Blvd., Ste. 220
Los Angeles, CA 90045
www.bulafiji.com

Finnish Tourist Board
655 Third Ave.
New York, NY 10017
www.goscandinavia.com

French Government Tourist Office
444 Madison Ave.
New York, NY 10022
www.francetourism.com

French Guiana
 French Government Tourist Office
444 Madison Ave.
New York, NY 10022
www.francetourism.com

Gabon Tourist Information Office
347 Fifth Ave., Ste. 810
New York, NY 10016

Gambia, Embassy of
1155 15th St. NW, Ste. 1000
Washington, DC 20005

Georgia, Embassy of
1511 K St. NW, Ste. 424
Washington, DC 20005

German National Tourist Office
122 E. 42nd St., 52nd Fl.
New York, NY 10168-0072
www.germany-tourism.de

Ghana, Embassy of
3512 International Dr. NW
Washington, DC 20008
www.ghana.com

British Tourist Authority
551 Fifth Ave., Ste. 701
New York, NY 10176-0799
www.visitbritain.com

Greek National Tourist Organization
645 Fifth Ave., 5th Fl.
New York, NY 10022

Grenada Board of Tourism
820 Second Ave., Ste. 9000
New York, NY 10017
www.interknowledge.com/grenada

Guadeloupe Tourist Office
161 Washington Valley Rd.
Warren, NJ 07059-7121
www.francetourism.com

Guam Visitors Bureau
1150 Marina Village Pkwy., Ste. 104
Alameda, CA 94501
www.visitguam.org

Guatemala Tourist Commission
299 Alhambra Circle, Ste. 510
Coral Gables, FL 33134

Guinea, Embassy of
2112 Leroy Pl. NW
Washington, DC 20008

Guinea-Bissau, Embassy of
1511 K St. NW, Ste. 519
Washington, DC 20005

Guyana, Embassy of
2490 Tracy Pl. NW
Washington, DC 20008

Haiti, Embassy of
2311 Massachusetts Ave. NW
Washington, DC 20008

Honduras Institute of Tourism
2100 Ponce de Leon Blvd., Ste. 1175
Coral Gables, FL 33134
www.hondurasinfo.htm

Hong Kong Tourist Association
590 Fifth Ave., 5th Fl.
New York, NY 10036-4706
www.hkta.org

Hungarian National Tourist Office
150 E. 58th St., 33rd Fl.
New York, NY 10155
www.hungarytourism.hu

Iceland Tourist Board
655 Third Ave.
New York, NY 10017
www.goscandinavia.com

Government of India Tourist Office
1270 Ave. of the Americas, Ste. 1808
New York, NY 10020
www.tourindia.com

Indonesia Tourist Promotion Office
3457 Wilshire Blvd., Ste. 104
Los Angeles, CA 90010

Iran, Interests Section of the Islamic Rep. of
2209 Wisconsin Ave. NW
Washington, DC 20007

Iraqi Interests Section
1801 P St. NW
Washington, DC 20036

Irish Tourist Board
345 Park Ave.
New York, NY 10154-0037
www.ireland.travel.ie

Israel Ministry of Tourism
800 Second Ave., 16th Fl.
New York, NY 10017
www.goisrael.com

Italian Government Tourist Board
630 Fifth Ave., Ste. 1565
New York, NY 10111

Jamaica Tourist Board
801 Second Ave., 20th Fl.
New York, NY 10017
www.jamaicatravel.com

Japan National Tourist Office
624 S. Grand Ave., Ste. 1611
Los Angeles, CA 90017
www.jnto.go.jp

Jordan Tourism Board
3504 International Dr. NW
Washington, DC 20008
www.jordanembassyus.org

Kazakhstan, Embassy of
3421 Massachusetts Ave. NW
Washington, DC 20007

Kenya Tourist Office
424 Madison Ave., Ste. 1401
New York, NY 10017
www. africavacation. com/kenya

Korea, Embassy of
2450 Massachusetts Ave. NW
Washington, DC 20008
www.knto.or.kr

Latvia, Embassy of
4325 17th St. NW
Washington, DC 20011
www.seas.gwu.edu/guest/latvia

Lesotho, Embassy of
2511 Massachusetts Ave. NW
Washington, DC 20008

Lithuania, Consulate General
3236 N. Sawtooth Ct.
Westlake Village, CA 91362

Luxembourg National Tourist Office
17 Beekman Pl.
New York, NY 10022

Macau Tourist Information Bureau
P.O. Box 350
Kenilworth, IL 60043-0350
www.macau.tourism.gov.mo

Macedonia, Embassy of
3050 K St. NW, Ste. 210
Washington, DC 20007

Madagascar Tourist Office
124 Lomas Santa Fe Dr., Ste. 206-B
Solana Beach, CA 92075
www.embassy.org/madagascar

Malawi, Embassy of
2408 Massachusetts Ave. NW
Washington, DC 20008

Tourism Malaysia
818 W. Seventh St., Ste. 8046
Los Angeles, CA 90017
www.tourism.gov.my

Maldives, Permanent Mission of
820 Second Ave., Ste. 800C
New York, NY 10017

Mali, Embassy of
2130 R St. NW
Washington, DC 20008

Malta National Tourist Office
350 Fifth Ave., Ste. 4412
New York, NY 10118
www.visitmalta.com

Marshall Islands, Embassy of
2433 Massachusetts Ave. NW
Washington, DC 20008

Martinique Promotion Bureau
444 Madison Ave., 16th Fl.
New York, NY 10022
www.francetourism.com

Mauritania, Embassy of
2129 Leroy Pl. NW
Washington, DC 20008

Mauritius, Embassy of
4301 Connecticut Ave. NW, Ste. 441
Washington, DC 20008

Mexican Govt. Tourist Office
405 Park Ave., Ste. 1401
New York, NY 10022
www.mexico-travel.com

Destination Micronesia
300 N. Continental Blvd. Ste. 600
El Segundo, CA 90245

Moldova, Embassy of
2101 F St. NW
Washington, DC 20008

Monaco Govt. Tourist and Convention Bureau
565 Fifth Ave.
New York, NY 10017
www.monaco.mc/usa/

Mongolia, Embassy of
2833 M St. NW
Washington, DC 20007

Moroccan National Tourist Office
20 E. 46th St., Ste. 1201
New York, NY 10017
www.kingdomofmorocco.com

Mozambique, Embassy of
1990 M St. NW, Ste. 570
Washington, DC 20036

Myanmar, Embassy of
2300 S St. NW
Washington, DC 20008-4089
www.myanmar.com

Namibia, Embassy of
1605 New Hampshire Ave. NW
Washington, DC 20009

Nepal Tourism Office
819 S. Federal Hwy., Ste. 103
Stuart, FL 34994
www.undp.org/missions/nepal

Netherlands Board of Tourism
355 Lexington Ave.
New York, NY 10017
www.goholland.com

Destination New Caledonia
9454 Wilshire Blvd., Ste. 715
Beverly Hills, CA 90212

New Zealand Tourism Board
501 Santa Monica Blvd., Ste. 300
Santa Monica, CA 90401
www.nztb.govt.nz

Nicaragua, Embassy of
1627 New Hampshire Ave., NW
Washington, DC 20009

Niger, Embassy of
2204 R St. NW
Washington, DC 20008

Nigeria, Embassy of
1333 16th St. NW
Washington, DC 20036

North Korean Mission to the UN
820 Second Ave., 13th Fl.
New York, NY 10017

Northern Ireland Tourist Board
551 Fifth Ave., Ste. 701
New York, NY 10176
www.ni-tourism.com

Norwegian Tourist Board
655 Third Ave.
New York, NY 10017
www.goscandinavia.com

Oman, Embassy of
2535 Belmont Rd. NW
Washington, DC 20008

Pakistan, Embassy of
2315 Massachusetts Ave. NW
Washington, DC 20008

Palau, Embassy of
1150 18th St. NW, Ste. 750
Washington, DC 20036

Panama, Embassy of
2862 McGill Terr. NW
Washington, DC 20008

Papua New Guinea, Embassy of
1615 New Hampshire Ave. NW, Ste. 300
Washington, DC 20009
www.airniugini.com.pg

Paraguay, Embassy of
2400 Massachusetts Ave. NW
Washington, DC 20008

Peru, Embassy of
1700 Massachusetts Ave. NW
Washington, DC 20036

Philippine Dept. of Tourism
3660 Wilshire Blvd., Ste. 825
Los Angeles, CA 90010

Polish National Tourist Office
275 Madison Ave., Ste. 1711
New York, NY 10016
www.polandtour.org

Portuguese National Tourist Office
590 Fifth Ave., 4th Fl.
New York, NY 10036
www.portugal.org

Puerto Rico Tourism Co.
575 Fifth Ave., 23rd Fl.
New York, NY 10017

Qatar, Embassy of
4200 Wisconsin Ave. NW, Ste. 200
Washington, DC 20016

Romanian National Tourist Office
14 E. 38th St., 12th Fl.
New York, NY 10016
www.rezq.com/ont

Russian Travel Bureau
225 E. 44th St.
New York, NY 10017
www.russiatravel.com

Rwanda, Embassy of
2141 Wisconsin Ave. NW, Ste. C1
Washington, DC 20007

St. Barts
    French West Indies Tourist Board
444 Madison Ave.
New York, NY 10022
www.francetourism.com

St. Kitts and Nevis Tourist Office
414 E. 75th St., 5th Fl.
New York, NY 10021
www.stkitts-nevis.com

St. Lucia Tourist Board
820 Second Ave., 9th Fl.
New York, NY 10017
www.st-lucia.com

St. Maarten Tourist Office
675 Third Ave., Ste. 1806
New York, NY 10017
www.st-maarten.com

St. Martin Tourist Office
10 E. 21st St.
New York, NY 10010
www.francetourism.com

St. Vincent and Grenadines Tourist Office
801 Second Ave., 21st Fl.
New York, NY 10017

Samoa, Permanent Mission of
820 Second Ave., Ste. 800
New York, NY 10017

San Marino, Consulate General of
1899 L St. NW, Ste. 500
Washington, DC 20036

Sao Tome and Principe, Permanent Mission of
122 E 42nd St., Rm. 1604
New York, NY 10168

Saudi Arabian Information Office
601 New Hampshire Ave. NW
Washington, DC 20037

Senegal, Embassy of
2112 Wyoming Ave. NW
Washington, DC 20008

Seychelles Tourist Office
235 E. 40th St., Ste. 24A
New York, NY 10016

Sierra Leone, Embassy of
1701 19th St. NW
Washington, DC 20009

Singapore Tourist Promotion Board
8484 Wilshire Blvd., Ste. 510
Los Angeles, CA 90211
www.singapore-usa.com

Slovak Republic, Embassy of
2201 Wisconsin Ave. NW, Ste. 250
Washington, DC 20007
www.inx.net.matica

Slovenian Tourist Office
345 E. 12th St.
New York, NY 10003

Solomon Islands, Permanent Mission of
820 Second Ave., Ste. 800
New York, NY 10017

Somalia, Permanent Mission of
425 E. 61st St., Ste. 702
New York, NY 10021

South African Tourism Board
500 Fifth Ave., 20th Fl.
New York, NY 10110
www.travelfile.com/get?satour

Spain, Tourist Office of
666 Fifth Ave., 35th Fl.
New York, NY 10022
www.okspain.org

Sri Lanka, Embassy of
2148 Wyoming Ave. NW
Washington, DC 20008
www.slembassy.org

Sudan, Embassy of
2210 Massachusetts Ave. NW
Washington, DC 20008

Suriname, Embassy of
4301 Connecticut Ave. NW, Ste. 108
Washington, DC 20008

Swaziland, Embassy of
3400 International Dr. NW, Ste. 3M
Washington, DC 20008

Swedish Travel and Tourism Council
655 Third Ave.
New York, NY 10017-5617
www.goscandinavia.com

Switzerland Tourism
608 Fifth Ave.
New York, NY 10020
www.switzerlandtourism.com

Syrian Arab Republic, Embassy of
2215 Wyoming Ave. NW
Washington, DC 20008

Tahiti Tourisme
300 Continental Blvd. Ste. 180
El Segundo, CA 90245
www.tahiti-tourisme.com

Taiwan Visitors Association
1 World Trade Center, Ste. 7953
New York, NY 10048
www.tbroc.gov.tw

Tajikistan, Permanent Mission of
136 E. 67th St.
New York, NY 10021

Tanzania, Embassy of
2139 R St. NW
Washington, DC 20008

Thailand, Tourism Authority of
5 World Trade Center, Ste. 3443
New York, NY 10048
www.tourismthailand.org

Togo, Embassy of
2208 Massachusetts Ave. NW
Washington, DC 20008

Tonga Consulate General
360 Post St., Ste. 604
San Francisco, CA 94108
www.vacations.gov.to

Trinidad and Tobago, Embassy of
1708 Massachusetts Ave. NW
Washington, DC 20036

Tunisia, Embassy of
1515 Massachusetts Ave. NW
Washington, DC 20005

Turkish Tourist Office
821 UN Plaza, 4th Fl.
New York, NY 10017
www.turkey.org/turkey

Turkmenistan, Embassy of
2207 Massachusetts Ave. NW
Washington, DC 20008

Turks and Caicos Tourist Office
11645 Biscayne Blvd., Ste. 302
N. Miami, FL 33181
www.turksandcaicostourism.com

Uganda, Embassy of
5911 16th St. NW
Washington, DC 20011

Ukraine, Trade Mission of
3350 M St. NW
Washington, DC 20007

United Arab Emirates, Embassy of
1255 22nd St. NW, Ste. 700
Washington, DC 20037

U.S. Virgin Islands Dept. of Tourism
1270 Ave. of the Americas
New York, NY 10020
www.usvi-online.com

Uruguayan Tourism Office
1077 Ponce de Leon Blvd.
Coral Gables, FL 33134
www.turismo.gub/uy

Uzbek Tourism
60 E. 42nd St., Ste. 2308
New York, NY 10165

Vanuatu, Mission of
866 UN Plaza, 10th Fl.
New York, NY 10017

Venezuela, Embassy of
1099 30th St. NW
Washington, DC 20007
www.venezuela.mit.edu/consulado.sfo

Vietnam, Embassy of
1233 20th St. NW, Ste. 501
Washington, DC 20036
www.vietnamembassy-usa.org

Yemen, Embassy of
2600 Virginia Ave. NW, Ste. 705
Washington, DC 20037

Yugoslavia, Embassy of the Fed. Rep. of
2410 California St. NW
Washington, DC 20008

Zambia National Tourist Board
800 Second Ave.
New York, NY 10017

Zimbabwe Tourist Office
1270 Ave. of the Americas, Ste. 2315
New York, NY 10020

APPENDIX **C**

Research Resources

Print

- *The Weissmann Travel Reports* is one of the most comprehensive geography reference tools anywhere. Even the world's most obscure countries receive pages of treatment. Every office that deals with travel should have a copy of this rich source of geographic wisdom or should subscribe to its electronic version.

- *The World Travel Guide* is a 1,200-page single-volume book that gives enormous detail—including information for business travel—about virtually every nation on earth. Its color layout is impressive. Also a "must" research tool.

- *The Star Service* analyzes hotels across the world in extreme detail. *The Official Hotel Guide (OHG)* and *The Hotel and Travel Index* both give information on thousands of hotels.

- *Travel guidebook series:*
  - **Birnbaum**, **Fodor**, **Frommer**, and **Fielding** are fine all-purpose guides. Several of these publishers also have created separate lines of guides for more budget-minded clients.
  - **Berlitz Pocket Guides** manage to compress an amazing amount of detail into their compact books.
  - **The Lonely Planet Series** takes a somewhat counter-culture look at places many other guidebooks neglect.
  - **Access** and **Michelin Guides** stress history, art, and architecture. Their beautiful graphic presentation makes them especially easy to consult.
  - **Insight Guides** also examine the history and culture of a destination, but with the added benefit of high-quality color photographs.

- **The Let's Go** and **Rough Guide** series treat the particular needs of student, budget, and independent travelers.

- *The Eurail Guide* contains handy descriptions of railroad routes—not only for Europe, but for many other countries.

- **The OAG Travel Planner** is a compact reference book that gives much information that other sources miss—such as golf course locations, airport maps, transfer services, and facilities for the physically challenged.

- *The Destination Specialist Series*, created by the Institute of Certified Travel Agents, is an admirable group of texts that focus on destinations. At the moment, eleven volumes exist: **North America**, **Western Europe**, **the Caribbean**, **the Pacific Rim**, **Latin America**, **Africa**, **Corporate Travel Geography**, **Specialty Travel**, **Eastern Europe**, **China**, and **Hawaii**.

- *The World Factbook*, published by the Central Intelligence Agency, is a little-known book that contains a wealth of information at a surprisingly affordable price.

- **Travel trade magazines** (such as *TravelAge*, *Travel Agent*, *Tour and Travel News*, *Cruise and Vacation Views*, and *Travel Weekly*) and tourist bureau materials are often excellent sources of up-to-date information. Tourist bureau addresses can be found in Appendix B.

- **Health and Political Advisories** are regularly issued by the U.S. State Department. You should consult them whenever foreign travel is involved.

Distributors of Travel Videos

These companies specialize in distributing destination travel videos to the general public. You may wish to contact them to be placed on their mailing lists; many of their cassettes may also be rented from major video chains, such as Blockbuster.

AAA Video Services
695 S. Colorado Bl., Ste. 270
Denver, CO 80222
Tel: 800-875-5000

Forsyth Travel Library
226 Westchester Avenue
White Plains, NY 10604
Tel: 800-FORSYTH

International Video Network
2242 Camino Ramon
San Ramon, CA 94583
Tel: 800-669-4486

Questar Video, Inc.
680 N. Lakeshore, Ste. 900
Chicago, IL 60611
Tel: 800-633-5633

Travelview International
10370 Richmond Ave., #550
Houston, TX 77042
Tel: 800-862-1306

Vacations on Video
7741 E. Gray Rd.
Scottsdale, AZ 85260
Tel: 602-483-1551

APPENDIX D

Films

Sometimes the ambiance of a place is just around the corner, at your neighborhood video store. Below is a list of films that capture the essence of—or even spoof—their locations. Historical films are, for the most part, excluded. Those rated "R" are indicated accordingly.

Baltimore	*Diner* (R)	Australia and New York City	*Crocodile Dundee*
Hawaii	*Blue Hawaii*	Austria	*The Sound of Music*
Hawaii	*Hawaii*	Austria (Vienna)	*The Third Man*
Hawaii	*Hawaiians*	Bermuda	*The Deep*
Hollywood	*The Player*	Botswana	*The Gods Must Be Crazy*
Hollywood	*Sunset Boulevard*	Canada	*Canadian Bacon*
Hollywood	*The Day of the Locust*	China	*Shoes of the Fisherman*
Las Vegas	*Viva Las Vegas*	China	*The Last Emperor*
Las Vegas	*Leaving Las Vegas*	France (Paris)	*A Little Romance*
Las Vegas	*Honeymoon in Vegas*	France (Paris)	*Forget Paris*
Los Angeles	*L.A. Confidential* (R)	France (Paris)	*Love in the Afternoon*
Los Angeles	*L.A. Story*	France (Paris)	*Paris When It Sizzles*
Los Angeles	*Chinatown* (R)	France (Paris)	*How to Steal a Million*
Los Angeles and New York	*Annie Hall*	France (Paris)	*French Kiss*
Miami	*Miami Rhapsody* (R)	France (Paris)	*An American in Paris*
Miami	*Miami Blues* (R)	France (Paris)	*Charade*
New Orleans	*A Streetcar Named Desire*	France (Paris)	*Gigi*
New Orleans	*The Big Easy* (R)	Greece (Crete)	*Zorba the Greek*
New York City	*Manhattan*	India	*Heat and Dust* (R)
New York City	*The Age of Innocence*	Italy (Assisi)	*The Assisi Underground*
New York City	*On the Town*	Italy (Rome)	*La Dolce Vita*
New York City	*After Hours*	Italy (Rome)	*Two Weeks in Another Town*
New York City	*Cocktail*	Italy (Rome)	*Roman Holiday*
New York City	*The Clock*	Italy (Venice)	*Don't Look Now* (R)
North Dakota	*Fargo*	Italy (Venice)	*Summertime*
Pennsylvania Dutch Country	*Witness*	Scotland	*Braveheart*
San Francisco	*Bullitt*	Wales	*The Englishman Who Went Up a Hill but Came Down a Mountain*
San Francisco	*Vertigo*		
St. Louis	*Meet Me in St. Louis*		
Washington, D.C.	*All the President's Men*		

Index

C

H

N

T